Parenting in Contemporary Society

FOURTH EDITION

TOMMIE J. HAMNER

University of Alabama

PAULINE H. TURNER

University of New Mexico

ALLYN AND BACON

Boston   London   Toronto   Sydney   Tokyo   Singapore

Series Editor: Jeff Lasser
Editiorial Assistant: Susan Hutchinson
Marketing Manager: Caroline Croley
Editorial–Production Service: Matrix Productions Inc.
Composition and Prepress Buyer: Linda Cox
Manufacturing Buyer: Suzanne Lareau
Cover Administrator: Linda Knowles
Electronic Composition: Omegatype Typography, Inc.

Library of Congress Cataloging-in-Publication Data

Hamner, Tommie J.
 Parenting in contemporary society / Tommie J. Hamner, Pauline H. Turner.—4th ed.
  p.   cm.
 Includes bibliographical references and index.
 ISBN 0-205-29646-7
  1. Parenting.   2. Parenting—Study and teaching.   3. Family.   4. Child rearing.
 I. Turner, Pauline H.   II. Title.

HQ755.8 .H35   2001
649'.1—dc21
                                                                00-042048

Printed in the United States of America

10 9 8 7 6 5 4 3   05 04 03

Photo Credits: Will Hart: pages 1, 68, 162, 260, 342; Will Faller: pages 33, 109; Robert Harbison: pages 135, 302; Michael Newman/PhotoEdit: page 201; Jim Pickerell/Stock Boston: page 371; Brian Smith: page 405; Jeanne A. Smith: pages 5, 19, 38, 150, 169, 306, 311, 346, 416; Carolyn L. Smith: page 364; Steven Heifetz: page 424. The rest of the photographs were taken by the authors.

CONTENTS

PART II
PARENTING: DIVERSE FAMILY TYPES

PREFACE

This book was written to acquaint upper-level undergraduate and graduate students with parenting in three major areas: (1) concepts, challenges, and changes; (2) diverse family types; and (3) risks and alternatives. Although it is specifically designed as preparation for students who will enter a profession requiring them to work with parents directly, the book also provides useful information in developing life skills. Thus, this book should be helpful to students preparing for teaching, social work, other human-service professions, health professions, and mental-health professions—and to parents themselves.

The fourth edition is even better than the first three. We have made significant revisions to most sections and have included new topics of interest. This book does not take a "cookbook" approach to parenting. We believe that there is no "recipe" for effective parenting behavior but instead that there are a number of strategies, skills, insights, and resources that can assist parents. Therefore, the topics selected represent those we believe to be the most relevant contemporary issues facing both parents and the professionals who work with them. We have included classical and current research, but we have attempted to emphasize the practical application of research and the implications for parenting and parent education.

Part I, "Parenting: Concepts, Challenges, and Changes," consists of the first five chapters. The first chapter introduces a variety of relevant concepts, discusses the need for parent education, and explores the determinants of parenting behavior. Chapters 2, 3, and 4 are companion chapters that discuss the changing nature of parenting throughout the life cycle, from infancy through old age, emphasizing the reciprocal nature of the parent-child relationships. The needs of parents, as well as those of children, at all stages of development are examined. Chapter 5 describes, compares, and evaluates the major contemporary strategies of parenting that many parents use to assist them in becoming more effective parents.

Part II, "Parenting: Diverse Family Types," is one of the unique features of this book. Chapter 6 discusses parenting in diverse cultures and includes sections on socioeconomic differences, African American families, Mexican American families, Native American families, and Asian American families, noting similarities and differences among the different cultures. Chapters 7 and 8 examine parenting in diverse families. The structural variations—single-parent families and stepfamilies—are examined in relationship to adjustment for both parents and children, and the lifestyle variations include dual-career and dual-earner families, cohabiting families, and gay and lesbian families.

Part III, "Parenting: Risks and Alternatives," begins with Chapter 9, which deals with parenting in high-risk families with teenage parents, abusive parents, and homeless families. Parenting exceptional children is the topic for Chapter 10. Parents of children with exceptionalities share many common challenges, but each type of disability presents additional unique challenges. These are described in the chapter, which also includes a section on the characteristics of resilient children.

Another distinctive section of the book is Chapter 11, which explores alternatives to biological parenthood: adoptive parenthood, parenting through assisted reproduction (artificial insemination by donor, in vitro fertilization, surrogate mothers, etc.), and foster parenthood. The concluding chapter is devoted to child care and early education, extremely timely issues. It describes types of programs, examines both infant care and children in self care separately, discusses the importance of quality care, examines the effects of child care on children, and outlines other preschool programs.

Keeping the book a manageable length has been a monumental task for us. Sometimes we only scratch the surface, and we regret that space limitations prevented a more in-depth discussion of certain topics. Other sections are necessarily limited by a paucity of relevant research, particularly the sections on cohabiting parents, gay and lesbian parents, and assisted reproduction. We hope that the inclusion of these topics will stimulate further research.

We are indebted to all the members of our family who so patiently endured the writing of this fourth edition, which often resulted in a neglect of other family responsibilities. Pauline is especially grateful to her husband, David Hamilton, who provided encouragement and support every step of the way, and who did far more than his share of household duties to permit sufficient writing time.

We also acknowledge with gratitude the reviewers of this edition: Patricia J. Otis, Kirkwood Community College, Cedar Rapids, Iowa; and Cheryl Robinson, The University of Tennessee at Chattanooga.

Two problems continued to perplex us in the preparation of this book. The first was how to use a nonsexist pronoun in referring to the child. Rather than using either he/his or she/her exclusively, we chose to alternate the use of the masculine and feminine. We hope this practice reflects our desire to treat all children equally.

Finally, since there was no senior or junior author, we wondered how to resolve the issue of whose name should appear first. Since we are sisters from a closely knit family, we worked together on this book in an unusually cooperative way. Neither feels she did more than her share. Therefore, we have chosen to have our names appear in alphabetical order, coincidentally in order of our birth.

Tommie J. Hamner
Pauline H. Turner

CHAPTER 1

Parenting in Perspective

A distinctive feature of our high-tech society is the growing recognition that parenthood can be a choice rather than an inevitable event. No previous generation has been as free to choose. Parallel to the development of this freedom has been the increasing realization of the necessity of choosing wisely. As the pressures and demands of the parenting role have become more complex, the decision to delay parenthood or to remain childless has become more realistic for some; for others it has become necessary to rely on formal and/or informal support systems once parenthood is assumed.

This book is aimed at assisting those students who are prospective parents and those who are already parents in exploring the concepts of parenting so that they might develop the skills necessary for effectiveness in their roles. In addition, the information should provide people in, or desiring to enter, the helping professions with some suggestions for becoming more effective in working with parents.

A logical place to begin is to clarify the various concepts involved in the areas of parenting. We will then review what has occurred in the past, assess the present, and look briefly at the challenges for the future.

CONCEPTS OF PARENTING

Parenthood

To many, it would seem foolish to define the concept of parenthood. After all, it has been with us since Adam and Eve. But with the complexity of society and the many variant lifestyles, the term *parenthood* has been expanded. Although in the past parenthood meant that a person was responsible for biologically reproducing a child, today many kinds of individuals can be called parents. The dictionary points out that a person is a parent if he or she has produced the offspring or has the legal status of a father or a mother. The term *parent* comes from the Latin word *parens,* meaning "give birth." The synonym for *parent* provided by the dictionary is *parenthood.*

Motivations for Parenthood. Most research documents the pronatalism evidenced in contemporary society. It is estimated that only 10 percent of the population plan to remain childless (Seccombe, 1991). Census figures indicate that although the total number of families has increased steadily since 1980, the number of families without children also has increased comparably. However, Brems and Sohl (1995) found that 15.6 percent of the college students in their study indicated that they were not interested in becoming parents. Calvert and Stanton (1992) found that 89 percent of the adolescents they interviewed planned to be parents. Boys and girls were equally committed to parenthood.

Economic contributions of children to the family may be ruled out as a motivation for parenthood, for children today are an economic liability rather than an asset. The amount that parents spend in rearing a child from birth to 18 years of age varies according to income level, marital status, and geographic location. As children grow from infancy through adolescence, the amount spent each year changes. Table 1.1 provides the estimated average total expenditures, based on 1991 figures, for rearing a child to age 18 by family structure, income, and category of expenditure. Since many children are in college or pursuing some technical training at age 18, the cost probably would be much higher—as much as $300,000 if a private college education is provided (U.S. Department of Agriculture, 1992).

Why, then, do so many individuals become parents? For some, pregnancy is planned—an overt decision is made. For others, although they plan sometime in the future to become parents, the pregnancy is an accident due to failure of, improper use of, or neglect to use contraceptives. Ignorance as to how and when conception occurs also may be the reason for pregnancy.

Developmental theorists have emphasized that when individuals reach adulthood, there is a desire to care for others by having children and assuming the parenthood role (Erikson, 1963), thereby developing a sense of generativity. Gerson, Berman, and Morris (1991) found that the 20- and 30-year-old individuals in their study were highly

TABLE 1.1 Expenditures on a Child by Families, 1991

EXPENDITURE	INTACT FAMILIES WITH INCOMES LESS THAN $31,200	INTACT FAMILIES WITH INCOMES $31,200 TO $50,000	INTACT FAMILIES WITH INCOMES OVER $50,000	SINGLE-PARENT FAMILIES
Housing	$30,420	$ 41,100	$ 62,820	$31,110
Food	18,390	22,950	27,840	18,120
Transportation	14,430	22,260	29,460	22,890
Clothing	8,220	10,380	12,540	6,990
Health Care	4,590	5,850	7,260	3,030
Education, Child	13,530	22,350	35,460	12,000
Total	$89,580	$124,890	$175,380	$94,140

Source: U.S. Department of Agriculture, ARS, Family Economics Research Group. (1992). Expenditures on a child by families, 1991. In J. Courtless (Ed.), *Family Economics Review, 5*(1), 34.

motivated toward parenthood, with the younger subjects being significantly more motivated than the older ones. Even though some individuals can achieve this sense of generativity in other ways, such as teaching or engaging in social services, parenthood appears to be the primary vehicle.

Another explanation for the high level of motivation to become parents is that individuals' attitudes toward parenthood have significant early antecedents. These attitudes are present long before one is able to have children. The reasons people may verbalize regarding the desire to be parents are likely to be closely associated with the experiences they had as children.

The subjects in the Gerson et al. (1991) study saw parenthood as a way to contribute to society, achieve immortality, experience love and life's fuller meaning, remember and reexperience their own childhood, achieve sex-role fulfillment, fulfill the desire to nurture, stimulate feelings of pride, and achieve personal growth. Further, parenthood was viewed as insurance during old age and as beneficial to the husband-wife partnership. Brooks (1991) reported on a survey that indicated the most frequent reason for having children given by men and women, parents, and nonparents, of all ethnic backgrounds, was a desire for love, interpersonal satisfactions, and close ties to others. A child was

seen as a defense against loneliness, isolation, and anonymity.

Transition to Parenthood.   Throughout life, individuals enter a state of transition, moving from the developmental stage of childhood to adolescence, from youth to adult status, from single to married, from married to single, from a nonparent to a parent, and so on. To say the least, life will never be the same after the birth of a baby. An old way of life must be ended and a new one begun. In some research on the process of becoming a parent, new parenthood has been conceptualized as a crisis. More recent research has viewed the addition of a baby to a couple's life as a transition rather than as a crisis.

The transition to parenthood is widely recognized to be a time of dynamic change in the family system. Cowan and Cowan (1995), in an extensive review of the literature, concluded with confidence that the transition to parenthood constitutes a period of stressful and sometimes maladaptive change for a significant proportion of new parents. It is clear that a substantial number of new mothers and an unknown number of new fathers are in acute emotional distress during the family-formation period. The Cowans found that 30 percent of both mothers and fathers experienced symptoms of depression and negative mood and that postpartum distress continued for some years. Kalmuss, Davidson, and Cushman (1992) found that one-fourth of their sample of new mothers experienced a difficult transition to parenthood. Respondents were the most negative about the amount of stress in their everyday lives; nearly two-thirds of these new mothers reported experiencing some or a great deal of stress.

Cowan and Cowan (1995) proposed that significant changes occur in each of five family domains: the quality of the new parents' family of origin, the quality of the new parents' relationship as a couple, the quality of the relationship that each parent develops with the infant, the balance between life stress and social support in the new family, and the well-being or distress of each parent and child as an individual. Inner psychological and interpersonal changes in both partners' relationship with their parents occur; sometimes these changes result in closer relationships and sometimes in more distant ones. The new family becomes organized around each parent's relationship with the child, and the quality of this relationship changes quickly, especially in the early months after childbirth. New mothers and fathers describe shifts in their friendship networks and their connection to work outside the home that make it increasingly difficult to juggle the competing demands of work and family life or to preserve time for friendship and leisure. Although some theorists have claimed that personality changes accompany the transition to parenthood, few studies have examined this claim. More certainly, the onset of parenthood brings with it not only a new identity as parent but also a rearrangement of parents' investment in their other roles—son/daughter, partner, lover, worker, friend.

The early postpartum period involves significant changes in daily routines, performance of unfamiliar tasks, and increased fatigue (Alexander & Higgins, 1993). Time has been mentioned by parents as the most changed aspect of life following the birth of a baby. Parents complain about their lives being more hectic and find that sleep time, television time, communication time, sex time, and even bathroom time are in short supply. The transition to parenthood makes family members more aware of their schedules. What has been taken for granted can no longer be. The new parents are much more aware of the clock, which, in turn, makes them feel that they are constantly running out of time. The degree of commitment to performing certain tasks also is a factor in how new parents perceive time. An overcommitment to motherhood, "being consumed" by the baby and the house, would cause the new mother to feel overwhelmed by a lack of time. The addition of a new child demands a new balance among work, home life, social life, and married life.

Kalmuss and associates (1992) examined the violated parenting expectations of a group of women birthing their first child. The women were interviewed before birth and again at 1 year postbirth. The results indicated that the women's expectations about how parenting would affect their lives and how they would fare in the maternal role did not match their experiences. In general, women expected things to be better at 1 year postbirth than they were. These discrepancies significantly affected the ease of adjustment to motherhood. Adjustment was more difficult when expectations exceeded experience in the following domains: relationship with spouse, physical well-being, maternal competence, and maternal satisfaction. In addition, high expectations regarding child-care assistance from the spouse and support from the extended family were associated with a more difficult period of adjustment to parenthood regardless of the amount of support actually received.

The effect of a new baby on the marital relationship and the differences between the perceptions of husbands and wives has received considerable attention (Belsky, Youngblade, Rovine, & Volling, 1991; Cowan & Cowan, 1995; Hock, Schirtzinger, Lutz, & Widaman, 1995). The parental role is highly compelling; one's sense of self as parent increases, especially for women from pregnancy to more than a year after childbirth, and the salience of other roles, such as marriage partner, decreases (Alexander & Higgins, 1993). These researchers found that following the birth of the baby, feelings of love for the spouse decline, ambivalence about the marriage increases, communication decreases, marital satisfaction decreases, and conflicts increase.

Cowan and Cowan (1995) found significantly more negative changes in the marital relationships of new parents than in those of childless couples, and decline in marital quality was greater in older, longer-married new-parent couples. Negative changes in marital quality seem to be experienced by a significant proportion of couples—as high as 59 percent in some studies. Some evidence indicates that the peak of marital adjustment is at 1 month postpartum and that by 6 months changes in the relationship are apparent. This decline continues for the first 2 or 3 years following the birth and is experienced by both husbands and wives, with wives displaying a higher marital adjustment than husbands (Wallace & Gotlib, 1990). At least 20 research studies in different locales have replicated findings of conflict and decline in marital satisfaction during the transition to parenthood (Cowan & Cowan, 1995).

The most serious effect of decline in marital adjustment is on the parent-infant relationship.

Belsky et al. (1991) found that father behavior and especially child behavior with the father were affected by marital change. Neutral or positive marital change in the case of husbands was associated with positive child behavior and positive and facilitative paternal behavior, whereas marital decline was associated with intrusive fathering and negative child behavior. Spousal conflict was associated with negative child behavior during mother-infant interactions. Belsky and Rovine (1990) found that women whose love declined and whose ambivalence and experience of conflict increased described their babies at 3 months as being more irregular in their daily rhythms of eating and sleeping than those who reported that their marriage had improved following the birth of the baby. Data indicate, however, that mother-infant relationships are not as likely to be negatively affected by a decline in marital satisfaction as father-infant interactions, suggesting that women may be more able than men to maintain boundaries between their relationship with their spouse and that with their children.

Hock et al. (1995) found that women with high levels of depression during pregnancy also

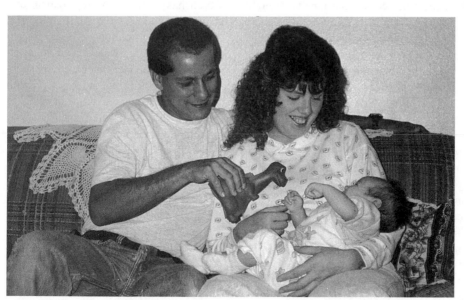

The transition to parenthood represents a dynamic change in the family system.

had the highest levels of depression when their infants were 9 months of age. Further, they found that both low marital satisfaction and more traditional sex-role attitudes with regard to marriage roles were risk factors for depressive symptoms. Alexander and Higgins (1993) found that women embracing a traditional role were more likely to think about themselves, including their role as spouse, in terms of their social responsibilities, and they experienced less marital stress than nontraditional women after becoming parents. In contrast, nontraditional women who emphasized their personal aspirations and their own ideals found that becoming a parent disrupted the attainment of preparenthood personal goals. Thus, they were more likely than traditional women to experience dejection-related suffering after childbirth, especially if they had been married a long time before the onset of parenthood and/or had a difficult child.

Cowan and Cowan (1995) noted that a baby's arrival is unlikely to destroy extremely well functioning marriages *or* to generate closer, more satisfying relationships between already troubled partners. They concluded that parents' individual symptoms, life stress, social support, and marital adjustment measured before birth account for a substantial portion of the variance in both men's and women's adaptation to parenthood. Particularly at risk for a difficult transition to parenthood are parents who already are troubled before the onset of parenthood, teenagers becoming parents, and families struggling with the added stress of living in poverty or having a child with medical or psychiatric disabilities. It is important to note that parents' well-being or distress during the family-making period is a precursor of their children's academic achievement, success with peers, and behavior problems in elementary school.

Few studies have included the role of the infant in the transition to parenthood, but it has been assumed that the infant contributes equal stress to both parents. Infant crying, irritability, and colic have been linked to depression, helplessness, anger, exhaustion, and rejection of the infant (Isabella & Belsky, 1985; Wilkie & Ames, 1986). Clearly it is logical to assume that the feelings and behaviors a passive, easy-to-soothe, cuddly baby elicits from his parents are very different from those elicited by a crying, difficult-to-satisfy baby. Interestingly, Wilkie and Ames found that infant crying had a greater effect on fathers than on mothers. Infant crying caused mothers to rate their infants more negatively, but crying did not affect mothers' feelings of adequacy. For fathers, however, infant crying was associated with greater anxiety, more concern about lifestyle changes, and rating themselves and their wives as low in potency.

Satisfaction with Parenthood.   As noted earlier, a large percentage of people desire to and do become parents. It can be assumed that those who deliberately decide to have children anticipate the rewards to outweigh the costs and the satisfactions to surpass the dissatisfactions, making the long, arduous, and challenging efforts of parenting personally worthwhile (Thoits, 1992). Nearly all Americans choose parenthood in spite of the continuous flow of evidence that suggests that the expected lofty satisfactions often remain unfulfilled.

Research on role identity demonstrates that parenthood is more salient than marriage and employment as a source of identity. Whereas considerable research has focused on employment and marital satisfaction and on the parent-child relationship, relatively little attention has been given to satisfaction with parenting. This lack of attention might be attributed to the fact that parenting satisfaction is less likely than marital or job satisfaction to predict role tenure (Rogers & White, 1998).

Variables that have been found consistently to relate to parenthood satisfaction may be found in the Highlights. These include parental gender, degree of commitment to the role, certain child characteristics, marital satisfaction of both parents, educational level, and family structure.

When examining satisfaction with parenthood in three family structures (first-married biological parents, remarried parents with biological children, and stepparents), Ishii-Kuntz and Ihinger-Tallman (1991) found substantial differences among the three groups. First-married biological parents expressed the most parental satisfaction, followed by

HIGHLIGHTS

Satisfaction with Parenthood

VARIABLE	FINDINGS
Role commitment	Parents more committed to the role of parenting receive greater satisfaction than those less committed.
Role overload	Multiple roles (wife, mother, employee) create stress and reduce satisfaction.
Role orientation (traditional vs. modern)	Parents who view themselves in the traditional, authoritarian parental role may experience greater satisfaction than those who evaluate their adequacy according to the more modern role, which emphasizes interpersonal warmth and tolerance.
Gender of parent	Women may experience greater parental role fulfillment than men do, but they also perceive parenthood to be more restrictive and burdensome.
Educational attainment	Level of education may be correlated negatively with parental satisfaction. The better educated tend to acknowledge the negative aspects of parenthood more often than the less educated do. Parenthood does not appear to be the pivotal focus of life for those with college educations as it is for those with less education.
Marital satisfaction	Greater marital satisfaction usually leads to greater satisfaction with parenthood. This relationship is more significant for men than for women.
Income	Greater economic resources lead to greater satisfaction with parenthood.
Employment status	For women, preferred work or nonwork roles may influence the degree of satisfaction with the maternal role. Women who achieve desired employment status may experience greater satisfaction than those unable to do so.
Marital status	Simple biological parents usually express the greatest satisfaction, followed by single parents, with stepfamilies expressing the least satisfaction.
Age at parental onset	Older, more mature parents tend to report higher levels of parental satisfaction.
Child characteristics	
Biological vs. step	Parents living with their biological children are more satisfied than those in remarried families. Stepmothers report lower satisfaction than stepfathers.
Age and number	More children and the presence of preschool children are associated with lower satisfaction.
Living arrangements	Satisfaction is higher when parents live in the same household with their biological children.
Personality and health	Satisfaction is lower if children are difficult or have severe health problems.
Stage in life cycle	The first stage of parenting, representing the transition from nonparenting, seems to be the most intense for both positive and negative effects. Parents report the greatest degree of satisfaction during the earliest stage of parenthood and the least satisfaction in the stages when children are adolescents and adults.

Source: Adapted from Goetting, A. (1986). Parental satisfaction. *Journal of Family Issues, 7*(1), 83–109; Rogers, S., & White, L. (1998). Satisfaction with parenting: The role of marital happiness, family structure, and parents' gender. *Psychological Quarterly, 55,* 236–256.

remarried biological parents. Stepparents experienced the lowest satisfaction with parenthood.

Recent studies on satisfaction with parenthood have reinforced findings from earlier research. Using data from a nationally representative sample, Rogers and White (1998) found that marital happiness was the strongest predictor of parenting satisfaction. Respondents with noncustodial minor children and parents of stepchildren reported significantly less parental satisfaction than biological parents who resided with their children. Fathers reported significantly lower parental satisfaction than mothers. Contact with one's own parents did not affect satisfaction with parenting.

These researchers also found that the positive effect of marital happiness was significantly stronger for men than for women. Their findings supported the fact that satisfaction varies with family structure. However, this study differed from previous studies in that single parents reported lower parental satisfaction than stepparents, and stepfathers were more dissatisfied than stepmothers. Having more children in the household was associated with lower parental satisfaction, but having male children increased fathers' satisfaction. The authors concluded that parental satisfaction was most affected by three factors—marital happiness, family structure, and parents' gender—that have both independent and interactive effects on satisfaction. To a lesser extent, satisfaction was related to the number and age of children, parents' social class, and parental employment patterns.

Although most studies have shown that marital happiness is an important variable in parental satisfaction, Kurdek (1996), in a longitudinal study, found little evidence of spillover effects between the two. He concluded that parenting satisfaction and marital satisfaction are distinct from each other and may be unrelated because satisfaction with each role involves nonoverlapping sets of perceived rewards, perceived costs, and expectations. Although fathers and mothers in this study did not differ in their levels of parenting satisfaction, they did show different patterns of change. Fathers, particularly, showed low parental satisfaction during the child's infancy but recovered

quickly, whereas mothers reported decreases in parental satisfaction through 3 years postpartum.

Delayed Parenthood.   Women are waiting longer to initiate parenthood. As noted in Table 1.2, births to women younger than 30 have gradually declined, and births to women from 30 to 45 have increased significantly since 1980 (U.S. Bureau of the Census, 1997). With the help of contraceptives, women are able to select the time they initiate childbirth and child rearing. Although data on first births for men have not been collected in national surveys, the data on total first births indicate that the age of first fatherhood also has increased (Garrison, Blalock, Zarski, & Merritt, 1997).

Factors that potentially contribute to these trends may include the following: demographics (declining fertility rate, postponement of marriage, marital dissolution rate, increase in childlessness); medical issues (reliable contraception and painless sterilization, sophisticated infertility treatments, better prenatal and neonatal care, greater acceptance of midlife pregnancy by the medical community); political events (the civil rights movement, the women's movement); educational opportunities (more education and labor-force participation, particularly for women); economic issues (unemployment, recurrent recessions, and a decrease in real income); and antinatalist forces and changing societal attitudes and values. Demographic information indicates that in the United States, age and timing patterns of first parenthood differ by characteristics such as gender, race, social class, and geographic region, with (a) men becoming parents later than women, and (b) rural, poor people of Black or Hispanic origin becoming parents sooner than urban, more affluent people of White or Asian origin (Garrison et al., 1997).

Gerson and associates (1991) found that older women experience the same amount of apprehension as younger women in anticipating the demands of parenthood and careers. They concluded that the recent trend toward delayed parenthood may not necessarily reflect the right time to have children, but the last time possible. Even though it is more difficult for older women to successfully

TABLE 1.2   First Births and Age*

AGE	1980	1991	1992	1993	1994
10–14 years	1.1	1.4	1.4	1.4	1.4
15–19 years	53.0	62.1	60.1	59.6	58.9
20–24 years	115.1	115.9	114.6	112.6	111.1
25–29 years	112.9	118.2	117.4	115.5	113.9
30–34 years	61.9	79.5	80.2	80.8	81.5
35–39 years	19.8	32.0	32.5	32.9	33.7
40–45 years	3.9	5.5	5.9	6.1	6.4
45–49 years	0.2	0.2	0.3	0.3	0.3

Source: U.S. Bureau of the Census. (1997). *Statistical abstract of the United States: 1997* (117th ed.). Washington, DC: U.S. Government Printing Office.
*Per 1,000 women.

conceive and the risk of both miscarriage and malformations increases in cases of spontaneous conception, with proper screening there is little obstetric risk in pregnancies resulting from donor oocytes. Further, there is little evidence to support an increase in obstetric or perinatal mortality if pregnancy is successfully established in women in their late thirties (Bowman & Saunders, 1995).

Garrison et al. (1997) assessed 69 families in which mothers had their first child after the age of 35 and found that, with few exceptions, parents who delayed childbearing were more satisfied and less stressed and reported better functioning than mothers who conceived early. Perhaps adults who delay parenthood are better prepared to be parents and adapt more easily to parenthood; or, it may be that parents who delay parenthood have different expectations, and these expectations moderate their experiences. The parents in this study had notably higher levels of educational attainment and somewhat higher family incomes than parents in the general population. These researchers concluded that there is no conclusive evidence that parental age, in and of itself, predicts the manner in which a couple tends to experience parenthood.

Whereas the impact of delayed motherhood has been examined by many scholars during the last decade, fewer researchers have focused on the impact of delayed fatherhood. Heath (1994) compared father-child relationships of late-time fathers (older than 35 at child's first birth) and on-time fathers. Late-time fathers were found to spend more time in leisure activities with their children, to have higher expectations for their children's behavior, and to be more nurturant toward their children. These fathers also had fewer total children, more marriages, and significantly greater incomes than on-time fathers, but they did not differ in educational level or socioeconomic status. This researcher concluded that late parenthood may be beneficial for children and their fathers.

Parenting

The term *parenting,* which has become rather common, is one to which some object. Strict grammarians object because a noun has been made into a verb; others object because a social relationship is made to sound like a motor or technical skill—something that can be taught and practiced, that can be analyzed and improved—such as knitting or table manners. The concept of parenting has been defined as the process or the state of being a parent (Brooks, 1991). Brooks pointed out that parenting is a process that includes nourishing, protecting, and guiding the child through the course of development. In this process, parenting is a continuous series of interactions between parent and child, and these interactions change both partners. This process or state of being has been extended to actions performed by a variety of people—parents, siblings, peers, relatives, teachers, friends, and others—that influence and guide the physical, social, emotional, and intellectual development of individuals. These actions result in a nurturing and caring relationship between human beings, whatever their age or kinship.

Mothering.   Although parenting has been defined as the process or state of being a parent, the processes of mothering and fathering have traditionally been somewhat different. Dictionaries have produced some interesting concepts of mothering, ranging from "the biological process of giving birth" to "exercising control over and responsibility for one's young." The phrase "exhibiting kindliness and affection" and vague references to "demonstrating the qualities of a mother" also appear. Mothering, then, may be viewed as simply possessing the biological and/or legal status of mother, the process of performing a social role, or engaging in behavior that facilitates the growth and development of one's children. Obviously each of these concepts has vastly different implications. Nevertheless, there is nothing simple or straightforward about mothering.

Oberman and Josselson (1996) suggested that mothers struggle to balance a set of polarities/tensions: loss of self versus expansion of self; omnipotence versus liability; life-destroying versus life-promoting behavior; maternal isolation versus maternal community; cognitive strategies versus intuitive responses; and maternal desexualization versus maternal sexualization. Although women often experience increased self-esteem as a result of becoming mothers, they may be ambivalent about the loss of some aspects of their former lives. Motherhood requires the adjustment of identity. Further, coming to terms with the omnipotence of the motherhood myth may be a struggle. Maternal power is felt as a woman meets the needs of a helpless infant, but at the same time, it may be a burden. Most new mothers are not completely isolated, but becoming totally immersed in a maternal community can occur at the other extreme. Motherhood also encompasses the extremes of using cognitive strategies to provide for the protection and care of the child and making decisions based on intuition and emotion. These modes of reacting to children are sustained throughout the mothering experience. Hence, mothers experience these and other conflicting emotions on a continuous basis as they go about their daily activities of caregiving.

However one chooses to conceptualize the term, it seems reasonable to assume that optimal mothering contributes to the optimal development of children. Competent infants are likely to have mothers who are conscious of their role in providing for their children's intellectual and social needs and who provide them with more than nurturant physical care.

Historically, the Madonna/child image that implies a cultural ideal of a unique dyadic relationship between mother and child has been prevalent. For some this dyad represents an instinctive drive or a biologically predestined relationship, with the implication that mothering is a "natural" phenomenon. Although this notion is currently rejected by most sociologists, psychologists, and biologists, there still remains a certain mystique with respect to the exclusiveness of the mother-child relationship. The biological fact of female pregnancy and childbirth contributes to the greater emphasis on mothering as opposed to fathering. Researchers stress that mothering, particularly in some cultures, is the primary role for which females have been socialized. Mothering as one of life's roles remains significant for women and for their children, but our conceptions of mothering have changed. Nonetheless, the role remains charged with guilt and surrounded by controversy, both stemming from children's dependency and great need for maternal care.

In the past, mothers, especially those employed full-time, were blamed for most of their children's emotional ills. In light of the women's liberation movement, the large number of mothers in the workforce, and the increase in the number of single and adolescent mothers, one wonders why, if the blame is warranted, we do not have a nation of neurotic children. Nevertheless, there is ample evidence to support the notion that the mother's role is a critical factor in the child's overall development, especially during the early years. One should be aware, however, that competence in children almost certainly has multiple causes and that there appear to be few absolutes in mothering. Numerous genetic and environmental factors impinge on the mother-child relationship. Research, however, does suggest that there are certain behavioral and attitudinal traits of mothers and certain environmental conditions that mothers can provide to enhance the optimal development and competence of their children.

Research Related to Mothering.   Much of the literature of the 1970s and 1980s related to mothering and its effects on children emphasized mothering during infancy, especially the process of attachment. The work of Klaus and Kennell (1982) described the development of attachment from mother to infant:

> *This original parent-infant tie is the major source for all the infant's subsequent attachments and is the formative relationship in the course of which the child develops a sense of himself. Throughout his lifetime the strength and character of this attachment will influence the quality of all future bonds to other individuals. (p. 3)*

Klaus and Kennell contended that the following principles contribute to the mother's attachment to her infant: close skin-to-skin contact with the infant for the first 45–60 minutes after birth; the infant's response to the mother by some signal, such as body or eye movement; witness of the birth process by mothers in a state of alertness; and the difficulty a mother has attaching herself to an infant when she is under stress.

The healthy bonding process of mothers to infants seems to make possible a healthy attachment of infant to mother. In some of the now classic studies on attachment, it was reported that an infant became optimally attached to only one person at a time (the concept of monotropy) and that person was usually the mother. The literature emphasized the dangers of separation of mother and infant, especially during the last half of the first year, when the attachment process was paramount in the child's development. There was disagreement as to the extent of harm a child would experience as a result of prolonged separation and whether this harm would be temporary or permanent. As infant child care became a necessity, one of the primary criticisms was that placing an infant in substitute care would interrupt the attachment process, and some authors equated it with the devastating effects of prolonged or total separation. Subsequent studies, however, examined other factors, such as the time and duration of separation, the quality of care received by the child, and the possibility of multiple attachments. These studies found essentially no differences in child-mother and mother-child attachment patterns between home-reared and day-care infants. In the 1990s the issue of the impact of early and prolonged out-of-the-home infant care on infant-mother attachment resurfaced (Belsky, 1991). Some researchers once again contended that out-of-home care of more than 20 hours per week is related to insecure attachment, but there is lack of consensus among experts regarding this issue. (See Chapter 12.)

Although the issue of the impact of prolonged out-of-home care on the infant-mother attachment may never be resolved fully, the topic of attachment has generated significant research, as well as theoretical controversy for the last 25 years. A significant amount of the research consistently has linked maternal sensitivity in the first year to child security. Evidence from numerous studies indicates that security is associated with prompt responsiveness to distress, moderate and appropriate stimulation, and interactional synchrony, as well as warmth, involvement, and responsiveness. Insecure attachments are related to intrusive, excessively stimulating interactional styles or to unresponsive, underinvolved caregiving. These findings have been generated from samples of a variety of family types.

Apparently, the security of attachment during infancy has long-range implications. Longitudinal research indicates that secure infants differ from their insecure counterparts as they grow up. Preschool children with secure-attachment histories were found to be more skilled in solving challenging problems, seeking maternal assistance in the face of challenges, and tolerating frustration. Further, in a nursery setting, 3-year-olds with secure-attachment histories were found to exhibit more peer leadership and less social withdrawal and hesitation, greater self-confidence and curiosity about new things, and more sympathy to the distress of others than agemates judged earlier to be insecure in their relationships with their mothers. Another study showed that 4- and 5-year-olds, previously rated securely attached, were rated by their teachers as more competent with peers and more liked by their classmates. Later, when secure infants entered school, it was found that they were less likely to be judged by parents and/or teachers to have serious behavior problems than children with insecure-attachment histories. It was concluded by Belsky (1991) that the data, in the main, consistently document associations between early infant-mother attachment security and subsequent competence. Belsky (1991) cautioned, however, that infant-mother relationship patterns cannot be assumed to function independently of subsequent relationship experiences. Mother-child relationships established in infancy are mediated, at least in part, by ongoing experiences with the mother and with others. Preschoolers with secure-infant histories who did not receive continued maternal support and school-age children with negative environmental factors (such as stress, few friends) were likely to develop behavior problems. In other words, continuity from early relationship history to subsequent socioemotional functioning was a function of intervening social experiences.

Particularly impressive is the evidence that high levels of observed maternal positive involvement (affectionate contact, verbal stimulation) during the first 2 years of life forecast low levels of mother-reported behavior problems at age 4, and the data demonstrating that maternal acceptance and responsiveness during the infant and toddler years predict high levels of consideration at age 10 (Belsky, 1991). The findings that third graders who experienced rejecting, authoritarian parental care and/or who failed to identify with their parents had higher levels of depression at age 19 and evidenced lower levels of ego development when followed up at age 30–31 clearly suggest that the effects of emotionally supportive and unsupportive care may extend well beyond childhood (Dubow, Huesmann, & Eron, 1987).

Research has suggested further that the seeds of compliance, cooperation, or antisocial behavior are sown in early childhood. For example, in one study, mothers of preschoolers who proactively engaged their young children in interesting materials before they started to play with off-limits objects induced more compliance than did mothers who simply rejected in every instance their children's handling something that was forbidden (Holden & West, 1989). Parpal and Maccoby (1985) found that when mothers followed the children's lead by responding to what they did, greater compliance subsequently resulted than when they simply engaged in free play in which the mother was more directive and less responsive. Rocissano, Slade, and Lynch (1987) found that mothers who were skilled in following their toddlers' leads in play and thus fostered more synchronous exchanges had children who were more responsive to and compliant with maternal directions. Mothers who engaged in direct control strategies and frequently reprimanded their preschoolers were more likely to have children who defied them, whereas agemates whose mothers used indirect and persuasive strategies (such as indirect commands and explanations) were more likely to negotiate with their mothers in the face of conflict (Kuczynski, Kochanska, Rodke-Yarrow, & Girniss-Brown, 1987). Considered together, these studies and others suggest that age-appropriate, sensitive care that fosters long-term harmony in adult-child relationships and maintains children's inherent motivation to attend to and cooperate with the desires of adults, especially parents, reduces the likelihood of noncompliant behavior, aggression with peers, low self-esteem, and academic problems as the child reaches school age and adolescence.

Mothers also seem to be important in language development. Research shows that the words mothers speak to their young children are picked up by them. Morphemes that are more frequent in the mother's language and acoustically distinct to the child appear earlier than usual in the child's speech. This suggests that young children are tuned in to the qualities of "motherese"—the special speech register adults use when talking to children, consisting of short simple sentences, frequent repetitions, high pitch and exaggerated pitch contours, and emphasis on the here and now. Researchers have found significant correlations between children's language gain and mothers' verbal input (number of utterances, noun phrases per utterance, number and percent of "wh——" questions, and other kinds of questions and directives), verbal prodding (accepting the child's language and asking questions that demand sentences as answers), and simple expansions of children's utterances (Clarke-Stewart, 1988).

Mothers' knowledge about child development and concepts of child rearing appear to have positive outcomes for children. Benasich and Brooks-Gunn (1996) conducted a longitudinal study of low-birth-weight, preterm infants to determine the effects of maternal knowledge of child development and concepts of child rearing on the quality of the home environment and child cognitive and behavioral outcomes. Data were gathered at birth and when the children were 12, 24, and 36 months of age. Overall, measures of maternal knowledge of child development and concepts of child rearing at 12 months were found to predict home environment, number of child behavior problems, and child IQ at 36 months to a small but significant extent. Data revealed that maternal knowledge was associated with home environment over and above socioeconomic status and that maternal knowledge continued to be important in the structuring of the environment when the child was 3 years old. These data suggested that maternal knowledge about child development and concepts of child rearing provides a pathway through which the home environment is structured by the mother, which, in turn, influences child outcomes. Maternal characteristics such as more education, higher income, and fewer children in the household predicted the quality of the home environment. Overall, the data

suggested that the causal chain from maternal beliefs and home environment to cognitive and behavioral outcomes might vary as a function of ethnocultural systems.

It is important to note that researchers cannot make simple generalizations about a mother's influence on her child's development. More recent research indicates that parents' effects on children's development are complex. Further, the child herself and the socioemotional climate in the family interact to mediate parents' effects.

The Reciprocal Nature of Mothering. Perhaps the most important point regarding mothering is that maternal behaviors at every age level of the child are affected by the child's behavior and temperament—in other words, the relationship is always reciprocal. Classic research demonstrates

---

HIGHLIGHTS

Positive Characteristics of Mothering

INFANCY/TODDLERHOOD

> Healthy bonding
> Nurturance
> Acceptance
> Sensitivity
> Consistent and prompt responsivity
> Provision of appropriate play materials
> Avoidance of restriction and punishment
> High degree of verbal and physical interaction

PRESCHOOL

> Nurturance
> Acceptance
> Sensitivity
> Allowance of exploration/expression
> Reasoning and inductive discipline
> Use of elaborated language and teaching
> strategies
> Setting limits

SCHOOL AGE

> Nurturance but not restrictiveness
> Stimulation but not directiveness
> Responsiveness but not control

that infants differ from the moment of birth, as demonstrated when they were observed in hospital nurseries before environmental influences become so apparent (Brazelton, 1969; Chess & Thomas, 1973). Some cry a lot; others cry little. Some are easy to soothe; others are difficult. Some eat and sleep well; others seem to demonstrate rhythmicity only with great effort. Picture the mother of an "easy" baby who cries little, sleeps soundly, is socially responsive, and generally thrives. If she is awakened only once a night to feed and manages to get her chores done while the baby is sleeping, it appears obvious that she will have energy and enthusiasm for mothering and will interact with her baby in generally positive ways. Compare that picture with one of a mother who is awakened at midnight, 2:00 A.M., and 4:00 A.M. for feedings. Even after feeding, the baby continues to cry. Rocking, walking, singing, and patting do not seem to help. She becomes anxious and communicates that anxiety to her infant through her tone of voice, rigid body, and facial expressions. A vicious circle is set in motion, and her maternal behavior will be far from enthusiastic or energetic.

One final point should be made. Every reference to mothering or maternal behaviors in this section need not apply to only the biological or adoptive mother. Grandmothers, baby-sitters, child-care workers, nurses, and friends can all be effective "mothers." It would seem that all the variables of maternal behavior apply to both full-time and employed mothers and to the substitute caregivers as well.

A mother's love for her child is not necessarily a given. A variety of possible conditions are likely to affect mothering, including personality factors, such as depression, anxiety, mental illness, and simply insensitivity; environmental conditions, such as poverty, unemployment, and poor health; hormonal influences that occur in conjunction with childbirth; ignorance or lack of factual information concerning the development and behavior of children; and, most important, the mother's own developmental history of being mothered herself.

Research indicates that the quality of care mothers provide is related to their experiences in their own families of origin. Those who are secure in their relationships with their own parents are likely to rear infants who develop secure attachments to them, and are likely to provide emotional support and assistance when interacting with their young children. For a more in-depth discussion of the factors affecting mothering, see the section on Determinants of Parenting later in this chapter.

It is appropriate to destroy the motherhood myth that all normal women instinctively want, need, and will enjoy having children and that they are psychologically, mentally, and technically equipped to rear them. Probably the most important variable in mothering is the desire to be a mother and the satisfaction derived from it. The choice is available to most women and should be exercised. Many women today who are engaged in mothering do not value highly what they are doing, and it is abundantly clear to them that no one else values it either. If mothering is to achieve the status it deserves, mothers must be mothers by choice and not by cultural compulsion or accident. They must be provided with the tools needed to meet the responsibility with which they have been charged. They must be provided with an understanding of child development and emotional assistance that enables them to accept their own feelings and guide the behavior of their children in constructive ways.

Fathering.   Traditionally, *fathering* has been referred to in the context of being a biological contributor to the formation of a human organism. Even today dictionaries use *father* as a figurative definition for *creator* or *originator.* The conceptualization of the paternal role over the past century has occurred in three phases: the father as a breadwinner (before the 1940s); the father as a sex-role model (mid-1940s to mid-1970s); and the nurturant father (mid-1970s to the present). The perspective on fathering that emerged in the 1970s emphasized the notion that men are psychologically able to participate in the full range of parenting behaviors and described the benefits that would be derived by both parents and children if fathers took active roles in child care and child rearing. From this perspective, fathering, like mothering, must be viewed as a complex interactive process occurring between at least two people and influenced by a variety of genetic and environmental factors.

Goodnough and Lee (1996) noted that the traditional role for fathers remains pervasive, and the results of the Ivey (1995) study support this conclusion. Practicing counselors, social workers, psychiatrists, and psychologists were asked to rate two videotaped interviews—one that demonstrated a matriarchal style of family interaction and the other, a patriarchal style. Participants' perceptions of family functioning were lower for the mother-led families than for the father-led families. Fathers in patriarchal families were viewed as healthier than fathers in matriarchal families, especially by the practitioners with family histories of attitudes favoring elevated parental control of children.

Even though current research has begun to focus on face-to-face interactions with children, it is clear that the father's interactions with his children are tied to his success—real or perceived—as the breadwinner. It appears that feelings of failure in the breadwinning role are associated with demoralization for fathers, which causes relationships with children to deteriorate. It was not until the last quarter of the twentieth century that the term *fathering* began to appear in the literature in the context of a more direct psychological and physical role in the rearing of children. However, the emerging ideal of fatherhood for the twenty-first century is that fathers are equal co-parents (Doherty, Kouneski, & Kouneski, 1998).

McBride and Rane (1998) noted that fathers' roles in rearing their young children held the interest of researchers, practitioners, and families alike as the 1990s came to an end. Doherty et al. (1998) described a variety of influences on fathering, which include individual characteristics of fathers, mothers, and children; mother-father relationship variables; and larger contextual variables in the environment. See Highlights.

The new male parenting image has been labeled variously as the involved father, the nurturing father, and the emergent father (Goodnough & Lee, 1996), illustrating the growing perceptions and depictions of men both as inherently nurturant and as competent in nurturing roles. Further, research indicates that nurturant, competent involvement can have a positive impact on various aspects of development for children. Self-esteem, cognitive functioning, social competence, perception of body image, and adolescent and adult adjustment all seem to be positively affected by nurturant fathering. Overall, the existing literature suggests that the fathering role is in the midst of change. Whereas some men remain traditionalists, a growing number of others are more nurturant and involved while maintaining a secondary or "helping" role, and still others are committed to a fully involved and nurturing role in the development of their children.

Many fathers become involved with their children even before birth. The father's preparation for childbirth and his participation in labor and delivery has been an important change in the perspective on fathering. The long-term effects of preparation for childbirth and participation in labor and delivery on paternal attitudes and behavior have yet to be established. Only future longitudinal studies that include observations of fathers interacting with their children in naturalistic settings will provide these insights. The available evidence strongly suggests that there are at least significant short-term advantages for the father and the child as well as for the mother.

Research over the last two decades has noted several differences between mothering and fathering during the infancy period. Fathers spend considerably less time on the average with infants than mothers do, and this decreased time includes less one-on-one interaction, less accessibility, and less responsibility for the infant's care (Lamb & Oppenheim, 1989). When with their infants, mothers and fathers differ in their interactions. Mothers' interactions typically involve caretaking, but fathers' interactions typically involve play. Moreover, fathers play in a more physical, idiosyncratic, and emotionally arousing way, whereas mothers tend to play in ways that are less arousing, more verbal, and more often involve toys and conventional games such as peek-a-boo (Bridges, Connell, & Belsky, 1988).

Factors That Influence Fathering

CONTEXTUAL FACTORS

Institutional practices	Employment opportunities	Economics
Race/ethnicity	Resources and challenges	Cultural expectations
Social support		

FATHER FACTORS

Role identification	Employment characteristics	Skills
Commitment	Psychological well-being	Relations with own father
Knowledge		Residential status

CHILD FACTORS

Attitude toward father	Behavioral difficulties	Temperament
Gender	Age	Developmental status

MOTHER FACTORS

Attitude toward father	Employment characteristics	Support of father
Expectations of father		

CO-PARENTAL RELATIONSHIPS

Marital status	Dual vs. single earner	Mutual support
Custodial arrangements	Relationship commitment	Conflict
Cooperation		

Source: Doherty, W., Kouneski, E., & Kouneski, M. (1998). Responsible fathering: An overview and conceptual framework. *Journal of Marriage and the Family, 60,* 277–292.

Other research has provided evidence that fathers are as capable of providing care for infants as mothers are (Cox, Owen, Henderson, & Margand, 1992). However, even when fathers are involved in caretaking, differences persist between mothers and fathers. Fathers are less likely to hold, tend to, show affection toward, smile at, and vocalize to their infants whether they are highly involved in caretaking or not. Perhaps for this reason, infants show preferences for their mothers on attachment measures even though the fathers are highly involved in caretaking (Lamb & Oppenheim, 1989). When distressed, infants tend to direct more attachment-related behaviors (prox-

imity seeking and contact seeking) toward their mothers.

However, infants tend to direct more playful distal behaviors toward their fathers than toward their mothers. Such patterns of infant behavior suggest that the roles of attachment figure and playmate are conceptually distinct. Data provide support for the contention that the infant-father relationship is more centrally concerned with affiliative needs than with attachment needs (i.e., felt security). The father, as socializer and playmate, provides the infant with social and cognitive stimulation that is qualitatively distinct from that provided by the mother (Bridges et al., 1988).

There is an emerging body of theoretical and empirical work suggesting that the father-child relationship is a particularly important influence on the child's social relationship outside the family. For example, paternal physical activity with preschool children was found to be related to the children's positive social attributes as reported by teachers, particularly for boys. Studies with other age groups have found that paternal characteristics are related to the emotional quality of social interactions between infants and strangers and later with important members of the adolescent's social networks. Fathers, in essence, teach their children how to "get along" with friends and strangers outside the family. Through physical play with the father, the child learns how to interpret the affective communications of the parent as well as how her own emotional signals influence the behavior of the parent. This ability to interpret affective behaviors of interactive patterns correctly and to influence others through emotional signals is considered to be a major source of social competence (Bridges et al., 1988).

Whereas most of the early research on fathering focused on the benefits of father involvement, considerable current research has examined various aspects of father involvement: amount of involvement, types of involvement, determinants of involvement, and beliefs concerning involvement. Most researchers agree that men's participation in child rearing has changed at a slow but minimal rate over the past 25 years—overall, fathers still spend only about one-third the time with children that mothers do. Men apparently do not perceive the unequal distribution of time as problematic unless or until their wives put pressure on them. Further, evidence indicates that mothers and fathers assign different meanings to time they spend with their children (Daly, 1996). The following studies describe various aspects of father involvement.

Fathers' participation in child rearing has been classified into three categories: *interaction,* which is the one-to-one father-child relationship in activities such as playing and feeding; *accessibility,* which is the father's physical and/or psychological availability when not directly interacting; and *responsibility,* in which the father assumes direct responsibility for the child's welfare, such as making child-care or baby-sitting arrangements or knowing when the child needs to go to the pediatrician. Being "responsible" does not necessarily include direct interaction with the child, but responsibility includes the concern and/or contingency planning that may occur when the father has a schedule conflict (Lamb, Pleck, Charnov, & Levine, 1987). This multidimensional view of paternal involvement has been influential in recent research on father involvement and has been accepted as including the critical dimensions of positive fathering.

Further, Lamb et al. (1988) proposed a four-component model of the determinants of father involvement: motivation, skills and self-confidence, support, and institutional factors. They noted that the psychological importance of work to the father's sense of identity, as well as the objective constraints associated with the workplace, may be crucial to his level of involvement. Fathers' attitudes toward parenting and work are important correlates of their involvement.

McBride and Rane (1997) examined the perceptions and attitudes of fathers and mothers about their own and their spouses' parental roles and the relationships between these perceptions and attitudes and variations in fathers' actual involvement in child rearing. Their results showed that fathers spent an average of 1.9 hours per workday and 3.8 hours per nonworkday interacting with their children, whereas mothers spent an average of 2.9 and 3.9 hours, respectively. Fathers were accessible to their children for an average of 4.4 hours on workdays and 9.3 hours on nonworkdays, whereas mothers were accessible for an average of 7.1 and 10.4 hours, respectively. Obviously, the men in this study participated significantly less than their wives in child-rearing activities, which suggests that these fathers may not be meeting increased societal expectations for active paternal involvement and equitable co-parenting.

Analyses suggested that fathers with more favorable attitudes toward the paternal role were more involved in child-rearing activities. Thus, these beliefs may have served as motivation and encouragement to enable them to overcome the external constraints of work roles in order to be involved. Further, mothers' perceptions of their husbands' role investments were more closely related to actual fathering behaviors than fathers' perceived role investments were, whereas both husbands' and wives' perceptions of wives' role investments were closely related to actual mothering behaviors.

Interestingly, a high percentage of both mothers and fathers in this study reported that paternal role expectations for men had changed in recent years, and they viewed this change as positive. Whereas more than 90 percent of the participants agreed that society's expectations for the maternal role have changed, only a small percentage of both fathers and mothers viewed this change as positive.

McBride and Rane (1998) found that certain aspects of the parent alliance predicted father involvement. Parenting alliance is the capacity of a parent to acknowledge, respect, and value the parenting role and tasks of the partner. Involvement was related to fathers' perceptions of their wives' confidence in their parenting skills, whether or not they shared similar parenting philosophies with their wives and regardless of their wives' emotional appraisal of their parenting. These researchers noted that results were strongly suggestive of maternal gatekeeping as a significant factor in regulating the amount of father involvement in direct child care and responsibility for their preschool children.

Daly (1996) examined the meaning of time for fathers based on their descriptions of time use with their children. An economy of time seemed to serve as the central organizing principle for the family aspects of the participating men. The following themes emerged: The "good" father is one who spends time with his children, and this belief is governed by the presence of a temporal conscience; family time is treated as a commodity that is produced and expended; fathers experience struggles in their efforts to control family time. These men appeared to be caught in a dialectical

tension between wanting to spend time with their children and a set of ongoing time constraints that limited their ability to do so.

Fathers seem to have less confidence than mothers in their ability to parent. Wille (1995) examined gender differences in parenting roles, and results supported previous research: Mothers' child-care responsibilities are greater than fathers', and fathers are more involved when mothers work. Further, both mothers and fathers rate mothers as more confident than fathers in their ability to care for their infants, both in responsivity and in meeting infants' needs. Mothers rate fathers as having better parenting skills than fathers rate themselves.

Woodworth, Belsky, and Crnic (1996) examined father-toddler (15 to 33 months of age) relationships to determine types of interactive involvement. First-born sons and their fathers were assessed over a three-year period to determine intrusiveness, detachment, cognitive stimulation, and positive and negative affect that fathers displayed when attempting to manage their sons' behaviors. Fathers were judged as skillful in the relationship when they gave guidance to their children by offering explanations and justifications along with their directions, and less skilled when they expressed overt negative emotion or other forms of disgust, resentment, or impatience. Fathers who were more extraverted, less neurotic, more satisfied with their social support, and higher in social class were highly skillful in their efforts to control or manage their toddlers' behaviors. The reverse was true for fathers who made more unskilled attempts. Skilled fathers were sensitive, positive, and appropriately responsive during interactions with their toddlers. Child characteristics were not found to be predictive of fathers' parenting skills. Further, more extraverted men and men who reported more satisfaction with their social networks increased their proportion of skilled control efforts over time. It was concluded that the most influential factors on fathers' parenting behavior are personality characteristics, followed by sociocontextual factors. Child characteristics were the least influential.

The type of work that fathers perform may affect their children's development. An interesting study by Curtner-Smith, Bennett, and O'Rear (1995) found that fathers who engaged in more complex work were more likely than other fathers to value self-direction over conformity in their children. Complex work was defined as work that provides opportunities for self-direction and autonomy and requires initiative, thought, and independent judgment. In contrast, less complex work includes work with "things" rather than people, work that is routine, and work that provides little opportunity for self-direction and autonomy.

Further, fathers in more complex jobs had children who were rated as less aggressive by their mothers than the children of fathers who worked in less complex jobs. Fathers who strongly valued self-direction perceived their parenting as less restrictive than fathers who valued conformity over self-direction. Fathers perceiving themselves as nurturant had children with lower depression and aggression scores; those perceiving themselves as restrictive had more aggressive children, but restrictive parenting was not related to children's depression. Fathers with strong values of self-

direction over conformity and those engaged in nurturant parenting were more likely to have children with lower depression scores than fathers with opposing views.

The Reciprocal Nature of Fathering. We should emphasize here that, like maternal behaviors, paternal behaviors must be viewed in the context of reciprocity; that is, at every age level, the child's behavior influences the father's behavior. Fathers have been found to be less responsive to and affectionate toward their infants and young children who are perceived by them and by their mothers to be temperamentally difficult. Fathers are likely to use coercive measures in response to the frustration of a problem child (Simons, Whitbeck, Conger, & Melby, 1990).

It can no longer be said with any degree of conviction that fathers are the forgotten contributors to child development. First it seems clear that fathers do not necessarily take, and have not necessarily taken in the past, a back seat to mothers in exerting a positive and powerful influence over

The father-child relationship is an important influence on the child's social relationships outside the family.

their children—their influence has simply been less visible. Research indicates that children develop best when their fathers (as well as their mothers) combine warmth and nurturance with strength, protection, and specified limits. The combination of providing discipline with warm affection seems to facilitate creativity, independence, generosity, and sensitivity. It can be concluded that fathers undeniably play an important role in child development from infancy on through childhood and that the role of fathering has changed considerably over time.

The fatherhood myth is as ripe for destruction as the motherhood myth is. No longer can we afford to neglect the recognition of the impact of the father on his children's development, given the opportunity to do so and the prestige for fathering. We can liberate men from their traditional instrumental role and reward them for being expressive, toward both their wives and their children. We can integrate fathers not only into the role of child care but also into the role of child rearing, which means more than changing diapers and chauffeuring. We can apportion the joys and griefs of child rearing between men and women so that fathers are no longer second-class citizens as parents. We can strive for a new perspective that emphasizes equal parenting.

It is unfortunate that just as American society has come to believe in the importance of fathering, some experts argue that fathers, in general, are moving away from the center of family life rather than toward it. Hawkins (1992) has contended that potent forces exist to move contemporary fathers closer to the center of the family as long as the family remains intact. However, with the high divorce rate, this trend is increasingly unlikely. Evidence indicates that a countertrend—a disappearing act by fathers following divorce—is more the norm (Harris & Morgan, 1991). Fathers are increasingly absent from the homes in which children reside. Statistics on child-support payments and noncustodial-father visits suggest relatively weak links between fathers and their children (Hawkins, 1992).

Some researchers contend that although biological fatherhood is waning, sociological fatherhood appears to be waxing. Stepfathering and cohabitation have increased. Thus, it is conceivable

that men are still a significant part of children's lives, though it is unclear whether sociological links can be substituted for biological ties or how effectively the two compare. However, evidence suggests that remarriage rates are slowing down and that the interval between divorce and remarriage is lengthening. Therefore, more children experiencing divorce in the 1990s will not experience a remarriage (Hawkins, 1992).

However, inconsistent results have been found in the few studies that have focused on the effect of nonresidential fathers or father figures on children's functioning. Some evidence indicates that contact with absent fathers relates to higher self-esteem; lower depression and anxiety; and fewer child behavior problems, especially for boys. Coley (1998), using a sample of school-age children residing with unmarried mothers, found that children's social interactions with their absent fathers or nominated father figures were important predictors of healthy functioning in both behavioral and cognitive realms. Data from this study showed the importance of discipline from both nonresidential fathers and nonpaternal men. It was notable that the majority of nonpaternal men named by children in the study were not extended family relatives but, rather, partners or boyfriends of their mothers.

The assessment of fathering in the future must be made within a context in which the father and child are operating—that is, the family system and the larger social system—and through examining emergent conceptions of parenting in general. In Chapter 7, fathering in single-parent families and stepfamilies is discussed. A more detailed discussion of father involvement in child care and household labor is found in Chapter 8.

Similarities and Differences between Parenting and Other Roles. Parenthood is one of the most significant roles in our society and one that a large percentage of the population will assume. There are some unique features of the parenthood role that distinguish it from other adult roles.

First, women experience greater cultural pressures to assume the role of parent than men do. Early in life girls begin to be oversocialized toward parenthood. They are encouraged, and sometimes coerced, to play with certain toys, such as dolls, and to engage in household-type activities. Thus girls grow up to believe that adult status and fulfillment come from motherhood and child-rearing duties. Boys, on the other hand, are socialized toward occupational roles outside the home rather than for fatherhood, and they are provided with toys that stimulate action and aggression. Although these cultural stereotypes are less visible than they once were, they are still alive and well.

Second, the parenthood role is not always voluntarily assumed, as are other adult roles. A certain degree of freedom exists in selecting an occupation, becoming a spouse, or serving in leadership roles. Even though individuals technically have the choice of becoming parents, a variety of personal, religious, or moral reasons may preclude the use of contraceptives or other forms of birth control.

Third, the role of parenthood is irrevocable. Once one decides that a pregnancy is to be continued and birth occurs, it is difficult to abandon the commitment to be a parent. Although a child may be placed for adoption, this alternative is not psychologically easy, and it is not a widely socially acceptable practice. One can quit a job or even become an ex-spouse much more easily than one can give up the responsibility of parenthood.

Fourth, preparation for parenthood is poor as compared with preparation for other roles. Illustrations of this phenomenon include the paucity of educational experiences or training for parenthood through the educational system, the limited amount of preparation for parenting during pregnancy, the minimal guidance provided by the culture for successful parenting, and the abrupt transition to parenthood.

Fifth, parenthood is a developmental role—parents develop as children develop. The developmental needs and changes occurring in the parent affect parenting behavior. Further, the methods and techniques of guiding the child and providing for her needs change as the child develops. Coping with a 2-year-old is obviously very different from guiding an adolescent. The changing nature of parenting is discussed in subsequent chapters.

Determinants of Parenting Behavior. Traditionally, determinants of parenting behavior have been examined in isolation from one another and in a single direction. For example, since the 1960s considerable attention has been focused on differences in child-rearing patterns among low- and middle-income families, some implying that socioeconomic status per se could account for a large portion of the variance. In a similar manner, few studies have considered the role the child plays in influencing parental behaviors. More recently, research has addressed the numerous factors that affect parenting behaviors, including the child, and the factors interact in different ways for different families. Parenting behaviors, then, are the result of a complex network that is not yet clearly understood, especially with regard to the relative impact each dimension has on the child. Thus, the characteristics of the child, the parent (ontogenic development, personality, and psychological resources), and the social context in which the parent-child relationship is embedded interrelate to determine parenting behaviors (Belsky, 1991).

Child Characteristics. As noted earlier, the parenting process is a reciprocal one, and the child to some extent creates his own environment. This phenomenon began to reemerge in the research of the 1980s. Research focused on the dynamic features of the child's behavior, often conceptualized under the rubric of temperament, such as negative mood, high activity level, and inclination to disobey. Much evidence indicates that children with difficult behavioral characteristics evoke from parents "upper limit" control. Parents exhibit behaviors that attempt to reduce the child's aversiveness. It is clear that many parents and other adults react to disobedient, negative, and/or highly active children with negative, controlling behavior (Belsky, 1991), but research reveals that parents vary in their susceptibility to these child characteristics. Parent characteristics moderate the effect of child characteristics (Bugental, Blue, & Cruzcosa, 1989).

Parent Characteristics. The last decade or so of research has demonstrated clearly that the parent-child relationship is embedded in the life course of parents and must be considered in terms of their psychological attributes. Repeatedly, it has been shown that parents who are psychologically healthy and mature are more likely to provide the kind of care that promotes healthy psychological development in their offspring. It was found that parents who scored high on measures of ego development and ego strength behaved sensitively and responsively toward their infants, and developed feelings of confidence and control in their roles as parents (Cox, Owen, Lewis, & Henderson, 1989). Characteristics of the parent seem to be the most important determinants of parenting behavior because they exert both a direct influence on parenting and an indirect influence through their impact on marital relations, network relations, and occupational experiences (Woodworth et al., 1996).

General feelings of self-efficacy and self-control have been shown to be positively associated with a warm, accepting style of teaching preschoolers; and mothers and fathers who feel positive about themselves tend to communicate more effectively with their preadolescents and adolescents and seem to manage disciplinary situations well. Several researchers have found that mothers who are depressed tend to be less affectionate toward, responsive to, and spontaneous with their infants and to be irritable and punitive with their older children. Simons and associates (1990) found that constructive parenting was negatively related to individualistic values of both mothers and fathers.

The quality of care that parents provide is related to their experiences in their own family of origin. That is not surprising, since parental characteristics linked to parenting behaviors are themselves thought to result from their own developmental experiences (Belsky, 1991). The intergenerational nature of attachment has been the focus of several studies. These have shown that adults who are secure in their relationships with their own parents are most likely to rear infants who develop secure attachments to them (Van Ijzendoorn, 1992). Further, secure mothers were found to provide more emotional support and as-

sistance when interacting with their young children, were accepting of the individuality of their infants, had greater understanding for the developmental problems of their toddlers, and were more able to adjust the family routine to the special needs of 2-year-olds.

Van Ijzendoorn (1992) reported numerous studies documenting the intergenerational nature of parenting. He pointed out that the continuity of parenting is stimulated by the sharing of genes between generations, as well as by sharing the same physical and social circumstances. Living in the same neighborhood, or even in the same house, stimulates continuity and reinforces a certain interactional style sustained across the life course and even across generations.

However, the past need not be prologue. Adults who acknowledge and seem to have worked through the difficulties of their childhood may not inflict them on their own children. Research on nonrisk parents as well as those at risk indicates that a supportive relationship with a spouse or mate functions to prevent the intergenerational transmission of negative, rejecting, and insensitive maternal care (Belsky, Youngblade, & Pensky, 1990).

Another area in which parenting practices may reflect intergenerational influences is child abuse. It has been demonstrated that abusive parents are likely to have been abused themselves as children. Although it cannot be said that this is the only factor that contributes to child abuse, it appears to be a significant one.

Remarkably little is known about just how parenting is transmitted from one generation to the other. Learning to be a parent and to acquire a certain parenting style may be the outcome of modeling, coaching, or other cognitive processes. Since most of the research is correlational, it does not provide insight into the causal mechanism. Some research, especially that on transmission of attachment and on mitigating circumstances that lead to a different perspective, has shed some light on the causes of parenting behaviors, but more research that addresses the issue in a methodologically adequate manner is needed.

Social Context. Research dating back to the 1960s generally has indicated that parents, particularly mothers, who have more education and higher family incomes and whose husbands have more prestigious jobs are more involved with their children; are less controlling, restricting, and punishing; and are more affectionate toward and responsive to their offspring than are parents of lower socioeconomic status (Belsky, 1991; McLoyd 1990). Further, there are deleterious consequences of parental job and/or income loss.

The effects of the marital relationship on parenting have received substantial interest from researchers since the 1980s. Investigators have repeatedly found that spousal support of both the emotional (e.g., love and intimacy) and the instrumental (e.g., child-care tasks) variety is associated with enhanced parental performance of both mothers and fathers (Belsky, 1991). Simons et al. (1990) found that constructive parenting by mothers was positively affected by their levels of marital satisfaction. Mothers with satisfying marital relationships with their husbands were more available, sensitive, and responsive to the needs of their children than those mothers with low levels of marital satisfaction. There is some indication that patterns of fathering are more systematically related to patterns of marital adjustment or satisfaction than are patterns of mothering, probably because fathering is less scripted by social convention than is mothering. Simons et al. (1990) found that both a wife's beliefs and her values relate to the quality of her husband's constructive parenting practices. It appears that, at least in part, a husband's degree of involvement in the parenting process is a function of his wife's beliefs about what is necessary and important.

The relationship of social support to parenting also has been the focus of certain studies. For example, Crnic and Booth (1991) investigated mothers' and fathers' perceptions of the daily hassles of parenting and how the stress associated with these may be mediated by social-support networks. Both mothers' and fathers' perceptions of hassles were related to indices of support. Parental support moderated the adverse effects of minor stresses.

Family support was most helpful for mothers, whereas friendships were related to fewer hassles for the fathers. Thus, social support can function in a stress-buffering manner. It is also possible, however, that mothers who are sensitive and caring are those who are skilled in using support systems.

Ethnicity and religion also are factors that impinge on parenting behaviors. These variables, alone or in combination, play a role in the kinds of activities the family engages in, the limits set and the controls placed on children's behavior, and the set of expectations that parents hold for their children. Some of these will be discussed in more detail later. Not only do cultural and religious values affect parental behaviors, but also, in many cases, stereotyping, discrimination, and prejudice against certain minority groups complicate the child-rearing process.

Closely associated with social class, religion, and ethnicity is the peer value system, which influences attitudes toward parenting and personal expectations of children's behavior. With the decline of the extended family, increasing numbers of parents are being influenced in their parental attitudes and behavior by their peers. All too often a mother initiates toilet training, weans her baby, or uses corporal punishment because all her friends are doing it. Similarly, a father may play golf with the boys instead of going on a family outing because that is more acceptable to his peer group. This is not to say that the influence of the adult's peer group is always negative; surely peer groups provide models of positive parenting behaviors as well. Although parents generally are not as easily influenced by their peers as children are, most of them prefer not to be conspicuously different.

Other factors in the larger culture influence how parents behave. Some evidence indicates that parents' level of education in general, knowledge of child development or training in parenting skills, education for childbirth, and father involvement in labor and delivery contribute to more positive behaviors. Although these factors alone cannot guarantee an effective parent, we believe that future research will indicate that they are significant. This means that the larger culture must undergo a number of changes to make these experiences possible for all parents.

A final aspect of social context that should be considered is the family itself. Variables such as the family structure (one parent or two parents, nuclear family or extended), lifestyle, number and birth order of children, parents' ages and the age and sex of each child obviously affect parental behaviors. Since parenting in a variety of family structures and lifestyles will be discussed in Chapters 7 and 8, we will not treat the subject of single parents, adolescent parents, or homosexual parents here. But even in the traditional family, parents have been shown to interact with their children differentially based on sex, age, birth order, and number of children. Fathers appear to differentiate between the sexes to a much greater degree than mothers do. And, unquestionably, as the child gets older, parenting behaviors change in response to the child's needs as well as to the parent's. Chapters 2, 3, and 4 will explore this phenomenon more fully.

The media have a powerful effect on parenting. Approximately 99 percent of American homes have at least one television, a greater percentage than those having refrigerators and indoor plumbing, and many families have more than one set. The number of families with videocassette recorders (VCRs) is almost as high. Access to the Internet and its extensive resources is growing daily. It is not our intent, however, to present evidence concerning the effects of television, video, and the Internet on children. There are numerous studies that may be reviewed on that topic. We do believe, however, that the various forms of the mass media have a definite impact on both parents and how they interact with their children and thus determine to some extent parenting behaviors. It appears that the media frequently espouse values that conflict with parental values, especially in the areas of sex, drugs, violence, materialism, and hedonism. On the one hand, parental values probably are shaped partially by the mass media, but, on the other hand, conflicting values often result in negative parent-child interactions.

One of the most significant effects of television, video, and the Internet on parenting is the amount of time they consume in many families, resulting in a presumable decrease in time spent in interaction with children. Furthermore, television-watching parents provide the model for television-watching children. Thirty years ago, Bronfenbrenner (1971) suggested that turning on the television set can turn off the process that transforms children into people. A similar statement might be made about videos and computer games, which often serve as baby-sitters. Many parents do no not monitor their children's television viewing or electronic-game playing, or what they access on the Internet.

Parents are influenced, too, by other forms of mass media, particularly newspapers, magazines, pamphlets, and books, many of which contain material related to child rearing. It is hardly possible today to pick up a newspaper or buy a women's magazine without noticing at least one reference to parenting. Ann Landers has been the sole parent educator for many. With this deluge of information, much of it contradictory and confusing, parental behaviors have been significantly affected.

We wish to emphasize again that we do not take the view that the influences of the mass media are all negative. For example, some television programs and computer software provide materials that guide parents in skills to practice with their children. Television and the Internet are the media through which most parents in this country can be reached. It is sad to observe their underutilization for increasing effective parenting. It would be quite interesting to see what effects a media blitz on parent education would have on parenting behaviors.

Other forms of mass media (movies, for example) also may offer the parent insight into the nature of children's behavior and provide a model of effective interaction. Most certainly we would not discourage the distribution of printed materials to parents. For many, they are the major source of information on parenting and the written word is gospel. What we should realize is that these materials do have an impact on parental behaviors, and often what is reported in the media is distorted or taken out of context. Even in the professional literature there is no common agreement as to what constitutes a "good" parent and no recipes for successful parenting. It seems to us that parents need assistance in interpreting what they read and in applying it in their own lives.

Historically, printed materials have reflected the middle-class pattern of child rearing. Some attempts have been made in recent years to provide more appropriate materials for the undereducated—materials with more pictures and fewer words. But printed materials probably will continue to be more effective with the educated middle-class parent.

It seems reasonable to conclude, then, that all the mass media have an impact on parenting behaviors, but the exact nature of the influence varies among parents, depending on their exposure to other sources and the degree of credibility they associate with the media.

In summarizing the determinants of parenting behavior, the main point to make is that they are numerous. A parent's relationship with a given child may be influenced by her own ontogenic development, personality, and psychological resources; the marital relationship; social networks and support available to her; occupational experiences; other cultural forces such as educational level, income, peers, religious beliefs, and the mass media; and most significantly, the child herself. Though some of these determinants are modifiable, others are obviously inflexible, and the various factors operate together in an extremely complex manner. For a summary of determinants of parenting behavior see the Highlights.

Parent Education

The concept of parent education has existed for a long time. The term was used in this country as early as the 1920s. Recently, parent education has been used to include a variety of experiences to assist persons who are already parents to be more effective in their roles as well as to educate individuals who plan to be parents in the near or distant future.

There is greater consensus concerning what parenthood is than whether it requires any special

HIGHLIGHTS

Determinants of Parenting Behaviors

Child Characteristics
  Personality
  Mood
  Activity level

Parent Characteristics
  Mental health
  Psychological resources
  Family of origin

Cultural Context
  Socioeconomic status
  Level of education
  Marital relationship
  Social-support network
  Mass media

training. Parenthood is viewed by some as a profession, which may be defined as an occupation requiring special education or training. Though the assumption that once a child is born the mother miraculously knows how to care for him has been widely accepted, mothers have actually received training in their own homes throughout the ages.

In the Victorian age one would not have been confronted with multiple decisions related to parenthood, with the question of whether to become a parent, and with the multiple ways by which one could become one. For most people, once marriage occurred, parenthood followed. Parents earned admiration and respect if they produced a child every year or so for several years. After conception, decisions about pregnancy and childbirth were made based on the experience of previous generations. Once a child was born, infant-care routines that had been practiced for generations most often were adopted with little thought or discussion. In the absence of information about child rearing from books, television, or other forms of media, parents simply did the "natural" thing, and the "natural" thing was what one had observed or remembered from being parented in one's own home.

Today many mothers are combining parenthood with other roles and are unable to teach or demonstrate effective parenting skills to their children. Nearly two decades ago, LeMasters and DeFrain (1983) stated the following:

> It is usually assumed in our society that people have to be trained for difficult roles: most business firms would not consider turning a sales clerk loose on the customers without some formal training; the armed forces would scarcely send a raw recruit into combat without extensive and intensive training; most states now require a course in driver's education before high school students can acquire a driver's license. Even dog owners often go to school to learn how to treat their pets properly. This is not true of American parents. (pp. 75–76)

Although it will be some time—and maybe never—before all people receive formalized training for parenthood, the view that this role requires training is widely held by professionals working with families and by many parents themselves.

Part of the problem in training for parenthood is the necessity of developing a set of competencies or coming to agreement about what constitutes an effective parent. There is no doubt that individuals with a wide variety of personalities; value systems; interests; abilities; and physical, social, emotional, and intellectual characteristics can be effective parents. Further, parents from varying educational and socioeconomic levels may be equally effective. Although consensus may never be reached as to what an effective parent is and no recipe for rearing a child be developed, there is much that can be gained from research to assist parents in their tasks.

Early Parent-Education Efforts.   At the beginning of the twentieth century, many "experts" in the area of child study began to appear. The ideas of the parent-education movement for this period were described by Schlossman (1983):

> We thus see in early twentieth century parent education, as embodied in the work of the PTA, an intriguing balance of perspective between private domestic responsibility and public political activity, and a reliance on religion and maternal instinct, versus a reliance on science and formal instruction.... It is important to recognize the exist-

ence of this balance and these tensions in the theory and practice of parent education in the pre–World War I era. (p. 10)

During the decade of the 1920s, dramatic changes took place in the professional and public attitudes toward child-care practices. The parent-education movement, transformed into a "well-organized social movement" (Schlossman, 1976, p. 10), reached millions of people for the first time. Many programs and publications appeared, reflecting a new interest in the scientific aspect of child-care and parenting skills. The impact of science was noted by the disappearance of references to the Deity in the literature. Whereas mothers of the late Victorian era had put their faith in the Bible, the mothers of the 1920s relied on scientific information on nutrition and good habits to help them solve child-rearing problems. The vigorous interest in parent education during the 1920s was affected by the breaking down of the social and moral codes that had guided the behavior of the middle class for generations.

Further, there was great confidence in the ability of science to solve problems in all aspects of life (Schlossman, 1983). As the movement grew and as parenthood brought increasing frustration, the number of parent-education organizations increased. Between the 1930s and the 1970s, contemporary parenting programs emerged. As more and more research was conducted, programs were developed by such experts as Skinner, Spock, Ginott, and Dreikurs. Many concepts from these experts form the foundation for present parenting strategies.

A Rebirth.   In the 1960s and 1970s, and again in the 1990s, a renewed interest in parenting, combined with social and cultural changes in society, early-intervention research, certain political movements (women's movement, civil rights movement, and others), federal legislation, and increased interest on the part of parents themselves, served as the impetus for parent education. A proliferation of programs emerged during the 1960s and 1970s and were totally or partially funded by the federal government.

These efforts at family intervention were numerous and varied but were aimed primarily at changing parents' behavior rather than assessing parents' effects on children's development (Clarke-Stewart, 1988). Most researchers did not evaluate parents' and children's behavior before, during, and after program implementation, and despite the consistent finding that children's IQ scores rose over the course of these programs, how and why the gains occurred were not determined. The studies of training programs in child management skills for parents of normal children have generally been concerned with identifying the most effective program for changing parents' attitudes, not with assessing the long-term effects on children's behavior or competence. However, changing parents' attitudes and beliefs about children is the first step in changing behavior.

During the 1980s, research continued to demonstrate that parent education was beneficial to both parents and children. The following were among the outcomes reported for parent education: mothers' caregiving became more sensitive and their interactions with infants more developmentally appropriate as a result of participation in a parent-education program; mothers improved in social skills; mothers can be successful at teaching cognitive skills to their children; mothers gained confidence in and insight into their parenting role; and mothers became more accepting, understanding, and trusting of their children.

In the 1990s, parent-education programs were numerous and varied and were deemed as critical as ever. Funding sources were diverse—local, state, and federal agencies, as well as private entities, recognized the need for improved parenting. The reasons included the changing structure and functions of American families and the increased pressures on these families; the increase in the number of teenage parents; more women as major wage earners of their families; the reduction of the amount of time parents could devote to parenting; and the many myths and misconceptions that existed about parenthood. Further, reports from early-intervention studies underscoring the importance of parents in facilitating their chil-

dren's development, researchers' interest in family influences on child development, and contributions of social-support systems to the quality of child rearing illustrated the benefits of parent education.

With the recognition that America is "a nation at risk" with an educational system unable to meet the demands placed upon it, parent education and involvement have once again emerged as priorities, endorsed by both the public schools and the federal government. The first goal of the National Goals of Education developed at the National Educational Summit in 1989 was as follows: *By the year 2000 all children in America will start school ready to learn.* This goal has provided the impetus for programs to assist parents in getting children ready for school and reemphasizing the critical importance of early education as well.

Despite the profiles of success of parent-education programs in the 1980s and 1990s, the programs also drew criticism (Thomas, 1996). Critics claimed, for example, that simply providing parents with information about children's development and teaching parenting as a collection of skills are not likely to affect deeper, critical parental perspectives. Others have pointed out that typical programs are successful with only a narrow range of parents, that broader individual and family outcomes are rarely addressed, and that such programs fail to reflect newer, more complex and comprehensive perspectives of family and human development. Such criticisms have generated alternative ways of thinking about parent education. These alternative perspectives are typically broader and more comprehensive than conventional ones—focusing, for example, on the entire family system, self-psychology, and parent development.

One example of the attempt to broaden the perspective of parent education was a cognitive theory-based educational design for facilitating parent development and its implementation (Thomas, 1996). The program, entitled Reflective Dialogue Parent Education Design (RDPED), was implemented and tested at four different sites. The program assumed that parents who have reached higher levels in their own development have a wider repertoire for dealing with, and more complex ways of understanding, their children, their parenting role, and their parent-child relationships than parents who have not reached these developmental levels. Parents who are more emotionally and cognitively mature or advanced should be better able than less mature parents to support their children's development.

The program focused on parent awareness and interpersonal interaction themes, two aspects of parental development. Parent awareness is the cognitive structure that parents use in interpreting children's responses and behavior and in formulating policies to guide their actions. Interpersonal interaction themes were characterized as deep motivations and interests that generate, organize, and give meaning, pattern, and predictability to a person's priorities, goals, plans, and actions. Thomas used the patterns of sensitivity, responsiveness, reciprocity, and support as a cluster of related themes that, when reflected in parent-child interactions and in the orientations of parents, encourage children's development. Results following the 10-week program showed that parents had lower proportions of egoistic and conventional thinking and higher proportions of individualistic and analytic thinking. The researcher concluded that the program was successful in promoting development of parent awareness and encouraging development themes in participants.

Another unusual approach in assessing parent-education outcomes was used by First and Way (1995). Mothers wrote stories about their feelings and experiences during an 8-week community-based parent-education program. Analysis of the stories indicated that transformative learning occurred—learning that seeks to raise consciousness regarding personal and societal oppression and serves to foster emancipatory action that may enhance development. The researchers concluded that the parenting class helped the participants to see their lives in fundamentally different ways. It motivated them to begin to question their basic beliefs and assumptions about fundamental parenting issues such as problem solving, communication, and discipline patterns.

Beginning in the 1980s a move began toward the development of family support programs—a broad approach focusing on all aspects of family life. Emphasis was placed on prevention rather than on repair. Three distinct trends in family support programs seem to be evident. First, comprehensive programs that include children and their families and that are usually initiated either before or soon after children are born address education, job training, parenting skills, child development and early education, health and mental health, and social services. Second, partnership and collaborative efforts have been developed between and among families, schools, the business community, and health and social-service agencies. Finally, a third approach consists of community-based efforts to identify the unique needs of citizens and families in the community and foster collaboration with a variety of entities to meet identified needs.

Partnerships and collaborative efforts imply close cooperation among the parties involved and a sharing of rights and responsibilities. Data suggest that when parents become partners with schools, and when agencies collaborate with one another, the needs of children and families are met more effectively, better relationships develop, and feelings of family empowerment increase. Long-range goals for the optimal development and functioning of children and families characterize many comprehensive programs. Most often an attempt is made to bring together family and community resources to achieve goals. Substantial evidence has indicated that when early childhood programs and schools initiate active collaboration with parents, everyone benefits—children perform better in school, parent-child relationships improve, and parents and teachers communicate. In short, parents and teachers become partners in the care and education of children. Further, collaborative efforts often provide a mechanism for preventing child abuse and juvenile delinquency. There is a growing recognition that both collaborative and comprehensive programs are more effective if begun early and extended over time (Turner, Hamner, & Orell, 1993).

The Future. It remains to be seen what the new millenium will bring for parent education. It is likely that programs will have a broad focus aimed at changing the lives of parents and children. A continuation of comprehensive, community-based family support programs, and parent education and involvement will be part of these efforts—a significant part, we hope. The emphasis still must be on meeting the needs of individual children and families. Research clearly shows that participation and involvement in parent training and the effects and effectiveness of parent-training programs depend on various traits and circumstances of the parents: their education, ethnicity, attitudes and beliefs, personalities, goals, degree of social support, and stress.

SUMMARY

Concepts of parenthood, parenting, and parent education have existed since biblical times. Both mothers and fathers have been shown to contribute significantly to the development of their children, but the interpretations of their roles have changed significantly, thereby bringing change in both the form and the content of parent education.

The beginning of the modern era of parent education has been placed at the beginning of the nineteenth century, when publications on child rearing began to appear and when organizations emphasizing education and support for parents emerged. The twentieth century saw the major impetus for parent education in the 1920s and the 1960s. The complex technological and rapidly changing society of the twenty-first century necessitates continual support for parents.

The need for education for parenting in contemporary society is supported by the prevalence of myths about parenthood and children, by the changing nature of the family itself, and by the lack of sufficient and reliable guidelines for effective parenting. Even though education for parenthood appears to be a necessity, it is important to understand that parenting behaviors result from a complex network of variables that includes child characteristics, parent characteristics, the social context of families, and the mass media.

REFERENCES

ALEXANDER, M., & HIGGINS, E. (1993). Emotional trade-offs of becoming a parent: How social roles influence self-discrepancy effects. *Journal of Personality and Social Psychology, 65*(6), 1239–1269.

BELSKY, J. (1991). Parental and nonparental child care and children's socioemotional development: A decade in review. In A. Booth (Ed.), *Contemporary families: Looking forward, looking back* (pp. 127–140). Minneapolis: National Council on Family Relations.

BELSKY, J., & ROVINE, M. (1990). Patterns of marital change across the transition to parenthood: Pregnancy to three years postpartum. *Journal of Marriage and the Family, 52*(1), 5–19.

BELSKY, J., YOUNGBLADE, L., & PENSKY, E. (1990). Child-rearing history, marital quality, and maternal affect: Intergenerational transmission in a low-risk sample. *Development and Psychopathology, 1*(1), 291–304.

BELSKY, J., YOUNGBLADE, L., ROVINE, M., & VOLLING, B. (1991). Patterns of marital change and parent-child interaction. *Journal of Marriage and the Family, 53*(2), 487–498.

BENASICH, A., & BROOKS-GUNN, J. (1996). Maternal attitudes and knowledge of child-rearing: Associations with family and child outcomes. *Child Development, 67,* 1186–1205.

BOWMAN, M., & SAUNDERS, D. (1995). Are the risks of delayed parenting overstated? *Human Reproduction, 10*(5), 1035–1036.

BRAZELTON, T. B. (1969). *Infants and mothers: Differences in development.* New York: Dell.

BREMS, C., & SOHL, M. (1995). The role of empathy in parenting strategy choices. *Family Relations, 44,* 182–194.

BRIDGES, L., CONNELL, J., & BELSKY, J. (1988). Similarities and differences in infant-mother and infant-father interaction in the strange situation: A component process analysis. *Developmental Psychology, 24*(1), 92–100.

BRONFENBRENNER, U. (1971). Who cares for America's children? *Young Children, 26*(3), 157–163.

BROOKS, J. (1991). *The process of parenting* (3d ed.). Palo Alto, CA: Mayfield.

BUGENTAL, D., BLUE, J., & CRUZCOSA, M. (1989). Perceived control over caregiving outcomes: Implications for child abuse. *Developmental Psychology, 25*(4), 532–539.

CALVERT, B., & STANTON, W. (1992). Perceptions of parenthood: Similarities and differences between 15-year-old girls and boys. *Adolescence, 27*(106), 315–329.

CHESS, S., & THOMAS, A. (1973). Temperament in the normal infant. In J. Westman (Ed.), *Individual differences in children* (pp. 83–103). New York: Wiley.

CLARKE-STEWART, K. (1988). Parents' effects on children's development: A decade of progress? *Journal of Applied Developmental Psychology, 9*(1), 41–84.

COLEY, R. (1998). Children's socialization experiences and functioning in single-mother households: The importance of fathers and other men. *Child Development, 69*(1), 219–230.

COWAN, C., & COWAN, P. (1995). Interventions to ease the transition to parenthood: Why they are needed and what they can do. *Family Relations, 44,* 412–423.

COX, M., OWEN, M., HENDERSON, K., & MARGAND, N. (1992). Prediction of infant-father and infant-mother attachment. *Developmental Psychology, 28*(3), 474–483.

COX, M., OWEN, M., LEWIS, J., & HENDERSON, V. (1989). Marriage, adult adjustment, and early parenting. *Child Development, 60*(5), 1015–1024.

CRNIC, K., & BOOTH, C. (1991). Mothers' and fathers' perceptions of daily hassles of parenting across early childhood. *Journal of Marriage and the Family, 53*(4), 1042–1050.

CURTNER-SMITH, M., BENNETT, T., & O'REAR, M. (1995). Fathers' occupational conditions, values of self-direction and conformity, and perceptions of nurturant and restrictive parenting in relation to young children's depression and aggression. *Family Relations, 44,* 299–305.

DALY, K. (1996). Spending time with the kids, meanings of family time for fathers. *Family Relations, 45,* 466–476.

DOHERTY, W., KOUNESKI, E., & KOUNESKI, M. (1998). Responsible fathering: An overview and conceptual framework. *Journal of Marriage and the Family, 60,* 277–292.

DUBOW, E., HUESMANN, R., & ERON, L. (1987). Childhood correlates of adult ego development. *Child Development, 58*(3), 859–869.

ERIKSON, E. (1963). *Childhood and society.* New York: Norton.

FIRST, J., & WAY, W. (1995). Parent education outcomes: Insights into transformative learning. *Family Relations, 44,* 104–109.

GARRISON, M., BLAOCK, L., ZARSKI, J., & MERRITT, P. (1997). Delayed parenthood: An exploratory study of family functioning. *Family Relations, 46,* 281–290.

GERSON, M., BERMAN, L., & MORRIS, A. (1991). The value of having children as an aspect of adult development. *Journal of Genetic Psychology, 152*(3), 327–339.

GOETTING, A. (1986). Parental satisfaction. *Journal of Family Issues, 7*(1), 83–109.

GOODNOUGH, G., & LEE, C. (1996). Contemporary fatherhood: Concepts and issues for mental health counselors. *Journal of Mental Health Counseling, 18*(4), 333–346.

HARRIS, K., & MORGAN, S. (1991). Fathers, sons, and daughters: Differential parental involvement in parenting. *Journal of Marriage and the Family, 53*(3), 531–544.

HAWKINS, A. (1992). Critical components or peripheral parts? Fathers in and out of families. *Family Perspective, 26*(2), 219–234.

HEATH, T. (1994). The impact of delayed fatherhood on the father-child relationship. *Journal of Genetic Psychology, 155*(4), 511–531.

HOCK, E., SCHIRTZINGER, M., LUTZ, W., & WIDAMAN, K. (1995). Maternal depressive symptomatology over the transition to parenthood: Assessing the influence of marital satisfaction and marital sex role traditionalism. *Journal of Family Psychology, 9*(1), 79–88.

HOLDEN, G., & WEST, M. (1989). Proximate regulation by mothers: A demonstration of how differing styles affect young children's behavior. *Child Development, 60*(1), 64–69.

ISABELLA, R., & BELSKY, J. (1985). Marital change during the transition to parenthood and security of infant-parent attachment. *Journal of Family Issues, 6*(4), 505–522.

ISHII-KUNTZ, M., & IHINGER-TALLMAN, M. (1991). The subjective well-being of parents. *Journal of Family Issues, 12*(1), 58–68.

IVEY, D. (1995). Family history, parenting attitudes, gender roles, and clinical perceptions of family and family member functioning: Factors related to gender inequitable practice. *The American Journal of Family Therapy, 23*(3), 213–226.

KALMUSS, D., DAVIDSON, A., & CUSHMAN, L. (1992). Parenting expectations, experiences, and adjustment to parenthood: A test of the violated expectations framework. *Journal of Marriage and the Family, 54*(3), 515–526.

KLAUS, M., & KENNELL, J., (1982). *Parent-infant bonding.* St. Louis: C. V. Mosby.

KUCZYNSKI, L., KOCHANSKA, G., RODKE-YARROW, M., & GIRNISS-BROWN, D. (1987). A developmental interpretation of young children's noncompliance. *Developmental Psychology, 23*(1), 1–8.

KURDEK, L. (1996). Parenting satisfaction and marital satisfaction in mothers and fathers with young children. *Journal of Family Psychology, 10*(1), 331–342.

LAMB, M., & OPPENHEIM, D. (1989). Fatherhood and father-child relationships: Five years of research. In S. Cath, A. Gurwitt, & L. Gunsberb (Eds.), *Fathers and their families* (pp. 11–26). Hillsdale, NJ: Erlbaum.

LAMB, M., PLECK, J., CHARNOV, E., & LEVINE, J. (1987). Effects of increased paternal involvement on fathers and mothers. In C. Lewis & M. O'Brien (Eds.), *Reassessing fatherhood: New observations on fathers and the modern family* (pp. 107–125). London: Sage.

LEMASTERS, E, & DEFRAIN, J. (1983) *Parents in contemporary America.* Homewood, IL: Dorsey.

McBRIDE, B., & McBRIDE, J. (1990). The changing roles of fathers: Some implications for educators. *Journal of Home Economics, 82*(3), 6–11.

McBRIDE, B., & RANE, T. (1997). Role identity, role investments, and paternal involvement: Implications for parenting programs for men. *Early Childhood Research Quarterly, 12,* 173–179.

McBRIDE, B., & RANE, T. (1998). Parenting alliance as a predictor of father involvement: An exploratory study. *Family Relations, 47,* 229–236.

McLoYD, V. (1990). The economic hardships of black families and children: Psychological distress, parenting, and socio-emotional development. *Child Development, 61*(2), 311–346.

OBERMAN, Y., & JOSSELSON, R. (1996). Matrix of tensions: A model of mothering. *Psychology of Women Quarterly, 20,* 341–359.

PARPAL, M., & MACCOBY, E. (1985). Maternal responsiveness and subsequent child compliance. *Child Development, 56*(5), 1326–1334.

ROCISSANO, L., SLADE, A., & LYNCH, V. (1987). Dyadic synchrony and toddler compliance. *Developmental Psychology, 23*(5), 698–704.

ROGERS, S., & WHITE, L. (1998). Satisfaction with parenting: The role of marital happiness, family structure, and parents' gender. *Journal of Marriage and the Family, 60,* 293–308.

SCHLOSSMAN, S. (1976). Before home start: Notes toward a history of parent education. *Harvard Educational Review, 46*(3), 436–467.

SCHLOSSMAN, S. L. (1983). The formation era in American parent education: Overview and interpretation. In R. Haskins & D. Adams (Eds.). *Parent education and public policy* (pp. 7–36). Norwood. NJ: Ablex.

SECCOMBE, K. (1991). Assessing the costs and benefits of children: Gender comparisons among childfree husbands and wives. *Journal of Marriage and the Family 53*(1), 191–202.

SIMONS, R., WHITBECK, L., CONGER, R., & MELBY, J. (1990). Husband and wife differences in determinants of parenting: A social learning and exchange model of parenting behavior. *Journal of Marriage and the Family, 52*(2), 375–392.

THOITS, P. (1992). Identity structures and psychological well-being: Gender and marital status comparisons. *Psychological Quarterly, 55,* 236–256.

THOMAS, R. (1996). Reflective dialogue parent education design: Focus on parent development. *Family Relations, 45,* 189–200.

TURNER, P., HAMNER, T., & ORELL, L. (1993). *Children and families in New Mexico* (Background Report for New Mexico First). Albuquerque: College of Education.

U.S. BUREAU OF THE CENSUS. (1997). *Statistical abstract of the United States: 1997* (117th ed.). Washington, DC: U.S. Government Printing Office.

U.S. DEPARTMENT OF AGRICULTURE, ARS, FAMILY ECONOMICS RESEARCH GROUP. (1992). Expenditures on a child by families, 1991. In J. Courtless (Ed.), *Family Economics Review, 5*(1), 33–36.

VAN IJZENDOORN, M. (1992). Intergenerational transmission of parenting: A review of studies in nonclinical populations. *Developmental Review, 12*(1), 76–99.

WALLACE, P., & GOTLIB, I. (1990). Marital adjustment during the transition to parenthood: Stability and predictors of change. *Journal of Marriage and the Family, 52*(1), 21–29.

WILKIE, C., & AMES, E. (1986). The relationship of infant crying to parental stress in the transition of parenthood. *Journal of Marriage and the Family, 48*(3), 545–550.

WILLE, D. (1995). The 1990s: Gender differences in parenting roles. *Sex Roles, 33*(11/12), 803–817.

WOODWORTH, S., BELSKY, J., & CRNIC, K. (1996). The determinants of fathering during the child's second and third years of life: A developmental analysis. *Journal of Marriage and the Family, 58*(3), 679–692.

CHAPTER 2

The Changing Nature of Parenting:
Infancy and Early Childhood

The role of parent is one of several adult roles achieved by a large number of men and women in society today. However, parenting has unique features, which we described in Chapter 1, in arguing for the need for education for parenting. In light of these features, it is no wonder that parents feel confused and even overwhelmed, particularly with the birth of the first child.

A number of factors have an impact on the specific nature of the parent's role. We discussed in Chapter 1 the characteristics of, and differences between, mothering and fathering. However, many contemporary parents have become more androgynous, thereby minimizing many of the traditional differences between the roles of mothers and fathers. Fathers classified as androgynous have been found to carry out more child-care tasks and interact more with their children than fathers who are rated as masculine. Other studies have indicated that fathers who participate more extensively in child rearing also are more nurturant and sensitive.

Number and spacing of children also affect the parenting role. As more children are added to the family, the nature of parent-child relationships is altered. In fact, the birth of each sibling may represent a developmental crisis for some families. Considerable research has shown that parent-child interactions are different in a variety of familial contexts—for example, mother and child, mother-father-child, mother and two children.

Family size, too, affects parenting style. It has been noted that children with few siblings have more parental resources available to them than children with many siblings, and the resources available seem to benefit children more. Further, number of siblings is related to academic achievement, with children from smaller families outperforming children from larger families in grades and in math and reading achievement test scores (Downey, 1995), presumably because parental resources are diluted. Further, children in larger families experience more overt conflict but more emotional closeness (Newman, 1996), both of which affect parenting behavior.

The structural makeup of the family is still another condition that affects the parenting role. Children reared in intact nuclear families are likely to have different relationships with their parents than children reared in extended families, single-parent families, or in stepfamilies. As children develop from infancy through adolescence, the changes in their developmental characteristics bring about changes in the parenting role. Traditionally, professionals have studied the effects of inadequate parenting on the development of the child and have ignored the significance of the interaction between the parent and the child within the context of the contributions that each makes to the other in shaping behavior.

PARENTS AND INFANTS

Parents as Caregivers

The term *caregiver* has been used in the literature to refer to the person or persons responsible for providing primary care of the infant or young child. Its use implies that males are as capable of giving care as females are and that persons other than biological parents frequently are significant caregivers. Most of the recent research indicates that infants may attach and adapt to more than one significant caregiver, as long as the number remains small and the adults are consistently responsive in the kind of care they provide. Of particular interest has been the father as caregiver and the infant's interactions with him. Fathers appear to be capable of nurturant behavior toward their infants and are strongly interested in them, although they engage in less caretaking and more play with them than mothers do.

The traditional, noninvolved "breadwinner" image of the father has changed for many families into the image of an actively involved father who is willing to assume some caretaking responsibility for his children soon after birth. The combination of a playful father and a responsive, verbal mother provides significant facilitation of cognitive development.

It is our position that a number of people can be effective caregivers for infants—mothers, fathers, grandparents, child-care workers, older siblings, and friends. It is on the parents, however, that we wish to focus here. Although caregiving by the parents may be supplemented by others when neither partner devotes full time to the care of the infant, we want to emphasize the quality rather than the quantity of parental caregiving activities. The kind of parent-child transaction that seems to promote competence has less to do with the amount of time a parent spends with a child than with the quality of the transactions, which, after all, may consume relatively little time in the course of a day. Further, studies have suggested that supplemental caregiving in a high-quality environment does not seem to interfere with the secure attachment process between infants and their parents. Therefore, we will consider the parents as primary caregivers of their infants, whether or not the infant receives supplemental care.

In most cases when an infant is born, her needs for mothering exceed the mother's need for the child. This fact necessitates reduction of a woman's, and many times a man's, involvement in nonfamily interests and social roles. With the decline of accessible extended families, most young parents today have little physical or emotional support for the awesome task that faces them. They are prepared poorly, at best, to cope with the strain of the sudden demands placed upon them. The infant is helpless and dependent on caregivers for all her needs. Her parents assume the roles of protectors and providers. Parents, who are accustomed to freedom, suddenly find themselves unable to go shopping, visit friends, or take weekend trips without considerable preparation and adaptation. Further, during the first few months, the infant's capabilities are unfolding so rapidly that parents' behavior must continually change to meet the baby's needs.

Initial caregiving consists primarily of the provision of life support and protection. The pregnancy, the infant's physical appearance, the helpless thrashing movements, as well as the fact that the infant's sensory and motor system matches that of the mother, all contribute to maintaining the caregiving system.

At least three major factors appear to influence relationships between parents and infants: (1) the quality of the parents' own early experiences—the care each received as a child; (2) the conditions of the present situation—family stability or marital discord, job security, health, degree of stress in daily lives, and so on; and (3) the characteristics of the infant himself (Eiden, Teti, Corns, 1995; Fox, 1995). Parental attitudes and accuracy of perceptions about the baby's characteristics and needs are additional influences. Some studies have shown that the infant's behavior is related to the mother's and the father's expectations—for example, what they believe the infant can do.

When we examine the parent-infant relationship from the perspective of what the infants themselves contribute, it is clear that infants differ from the beginning in their responses to the environment. Brazelton's classic book *Infants and Mothers: Differences in Development* (1969) described the normal developmental paths of three very different infants as well as the different ways in which they affected their environments. His portraits of Daniel, Louis, and Laura illustrated that normal babies differ from the beginning in their level of activity, their adaptability, their biological rhythmicity, and their general responsiveness to their environments.

Studies have shown that the more difficult the child is temperamentally, the less responsive the mother is likely to be. A classic longitudinal study described *easy babies, difficult babies,* and *slow-to-warm-up babies*—a description of the different temperaments of babies based on nine traits, thought to be largely innate (Thomas & Chess, 1977). Difficult babies cry a lot and have irregular schedules. They are difficult to soothe and do not adapt easily to new people and situations. These babies do not fare well with impatient, unresponsive mothers, but they may, in fact, contribute to their mothers' impatience and unresponsiveness. "Goodness of fit" does not occur in such cases between mother and infant, and synchrony (reciprocal, mutually rewarding interaction) is difficult to achieve. Babies further contribute to the parent-child interaction by their state of awareness—that is, whether they are asleep, awake, drowsy, or alert; by the types of signaling they demonstrate through vocalizing, touching, or looking; by the amount of attention they seek; and by the extent of responsiveness they demonstrate. Brazelton (1995) noted that there were several "touchpoints" during the period of infancy for most families. These are points at which a change in the family system is brought about by the baby's spurt in development. Just before each developmental spurt, the baby experiences a brief but predictable period of disorganization, which parents may view as regression or problem behavior. Really, it represents a period of reorganization before the next spurt in development. For example, nearly 85 percent of U.S. infants between 3 and 12 weeks of age are fussy at the end of each day, which seems to be a necessary organizing period for them. Often parents become anxious or feel incompetent if they are unable to soothe the baby.

Three other touchpoints occur during the first year. The first is between 6 and 8 months when the baby begins to sit alone, crawl, handle food with a pincer grasp, and show stranger anxiety and separation anxiety. The second occurs at approximately 10 months when the baby tries to get out of her crib and shows a desire to stand alone and walk holding on. The final touchpoint occurs around 1 year of age, or when the baby shows awareness of his independence by walking unassisted and begins to test limits and refuse proffered food. During all these periods of disorganization, infants can challenge their parents' patience, thus creating tension that can affect the parent-child relationship. By predicting these touchpoints and recognizing them as natural aspects of development, parents can reduce their anxieties and support the baby's development.

It seems obvious, then, that the infant is no mere passive recipient of stimulation who is controlled by the adults in her environment but is an active participant in her own development, and her unique manner of participation is a critical factor in the kind of parenting behaviors she receives. Competent caregiving lays the foundation for social interactions, reciprocal communication and signaling, and the development of special skills during the period of infancy.

Establishing Basic Trust

Erik Erikson (1963) described the stages of the life cycle and the psychosocial development of the ego. Erikson conceived of each stage as being marked by an issue or a "crisis" to connote an emphasis in the individual's life. The first of these stages, occurring from birth to about 1 year, is defined as trust versus mistrust. The degree to which the child comes to trust the world, other people, and himself depends to a considerable extent on the quality of care that he receives. The infant whose needs are met when they arise; whose discomforts are quickly removed; and who is cuddled, fondled, played with, and talked to develops a sense of the world as a safe place to be and of people as helpful and dependable.

When, however, the care is inconsistent, inadequate, and rejecting, it fosters a basic mistrust, an attitude of fear and suspicion on the part of the infant toward the world in general and toward people in particular, that will carry through to later stages of development. Erikson did not believe, however, that the problem of basic trust versus mistrust was resolved once and for all during the first year of life; rather, it arises again at each successive stage of development. If basic needs are not met, the child feels somehow empty, cheated, at a loss, and ill at ease with others and with herself.

How can a sense of basic trust be fostered? The newborn comes equipped with one major means of communicating with others in the environment—crying. At first, parents must infer what the infant is attempting to communicate with his cries. They check his diapers, feed him, change his positions, rock him, or do whatever it takes to relieve his distress. In essence, parents are at the mercy of the infant's cries.

It is not long, however, until parents begin to distinguish a hunger cry from a distress cry and can attend to these with less trial-and-error behavior. There has been some controversy concerning how much attention should be given and how quickly parents should respond to infant crying.

Nearly 30 years ago, Bell and Ainsworth (1972) found that infants who have an early history of delay on the part of the mother in responding to crying tend later to cry for longer periods than do infants with a history of less delay. In other words, the consistency and promptness of maternal response during the first 3 months (or its absence) affects the pattern of later infant crying. Moreover, they found that infants whose cries had been neither ignored nor responded to with undue delay developed modes of communication other than crying. Thus, a baby whose experience has been that his mother responds to his signals with consistency and promptness learns to expect that signaling—and, later, communication—is effectual and not merely that there will be a response to crying. (Fathers were not involved in this study, but we assume that these conclusions would apply to them as well.)

Although there are those who are still convinced that if a mother or a father attends to crying, the infant will be reinforced and thus cry more, we believe that Bell and Ainsworth's conclusions are still valid. Prompt attention to crying during the early months is one way of facilitating the basic trust that Erikson believed to be so important. Moreover, the repeated pattern of infant crying and parental responding is critical for the development of early communicative skills, early expectencies, and secure attachments (Green, Gustafson, & McGhie, 1998).

Equally important as prompt, consistent attention to the infant's needs is the maintenance of an orderly, predictable environment. The infant at birth does not view herself as a separate entity from others in the environment. In fact, at first, everyone and everything is an extension of herself. A critical task of the period of infancy is to develop a sense of self and of others as separate from self. This task is related in a complex way to establishing a sense of basic trust.

In the beginning, much of the infant's world is bound to his physiological needs. If he is fed when he is hungry, changed when he is wet, helped to sleep or rest when he is tired, and cared for by the same few people whom he eventually comes to recognize as significant, then his day-to-day environment becomes predictable, orderly, and consistent. He comes to know that certain things happen at particular times and that familiar people come when he needs them. He learns to recognize, too, the particular patterns of responses of his special caregivers—their tones of voice, their odors, and

the way their bodies feel when he is held close. All these consistent, predictable subtleties help him to learn who he is and that he can depend on others for his safety.

Trust is built also from the child's own behavior; that is, she begins to view herself as competent by her ability to act on her environment and her success in eliciting certain responses from her caregivers. If, however, the infant is cared for by a number of different people; if there is no predictability in her feeding, sleeping, or being played with; and especially if she is neglected or abused, then her sense of basic trust in herself as competent and in others as dependable will be impeded.

Attachment

Profoundly related to a sense of trust during the first year is the security of attachment the infant develops for his mother and other primary caregivers. *Attachment* refers to the special bond that the infant forms with significant adults in his life. It is the enduring relationship that persists in the face of transitory fluctuations in interactive behavior. In fact, some experts regard attachment as encompassing the totality of the infant-parent relationship, expressed in a range of interactive contexts (Pederson & Moran, 1996).

_____ TIPS _____

For Parents of Infants

Hold and cuddle the infant often—it won't spoil her!

Talk and sing to the infant frequently.

Respond promptly and consistently when the infant cries, and when he is older, he will cry less.

Maintain a predictable schedule for eating, sleeping, playing, but take cues from the infant.

Provide appropriate stimulation that is timely and reciprocal.

Balance the infant's day with interactive play and exploration of her environment.

Use routines (bathing, dressing, feeding) as language-learning experiences.

A sense of trust is crucial for the formation of this special relationship. Biological and environmental factors work interdependently to facilitate the infant's attachment to significant others. Maternal sensitivity and responsivity are the central features that foster secure attachment. Sensitivity is the mother's ability to perceive the infant's signals accurately and the ability to respond to them promptly and appropriately (DeWolff & van Ijzendoorn, 1997). Specifically, mothers who foster security are more responsive to their infants' cries, are more affectionate and tender, are more positive in affect, and interfere less often in their infants' ongoing behavior (Isabella & Belsky, 1991). Other variables that seem to affect security of attachment are mutuality and synchrony; stimulation; positive attitude; emotional support (DeWolff & van Ijzendoorn, 1997); and child characteristics such as temperament (Fox, 1995), gender (with a greater likelihood for insecure attachment in boys), and affect (Fish & Stifter, 1995).

The attachment relationship is critical to the subsequent cognitive and socioemotional development of the child. There are clear links between infant attachment and social competence through adolescence. In general, children with secure-attachment histories are more affectively positive and less affectively negative in peer interactions; they participate more actively in the peer group; they are rated as more popular; and they form deeper friendships. It is believed that a person's propensity to seek individuated relationships throughout life and the capacity to sustain them is critically related to the attachment relationships in infancy and early childhood (Belsky, Grossman, Grossman, & Scheuerer-Englisch, 1996).

Typically, attachment of infant to parent is assessed between 12 and 15 months of age in a laboratory setting called the Strange Situation, which consists of a series of brief episodes with presence/absence of the parent and presence/absence of a stranger. The infant's response to stress induced by the novelty of the context and the departure of the parent is used to assess the security of attachment. However, it is the infant's behavior toward the parent upon reunion that is the most important vari-

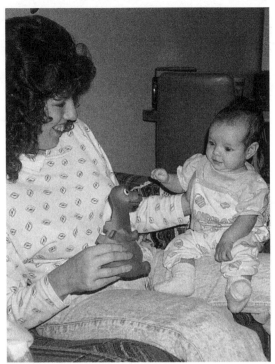

Maternal sensitivity is the central feature that fosters an infant's secure attachment.

able. Recently, however, researchers have designed and tested a home-based attachment relationship classification system that lacks the deliberate distress-inducing elements of the Strange Situation, which also seems to accurately distinguish between secure- and insecure-attachment patterns (Pederson & Moran, 1996).

Both the Strange Situation and home-based assessments yield classifications of infants into 3 major categories: secure, insecure-avoidant, and insecure-resistant. Infants rated as secure use their parents as a secure base from which to explore the novel environment, and the parent's response to the infant's signals is appropriate and predictable—the parent and the child's behavior are in harmony. Secure infants seek comfort from their parents when distressed, such as upon the parent's return after separation in the Strange Situation (Pederson & Moran, 1996).

Infants classified as insecure-avoidant tend to be relatively independent of their parents and display little proximity seeking. Typically, parents display inconsistent behavior, being at times surprisingly attentive to their infants' signals and at other times surprisingly inattentive. Infants may actively seek comfort from their parents, but when they are successful at gaining attention, they become fussy and hostile (Pederson & Moran, 1996). Overinvolved and intrusive parents also foster insecure ambivalence by leading their infants to develop defenses whereby they shut down from within. Insecure-avoidant behavior, then, is a self-protecting strategy for parental insensitivity and intrusiveness.

Infants classified as insecure-resistant, on the other hand, have parents who are underinvolved. The parent's behavior is unresponsive, such as delay in responding to the infant's cries. These infants tend to be distressed by separation from their parents in the Strange Situation and to seek contact during reunion but appear to be inconsolable (Steele, Steele, & Fonagy, 1996). Recently, some researchers have added a fourth category of attachment, disorganized, to describe infants who, because of their atypical responses to the Strange Situation, do not seem to fit into any of the three major classifications.

Although the bulk of research on attachment has focused on the mother-child relationship, research on father-infant attachment is growing, and a handful of studies has examined attachment of infants to other primary caregivers, such as childcare personnel. A meta-analysis of studies on infant-father attachment shows that the percent of infants securely attached to their fathers is roughly equal to the percent securely attached to their mothers—approximately two-thirds of all infants studied. However, the association between paternal sensitivity and infant attachment is somewhat weaker and less consistent than that association for mothers and infants. The tentative conclusion is that fathers shape their infants' attachment to a lesser extent than mothers do, and the transmission mechanisms are largely unknown. It has been suggested that fathers may compensate for their relative lack of influence indirectly through their impact on mothers' attachment and sensitivity (van Ijzendoorn & DeWolff, 1997).

To what extent are attachment patterns to the mother related to attachment patterns to the father? The research findings on this issue are mixed. Some researchers have found that infant attachment security does not generalize across relationships within the family system; that is, attachment security is relationship-specific (van Ijzendoorn & DeWolff, 1997). Other studies have found significant concordance (agreement in attachment classifications) between parents; that is, infants classified as secure with their mothers were likely to be classified as secure with their fathers, and those classified as either insecure-avoidant or insecure-resistant were likely to receive that classification with both parents. These researchers concluded that this concordance is due to the combined influences of the child's temperament and the parents' shared behaviors and values (Fox, 1995; Steele et al., 1996).

A relatively recent line of research has investigated the transmission of attachment patterns across generations. Using the Adult Attachment Inventory (AAI), mothers' or fathers' relationships with their own primary caregiver(s) during their early childhood are assessed. Parents are then asked to describe their relationship with their parents and to provide specific memories to support global evaluations, including experiences of rejection, distress, hurt, loss, abuse, and separation. They are then classified into the secure (autonomous) or one of the insecure (dismissing or preoccupied) groups, depending on the clarity, coherence, completeness, and orderliness of their narratives.

One study found a significant relationship between both mothers' and fathers' attachment and their infants' attachment classifications—that is, between secure and autonomous and between insecure-avoidant and dismissing—but no significant association was found between either mothers' or fathers' preoccupied classification and their infants' insecure-resistant classification. However, mothers who were classified as unresolved on the AAI with respect to past loss or trauma were likely to have infants who showed a disorganized pattern of behavior on the Strange Situation. Further, the data showed an apparently greater influence of the mother as opposed to the father upon infant-parent attachment (Steele et al., 1996). Another study (Eiden et al., 1995) found similar results: a match between mother and child attachment classifications of secure/insecure in 73 percent of the dyads. These data lend support to the notion of the intergenerational transmission of attachment patterns.

The importance of secure attachment cannot be overstated. As the infant's first primary socioemotional relationship, secure attachment lays the foundation for future positive relationships with peers, siblings, romantic partners, spouses, and, ultimately, one's own children. The quality of the parent-child relationship during the first year plays the primary role in this important process.

Developing Reciprocity

It should be obvious now that the parent-infant system is reciprocal in nature, with the behavior and characteristics of one influencing the behavior and characteristics of the other. Since much more has been written about mother-infant reciprocity than father-infant, we will focus on the mother-infant dyad. However, we want to emphasize that we believe the same sort of reciprocity can be developed between a father and his infant and between any other caregiver and an infant.

Reciprocity has been defined as a parallel waxing and waning of each partner's level of arousal, the degree of positive or negative involvement at given points during interaction (Brazelton, Koslowski, & Main, 1974). Similar concepts are those of *synchrony* and *mutuality*. Synchrony refers to the extent to which the mother-infant interaction is reciprocal and mutually rewarding. On the other hand, asynchronous interactions are those that are represented by one-sided, unresponsive, or intrusive behavioral exchanges. Positive mutuality includes positive exchanges in which mother and infant attend to the same thing, mutual gazing, mothers' skillful modulation of babies'

arousal, and active maintenance of the interaction (DeWolff & van Ijzendoorn, 1997).

Mother-infant reciprocity, however, appears not to be a phenomenon brought about solely by "good" mothering but, rather, by a process of mutual adaptation between mother and child. Both learn to recognize cues, signals, or patterns of specific behaviors and characteristics of each other in numerous situations. This sort of mutual adaptation begins in the prelinguistic phase and, in time, allows each partner to communicate to the other her involvement in the interaction.

In keeping with Brazelton's notion of level of arousal, both mother and infant contribute to the maintenance of an optimal level. Sensitive mothers provide appropriately timed stimulation for their infants; that is, they take cues from the infant—whether she is alert or drowsy, what stimuli she is attending to, and what signals she is sending. These mothers are neither intrusive nor unresponsive. They respond contingently to the baby's behavior. They reduce or stop stimulation, when appropriate, to allow the infant a brief period to withdraw and reestablish equilibrium. By the same token, babies seek stimulation when they desire it, they create or prolong pleasant situations, and they avert their gaze or turn their heads when stimulation is too overwhelming. Thus, the two partners work together to regulate the reciprocal interaction.

The development of reciprocity and the goodness of fit during the first 6 months of life facilitate the infant's learning to separate himself from others in his environment. The infant learns which behavior patterns represent "Mother" and thereby can distinguish her from others in the environment. Reciprocity fosters a sense of competence in that the child learns that he can influence how others behave toward him. During the last half of the first year, the infant's behaviors signal a preference for particular types of responsiveness instead of generalized responsiveness. He begins to anticipate his mother's actions in response to his own and initiates interactive sequences or alters interaction the mother has initiated in order to better suit his own needs and devices. The development of a system of communication is determined to a large extent by the manner in which the mother has responded to the infant's signals in the earlier months.

It appears that the development of reciprocity in the early months and the maintenance of reciprocal relationships in later months are both critical to healthy development. It is clear that both mother and infant either facilitate or impede this progress. Either an unresponsive baby or an unresponsive mother can interfere with the development of reciprocity, as can an overly intrusive mother who seldom gives her infant opportunity to initiate interaction.

Brain Development and Infant Stimulation

Only within the last quarter of the twentieth century was significant attention given to any aspect of infant care other than caring for physical needs. The influence of Piaget, the development of infant child-care centers, and convincing research concerning the importance of the first 2 or 3 years of life led to much more emphasis on optimal experiences during the period of infancy. The most exciting and revealing recent research has been conducted not by psychologists or educators but by neuroscientists. This research on the brain development of fetuses, infants, and children has found that the electrical activity of young brain cells actually changes the physical structure of the brain. Connections between the brain cells at birth explode over the first few months of life, reach their peak at about age 2, and remain at that level until approximately age 10. Spontaneous bursts of electrical activity strengthen some connections, whereas others, not reinforced by activity, become weak and atrophy.

What triggers these bursts of electrical activity?—Sensory experiences and stimulation. Children who are deprived of stimulating environments have brains that suffer. For example, children who do not play much or who are seldom touched by adults have been found to develop brains as much as 30 percent smaller than normal for their age

(Nash, 1997). It is repeated positive experiences that wire a child's brain—for vision, for emotions, for language, for movement—by providing a variety of experiences, including interesting things to look at; loving and responsive care; talking, singing, and reading; space and objects to explore.

Parents even play a role in wiring the brain for subsequent responses to stress. For example, Dr. Bruce Perry at Baylor University has found that children who are abused early in life develop brains that are attuned to danger. Early experiences of stress form a sort of template around which later brain development is organized. In addition, infants reared by depressed mothers show significantly reduced activity in the area of the brain that serves as a center for happiness and joy. Sad experiences produce sad brains (Nash, 1997).

Beginning at about age 10, the brain discards or destroys its weakest connections, preserving those that have been strengthened by repeated experience, either positive or negative. These findings emphasize the importance of early experiences and their impact on later development. It places an enormous responsibility on parents and other primary caregivers of infants to provide appropriate, timely, and reciprocal stimulation.

Parents provide stimulation in two ways: by structuring the environment to facilitate sensorimotor activities and by interacting directly with their infants. There is an abundance of research relating to the sensory equipment of infants and their preferences in attending to certain types of stimuli. For the sake of brevity, we will attempt to summarize and interpret the results in a practical way that relates to parenting.

It is now known that infants can see from the moment of birth but their focus and coordination are immature. Visual stimulation should consist of bright colors, light-and-dark contrasts (stripes, bull's-eye patterns, and geometric shapes), objects that move, and contoured surfaces. Although familiarity is important in the early months, within 5 or 6 months infants seem to prefer attending to moderately discrepant or complex stimuli. The human face is a favorite object for attention; it is contoured, it moves, and it talks. Close face-to-face gazing and vocalizing provide opportunities for significant visual, auditory, and even tactile stimulation. Frequent changes in position—from back to stomach, from crib to pallet, and from infant seat to swing—provide infants with different vantage points of vision and the variation they seek. Instead of Mother Goose wallpaper that the infant must look at for 3 to 6 years, we recommend the use of pictures, posters, mobiles, and collages that can be changed frequently as the infant seeks novelty and variation.

For auditory stimulation, vocalizing (imitating coos and babbles, talking, singing) is of utmost importance. The amount and the type of language used in the home during the period of infancy has been shown to be a critical factor in the child's later intellectual development. Exposure to music (all types), daily sounds in and out of the house, and reading regularly to the baby all help to provide auditory stimulation. It should be emphasized, however, that control of noise and distraction is important. Infants who are bombarded with noise (constant television, radio, shouting, and general commotion) learn to tune out the distractions and may have difficulty later in auditory discrimination and attention.

Of all the types of sensory stimulation, tactile stimulation seems to be the most important for healthy development. The sense of touch is the most highly developed sense at birth, having functioned prenatally longer than the other senses. Holding, cuddling, stroking, rocking, and movement have been shown to be essential. Other forms include massaging and bathing. Caregivers can provide these kinds of stimulation during feeding, changing, and other routine activities. Mothers who prop bottles or who put their babies to bed with a bottle not only are depriving them of a sense of warmth and closeness but also are depriving them of critical visual, auditory, and tactile stimulation. Toys that have varied textures (soft, slick, flexible, and rigid) also provide diverse tactile experiences. Variations in flavors and textures of foods provide stimulation for taste and smell.

Eye-hand coordination can be enhanced by crib toys and cradle gyms; by encouraging participation in feeding; by placing toys slightly out of reach when infants are old enough to move their bodies in an effort to retrieve them; and by providing objects that can be banged, thrown, or dumped and filled.

If the parent creates an interesting, stimulating environment, much of the infant's learning will be self-initiated. On examining Piaget's description of the growth of intelligence during the period of infancy, it becomes even more clear that the environment does not mold the child's behavior by simply imposing itself on a passive infant. Rather the infant seeks contact with her environment; she searches for environmental events to happen and seeks increased levels of stimulation and excitation. The infant interprets events in her environment and gives them meaning and consequently produces specific behaviors (Piaget, 1952).

The sensitive caregiver encourages action cycles with the infant by observing his moods, knowing what is interesting to him and learning what his skills are, giving him a chance to practice the familiar, and then challenging him to extend his skills in new directions with moderately novel materials and behaviors.

It is important, then, to balance the infant's day with self-initiated, independent activities for which the parent has set the stage and with interactive games or exchanges. An effort should be made to keep these interactions spontaneous, fun, and

HIGHLIGHTS

Ways to Provide Infant Stimulation

Visual—bright colors, light-dark contrasts, movement, contour, facial expressions
Auditory—talking/singing, reading, rattles, music, household sounds
Tactile—holding/cuddling, stroking, rocking, bathing, textured toys
Eye-hand coordination—crib toys, mobiles, holding toys about 7 inches away

consistent with the needs of both parent and child, striving for high mutuality.

In conclusion, infant stimulation needs to be varied, appropriately timed, linked to the infant's actions, and presented in a context of basic trust, remembering always that quality of stimulation is more important than quantity. We believe that if this task is accomplished, along with establishing basic trust, developing secure attachments, and developing reciprocity, the infant will have the best possible start in life.

PARENTS AND TODDLERS

The Parents' Roles as Protectors

Each phase of the parent-child interaction can alter the status of a child so that during the subsequent phase of interaction the child stimulates the parent in a different way or reacts differently to parent behavior. In turn, parents discover that previous behaviors are no longer appropriate, and they are faced with finding new ways of guiding and interacting with the child.

As the child becomes mobile, the role of the parent gradually takes on the new dimension of protector. The once dependent, "helpless" child is transformed into an active, tireless, and curious toddler. Suddenly she can see the top of the table, reach the magazines or ashtrays, flush toys down the toilet, drink from the pet's bowl, and perform a host of other activities that are fascinating to her growing curiosity. These behaviors are related to the fact that the toddler no longer needs hands to assist with locomotion and is free to feel and touch things that are attractive. First-time parents (and grandparents who have forgotten) are astonished at the ingenuity toddlers employ to satisfy their curiosity.

As protectors, parents must provide the safest possible environment for toddlers to exercise their growing autonomy and increased capacity for learning. The house and yard must now be accident-proofed. Glass, nails, and other sharp objects outdoors should be discarded; fences and gates need to be secure; and outdoor equipment should

be safe and in good repair. In the bathroom, all medicines should be locked and glass objects put out of the toddler's reach or put away entirely. In the kitchen, breakable items should be removed from lower cabinets, and all detergents, bleaches, and cleaning supplies should be stored in an inaccessible place. Many parents find that specifying a low cabinet especially for toddlers with metal or plastic utensils that they can bang and stack relieves parents and children of much tension. If parents are consistently firm about restricting the child to one cabinet, he soon learns to leave the others alone.

The remainder of the house (living room, bedrooms, and so on) should be accessible to the child to expand her space and possibilities for learning experiences. However, for a time everyone will be happier if breakable, fragile, or precious items are put away. In addition, it frequently is necessary to put safety devices in electrical outlets and put gates across entrances and exits to stairways. The argument from some is, "But he has to learn sometime." Yes, he has to, and he will. Obviously, parents cannot be expected to put away every lamp, get rid of all their plants, and eat off paper plates until their child gets older. Our point is that there will still be plenty of "no's" around that are necessary, and the child will have ample opportunity to learn that there are some things that are not meant for him without inviting temptation with other things that can easily be put away.

No matter how carefully parents accident-proof the house and yard, the precocious toddler always finds that one button under the carpet that she can swallow or climbs up on the kitchen cabinet to obtain the aspirin bottle on the top shelf. This means that, in addition to taking all the necessary precautions, parents must keep a constant watchful eye on the toddler's whereabouts and provide maximum supervision (as distinguished from interference) at all times.

For many parents the transition from caregiver (which does not cease altogether) to protector is a difficult one. First, they are not prepared for the safety measures they must take, and many learn through unfortunate experiences. Accidental poisoning is one of the leading causes of death during the first 2 years of life. Second, parents find that the care of a toddler is physically exhausting, so that they have little energy left to devote to social activities or to attending to the needs of their spouses. And finally, they find themselves becoming irritable at having to play the role of a police officer, and they long for the days when they could put the young baby in the crib or in the highchair and he would stay there.

Co-parenting can be supportive (one parent supports the other's goals, desires, or intentions) or unsupportive (one parent undermines the other's goals, desires, or intentions) or unsupportive-emotional (unsupportive accompanied by negative emotion). A recent study (Belsky, Crnic, & Gable, 1995) that examined relationships between parents and their first-born male toddlers found that supportive co-parenting was less frequent and unsupportive co-parenting more frequent when spouses differed from each other in several psychological domains (e.g., extraversion, neuroticism, and interpersonal affect) but not when they differed demographically (e.g., age, education) or in child-rearing attitudes. Further, the adverse effects of these differences were significantly greater when mothers and fathers were more stressed—that is, when they experienced many daily hassles. Therefore, spousal differences serve as a vulnerability factor with regard to unsupportive co-parenting, especially that which is accompanied by negative emotion.

Coping with Growing Autonomy

More difficult for parents, perhaps, than fulfilling the role of protector is coping effectively with the child's growing autonomy. The years from 1 to 3 constitute for the child a declaration of independence (Brazelton, 1974). Stage 2 in Erikson's theory of psychosocial development is described as autonomy versus shame and doubt. The child takes pride in her new accomplishments of walking and climbing, opening and closing, dropping, pushing

and pulling, and holding on and letting go. She wants to do everything for herself, from turning off the light switch to flushing the toilet.

If parents recognize the young child's need to do what he is capable of doing at his own pace and in his own time, the toddler develops a sense that he is able to control his muscles, his impulses, himself, and, not insignificantly, his environment. The phrase "Me do it" is familiar to most parents who have experienced the endless patience required to let the child dress himself in the morning, pour his own milk, or put away his toys. Erikson believed, however, that if caregivers are impatient and do for the child what he is capable of doing himself, they reinforce a sense of shame and doubt. When caregiving is consistently overprotecting or critical or harsh and unthinking, the child develops an excessive sense of doubt about his abilities to control his world and himself and develops shame with respect to other people.

Evidence shows that resistant and angry child behavior peaks during the second year and then begins its decline thereafter. In fact, mothers and fathers have been shown to react more positively to 12-month-olds than to 18-month-olds, and parents' self-rated enjoyment of parenting declines from 18 to 24 months. Many parents resist their toddlers' strivings for autonomy, and/or they have limited skill in managing effectively the child's emerging developmental advances (Belsky, Woodworth, & Crnic, 1996). Studies have shown that about 65 percent of parent-child interactions at age 2 are parental prohibitions, and parents have been found to interrupt their toddlers every 6 to 8 minutes to induce them to change their behavior (Baumrind, 1996).

This striving for autonomy in toddlers often is coupled with open negativism toward the parents. With toddlers' "no's," they establish themselves as separate from their parents. They learn what parents expect of them and how parents will act in response to them. Parents can minimize setting themselves up for a "no" from the child by phrasing statements in the form of expectations rather than choices when choices are not intended. For example, if a parent expects the toddler to go to bed, she should not say, "Do you want to go to bed now?" Instead she should say, "It's bedtime."

Setting Limits. There is no question that once children become mobile, parents must set firm limits and enforce them consistently in a loving manner. Either extreme in the setting of limits at this stage will interfere with healthy development. The most important limits have to do with the child's own safety and well-being—she does not go into the street, she does not eat the pet food, she does not climb on objects that are not sturdy or safe, she does not touch hot objects. The newfound freedom of the toddler carries with it potential danger, making the setting and maintenance of limits necessary. The purpose of external control (aside from safety) at this point is to make it possible for the child to know how and when to control herself. Erikson (1963) believed that a lasting sense of goodwill and pride derives from a sense of self-control without loss of self-esteem.

The evidence that toddlers between the ages of 1 and 3 actually comply with parental requests between 43 percent and 70 percent of the time suggests that the "terrible twos" may not actually be so terrible! However, socioeconomic status of the family is related to the degree of toddler compliance. More advantaged families experience more child compliance, lower levels of reprimands and authoritarian reactions to misbehavior by mothers, and a lower incidence of behavior problems (Belsky et al., 1996).

Temper Tantrums. More severe forms of negativism are manifested by toddlers in their frequent temper tantrums, which occur normally because wishes or desires for independence are thwarted. They are perpetuated by the parents who either force a contest of wills or give in to toddlers' desires. Neither technique is appropriate. Contests of wills may be avoided by making expectations simple, clear, and consistent. When children test these expectations, parents can assist cooperation by reinforcing verbal requests by physical contact (tak-

ing the child by the hand and leading him in the desired direction), modeling the expected behavior for the child, and offering legitimate choices so that he can exercise his independence—what kind of juice he wants, which book he wants to read, or which shirt he wants to wear. If all this fails and a tantrum ensues anyway, then the worst possible behavior is for the parent to give in to the child's wishes, if it is clear that those wishes are inconsistent with the limits the parent already has set. Consistent failure to pay attention to tantrum behavior usually serves to reduce it in normal, healthy children. Parents fail to reinforce it not only by not giving in but also by withdrawing attention from the tantrum and refusing to allow the child to harm himself, others, or property. It may be necessary to remove the child from the immediate environment in order to remove reinforcing agents.

Belsky and his associates (1996), in their research with families and their first-born male toddlers, identified a group of families who seemed to be having more difficulty than others managing their children. The families in the "most troubled" group were more likely to rely on basic control techniques (directives and prohibitions) and least likely to couple these control efforts with guidance (simple declaratives accompanied by reasons or explanations). Their children were the most defiant and subsequently experienced the most escalation of negative affect by parents. Further, these children demonstrated more aggression and acting out, and their parents reported more daily hassles. These investigators found that, in addition to low socioeconomic status, families likely to be "most troubled" were characterized by more support for and less interference with the fathers' work; had both mothers and fathers who were less social, more negative, and less friendly; and had both mothers and fathers who were least satisfied with the social support they were receiving. The strong associations with fathers' characteristics were surprising. The authors raised the important question of whether trouble in the second year forecasts further trouble in child rearing. Some experts have speculated that the parent-child interaction during toddlerhood represents a critical period for patterns that persist in the future. If such is the case, it seems that parents with toddlers should be targeted for family support and parent-education programs that might offset future problems.

We can conclude that the growing sense of autonomy in the toddler, although it is a necessary stage of healthy development, may be extremely frustrating for both parent and child. Parents need to recognize normal developmental behavior and not allow themselves to be threatened by negativism and sometimes lack of compliance. At the same time, they need to set firm limits, consistently maintain them, and provide simple reasons and explanations for required behavior. Appropriate techniques of guidance are those that allow the child choice of action and emphasize the positive rather than the negative. Opportunities for positive interaction and patience in providing independence training in self-help skills also are important. Parents should recognize an appropriate balance between too little and too much autonomy and facilitate self-control without causing the child to lose her self-esteem.

Providing Learning Experiences

Self-Help Skills.   The first area in which a parent can provide learning experiences for the toddler is in self-help skills. Even before toddlers begin to walk, they indicate a readiness to feed themselves. They can handle finger food, and they like to try to spoon foods into their mouths, often with the result that less ends up in the mouth than on the face, in the hair, and on the highchair tray. However, the wise parent picks up the child's cues that he is ready, even though his coordination may not be equal to his desire for independence. Some parents find it easy to give the baby a spoon or a piece of finger food and alternate feeding him with his own attempts. This gets the job done and allows the child to be involved in the interaction and practice his rudimentary skills. Later, when he is old enough to eat at the table with the family and to eat family food, the parent can gradually reduce assistance but keep a watchful eye to help when it is

needed. There is no need for a parent to go into orbit over a mess of peas on the floor or applesauce in the hair. The child himself can help clean the table, the floor, and himself when the meal is over.

Somewhat later the child repeats her "Me do it" in connection with dressing. A compromise may be reached between parent and child by allowing the child to do simple things such as pulling up her pants, putting on her socks, and zipping her jacket after the parent has gotten the zipper on the track. Simple clothing that the child can manipulate (large buttons, no straps to cross or pull over the shoulders, and shoes that do not need to be tied or buckled) make the task easier for the child and save the parent a lot of frustration. Pants that can be pulled up and down are especially important during the toilet-training phase. No one can expect a young child who waits until the very last minute to wait even longer until her belt is unbuckled or her straps are unsnapped.

Toilet Learning.   Toilet learning in the United States perhaps has caused parents more frustration than any other experience of child rearing. Parents indicate a desire for more information on the subject (Gross & Tucker, 1994). The degree of attention it receives in the literature varies with changing attitudes of the culture, which have come full circle from rigid to laissez-faire to permissive and all the way around again. However, in our present society there is no urgency in accomplishing toilet training; we can wait for the child to learn at his own pace. We are emphasizing "developing strong individuals who make their own choices in childhood, as preparation for an adulthood fraught with choices. To treat toilet training differently from all of the child's other tasks places undue emphasis on it" (Brazelton, 1974, pp. 143–144). This statement by Brazelton is still relevant today. Because this area has caused so much parental frustration, it often serves as a basis for conflict between parent and child that is not resolved easily. If we view the toilet-training process as an important learning experience for the child rather than a contest of wills, then perhaps conflict can be minimized.

The child indicates to his caregiver that he is ready for assistance in learning to control his bodily functions, first by demonstrating regularity in bowel movements and later in frequency of urination, followed by the child's understanding that dirty or wet pants are related to an act that he himself has performed. Finally, language skills to communicate the need to go to the bathroom signal the readiness for transition from diapers to training pants, at least during waking hours. If parents are alert to these cues, assist the child by providing simple clothing and accessibility to toileting facilities, and have infinite patience, the process will proceed smoothly (but perhaps not quickly by parental standards). A positive, reinforcing, patient attitude on the part of the parent will help the child to gain a sense of autonomy, whereas a critical, harsh, and impatient attitude will promote a sense of doubt and shame and a loss of self-esteem.

The developmental step of toileting should be treated like all others, such as feeding oneself or making choices about clothing, so that parents should wait for the child to learn at her own pace. If it is treated differently from the child's other tasks, then undue emphasis is placed on it. If it becomes a focus for attention, the child may use it for rebellion and negativism, and the child's determined strength will usually win. After all, urinating and defecating at the appropriate time and place is the *one* thing a parent cannot force the child to do. Constipation, wetting pants after being removed from the toilet, denying the need and then demonstrating it, or hiding in a corner to produce a bowel movement may be signals of too much parental control.

Further, the child's motivation and autonomy are of primary importance to any real success in toilet learning. Viewing toilet training as a learning experience within the context of acceptance, the child will get pleasure and excitement from mastering each step himself.

Social and Intellectual Learning. Aside from encouraging independence in self-help skills as learning experiences for the toddler, there seem to be four other areas of learning that are critical dur-

_____ **TIPS** _____

For Parents of Toddlers

Child-proof the environment by being sure it is safe.

Provide space and stimulating materials for play and exploration.

Give the toddler opportunities for making simple choices—e.g., "Do you want orange juice or apple juice?"

Set simple, appropriate limits and consistently enforce them.

Ignore temper tantrums unless the child is hurting herself or damaging property.

Promote independence by letting the child do things for himself—e.g., eating, dressing.

Avoid power struggles.

Initiate toilet learning when the child demonstrates that she is ready; be calm and patient with toilet accidents.

Recognize that toddlers are unable to "share."

Encourage rather than discourage curiosity.

Support language development by repetition, expansion, and modeling.

ing this period: the acquisition of social skills, language, the development of curiosity, and the formation of the roots of intelligence. In the first area, toddlers need exposure to interactions with other children their own age. Frequently, parents choose to place toddlers in a play group or a child-care center at this time so that they can learn such rudimentary skills as waiting one's turn, sharing toys and equipment, delaying gratification, and getting along well in groups. Some research suggests that toddler play groups have a positive impact on parent-child relations as well as on the child herself.

Children who do not have play-group, nursery-school, or child-care experience at the toddler stage need the opportunity to interact with their peers. Parents frequently can encourage neighborhood gatherings or associations with children of other friends. However, toddlers frequently treat their peers as objects rather than as persons, especially in the beginning stages of association. The

"Me do it" phrase mentioned earlier in this section is indicative of the egocentric nature of the young child. The "No, mine" protest that is familiar to all of us further emphasizes the immaturity of the toddler's understanding of social interaction. And the toddler's grabbing, pulling, biting, hitting, and so forth, are in part due to egocentricity and in part due to lack of language skills that older children use when cooperating in play.

The learning of appropriate social skills requires a patient adult who recognizes the child's immature level of development and therefore does not place too many demands on him to "be nice" or to "share the toys" or to wait too long. The wise parent or teacher duplicates toys and activities to minimize conflict over any special one; uses distraction and offers alternatives; and, most important, models appropriate social behavior for the child.

An extremely important event in the life of the toddler is the rapid development of language. From 18 months to 3 years, the average vocabulary of a child leaps from approximately 20 to 22 words to 900 words. Naturally, the child understands far more words than she uses. The parent's role in language development includes labeling familiar objects and events; expanding on the child's telegraphic speech; reinforcing language attempts; and, most important, modeling. Numerous studies have indicated that a child's language development is correlated closely with the quantity and quality of language used in the home. Further, children learn early language from adults, not from other children. The degree to which a parent talks *with* the child; asks questions as well as answers hundreds of *whys, whats,* and *hows;* reads to the child; and considers language as a valued tool for intellectual development relate to early language facility in the child.

The development of curiosity and the formation of the roots of intelligence during the toddler stage are related closely to language development. Even before the toddler has the language to ask questions, he demonstrates his curiosity by using the senses of touch, taste, smell, vision, and hearing. These senses, coupled with the ability for independent locomotion, provide important cues

about his expanded world and assist him in the formation of rudimentary concepts related to color, shape, size, weight, distance, and causality. As he acquires greater language facility, he is able to expand his concepts by attaching labels to them.

For the child to develop optimally intellectually and to satisfy curiosity, parents need to provide a variety of objects and experiences in a safe environment. Ample space in and around the house for the child to explore and experiment; rotation of toys and books; and excursions to the supermarket, the shopping center, the library, the zoo, and numerous other interesting places provide invaluable learning experiences. Parents need to be careful to avoid structured, didactic "lessons" that have preconceived expectations for performance and to encourage spontaneous, natural learning experiences from which the child is able to draw a wide variety of learning, based on her own interests and motivations. For example, a toddler with a coffee can full of objects from around the house will spend hours filling the can, dumping it, filling it again, and so on. From this experience she is learning something about size, shape, weight, color, and cause-and-effect relationships. With the parent's verbal interaction, she is also learning that a particular word stands for a particular object. Besides, she is probably having much more fun than a toddler whose mother is trying to teach her the alphabet or how to use the computer.

Put another way, the most important learning experiences for the toddler are those that are intellectual in nature and those of discovery. The role of the parent in discovery learning essentially is to structure the environment so that discovery can occur—that is, the parent provides the materials and the experiences and interacts with the child both verbally and physically when appropriate. As in earlier infancy, there should be a balance between self-initiated and self-sustained activity by the child as well as parent-child interaction. In this way the child controls much of his own learning within a framework provided by the parent.

Confidence in Parenting Toddlers. The toddler period represents a time when multiple aspects of development seem to explode—motor skills, language, curiosity, self-help skills, self-awareness, independence—and many parents experience stress in coping with such rapid changes, especially growing autonomy. Both fathers and mothers express a desire to know more about specific issues related to this stage of development. Mothers with more difficult children tend to feel less confident and tend to be at increased risk for depression; they feel ineffective managing their children's behavior in the face of friends and family members who expect them to be competent (Gross & Tucker, 1994). The previous investigators found that both mothers and fathers who perceived their toddlers to have more intense behaviors and more difficult temperaments had significantly lower parenting confidence. For mothers only, perception of more problematic toddler behaviors and more depression were linked to lower parenting confidence. The issues about which both mothers and fathers wanted more information, in addition to toilet learning, included temper tantrums, language development, bedtime struggles, peer relations, and limit setting. The authors concluded that when "the child's behavioral difficulty is pervasive, all parenting tasks become more difficult, leading to lowered confidence among fathers… [and] mothers" (p. 34).

PROGRAMS FOR PARENTS OF INFANTS AND TODDLERS

There is no consensus about the most effective form or timing of parent education. It seems, however, that parent-education programs for the parents of very young children are particularly important for two reasons. First, it is assumed that a person is most motivated when he or she *is* a parent or is about to become a parent. Further, parents have a more realistic orientation to some of the problems of parenthood than potential parents have and thus will reap more benefits from a program that is directed toward their current needs. Second, the emphasis that has been placed on the importance of environmental experiences for brain development in the early years and their

implications for the child's further development would seem to suggest the need for early intervention and support for parents. In fact, it has been said of parent-education programs that the earlier the better; the longer the better; the more consistent the better.

Formal early parental support was part of most of the federally funded children's programs in the late 1960s and 1970s. During the 1980s and the first half of the next decade, little public money was targeted to parents of very young children except for those at risk for abuse and neglect.

Recently there has been renewed interest in home-visiting programs for new parents, which currently serve a variety of populations and achieve many different goals. Home visiting is not a single, specific, uniformly defined service but, rather, a strategy for service delivery—it brings services to a family rather than requiring the family to come to the service providers. Programs target primarily pregnant women and/or families with young children up to 3 years of age. The goals of the programs range from a single goal, such as preventing low birth weights, to multiple goals, such as promoting a child's physical health and cognitive development and preventing child abuse. Still others take an even more comprehensive approach, seeking to address the needs of other family members. Some programs target specific populations, such as pregnant teens or families at risk for child abuse and neglect, whereas other programs are universal—that is, open to any family who wishes to participate (Gomby, Larson, Lewit, & Behrman, 1993). One example of a universal program is the Parents as Teachers program (see Chapter 5), which is widely used across the nation.

A 1994 survey (Wasik & Roberts) of nearly 2,000 home-visiting programs found significant diversity among and within program types. Somewhere between 20 percent and 34 percent of programs reported hiring both professional and paraprofessional staff. However, staff reported receiving very little ongoing training or supervision, and they rarely were provided with written materials to use with parents. The authors concluded that these gaps were of serious concern because of the stressful nature of the work and the wide range of knowledge and skills needed.

Olds and Kitzman (1993) conducted an extensive review of the effectiveness of home-visiting programs in improving the lives of children and families. Their results were mixed. Programs for parents of preterm and low-birth-weight newborns have been remarkably successful in promoting effective prenatal caregiving and children's intellectual functioning, but programs designed to *prevent* preterm delivery and low birth weight have been disappointing. The outcomes of programs designed for low-income parents have been inconsistent. Those programs that were comprehensive in nature, that began when the mother was pregnant, and that employed professionals or highly trained staff as home visitors had the most positive results. Though not experimental in nature, recent evaluations of the Parents as Teachers program indicate that both parents and children benefit—children, by demonstrating once they are in school advanced academic skills when compared with nonparticipants, and parents, by being more involved than nonparticipating parents in their children's schooling.

Though little federal support has existed for parent education since 1980, many hospitals and birthing centers offer classes for new parents, and ever increasing numbers of schools use the Parents as Teachers program. Hospital-based new-parent classes most often emphasize the practical aspects of parenting, such as feeding, bathing, soothing, and health-related issues. Although discussion of these daily routines may be useful to first-time parents, more in-depth exposure to the psychological aspects of parenting would be desirable. Existing programs normally are limited to the first few days after birth or, at best, to the first few weeks, and they seldom are led by psychologists or child-development specialists. Most parents who participate are from the middle class.

There are several impediments to the success of education and support programs for parents of infants. The first is the reluctance of parents to admit to nonmedical concerns or problems with their babies. This reluctance is compounded by the lack of specialized training of well-intentioned social-service and health professionals who imply that "nothing is wrong" to parents who do seek help. Second, even if individual or group sessions for parents are available, they often do not accommodate working parents or make provisions for including care of infants. Parent group sessions seem to be more effective when the infants participate in a concurrent but separate program (McKim, 1987). Finally, parents who most need help are not receiving it. The lack of time, energy, motivation, and resources frequently prevents single parents, families with babies with disabilities, working parents, and parents of "difficult" babies from participating in programs or seeking support services.

Further, parents of different socioeconomic levels may have different needs. It has been found that socioeconomic status (SES) is an important variable in the relationship between parenting knowledge and quality of stimulation in the home. Low SES mothers' perceptions about the influences of infant caregiving practices on infants' well-being were directly related to the quality of the home environment, and the quality of stimulation in the home was, in turn, directly related to infants' performance on the Griffiths Mental Development Scale (Parks & Smeriglio, 1986). These results suggest that parenting education groups for low-income parents should emphasize the importance of caregiving practices for specific developmental outcomes.

As children develop from infants to toddlers, the support needs of parents change, and the emphasis of programs must reflect this change. For example, program content should include such topics as toilet learning, behavior problems, ways of coping with growing autonomy, management techniques, and training in self-help skills. Even though for many parents toddlerhood presents special challenges, few programs currently focus on this particular developmental period.

In summary, the following issues need to be considered in developing programs for parents of infants and toddlers: (1) training professionals to be sensitive to and skillful in counseling about the daily issues and adjustments of parents of young infants; (2) designing long-term programs that emphasize the psychological aspects of parenting children during the first 3 years of life; (3) considering the particular needs of parents of different socioeconomic levels in developing program content; (4) designing programs that have immediate relevance for age-related development; and (5) using delivery systems, such as television, that reach a broader range of parents, particularly those who are the most in need.

PARENTS AND PRESCHOOL CHILDREN

The Parents' Roles as Nurturers

Nurturance is affectionate care and attention. According to Webster's (1994), to nurture is "to educate or to further the development of...." These definitions aptly describe the chief role that parents assume as their children move into the preschool period. Nurturance can be provided by both mothers and fathers. Although the child's environment still must remain safe and protective, preschool children do not need the constant watchful eye of parents that was so necessary for a toddler. To discover the optimal amount of supervision without interference, assistance without indulgence, and warmth and love without suffocation is difficult for many parents. They find that their need to be needed is still very strong, and some find it difficult to meet that need in a way that is healthy for both themselves and their children.

It is during the preschool period that many mothers immerse themselves in the parenting role. Young children are loud, intrusive, and demanding of their parents' attention, time, and energy. Adults find themselves continually interrupted in conversations, visited by their children in the bathroom, and irritable at the consistent elevated noise level and disarray of the house. Further, the preschool child seems to alternate between behavioral extremes—that is, phases of cooperative, compliant behavior alternate with phases of resistant, negative behavior, coupled with emotional extremes of shyness and aggressiveness. These inconsistent behaviors puzzle many parents and often cause them to question their methods of dis-

cipline, which may result in vacillation between freedom and control.

Warmth refers to the parents' emotional expression of love. Children of parents with warmth and empathy are motivated to participate in cooperative strategies, and these parental characteristics are associated with children's internalization of moral values. Conversely, a predominance of parental negative affect is associated with defiance and hostile aggression in children (Baumrind, 1996).

It is likely that a child's perception of the emotional climate that exists within the home is of far greater consequence in healthy development than the specific behaviors of the parents. Further, consistency in the kind of discipline used by parents, how it is administered, and in what context (Baumrind, 1996) seem to be more influential in facilitating healthy development than the specific type of discipline used. If parents have not agreed already on the goals and values they have for their children, it is critical that some agreement be reached at this point. Belsky et al. (1995) reported research noting that spousal disagreements about child-rearing attitudes and values when children were 3 years old predicted both child behavior problems 2 years later and marital dissolution 7 years after that. Other research has shown that such disagreements forecast psychological and behavioral development when children are as old as 18.

Another study examined the relationship of parental disputes about child rearing and the behavior of preschool boys. Seven types of negative behavior were included: being sneaky, hurting others, being rude or using unacceptable language, annoying or teasing others, breaking things, approaching trouble others have started, and disobeying or ignoring parents' rules. Disagreements between a child's parents about child rearing predicted six of the seven behaviors in 3- to 6-year-old boys. This aspect of the marital relationship was more reliable than global marital adjustment in predicting behavior problems (Jouriles et al., 1991).

However, children can adjust to some differences in the behavior of parents (Daddy reads to me, Mommy bathes me). They find it much more difficult to adjust to disputes about long-term goals and values. Each parent is different and will interact with the child in ways that are unique to his or her own style, but consistency in making and enforcing rules and a common agreement as to whether discipline will be permissive, authoritative (democratic), or authoritarian will offer the young child the consistency that is vital to her growing sense of competence. Children need to know that behavior allowed today will not lead to punishment tomorrow; behavior approved by mom is also approved by dad. They need the comfort that parents do not respond to children from whim but from some sense of consistency, both within the individual parent and between the parents.

A strong love relationship between the parents at this time facilitates their roles as nurturers of their children. Respect for each other and respect for their children as individuals creates a positive emotional climate in the home. Furthermore, love and respect of parents for each other is an effective tool for facilitation of the identification process in the late preschool period.

One major consideration in providing nurturance is knowing how to establish limits and achieve responsible behavior in young children without threatening their sense of autonomy and initiative.

Discipline versus Punishment

One of the major concerns that parents of young children face is how much or how little to "discipline" their children. Unfortunately, in our society the terms *discipline* and *punishment* often are used synonymously. When someone says, "What that child needs is discipline," usually it means that the child needs punishment, most often physical in nature. In fact, however, the term *discipline* derives from the Latin word *discipula,* which refers to one who receives instruction from another—a follower. When the word is used in its exact context, then, a system of discipline should imply a broad positive system of guidance of the young child, with the particular methods of punishment used being only a minor aspect of that system.

TIPS

For Parents of Preschoolers

Supervise the child without interfering with his activities.

Establish limits without threatening the child's sense of initiative.

Use authoritative discipline—e.g., reasoning, explanations, and a combination of responsiveness and appropriate control.

Use inductive discipline; i.e., focus on the "how" rather than the "what" of behavior.

Use natural and logical consequences rather than aversive punishment.

Promote a positive self-concept.

Encourage self-initiated activities and exploration of the environment.

Read to the child every day.

Listen and respond to the child's endless questions.

Provide appropriate play materials to facilitate learning.

Provide opportunities for the child to play and interact with peers.

More than 30 years ago, Diana Baumrind (1966) described three prototypes of adult control that still are referred to frequently in the literature as discipline systems. Recently she revisited her earlier work, and again she emphasized that either extreme in the discipline controversy (permissive or authoritarian) results in negative child outcomes, whereas the authoritative model rejects both extremes (Baumrind, 1996). (See Highlights for the three prototypes.) Whereas authoritarian parents place obedience as the cornerstone in the foundation of character, permissive parents are child-centered, high on responsiveness, and low on demandingness. The authoritative model, on the other hand, views behavior compliance and psychological autonomy as interdependent rather than as mutually exclusive. Children are encouraged to respond in prosocial ways *and* to reason autonomously about moral problems. Further, they are expected to respect adult authority *and* learn how to think independently (Baumrind, 1996). Parents

HIGHLIGHTS

Prototypes of Parental Discipline

TYPE	PARENTAL CHARACTERISTICS
Permissive	Nondamanding and responsive
	Nonpunitive, accepting, and affirmative
	Little constraint or inhibition
	High persuasion
	Avoids exercising control
	Obedience to externally defined standards not valued
	Consults child on family decisions
	Uses reason and manipulation rather than power
Authoritarian	Demanding and nonresponsive
	Uses set standard of conduct to control and shape child
	Values obedience
	Uses punitive, forceful measures
	Restricts autonomy
	Curbs child's self-will
Authoritative	Demanding *and* responsive
	Rational, issue-oriented
	Values both autonomous reasoning and conformity
	Uses firm control contingently
	Emphasizes discussion, explanation, clear communication
	Uses reason, power, reinforcement in shaping behavior

Source: Baumrind, D. (1996). The discipline controversy revisited. *Family Relations, 45* 405–414.

who are warm and nurturant, who use reason and explanations for required behavior, who set and maintain reasonable limits with appropriate levels of control, and who provide a balance between the values of autonomy and conformity provide the best possible environment for children, who demonstrate positive outcomes in almost every area of behavior and development from preschool through adolescence. Parents who exercise no control and exert few or no demands on children generally produce children who have no framework for developing self-discipline or no guidelines for making decisions. Finally, parents who use power-asser-

tive techniques to control their children's behavior (e.g., physical punishment, threats, belittling, and directives given with little or no justification) produce children who are aggressive and hostile.

Authoritative parental style is associated with more positive child interactions with peers and more positive interactions between siblings. For example, it was found that mothers' ability to support their preschool children, to create appropriate structure and limits, to allow autonomy, and to avoid hostility predict socioemotional competence in peer interactions, whereas lack of support and autonomy predict sadness and feelings of rejection, especially for preschool girls (Denham, Renwick, & Holt, 1991). Mothers' encouragement of curiosity and openness, their reference to social rules and the feelings of others, and sensitivity in responding to children's needs also predict cooperative and friendly sibling relationships. Interestingly, early parent-child interactions apparently continue to influence children's development, even if the caregiving environment changes over time. For example, one study found that when mothers were intrusive and overcontrolling when the child was 3 years old, this behavior was related to high levels of sibling conflict and aggression 3 years later. In addition, early facilitative and affectionate fathering was associated 3 years later with prosocial interaction among peers (Volling & Belsky, 1992).

Inductive Discipline.   Inductive discipline focuses on encouraging the young child to take into account the potential effects of his behavior on other people and on himself when making decisions about what he will and will not do. This approach is most often combined with an authoritative style of parenting. The inductive parent emphasizes process goals, stressing the "how" rather than the "what" of behavior. This procedure is in contrast to the parent telling the child that certain behaviors are good and others are bad, which is more likely to produce unnecessary feelings of guilt and shame. It is important to show children why their present behavior pattern is inappropriate, showing them how to act instead, and demonstrating the expectation that they will change their behavior in the desired direction. Parents who use inductive, rational disciplinary techniques often have children who are less likely to violate prohibitions than other children are.

A recent study found very high prevalence and chronicity rates of spanking young children. Well over 61 percent of mothers of preschool children reported spanking their children within the last week, with a mean of about 3 spankings that week, sug-

Mothers' ability to support their preschool children predicts socioemotional competence in peer relations.

gesting that children 3 to 5 years of age are spanked about 150 times each year. Significant relationships were found between low socioeconomic status and both prevalence and chronicity of spanking. More sons than daughters were spanked, and African American mothers spanked more than other mothers did. Rural mothers, young mothers, and Protestant mothers spanked more than urban, older, and Catholic mothers. The authors concluded that these data suggest a serious threat to the well-being of children because spanking increases the chances of both physical aggression and delinquency and is associated with depression, spouse abuse, and reduced occupational achievement in adulthood (Giles-Sims, Straus, & Sugarman, 1995).

The findings of Day, Peterson, and McCracken (1998) were consistent with those of Giles-Sims et al. (1995) in confirming that spanking is a common occurrence in families with young children, with fathers spanking less than mothers. The strongest and most consistent predictors of parental spanking, though, in their study were the personal characteristics of parents (young age and conservative religious ideology) and perceived characteristics of the child (whether the child was difficult and whether he or she was competent). They pointed out, however, that different family structures and characteristics lead to wide variations among families in the incidence and intensity of spanking behavior.

It also is important to note that socialization practices vary across cultures, and children generally accept most normative practices. Chapter 6 discusses cultural variations in parenting in some depth. Baumrind (1996) noted that cultural differences in socialization practices, including discipline, often reflect adaptive solutions to problems posed by particular environments. Some practices judged to be overly restrictive in a benign middle-class environment actually may provide appropriate supervision and support in a more impoverished and/or dangerous environment. In fact, the relationship between spanking and aggression has been found to be negative in at least one sample of African American families and generally positive in Anglo-American families (Baumrind, 1996).

Natural and Logical Consequences. Rudolf Dreikurs was noted for his approach to discipline through the use of natural and logical consequences (Dreikurs & Grey, 1968), and this approach is still widely used today. Natural consequences are those that occur naturally from behavior; for example, the child who refuses to eat goes hungry. Logical consequences are those that are assigned by the parent to express the reality of the social order, not of the person; for example, a child who is disturbing the rest of the family at mealtime is given the choice to settle down or to leave the table.

Some advantages of using natural and logical consequences rather than relying on reward and punishment were pointed out by Dinkmeyer, McKay, and Dinkmeyer (1997) in their parent-education program, Systematic Training for Effective Parenting. (See Chapter 5.) First, this approach holds children, not their parents, responsible for the children's behavior; second, it allows children to make their own decisions about what courses of action are appropriate; and, third, it permits children to learn from the (impersonal) natural or social order of events rather than forcing them to comply with the wishes of other people. When parents apply natural and logical consequences, the consequences must be sensible and logically related to the behavior, and children must see them as logical. In addition, choices are essential. Alternatives are proposed by the parent, and the parent accepts the child's decision. Then the child makes a choice without external pressure. The parent should be both firm and kind, with firmness referring to following through with the behavior and kindness referring to the tone of voice and manner in which choices are given to the child. Finally, the parent must separate the deeds from the doer; that is, the parent's action must be based on respect for the child as a person separate from her deeds.

It appears difficult for many parents to use natural and logical consequences, first, because parents do not like to see their children suffer from some of the consequences, and, second, because they become discouraged if they do not see changes in the child's behavior right away. Encouragement is implicit in this approach, and, if the parent is patient and consistent, children will learn to accept responsibility for their own behavior in a way that conveys mutual respect and avoids power struggles.

Guidelines for the Use of Punishment.   We have thus far focused on the characteristics of authoritative and inductive parental styles, as well as the use of natural and logical consequences as alternatives to punishment. All punishment can be conceived as power assertion, for it is the parent who uses his or her power to determine the punishment and carry it out. Mild punishment that is not physical or psychological in nature, however, has fewer negative consequences for the child than spanking, belittling, threatening, and so on, especially if it is administered by a parent who is loved and respected. Arbitrary reliance on aversive discipline is the critical factor that results in harm to children or failure to obtain their compliance (Baumrind, 1996). A clear distinction must be made between punishment that is perceived by the child as being just, deserved, and administered in a warm, loving environment, and punishment that is perceived as harsh, unjust, and administered in a restrictive, rejecting environment. If all else fails and a parent feels he or she must punish a child, considerable thought should be given to the form that punishment takes, the frequency with which it is used as a means of control, and the context in which it is administered. Before punishment is administered, the child should know clearly the expectations for his behavior and the consequences that will occur if those expectations are unfulfilled.

When the parent deems it advisable to administer punishment for a given act, several conditions should be met. First, the punishment should follow the act immediately. If a mother, for example, says, "Wait until your father gets home; he will spank you," then two significant things are happening to the child—first, he is learning to fear his father and dread his coming home, and, second, he really is being punished all day because he has to live with the threat until his father comes home. Punishment is more effective at suppressing children's rule-breaking behavior when it is administered without delay.

Second, the punishment must be deserved and understood. Often there are extenuating circumstances that cause misbehavior. The parent needs to take the time to assess the circumstances surrounding the misdeed in order to decide if, in fact, mild punishment is warranted. Children are affected negatively by punishment that they perceive as unfair far longer than they are affected by punishment that they believe they deserve. Further, children need to know exactly what they are being punished for, particularly in the case of preschool children, whose memories are short and whose conceptions of right and wrong are different from adults' because of their premoral characteristics (Kohlberg, 1975). An explanation of the misbehavior and the punishment, and inductive discipline, accompanied by a suggestion of a more acceptable act, will in the long run be more effective and more humane.

Third, the punishment must be related to the act. If, for example, the preschool child colors on the wall, perhaps the most effective punishment is having her scrub it off and put away the crayons for a while. Or if she continues to be aggressive in a hostile way to a friend, she should be deprived of the opportunity to play with that friend for a brief period of time. In this way the child associates the punishment with the act and is likely to have clearer understanding of the forbidden behavior. On the other hand, if global punishments such as spanking, sending the child to her room, or not allowing television watching are used for *all* forms of misbehavior, the child has more difficulty learning appropriate forms of behavior.

Finally, the punishment should be administered within the context of a supportive parent-child relationship. Parents should attempt to remain as objective as possible and refrain from venting their own anger at the child's expense. One of the major disadvantages of spanking or other forms of corporal punishment is that normally they serve as a vehicle for the release of parental feelings as opposed to helping the child learn appropriate behavior. But even more distastefully, the parent is modeling aggressive, angry behavior for the child and is, in effect, telling him that it is all right for a person to hit another person when he becomes angry. If the parent remains calm and focuses on the behavior of the child instead of the child himself, then the child's self-respect is not damaged in the process of facilitating acceptable behavior. The child needs to know that he has or can develop the necessary skills to manage his own affairs.

The frequency with which punishment is used as a form of control also is of primary importance. If parents use it judiciously and concentrate on achieving compliance with their standards by using explanations, reason, and external reinforcement, it may be possible to obtain obedience and self-correction without stimulating self-punitive reactions. It should be considered, however, that children often influence parental behavior as strongly as parents influence children's behavior. Some researchers have suggested that assertive, irritable children may "train" their parents to use upper-limit controls of physical punishment, hence producing a positive correlation between punishment and aggression.

Self-Concept

It appears that one of the most significant results of nurturance during the preschool period is the building of a healthy self-concept in young children. Self-concept is believed to be intimately related to the individual's interactions with significant others in her social world. Based on significant research, we can make three assumptions concerning the development of the self-concept: first, the self-concept is learned; second, the self-concept is learned early within the socialization process of the family; and, third, the self-concept is a powerful determinant of behavior.

Early Beginnings. The current literature suggests that the first step in self-awareness during the period of infancy is both affective and cognitive. The infant has experiences that help him to learn that he is separate and distinct from the objects in his environment. As people and more objects are introduced, he develops an awareness of others and a sense of basic trust, which has been

discussed in an earlier section. As an active, curious, striving individual, he develops a sense of competence about his ability to effect changes in the environment and in the behavior of others. These views of the infant support the notion that self-concept begins to be learned in the period of infancy within the context of the family. The preschool period, then, seems to be a critical time for the validation of these early impressions that the child has in regard to himself.

Early researchers on self-concept (e.g., Coopersmith, 1967; Sears, 1970) established the fact that parental warmth, acceptance, and respect for the child, supported by a limit-setting democratic parenting style, resulted in children with high self-esteem, whereas lack of affection, lack of regard, and the use of severe punishment resulted in lower self-esteem. Further, they concluded that parents of children with high self-esteem are concerned with and attentive to their children, that they structure the world of their children along the lines they believe to be appropriate, and that they permit relatively great freedom within the structure they have established. Other, more recent, studies have supported these researchers' findings.

One study examined the determinants of home environments on preschool children. The results indicated that in addition to maternal age, education, and ethnicity, self-esteem and the locus of control of mothers are the most critical predictors for home environments. Mothers who perceive that they control their own life chances may consciously create stronger home environments than mothers for whom life events, likely extending into household circumstances, appear less within their control. Mothers with stronger self-esteem seemed to attempt to impart these feelings of competence and self-worth to their children, in part by providing a strong home environment (Menaghan & Parcel, 1991).

Aspects of Self-Concept. Traditionally, the two aspects of the child's self-concept that have been emphasized are a sense of belonging and a feeling of worth. Although these are no doubt critical to the child's overall feeling of self-esteem, the more recent examination of the child's perceived behavioral competencies is consistent with the view of the child as an active participant in her overall development. It appears that the young child's ability to interact successfully with her environment is a vital aspect of her development of a positive sense of self-worth.

The characteristics of authoritative and inductive parents previously discussed contribute to young children's competence. Baumrind (1996) defined competence as "effective human functioning in attainment of personally desired and culturally valued goals" (p. 406). Earlier (1967) she had concluded that parents of the most competent and mature children were firm, loving, demanding, and understanding. Parents of disaffiliative children were firm, punitive, and unaffectionate. Mothers of dependent, immature children lacked control and were moderately loving; fathers of these children were ambivalent and lax. Further examination of the same data revealed that parental acceptance and warmth were not enough to promote prosocial and competent behavior in children. Rather, there appeared to be an interaction between parental warmth and control. Other studies have indicated a relationship between the self-concepts of parents and those of their children. See the Highlights for a summary of parenting behaviors that promote positive self-concepts.

By kindergarten, children's close friends, especially those who offer personal support (i.e., validation) and interpersonal aid, also have been shown to enhance children's feelings of competence and security in school. Validation by close friends appears to be a significant factor in self-concept, since affirmation helps to maintain an image of oneself as competent (Ladd, Kochenderfer, & Coleman, 1996).

Self-Concept as a Determinant of Behavior. Abundant evidence suggests that a child's self-concept is a powerful determinant of his behavior. A correlation exists between self-concept and achievement as early as kindergarten, though this relationship becomes more prominent during the school-age period. In fact, an individual's chances for success increase as his self-esteem increases. Preschool children with poor self-concepts may be overly cautious when attempting new tasks, fearing failure. They may appear anxious, defensive, and withdrawn. Their lack of confidence may result in unpopularity with their peers. Although self-concept changes over the course of development—for better or for worse—the preschool period is a crucial time for observing behaviors that might suggest a poorly emerging self-concept.

Correlates of Self-Concept. It seems, then, that the conditions that appear necessary for the development of a positive self-concept (a sense of belonging, a feeling of worth, and a sense of competence) are the following: parental responsiveness and acceptance; a democratic parenting style that sets clearly defined limits but allows unrestricted freedom within those limits; opportunities for the child to construct her own knowledge of herself and others; and, finally, a reciprocal parent-child relationship that is permeated with mutual respect. Toward the end of this period, close peer friendships that are validating also can enhance one's sense of self. The child who has come to value herself under these conditions has a firm base from which to venture forth and try her hand at new learnings. During the preschool period the child begins to judge her self-worth partly on the basis of her competence with adults. This sense of competence has considerable implications for her later adjustment and achievement.

Developing a Sense of Initiative

Erikson (1963) described the third stage in psychosocial development as initiative versus guilt. This stage has its beginning in the latter part of the third year after the child has attained proficiency in walking and feeding himself. Basic motor skills and bowel control have become relatively automatic. The child's attention, no longer needed to develop and control these activities, is now free to add a new dimension to his newly achieved muscular autonomy. He now directs his attention away from his own bodily functions and toward increas-

Parenting Behaviors That Promote Positive Self-Concepts

The parent...

Shows warmth for, acceptance of, and respect for the child

Shows concern for and attentiveness to the child

Provides an environment appropriate for the child

Allows the child freedom within established structure

Provides an environment for successful interaction

Exhibits consistent love, conscientiousness, and security in handling child

Maintains high nurturance, high control, and high demands

Has clear expectations

Makes firm demands coupled with understanding

Has a positive self-concept

---

ing participation in his social environment, largely the basic family but also, to some extent, other adults and peers.

The young child at this stage thus can initiate motor activities of various sorts on her own and no longer merely responds to or imitates the actions of others. The same holds true for her language and fantasy activities. Whether the child will leave this stage with a sense of initiative far outbalancing a sense of guilt depends to a considerable extent on how her parents respond to her self-initiated activities. Children who are given freedom, opportunity, and encouragement to initiate motor play, to ask questions, and to engage in fantasy play activities will have their sense of initiative reinforced.

On the other hand, conscience is beginning to develop, and the child begins to understand the difference between right and wrong and pleasing and displeasing his parents. If he thinks that his motor activity is bad or dangerous, that his questions are a nuisance and that his play is silly or a waste of time, then he may develop a sense of guilt over self-initiated activities in general that will persist through later life stages.

Further, the child of this age becomes increasingly aware of a sex difference between mother and father figures and learns that he or she is "like" the parent of the same sex. This early awareness forms the basis of the child's first identification. The perception of similarity causes the child to consign to himself similar privileges and strivings to the like-sex parent.

Erikson (1963) described this stage as one of mutual regulation between the child and family: "Where the child, now so ready to over-manipulate himself, can gradually develop a sense of moral responsibility, where he can gain some insight into the institutions, functions, and roles which will permit his responsible participation, he will find pleasurable accomplishment in wielding tools...in manipulating meaningful toys...and in caring for younger children" (p. 256).

Children who are encouraged, or at least allowed, to explore their environment tend to become eager and carefree about initiating such exploration, whereas children who are overprotected from or punished for such exploration of their environment tend to become inhibited. If parents consistently are harsh, young children may develop strong guilt feelings and inhibitions, becoming very dependent and unable to take new initiatives without experiencing anxiety.

Implications of Initiative. The implications of these developmental characteristics for parents seem obvious. First, preschool children will need the space, the opportunity, and the tools for initiating motor activity. Outdoor space and equipment for climbing, swinging, riding, jumping, and simply running and shouting will allow children to use new capacities and develop skills. As skills are developed and practiced, the child gains a sense of self-confidence and competence and extends these skills into more elaborate forms of play that frequently include fantasy. (For example, the tricycle becomes the fire engine and the climbing structure becomes the firehouse.) Initiative can be further reinforced by allowing children space and opportunity indoors to engage in both fantasy and real-life activities. Parents who are overly fastidious about keeping the house in order frequently restrict children to such a degree that they are unable to initiate activities for fear of displeasing parents. Impatient parents often do not allow the child to assume the initiative in routine household chores because their expectations far exceed the child's skills.

Second, intellectual initiative can be fostered by parents' both answering and asking questions. The *whos, whats, whys,* and *hows* of the child may seem endless, but the patient responses of parents encourage further exploration and curiosity—and result in the child's valuing the pursuit of knowledge. Questions from parents that encourage the child to think on higher cognitive levels, such as problem-solving and inference questions, lay the foundation for future intellectual curiosity. Regular reading to the child fosters early language development and introduces new words and concepts.

Finally, providing play materials that encourage fantasy and imagination allows the child to try out a range of life roles and to come to grips with reality. The testing of roles indicates that the child is attempting to identify with her own appropriate role and should not be viewed by the parent as silly or inappropriate behavior. Fantasy also is a vehicle for the expression of feelings and conflicts that the young child needs to work out.

Children who resolve the conflict between initiative and guilt successfully will learn to control their behavior and respect social conventions and moral responsibilities. At the same time, they will not lose their psychological freedom to assume initiatives and the responsibilities that come with them. Conversely, children who fail to resolve this conflict successfully will tend to emerge with overly strong and inflexible consciences that inhibit them from taking initiative in ambiguous situations in which they are not sure that they are safe from disapproval.

Providing Learning Experiences

The emphasis on the first 6 years of life as being critical for learning experiences that determine later development have led many parents to be concerned about providing materials and opportunities for learning during the early years. It is true that learning occurs rapidly in the early years. For example, children learn a second language much faster during the preschool period than during adolescence or adulthood—but not by drill and rote repetition. In fact, young children learn in very different ways from older children and adults. They learn by having direct, concrete, relevant experiences with the physical environment, by experimentation, and by discovery. They also learn by having rich, stable relationships with adults.

Much of what we have already discussed in this section—methods of discipline, the building of a healthy self-concept, and developing initiative—can hardly be separated from providing optimal learning experiences. A child who is nurtured, who is given freedom to explore and initiate, and who feels good about himself as a person and a family member will be inspired to learn in keeping with his potential. The young child learns from every event in which he participates—his peers, his play, and his everyday interaction with his environment, especially if his parents and teachers are responsive to his interests and inquiries. Warmth, nurturance, and responsiveness are prerequisites for effective learning experiences during the preschool years.

Studies have found that cognitive development is influenced both by direct effects on cognition and by indirect efforts through alterations in self-concept, aspirations, attitudes toward learning, and styles of interaction with other people.

In addition to a positive social and emotional climate that facilitates the natural learning process, other aspects of the home environment can enhance the learning process for young children.

Research repeatedly has found that parents' educational level shows a strong relationship to children's IQ, and some studies have found a same-sex relationship; that is, mothers' educational level correlates with their daughters' IQ, and fathers' educational level correlates with sons' IQ. Other aspects of the home environment shown to affect children's cognitive development and later school success include the amount of reading materials available (and read!), variety in daily stimulation, and provision of appropriate play materials.

Play and Learning. Through play, young children learn in a way that no one can teach them. Play is the major vehicle for learning during the early childhood years, and preschoolers like to "mess and manipulate." They learn about their physical world by touching, examining, testing, exploring, evaluating, and imagining. Raw materials such as sand, dirt, water, paints, clay, and even mud allow children sensory experiences that are vital for the formation of basic concepts about their world that facilitate later academic learning. Experience with pets and plants helps them to understand growing and living things. Cooking experiences lay the foundation for scientific concepts. Short trips away from home (to museums, parks, shopping centers, farms, libraries, airports, and concerts) help them to understand how their culture operates. And reading a variety of books to children helps to instill an early love of the printed word.

Many parents and preschool teachers introduce children to computers during this stage. Over the years, software appropriate for preschool children has improved dramatically. When children are able to start the computer, load the software, interact with the software, and exit the program—all without continual adult help—then they probably are interested and ready for computers. A word of caution: Computers should be used like any other activity with preschool children—as a choice among many in which children can participate. Because of diverse interests and skills between the ages of 3 and 6, all preschool children will not be interested in computers, just as all children are not interested in collecting bugs. Often younger chil-

dren become interested in computers by watching older children or adults interact with them. A sensible "take it or leave it" attitude by parents of preschool children seems warranted. Children will become computer literate either when they become interested or when they are required to do so in an academic setting later on.

Perhaps the most important ingredient for learning experiences is people. A loving, caring adult who is available to the child to answer her questions, to engage her in imagination and fantasy, to introduce her to new words and ideas, and to pick up on her cues of curiosity cannot be replaced by dozens of toys or daily field trips. The adult who structures the environment so that learning will occur, who allows the child freedom and encouragement for exploration, and who interacts with her in a warm, accepting manner will provide the most important learning experiences of all.

Adults, both parents and preschool teachers, can scaffold children's learning by anticipating the child's developmental readiness for new ideas and experiences and responding at the appropriate time. Years ago, Lev Vygotsky, a prominent developmental psychologist, talked about the child's Zone of Proximal Development—that small area just beyond a child's demonstrated level of development that a child can move toward with adult guidance. Adults who are sensitive to children's cues can extend children's development into that proximal zone.

Appropriate Play Materials. The provision of appropriate play materials is an important consideration in facilitating play and learning, partly because parents want to provide toys that stimulate learning and partly because, over a period of time, toys represent a real investment. For this reason toys during the preschool period should be selected with care. Basic guidelines for toy selection are summarized in the Highlights.

If parents follow these basic guidelines and do not succumb to the persuasive advertising of the media, toys can provide valuable learning experiences for young children. It should be remembered, however, that the best toys in life are free.

Guidelines for Toy Selection

Toys are. . .

   Appropriate to child's developmental level—challenging but not frustrating
   Versatile—variety of uses (Legos, blocks, Tinker Toys)
   Durable—outlast child's desire to play with them
   Encourage active participation rather than passive observation
   Aesthetically pleasing
   Safe

Common household items such as pots and pans, measuring spoons and cups, coffee cans filled with odds and ends, nesting cans or boxes, blocks made from milk cartons or cigar boxes, and plastic bottles with screw-on caps provide hours of creative play in which children can extend and elaborate on their skills. It cannot be overemphasized that optimal learning can occur in the home without a big investment in "educational" toys. Almost any toy can "teach" if parents take the time to use it to arouse the child's interest and curiosity and if it provides for social interaction between parent and child.

PROGRAMS FOR PARENTS
OF PRESCHOOL CHILDREN

Parent involvement and/or parent education was a requirement of the federally funded preschool programs in the late 1960s and 1970s. More than any other Great Society program of the Johnson administration, Head Start translated the parent-participation principle into specific guidelines. Formalized parent-education programs in conjunction with other forms of parent participation and involvement have always been an essential component of Head Start. Since Head Start was the only early-intervention program to survive the federal budget cuts of the 1980s and 1990s, few formalized parent-education programs for parents of young children currently exist. However, a few nursery schools and child-care centers provide some form of parent support or education in conjunction with

their children's program. These efforts tend to be more common among nonprofit programs, those serving largely low-income parents, and university-based laboratory programs. Further, the efforts tend to be directed toward one-shot speakers or workshops led by community professionals rather than toward a series of formalized instruction for parents. In metropolitan areas, some agencies provide commercially produced programs such as STEP or Active Parenting (see Chapter 5), and normally these serial-session programs require a fee, sometimes not inconsequential.

Unfortunately, little empirical research has been conducted on the effectiveness of parent education, with a few exceptions. One exception is parents of children in Head Start, who have cited numerous benefits, both personal and parental, as a result of their involvement. Other program evaluations in the 1970s indicated at least short-term effectiveness regarding the child's performance on standardized measures; parent attitudes; and, less often, parent behaviors. However, few definitive answers have been provided regarding the best method of delivery, the role of the parent educator, how to reach the parents who are most in need, and whether efforts have had lasting effects on parents and their children.

Conventional wisdom implies that parents of all races, all socioeconomic levels, all ages, and both genders can profit from support and education, especially during their children's early years, but programs obviously need to be designed individually. Powell (1986) stated that "There is no convincing evidence that one particular program is significantly more effective than another" (p. 49), and today there is still no evidence favoring a particular program.

Further, he concluded that perhaps the primary functions of a parent-education curriculum are to stimulate parents to more closely examine their relationship with their children and to encourage interaction among parents. Therefore, few generalizations can be made regarding the content of such efforts. However, the trend during the 1990s was toward broad-based family support programs that emphasized support rather than intervention.

The most common vehicles of delivery for education for parents of preschool children in the 1990s were preschool/child-care settings and churches. Clearly other agencies (hospitals and social-service agencies) also have been involved, but parents are more likely to participate in such programs if they have established some social relationship with other participating parents.

The following guidelines may be useful in developing support/education programs for parents of young children:

1. Assess the demographic characteristics of the parent population (age, level of education, number of children, socioeconomic status, marital status, and so on). Programs for middle-class parents may not be effective with low-income parents; programs for two-parent families may be ill-suited for single parents.

2. Utilize parent input, if possible, when determining content so that it has relevance for the population it is designed to serve. Participation is likely to be greater if parents are involved in the decision making.

3. Plan programs around the convenience of parents (in a child-care setting, a potluck supper at closing time followed by a program is likely to draw greater participation than a later event).

4. Provide child care and transportation, if necessary, and keep the program brief.

5. Plan programs in which sessions can be either discrete or serial. Working parents are reluctant to make long-term commitments.

6. Avoid "patronizing" parents. Accept and emphasize parents' roles as primary educators for their own children.

7. Use a variety of methods of delivery—speakers, discussion leaders, peer-led support groups, reading material, video and television, and so forth.

8. Be flexible in both program content and format of presentation.

9. Offer information within a supportive context rather than in a threatening one. Strive to view parents as partners.

Because the early-childhood years are so important for laying the foundation for later development and because parenting today is so complex, careful, well-planned programs that support and enhance parents' roles are essential.

DEVELOPMENTAL NEEDS OF PARENTS

Erikson (1963) described the seventh stage in his theory of psychosocial development as generativity versus self-absorption. *Generativity* is defined as the interest in establishing and guiding the next generation, or a sense of caring for others or becoming involved with creative production. Erikson believed that people are "triggered" by physical, psychological, and social stimuli to develop this sense of generativity. The parenting role is one of the major vehicles for facilitating a sense of generativity, and it allows parents to manifest what Erikson believed is an inborn desire to teach.

With the birth of their first child, most parents begin to develop their sense of generativity as their infant begins to develop a sense of basic trust. Mature first-time parents are probably better able to mesh their needs with those of the infant than younger, less mature parents are. Other factors, such as marital status, economic condition, career involvement, and availability of support systems, also affect the developmental needs of parents of infants and determine how effectively those needs are fulfilled. For example, the normative family sequence is marriage and then parenthood. For individuals who give birth out of the conventional sequence, the risk for negative outcomes is increased. Especially for young people, precocious parenthood, with associated responsibility and social stigma, adds to their life stress and/or their difficulties in marital adjustment should they choose to marry (Aldous, 1990).

The transition to the birth of their first child, in any event, represents a significant change in the lifestyle of most mothers and fathers and for some may even constitute a major crisis. Roles and relationships that precede parenthood often are altered. Time and resources must be reallocated. The demands of the infant result in less leisure time for the parents, and they juggle multiple responsibilities. Several research studies have suggested that a decline in marital satisfaction may begin shortly after the birth of the first child and continue to decline throughout the child-rearing years (Heidemann, Suhomlinova, & O'Rand, 1998), with the decline being greater for women than for men. If this is so, then it appears that the obligations and responsibilities of parenting for many families take precedence over those related to the marriage. This, in turn, would suggest that having children is a detriment to the marriage relationship rather than a support for it. In spite of these potential stresses, there usually is a mutual interdependence of the infant's needs and the parents' needs to be needed, so that each serves as a source of stimulation for development and socialization of the other. Family researchers have discussed the concept of "critical role transitions," one of which is first parenthood. These transitions are characterized by initial disarray, followed by a period of reorganization in which families establish more stable interaction patterns demanded by the new time period (Aldous, 1990).

Adjustment to later-born infants in some ways is easier for parents. They feel more secure in their parenting skills and less anxious about the baby's development and often are more relaxed in their interactions. On the other hand, multiple children may present special problems to parents, such as economic stress, sibling rivalry, access to quality child care, and lack of time and energy to meet the needs of each child. With the birth of each subsequent child, parents are faced with a new adjustment. The extent of these adjustments depends on a number of factors, such as whether the births were planned, the spacing between children, whether the mother is employed, the support systems available to the family, and the father's availability for participation in child care and work at home. Further, parents must meet the developmental needs of their children at different stages of development while taking into account their own needs.

When the child becomes a toddler, it is more difficult for parents to include him in adult activities and sometimes more difficult to obtain reliable baby-sitters. However, recognizing the importance of early experiences, parents often neglect their own personal needs for privacy, for socializing with other adults, and for developing interests outside the family. Their developing sense of generativity, then, is confined solely to the process of parenting, as opposed to including other activities that contribute to becoming a fully functioning human being. Traditionally, this has been truer for mothers than for fathers. However, in families where both parents are employed and share somewhat equally in child-rearing responsibilities, there hardly seems to be enough time for either parent to meet the children's needs, the spouse's needs, and one's own personal needs. The end result for parents often is fatigue, a sense of isolation from their peer group, and growing dissatisfaction with the marriage relationship.

Throughout the preschool years, the issues of child care, balancing work and family demands, and maintenance of self continue to loom large for parents. The research on marital satisfaction serves as an indication that adults need to be aware of the stresses that begin during the childbearing years. This awareness can assist parents in making an effort to meet their own personal needs and in maintaining the marriage relationship. It seems that our culture has made many parents feel entirely responsible for their children's behavior and development, and if they do not create a child-centered family and sacrifice their own needs, they feel as if they are bad or inadequate parents.

It has been emphasized throughout this chapter that parent-child relationships are reciprocal. No doubt parents face many responsibilities and challenges in providing the best possible environment for their children; in turn, children can and should assume their share of responsibility to the family. If each family member is viewed as having rights and status, then adults need not always sacrifice their own needs for those of their young children. When they do, they find that their overall relationship with their children gets worse instead of better. Children quickly learn to depend totally on their parents for everything, and parents, in turn, come to experience hostility toward their children for being unable to fend for themselves.

To minimize some of the stresses of parenting during the early years, parents need to balance their needs with those of their children—for example, by taking occasional trips alone as well as with the children, interacting socially with adult friends as well as families that include children, developing interests or hobbies with peers outside the family, and making some household rules that ensure a degree of privacy. These arrangements not only strengthen personal and marital development but also foster a sense of autonomy and initiative in the children.

SUMMARY

Parenting infants, toddlers, and preschool children is a challenging task. During the first 6 years of life, a child evolves from a "helpless" infant who cannot turn over in his crib to a curious toddler emptying every available drawer and cabinet, and, finally, to an intrusive preschooler who asks questions constantly and has endless energy. To be sure, parents are the most influential people in the lives of these children, and early parental influences will be felt for many years to come.

On the other hand, parents assume the parental function rather abruptly, and their role changes from caregiver to protector to nurturer in a remarkably short time. The reciprocal interaction between parents and children that has been established will remain fairly consistent throughout the parenting years as parents and children continually respond to one another's needs and behaviors. And parents will experience developmental changes equal in importance to those of their children.

REFERENCES

ALDOUS, J. (1990). Family development and the life course: Two perspectives on family change. *Journal of Marriage and the Family, 52*(3), 571–583.

BAUMRIND, D. (1966). Effects of authoritative parental control on child behavior. *Child Development, 37*(4), 887–907.

BAUMRIND, D. (1967). Child care practices anteceding three patterns of preschool behavior. *Genetic Psychology Monographs, 75,* 43–88.

BAUMRIND, D. (1996). The discipline controversy revisited. *Family Relations, 45,* 405–414.

BELL, S. M., & AINSWORTH, M. D. (1972). Infant crying and maternal responsiveness. *Child Development, 43,* 1171–1190.

BELSKY, J., CRNIC, K., & GABLE, S. (1995). The determinants of co-parenting in families with toddler boys: Spousal differences and daily hassles. *Child Development, 66,* 629–642.

BELSKY, J., GROSSMAN, K., GROSSMAN, K., & SCHEUERER-ENGLISCH, H. (1996). Continuity in parent-child relationships from infancy to middle childhood and relations with friendship competence. *Child Development, 67,* 1437–1454.

BELSKY, J., WOODWORTH, S., & CRNIC, K. (1996). Trouble in the second year: Three questions about family interaction. *Child Development, 67,* 556–578.

BRAZELTON, T. B. (1969). *Infants and mothers: Differences in development.* New York: Dell.

BRAZELTON, T. B. (1974). *Toddlers and parents: A declaration of independence.* New York: Dell.

BRAZELTON, T. B. (1995). Working with families: Opportunities for early intervention. *Pediatric Clinics of North America, 42*(1), 1–9.

BRAZELTON, T. B., KOSLOWSKI, B., & MAIN, M. (1974). The origins of reciprocity: The early mother-infant interaction. In M. Lewis & L. Rosenblum (Eds.), *The effect of the infant on its caregiver* (pp. 49–76). New York: Wiley.

COOPERSMITH, S. (1967). *The antecedents of self-esteem.* San Francisco: W. H. Freeman.

DAY, R., PETERSON, G., & McCRACKEN, C. (1998). Predicting spanking of younger and older children by mothers and fathers. *Journal of Marriage and the Family, 60,* 79–94.

DENHAM, S., RENWICK, S., & HOLT, R. (1991). Working and playing together: Prediction of preschool social-emotional competence from mother-child interaction. *Child Development, 62*(2), 242–249.

DEWOLFF, M., & VAN IJZENDOORN, M. (1997). Sensitivity and attachment: A meta-analysis on parental antecedents of infant attachment. *Child Development, 68*(4), 571–591.

DINKMEYER, D., MCKAY, G., & DINKMEYER, D. (1997). *The parents' handbook* (A part of the complete STEP Program). Circle Pines, MN: American Guidance Service.

DOWNEY, D. (1995). When bigger is not better: Family size, parental resources, and children's educational performance. *American Sociological Review, 60,* 746–761.

DREIKURS, R., & GREY, I. (1968). *A new approach to discipline: Logical consequences.* New York. Hawthorne.

EIDEN, R., TETI, D., & CORNS, K. (1995). Maternal working models of attachment, marital adjustment, and the parent-child relationship. *Child Development, 66,* 1504–1518.

ERIKSON, E. (1963). *Childhood and society.* New York: Norton.

FISH, M., & STIFTER, C. (1995). Patterns of mother-infant attachment: A cluster-analytic approach. *Infant Behavior and Development, 18,* 435–446.

FOX, N. (1995). Of the way we were: Adult memories about attachment experiences and their role in determining infant-parent relationships: A commentary on Ijzendoorn (1995). *Psychological Bulletin, 117*(3), 404–410.

GILES-SIMS, J., STRAUS, M., & SUGARMAN, D. (1995). Child, maternal, and family characteristics associated with spanking. *Family Relations, 44,* 170–176.

GOMBY, D., LARSON, C., LEWIT, E., & BEHRMAN, R. (1993). Home visiting: Analysis and recommendations. *The Future of Children: Home Visiting, 3*(3), 6–22.

GREEN, J., GUSTAFSON, G., & MCGHIE, A. (1998). Changes in infants' cries as a function of time in a cry bout. *Child Development, 69*(2), 271–279.

GROSS, D., & TUCKER, S. (1994). Parenting confidence during toddlerhood: A comparison of mothers and fathers. *Nurse Practitioner, 19*(10), 25–34.

HEIDEMANN, B., SUHOMLINOVA, O., & O'RAND, A. (1998). Economic independence, economic status, and empty nest in midlife marital disruption. *Journal of Marriage and the Family, 60*(1), 216–231.

ISABELLA, R., & BELSKY, J. (1991). Interactional synchrony and the origins of infant-mother attachment: A replication study. *Child Development, 62*(2), 373–384.

JOURILES, E., MURPHY, C., FARRIS, A., SMITH, D., RICHTERS, J., & WATERS, E. (1991). Maternal adjustment, parental disagreements about child rearing, and behavior problems in boys: Increasing the specificity of the marital assessment. *Child Development, 62*(6), 1424–1433.

KOHLBERG, L. (1975). The cognitive developmental approach to moral education. *Phi Delta Kappan, 56*(10), 670–677.

LADD, G., KOCHENDERFER, B., & COLEMAN, C. (1996). Friendship quality as a predictor of young children's early school adjustment. *Child Development, 67,* 1103–1118.

MCKIM, M. (1987). Transition to what? New parents' problems in the first year. *Family Relations, 36,* 22–25.

MENAGHAN, E., & PARCEL, T. (1991). Determining children's home environments: The impact of maternal characteristics and current occupational and family conditions. *Journal of Marriage and the Family, 53*(2), 417–431.

NASH, M. (1997, February 3). Fertile minds. *Time,* pp. 49–56.

NEWMAN, J. (1996). The more the merrier? Effects of family size and sibling spacing on sibling relationships. *Child Care, Health and Development, 22*(5), 285–302.

OLDS, D., & KITZMAN, H. (1993). Review of research on home visiting for pregnant women and parents of young children. *The Future of Children: Home Visiting, 3*(3), 53–94.

PARKS, P., & SMERIGLIO, V. (1986). Relationships among parenting knowledge, quality of stimulation in the home and infant development. *Family Relations, 35,* 411–416.

PEDERSON, D., & MORAN, G. (1996). Expressions of the attachment relationship outside of the Strange Situation. *Child Development, 67,* 915–927.

PIAGET, J. (1952). *The origins of intelligence in children* (M. Cook, Trans). New York: Norton.

POWELL, D. (1986). Parent education and support programs. *Young Children, 41,* 47–53.

SEARS, R. (1970). Relation of early socialization experiences to self concepts and gender role in middle childhood. *Child Development, 41,* 267–289.

STEELE, H., STEELE, M., & FONAGY, P. (1996). Associations among classifications of mothers, fathers, and their infants. *Child Development, 67,* 541–555.

THOMAS, A., & CHESS, S. (1977). *Temperament and development.* New York: Brunner/Mazel.

VAN IJZENDOORN, M., & DEWOLFF, M. (1997). In search of the absent father—Meta analyses of infant-father attachment: A rejoinder to our discussants. *Child Development, 68*(4), 604–609.

VOLLING, B., & BELSKY, J. (1992). The contribution of mother-child and father-child relationships to the quality of sibling interaction: A longitudinal study. *Child Development, 63*(5), 1209–1222.

WASIK, B., & ROBERTS, R. (1994). Home visitor characteristics, training, and supervision: Results of a national survey. *Family Relations, 45,* 405–414.

WEBSTER'S NEW ENCYCLOPEDIC DICTIONARY. (1994). New York: Black Dog & Leventhal.

The Changing Nature of Parenting:
Middle Childhood and Adolescence

The transition of a child from total physical and psychological dependency to self-sufficiency and independence occurs gradually. Starting school, however, is an early major step in the process. Patterns of interaction established during the early years continue to influence children as they progress in school. The reason is twofold: Many of the behaviors of children already have been shaped, and the same child continues to interact with the same parents. Although we are emphasizing the developmental relationship that occurs between parent and child and the reciprocal nature of that relationship, it is nevertheless safe to assert that once patterns of family interaction are established, they tend to persist. Change occurs gradually as components of the family system change.

The general pattern of stabilization that occurs during the school years makes this period critical. From observations during middle childhood, one can predict with moderate accuracy what the young adult will be like. Personality develops during the school-age years in important ways, and personality attributes stabilize into something similar to their adult form somewhere between the ages of 6 and 10. In addition, a wide range of competencies develop rapidly. Middle childhood, then, is a period of active development involving expansion and integration of social, affective, and cognitive phenomena.

PARENTS AND SCHOOL-AGE CHILDREN

The Parents' Roles as Encouragers

As a child develops from infant to toddler to preschooler to school age, the parent's role changes from caregiver to protector to nurturer and, finally, to encourager. With growing competencies and an emerging sense of individuality, the child gradually decreases conformity to parents and increases conformity to peers.

School offers children alternative sources of rewards and evaluations while simultaneously adding pressure that may increase anxiety, because of the evaluative relationship that develops between children, teachers, and peers. Because this is

so, children must develop a system for dealing with occasional incompetencies, failures, and rejection by friends. Thus, the role of the parent as encourager becomes crucial. Further, encouragement appears to be the most corrective influence on behavior during this period. Although nurturance still is a necessary ingredient in the parent-child relationship, normally it is manifested in different ways. It is sometimes difficult for a mother to accept the fact that her child no longer wants to be kissed good-bye in the presence of friends or for a father to understand why his son would rather skateboard with his neighborhood friends than go on a family picnic. The nurturance that is expressed, then, may be more in a psychological than in a physical form.

It is true, however, that some parental attitudes and practices will carry over into the school-age years. Certain forms of punishment, feelings of love and affection, reasoning, and decision making are among the attitudes and practices that are likely to continue, perhaps in a different form or to a different degree. But as interaction between parent and child becomes more psychological and less physical and as children are exposed to a wider range of significant other people and experiences, the parent finds himself in the encouraging role more and more frequently. The necessity for this should become obvious in the following sections.

Parenting Styles and Practices

It appears that parenting styles and practices during middle childhood have far-reaching impact on the child's life. For example, Pettit, Bates, and Dodge (1997) examined the impact of supportive parenting on children's school adjustment over a 7-year period. Five hundred eighty-five children and parents were assessed when the children were 5 years old, when they were in kindergarten, and in every grade thereafter through grade 6. Parental proactive teaching, calm discussion in disciplinary encounters, warmth, and interest and involvement in the child's peer activities were the aspects of parenting that predicted children's behavioral, social, and academic adjustment in both kindergarten and grade 6. Each kindergarten adjustment outcome was associated with multiple supportive parenting variables, which then predicted changes in children's academic performance from kindergarten to grade 6. These predictive relationships were of modest magnitude, but they suggested that early positive and supportive parenting qualities may play a distinct role in promoting children's school adjustment.

Supportive parenting also was found to buffer some of the developmental risks associated with early family adversity. Supportive parenting was most strongly related to child adjustment in grade 6 for those children who had been reared in single-parent and/or low socioeconomic-status families in their early years. This finding suggests that supportive parenting may serve as a protective factor against the risks associated with certain types of family adversity.

Good communication during middle childhood is a key component in parent-child relationships and sets the stage for continued communication throughout adolescence. Fitzpatrick, Marshall, Leutwiler, and Krcmar (1996) assessed the relationship of various family communication environments of children in grades 1, 4, 6, and 7 to children's self-restraint and social withdrawal. Based on a "talking picture books" approach, in which children listened to dialogues and examined cartoon pictures depicting different families, children identified their families as (a) pluralistic (high conversation and low conformity), (b) consensual (high conversation and high conformity), (c) protective (low conversation and high conformity), or (d) laissez-faire (low conversation and low conformity). Results revealed an interaction among family type, gender, and grade level for both social withdrawal and social self-restraint. Variability across grade levels within family types was found for boys, but the only girls who showed variability were those from laissez-faire families, suggesting that the effects of family communication environments are stronger for boys than for girls. Further, results suggested that peer rejection may be related to lack of self-restraint for boys and to social withdrawal for girls. Like other research, this study shows the inter-relationships among certain aspects of parenting style and child characteristics (e.g., gender, age) in affecting children's behavior.

In Chapter 2 we differentiated between discipline and punishment. If discipline is viewed in its broadest context of positive guidance, then it becomes obvious that the discipline system gradually changes as children reach school age and as parents' own needs change.

Parents continue to serve as strong models and reinforcing agents for their children's behaviors, but the range of behaviors and attitudes to which children are exposed on entering school becomes far greater. Children may begin to question the values their parents hold and become far more inclined to model behaviors of their peers or, occasionally, other adults whom they admire. Parents may find themselves applying different consequences for behavior simply because they are either more effective or more suited to the child's developmental level. For example, withholding privileges becomes a common technique for achieving desired behavior for many parents, whereas isolation for undesirable behavior may become less common. Reasoning and explanation may be used more frequently simply because the parent believes the child of school age is more capable of responding to such techniques than the toddler or the preschooler. The use of natural and logical consequences, as described in Chapter 2, seems to be especially effective in achieving acceptable behavior, particularly if the parent has established an early pattern of using the techniques.

Three major categories of child-rearing practices and their effects on children were first described by Hoffman (1970) (see Highlights) and are still cited in contemporary discussions of parenting styles. These categories seem especially applicable to school-age children. Hoffman contended that both power-assertion and love-withdrawal techniques are punitive in nature. Further, power assertion is not associated with positive conscience development, whereas induction, at least for mothers and children, shows a positive relationship with conscience development. Parents who use love-withdrawal techniques will likely

HIGHLIGHTS

Types of Child-Rearing Practices

POWER ASSERTION

Attempts to control children by exercising power of a superior nature, either physical or control of resources (spanking, deprivation of privileges/objects, grounding, withholding meals, or threats of punishment)

LOVE WITHDRAWAL

Direct expression of anger and/or disapproval without use of power; love is conditional on child's behavior

INDUCTION

Provision of reasons or explanations to describe desirable behavior; emphasis of impact of behavior on self and others

Source: Hoffman, M. L. (1970). Moral development. In P. Mussen (Ed.), *Carmichael's manual of child psychology* (Vol. 2, 3d ed.). New York: Wiley.

---

produce more anxious children who are more susceptible to adult influence than other children are. Krevans and Gibbs (1996) found that parents' use of inductive, as opposed to power-assertive, discipline was related to children's prosocial behavior. Children of inductive parents were more empathic, and more empathic children were more prosocial. The one component of inductive discipline that was most strongly related to children's prosocial behavior was the expression of disappointment. Only for those children who scored high on empathy did guilt predict prosocial behavior. Girls were found to be more empathic and more prosocial than boys.

All parents, however, do not use inductive techniques, even when their children are school age. For example, Day, Peterson, and McCracken (1998) investigated spanking as a discipline strategy. They found that spanking is still a common occurrence in families. Boys are spanked more frequently than girls; mothers spank more frequently than fathers; children older than 7 are spanked less frequently than younger children; Black mothers, but not Black fathers, tend to spank more frequently than White mothers; and parents who view the child as competent and not difficult spank less. Further, certain parental attributes and ideology

(such as poor mental health, lower educational level, being older, and conservative religious orientation) predicted greater use of spanking. Usually, as parents acquire greater experience in child rearing, they will be more likely to demonstrate alternative forms of firm control, such as reasoning or the deprivation of privileges, which diminish the need for spanking as a disciplinary style. These researchers estimated that 2–5 percent of parents use harsh physical punishment even when the child gets older, and these are the parents who should be targeted for intervention.

Parenting style has been found to relate to school adjustment, academic achievement, and self-concept. Bronstein et al. (1996), using family reports and observations over a 3-year period, examined family factors relating to children's adjustment during the middle-school years. Children and parents were assessed when the children were in the fifth, sixth, and seventh grades. Results showed that supportive and aware parenting, characterized by affection, approval, attentiveness, responsiveness, guidance, and receptivity to emotions, was associated with fifth-grade girls' and boys' more positive self-concept, higher academic achievement, and greater popularity with their peers, as well as with lower incidence of psychological and behavioral problems in the following year. In addition, the relationship between the positive parenting measures and adjustment outcomes was stable over time; that is, fifth-grade parenting was, for the most part, similarly correlated with the same adjustment measures obtained in the seventh grade.

As predicted, more problematic parental behaviors were associated with negative adjustment outcomes. Further, parenting practices were related to eventual improvements in girls' and boys' adjustment over the transition to middle school, including better academic performance, decreased incidence of psychological and behavior problems, and increased peer popularity. Aware parenting was particularly salient for boys, in that it appeared to be associated with decreased externalizing behavior, whereas for girls, it appeared to serve as a buffer against a decline in self-esteem. Problematic parenting behaviors tended to be associated with negative changes in adjustment over time for both boys and girls.

Another study examined parenting style and children's interactions with their peers. Children of more power-assertive (less inductive) mothers were more rejected and less accepted by their peers. Maternal and paternal induction is linked to children's positive peer interactions, whereas power assertion is linked to hostile interactions with peers (Hart, DeWolf, Wozniak, & Burts, 1992).

Some research has emphasized that parental use of reasoning that induces children to take the perspective of others cognitively—to focus on the other person's needs rather than one's own—generally is positively associated with children's empathy and their prosocial behaviors, such as comforting, sharing, and helping, which contribute to positive peer interactions. On the other hand, parental demands for children to control their own feelings and emotional displays are likely to lead children eventually to experience anxiety while trying to mask facial displays (Eisenberg et al., 1992).

Secure attachment to parents, established during infancy, seems to have long-term effects on children's behavior. Moss, Rousseau, Parent, St. Laurent, and Saintonge (1998) examined the predictive validity of school-age attachment, mother-child interaction, and maternal self-reports in explaining teacher-reported behavior problems. Participants were 121 children between the ages of 5 and 7 and their mothers. Results of the study suggested that school-age attachment significantly predicted teacher-reported behavior problems at the transition to school and two years later. When compared with the secure group, insecure-attachment groups were more likely to manifest behavior problems. Insecure controlling/other and younger ambivalent children were more likely to demonstrate higher levels of externalizing and other problem behaviors. Further, these researchers found that problem behaviors during the early years continued into the school years. The findings of these researchers supported previous studies of associations between disorganization and behavior problems.

In another study Booth, Rubin, and Rose-Krasnor (1998) tested several hypotheses relating children's attachment security during the preschool years to their perceptions of emotional support from their mothers and best friends and to social-emotional adaptation during middle childhood. Results indicated that attachment security at age 4 was positively related to children's perceptions of maternal emotional support at age 8. Specifically, attachment security was related to the children's ranking of their mothers as sources of support relative to other members of the support network. Children who are securely attached in the preschool years (i.e., who experience their mothers as a supportive presence) are likely, in middle childhood, to view their mothers as important sources of emotional support. Contrary to expectations, securely attached children were no more likely than insecurely attached children to include their best friends in their emotional support network. Girls who were insecurely attached to their mothers were more likely to turn to sources of support outside their immediate families than were girls who were securely attached. Perceptions of support from the mother were not related to social-emotional adaptation, but support from the best friend was related to these outcomes. Further, socially competent behavior with peers was linked to perceptions of emotionally supportive connections with best friends.

However, among insecurely attached children, the greater the reliance on best friends for emotional support, the greater the externalizing problems. In general, perceiving that one's best friend is a potential source of emotional support may indicate a certain degree of social competence and maturity, but excessive reliance on the friend for support may have negative consequences. The friendships of rejected children are less emotionally supportive and more negative than the friendships of other children. The results indicate the complexity of family-peer links in middle childhood.

It is clear that parenting style and behavior during middle childhood have an impact on children's school adjustment, achievement, and peer interactions. Correlations between parents' behaviors and children's attributes are already evident before children reach school age. Differences among children of permissive, authoritative (democratic), and authoritarian parents also are evident. (See Chapter 2.) These relationships continue to exist throughout the period of middle childhood.

As children gradually decrease their conformity to parents and increase their conformity to peers, many parents experience new problems in the relationships with their children. Some of the common problems that parents face with school-age children are identified in the Highlights. If these problems can be faced factually, realistically, and unemotionally with reasonable, firm limits imposed that are understood by the child, then nagging and power struggles can be avoided. Even if children cannot have a choice in the solution to a problem, they can have a voice in its solution.

Common Problems for Parents of School-Age Children

Lying	Television
Stealing	Bedtime
Rudeness	Allowance
Irresponsibility	Sex education
Homework	Drugs

In summary, parenting style during middle childhood continues to be important for healthy development and adjustment. Discipline seems more effective if it is inductive, is encouraging rather than punitive, and includes limits that are reasonable and understood. Promoting mutual respect while gradually encouraging greater independence and self-discipline are important goals at this time. Finally, studies have indicated the importance of consistent discipline. Children who receive consistent feedback from socializing agents are able to form reliable expectations about the consequences of their behavior and therefore modify behavior accordingly.

Developing a Sense of Industry

The fourth stage in Erikson's (1963) theory of psychosocial development is industry versus inferiority and spans the school-age period, from approximately 6 through 11 years of age. The school-age child shows unceasing energy toward investing all possible efforts in producing. On the other hand, there is a pull toward an earlier level of lesser production. Because he still is a child, there are fears of inferiority that he tries to overcome by diligently engaging in opportunities to learn by doing. He works incessantly on expanding bodily, muscular, and perceptive skills as well as on expanding knowledge of the world around him. A concern with how things are made, how they work, and what they do predominates. It is the age of collections, long-term projects, and "making a mess." The child's peers become far more significant to him at this phase, and he tries to relate to and communicate with them. He feels a strong need for a sense of accomplishment and will ward off failure at almost any price. Acceptance by his peers is critical for his ego development.

The sense of competence at this stage is the sense of oneself as capable and able to do meaningful tasks. It includes taking on tasks and projects because of a basic interest in doing them and in working to complete them to achieve satisfaction from the results. When the child's use of her expanding skills and competencies meets with success, when she receives support and approval from parents, peers, and teachers, then she will develop a sense of industry. But if there are repeated experiences of failure and disapproval, the sense of inferiority will predominate.

Erikson believed that many of the attitudes toward work and work habits that are exhibited later in life are formed during this period. It is important that both teachers and parents provide many opportunities for the child to succeed at a variety of work experiences. Since children are striving to accomplish a sense of industry, they are work-oriented. Attention should be given, both at home and at school, to the establishment of positive work habits—doing one's best, appropriate standards for work attempted, and so on.

Play continues to be important. Many pursuits are segregated by gender. Children begin to see their families as representatives of society and begin to measure them against other representatives. Parental identification is established, and the child forms relationships with other adults—teachers, relatives, family friends, and recreational leaders. Therefore, social institutions other than the family come to play a central role in the child's develop-

ment. Thus, the achievement of a sense of industry does not depend solely on the caretaking efforts of the parents.

During the sense-of-industry stage, the child becomes capable of deductive reasoning and of playing and learning by rules. New words and ideas are learned from peers and are tried out at home. Children begin to compare their own homes with those of their peers. The assumption that adults are not very bright becomes apparent when children use new reasoning skills at their command and catch adults in errors of reasoning or fact. If parents see the child's behavior as being silly, then a sense of inferiority may be established.

Building a Healthy Self-Concept

The discussion in Chapter 2 pointed out the three basic dimensions of self-concept: a sense of belonging (that is, the individual perceives himself as part of a group and is accepted and valued by the other members of that group); a sense of worth (that is, the individual perceives himself as a "good" or worthy person); and a sense of competence (that is, the individual perceives that he is

Attitudes toward work are formed during the school-age period.

successful at doing things well). We have further noted that parenting style and the quality of interactions between parents and children are significantly related to the child's development of a healthy self-concept.

Ketsetzis, Ryan, and Adams (1998) examined the direct and indirect associations among general family relationships, school-focused parent-child interactions, child personal characteristics, and school adjustment with 161 fourth- and seventh-grade children, their parents, and teachers. Results indicated that child characteristics (exclusive of self-esteem) demonstrated the most consistent and direct association with school social adjustment. However, a variety of parent-child interaction factors and family-life factors also were found to predict adjustment indirectly. For example, pressuring mothers of fourth graders, even in the context of supportive fathering, had children who demonstrated more externalizing behaviors. Overall, parental pressure decreased self-esteem, but parental support increased it. Support for seventh graders by both mothers and fathers promoted assertiveness and tolerance of frustration in their children.

The researchers concluded that excessive parental pressure for school success is associated with decreased levels of children's self-esteem, frustration tolerance, and intellectual effectiveness. Another recent study by Franco and Levitt (1998) confirmed that parental support enhances children's self-esteem. These researchers further found that parental support contributed indirectly to the quality of the child's best friendship, which, in turn, contributed further to self-esteem.

It seems obvious, then, that parental attitudes and behaviors, and the quality of the parent-child relationship begin very early to have a strong impact on how the child views herself. The school-age child's sense of self is very much a reflection of the success of her interactions with others, especially her parents. Other factors related to self-concept during the school years are summarized in the Highlights.

There has been much discussion concerning the relationship between self-concept and aca-

HIGHLIGHTS

Other Factors Related to Self-Concept during School Years

Physical appearance (body image)
Anxiety level
Competence (especially academic)
Peer acceptance
Size of family
Ordinal position

demic achievement. Which is the cause of the other is not always clear; however, there is ample evidence to suggest that positive self-concept is related to high academic achievement during the school-age years (Chapman, Lambourne, & Silva, 1990). Low self-concept and low academic achievement interact and feed back negatively on each other. Since parental acceptance and support seem to be relevant factors in the child's self-concept, this dimension of parent behavior should be related to the child's academic performance.

However, the child plays a role, too, in the view of himself. Children will behave in ways consistent with the ways they see themselves. If a child feels he is worthless, he will expect others to treat him as worthless. Since children cannot be viewed as simply mirror images of external events but as active, striving, learning individuals, self-esteem represents the child's unique organization of his own genetic makeup, the evaluations made of him by significant adults, and the feedback he receives from his world. There seems to be a downward trend in self-concept as children enter school because of the increased sources of evaluations by teachers and peers, but by fifth grade the trend climbs upward. Since, however, the school-age child is more independent and increasingly in charge of himself, more and more evaluations of behavior are self-evaluation, and a larger percentage of his rewards will be self-rewards. It seems important, then, for parents to help children identify their strengths and reward themselves for those while minimizing negative evaluations of weaknesses.

In summary, the role of the parent in developing a healthy self-concept in the child during middle childhood, just as in infancy and early childhood, remains crucial. The same parental characteristics and behaviors that were mentioned in Chapter 2 in relation to early childhood also are important in middle childhood.

Peer Relationships

We have previously noted that peer relationships take on new importance for school-age children, and conformity to peer standards increases gradually over this period of development. It is extremely important that the child be a part of a peer group. Newcomb, Bukowski, and Pattee (1993) conducted a meta-analysis review of peer relations of children in different sociometric status groups (popular, rejected, neglected, controversial, and average). These researchers found that popular

---

TIPS

For Parents of School-Age Children

Use supportive parenting practices and inductive discipline.

Set reasonable limits that are mutually understood.

Maintain effective communication with children.

Recognize the vulnerability of the child's self concept as he is exposed to a variety of evaluative adults and peers.

Provide support and encouragement for the child's efforts rather than pressuring her to achieve.

Support the child's interests in leisure activities without imposing parental interests/standards.

Monitor and supervise children's activities and their friends.

Provide the child with learning experiences and opportunities both inside and outside the home.

Recognize the importance of peer-group norms and acceptance without relinquishing monitoring and supervision. Don't sweat the small stuff!

Be patient during the preadolescent's transition from adult code to peer code.

---

children were liked and accepted by their peers, with whom they experienced close, mutual, dyadic relationships. They also evidenced better social problem-solving skills, positive social actions, positive social traits, and friendship relations than average children. Although popular children appear to be able and willing to be assertive/aggressive, their behavioral repertoire is made up primarily of socially skilled behaviors that lead to positive outcomes. Further, popular children have a low level of disruptive aggressive behavior.

On the other hand, rejected children were found to be more aggressive and withdrawn and less sociable and cognitively skilled than average children. Aggressiveness is exhibited in disruptive and negative behavior, including physical aggression. Rejected children lack positive qualities to balance their aggressive behavior and are seen as lacking positive social actions, positive social traits, and friendship relations. Being rejected often leads to isolation and ostracism, which places these children at risk for psychological disturbance in adolescence and adulthood. Socially neglected children were found to be less aggressive and less social than average children. They rarely demonstrate disruptive behaviors, but they demonstrate fewer positive traits than average children. These children may not be drastically socially inept, but they lack visibility in the peer group. However, they are not at serious risk for poor outcomes.

Children labeled as controversial in sociometric status were indeed controversial in that they showed characteristics of both rejected and popular children. Like rejected children, they demonstrated higher levels of aggression than average children. At the same time, they showed more sociability than average children. Although often disruptive, controversial children have significantly better cognitive and social actions than rejected children, and have positive social traits and friendship relations equal to those of popular children.

Kupersmidt, Griesler, DeRosier, Patterson, and Davis (1995) explored the impact of ethnicity, income, and structural characteristics of families and neighborhoods on childhood aggression and peer relations in children from second through fifth grade. Findings supported the notion that the neighborhood context is associated with childhood aggression and peer relations over and above family characteristics. In low-SES neighborhoods, parental supervision often is lacking. Unsupervised wandering, a natural consequence of low supervision, in combination with children's association with a deviant peer group, best predicted delinquent behavior. In addition, boys living in low-SES neighborhoods were more likely to be recruited for membership in antisocial gangs than children living in middle-SES neighborhoods. The neighborhood context, then, plays an important role in the development of peer relationships. Middle-income White children living in middle-SES neighborhoods had significantly more playmates than other children. Children who lived in physically unsafe neighborhoods with drugs and crime had fewer friends than those living in safe neighborhoods, perhaps partly because of more restrictive parental behavior in efforts to ensure children's safety. Results showed that boys and girls functioned similarly irrespective of their neighborhood surroundings. The only consistent finding surrounding gender was that boys were more aggressive and delinquent and had more conflict in their relationships than did girls.

Most parents are concerned about the characteristics of their children's peer groups, and this concern is valid. Peer groups exert considerable pressure on children to conform to the group's standards. Parents need to know the children constituting the peer group and their families by inviting their children's friends into their homes and communicating with their parents. Careful monitoring and supervision of children's activities and friends, especially as they approach adolescence, is important. However, some research has shown that social networks and friendships during middle childhood wax and wane in strength, depending on the centrality of the group and the status of the group member (Cairns, Leung, Buchanan, & Cairns, 1995).

Providing Learning Experiences

Even though the child has entered the structured learning environment of the school, the home continues to be an important learning laboratory. When describing the growing sense of industry earlier in this chapter, we stated that the school-age child is concerned with how things are made, how they work, and what they do. Further, the child works to expand both her body skills and her perceptual skills. The role that parents play in structuring the home environment to permit these capacities to develop and in assisting and encouraging the child to pursue relevant out-of-home, out-of-school activities is extremely important. Therefore, we will discuss learning activities during middle childhood from two perspectives: (1) those that occur out of the home and out of the school (commonly labeled as extracurricular activities) and (2) those that occur mostly in the home or with the family.

The importance of play during middle childhood cannot be overemphasized, since it provides the child with situations in which he can test himself, work out feelings, experiment with roles, learn rules and expectations, and develop and practice skills that will be important for adult life in society. Many of these goals are achieved by play involving peers or by team efforts.

Out-of-Home Learning Experiences.   Aside from peer-group interaction within the normal course of a school day, children have an opportunity to achieve group status as well as to broaden their scope of learning through organized out-of-home activities. These usually fall into the following categories: sports (soccer, football, baseball, basketball, gymnastics, swimming, tennis, and so forth); music/dance/drama/crafts; Cub Scouts, Boy Scouts, Brownies, Girl Scouts, or Campfire Girls; church activities; and camps.

Clearly there are both advantages and disadvantages to children being involved with such activities. The advantages are relatively obvious: Children begin to associate and identify with unrelated adults who are important socializing agents for them; children extend their peer interactions beyond the classroom and are frequently exposed to children from a variety of cultural backgrounds; children can spend time with other children who share their interests; children learn to develop a team spirit; children can develop and practice their growing bodily and perceptual skills within the context of a group setting; children can learn to play by rules and how to be good winners and good losers; children can establish status in the group; and children can expend energies in playing.

The disadvantages may not be quite so obvious to parents. First, many parents fall into the "more is better" trap or the "my child is busier than your child" syndrome when planning for the child's out-of-home activities. In their desire to develop well-rounded children, some parents overenroll their children in "classes," so that there is little time left for meaningful interaction or for children to pursue other interests.

The second major disadvantage is that parents may actually coerce children to be involved in an activity simply because the parents themselves enjoy it. A typical example is the "jock" father who almost literally forces his son into sports. When children are not genuinely interested in an activity, the activity will not provide effective learning experiences for them.

Finally, the competitive aspect of organized sports may overshadow their inherent learning potential. We have attended Little League baseball games that could compare to the stress and tension of the World Series. The desire to win superseded any effort to help children develop and refine skills

or to teach the rules of cooperation. Further, the models presented by both coaches and parents were ones of competition and aggression rather than of cooperation. Parents need to examine the competitive aspects of such organized groups and identify the potential for positive development that accompanies them.

It is not our intention to minimize the importance of extracurricular activities for school-age children, but we do wish to encourage parents to follow the guidelines in the Highlights. If these guidelines are followed, out-of-home activities can provide a source of valuable learning for children.

In-Home Learning Activities.   Two types of family activities that can provide valuable learning experiences for school-age children are those that are planned and organized and those that are unplanned or spontaneous. Organized activities include vacations; camping, picnicking, or hiking; going out to dinner, parks, movies, museums, and cultural events; attending sports events or amusement parks; and shopping. Naturally, these activities offer a wide range of learning experiences for children. They give families opportunities to share common interests, to be together away from a usually hectic home schedule, and to share new experiences. Often it is difficult to plan such activities so that every family member enjoys them equally. As children reach middle childhood, they develop new interests and an increasing sense of individuality. Therefore, organized activities should be planned with the interests of each family member in mind. The favorite activities of individual chil-

---

HIGHLIGHTS

Guidelines for Choosing Out-of-Home Activities for School-Age Children

Examine alternatives carefully. Consider time commitment, competitive aspects, and characteristics of participating adults and children.
Determine child's interest and "fit" between activity and development level.
Give encouragement and guidance as child selects his or her own activities.
Select judiciously; do not overcommit child's time.
Help child select activities in which he or she can be successful.

dren might be combined or alternated. Or perhaps some family members might engage in activities together while the rest of the family participates in another activity.

Equally important as organized activities are those that occur spontaneously in the home, such as games, hobbies, family projects, and reading or talking together. Unplanned and unorganized leisure time with children may yield the fondest memories for children as well as stimulating learning. It has been said that there is math in the bathroom and science in the sink, and parents who take advantage of these opportunities stimulate learning in the home for their children.

Parents who make arrangements for their children to be involved in an array of enriching social and cultural experiences during the elementary years have children who perform better on achievement tests and who are rated as more task-oriented and better adjusted by their teachers. Further, parental involvement with children is consistently related to child competence throughout the child's development.

Frequently public schools will prepare materials that can be used in the home to support academic performance or provide ideas for activities parents and children can do together. An activity may be simple as "Take a walk with your child and listen for different sounds" or as complicated as a science experiment or writing a story.

There is no consensus among experts on the role parents should play in the child's "homework." Clearly a child's homework is her responsibility, not her parents'. If one subscribes to the use of natural consequences, then the child who does not complete her homework assignments will suffer the natural consequences of not doing well in school. A "hands-off-the-homework" approach is difficult for many parents who see their role as assisting the child in her learning experiences. Probably the more sensible and effective approach is to encourage and assist when necessary but refuse to assume responsibility for its completion. How does one accomplish this? First, parents can create a home environment that is conducive to study; a quiet time and place for children to work;

a flexible schedule to allow enough time for work; resources (newspapers, books, magazines, dictionaries, encyclopedias) to assist in the completion of assignments; encouragement and assistance in areas in which the child seems to be having problems; and elimination of nagging.

It is critical that parents and teachers establish partnership relationships if children are to receive maximum benefit from school. If a child is having learning difficulties, on the advice of the teacher parents may need to secure tutoring for the child in some academic area. If parents and teachers work together, realistic expectations can be determined and a plan of action initiated.

Issues that commonly divide parents and their school-age children are television viewing and playing video games—when, how often, and what kind. Clearly how these activities influence children is an issue that has attracted much attention in recent years. For example, studies have indicated that the effects of television watching are evident in children's play and fantasy behavior as well as in everyday behavior and personal interactions. However, mediating factors such as personality characteristics, IQ, and social class begin to interact with television viewing during the preschool period and continue to do so into school age. Although some of the child's behaviors that appear to be related to television are negative—that is, aggression or sex-role stereotypes or standards—others may be positive, such as indicating greater knowledge of public affairs and current events. The proliferation of video games is relatively recent, and little or no research exists on their impact on children. However, common sense dictates that they be monitored (for content) and regulated (for frequency) by parents.

Whatever rules parents make about television watching and video games should be reasonable and enforceable. For example, it is rather difficult for a parent to forbid television viewing and video games when there is no adult present to enforce such a rule. It probably is a good idea for parents to be thoroughly familiar with the content of programs and games before setting limits on content and frequency. Avoiding stimulating programs and games just before bedtime will help the child relax. Parents and children need to develop mutual reasonable solutions and avoid power struggles over the issue. It seems apparent, however, that parents who are addicted to television and/or video games will produce children who are addicts.

One of the major criticisms of too much television viewing and/or playing of video games is that it reduces the level of conversation within the family. Surely one of the most valuable learning experiences for children is conversation with other family members. Most conversation is spontaneous, centering on specific interests or activities that occur at a given moment. One child whose parents had designated the evening meal as the specific time for conversation in the family felt so frustrated that conversation became less frequent. Parents should value spontaneous moments to such an extent that enough time is left in organizing individual and family schedules to preserve them.

In summary, the school-age years continue to be an important stage during which learning experiences outside the school play a crucial role in the child's development. Parents can enhance learning by creating a home environment that is conducive to learning, by helping the child select extracurricular activities that promote overall adjustment and development, and by helping the child achieve a mix of peer and family activities that is acceptable to both parents and children.

SPECIAL CHALLENGES OF PREADOLESCENCE

Preadolescence is a period of transition between childhood and adolescence, roughly spanning the years between 9 and 13 and fifth or sixth grade through eighth grade. This transition period is the one about which the least is known. One thing is clear—the role parents play during this period of development is crucial but confusing and sometimes unstable, vacillating between encourager and counselor. Obviously, because peer identification is paramount, preadolescents still need the encouragement from their parents that was so necessary during middle childhood. Loyalty to gangs is evident, but rejection by the peer group can threaten the self-concept. It can, in fact, cause the preadolescent's world to disintegrate. Team sports are popular at this time, and those children who do not excel in these areas need encouragement from parents to pursue other activities that will facilitate acceptance by the peer group.

Awkwardness, restlessness, and laziness are common characteristics of preadolescents as a result of rapid and uneven growth. Accompanying behaviors may include excessive criticism, unpredictability, rebellion, and lack of cooperation in the home setting. These on-and-off behaviors may result in rejection of adult standards, and they make the parenting role a difficult one. In addition to encouragement, parents need to understand the physical and emotional changes that are about to come and understand and accept peer-group pressure. Counseling the child, without undue pressure, in the move toward greater independence and increased responsibility is a role that parents will begin to assume and one that will flourish as the child moves into adolescence. Condemnation of the child's choice of friends (inevitably, ones who are rejected by the parents), nagging about keeping appointed meal times and failure to do chores, and "talking down" as one might do to a younger child are nonproductive forms of parental behavior. Warmth; affection; a sense of fairness; and, most of all, a sense of humor and being a good sport are necessary for parents to survive.

Vuchinich, Angelelli, and Gatherum (1996) examined the factors associated with, and the nature of the changes in, the quality of family problem solving during preadolescence. As predicted, the effectiveness of family problem solving deteriorated during preadolescence, probably because of the increase in preadolescent striving for autonomy that leads to difficulties with parents. In general, preadolescents became more negative over the 2-year span of the study, especially in discussion of parent-selected topics. Families with preadolescent females had significantly less effective problem solving than families with preadolescent males.

Preadolescents appear to be particularly vulnerable to family disruption. Coughlin and Vuchinich (1996) examined aspects of the family experience of White males at age 10 as predictors of police arrest by age 17. These researchers found clear evidence that experiencing a stepfamily or a single-parent family in preadolescence is associated with a substantially higher risk of arrest, even after controlling for other key predictors. Children in these families were more than twice as likely to be arrested by age 14 as were children with two biological parents in residence. Good peer relations at age 10 had significant protective effects against arrest by age 17 for boys in all family structures. But the effects of family problem solving differed markedly across family structure. In stepfamilies, effective problem solving in preadolescence reduced the odds of arrest by about half; in families with two biological parents, there was no significant effect. However, in single-parent families, oddly enough, effective problem solving more than doubled the risk of arrest in adolescence. It could be that negative mother-son relationships following divorce created the basis for adolescent problem behavior.

Hierarchical analysis consistently showed that good parent-child relations and discipline practices had significant protective effects as long as peer relations and antisocial characteristics were not taken into account. But when these variables were included, the parent-child relationship and discipline effects disappeared. There was clear evidence that family factors were more influential in predicting delinquency that began by age 14 than delinquency that began between ages 14 and 17.

Further evidence of the impact of preadolescence on later development was found by Bagwell, Newcomb, and Bukowski (1998), who examined the contribution of friendship during preadolescence to adjustment in early adulthood. Results showed that adult life status, perceived competence, and psychological symptoms were significantly associated with peer relations in preadolescence. Both having a mutual friend in fifth grade and low levels of peer rejection predicted successful adjust-

ment in life status. Peer rejection in fifth grade, however, was highly related to antisocial outcomes across adolescence and adulthood, including greater distress from psychopathological symptoms..Further, general self-worth was predicted by friendship status.

Finally, transition from elementary to middle school often has an impact on the adjustment and achievement of preadolescents. Fenzel (1992) investigated the effects of relative age among students in grades 6 through 8 who made the transition from elementary to middle school on self-esteem, role strain, grade point average, and anxiety. In all cases, being relatively older than classmates provided adjustment benefits. However, older age relative to classmates at this transition resulted in higher self-esteem and less strain for girls only. Younger students whose fathers held college degrees achieved a full point higher in their grade point average than did younger students whose fathers had not completed college; these same students reported less strain related to schoolwork demands and teachers' and parents' expectations. Therefore, relatively younger students whose parents are not highly educated may be doubly disadvantaged with respect to school-related adjustment indicators of strain and grade point average. Relative age effects do not seem to disappear after the primary school years but may continue into fifth and sixth grade.

Preadolescence represents a transition from the adult code of the parent to the peer code—a transition from dependence to independence, which will ultimately lead the child at adolescence into identity formation. The group phenomenon, or clique and gang formation, during preadolescence is essential to the child's later functioning as a citizen in society. However, the more the "gang" character is subversive of certain adult standards, the more thoroughly it is enjoyed by the child. In many cases, then, the peer code may be diametrically opposed to the adult code. Some examples include the values of cleanliness, good grades in school, obedience to adults, dress codes and hairstyles, and dirty jokes and/or language. What is labeled "good" or "bad" behavior by parents may be labeled exactly the opposite by peers. Often the peer-group behavior or code is unspoken but nevertheless strongly implied.

The change from adult code to peer code is not an easy process for a child, and it may be accompanied by conflict. Although the preadolescent wants and needs to be admired and respected by his friends, he is still loyal to his family and does not want to be misunderstood by them or make them unhappy. One the other hand, if he pleases his parents and they accept him, he may run the risk of being called a "sissy" or a "coward" by his friends.

Perhaps the most difficult adjustment that parents must make when their children are preadolescents is that of understanding and accepting the child's rejection of adult standards and her loyalty to peers. Although most parents *want* their children to be independent, they wish it could be done less painfully. They wish they could impart the wisdom of experience to their children. Parents may feel guilty because they think that they have failed—otherwise the child would not reject them. The child, in turn, may feel guilty because she does love her parents but cannot bear to lose face with her friends. The resolution of this crisis is an important factor in parent-child relationships at this time. A satisfactory resolution will determine, to some extent, how parents deal with the so-called midlife crisis.

PROGRAMS FOR PARENTS OF SCHOOL-AGE CHILDREN

The older the child, the fewer the programs that exist for parents. Therefore, parent-education programs for those with infants and preschool children far outnumber programs for those with school-age children. As a society we have assumed that parents with young children need more support and assistance than those with older children. We also have assumed that parent behaviors and attitudes are resistant to change and we should therefore focus on early parental behavior. Although a variety of agencies—including churches, mental-health clinics, and family-counseling

agencies—have made sporadic attempts at education for parents of school-age children, the most consistent efforts have been through the public education system.

Parent Involvement in the Schools

Efforts to involve parents in school programs are not new. Since the founding of the National Congress of Mothers in 1897, which became the PTA (Parents and Teachers Association) in 1924, attempts to create links between home and school have been evident. A variety of approaches have been used, including parent-teacher conferences, involving parents in fund-raising and open houses, and utilizing parents as volunteers in the classroom and as tutors either at home or in the school. These activities have been most successful with middle-class mothers, with little involvement of fathers or working-class parents, except in Chapter I programs (see following discussion). It has been assumed that this kind of involvement contributes to greater adjustment and achievement of children and improved attitudes on the part of parents.

Even so, parent involvement in the schools has left much to be desired, sometimes reaching the point of hostility between parents and school personnel. It is not unusual for teachers to complain that parents have little interest in their children, leaving the business of child rearing to the schools, and, on the other hand, to resent parents' intrusion into the classroom. Parents, too, may insist that teachers are poorly prepared and assert their perceived parental rights to determine school curricula. Of course, the success with which these issues are resolved varies from teacher to teacher, school to school, and district to district. The rebirth of the "back to basics" movement of the 1980s, however, resulted in state legislation allowing home education and a greater proportion of parents educating their children at home because of dissatisfaction with both the content of public school curricula and the degree of parental input into curriculum decision making. The issue of parental versus institutional rights in public education is far from resolved.

The importance of parent involvement in the schools has reemerged in recent years as public schools have been increasingly attacked for their failure to educate children properly. However, since much of the emphasis has been placed on the early-childhood period, few successful models have been implemented and tested. Professionals and parents alike are nonetheless renewing their interest in finding ways to work together for the benefit of school-age children.

Chapter I Programs

Public schools are eligible to receive Chapter I funds under the Elementary and Secondary Education Act to develop stimulating and remedial education for low-income children in order to achieve the goals of grade-level proficiency of children, education for their parents, and greater involvement of parents in the education of their children. Many of these programs exist throughout the country, and activities vary according to the needs of the parents in the community where the program is located. Parents and teachers collaborate on the design and implementation of Chapter I programs. The goal of Chapter I programs is to equip parents to become more effective partners in their children's educational experience (Turner, Hamner, & Orell, 1993).

There are four major capacities in which parents have been involved: (1) as observers or learners, (2) as participants in school activities, (3) as volunteers in the classroom, and (4) as participants on school advisory committees. The major purpose of involving parents as observers or learners is to enable them to increase their understanding of themselves, their children, and/or the school program. These efforts have been most successful when parents perceive that the information offered is vital to learning, or to their child's interests, or when the programs are aimed specifically at parent interests and needs.

A lesser degree of involvement has occurred when parents are participants in school activities that are peripheral to the classroom, such as supervising after-school clubs, producing newsletters, and assisting in the school library. Research has shown that children in Chapter I programs with high parent involvement in these types of activities make significant achievement gains, but variables other than parent involvement may have accounted for the improvement. Parents, however, have reported increased self-esteem and better understanding of school programs.

The use of parents as volunteers in the classroom has been minimal in Chapter I programs. In those instances in which it has occurred, parents have reported improved self-image and greater understanding of the curriculum and the teacher's problems. No data are available on the relationship between this type of involvement and children's achievement.

In general, there has been a low level of involvement of parents in the school advisory committees of Chapter I programs. Often administrators have not encouraged participation at this level, and confusion has existed over role responsibilities. The effects of such participation, where it has occurred, on student achievement, on the school program, and on the parents themselves have not been definitively shown by the research.

Parent Education via the Child's School

In some instances the school has been a vehicle for the delivery of more formalized parent education, although this practice is not commonplace. Several school districts have provided STEP (Systematic Training for Effective Parenting) or Active Parenting Today classes to parents, with moderate success. One district with which we are familiar sponsors a yearly mini–parent conference on a Saturday, which includes a keynote speaker and a variety of workshops led by community professionals. Other school districts offer similar programs using different contemporary strategies or a combination of two or more. These programs represent more of an attempt to meet the needs of parents in the community than to test empirically the effectiveness of such programs as it relates to the child's behavior and achievement in the school setting. As with efforts toward achieving parental involvement in school programs, most participating parents have been middle class.

Even though education and support programs for parents whose children are in middle childhood are not numerous and research regarding the effectiveness of such programs is scarce, increased efforts should be made in this direction. The complexity of parenting in contemporary society suggests that parents are in need of such services. For example, drug use by school-age children is becoming a greater problem, early sexual activity is a concern for many parents, and the lack of accessibility to programs that provide before- and after-school supervision for children creates problems for working parents. Creative ways to reach parents and program content that focuses on current issues and concerns need to be developed.

DEVELOPMENTAL NEEDS OF PARENTS

The sense of generativity that was described in Chapter 2 continues to develop for parents as their children move from the preschool period into middle childhood. However, the need to care for others or to become involved with creative production may begin to be fulfilled in new or different ways. As children enter school and are absent from the home for large parts of the day and as they are developing a wider range of interests outside the home, mothers who have not already done so may return to school, obtain a job, or resume leisure activities after a long absence. These opportunities enable them to blend their parenting role with other roles that are related to developing a sense of generativity. However, as more women with very young children are entering the workforce or continuing with their education, the stereotype of the mother who stays home with her children until at least school age is rapidly disappearing. In any case, many parents do find that middle childhood, with its decreasing demands on physical care, allows them an opportunity for a wider variety of experiences to meet their developmental needs, whether they are employed outside the home or not. Socializing with other adults, time for privacy, and developing interests outside the family become a little easier. Fatigue may be somewhat

alleviated as children begin to contribute to household responsibilities.

However, several problems confront parents at this time. The first is the changing nature of the guidance that parents give children, which becomes less physical and more psychological. Parents identify with the disappointments their children feel when they fail at a task or are rejected by their peers. Often the pain is greater for the parents than it is for the children. Encouragement in the face of pain may be difficult for parents. Further, as children develop skills of logic and reason, parents have to find new ways of discipline that are effective. Parents, especially mothers, may be ambivalent toward the child's increasing self-sufficiency. If parents feel that peers, school, and other community relations detract from them, they may behave in ways that curtail children's activities outside the family.

Nevertheless, one of the biggest problems parents face when their children enter school is that of "letting go" to some degree. Although nurturance is still an important ingredient in the parent-child relationship, it is difficult for parents to accept the growing influence of peers and other adults. Their need to be needed is still quite strong. If, however, parents can develop outside interests while their children are expressing a growing need for individuality and peer relationships, letting go becomes somewhat easier. We remember the traumatic experience of leaving our children alone for the first time without a sitter. Of course, most children are ready for this experience before their parents are. We also remember the first time our children spent the night with friends or the first time they went to a movie without us. These experiences are part of the process of letting go and are necessary milestones in the lives of both parents and children. Parents who fail to encourage the child to develop independence and form new relationships contribute to poorly adjusted children and unhappiness for themselves.

Finally, parents may be preoccupied at this time with the direction their lives are taking. Are they satisfied with their jobs? Do they want more education? Is their marital satisfaction diminishing? The average length of marriage before divorce is about 7 years. This means that for many parents the beginning of the period of middle childhood or just prior is a critical period for maladjustment in marriage. Further, if the mother does return to work or school at this time, she may experience role strain that contributes to marital dissatisfaction. If parents can positively evaluate the direction their lives are taking, share the responsibilities of parenting and maintaining the household, and develop interests outside the family, then this role strain can be reduced. In addition, if they capitalize on the decreasing demands their children are making upon them, middle childhood can offer a period of satisfaction.

Again, it is important to emphasize the reciprocal character of the parent-child relationship during middle childhood. There seems to be a natural dovetailing of the developmental needs of school-age children and the developmental needs of parents at this time. Just as children are beginning to strive for greater independence and are moving toward stronger peer relationships, parents are beginning to reevaluate their lives and develop new interests. If equal attention is given to the needs of children and parents, the developmental tasks of all family members can be met with minimal stress. Both parents and children play a crucial role in the resolution of psychosocial crises, and the behavior of one member continues to influence the behavior of another. It seems that a mutually satisfying resolution of establishing a sense of industry for the parent results in an easier transition for both during the stages of preadolescence and adolescence.

PARENTS AND ADOLESCENTS

Many parents in Western society dread their children's approaching adolescence; at best they experience some degree of confusion in parenting an individual who is neither a child nor an adult. The persistent notion that parent-adolescent conflict is inevitable has contributed to the uncertainties of parents and their general lack of enthusiasm for this stage of development. Because of the biological, cognitive, and psychosocial changes that occur in adolescence and because of the rapid social changes occurring in our society, the concept of a

generation gap between parents and children is widespread. There are anthropological and sociological studies, however, indicating that adolescence itself does not universally represent a period of polarization and social difficulties. In fact, research over the past two decades has challenged the view of adolescence as a time of storm and stress (Gecas & Seff, 1991). Many adolescents feel respect and fondness for their parents; have value systems consistent with them; talk openly about special concerns and problems; and seek guidance on such issues as morality, education, career, and marriage.

There seems to be little consensus in our society, then, on the degree of conflict that occurs between adolescents and their parents and to what extent conflict is dependent on parenting behaviors, changes in adolescents' behaviors, or social changes. It seems reasonable to assume, however, that as children reach puberty, significant biological and cognitive changes affect behavior in such a way that parents themselves must make significant adjustments to their parenting roles.

Parent-Child Interactions

To understand the changing parental role, it is important to understand what is happening to the adolescent. First, there are obvious physical and hormonal changes that occur at puberty that affect adolescent behavior. A teenager can "go into orbit" over a few extra pounds or hair that is too curly, too straight, or too short. The psychosocial development of a sense of identity, which will be discussed in the next section, has important implications for adolescent behavior, especially when the idealism of the teenager is incompatible with the pragmatism of the parent. And finally, significant changes in cognitive development, often misunderstood by parents, help to explain adolescent behavior.

The Parents' Roles as Counselors.   Because of the developmental characteristics of adolescents, which often result in behaviors that are confusing and irritating, parents must once again change their roles. Although caregiving, nurturance, and encouragement continue to be important aspects of parental behavior, the primary role of the parent becomes that of counselor. An effective counselor has established positive communication with the counselled, and this aspect of the parent-child relationship is perhaps the most important ingredient.

Communication with one's child begins in the cradle. Parents begin to communicate with their infants by responding to a variety of behaviors, such as the touching of genitals or even crying. The parent's tone of voice, facial expression, and specific answers to a preschooler's questions further influence the direction a communication system will take. Tolerance of others' opinions and acceptance of school-age children's feelings and attitudes assist in keeping the channels of communication open. In short, by the time a child reaches adolescence, the communication system in the family can already be described as open or closed, determining how comfortable the teenager will feel in discussing openly his other concerns and problems with his parents. It is important to remember that adolescents may be overly sensitive to parental criticism and often misinterpret what parents say. They also may be more reserved, reclusive, and generally less communicative than when they were younger (Small & Eastman, 1991). Perceptions of parents and adolescents toward one another affect their communication style. Negative beliefs and attitudes toward one another predict negative communication behavior, and both positive and negative communication behaviors of parent-child pairs have been found to be highly interrelated (Reed & Dubow, 1997).

Self-concept appears to have an effect on communication patterns within the family. It has been suggested that those adolescents who have poor self-concepts perceive communication with their parents as significantly more nonconstructive than do adolescents with better self-concepts. Adolescents' feelings of "mattering" to their parents is associated with higher self-esteem (cited in Gecas & Seff, 1991).

Parenting Styles.   Parents struggle with finding the appropriate guidance techniques, yet the effects of past parent-child interactions and child-

rearing practices carry into adolescence. However, parental support appears to be one of the most important characteristics at this stage of development, relating positively to cognitive development, conformity to adult standards, moral behavior, internal locus of control, self-esteem, instrumental competence, and academic achievement. The greater the degree of parental support, the greater the adolescent's social competence (Gecas & Seff, 1991). The converse also seems to be true: Lack of parental support is related to negative socialization outcomes for teenagers, such as low self-esteem, delinquency, deviance, drug abuse, and other problem behaviors. Support includes general sustenance, physical affection, companionship, and sustained contact (Weiss & Schwarz, 1996).

The benefits of authoritative parenting that accrue before adolescence continue to hold throughout the teen years. Weiss and Schwarz (1996) examined the relationships of six parenting styles (authoritative, democratic, nondirective, nonauthoritarian-directive, authoritarian-directive, and unengaged) to adolescent behavior in four domains: personality, adjustment, academic achievement, and substance use. Adolescents from authoritative homes received the most or second most favorable scores in all areas assessed, but the differences were not statistically significant. Nondirective parenting resulted in almost as many positive outcomes as authoritative parenting. Unengaged parenting style was associated with the following characteristics: more nonconformity, maladjustment, domination, selfishness, lack of originality, and high consumption of alcohol.

Teens from authoritarian-directive homes were particularly weak in academic aptitude and achievement compared with children from nondirective or authoritative homes. Democratic and nondirective parenting seemed to be more effective for daughters than for sons, suggesting that sons may require more rules and limit setting than daughters to reach their full potential.

In another study Glasgow, Dornbush, Troyer, Steinberg, and Ritter (1997) found that authoritative parents were the most successful in fostering personal and social responsibility in adolescents without limiting their emerging autonomy. Adolescents exposed to nonauthoritative parenting styles were less inclined than adolescents with authoritative parents to view their academic achievements as the products of their own capacities and persistence. These students were more likely to emphasize either external causes for high school grades or low ability as the cause of poor grades. One study found an interesting relationship between authoritative parenting, peer influence, and adolescents' grade point average (GPA). Although the adolescents' GPAs were predicted by their friends' GPAs, perceptions of authoritative parenting moderated peer efforts, such that high and medium levels of authoritative parenting enhanced the positive effects of having high-achieving friends (Mounts & Steinberg, 1995).

Although authoritative parenting is characterized by a high degree of support and autonomy-granting in particular areas, it also is characterized by a certain amount of control. However, different types of control have different outcomes. Authoritarian or coercive control—based on threats, force, or physical punishment—has negative consequences, whereas authoritative or inductive control has positive outcomes. (The concepts of authoritative and inductive discipline have been discussed in previous sections.) Failure to distinguish between these two types of control has resulted in much confusion and inconsistency on the part of parents. Much of the conflict and stress of parent-adolescent interactions revolves around the issue of control, since teens usually want greater freedom and parents usually seek greater control. Parents have more influence over adolescents when they express a high level of support and exercise inductive control. In fact, by articulating clearly the societal or welfare concerns that complex issues raise, authoritative parents are likely to facilitate adolescents' understanding of the limits or boundaries of their personal restrictions. These parents maintain clear boundaries between moral, conventional, and personal issues, whereas authoritarian parents treat both moral and conventional issues as obligatory and legitimately subject to parental authority (Smetana, 1995).

Unfortunately, some authoritarian parents continue to use corporal punishment with adolescents. Straus and Yodanis (1996) found that parental corporal punishment during adolescence increases the probability of approving violence against one's spouse in adulthood, experiencing depression as an adult, and elevated levels of marital conflict. These three factors, in turn, led to increased probability of physically assaulting one's spouse, regardless of age, socioeconomic status, ethnicity, and whether one had witnessed violence between one's own parents. Aquilino (1997) provided further evidence for the continuity in parent-child relationships from adolescence into young adulthood, noting that the history of the parent-child relationship with respect to control and conflict set the stage for either intergenerational solidarity or a lack of solidarity in adulthood.

Peer Influence.   Inevitably in adolescence occasions will arise when parents and children will disagree about what is appropriate behavior. Because of the adolescent's desire to establish a sense of identity and increasing degrees of independence, peers will exert more influence than in the past. Friendship bonds are important for achieving the developmental tasks of adolescence (Giordano, Cernkovich, & DeMaris, 1993). When parents and peers are in agreement, a particular behavior in question is most likely to occur. If, however, parents and peers disagree, their respective influence varies with the issue involved and with the sex of the child. For example, in matters of finances, education, and career plans, adolescents are likely to seek advice or counsel from their parents. For the specifics of their social life (dress, dating, drinking, social events, and joining clubs), they clearly want to be attuned to the standards of their peers, suggesting equally important dual reference groups for teenagers.

However, many parents are concerned about the powerful influence peers have on adolescent behavior. Later in this chapter we will discuss peer influence on particular behaviors such as alcohol and drug use. It is important to remember that much research points out the interaction effects of parents and peers. It appears that certain adolescents are more likely to be susceptible to peer behavior, and susceptibility seems to vary with adolescents' perceptions of their parents' practices. Mounts and Steinberg (1995) noted that parenting style (i.e., authoritative parenting) encourages adolescents to be less susceptible to peer influences specifically when peers are engaging in unacceptable behavior. In contrast, when peers are engaging in adult-approved behaviors, adolescents from authoritative homes are more influenced by peer behavior than those reared in other types of homes, suggesting that parenting style can act as a buffer or as a facilitator of peer influence.

Cashwell and Vacc (1996) examined how family relationships and risk behaviors related to self-reported delinquency among adolescents. Results showed that being involved with deviant peers was the strongest direct predictor of adolescent delinquent behavior; adaptability of the family unit was the second strongest direct predictor. Overall, family cohesion provided the strongest familial influence because of its significant impact on peer-group choice. Living in a cohesive family reduces the likelihood of becoming involved with deviant peers, once again supporting the interactive nature of parental and peer-group influence on adolescent behavior.

Based on the evidence presented above, it appears that the parental role of counselor is characterized by allowing increasing independence by maintaining an atmosphere of warmth, affection, support, and understanding; by maintaining a positive communication system that involves self-disclosure and openness to feedback by both parents and adolescents; by limiting parental power and authority based on coercion; and by recognizing the influence of peers. If these conditions exist, adolescents who have previously internalized the values of their families and the larger society will, in most instances, continue to accept as legitimate the standards for behavior set by their parents.

Developing a Sense of Identity

The fifth stage of Erikson's (1963) theory of psychosocial development is identity versus role con-

_____ **TIPS** _____

For Parents of Adolescents

Maintain positive and open communication with the teen.

Let the teenager know that she matters to you.

Use inductive, authoritative discipline that combines the right amount of support and noncoercive control.

Maintain an atmosphere of warmth, acceptance, and understanding.

Recognize that the adolescent's quest for identity may manifest itself in cliques, fads, and experimentation with diverse ideologies.

Be alert to warning signs of gang activity and substance use.

Provide the adolescent with appropriate information and honest feelings about sexual activity. Be alert to warning signs of early sex.

Provide appropriate supervision and monitoring of teen's activities while respecting his right to a certain amount of privacy.

Obtain information on preventing substance use, gang activity, and early sexual activity.

fusion, which corresponds to adolescence. As the adolescent matures physiologically, she experiences new feelings, sensations, and desires; and as she matures mentally, she develops a multitude of ways of looking at and thinking about the world. Adolescents, in their crucial task of searching for identity formation, might be described as impatient idealists who believe there is little difficulty in realizing an imagined ideal. They become capable of constructing theories and philosophies designed to bring the varied and conflicting aspects of society into a harmonious whole.

By ego identity Erikson meant that, under a variety of circumstances, an individual's mind has a certain recognizable quality or character all its own, but in a certain measure it can be shared thoroughly with others. The adolescent's effort to formulate an identity involves the ego's ability to integrate the demands of the libido, the abilities he has developed from natural capacities, and the numerous opportunities offered by available social roles. Further, adolescence may be seen as a time when all the crises of the previous stages are re-lived, and those of future stages are rehearsed, as the individual integrates previously acquired iden-tifications with future aspirations into a cohesive ego identity. In Erikson's view, then, adolescence is a socially authorized delay of adulthood in which the individual has time to integrate himself into adulthood.

Adolescent identity strivings may result in the assumption of nonconforming roles, member-ship in cliques, adoption of faddish signs and styles that mark one as an "in-grouper," and/or ex-perimentation with diverse ideologies. In addi-tion, the sexual identity is rehearsed and tested during a period of first courtships. The final task for the adolescent is to bring together all the things she has learned about herself and to integrate all the images into a whole that makes sense as well as shows continuity with the past while preparing for the future. Erikson's discussion of identity, then, focuses on work, sex-role identity and sexu-ality, and ideology.

If a child reaches adolescence with a sense of trust, autonomy, initiative, and industry, then his chances of arriving at a meaningful sense of iden-tity are greatly enhanced. Preparation for a successful adolescence and the attainment of an in-tegrated psychosocial identity must, therefore, be-gin in childhood. On the other hand, failure to attain a sense of personal identity results in identity or role confusion, which has been associated with severe emotional upheavals and delinquency.

Questions have been raised concerning the differences between male and female adolescents in their evolution toward identity formation. It seems that the process of identity formation in males reflects the cultural expectations of auton-omy, personality differentiation, and success. For females, on the other hand, the process reflects the cultural expectation of establishing an intimate, caring relationship. Further, experiencing a crisis seems to be adaptive for males and maladaptive for females. Therefore, the literature suggests the ex-istence of traditional sex-role stereotypes in iden-tity formation, which may mean that a sense of

identity and a sense of intimacy are more clearly differentiated for males than for females.

Fairly consistent results have been found in studies relating to the parent-child relationship and its effect on identity formation in adolescence. A broad body of research supports the notion that positive family relations (e.g., those high in paren-tal support, communication, involvement, and in-ductive control) facilitate the development of ego identity in adolescence (Gecas & Seff, 1991). In-volved, supportive parents who use inductive con-trol and maintain good communication seem to produce high-identity adolescents who are inde-pendent and self-directed. Bhushan and Shirali (1992) examined the relationship of family func-tioning to identity achievement. They found that family cohesion and adaptability increased iden-tity development and facilitated more openness and fewer communication problems between par-ents and adolescents. It therefore appears that the nature and quality of the parent-child relationship is an important factor in how the adolescent re-solves the identity crisis.

Finally, the social milieu seems to affect the development of a sense of personal identity. When rapid social and technological changes occur that affect traditional values, the adolescent may have difficulty finding continuity between what he has learned or experienced as a child and what he is ex-periencing as an adolescent. The search for causes that give life meaning and direction may result in activism, cultism, or even affiliation with a gang. Another interesting notion is that the present need for longer periods of education for adolescents may limit their experiences with the outside world and cause them to remain economically dependent on parents at a stage when they want to be indepen-dent and work out their own identity.

The task of identity formation may be difficult for adolescents and trying for parents, but it is doubtlessly an essential task if the individual is ul-timately to function as a decision-making adult.

Gang Activity. Beginning in the late 1980s and continuing into the 1990s, juvenile gangs emerged as a major crime phenomenon. The systematic

Preadolescence represents a transition from dependence to independence, leading to identity formation in adolescence.

study of gangs dates back to the late 1920s, in which a sociological analysis suggested that gang membership was stimulated by residence in a slum community. Poverty-stricken environments were believed to produce negative values, beliefs, symbols, and behaviors that were internalized and transmitted by delinquent gang members to the next generation of young people (Adler, Ovando, & Hocevar, 1984). Since the 1950s, juvenile gangs have been portrayed as social forms concentrated primarily among poor, inner-city, minority male populations (Pryor & McGarrell, 1993). These gangs manifested themselves largely in urban schools. Recent evidence shows, however, that youth gangs can now be found in suburban and rural communities and schools, as well. Some evidence shows that gangs grow up almost spontane-

ously within schools, by default rather than design, and not by invasion into suburban and rural schools by urban gang members (Moriarty & Fleming, 1990).

All teenagers want their peers to accept and recognize them, and they will find a means of acceptance one way or another. During this period, "running in packs" is common behavior, and looking and acting like the rest of the group is important. Social groups of teenagers, then, do not necessarily constitute a gang, but when groups assault other students or create an atmosphere of fear and intimidation, they become gangs. Gang incidents include fights and disruptive behavior, threatening and menacing words, trespassing, defacement of structures with graffiti, carrying and using weapons, possession and use of drugs, and other juvenile offenses. However, gang activity varies considerably from region to region. In short, groups of teenagers reach gang status when their behavior, either individually or collectively, is disruptive, antisocial, or criminal (Trump, 1993).

Dishion, Andrews, and Crosby (1995) examined the close friendships of early-adolescent boys in relation to antisocial behavior. Results showed that many factors account for establishing friendship clusters, including geographical proximity, activity involvement, homophily, rejection by school peers, and academic failure. Relationships of antisocial dyads were somewhat low in quality, were of relatively short duration, were perceived by the boys as marginally satisfactory, and tended to end acrimoniously. Bossiness and coercive behavior, rather than the absence of positive behaviors, accounted for compromised relationship quality. Thus, antisocial friendships provided a context within which to practice coercion. Negative reciprocity across relationships and time was the best predictor of the boys' overall level of antisocial behavior. The researchers concluded that at the onset of adolescence, antisocial boys tend to coalesce into antisocial peer groups, and that if these friendships are rewarding the result will likely be deviant peer networks that are more satisfactory, more stable, and perhaps more maladaptive in the long run. On the other hand, improving children's performance in relationships early in development might promote friendships with prosocially skilled peers.

Poverty probably increases the risk for gang membership. Many researchers believe that regardless of social class, ethnicity, or geographical location, most children are vulnerable to gang membership and delinquent behavior. In fact, a growing number of affluent white youngsters have become attracted to gangs. The reasons for this include self-defense against established gangs, the allure of drugs and money, and the search for a sense of group identity. Young people often believe that gang membership can offer social and economic rewards such as power, status, money, security, friendship, and a substitute for the family (Trump, 1993). Gangs have been described as "or-

phan institutions"—when teens are not making it in other institutions (e.g., school and the working world), they turn to gangs with all their status, excitement, and money (Moriarty & Fleming, 1990).

Wang (1994) compared gang and nongang high school students on self esteem, racial attitudes, and self-professed role models. As predicted, both White and African American gang members had lower levels of self-esteem than their nongang peers, confirming self-esteem motivation theory that states that negative self-attitudes may prompt individuals to engage in deviant patterns of behavior. All students manifested negative racial stereotyping toward racial outgroups, and adolescents were more likely to name role models from their own racial group. Further, there was a tendency for gang members to name fewer role models than their nongang peers, and the absence of either a parent or a teacher as a professed role model was the best predictor of gang membership.

As early as the 1950s, studies suggested that gang affiliation was related to family variables. Gang-producing homes were believed to experience considerable psychological, cultural, and economic instability, which led to consequences such as divorce, absence of the father, out-of-wedlock births, and school dropouts. Later studies showed that Mexican American gang members in East Los Angeles came predominantly from families that had more involvement with law enforcement agencies, lower socioeconomic status, poorer housing, more alcoholism, and more family breakdown. A recent study of Mexican American families with 15-year-old male children in East Los Angeles found significant differences between gang-member families and non-gang-member families. Intrafamilial socialization, youth socialization, youth supervision, and display of affection were more negative in gang-member families. Gang-member families reported greater frequency of offspring or relatives who had spent time in jail, fewer joint family activities, less display of emotional warmth, greater incidence of having a son murdered in gang-related activities, and less likelihood of knowing their sons' friends.

The potential signs of gang affiliation are the following:

Colors: Choice of a particular color for gang members or specific brands or styles (e.g., hats, bandannas, jewelry, haircuts)

Graffiti: Unusual signs or symbols on public structures as well as on notebooks, papers, clothing, and walls

Tattoos: Symbols or names tattooed on arms, chest, or other body parts

Handsigns or handshakes: Unusual ways of signaling or greeting one another

Language: Uncommon terms, words, names, or phrases

Initiations: Suspicious or otherwise unexplained bruises, wounds, or injuries

Behavior changes: Sudden changes of mood or behavior, unexplained poor grades, and secretive friendships or meetings

Although any one or two of these behaviors alone does not indicate gang membership, several together may. Further, most of these outward signs are harmless enough by themselves, but it is the violence associated with gang membership that is alarming. Initiation into a gang frequently requires committing a violent or criminal act. Huff and Trump (1996) noted that very conservative estimates show that more than 16,000 gangs with more than a half-million members commit nearly 600,000 crimes per year. Further, youths are more likely to engage in delinquent behavior during periods of gang membership than either before or after their involvement. Criminal behavior of gang members significantly exceeds that of nongang youths, at-risk youths, or their peer groups. Reports from gang members have shown that more than half acknowledged that members of their gang assaulted teachers, about 70 percent reported assaults on students, more than 80 percent reported taking guns and knives to school, and more than 60 percent admitted selling drugs at school.

Overreaction to gang activity and resorting to extreme measures by either parents or school officials will do little to alleviate gang violence. Gang-prevention efforts should begin in the middle-school years or earlier. Community-wide efforts that help younger children do better in school and provide older children with training and jobs have been the most successful. Huff and Trump (1996) described two programs designed to reduce gang activity in the schools. In addition to enforcing restrictions on weapons, drug trafficking, and trespassers, preventive functions included staff, parent, and student gang-awareness and educational programs and working with community-wide initiatives, agencies, and officials to reduce gang activity and to identify youth alternatives to gangs. An evaluation of the programs showed that more than 8 in 10 students felt safe at school, fewer students were found to bring weapons to school, gang involvement stabilized, and fewer students reported having friends in gangs and spending time with gang members. The students recommended the following additional initiatives: more activities for young people, expelling or suspending any student who brought a weapon to school, getting parents more involved with their children at home and at school, getting teachers more involved with students they teach, improving school security, and developing programs to resolve conflicts between students.

Combatting gangs requires a three-pronged approach: being aware of what is going on with groups of young people; establishing rapport between schools, families, and community groups and agencies to seek common solutions; and enlisting the support of the children themselves to keep their schools and neighborhoods safe. Devising ways to keep students involved after school hours helps. Providing parent education about gangs is essential—helping them to recognize the early signs of gang involvement (Moriarty & Fleming, 1990). In some instances, it may be necessary to target the family as the agent for intervention, recognizing and incorporating the values held in a specific cultural group.

Rearing Adolescents in Contemporary Society

Teenagers in today's society experience more situations of stress and crises than teens did in the past.

In addition, parents are likely to feel less adequate and more anxious than when their children were younger. Though recent literature suggests that, traditionally, the degree of conflict between parents and adolescents and the extent of adolescent rebellion has been overstated, this period of development can be quite challenging for parents. Societal changes have contributed to this challenge in the following ways:

1. The lengthening of the period of adolescence has simultaneously lengthened the period of parental responsibility and of adolescent dependency, leaving many parents uncertain about how to rear teenagers.

2. The rapid rate of sociocultural change and competing sources of information and values have made it more difficult to prepare adolescents for adult roles.

3. A greater number of potentially dangerous activities, substances, and influences to which teenagers are exposed causes more worry and concern for parents.

4. Parents are more isolated and have fewer support networks to assist them in rearing adolescents in today's society.

5. The media's attention to problems of adolescents and conflicting advice from experts have led to confusion on the part of parents (Small & Eastman, 1991).

The structure of families with adolescent members varies considerably, and parents fulfill their roles in different ways. However, four major functions of families with adolescents have been identified: meeting basic needs, protecting adolescents, guiding and supporting development, and advocacy. Each of these functions will be discussed briefly.

Meeting Basic Needs. Having basic needs met is essential to healthy adolescent development. These needs include a secure place to live, adequate food and nutrition, clothing, and access to health and mental-health services and education. The ability of parents to provide these resources depends on the education, income, and health of the parents.

Protecting Adolescents. The kind of protection needed by adolescents differs from that needed by younger children. Adolescents are able to attend to their physical needs independently, but psychological needs remain. Parents provide protection to adolescents as they take on new responsibilities, such as driving and employment, and as they become exposed to a wider range of influences and potential dangers, such as alcohol, drugs, and sexual activity. This protective function is met through parental monitoring and teaching the teenager self-protection skills.

Monitoring refers to the parent's awareness and supervision of the teen's behavior and whereabouts, which has been shown to be an important factor in preventing problem behavior. It does not mean being overly intrusive; rather, parents must take a genuine interest in the lives of their children and set clear and reasonable rules for their behavior. Parental monitoring is not an easy task for employed parents as they attempt to balance the demands of work and family.

In addition to monitoring teens' behavior, parents have a responsibility to teach their children skills that will enhance their physical safety and psychological well-being. These adaptive skills may vary from culture to culture and from one neighborhood to another, but they normally include knowing how to respond appropriately in an emergency and how to resist peer pressure to engage in potentially harmful behaviors.

Guiding and Supporting Development. Parents have a responsibility to facilitate their teen's development in the following areas: social, emotional, cognitive, physical, moral, spiritual, sexual, cultural, and educational. This is accomplished by an appropriate balance of support and control, including demonstrating warmth, setting limits, engaging in positive communication, providing information, using reinforcement and appropriate sanctions, resolving conflict in healthy ways, and modeling the behaviors and values that are important to them. These characteristics are part of both an authoritative and an inductive style of interaction.

Advocacy.   As advocates, parents support their children and collaborate with other individuals, groups, and institutions that help to socialize teenagers. This advocacy function is important as adolescents face the multiple choices they must make in a rapidly changing society.

At least three groups of factors determine the ability of parents to fulfill these functions: their personal and psychological resources, the characteristics of the adolescent, and the contextual sources of stress and/or support. The first two will be discussed later in this chapter. The last group includes such factors as quality of the marital relationship, the parents' work situation, informal social networks, and the quality of the neighborhood (Small & Eastman, 1991).

Parent-Adolescent Conflict.   The degree of parent-adolescent conflict varies from culture to culture and from family to family. Culturally, conflict is greater in periods of rapid social change; familially, conflict is greater when there is a high degree of parental power and authority. Other factors that can contribute to conflict include expression of sexuality or the postponement of sexual expression, experimentation with alcohol and drugs, confusion about the adolescent's economic role, increasing independence from the family and yielding to peer pressure, the failure of schools to fulfill the adolescent's needs, pressure to choose a life occupation, and discord between parents and/or dysfunctional parental behavior. More specific differences occur between parents and teenagers in the areas of assuming responsibility, curfews, use of the car, academic performance, tidiness, dress and grooming, choice of friends, and so on.

Parental interest and involvement in the adolescent's activities, but not intrusion, seem crucial in preventing and resolving conflict. Simple attitudes and behaviors, such as the following, facilitate the teenager's perception of parental interest and involvement: knowing the names of the teenager's friends; being interested in where they go and what they do; welcoming friends into the home; participating (when appropriate) in school, athletic and social events; and showing tolerance for contemporary styles of dress, music, and harmless teen activities.

Parents can reduce conflict by being warm, accepting, nurturant, supportive, and autonomy-granting. When conflict does occur between parents and children, many parents try to resolve the conflict by exerting more power or control. Usually, this approach is counterproductive, resulting in more conflict.

A more effective approach for resolving conflict is to engage in joint decision making and to show respect for the opinions of teenagers. Mutual understanding and respect between parents and children, reasonable and consistent rule enforcement, as well as interest and involvement in the teen's activities, will facilitate resolution of

---

HIGHLIGHTS

Keys to Prevention and Resolution of Parent-Adolescent Conflict

Low degree of parental power and authority
Warmth, acceptance, nurturance, and letting go
Parental interest and involvement in the adolescent's activities
    Knowing names of friends
    Showing appropriate interest in the specifics of activities
    Participating in appropriate athletic and social events
Tolerance for contemporary styles of dress and music
Joint decision making
Respect for teen's opinions

minor differences and minimize conflict. Larger issues of morality or ideology may be more difficult to resolve.

Adolescents' Perceptions of Parents.   As we emphasized earlier, the teenager's perceptions of the parents' attitudes and behaviors are as important as the actual attitudes and behaviors. Several studies have shown that there may be discrepancies between what actually occurs and the teenager's perception as well as discrepancies between reported perceptions of the parents and reported perceptions of the adolescents.

In general, adolescents tend to perceive lower levels of intimacy and independence, greater differences in characteristics, and slightly higher levels of conflict with their parents than parents themselves perceive, but some evidence shows consistency between parents' and adolescents' perceptions. In one study, both mothers and fathers who perceived themselves as more competent parents had adolescents who reported more competent parenting (warm, accepting, and helpful) (Bogenschneider, Small, & Tsay, 1997). Positive affect by adolescents toward parents has been found to be associated with better psychological functioning of adolescents, whereas negative affect is associated with problematic psychological functioning. One study found that older adolescents tend to have more positive and fewer negative feelings about their mothers than about their fathers (Phares & Renk, 1998).

Several studies have indicated that relationships with the father are crucial for the healthy development of both adolescent boys and girls. Boys who receive less than adequate affection from fathers are less secure, less self-confident, and more distant from their fathers. Perceived parental hostility or mistreatment by young adolescents in one study predicted internalizing behaviors for both boys and girls and externalizing behaviors in boys. In fact, the influence of actual parental hostility and adolescent awareness of conflict frequency on psychological distress was entirely mediated by the adolescent's perception that she was being treated in a hostile fashion by her parents (Harold

& Conger, 1997). Therefore, adolescents' perceptions of parental behavior and attitudes of both mothers and fathers have direct effects on their own behavior.

Adolescent Sexuality

Parental influence on adolescent sexual behavior is presumed to begin in early childhood, but the effect of the parent-child relationship is not entirely clear. Although a poor parent-child relationship has been suggested as being linked to incidence of sexual intercourse, little evidence exists to show that a good parent-child relationship inhibits it. One aspect of a positive relationship is openness in communication. Almost all parents and their teenage children agree that teenagers should get full and accurate information concerning sex, contraceptives, sexually transmitted diseases, teenage pregnancy, and abortion, and that this information should come from parents. Further, both teenagers and parents are in favor of more open discussions concerning these topics. Nevertheless, many studies have noted that most parents do not discuss sexual topics with their children. Research has suggested that discussions of sexuality in the home seem to be related to the postponement of sexual activity and to the responsible use of contraceptives. Specifically, as the number of sex topics discussed by parents increased, the likelihood for engaging in intercourse decreased.

Adolescent females in the Hutchinson and Cooney (1998) study reported low to moderate levels of parent-teen communication about sex, with particularly low levels of father-teen communication. Participants reported that 74 percent of mothers and 21 percent of fathers had provided them with at least some general information on human sexuality. More than 55 percent of the young women reported that their mothers had provided them with some information on contraception/birth control, but only 20 percent of their fathers had done so. Similarly, nearly two-thirds of the mothers and only about one-third of the fathers had discussed with them risk-related topics such as postponing sex, sexual pressure from dating partners, and resisting sexual pressure. Only half of the mothers and one-quarter of the fathers had discussed sexually transmitted diseases, infection, and use of condoms with them.

Nearly half of the young women were uncomfortable discussing sexual issues with their parents. Almost all could name at least one issue about which they wanted further information from both their mothers and their fathers. Significantly higher levels of parental communication about sexual risk occurred with African American as opposed to White women. There was a positive association between parent-teen sexual communication and sexual attitudes and behaviors. Those receiving more information reported higher levels of condom use and greater sexual communication with their partners regarding sexually transmitted diseases and previous sexual history.

Raffaelli, Bogenschneider, and Flood (1998) found that gender was the only major demographic influence on whether sexual communication occurred between parents and their teens in grades 8 through 12. Consistent with other research, they found that teens were more likely to discuss sexual topics with their mothers than with their fathers and that daughters reported more sexual communication than sons. Two variables emerged as significant predictors of all discussion topics: More frequent communication about other topics predicted parent-adolescent communication about sex, and believing that the teen's friends were sexually active increased communication.

Even positive parent-child relationships do not guarantee adolescents' abstinence from sexual activity. Jaccard, Dittus, and Gordon (1998) investigated the agreement between mothers' and adolescents' reports of communication about sex, satisfaction with the parent-child relationship, maternal disapproval of adolescent sexual activity, and adolescent sexual behavior in a sample of African American adolescents 14–17 years of age and their mothers. Consistent with prior research, these researchers found that mothers tended to underestimate the sexual activity of their adolescents, both males and females. Whereas 58 percent of the sample of teens reported that they engaged in sex,

only 34 percent of the mothers thought this was the case. Mothers were more likely to underestimate the teens' sexual activity if they had not engaged in conversations about sex and if their teenagers were younger. Mothers who were more disapproving of teen sexual activity were more likely to judge their teens as not having had sexual intercourse. Contrary to expectations, maternal underestimation of sexual activity increased as the quality of the mother-teen relationship improved. The researchers concluded that it was important for mothers to show their strong disapproval of premarital sex and to recognize that a positive relationship with the child does not guarantee abstinence.

Several researchers have examined factors other than communication that appear to be related to teen sexual activity. Some of these warning signs are identified in the Highlights. As noted, a variety of social, psychological, and biological factors interact in ways that are complex. Both peer and familial behavior and attitudes appear to be important. Perkins, Luster, Villarruel, and Small (1998) examined the ecological risk factors associated with adolescent sexual behavior in three ethnic groups: White, African American, and Latino. They found that the risk factors related to sexual activity were at all three levels of the social ecology—individual, family, and extrafamilial. Several of the risk factors (e.g., age, alcohol use, and religiosity) have been identified in other studies. Physical abuse predicted sexual activity in Latino males, White males, and all the females, and sexual abuse predicted sexual activity for White males and for females from all ethnic groups. Further, a clear association between the level of negative peer-group characteristics and sexual activity emerged for all adolescents, regardless of ethnicity. Heavy alcohol use was associated with an increase in being sexually active by as much as 51 percentage points. Grade point average was a significant predictor of sexual activity in all ethnic groups for both genders. Time at home alone also predicted sexual activity, providing support for the contention that supervision is related to the sexual activity of adolescents.

These researchers unlike others did not find parental monitoring and family support to be asso-

HIGHLIGHTS

Warning Signs of Adolescent Sexual Activity

SOCIAL

Low level of religious orientation
Permissive societal social norms
Poverty and racism
Single-parent families
Peer-group pressure

PSYCHOLOGICAL

Use of drugs/alcohol
Poor educational achievement
Permissive parental attitude
Poor communication with parents
Risk-taking attitudes
Going steady, being in love
Low self-esteem, desire for affection, social criticism, passivity/dependence
   (females)
Aggression, high degree of interpersonal skills with opposite sex (males)
Poor emotional climate
Time alone at home

BIOLOGICAL

Older than 16
Early puberty

Source: Whitbek, L., Conger, R., & Kao, M. (1993). The influence of parental support, depressed affect, and peers on the sexual behavior of adolescent girls. *Journal of Family Issues, 14*(2), 261–278.

ciated with sexual activity for any of the ethnic groups, but school climate was a significant predictor for males but not for females. Similar risk factors were associated with sexual activity for all ethnic groups, except low religiosity, which varied by gender across the three ethnic groups. African American males reported the highest rate of sexual activity, regardless of risk factors. The results of cumulative risk analyses suggested that there is a relationship between the level of risk and the rate of sexual activity for adolescents regardless of ethnicity. Adolescents who were consistently in a low-risk category were less likely than those in the high-risk category to be sexually experienced.

Rodgers (1999) examined the parenting processes related to adolescent sexual risk-taking behaviors among sexually active White adolescent males and females. Parental communication about sexual matters and parental support were not directly associated with sexual risk taking except for sexually active adolescent males who discussed sexual issues with parents they perceived as unsupportive. Sexually active males and females with parents who monitored them were more likely to minimize their sexual risks than adolescents exposed to less parental monitoring. Hence, parental monitoring was a protective factor independent of parental support. The parenting strategy of psychological control (control through guilt) increased the odds of sexually active daughters demonstrating high-risk sexual behavior. Further, fathers' psychological control appeared to be more important than mothers' psychological control. Daughters who had been given the opportunity for autonomous thought by parents demonstrated greater likelihood of developing the psychological maturity and internalized moral reasoning necessary to make mature sexual decisions and to demonstrate low-risk sexual behaviors. Data revealed that risk-taking behaviors for daughters were more related to psychological than behavior control, whereas the reverse was true for sons. Females were more likely than males to equate emotional commitment or love to sexual intimacy and were less likely to have multiple sex partners.

In a sample of African American and Hispanic teens Miller, Forehand, and Kotchick (1999) found no differences in sexual activity between adolescents from a variety of family structures, but parental monitoring, communication, and attitudes were associated with adolescent sexual behavior. Parental monitoring across gender and ethnic groups consistently predicted less sexual activity (i.e., frequency of intercourse and number of sex partners) and greater condom use. Positive general communication between mother and adolescent was associated with less frequent intercourse and fewer sexual partners. It is important to point out that communication in general, not communication specifically about sex, was more strongly and consistently related to less sexual activity. Permissive maternal attitudes about adolescent sexual activity also related positively to the frequency of intercourse and the number of sexual partners. Family-process variables were related more often to the frequency of adolescent sexual intercourse and the number of sex partners than to age at first sex and percentage of times condoms were used.

Capaldi, Crosby, and Stoolmiller (1996) used event history analysis of male students in grades 6 through 11 to predict the timing of the onset of sexual intercourse. Parental transitions, antisocial behavior, and physical maturity predicted significantly early initiation of sexual activity. The number of parental transitions (divorce, remarriage), as opposed to family structure, was important. Previous research has shown that parental transitions are associated with parents' antisocial behavior and lack of involvement with and supervision of their children, as well as with boys' antisocial and delinquent behaviors. Antisocial behavior, deviant peer association, delinquent acts, and substance use were all predictors for early onset of sexual activity. These factors doubled in importance in the rate of initiation at grade 12. Further, physical maturity was found to be a significant factor in the initiation of sexual activity. This study also showed that boys who initiate sexual intercourse at early ages are less likely to comply with pregnancy- and disease-prevention procedures than older adolescent boys.

Tubman, Windle, and Windle (1996) examined precursors and correlates of sexual intercourse patterns among tenth- and eleventh-grade students. Data were collected at 6-month intervals over a 2-year time period. Most adolescents reported a persistent pattern of intercourse after initiation, with boys being overrepresented in the more sporadic intercourse patterns, and girls' activity more likely in the context of longer-term relationships. Adolescents characterized by earlier onset and more persistent patterns of sexual activity reported more depressive symptoms, more alcohol problems, delinquent activities, and lower GPAs than those older, as well as high levels of childhood and early-adolescent problem behaviors. However, overall, academic performance appeared to be independent of the onset of sexual behavior. The accelerated increase of delinquent activities occurring simultaneously with the onset of intercourse suggested that these behaviors may be manifestations of similar underlying developmental processes—the increasing importance of the peer group, greater integration into deviant peer networks, and/or the overt expression of autonomy from parents.

Nonmarital adolescent sexual activity is at an all-time high, but many teens do not use contraceptives. It has been reported that approximately 20 percent of single, sexually active women have never used contraceptives, but 40 percent always use them, leaving 40 percent who use them sporadically. About one-third of sexually active males aged 15–19 reported using condoms all of the time; about one-half used them sometimes; and under one-fifth never used them. The reasons given for failure to use contraceptives were numerous, including ignorance; religious beliefs; and sporadic, noncommitted relationships (Pleck, Sonenstein, & Ku, 1990, 1991).

It appears, then, that there are many variables that affect adolescent sexual activity, and some are outside the control of parents. Although it is not completely clear what the direct influence of parents is on teenage sexual activity, it does seem clear that a positive parent-child relationship—particularly open communication and full and accurate information from parents about sex, contraceptives, pregnancy, and so forth—facilitates responsible sexual behavior in adolescents.

Sexually Transmitted Diseases. Increased adolescent sexual behavior and the low rate of consistent condom use by teens make adolescents a high-risk group for sexually transmitted diseases. Gonorrhea and Herpes 2 continue as risks to individuals who have multiple sex partners, and AIDS has created a monumental health crisis (Schvaneveldt, Lindauer, & Young, 1990). Even though adolescents currently represent a small percentage of all diagnosed cases, it is likely that many current AIDS patients were originally infected as adolescents, because it takes 5 years or longer from infection to appearance of symptoms.

Because complications from AIDS often are fatal, the need for AIDS education is crucial. As of 1990, all states had either mandated or recommended AIDS education in the public schools, yet most of the programs did not integrate AIDS-preventive education within a comprehensive family-life education curriculum that provided a positive, life-affirming approach to sexuality and relationships. AIDS education should begin early, before children become sexually active, and it should be embedded within a holistic framework of healthy relationship values that include respectful regard for oneself, for one's partner, and for both genders. Parents should encourage children to ask questions, and discussions and explanations should be brief and simple, using accurate scientific and medical terminology without giving more detail than can be understood (Street & Isaacs, 1995).

Teenagers are more knowledgeable about AIDS than younger children. However, knowledge does not necessarily result in a decrease in risky behavior—information alone does not seem sufficient to bring about behavior change. It has been hypothesized that teens who have not achieved a stable sense of self may be less able to make a concrete decision to change their behavior in response to AIDS; those with a clear sense of identity may be more likely to value their mental and physical abilities, take precautions to protect themselves, and feel responsible for protecting others than those whose sense of identity is less clear (Jurich, Adams, & Schulenberg, 1992).

Even with college students, accurate knowledge about AIDS transmission does not seem to lead to the implementation of safer sexual practices. One study included 459 students in human sexuality classes. Results suggested that AIDS was not an issue of personal concern to most of these students. Further, misconceptions about the disease lingered into young adulthood. For example, almost one-third believed that AIDS could be contracted through casual contact such as in sharing eating utensils. Even though the students did not believe that people with AIDS should be isolated, less than half indicated their willingness to work alongside someone they knew was infected.

Well over three-fourths reported up to four sexual partners during the last year, but only a small group identified themselves as being at "high risk" for contracting the disease, even though only about half would very likely discuss condoms and fewer than one-fourth would ask new partners about intravenous drug use or other possible exposure to the virus. Only 5 percent indicated that they were very likely to have both themselves and a new sexual partner tested for AIDS before sexual intercourse. Finally, the majority of the students reported no change in their sexual activities as a result of AIDS awareness (Gray & Saracino, 1991).

These studies underscore the necessity for developmentally appropriate AIDS education, beginning with school-age children and extending into young adulthood. It is surprising that so little emphasis on prevention seems to come from the family. Apparently, information alone, either at home or at school, is insufficient. Efforts to implement preventive education in schools often have not been successful because they have been placed in the context of sexuality education, a controversial approach in many communities. Further, sexuality education is often narrow rather than comprehensive in its approach, focusing on the global objectives of preventing pregnancy and sexually transmitted diseases. A "just the facts" approach fails to take into account psychosocial factors in adolescent development, such as self-efficacy, accountability and responsibility, and willingness to take risks (Croft & Asmussen, 1992; Jurich et al., 1992).

Adolescent Substance Use

Adolescents use tobacco, alcohol, marijuana, stimulants, and other illicit drugs at alarming rates. In fact, children are introduced to a variety of drugs in elementary school, and the availability of drugs has become widespread. Despite the efforts to restrict young people's access to drugs and to keep schools and neighborhoods safe, the most pressing societal problem today is the combination of drugs and violence that threatens the lives and well-being of our children. The use of substances by teenagers can be conceptually perceived as one strategy to cope with adverse circumstances associated with inadequate family structure or lack of positive familial relationships. One recent study found positive relationships between harsh/inconsistent parenting and adolescent tobacco use, and negative relationships between nurturant/involved parenting behaviors and adolescent tobacco use. Recent statistics suggest that approximately 28 percent of high school students smoke and that 1 in 10 children was already smoking in middle school (Bynum, 2000). Though tobacco use may not necessarily lead to drug use, it appears to be part of a general syndrome of deviant or problem behavior that predicts increased risk for developmental difficulties throughout adolescence (Melby, Conger, Conger, & Lorenz, 1993).

Several studies have examined family variables that relate to substance use by teens. One significant risk factor for alcohol use is a drinking problem in the family. Equally important to the modeling function, parental support and responsiveness are key factors in preventing alcohol abuse. When adolescents perceive lower levels of family support, higher levels of alcohol consumption and cigarette use, as well as greater incidence of delinquent activity and depressive symptoms, are found (Bogenschneider, Wu, Raffaelli, & Tsay, 1998; Windle & Miller-Tutzauer, 1992). Lower family social support is perceived when the primary caregiver feels anxious and overly burdened by parental responsibilities (Windle & Miller-Tutzauer, 1992). Bahr, Maughn, Marcos, and Li (1998) found that the best predictor of adolescent drug use was lack of bonding with the mother, followed by family drug problems. Religious involvement also may be a protective factor that decreases the chance of adolescent substance use.

A number of researchers have found that parental monitoring, particularly monitoring by fathers, is a key predictor of substance use. However, Bogenschneider et al. (1998) argued against the proposition that parental monitoring consisting of tracking adolescents' whereabouts, discussing adolescents' plans, and becoming acquainted with adolescents' friends and their parents directly reduces substance use. Instead, they argued that parents influence peer orientation by being responsive and available to their adolescents, thus reducing the influence of peers.

Several studies have examined the effects of family structure on adolescent substance use. Barnes and Farrell (1992) found that after controlling for race/ethnicity, family structure did not predict regular drinking or deviance. On the other hand, Flewelling and Bauman (1990) found significantly higher levels of use of cigarettes, alcohol, and marijuana for children in nonintact families. A longitudinal study found that adolescents who experienced a divorce during adolescence had greater involvement with drugs than children who had experienced a divorce before adolescence and those who lived in intact families. When mothers remar-

Family Factors Influencing Adolescent Substance Use

Harsh and/or inconsistent parenting
Parental substance use
Low levels of family support
Lack of bonding to mother
Poor family functioning
Absence of parental monitoring
Family disruption and/or remarriage during adolescence

ried, female adolescents increased their drug involvement and male adolescents decreased their use (Needle, Su, & Doherty, 1990). Results from the National Household Survey on Drug Abuse confirmed that living with both parents decreases the risk of several types of drug use, from episodes of drunkenness to problem drug use. Further, adolescents in father-custody families showed significantly heightened risk of drug use, even after controlling for the effects of several demographic characteristics, family income, and residential mobility (Hoffman & Johnson, 1998). These data seem to suggest that the relationship between teen substance use and family structure is a complex one—depending on the gender of the child, the gender of the custodial parent, when the family disruption occurs, and whether the custodial parent remarries.

Interestingly, a survey of eighth graders conducted by the National Center on Addiction and Substance Abuse found that adolescents in small towns and rural America are 104 percent more likely than their peers in urban centers to use amphetamines, 50 percent more likely to use cocaine, and 34 percent more likely to smoke marijuana. The report urged the government to reverse the alarming trend by funding the war on drugs in nonmetropolitan areas ("Rural youths more...," 2000).

Important as family variables are, several studies have suggested that the strongest predictor of drug use for adolescents is the extent to which one's friends consume drugs. Bauman and Ennett (1994) noted that friends make drugs available to one another; friends model drug use by their friends; and peer-group support and norms favor drug use. Further, the role of drug use in friendship formation (selection) and attributing one's own behavior to the behavior of friends (projection) are factors that demonstrate the link between peers and substance use. Bahr et al. (1998) confirmed that adolescents who use drugs tend to have close friends who also use drugs.

Peer orientation, then, is a significant predictor of both drinking and other drug behavior and interacts with aspects of parenting. Bogenschneider et al. (1998) found that parenting practices influenced adolescents' orientation toward peers and that experiences in both the parent and the peer domains influenced the likelihood that teens would engage in substance use. For example, when mothers reported higher levels of responsiveness, adolescents reported lower orientation to peers, which in turn resulted in lower self-reported substance use. Further, when mothers were less disapproving of adolescent alcohol use in certain circumstances (e.g., at family celebrations, as long as drinking and driving do not occur, and/or when parents are present), maternal responsiveness was associated with less substance use. However, when mothers disapproved of adolescent alcohol use in every circumstance, maternal responsiveness was associated with more substance use. They concluded that there was a mutual, contingent, and interactive parent-peer linkage for adolescent substance use.

When the parent-child relationship is difficult, however, teenagers are likely to withdraw from the family and rely more heavily on the influence of peers. Adolescents who value peer opinions, as opposed to those of their parents, for important life decisions and values are at high risk for alcohol abuse, illicit drug use, and other problem behaviors (Barnes & Farrell, 1992). Further, drug-using adolescents are more likely to interact frequently with their friends and to be distant from their parents than nonusers are.

It is important to note that the parent-child system is bidirectional in influence processes. Teenagers may initiate problem behaviors that lead to negative parent socialization practices and negative family environments. Teen drug users spend less time on schoolwork, are more likely to skip school, and are less likely to get good grades. They are more involved in nonconforming acts, less likely to attend religious services, more likely to hold radical political beliefs, more likely to participate in more minor and major types of delinquent acts, and more likely to be depressed and dissatisfied with themselves. Finally, psychological distress is a significant precursor to greater drug involvement. To what extent these behaviors are the result of drug use and/or poor socialization practices or the cause of either or both is not clear.

It appears, then, that adolescent personality attributes, parental attitudes and behaviors, and peer orientation all have an impact on drug use. Thus, use may occur in the face of any one set of factors but is compounded by the interaction of all three. Some studies have noted a relationship between adolescent substance use and sexual activity (Rosenbaum & Kandel, 1990).

HIGHLIGHTS

Warning Signs of Possible Substance Use

Little time spent on schoolwork
Truancy
Poor grades
High involvement in nonconforming acts
Radical political beliefs
Participation in delinquent acts
Depression and dissatisfaction
Early sexual activity

Most drug-prevention programs have focused on the negative consequences of ingesting drugs. However, more broadly based programs that combine information with a focus on resisting peer influences and decreasing psychological distress are needed. Donaldson (1995) examined outcomes of school-based drug-prevention programs based on the social-influence model, which has had mostly positive effects. These programs reflect a broad and accurate understanding of why children and adolescents begin using alcohol and drugs with regard to peer and other social influences. The success of these programs is due primarily to enhancing an adolescent's ability to resist passive social pressure (e.g., social modeling and overestimation of peer use) rather than to teaching refusal skills to combat active social pressure (i.e., explicit drug offers from friends).

PROGRAMS FOR PARENTS OF ADOLESCENTS

Given the difficulties that many parents face at this particular stage in the life cycle, it is ironic that so few formalized parent-education programs exist specifically for parents of adolescents. It is true that many of the contemporary strategies of parenting described in Chapter 5 can be used with adolescents as well as with younger children. However, the majority of programs that use these strategies involve parents of children younger than adolescents. It is our contention that parents of adolescents are in critical need of some form of education, whether it be discussion groups, development of skills in behavior management, or an emphasis on maintaining positive communication.

Much of what currently exists for parents of adolescents is therapeutic in nature. Clinics sponsor parent-adolescent counseling sessions *after* the child is in trouble; mental-health agencies require parents and teenagers to participate in drug-abuse programs *after* the child's achievement begins to lag. There seems to be very little preventive parent education available anywhere. Parents do have a rather wide selection of printed materials to choose from regarding the characteristics of adolescence and suggestions for positive parent-adolescent interaction—newspaper articles, paperbacks, popular magazines, and so on. But there seems to be a void in support groups, discussion groups, and preparing parents for the changes that will occur in their own lives and those of their children when they reach adolescence.

Programs for parents of normal adolescents should focus on the biological and psychological changes occurring at this stage of development and ways to facilitate healthy development. Helping parents to fulfill more effectively their roles as counselors by, for example, practicing communication skills and developing a balance between freedom and responsibility for their children would seem to be helpful. Talking with other parents about current teenage trends in music, dress, and leisure activities may help parents to be more accepting. Making an effort to get acquainted with the parents of children's friends can provide a support network. Clearly there is a need for programs that are preventive in nature if parents are to facilitate successfully their offspring's transition from child to adult.

DEVELOPMENTAL NEEDS OF PARENTS

Until recently, little emphasis has been placed on adult development in the sociological and psychological literature. The crucial events of one's life were assumed to occur from birth through adolescence, virtually ending with the establishment of a sense of identity in late adolescence or early adulthood. After that a period of stabilization was believed to set in, characterized by relatively uneventful changes. Although earlier theorists such as Erikson, Havighurst, and Duvall described developmental changes or tasks throughout the life cycle, the concept of adult developmental crises was not emphasized. Recently, however, emphasis has been placed on adult development, beginning with marriage and proceeding through death. From the standpoint of parenting, these perspectives clearly indicate that significant changes occur in parents from the time their children are born until they "leave the nest" and that developmental crises occur for adults as well as for children.

Parents with teenagers have been described as approaching a time in their lives that may be as crucial as adolescence itself, quite apart from the fact that they are parents of teenagers. This period has been aptly termed "middlescence" by Gerald Nachman (1979). Normally it occurs between the ages of 35 and 45, with women experiencing it somewhat earlier than men. The midlife transition is the turning point between earlier and later periods of stability. It is the "deadline decade" in which men and women take a serious look at what they are and what they want to be—the gap between the ideal and the realized self—preoccupied with the realization that it is a last-ditch effort to close this gap. In other words, it is an authenticity or affirmation crisis, not completely unlike the identity crisis that the adolescent himself experiences. Preceding the transition to a period of restabilization in middle adulthood, there is a sense of constraint and oppression. For men and women who are employed, constraint and oppression may be experienced in work and, for both, perhaps, in the marriage and/or in other relationships. It is compounded by a feeling of bodily decline ("I'm not as attractive and appealing as I once was"), a recognition of one's mortality, a sense of aging, and a feeling that time is running out. These feelings are verified by the existence in novelty shops of materials to celebrate an "Over the Hill" party on one's fortieth birthday.

At the same time, adolescent children occupy their parents' time and thoughts less and less. Parents, particularly the mother, may be searching for something to fill the gap. Often the father in the midlife crisis who has neglected spending time with his child or children over the years begins to feel a sense of guilt. Many parents must reinvest in each other as companions, parents' authority over their children must be redefined, and there must be a gradual shift toward the child's financial and emotional independence.

When adolescents begin to leave home, somewhere between the ages of 16 and 22, parents may experience the "empty-nest" syndrome, and mothers and fathers may react to it in very different ways. Parents may need to evaluate their experiences and review their own strengths and weaknesses, followed by the formation of an adult-adult relationship with their children.

It is difficult to make generalizations concerning both the timing and the intensity of the midlife crisis. If there are several children in the family, the crisis may be delayed for those parents still actively rearing younger children, especially for women who experience a significant portion of their rewards from mothering. The intensity of the midlife crisis may be affected by the degree to which the marital relationship is satisfying and the degree to which the individual is satisfied with her life.

Another factor that may be related to the timing and intensity of the crisis is the structure of the family. In single-parent families, stepfamilies, or families that began when the parents were themselves teens, the nature of the midlife crisis may be quite different, since it is compounded by a host of other variables. If a single mother has had custody of her children for several years, she may have experienced the need for authenticity and affirmation much sooner than the "deadline decade." The noncustodial father may have separated himself from his child or children physically and/or psychologically long before they became teenagers, so that the "empty-nest" syndrome is not one with which he must cope. Parents in blended families have already experienced a reorganization process that may well ward off much of the stereotypic adjustment described as necessary in traditional nuclear families. Parents of teenagers who were teens themselves when their children were born may be in an entirely different stage of development from that of older parents. It is probably safe to assume that these families have experienced, over time, a higher degree of stress and a quest for identity that may be quite dissimilar to other families' experience.

Many parents, however, are experiencing a kind of identity crisis themselves at nearly the same time their teenagers are searching for a sense of identity. Much of the literature concerning parent-adolescent conflict has failed to recognize the implications of such a phenomenon.

Again we emphasize that there is a reciprocal relationship that is developmental in nature between parent and child at every stage. We must consider to what extent the developmental needs of parents affect, either positively or negatively, the parent-teen relationship, as well as to what extent teens contribute to the socialization of their parents.

It has been pointed out that the crises experienced by adults make it possible to effect changes in personality. A woman may become more assertive; a man may become more nurturant; and, more important, both men and women may come to love themselves more, that is, to learn to value those things in the self formerly devalued. The end result of the midlife crisis need not, then, have negative implications. Parents do have more time for self-development when their children are adolescents. More meaningful personal relationships can be developed; more creative endeavors can be demonstrated; greater participation in social and cultural activities can become possible. If parents take advantage of these alternatives, they provide their teenagers as well as themselves with opportunities for healthy growth. It is unfortunate that initially teenagers are generally insensitive to and intolerant of the developmental needs of their parents. It is inconceivable to them that parents share many romantic fantasies similar to their own. But when adolescents observe their parents reorganizing their life structure in a healthy way, the impact on their own growth process is phenomenal.

In summary, parents of adolescents demonstrate developmental needs that may be equal in importance to the developmental needs of adolescents. The interaction of parents and their children at this stage of development is influenced to a great degree by the needs of both and by the manner in which each seeks to satisfy his or her needs. If parents complete the development of a sense of generativity at this time and successfully regroup themselves, they will be able to move into their later years with a sense of integrity rather than a sense of despair.

SUMMARY

Parenting is a complex reciprocal relationship that manifests developmental change by all the individuals who are involved in the process. During the school years, children become exposed to a diverse social milieu, and their broader experiences necessitate adaptive parental patterns. Encouragement seems to be a crucial parental characteristic as children develop a sense of industry and a healthy self-concept. The vacillating, unstable behavior of preadolescents may cause parents some confusion as they attempt to demonstrate patience and understanding.

As adolescence ensues, the prevention and resolution of conflict become a primary task. Peer pressure may create differences over minor issues related to dress, punctuality, or assuming responsibility, but some parents experience especially grave concern over adolescent sexuality and/or drug and alcohol use. Increasing incidence of gang activity is an additional cause for concern. Positive communication, with parents assuming the role of counselor, seems to be a necessary ingredient for prevention of these problems.

Parents themselves have significant developmental needs as their children progress through latency and puberty, and recognition of these needs may offset some of the conflict that characterizes this period.

REFERENCES

ADLER, P., OVANDO, C., & HOCEVAR, D. (1984). Familiar correlates of gang membership: An exploratory study of Mexican-American youth. *Hispanic Journal of Behavioral Sciences, 6*(1), 65–76.

AQUILINO, W. (1997). From adolescent to young adult: A prospective study of parent-child relations during the transition to adulthood. *Journal of Marriage and the Family, 59,* 670–686.

BAGWELL, C., NEWCOMB, A., & BUKOWSKI, W. (1998). Preadolescent friendship and peer rejection as predictors of adult development. *Child Development, 69*(3), 140–153.

BAHR, S., MAUGHN, S., MARCOS, A., & LI, B. (1998). Family, religiosity, and the risk of adolescent drug use. *Journal of Marriage and the Family, 60,* 979–992.

BARNES, G., & FARRELL, M. (1992). Parental support and control as predictors of adolescent drinking, delinquency, and related problem behaviors. *Journal of Marriage and the Family, 54*(4), 763–776.

BAUMAN, K., & ENNETT, S. (1994, September). Peer influence on adolescent drug use. *American Psychologist,* pp. 820–822.

BHUSHAN, R., & SHIRALI, K. (1992). Family types and communication with parents: A comparison of youth at different identity levels. *Journal of Youth and Adolescence, 21*(6), 687–697.

BOGENSCHNEIDER, K., SMALL, S., & TSAY, J. (1997). Child, parent, and contextual influences on perceived parenting competence among parents of adolescents. *Journal of Marriage and the Family, 59,* 345–362.

BOGENSCHNEIDER, K., WU, M., RAFFAELLI, M., & TSAY, J. (1998). Parent influences on adolescent peer orientation and substance use: The interface of parenting practices and values. *Child Development, 69*(6), 1672–1688.

BOOTH, C., RUBIN, K., & ROSE-KRASNOR, L. (1998). Perceptions of emotional support from mother and friend in middle childhood: Links with social-emotional adaptation and preschool attachment security. *Child Development, 69*(2), 427–442.

BRONSTEIN, P., DUNCAN, P., D'ARI, A., PIENIADZ, J., FITZGERALD, M., ABRAMS, G., FRANKOWSKI, B., FRANCO, O., HUNT, C., & OH CHA, S. (1996). Family and parenting behaviors predicting middle school adjustment. *Family Relations, 45,* 415–426.

BYNUM, R. (2000, January 28). High school smoking drops. *Albuquerque Journal,* p. A12.

CAIRNS, R., LEUNG, M., BUCHANAN, L., & CAIRNS, B. (1995). Friendship and social networks in childhood and adolescence: Fluidity, reliability, and interrelations. *Child Development, 66,* 1330–1345.

CAPALDI, D., CROSBY, L., & STOOLMILLER, M. (1996). Predicting the timing of first sexual intercourse for at-risk adolescent males. *Child Development, 67,* 344–359.

CASHWELL, C., & VACC, N. (1996). Family functioning and risk behaviors: Influences on adolescent delinquency. *The School Counselor, 44,* 105–114.

CHAPMAN, J., LAMBOURNE, R., SILVA, P. (1990). Some antecedents of academic self-concept: A longitudinal study. *British Journal of Educational Psychology, 60,* 142–152.

COUGHLIN, C., & VUCHINICH, S. (1996). Family experience in preadolescence and the development of male delinquency. *Journal of Marriage and the Family, 58,* 491–501.

CROFT, C., & ASMUSSEN, L. (1992). Perceptions of mothers, youth, and educators: A path toward detente regarding sexuality education. *Family Relations, 41*(4), 452–459.

DAY, R., PETERSON, G., & McCRACKEN, C. (1998). Predicting spanking of younger and older children by mothers and fathers. *Journal of Marriage and the Family, 60,* 79–94.

DISHION, T., ANDREWS, D., & CROSBY, L. (1995). Antisocial boys and their friends in early adolescence: Relationship characteristics, quality, and interactional process. *Child Development, 66,* 139–151.

DONALDSON, S. (1995, September). Peer influence on adolescent drug use: A perspective from the trenches of experimental evaluation research. *American Psychologist,* pp. 801–802.

EISENBERG, N., FABES, R., CARLO, G., TROYER, D., SPEER, A., KARBON, M., & SWITZER, G. (1992). The relations of maternal practices and characteristics to children's vicarious emotional responsiveness. *Child Development, 63*(3), 583–602.

ERIKSON, E. (1963). *Childhood and society.* New York: Norton.

FENZEL, L. (1992). The effect of relative age on self-esteem, role strain, GPA, and anxiety. *Journal of Early Adolescence, 12*(3), 253–266.

FITZPATRICK, M., MARSHALL, L., LEUTWILER, T., & KRCMAR, M. (1996). The effect of family communication environments on children's social behavior during middle childhood. *Communication Research, 23*(4), 379–406.

FLEWELLING, R., & BAUMAN, K. (1990). Family structure as a predictor of initial substance use and sexual intercourse in early adolescence. *Journal of Marriage and the Family, 52*(1), 171–181.

FRANCO, N., & LEVITT, M. (1998). The social ecology of middle childhood: Family support, friendship quality, and self-esteem. *Family Relations, 47,* 315–321.

GECAS, V., & SEFF, M. (1991). Families and adolescents: A review of the 1980s. In A. Booth (Ed.), *Contemporary families: Looking forward, looking back* (pp. 208–225). Minneapolis: National Council on Family Relations.

GIORDANO, P., CERNKOVICH, S., & DeMARIS, A. (1993). The family peer relations of black adolescents. *Journal of Marriage and the Family, 55*(2), 277–287.

GLASGOW, K., DORNBUSCH, S., TROYER, L., STEINBERG, L., & RITTER, P. (1997). Parenting styles, adolescents' attributions, and educational outcomes in nine heterogeneous high schools. *Child Development, 68*(3), 507–529.

GRAY, L., & SARACINO, M. (1991). College students' attitudes, beliefs, and behaviors about AIDS: Implications for family life education. *Family Relations, 40*(3), 258–263.

HAROLD, G., & CONGER, R. (1997). Marital conflict and adolescent distress: The role of adolescent awareness. *Child Development, 68*(2), 333–350.

HART, C., DeWOLF, D., WOZNIAK, P., & BURTS, D. (1992). Maternal and paternal disciplinary styles: Relations with preschoolers' playground behavioral orientations and peer status. *Child Development, 63*(4), 879–892.

HOFFMAN, J., & JOHNSON, R. (1998). A national portrait of family structure and adolescent drug use. *Journal of Marriage and the Family, 60,* 633–645.

HOFFMAN, M. (1970). Moral development. In P. Mussen (Ed.), *Carmichael's manual of child psychology* (Vol. 2, 3d ed.) pp. 261–359). New York: Wiley.

HUFF, C., & TRUMP, K. (1996). Youth violence and gangs. *Education and Urban Society, 28*(4), 492–503.

HUTCHINSON, M., & COONEY, T. (1998). Patterns of parent-teen sexual risk communication: Implications for intervention. *Family Relations, 47,* 185–194.

JACCARD, J., DITTUS, P., & GORDON, V. (1998). Parent-adolescent congruency in reports of adolescent sexual behavior and in communications about sexual behavior. *Child Development, 69*(1), 247–261.

JURICH, J., ADAMS, R., & SCHULENBERG, J. (1992). Factors related to behavior change in response to AIDS. *Family Relations, 41*(1), 97–103.

KETSETZIS, M., RYAN, B., & ADAMS, G. (1998). Family processes, parent-child interactions, and child characteristics influencing school-based social adjustment. *Journal of Marriage and the Family, 60,* 374–387.

KREVANS, J., & GIBBS, J. (1996). Parents' use of inductive discipline: Relations to children's empathy and prosocial behavior. *Child Development, 67,* 3263–3277.

KUPERSMIDT, J., GRIESLER, P., DeROSIER, M., PATTERSON, C., & DAVIS, P. (1995). Childhood aggression and peer relations in the context of family and neighborhood factors. *Child Development, 66,* 360–375.

MELBY, J., CONGER, R., CONGER, K., & LORENZ, F. (1993). Effects of parental behavior on tobacco use by young male adolescents. *Journal of Marriage and the Family, 55*(2), 439–454.

MILLER, K., FOREHAND, R., & KOTCHICK, B. (1999). Adolescent sexual behavior in two ethnic minority samples: The role of family variables. *Journal of Marriage and the Family, 61,* 85–98.

MORIARTY, A., & FLEMING, T. (1990). Youth gangs aren't just a big-city problem anymore. *The Executive Educator, 12*(7), 13–16.

MOSS, E., ROUSSEAU, D., PARENT, S., ST. LAURENT, D., & SAINTONGE, J. (1998). Correlates of attachment at school age: Maternal reported stress, mother-child interaction, and behavior problems. *Child Development, 69*(5), 1390–1405.

MOUNTS, N., & STEINBERG, L. (1995). An ecological analysis of peer influence on adolescent grade point average and drug use. *Developmental Psychology, 31*(6), 915–922.

NACHMAN, G. (1979). The menopause that refreshes. In P. Rose (Ed.), *Socialization and the life cycle* (pp. 279–293). New York: St. Martin's.

NEEDLE, R., SU, S., & DOHERTY, W. (1990). Divorce, remarriage, and adolescent substance use: A prospective longitudinal study. *Journal of Marriage and the Family, 52*(1), 157–169.

NEWCOMB, A., BUKOWSKI, W., & PATTEE, L. (1993). Children's peer relations: A meta-analytic review of popular, rejected, neglected, controversial, and average sociometric status. *Psychological Relations, 113*(1), 99–128.

PERKINS, D., LUSTER, T., VILLARRUEL, F., & SMALL, S. (1998). An ecological, risk-factor examination of adolescents' sexual activity in three ethnic groups. *Journal of Marriage and the Family, 60,* 600–673.

PETTIT, G., BATES, J., & DODGE, K. (1997). Supportive parenting, ecological context, and children's adjustment: A seven-year longitudinal study. *Child Development, 68*(5), 908–923.

PHARES, V., & RENK, K. (1998). Perceptions of parents: A measure of adolescents' feelings about their parents. *Journal of Marriage and the Family, 60,* 646–659.

PLECK, J., SONENSTEIN, F., & KU, L. (1990). Contraceptive attitudes and intention to use condoms in sexually experienced and inexperienced adolescent males. *Journal of Family Issues, 11*(3), 294–312.

PLECK, J., SONENSTEIN, F., & KU, L. (1991). Adolescent males' condom use: Relationships between perceived cost-benefits and consistency. *Journal of Marriage and the Family, 53*(3), 733–745.

PRYOR, D., & MCGARRELL, E. (1993). Public perceptions of youth gang crime: An exploratory analysis. *Youth and Society, 24*(4), 399–418.

RAFFAELLI, M., BOGENSCHNEIDER, K., & FLOOD, M. (1998). Parent-teen communication about sexual topics. *Journal of Family Issues, 19*(3), 315–333.

REED, J., & DUBOW, E. (1997). Cognitive and behavioral predictors of communication in clinic-referred and nonclinical mother-adolescent dyads. *Journal of Marriage and the Family, 59,* 91–102.

RODGERS, K. (1999). Parenting processes related to sexual risk-taking behaviors of adolescent males and females. *Journal of Marriage and the Family, 61,* 99–109.

ROSENBAUM, E., & KANDEL, D. (1990). Early onset of adolescent sexual behavior and drug involvement. *Journal of Marriage and the Family, 52*(3), 783–798.

"Rural youths more likely to use drugs." (2000, January 28). *Albuquerque Journal,* p. A12.

SCHVANEVELDT, J., LINDAUER, S., & YOUNG, M. (1990). Children's understanding of AIDS: A developmental viewpoint. *Family Relations, 39*(3), 330–335.

SMALL, S., & EASTMAN, G. (1991). Rearing adolescents in contemporary society: A conceptual framework for understanding the responsibilities and needs of parents. *Family Relations, 40,* 455–462.

SMETANA, J. (1995). Parenting styles and conceptions of parental authority during adolescence. *Child Development, 66,* 299–316.

STRAUS, M., & YODANIS, C. (1996). Corporal punishment in adolescence and physical assaults on spouses in later life: What accounts for the link? *Journal of Marriage and the Family, 58,* 825–841.

STREET, S., & ISAACS, M. (1995). AIDS education for children: Fostering prevention through parent and family education. *Individual Psychology, 51*(2), 178–183.

TRUMP, K. (1993). Tell teen gangs: School's out. *The American School Board Journal, 180*(7), 39–42.

TUBMAN, J., WINDLE, M., & WINDLE, R. (1996). The onset and cross-temporal patterning of sexual intercourse in middle adolescence: Prospective relations with behavioral and emotional problems. *Child Development, 67,* 327–343.

TURNER, P., HAMNER, T., & ORELL, L. (1993). *Children and their families in New Mexico.* Albuquerque: New Mexico First.

VUCHINICH, S., ANGELELLI, J., & GATHERUM, A. (1996). Context and development in family problem solving with preadolescent children. *Child Development, 67,* 1276–1288.

WANG, A. (1994). Pride and prejudice in high school gang members. *Adolescence, 29*(114), 279–291.

WEISS, L., & SCHWARZ, C. (1996). The relationship between parenting types and older adolescents' personality, academic achievement, adjustment, and substance use. *Child Development, 67,* 2101–2114.

WHITBEK, L., CONGER, R., & KAO, M. (1993). The influence of parental support, depressed affect, and peers on the sexual behaviors of adolescent girls. *Journal of Family Issues, 14*(2), 261–278.

WINDLE, M., & MILLER-TUTZAUER, C. (1992). Confirmatory factor analysis and concurrent validity of the perceived social support-family measure among adolescents. *Journal of Marriage and the Family, 54*(4), 777–787.

CHAPTER 4

The Changing Nature of Parenting:
Later Life

The traditional concept of the role of parenthood has spanned the period from the birth of the first child through the adolescent period of the last child. Parenting, then, has been thought of as a 20- to 30-year commitment. Family relations research has consistently identified the stage when young adult children leave home as the "launching" stage and has referred to parents as experiencing the "empty-nest" syndrome after the departure of children from the home. Put another way, the period of childbearing is considered the expansion phase for families, and following the maturity of all the children, the family is said to be in the contracting stage.

Recent social changes, however, have contributed to a somewhat expanded conception of parenthood. These changes have resulted in children remaining in the parental home longer and, for some, returning to live, at least for a brief period. The period of active parenting (when parents are responsible for the physical and psychological well-being of their children) is differentiated from the period of adult parenting (when children have become mature enough to be physically and/or psychologically independent from parents) (Atkinson & James, 1991).

Further, grandparents have become more numerous because of greater longevity, and the roles of many grandparents have been altered as a result of divorce. Finally, greater longevity has also contributed to increased responsibility of middle-aged adults in providing assistance and care to their elderly parents. All these phenomena have had a significant impact on the changing nature of parenting, both for parents and for children. This chapter examines parenting in later life, grandparenting, and caring for elderly parents.

PARENTS AND ADULT CHILDREN

In the past in the United States, it has been the practice for young adults to be launched, or to leave the parental home, in their late teens or early twenties to establish homes of their own or to attend college. However, beginning in the 1980s and continuing until the present, more young adults have been living with their parents than at any other time since 1940, when the aftermath of the Depression resulted in a high unemployment rate, thus prohibiting young people from becoming financially independent.

Table 4.1 shows the total number of young adults and the percent living with their parents in 1980, 1990, and 1996. As noted, in 1996, 58 percent of male and 47 percent of female children 18 to 24 years of age lived with their parent(s). But even more surprising, 15 percent of male and 8 percent of female adult children 25 to 34 years of age also lived with their parents. Particularly noteworthy is the increase from 1980 to 1996. It has been estimated that one of seven parents older than 65 still has at least one adult child living at home. Not only are adult children remaining at home

TABLE 4.1   Young Adults Living with Parents: 1980, 1990, 1996

LIVING WITH PARENTS AND SEX	PERSONS 18 TO 24 YEARS OLD			PERSONS 25 TO 34 YEARS OLD		
	1980	*1990*	*1996*	*1980*	*1990*	*1996*
Total (1,000)	29,122	25,310	25,158	36,796	43,240	41,389
% Distribution	48	53	53	9	12	12
Male	54	59	58	11	15	15
Female	43	48	47	7	8	8

Source: U.S. Bureau of the Census. (1997). *Statistical abstract of the United States: 1997* (117th ed.). Washington, DC: U.S. Department of Commerce.

longer, but also they are more likely to return after the first and subsequent departures (Mitchell & Gee, 1996).

There are several reasons for adult children remaining and returning home: increased age at first marriage; economic circumstances, such as the high cost of living and high youth unemployment rates; the need for more education for career placement; lack of financial aid for postsecondary programs or college; ambivalence about the capacity to assume adult roles; and increase in divorce (Mitchell & Gee, 1996).

The marital status of parents and the gender of single parents are related to the likelihood of having adult children living in the home. Married parents are more likely to have co-resident adult children; single mothers are next mostly likely; and single fathers are the least likely to have adult children living with them. The remarriage of parents also decreases the likelihood of co-residence (Aquilino 1990, 1991). Like previous researchers, White and Rogers (1997) found that the odds of co-residence of adult children and their parents were significantly higher when parents had less education, when parents had been continuously married, when children were divorced or had never married, or when children were younger. The quality of past family life and whether parents wanted to have their children out of the house were unrelated to co-residence.

Goldscheider and Goldscheider (1998) examined the life-course transitions of children leaving and returning home and the impact of parental family structure on the timing of these events. Results showed that living in any form of nontraditional family reduced the likelihood of young adults leaving home for college and increased the likelihood of leaving home early and not returning. The most powerful predictors were gaining a stepparent and stepsiblings, particularly during adolescence. Leaving home to form a nontraditional family via cohabitation or single parenthood also was a strong predictor. Results suggested that the timing of "nest-leaving" and the reasons for leaving home reflect parental investment in children. Having two parents in a stable family structure,

having parents with more resources, and having fewer siblings appear to facilitate children's mature launch into adulthood. Adult children who have had different experiences during childhood, particularly disruptions during adolescence, often leave home at an early age any way they can and are likely to move into relationships that provide less support and less stability.

Based on the above data, it seems that the 1980s marked for many families the beginning of a period when the launching stage was postponed or when the child-rearing stage was resumed as the adult-rearing stage after a brief empty-nest period. This phenomenon has been referred to as "the cluttered nest" or the "elastic nest," which stretches and contracts. Adult children as co-residents have been referred to as the "baby boomerangers" (Atkinson & James, 1991; Mitchell & Gee, 1996).

Interestingly, there is an inverse relationship between the extent to which young adults live with their parents and the birthrate of the preceding decade or two. The tendency toward having smaller families seems to be simultaneous with the tendency for young adults to remain in or return to the parental home, and these trends are likely to continue.

Parenting Young Adult Children

Though recent attention has been given to adult development, little has been given to parenting young adult children. Adult children are considered to be those 18 years of age or older, married or single, living in or out of the parental home. The time at which "young adult children" cease to be young is clearly debatable. For convenience' sake, children referred to here are those between 18 and 29 years of age. In the United States, "coming of age" is not noted by any particular rite of passage, but becoming eligible to vote—and, for men, becoming eligible for military service—signify in our society legal status as an adult. By law parents are no longer responsible for their offspring after their eighteenth birthdays. According to Bernard (1975), "In the name of tidiness,... motherhood ought to end when children leave home" (p. 133).

However, the truth is that, for many, parenting continues for years to come, even until death of the parent or the child. There are few norms governing familial relationships in adulthood, but adult parenting usually is characterized by more equal relationships between parents and children (Atkinson & James, 1991).

Adult Children Living at Home. A national survey found that parental satisfaction with the co-residence of their adult children (ages 19–34) was highly related to the degree of parent-child conflict and to the level of positive social interaction between parent and child. Children's financial dependency and unemployment were associated with increased parent-child conflict, as was the presence of grandchildren who lived in the home with a divorced parent. School enrollment was weakly related to more positive parental perceptions of co-residence. Age of the adult child did not affect parental satisfaction, but the child's progress in the transition to adulthood was a strong force in shaping parent-child relationships. Mothers generally reported greater enjoyment than fathers of their adult co-resident children, and greater involvement seems to occur more often with daughters than with sons. Mitchell and Gee (1996) found that mothers reported such positive aspects of having a child at home as companionship, friendship, and emotional support. Parental satisfaction seems to be highest when parents are involved with adult children in pleasurable activities and when adult children are more self-sufficient. Interestingly, parents with more education and higher incomes reported more negative effects of co-residence of adult children than parents with less education and income. It may be that this stems from middle-class parents' higher expectations for self-development and life opportunities during their midlife stage (Aquilino, 1991; Aquilino & Supple, 1991).

The most typical adult child who resides at home is one who is continuing his schooling at a college or university or at a vocational school within commuting distance of the parental home. There are, however, young adults who are not in school who continue to live at home, most of whom are employed or seeking employment. In either case parents are faced with the task of interacting with offspring over whom they have little control and who generally have a different lifestyle from that of their parents. The rules and regulations that governed the period of adolescence and the nature of interactions are no longer appropriate, but daily proximity forces intrusion of one lifestyle on the other. The need for independence among young adults is widely recognized, but the need for independence on the part of middle-aged parents often is ignored (Thompson & Walker, 1984). For some adult children, it may be easy to slide back into old roles of dependence, asking for advice or having parents prepare meals or do laundry for them.

One of the major issues in households with adult children seems to be lack of privacy; interference with parents' social life and privacy seems to be greatest in the case of co-resident adult children ages 25–29. (See Highlights for other issues.) This age group is associated with a sizable increase in the unanticipated return of previously independent children, primarily because of marital dissolution (Aquilino, 1991). Unless the living quarters are spacious, neither parents nor children can maintain independent, private lives. Coming and going, entertaining friends, use of leisure time, and even eating habits must be inflicted on other members of the family. Young and older adults often differ significantly in their choice of music, food, and clothing, and their schedules of sleeping, working, studying, and eating may not coincide. Therefore compromises must be made if conflict is to be avoided.

Mitchell and Gee (1996) found several parent and child variables associated with marital satisfaction among parents with co-residing adult children. Parental variables included being first-time married parents as opposed to having been divorced and remarried and being in good to excellent health. More striking findings, however, were the relationships to child variables. Parents were 10 times more likely to experience marital satisfaction if the child had returned home only once rather than three or more times. It appeared that

HIGHLIGHTS

Issues in Parenting Live-In Adult Children

LIFESTYLE DIFFERENCES

Listening to music
Coming and going privately
Entertaining friends
Using leisure time
Eating and dressing

DIVISION OF LABOR

Doing the laundry
Preparing the meals
Maintaining the household

ECONOMIC ISSUES

Providing financial support
Providing room and board

RULES AND REGULATIONS

Curfews
Use of car and other family possessions
Use of alcohol/drugs

---

parents were willing to accept one or two returns, but a pattern of bouncing back and forth apparently strains family relationships, thus diminishing marital satisfaction for the parents. Further, parents were more satisfied with their marriages when children left home to become independent, presumably permanently, than when they left home temporarily for work or school. Finally, children's relationships with their mothers during co-residence significantly influenced parental marital satisfaction. Parents were significantly more satisfied with their marriages when the returned children had excellent relationships with their mothers than when they had poor relationships. However, children's relationships with their fathers did not predict marital satisfaction.

The pattern of aid between generations has been the focus of some research, which suggests that there is a shift in the pattern as parent and child grow older. In the early years and continuing through the child's young adult stage, the flow of material assistance is from the parent to the child. This pattern reverses as the young generation reaches middle age and the parent becomes elderly. The same pattern persists in the provision of nonmaterial aid.

White and Rogers (1997) found that co-residence appears to increase the exchange of resources between parents and adult children, but the exchange occurs at some cost to relationship quality. Co-residing children exchange significantly more help with their parents than children who do not live with their parents. The further away the child is from the parent, the less the exchange. Although they exchange more and perceive more support from parents, co-resident children, on the average, evaluate their affective relationships with parents more negatively than children who do not live with their parents. The impact of co-residence, however, varies significantly, depending on the characteristics of children and specifically on their place in the transition to adulthood. According to children's reports, co-residence is a more positive experience when children are older, in school, and employed. Further, this research suggested that both support and stress are greater under conditions of co-residence.

The issue of the division of labor may then arise. For example, do parents continue to do laundry for their adult children? Do they prepare meals for them? Buy their clothes? Are adult children expected to participate in the maintenance of the home? If so, how and to what extent? One of the patterns of adult children who reside with their parents is that of "star boarder"—goods and services are provided by the household, but the adult child shows little support for or participation in family activities (Atkinson & James, 1991).

Parents interviewed in a national study complained that children did not provide much help with housework (Aquilino, 1991). The fact that more male than female adult children live with their parents suggests that sons continue to rely on their parents, especially their mothers, to perform stereotyped gender-related activities. However, we suspect that whether the child is in school or is employed, or both, and whether the parents are employed determines to some extent the expectations parents have of their children.

The related issue of financial aid raises similar conflicts. Does the adult child pay rent? Does she contribute to the purchase of food? Does she pay for her own health and car insurance? Has she begun a savings account? What kind of financial assistance does she get from her parents, if any? Again, financial issues seem to be related both to whether the young adult is employed or is in school and to the economic status of the parents. Many parents, if they are willing and able, subsidize their children's room and board as well as their tuition and books as long as they are actively pursuing an education. Some parents place a time limit on these kinds of subsidies.

The national study previously mentioned found that children's effects on financial well-being were mostly negative among 19- to 21-year-olds, an age group that is most likely to be attending school, and were consistently more positive for parents with older adult children (Aquilino, 1991). Goldscheider and Goldscheider (1991) found that African American parents invest less than White parents in the educational expenses of their children beyond high school, and this level of investment solely reflects the much lower family income of African Americans and the lower educational attainment of African American mothers. Most parents expect some financial contribution from their live-in children if they are employed full-time, but Aquilino (1991) found that children's room-and-board payments did not affect parental satisfaction with co-residence. However, parents' out-of-pocket expenses did. Most young adults desire to form their own homes independently once they become financially self-sufficient. However,

moving out of the parental home may result only in returning later, only to move out once more. This is not an uncommon occurrence because of the fluctuating economic status of young adults.

Finally, the issue of rules and regulations looms large for many families with adult children at home. To what extent do parents have a right to know where their children are, when they will be home, and whom they are with? Should parents set down rules about dress, socializing with friends, use of parents' possessions, and the use of alcohol and drugs? Most parents feel the need to apply rules that make their own lives more comfortable, yet they feel guilty that they are not accepting their child's level of maturity and sense of responsibility. Creating an atmosphere of peaceful coexistence while maintaining mutual respect often is difficult. There actually is no magic solution to this dilemma. Each party must be sensitive to the feelings and expectations of the other, and, no doubt, compromises must be made by all.

Using Erikson's framework, most parents of young adult children are completing their stage of generativity and moving toward the final stage of integrity versus despair. At the same time, their offspring are seeking to achieve a sense of intimacy, beginning to think about establishing their own homes and families. Unlike the develop-

---

TIPS

For Parents of Adult Children

Examine feelings about the child's returning home. Have a meeting with the child:

To explore parents' and child's feelings; use "I" or "we" messages and active listening.

To ascertain each person's expectations; use problem solving if problems arise regarding expectations.

To determine the child's long-range goals and how each can work toward accomplishing them.

Remember that the child is an adult—speak in an adult manner and demonstrate respect for another adults' opinions and behavior.

mental reciprocity between parents of younger children (generativity stage) and the children themselves (initiative and industry stages), this period of the life cycle does not lend itself well to complementarity. As a result, the conflicts previously discussed would not seem surprising. In fact, one study found that 42 percent of the middle-aged parents surveyed reported serious conflicts with at least one of their resident adult children (Clemens & Axelson, 1985), and a more recent study reported that only one-quarter of the parents approved of their adult children moving in with them (Aquilino & Supple, 1991).

Adult Children Living Away from Home. Aldous (1985) pointed out that when children leave home to establish financial independence and to begin their own families, parental solicitude does not stop. In other words, there is no such thing as a "postparental" period. However, relationships between parents and their adult children are perhaps less stressful once children leave the parental home permanently, because the conflicts that arise from attempting to mesh two different lifestyles are absent. Nevertheless, children may still be dependent on parents economically and/or emotionally. Parents, too, may have difficulty in resolving their emotional dependency on their children. Rarely has parent-child attachment been studied when children reach adulthood; it has been speculated that emotional dependencies are more balanced in adulthood than in early parent-child relationships when the child is more dependent on the parent (Thompson & Walker, 1984). Still later an imbalance may occur in the other direction as aging parents become more dependent—physically, economically, and psychologically—on their mature children.

Recent evidence suggests that most parents and adult children have regular contact with one another. Seventy-five percent of the parents who have nonresidential children older than 16 have reported seeing their children at least once a week or more often; only 1 percent have reported never seeing their children. Furthermore, fairly positive relationships between parents and children are reported.

The nature of the relationships between parents and their adult children depends to some extent on the marital status of the parent(s) and the marital and parental status of the children, but the results of studies show inconsistencies. Aldous (1985) reported that parents and daughters are more involved with each other's lives than parents and sons are. However, parents show greater solicitude for their divorced adult children who have children than for other children. They are more likely to provide child care for these grandchildren, to give comfort to their own divorced children, and to help them with housework.

Participants in the Coleman, Ganong, and Cable (1997) study believed strongly that mothers as opposed to mothers-in-law should provide assistance to their daughters in time of need. They also felt that mothers are obligated to their daughters more than to their grandchildren, but it was the grandchildren to whom mothers-in-law should be obligated rather than to their daughters-in-law.

Other studies have shown, however, that divorced children receive less support from parents and experience more strain in relationships with them than married children (Umberson, 1992).

White (1992) found that parental divorce and remarriage were associated with significantly less social, instrumental, and financial support to adult children. In the case of divorce, this reduced support characterizes both mothers and fathers. The reduced financial support to children can be accounted for by the lower earnings and assets and greater obligations of divorced parents, but the reduced support in other areas appears to be the result of lower parent-child solidarity. It seems, then, that structural circumstances influence the quality of relationships and the degree of intergenerational transfers between adult children and their parents (Umberson, 1992).

Transfer of aid among the generations is never really symmetrical: It is transferred from parent to child. Only by grown children transferring to their own children is there any balancing of material and emotional investment. Transfer of aid was examined in two generations of mother-daughter relationships (Thompson & Walker, 1984). Most of the youngest generation of daughters (who were university students) were single. The investigators found, not surprisingly, that nonreciprocity existed in the transfer of aid: The mothers essentially were the givers, and the daughters were the receivers. They concluded that these young adult women could invest only upward to their parents—neither horizontally to their husbands nor downward to their children. Again, marital status of parents seems to be a factor. Some research reported greater closeness and reciprocity of aid between mothers and their young adult daughters when the mothers were widowed as opposed to married. It may be the family member in the nonreciprocating position (receiving but not giving help) who avoids contact with kin; the nonreciprocated giver (giving but not receiving help) does not.

Finally, proximity of parents to their adult children is clearly a pivotal factor. Geographical distance affects the frequency and type of communication, the exchange of aid, the degree of independence, and the differences that may arise over conflict in lifestyle.

In sum, it seems apparent that relationships between mature adults and their adult children, whether the children are living at home or not, are complex and little understood. Although we suspect that there is great diversity in the degree and extent of contact and in the transfer of aid, goods, and services, few generalizations can be made, and few guidelines can be established. Therefore it appears that an interesting and promising area of research would be the relationship between parents and their adult children.

GRANDPARENTING

Until very recently there has been little theoretical foundation for the dynamics of grandparenthood, but the topic is stimulating interest in both the scholarly and the popular areas. Our perceptions about grandparents have changed radically over the years. The perception of the grandmother, for example, in the late 1800s was one of a kindly, elderly, somewhat frail, gray-haired woman sitting in a rocking chair by the fire. Pruchno and Johnson

(1996) observed that grandparenting is about generations but not necessarily about old age. Today grandmothers range in age from their thirties to their hundreds, and the "typical" grandmother is a middle-aged active woman, most likely dressed for work or a tennis game. There is no uniform, consistent picture of grandparents; rather, there is a great heterogeneity and diversity.

Several social changes have contributed to these broader perceptions and renewed interest. Greater longevity is permitting a longer period of grandparenthood and even great-grandparenthood, and those who are living longer are not as likely as before to suffer limitations of daily living. Attention has been focused on grandparenting partly because of increases in maternal employment (and the corresponding demand for child care) and increases in multigenerational households resulting from teenage childbearing, single parenthood, and poverty. Further, smaller, more closely spaced families have resulted in little overlap between the cycles of parenting and grandparenting, so that the two roles are more sharply differentiated. Third, geographic mobility of young families makes it difficult for some grandparents to assume active roles (Baydar & Brooks-Gunn, 1998; Pruchno & Johnson, 1996).

Grandparents are more prevalent today than ever before. An estimated three-quarters of adults will live to be grandparents. Ninety-four percent of older adults with children are grandparents, and nearly 50 percent are great-grandparents. Most middle-aged people become grandparents near the age of 45. One recent estimate places nearly half of grandparents at younger than age 60, one-third at younger than age 55, and one-fifth at age 70 or older. And, because of changed family configurations through divorce or remarriage, the "new" grandchild can be an infant or a retiree. As mentioned earlier, the grandparent role has been extended, and it is not uncommon for women to be grandmothers for more than four decades, or as much as 50 percent of their lives (Giarrusso, Silverstein, & Bengston, 1996; Pruchno & Johnson, 1996).

The passage to grandparenthood has been called a "countertransition" because it is brought about by the transition of another family member

(Pruchno & Johnson, 1996). It has been noted that grandparenthood is not self-initiated or voluntary, as most other adult roles are. Therefore, the transition into the role may be more difficult for some. Specifically, Bengston (1985) found that the transition to grandmotherhood was more easily accepted if it was perceived as occurring "on time" rather than "early." Other research shows that there is a similar "on-time" phenomenon for grandfatherhood (Baronowski, 1990).

Content and Meaning of the Grandparent Role

Grandparenthood, as a derived status, is only weakly regulated by social norms. Therefore, grandparent roles are ambiguous and vary in both form and function. The social and legal rights and obligations of grandparents are not at all clear. With few normatively explicit expectations for their role behaviors, the type and level of grandparent involvement often are matters for family negotiation (Pruchno & Johnson, 1996). In fact, there is no single "grandparent role," but there are multiple ways to be grandparents and a variety of reasons that grandparents assume different roles (Giarrusso et al., 1996).

Grandparent roles and styles differ across individuals, across the life span of grandparents, and across the life span of grandchildren. For example, grandparents are influential in the family's social construction of its history, and they serve as historians, mentors, role models, wizards, or nurturers (Bengston, 1985). Cherlin and Furstenberg (1985) described three relationship dimensions of grandparents: exchange of services with grandchildren, influence over grandchildren, and frequency of contact. Across these dimensions, grandparents range from significantly involved with their grandchildren to somewhat detached. Giarrusso et al. (1996) noted that grandparents/great grandparents and their grandchildren are linked through interactions, through sentiments, and through exchanges of support.

Grandparents' roles change as they and their grandchildren develop. Younger grandmothers may be fulfilling multiple roles, such as caring for their own children, their aging parents, and their grandchildren. They may have neither the time nor the desire to assume the conventional role of grandmother (Emick & Hayslip, 1996). When the grandchildren are young, grandparents may be more supportive and authoritative through providing more caregiving and helping services. Shared leisure activities may account for a large portion of contact between the generations during this time. As grandchildren enter adolescence, however, these roles and activities give way to mutual assistance, advice giving, and discussion of problems.

A few studies specifically have examined relationships between adolescent and adult grandchildren and their grandparents. Adolescence, with its emphasis on identity formation, may be a time when contact with grandparents can be especially helpful because grandparents' historical accounts of familial/cultural events might provide a sense of continuity to the adolescent's life by merging her familial past with the future (Creasey & Koblewski, 1991). Although actual contact with grandparents tends to decrease throughout the life span, grandchildren's desire for contact over the course of adolescence does not decline; grandparents still are viewed as important attachment figures. A study of older adolescents and their grandparents found that grandparents were not seen as major targets for intimacy and did not provide significant instrumental aid, but grandchildren reported mutual love and respect and very low levels of conflict with their grandparents. The researchers concluded that most grandparents continue to play a relatively active role within their adolescent grandchildren's social networks (Creasey & Koblewski, 1991).

In fact, adult grandchildren report that their relationships with their grandparents are close and enduring, and these ongoing relationships often include high levels of association. When asked to choose a grandparent with whom they had the emotionally closest relationship, respondents in one study were more likely to pick a grandmother—especially the maternal grandmother—than a grandfather, regardless of their own sex. Further, they found that time spent in an extraordinary relationship, such as that of a grandparent acting as

Most grandparents report that their lives have changed for the better as a result of grandparenthood.

surrogate parent for a grandchild, fixed a permanent attachment between the generations. Finally, men and women alike noted that as they had grown to adulthood, they were more likely to appreciate their grandparents (Hodgson, 1992).

Parental marital status does not appear to be a major determinant of adult grandchildren's perceptions of the role behaviors of their grandparents or the importance of grandparent/grandchild relationships. Cogswell and Henry (1995) reported that grandparents were equally important to adult children whose parents were divorced and to those who came from intact families. There were no differences in maternal or paternal grandparents' involvement in instrumental roles, such as shared activities, financial assistance, or caretaking. However, grandchildren from divorced families reported greater expressive role performance by maternal grandmothers than did grandchildren from intact families.

An interesting study by King and Elder (1997) found that grandparents who had known their own grandparents as children, as opposed to those who had not, participated in more activities with their grandchildren, provided more instrumental assistance, were more likely to play the roles of mentor and companion, felt that they knew their grandchildren better, and were more likely to talk to their grandchildren about problems and plans for the future. Grandparents who had lived with a grandparent while growing up were more likely than others to discuss their grandchildren's futures with them.

Grandparents as Caregivers.   One of the most important and visible functions of grandparents, particularly grandmothers, is that of caregiving. Most grandparents provide some level of caregiving—from occasional baby-sitting to daytime care—while mothers work. Investigations carried out in a number of industrialized countries with different family cultures indicate that many working mothers with children younger than age 3 use grandmothers as either principal caregivers or part-time caregivers to supplement other forms of extrafamily care, such as child-care centers or baby-sitters. Although child care by grandmothers is an ancient social phenomenon, changes in family patterns and women's attitudes toward care within the family have affected the meaning assigned to grandchild care by modern grandmothers (Gattai & Musatti, 1999). Baydar and Brooks-Gunn (1998) found that 43 percent of grandmothers helped to provide care for their grandchildren on a regular basis, almost four times the percent of grandparents who are primary caretakers of their grandchildren. Grandparent caregiving is particularly common in low-income inner-city areas, where between 30 and 50 percent of children are cared for by grandparents (Minkler & Roe, 1996). Fuller-Thomson, Minkler, and Driver (1997) found that African American grandparents, young grandparents, and grandparents with multiple grandchildren were more likely to be primary caregivers than grandmothers from other groups. Ninety percent of the grandparents in their study had never been primary caregivers, but most provided care on an occasional basis.

Gattai and Musatti (1999) explored the psychological and relational aspects of grandmother involvement in child care from the grandmothers' points of view. Involvement in child care varied considerably—from full-time during mothers' working hours, to a few hours a day while mothers worked part-time, to extending a child-care center's or a baby-sitter's hours, to occasional involvement. Both paternal and maternal grandmothers described strong love relationships, or actual bonds, with their grandchildren. They insisted that these feelings were unique, different from other feelings of love for their spouses and children. Feeling less responsibility for their grandchildren than for their own children provided these grandmothers free rein to give affection to their grandchildren. Further, caregiving elicited memories of caring for their own children and difficulties in reconciling work and child care, and often the involvement reestablished loose links with their own children. Grandfathers' roles were minimal—sharing moments of play and walks with the grandchildren and relieving grandmothers when they had household tasks to perform. These grandfathers did not form deep,

stable relationships with their grandchildren, and they tended to ignore the children's lack of autonomy and need for care.

Whereas grandparents typically do not provide full-time child rearing, some grandmothers accept surrogate roles when there has been a major crisis precipitated by divorce, drug abuse, alcoholism, teenage pregnancy, parental abuse, or separation from or abandonment of children by their natural parents. These intergenerational households have been referred to as "skip-generation" households (DeParle, 1999). In 1991, approximately 3.2 million, or a conservative estimate of 5 percent, of children younger than 18 were residing with grandparents. In at least one-third of these households, neither parent was present (Emick & Hayslip, 1996). DeParle (1999) noted that, according to the Census Bureau, the number of children in their grandparents' care had increased by 50 percent in the decade of the 1990s. This increase is directly related to the welfare-reform legislation passed by Congress in 1996. As welfare rolls shrank, grandmothers were pressed into action, and approximately 1.4 million children were living with their grandparents without a parent present before the decade ended. Of these grandparents, 57 percent were poor, 46 percent lacked a high school education, and only one-third were employed. In addition, 53 percent were Black, 28 percent were White, and 16 percent were Hispanic. Forty-one percent were younger than age 54.

For these women, grandparenting is "second-time-around parenting." How do these children and their grandparents fare? What problems do these grandparents face, and how do they feel about their roles? Studies show that most grandparents rearing grandchildren accept the task willingly. Indeed, they often intervene to provide a safe environment for children. However, some studies have found that custodial grandparents have a variety of problems. For example, grandparents have been found to score low on psychological and overall well-being. Many frequently feel depressed or anxious; they suffer from insomnia, hypertension, back and stomach problems, and other conditions that may be caused by the physical demands of the new role (Minkler & Roe, 1996; Pruchno & Johnson, 1996). Baydar and Brooks-Gunn (1998) found that approximately 25 percent of their national sample of grandmothers could be classified as depressed. In one study, more than one-third reported a decline in their health status, and many reported having missed a recent doctor's appointment because of demands of caregiving. Increases in alcohol and cigarette consumption also have been observed (Minkler & Roe, 1996; Pruchno & Johnson, 1996). In the Emick and Hayslip (1996) study, two-thirds of the grandparents were actively concerned about their health, especially those caring for children with disabilities.

More than half of custodial grandmothers are low-income. For younger grandparents, assuming the caregiving role often means quitting a job, decreasing work hours, or making job-related sacrifices that jeopardize their economic situations. Retired or nonworking caregivers also frequently suffer financially from the decision to become full-time caregivers. Many have no savings as cushions and have to stretch already inadequate Social Security checks even further. Some grandparents report selling their cars, giving up "luxuries," making clothing sacrifices, and so forth to cope financially with their new roles.

The negative economic consequences experienced often are compounded by a lack of adequate governmental assistance. In most states, government policy differentiates between grandparents rearing their own grandchildren and foster care. Grandparents may qualify for low, and often stigmatizing, welfare payments but usually not for the substantially higher government compensation afforded to foster parents. In one state, grandmothers receive $215 per month for every grandchild in their care. Furthermore, they are not eligible for such benefits as psychological counseling or clothing allowances routinely made available to foster parents. These grandmothers need easier access to payments and more social services to keep their grandchildren out of foster care. Thus, it is not surprising that grandparents often feel like "second-class" citizens in the eyes of a government that penalizes them for stepping in and rearing some of the nation's most vulnerable children (DeParle, 1999; Minkler & Roe, 1996).

Besides health and economic costs, grandparents often face diminished social support. Some grandmothers in the Minkler and Roe (1996) study reported that parenting responsibilities limited their social roles, isolated them from friends, and gave them less time with other family members. Younger grandmothers who had to quit their jobs and leave behind valued social ties were the most isolated. However, grandmothers in the Baydar and Brooks-Gunn (1998) study reported a variety of social roles. Even though more than one-third were working, 65 percent reported that they had participated in at least one social organization several times a year or more often. Nevertheless, one-third had no contact with social or community organizations.

Little research has focused on the effects on children of being reared by grandparents. Most custodial grandparents assume the care of their grandchildren because of the parents' inability to care for them. Thus, although studies have shown that many of the children reared by grandparents exhibit behavioral or emotional problems and are treated in mental-health centers, it is unclear whether these problems result from disturbances in their families of origin or from residence with grandparents. When the child's parent(s) resides with or near the child, both children and adults may suffer role confusion. Too many potential caregivers may lead to the presumption that someone else has performed a specific child-care duty, and grandchildren may subsequently suffer. Children reared by grandparents have been found to be poorer students academically but less likely to experience behavioral problems in school. Further, they were healthier than were children reared by single biological parents. Children reared by older grandparents seemed to be better students than those reared by younger grandparents (Emick & Hayslip, 1996). However, Pruchno and Johnson (1996) noted that children reared solely by their grandparents fared quite well relative to children in families with one biological parent present. Furthermore, they were not significantly different, except in academic performance, from children reared in traditional families.

Baydar and Brooks-Gunn (1998), using a national sample, established profiles of grandmothers who help care for their grandchildren. Age was found to be significantly associated with grandmothers' caregiving. The odds of providing care for grandchildren increased with age, peaking at age 67 and then declining. The larger the number of grandchildren, the more likely the grandmothers were to provide care. Grandmothers living with their husbands were significantly more likely to provide care than those living in households with other individuals, and grandmothers who had a grandchild living in the household were more than twice as likely as others to provide care. In this study, grandmothers with more education were more likely to help provide care than those with less education. This profile is strikingly different from that of grandmothers who are raising their grandchildren.

Variables Related to Grandparenting

Several variables have been identified that seem to affect the style of grandparenting (see Highlights). The first of these is *gender*. Women outlive men by about 8 years, so that the oldest member of the family lineage is likely to be female. Therefore, most grandfathers are likely to be married, and a greater proportion of grandmothers are likely to be widowed. Perhaps that is the reason that grandmothers have been studied in more depth than grandfathers have. Another factor that influences grandparent-grandchild relationships is the *geographic distance* separating them. Proximity has been cited as one of the strongest predictors of the grandparent-grandchild relationship. Evidence suggests that movement of older people to retirement communities reduces in-person contact between grandparents, their adult children, and grandchildren. The "boomerang" generation of adults might maintain or strengthen their relationships with grandparents by virtue of living with parents who facilitate extended intergenerational involvement.

Ethnicity is another factor related to grandparenting style. Research on intergenerational living arrangements, expectations, and circumstances of custodial grandparents has emphasized the need to examine ethnicity and social class in studies of grandparenting. There is some evidence that acculturation—the adoption of mainstream values, language, and practices—creates a cultural gulf between generations in Hispanic families. Spanish-language compatibility between grandparents and grandchildren has predicted the amount of contact between them, underscoring the importance of cultural affinity in structuring intergenerational relations. Studies of White grandparents have focused on describing different types of grandparents and examining the meaning of the grandparent role, whereas studies of Black grandparents have focused on grandparents as parent substitutes. Grandparenting seems to have a more central role for African American men than for male members of other ethnic groups, and grandparenthood is more important to rural Black grandfathers than to rural White grandfathers (Pruchno & Johnson, 1996).

Black grandmothers play a critical role in child-rearing and parenting support, with grandmother involvement being a common response to family transitions and family crises, such as teen pregnancies, drug addiction, incarceration, or physical or mental illness (Hunter, 1997). Several studies have suggested that custodial Black grandmothers are in a double bind, both physically and emotionally. Whereas they may resent the demands of their new roles as parent surrogates, they nevertheless find assumption of those roles preferable to giving up their grandchildren to foster care. If grandparents are caring for their adult children, other frail family members, and their grandchildren, they are likely to suffer role overload. Many are employed, and caregiving seriously undermines their ability to earn a living and leaves no time for themselves (Emick & Hayslip, 1996).

Black grandparents rarely demonstrate a passive style of grandparenting, with most having an "authoritarian" or "influential" style that involves high levels of support and/or a "parentlike" influence. Black children are more likely than White children are to view grandmothers as more influential in teaching lessons about life, morality, the importance of learning, and religion.

Hunter (1997) found that grandmothers were the most frequently nominated source of parenting help among African American mothers and fathers, especially in the rural South. For fathers, being employed and family proximity significantly increased reliance on grandmothers for parenting support, and married fathers relied on grandmothers almost as much as unmarried fathers did. For women, parenting alone, being a young parent, and having fewer economic resources were associated with receiving parenting assistance from grandmothers. The researcher concluded that grandmothers are central to the child-rearing system of many Black families. Further, she suggested that the significant changes in marital status of Black adults and shifts in family structure increase the likelihood that young adult parents will continue to need the help of grandparents to provide parenting support, economic resources, and housing. Indeed, in 1990 more than 12 percent of Black children lived in households with grandparents, with or without their parents.

Finally, family disruption, especially the *divorce* of adult children, has been found to have substantial, often profound, effects on grandparents. Divorce may alter the normative, voluntaristic nature of the grandparent role, and the nature, type, and amount of interaction may either significantly increase or decrease.

Clingempeel and his associates (1992) noted that children living in mother-custody single-parent families are likely to have more contact and closer emotional relationships with maternal grandparents than children living with both biological parents. These grandparents also are more likely to engage in more parentlike behavior with their grandchildren. The data from this study showed that significant stressors in the middle generation engendered greater grandparent involvement following divorce. However, upon the remarriage of the custodial mother, grandparents tended to retreat to predivorce levels of contact and emotional involvement. These findings were more significant for grandfathers than for grandmothers. Thomas (1990) noted the double bind that these grandparents may experience: Divorced mothers may value the practical and psychological support grandparents can offer in child rearing, but at the same time, they expect grandparents to refrain from interfering in the rearing of grandchildren—a conflict between the need for assistance and the desire for autonomy.

Divorced daughters are reported to receive more grandparental help than any others. It has been suggested that the adult child's need for parental attention as reflected by his or her marital and parental status constitutes part of the explanation for intergenerational contacts (Aldous, 1985). The downside of that phenomenon, then, often is reflected in the experience of the paternal grandparents.

Relationships with paternal grandparents for children in mother-custody families may be disrupted following divorce (Thomas, 1990). Geographic mobility may be a factor, since custodial mothers often move following divorce. Frequent, consistent relationships with the noncustodial father are likely to facilitate continuing relationships with paternal grandparents, especially if they live in close proximity. However, for many paternal grandparents, only legal action guarantees that they will maintain regular contact with their grandchildren after their sons' divorces.

Grandparent visitation laws, which grant grandparents legal standing to petition for legally enforceable visitation with their grandchildren—even over parental objections—have been passed in all 50 states. The impetus for these statutes was the severing of grandparent-grandchild relationships following the death or divorce of the custodial parent, usually, but not always, the mother. The award of visitation rights depends in most states on a judicial determination of the child's "best interests." Despite the positive role that grandparents can play in facilitating the healthy development of grandchildren, intergenerational conflict as a result of a visitation dispute can victimize grandchildren, and the ensuing long-term consequences are unknown. Clearer guidelines for "best interests" are needed, and more data on what happens in families following a judicial award of visitation privileges is essential (Thompson, Tinsley, Scalora, & Parke, 1989).

Only within the past 5 years has attention to *stepgrandparents* been found in the research literature. The high rates of divorce and remarriage have increased dramatically a child's chances of having both grandparents and stepgrandparents, and sometimes ex-stepgrandparents. A study of young adult college students assessed relationships with stepgrandparents and found that stepgrandchildren maintained contact with their stepgrandparents beyond high school, and the majority of young people desired more contact. Almost half rated their relationships with stepgrandparents as important, though the relationship strengths were rated as moderate. Stepgrandchildren perceived the relationship as both personal and social, and they expected little from their stepgrandparents beyond gift-giving. It has been suggested that the older the child is when he becomes a stepgrandchild, the less important the relationship will be. Other variables, such as the prestige of the biological father and the stepfather, distance between stepgrandchildren and their stepgrandparents, acquisition of the stepgrandparents through death or divorce, satisfaction with the remarriage of the biological parent, and maternal or paternal lineage of the stepgrandparents all were related to the stepgrandchild-stepgrandparent relationship (Trygstad & Sanders, 1989).

It was found that these young adults had considerably more contact with their grandparents than with their stepgrandparents, and relationships with their grandparents were rated as stronger than those with their stepgrandparents. Further, the young adults' expectations of their grandparents exceeded their expectations of their stepgrandparents. It appears that stepgrandparents can play an important role with their stepgrandchildren, but the relationship does not replace the relationship with the children's grandparents (Sanders & Trygstad, 1989).

Grandparents influence their grandchildren in many ways. Influence can be described as *indirect* and *direct*. Much of grandparental influence on children is indirect, mediated through the parents, taking the form of emotional and material assistance, child-rearing controls, and role modeling. Grandparents may influence their grandchildren indirectly through their individual relationships with the parents and their impact on the marital adjustment of the parents, and this influence may be either positive or negative. Grandparents are not limited to indirect influences. Four kinds of direct influences have been described in the literature: cognitive and social stimulation, direct support, modeling, and participation in mutual activities. These influences are exercised through many different face-to-face interactions between grandparents and grandchildren. The most direct influences of grandparents probably occur in families in which grandparents become primary caregivers of their grandchildren.

Support for Grandparents.   As interest in grandparent caregiving has grown, community interventions and service programs to assist relative caregiving have increased. More than 300 support groups all over the United States provide opportunities to share feelings and concerns while giving and receiving informational support about resources and methods for coping with the new caregiving role. These support groups are of two kinds: informal, which often are held in a grandparent's home, and formal, which are sponsored by a health or social-service agency, a church, a school, or some other organization (Minkler & Roe, 1996).

Comprehensive programs generally offer a range of services, such as individual counseling, parenting classes, and supportive services for children. Peer training, respite care, and legislative advocacy of the rights of grandparents rearing children are among other activities provided. Some programs meet specific needs of parents, such as bus transportation for grandmothers and young children in their care so that they may visit incarcerated mothers, play-therapy sessions for young children prenatally exposed to crack cocaine, and "warm line" telephone support.

Coalitions have been developed to influence legislative changes needed to address the needs of grandparent-headed families. The Grandparent Information Center in Washington, D.C. provides information and referral for grandparents nationwide. It also publishes a newsletter three times annually and "tip sheets" on how to start support groups, plus other topics of interest (Minkler & Roe, 1996). The visibility of grandparenthood has been facilitated by the proclamation of Grandparents Day (the first Sunday after Labor Day).

Grandparents: A Potpourri

It is easy to see that grandparents come in all ages, represent all vocations, have few to many grandchildren and possibly great-grandchildren, have varied frequencies of contact with their grandchildren, and demonstrate a wide variety of grandparenting styles. Evidence indicates that grandparents exert significant influence over their grandchildren.

Whatever grandparenthood represents, an individual's expectations are, no doubt, derived from his own parents and grandparents. Maintaining a sense of family continuity may be the most significant role of grandparents, who are crucial as transmitters of culture and history and are functionally necessary to ensure adequate socialization of the young. Younger generations, then, socialize elders by needing, receiving, and incorporating their knowledge and experiences into their life space (Robertson, Tice, & Loeb, 1985).

Before leaving the subject of grandparents, we should note that more than 40 percent of individuals older than 65 have great-grandchildren, yet little research exists concerning the nature of the relationship between great-grandchildren and their great-grandparents. Some evidence suggests that the role of great-grandparent is more remote than that of grandparent, possibly because of distance and advancing age. Yet young adults who have great-grandparents tend to have more positive views of the aged, and great-grandparents seem to value the sense of familial immortality and vitality that great-grandchildren contribute to their lives. Because the role of great-grandparent is twice mediated—through two generations of parents—the norm of noninterference is probably stronger (Doka & Mertz, 1988).

A great-grandparent study found that 93 percent responded very favorably to their new status and gave great emotional significance to the role. The important aspects of the great-grandparenthood role were personal and family renewal, diversion provided by their great-grandchildren, and a mark of longevity. Seventy-eight percent of the great-grandparents were described as "remote," with limited and ritualistic contact with their great-grandchildren, usually around holidays and family celebrations. Some viewed limited contact as an advantage because of their impatience with young children. Thirty-five percent of the great-grandparents were described as "close," since they saw their great-grandchildren at least once a month, spoke at least once a week with their parents, often baby-sat, and participated with them in shopping and leisure activities. These great-grandparents tended to be somewhat younger and on the maternal rather than the paternal side. Proximity was a necessary, but not a sufficient, condition for close relations. It seemed that these great-grandparents had lived in times of significant family change, experiencing significant family crises, but they adapted to new situations and changed circumstances (Doka & Mertz, 1988).

In sum, the literature on grandparenting repeatedly stresses the changing perceptions of grandparenthood and the heterogeneity among grandparents. Yet the norms for grandparent behavior are ambiguous at best, and the rights and responsibilities are poorly articulated. There are symbolic dimensions of grandparenthood as well as different styles and typologies of grandparenting.

Grandparents differ on a number of dimensions by gender; by kin position; by geographic distance from grandchildren; by ethnicity; and by experiences of family disruption, especially divorce. Nevertheless, most grandparents view their lives as being enriched by having grandchildren.

Giarrusso et al. (1996) reiterated the lack of research on great-grandparenting. However, they stated that what is known suggests much similarity between the experiences of being a grandparent and being a great-grandparent. The immediate future is likely to see more in-depth research on grandparenthood, more intergenerational programs, and more social policy related to the preservation of intergenerational contacts. As more people become grandparents and live longer to enjoy the role, grandparenting will once again come of age.

CARING FOR ELDERLY PARENTS

The final stage in Erikson's stages of psychosocial development occurs when individuals approach old age. This stage, integrity versus despair, represents a time in which people reflect on their lives—it is hoped, with a sense of satisfaction. For most extended families, it is at this point in the life cycle that child-rearing and parenting demands decrease or cease and caring for elderly parents increases. Some sociologists have maintained that there is, in fact, a role reversal as the middle-aged adult child becomes "parent" to her own parents when the burden of care shifts to the middle generation. Other sociologists have maintained that the role-reversal model is far too simplistic to explain the relationships between adult children and their aging parents, and still others suggest that role reversal is pathological.

Clearly a shift in dependency needs occurs. In fact, the years between 40 and 60, in which people often find themselves coping simultaneously with the demands of children and their own parents, was first referred to in 1979 as the "sandwich generation." Because parent care almost always is provided by a daughter (and to a lesser extent by a daughter-in-law), women in this sandwich generation have been referred to as "women in the middle"

(Noelker & Wallace, 1985). These "women in the middle" are more likely to provide care to their mothers, so that both the givers and the receivers of this care are overrepresented by women (Marks, 1996). For the first time in history, an individual is likely to spend more years as an adult child with living parents than as a parent of a child younger than 20 (Stein et al., 1998). Thus, grandparenting and great-grandparenting will become more prevalent.

Roles as caregiving daughters and daughters-in-law to dependent older people have been added to their traditional roles as wives, homemakers, mothers, grandmothers, and workers. Recent evidence suggests that, in spite of increased labor force participation by women, few significant changes in the household division of labor have occurred (see Chapter 8). Rather than a redivision of domestic tasks between husband and wife being made, the length of the wife's work week has increased, and daughters respond to the needs of their impaired elderly parents by allocating less time to leisure (Marks, 1996; Mui, 1995). Several demographic trends have been cited as reasons for this relatively new role: The decreased birthrate has resulted in fewer children to provide elderly care; as people are living longer, the population of elderly people has increased, especially those who live into their eighties and nineties; and geographic mobility has resulted in fewer adult children living near their elderly parents, who consequently assume most or all of the responsibilities of care.

Parent care has been conceptualized from a life-span perspective, likening it to child rearing. In the early part of the life span, parents provide the necessities for the child's survival—food, clothing, shelter, love, and guidance. During this time there is an imbalance in the exchange of help in favor of the child, often resulting in parental sacrifices. The child, it is hoped, develops the basic attachment that provides the foundation for later relationships. When the child reaches young adulthood, the exchange of help becomes more balanced, especially if the young adults have children of their own. Middle-aged parents may provide babysitting, help with finances, and so forth, and young adults may assist their parents with transportation, household and yard maintenance, and so forth. In the latter part of the life span, the exchange of help often shifts in favor of the elderly parent, when parent caring is essential for survival of the elderly. Viewed this way, parent caring and child rearing become intricately related (Krause & Haverkamp, 1996).

Several investigators, however, have noted demographic trends that threaten to disrupt this cycle of caregiving. First, the increasing number of women in the workforce limits the resources (time and energy) that middle-aged adults may need to invest in elderly care. Second, since elderly parents are living longer, they are more apt to have chronic health conditions that require more intensive care. Third, divergent family forms (single parenting, remarriage, cohabitation, gay marriages, and so on) may disrupt the helping relationships between adult children and their parents (Marks, 1996). Finally, geographic mobility alters the form of communication and the kind of assistance given.

In spite of these demographic changes and contextual variables, most of the data suggest that both the ideology and the practice of familial responsibility for the elderly persist. Older people still tend to live near (but rarely with) at least one child, interact frequently with their children, and often are involved in exchange of mutual aid with their adult children. The notion that older people are alienated from their children, then, appears to be a myth (Lin & Rogerson, 1995).

Types of Parent Care

Walker, Pratt, and Eddy (1995) distinguished between the concepts of caregiving and providing aid. Caregiving reflects dependence on another person for any activity essential for daily living, including instrumental activities (e.g., laundry, meal preparation, and certain aspects of health care). Caregiving encompasses assistance beyond the aid provided to physically and psychologically healthy parents. For example, getting an item from the grocery store is considered intergenerational aid exchange rather than caregiving unless the parents are unable to shop independently. Providing aid to elderly parents

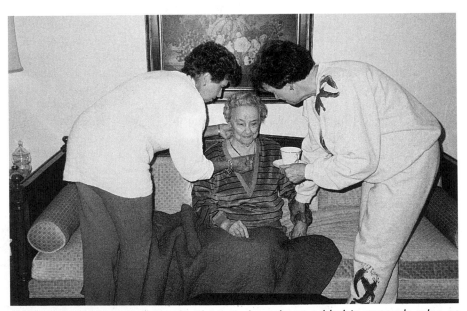

Roles as caregivers to dependent parents have been added to women's roles as spouses, mothers, and workers.

is more common than providing care. Compared with husbands and sons, wives and daughters provide more aid, as well as more caregiving, to elderly parents.

Previous studies have examined the types of assistance and aid given to elderly parents by their adult children as well as the degree of contact between them. However, most have failed to differentiate among contact, aid, and intimacy, assuming that the quantity of interaction is the same as the quality and that material exchange is the same as emotional exchange. However, evidence suggests that contact does not necessarily imply intimacy and that family members can feel close to one another without frequent contact, although some contact may be necessary to maintain intimacy.

Numerous studies have found that caregiving daughters provide more hands-on help (e.g., transportation, household chores, laundry, meal preparation, personal care) than caregiving sons. The literature consistently suggests that women provide 70–80 percent of care to their elderly parents, but men are equally likely to provide financial aid and bureaucratic mediation (e.g., obtaining information, negotiating with service providers). Further, caregiving daughters are more likely than sons to involve siblings in decisions about care for their mothers.

Recent research, however, has begun to examine aspects of male caregiving (Mui, 1995). Caregiving sons receive more support from their spouses than caregiving daughters do, and they are less likely than daughters to make sacrifices to provide care. Daughters who provide care report more neglect of other family responsibilities and more negative effects on their future plans and leisure time than sons report. Married daughters expect little from their husbands, and they view their husbands as supportive as long as they neither resent nor interfere with their caregiving activities (Walker et al., 1995). Actually, male caregivers constitute a sizable portion of the total population. Marks (1996), using a national sample, found that one in seven men is a caregiver, but not all the men in the sample were caring for elderly parents. He

noted that there are differences in the way sons and daughters approach caregiving, the roles they play, and the impact of the caregiving experience on their lives.

Halpern, Shroder, and Citera (1996) examined the accuracy of adult children's perceptions of their elderly parents' concerns. They found that elderly parents and their adult children agreed on the needs that were most important. Both ranked health-related needs highest and emotional-support needs next. Both sons and daughters more accurately estimated fathers' concerns than mothers', and middle-born children more accurately predicted parents' concerns than youngest or oldest children. Adult children were most accurate when their parents lived in retirement communities, whereas children sharing households with their parents tended to overestimate parental concerns. The authors concluded that moderate involvement with elderly parents leads to more accurate predictions of their needs.

Variables Related to Aid and Contact

Obviously, the frequency and type of aid and contact provided by middle-aged children to their parents vary. Parents who are older, widowed, have low incomes, and are in poor health tend to expect and receive more aid from their offspring (Hamon, 1992).

Demographic characteristics of children also affect aid and contact: employment status, age, marital status, geographic proximity, and life changes. Employment status has been found to interact with gender. Marks (1996) found that women who worked more than 45 hours per week were more likely to provide care than men who worked the same amount of time. Employed caregiving daughters gave approximately the same amount of care as those daughters who were not employed. Employed sons, however, gave less care than unemployed sons. Women, particularly women of color, were more likely than men to quit work in order to give care (Walker et al., 1995). Kaufman and Uhlenberg (1998) found that increasing work hours improved sons' relationships with their fathers, but daughters' relationships deteriorated when they increased their work hours and improved when they decreased the amount of work. According to Marks (1996), a woman's likelihood of being a caregiver is significantly higher between ages 35 and 74 than between ages 19 and 34. Between 35 and 49 there is approximately a 50 percent chance of being a caregiver, increasing to 65 percent between the ages of 50 and 64. Separated and divorced men and women and widowed women were significantly less likely to be caregivers than were men and women in their first marriages.

Geographic distance between elderly parents and their adult children is another factor that affects the frequency and type of intergenerational care. Lin and Rogerson (1995) found that most elderly parents have at least one child living within 5 miles of their residence. Approximately 25 percent have their closest child within one mile. Daughters in this study, contrary to expectation, lived no closer than sons to their parents. Parents older than age 80 lived closer to their children than younger parents did. Widowed mothers tended to live near a daughter, and married couples lived in closer proximity than divorced or separated parents. Children, especially female, whose elderly parents reside with them spend considerably more time in caregiving activities than those whose parents do not live with them. Kaufman and Uhlenberg (1998) found that an increase in geographic distance between elderly parents and children increased the likelihood of a decline in the relationship between sons and mothers, but distance seemed to lead to improved relationships between daughters and both parents.

These researchers also noted that life changes for both parents and children had adverse effects on the parent-child relationship. For example, when parental health declined, the relationship between daughters, but not sons, and their parents deteriorated. Disruption of the marriage of either parents or children can induce stress that changes parent-child relationships. A parent's divorce, particularly, leads to deterioration in relationships with the father, who is usually blamed by both sons and daughters. Effects are stronger for father-son relationships, especially if the son is expected to assume part of the father's role in the family. Problems in the child's marriage also may bring tensions into other family situations or result in the child's neglect of other family obligations. An adult child's divorce does not negatively affect a son's relationship with his parents, but it has a strong negative effect on a daughter's relationships with her parents. Having additional family members seems to help mediate deteriorated child-parent relationships. These researchers concluded that intergenerational relationships are vulnerable to the stresses and strains produced by life changes that affect either generation.

Qualitative Aspects of Parent Care

Several researchers have examined the affective impact of interactions between adult children and their parents. Krause and Haverkamp (1996) used attachment theory to describe adult children's motivation to provide care to their parents. According to this theory, attachment to one's parents endures throughout the life span and is expressed by the extent to which children maintain proximity to and contact with their parents. They found that these feelings of attachment not only predicted present behavior but also had a significant influence on the

HIGHLIGHTS

Variables Related to Aid and Contact between the Elderly and Their Children

Degree of limitation of the elder
Gender of the children
Marital status of the elder
Marital status of the children
Employment of the children
Geographic distance between the elder and the children
Living arrangements

commitment for future help. In addition, a sense of filial obligation tended to increase the adult child's attachment behaviors. Apparently, adult children increase their attachment behaviors to their parents in later life as the first signs of decline begin to appear and at a point before actual help may be needed.

Szinovaez (1997) examined intergenerational solidarity and the role of childhood experiences in the likelihood of co-residence of adult children and their elderly parents. Intergenerational solidarity reflects a strong sense of permanence, moral obligation, cohesion, and mutual trust that evolve from permanence and established family rituals and traditions. This concept implies that contacts and supports among kin are based largely on feelings of obligation (normative solidarity). Generalized exchange principles may manifest themselves in parent-child relationships in a dual manner. First, parents' support of their children during childhood and adolescence should enhance the children's feelings of obligation toward older parents (delayed reciprocity). Second, parents' contributions to other kin, especially their own parents, should increase children's feelings of obligation toward their parents, as well as toward their children (transferred reciprocity). By enhancing normative solidarity, both delayed and transferred reciprocity should culminate in more support to older parents (functional solidarity). Further, an atmosphere of permanence and trust would promote positive interaction styles and development of attachment (affectional solidarity). These relationship characteristics can be expected to be reenacted in later parent-child interactions.

However, Szinovaez (1997) noted that childhood experiences could interfere with the development of intergenerational solidarity. Individuals who grew up in single-father households were the least likely to endorse parental co-residence. Apparently, exposure to a female role model is essential for developing normative solidarity, and even a stepmother is sufficient for developing normative solidarity. Men who grew up with single mothers espoused stronger feelings of obligation to take parents into their homes than men from two-parent families. On the other hand, living with a remarried mother had a negative effect on men's normative solidarity. Living in traditional extended families (i.e., two biological parents and grandparents) was found to enhance the endorsement and implementation of parental co-residence among women but not among men.

Race and ethnicity also relate to normative solidarity. Both African Americans and Hispanics were more likely to express positive attitudes toward co-residence than Whites, and Asians had the most positive attitudes of all subjects. For women, age, number of brothers, and income were significantly related to their attitudes toward co-residence. Women who were near the age at which they might experience parental co-residence were the most hesitant about the arrangement. Those with brothers and higher incomes had more negative attitudes, suggesting that adult children who can afford alternative arrangements were less likely to endorse parental co-residence. The availability of siblings (both male and female) seems to lead to dispersion of the responsibility for parents, reducing the probability of co-residence. Finally, parents' needs—especially financial resources, health, and marital status—had a strong influence on parental co-residence for women.

Stein et al. (1998) examined the motivations of adult children for caring for elderly parents. They found that feelings of obligation were more important than feelings of affection and general attitudes about filial responsibility combined. However, obligation was more strongly associated with affection than with filial responsibility. Adult children with only one living parent reported feelings of more obligation. Overall, women experienced greater feelings of obligation than men did. Specifically, female children felt more obligation to maintain contact, to participate in family rituals, to provide assistance, to avoid conflict, and to engage in personal sharing with their parents. Like many other aspects of family relationships, parental obligation is an issue primarily for women.

Another issue related to intergenerational interaction is the effect of aid and contact on the psychological well-being and morale of older people. Earlier research indicated the absence of a correlation between interactions with adult children and feelings of well-being among the elderly. Some investigators have argued that because of the imbalance in the exchange of aid (more flowing *from* the adult child *to* the older parent), low morale and depression result. Other researchers have found that the impact of helping others had a significant positive impact on older people. Further, the inability of elders to reciprocate rather than the need for assistance (dependency) undermined the morale of the older people. However, other studies have failed to support a positive relationship between the frequency of the interaction and the morale, and imbalances in aid exchange do not seem to have negative consequences for either partner's perception of attachment.

Some researchers have suggested that the elderly engage in a deliberate strategy of reciprocation to build and maintain their interpersonal relationships, and some are able to compensate for declines in health and/or income that may interfere with their ability to provide aid. The majority of both mothers and daughters in a study conducted by Walker, Pratt, and Oppy (1992) perceived that mothers gave aid to daughters in return for the help mothers received, and the most common type was love. Other types of maternal aid included information, advice, and money, all of which were reported by daughters as being valuable to them. Assistance from the elderly parent was found to reduce caregiver stress, even when the parent was somewhat impaired, either physically or cognitively (Starrels, Ingersoll-Dayton, Dowler, & Neal, 1997).

Luescher and Pillemer (1998) noted that caring for elderly parents involves conflicting norms, leading to ambivalence. For example, on the one hand, caregiving is humanizing, meaningful, and fulfilling. On the other hand, many caregiving tasks are boring and repetitive. Conflicting emotions such as affection and resentment toward one's elderly parents may be experienced frequently, and the parents themselves experience conflicting emo-

tions. Although they expect support from their children, they also feel guilty and helpless if they are unable to reciprocate in some way.

Outcomes of Parent Care

Numerous studies have documented that caring for aging parents can result in stress and strain for the adult children providing the care. Negative outcomes for caregivers have been reported in the areas of household performance, employment, participation in social activities, marital satisfaction, and health and well-being (Hoyert & Seltzer, 1992; Marks, 1996; Mui, 1995; Starrels et al., 1997; Walker et al., 1995). Most studies indicate that caregiver strain is more prevalent for women than for men. Women's involvement in multiple roles—mother, spouse, employee, and caregiver—creates overload, conflict, and anxiety. Female caregivers with competing obligations and responsibilities struggle with setting priorities and deciding how to divide their time, energy, and financial resources between older parents and their families. Some women who face these competing demands do not decrease the extent of parent care; rather, they sacrifice their leisure activities to assume the additional burden (Marks, 1996; Mui, 1995).

In fact, the most pervasive outcome of caregiving is the emotional strain on caregivers, particularly daughters. Stress for women may be related to the significantly greater amount of care they provide and/or their expectations of freedom from family and household responsibilities in later years of life. Apparently, men are better able to distance themselves emotionally from their parents while providing informal care, and they are more likely than daughters to use formal services to help with caregiving (Mui, 1995; Walker et al., 1995). Other outcomes include poor health, interference with personal and social lives, and employment adaptations.

Mui (1995) found that caregiving daughters, as compared with sons, reported poorer health, less respite support, higher levels of caregiving role involvement, and more interference in their personal and social lives. The level of daughters' emotional strain was associated with being White, with poor parent-daughter relationships, with interference in their personal and social lives, and working conditions. For sons, the sources of emotional strain were parents' disruptive behaviors, fewer secondary helpers, and interference in their personal and social lives. Overall, the results of this study suggested that the perceptions of emotional strain are most affected by the meaning of the caregiving role and the resources available to the caregiver rather than the condition of the elderly person. Further, it is not the extent of caregiving that determines the level of emotional strain but, rather, the caregiver's beliefs or perceptions about the interference of caregiving with his or her personal and social life.

However, Starrels and associates (1997) found that the elder's cognitive-behavior impairment affected caregiver stress for both male and female children. Clearly, more physical limitations and problems demanded more caregiving tasks. Further, the elder's degree of impairment had indirect effects on caregiver stress when fewer resources were available from the elder and when the caregiver took more time off work.

Adults, particularly women, who care for elderly parents make many employment adaptations—working fewer hours, arranging work schedules, taking time off without pay, arriving late or leaving early, taking personal or sick leave, refusing jobs or promotions, taking leaves of absence, and resigning from their jobs. Absenteeism has been found to be the most negative work-related outcome of elder caregiving.

Both caregiving men and women report poorer health than other adult children do, even when age, education, and income have been controlled (Marks, 1996). Although some studies have found that caregiving is related to increased depression, Walker et al. (1995) noted that the vast majority of caregivers do not have clinical levels of depression.

The caregiving arrangement whereby two generations share the same household seems to be particularly fragile and vulnerable to disruption. Research has indicated that outcomes are more negative for co-residing caregivers than for those living independently (Hoyert & Seltzer, 1992). In-house caregivers have described rigidly scheduled lives, little freedom, and few benefits (Walker et al., 1995). The longer the period of caregiving, the greater the negative outcomes (Hoyert & Seltzer, 1992). Increased sources of respite and support can relieve emotional strain and improve the health of caregivers.

Though the literature has focused on negative outcomes for caregivers, some researchers have noted positive outcomes. Walker et al. (1995) felt that sampling problems in conducting research might have misrepresented the nature of outcomes for caregivers. In fact, it has been reported for both African Americans and Whites that increased levels of caregiving result in more significant outcomes, both positive and negative. For example, caring for elderly parents may magnify financial problems and interrupt careers, but at the same time, it brings emotional satisfaction. Caregivers have reported receiving valuable instrumental and socioemotional aid from their dependent mothers. Walker et al. (1995) concluded that family caregiving is complex, and future research should focus on a broad relational and sociocultural context to reflect this complexity.

In sum, caring for elderly parents is a common phenomenon in contemporary society, despite the increase of women in the workforce, geographic mobility, the declining birthrate, and divergent family structures. Most elderly people desire to remain independent for as long as possible, and therefore few share the same households with their adult children. Nevertheless, for most families, contact is maintained in various forms, and aid and assistance are exchanged between generations.

In contemporary society there is a fair amount of both social and legal consensus about the roles of parent and child: Parents are to provide affection, physical care, recreation, and socialization to their children; children are to respect and obey their parents, do well in school, and develop social skills. No such clear parameters exist for the period when both child and parent are adults (Mancini & Blieszner, 1991).

There are few norms to guide relationships between these two generations of adults, but it does appear that attachment to each other is sustained throughout the family life cycle. The perceptions of the qualitative aspects of these relationships seem to be more significant than the frequency of contact and assistance. Stress and strain of at least a moderate level may result for adult caregivers, and the inability of elders to reciprocate caregiving may result in lower morale. Although these relationships may be likened to parenting, most research indicates that role reversal should be avoided. Adult day-care and recreational programs in senior-citizen centers provide some assistance in care of the elderly, but most agree that these services are inadequate to meet current needs.

SUMMARY

Parenting is a process that begins with the birth of the first child and continues through the maturity of all children in the family. As children develop from one major stage to the next, their needs and behavioral characteristics change. Similarly, as parents progress through the stages of adulthood, their developmental needs change, as well.

Throughout the life cycle the process of parenting is a reciprocal one. Each child affects the behavior of each parent, and each parent affects the behavior of each child, so that multidimensional relationships occur. When children are young, they are dependent on parents. As they approach adulthood, dependency needs become more balanced, and patterns of aid become more reciprocal. As parents approach later life, needs change, so that elderly parents become more dependent on their children. In a sense, the process of parenting has come full circle.

An intervening stage in this process, for most families, is that of grandparenting. There is great heterogeneity and diversity in today's grandparents, and their rights and responsibilities are not well articulated. Because grandparenthood is not self-initiated or voluntary, it differs from parenthood and other adult roles. But for many, it represents an opportunity to relive parenthood, or to have a second chance at it. Like parenting adult children and caring for elderly parents, grandparenting has few norms to guide relationships.

REFERENCES

ALDOUS, J. (1985). Parent-adult child relations as affected by the grandparent status. In V. Bengston & J. Robertson (Eds.), *Grandparenthood* (pp. 117–132). Beverly Hills: Sage.

AQUILINO, W. (1990). The likelihood of parent-adult child coresidence: Effects of family structure and parental characteristics. *Journal of Marriage and the Family, 52*(2), 405–419.

AQUILINO, W. (1991). Predicting parents' experiences with co-resident adult children. *Journal of Family Issues, 12*(3), 323–342.

AQUILINO, W., & SUPPLE, K. (1991). Parent-child relations and parents' satisfaction with living arrangements when adult children live at home. *Journal of Marriage and the Family, 53*(1), 13–27.

ATKINSON, A., & JAMES, D. (1991). The transition between active and adult parenting: An end and a beginning. *Family Perspective, 25*(1), 57–66.

BARANOWSKI, M. (1990). The grandfather-grandchild relationship: Meaning and exchange. *Family Perspective, 24*(3), 201–215.

BAYDAR, N., & BROOKS-GUNN, J. (1998). Profiles of grandmothers who help care for their grandchildren in the United States. *Family Relations, 47,* 385–393.

BENGSTON, V. (1985). Diversity and symbolism in grandparental roles. In V. Bengston & J. Robertson (Eds.), *Grandparenthood* (pp. 11–25). Beverly Hills: Sage.

BERNARD, J. (1975). *Women, wives, mothers.* Chicago: Adeline.

CHERLIN, A., & FURSTENBERG, F. (1985). Styles and strategies of grandparenting. In V. Bengston & J. Robertson (Eds.), *Grandparenthood* (pp. 97–116). Beverly Hills: Sage.

CLEMENS A., & AXELSON, L. (1985). The not-so-empty nest: The return of the fledgling adult. *Family Relations, 34*(2), 259–264.

CLINGEMPEEL, G., COLYAR, J., BRAND, E., & HETHERINGTON, M. (1992). Children's relationships with maternal grandparents: A longitudinal study of family structure and puberal status effects. *Child Development, 63*(6), 1404–1422.

COGSWELL, C., & HENRY, C. (1995). Grandchildren's perceptions of grandparental support in divorced and intact families. *Journal of Divorce & Remarriage, 23*(3/4), 127–150.

COLEMAN, M., GANONG, L., & CABLE, S. (1997). Beliefs about women's intergenerational family obligations to provide support before and after divorce and remarriage. *Journal of Marriage and the Family, 59,* 165–176.

CREASEY, G., & KOBLEWSKI, P. (1991). Adolescent grandchildren's relationships with maternal and paternal grandmothers and grandfathers. *Journal of Adolescence, 14*(4), 373–387.

DEPARLE, J. (1999, February 21). As welfare rolls shrink, load on relatives grow. *The New York Times,* pp. 1, 20.

DOKA, K., & MERTZ, M. (1988). The meaning and significance of great-grandparenthood. *The Gerontologist, 28*(2), 192–197.

EMICK, M., & HAYSLIP, B. (1996). Custodial grandparenting: New roles for middle-aged and older adults. *International Journal of Aging and Human Development, 43*(2), 135–154.

FULLER-THOMSON, E., MINKLER, M., & DRIVER, D. (1997). A profile of grandparents raising grandchildren in the United States. *The Gerontologist, 37,* 406–411.

GATTAI, F., & MUSATTI, T. (1999). Grandmothers' involvement in grandchildren's care: Attitudes, feelings, and emotions. *Family Relations, 48,* 35–42.

GIARRUSSO, R., SILVERSTEIN, M., & BENGTSON, V. (1996, Spring). Family complexity and the grandparent role. *Generations,* pp. 17–23.

GOLDSCHEIDER, F., & GOLDSCHEIDER, C. (1991). The intergenerational flow of income: Family structure and the status of black Americans. *Journal of Marriage and the Family, 53*(2), 499–508.

GOLDSCHEIDER, F., & GOLDSCHEIDER, C. (1998). The effects of childhood family structure on leaving and returning home. *Journal of Marriage and the Family, 60,* 745–756.

HALPERN, J., SHRODER, M., & CITERA, M. (1996). Perceptions by adult children of elderly parents' needs. *Psychological Reports, 78,* 571–577.

HAMON, R. (1992). Filial role enactment by adult children. *Family Relations, 41*(1), 91–96.

HODGSON, L. (1992). Adult grandchildren and their grandparents: The enduring bond. *International Journal of Aging and Human Development, 34*(3), 209–225.

HOYERT, D., & SELTZER, M. (1992). Factors related to the well-being and life activities of family caregivers. *Family Relations, 41*(1), 74–81.

HUNTER, A. (1997). Counting on grandmothers: Black mothers' and fathers' reliance on grandmothers for parenting support. *Journal of Family Issues, 18*(3), 251–269.

KAUFMAN, G., & UHLENBERG, P. (1998). Effects of life course transitions on the quality of relationships between adult children and their parents. *Journal of Marriage and the Family, 60,* 924–938.

KING, V., & ELDER, G. (1997). The legacy of grandparenting: Childhood experiences with grandparents and current involvement with grandchildren. *Journal of Marriage and the Family, 59,* 848–859.

KRAUSE, A., & HAVERKAMP, B. (1996). Attachment in adult child–older parent relationships: Research, theory, and practice. *Journal of Counseling & Development, 75,* 83–91.

LIN, G., & ROGERSON, P. (1995). Elderly parents and the geographic availability of their adult children. *Research on Aging, 17*(3), 303–331.

LUESCHER, K., & PILLEMER, K. (1998). Intergenerational ambivalence: A new approach to the study of parent-child relations in later life. *Journal of Marriage and the Family, 60,* 413–425.

MANCINI, J., & BLIESZNER, R. (1991). Aging parents and adult children: Research themes in intergenerational relations. In A. Booth (Ed.), *Contemporary families: Looking forward, looking back* (pp. 249–264). Minneapolis: National Council on Family Relations.

MARKS, N. (1996). Caregiving across the lifespan: National prevalence and predictors. *Family Relations, 45,* 27–36.

MINKLER, M., & ROE, K. (1996, Spring). Grandparents as surrogate parents. *Generations,* pp. 34–38.

MITCHELL, B., & GEE, E. (1996). "Boomerang kids" and midlife parental marital satisfaction. *Family Relations, 45,* 442–448.

MUI, A. (1995). Caring for frail elderly parents: A comparison of adult sons and daughters. *The Gerontologist, 35*(1), 86–91.

NOELKER, L., & WALLACE R. (1985). The organization of family care for impaired elderly. *Journal of Family Issues, 6*(1), 23–44.

PRUCHNO, R., & JOHNSON, K. (1996, Spring). Research on grandparenting: Review of current studies and future needs. *Generations,* pp. 65–70.

ROBERTSON, J., TICE, C., & LOEB, L. (1985). Grandparenthood: From knowledge to programs and policy. In V. Bengston & J. Robertson (Eds.), *Grandparenthood* (pp. 211–224). Beverly Hills: Sage.

SANDERS, G., & TRYGSTAD, D. (1989). Stepgrandparents and grandparents: The view from young adults. *Family Relations, 38*(1), 71–75.

SCHWARTZ, A. (1979). Psychological dependency: An emphasis on the later years. In P. Ragan (Ed.), *Aging parents* (pp. 116–125). Los Angeles: University of Southern California Press.

STARRELS, M., INGERSOLL-DAYTON, B., DOWLER, D., & NEAL, M. (1997). The stress of caring for a parent: Effects of the elder's impairment on an employed adult child. *Journal of Marriage and the Family, 59,* 860–872.

STEIN, C., WEMMERUS, V., WARD, M., GAINES, M., FREE-BERG, A., & JEWELL, T. (1998). "Because they're my parents": An intergenerational study of felt obligation and parental caregiving. *Journal of Marriage and the Family, 60,* 611–622.

SZINOVAEZ, M. (1997). Adult children taking parents into their homes: Effects of childhood living arrangements. *Journal of Marriage and the Family, 59,* 700–717.

THOMAS, J. (1989). Gender perceptions of grandparenthood. *International Journal of Aging and Human Development, 29*(4), 269–282.

THOMAS, J. (1990). The grandparent role: A double bind. *International Journal of Aging and Human Development, 3l*(3), 169–177.

THOMPSON, L., & WALKER, A. (1984). Mothers and daughters: Aid patterns and attachment. *Journal of Marriage and the Family, 46*(2), 313–322.

THOMPSON, R., TINSLEY, B., SCALORA, M., & PARKE, R. (1989). Grandparents' visitation rights: Legalizing the ties that bind. *American Psychologist, 44*(9), 1217–1222.

TRYGSTAD, D., & SANDERS, G. (1989). The significance of step-grandparents. *International Journal of Aging and Human Development, 29*(2), 119–134.

UMBERSON, D. (1992). Relationships between adult children and their parents: Psychological consequences for both generations. *Journal of Marriage and the Family, 54*(3), 664–674.

U.S. BUREAU OF THE CENSUS. (1997). *Statistical abstract of the United States: 1997* (117th ed.). Washington, DC: U.S. Department of Commerce.

WALKER, A., & PRATT, C. (1991). Daughters' help to mothers: Intergenerational aid versus caregiving. *Journal of Marriage and the Family, 53*(1), 3–12.

WALKER, A., PRATT, C., & EDDY, L. (1995). Informal caregiving to aging family members: A critical review. *Family Relations, 44,* 402–411.

WALKER, A., PRATT, C., & OPPY, N. (1992). Perceived reciprocity and family caregiving. *Family Relations, 41*(1), 82–85.

WHITE, L. (1992). The effect of parental divorce and remarriage on parental support for adult children. *Journal of Family Issues, 13*(2), 234–250.

WHITE, L., & ROGERS, S. (1997). Strong support but uneasy relationships: Coresidence and adult children's relationships with their parents. *Journal of Marriage and the Family, 59,* 700–717.

CHAPTER 5

Becoming a More Effective Parent: Contemporary Strategies

Because of the eagerness of parents for support and guidance in rearing their children, a number of strategies for child rearing have evolved over the last two decades to help parents become more effective. Most have been reflective of the social nature of our society at the time and therefore have been discarded as they have become inappropriate or inconsistent with prevailing attitudes and practices. Many strategies have been introduced to parents simply by the publication of books designed specifically for them. Others have been more formalized in the sense that they have been "taught" to parents by professionals. More recently, strategies have been developed in kits, books, and/or videos intended to be taught to parents in the workshop format over a specified period of time, usually no longer than 6 to 8 weeks.

This chapter discusses some of the contemporary strategies for parenting that are used by schools, agencies, churches, and other groups to help parents become more effective:

1. Systematic Training for Effective Parenting (STEP)—developed by Dr. Don Dinkmeyer and Dr. Gary McKay and based on the work of Dr. Rudolf Dreikurs and Dr. Alfred Adler.
2. Active Parenting TODAY—developed by Dr. Michael Popkin, based on ideas proposed by Dr. Alfred Adler, Dr. Rudolf Dreikurs, and Dr. Carl Rogers.
3. How to Talk So Kids Will Listen—developed by Ms. Adele Fabish and Ms. Elaine Mazlish and based on work of Dr. Haim Ginott.
4. Parents as Teachers—developed by The National Parents as Teachers Center; a home-visitation program for mothers and children from birth through age 4; designed to help mothers promote development in language, social, and cognitive areas.
5. Nurturing Programs—implemented through Family Development Resources; home- and group-based programs for parents and children from birth through adolescence, with special programs available for Hispanic, foster, adoptive, and teen parents, and for par-

ents of children with special needs; designed to treat and prevent child and adolescent maltreatment.
6. Assertive Discipline—developed by Lee and Marlene Canter, based on their earlier success with this model in school classroom management.
7. The National Extension Parent Education Model—developed by Charles Smith, Dorothea Cudaback, Wallace Goddard, and Judith Myers-Wall to be used by extension specialists and other professionals in parenting programs.
8. Partners for Fragile Families—developed by Pamela Wilson and Jeffery Johnson; addresses young fathers' real experiences and provides support, information, and motivation on issues involving parenthood, relationships, sexuality, employability, and manhood.
9. Growing Together—developed and disseminated by American Guidance Service to meet the needs of at-risk teen mothers; focuses on practical methods to help young parents cope with their own needs and those of their infants.
10. Achieve! Success for Young Fathers—developed and disseminated by American Guidance Service for teen fathers; includes information for those not married and not living with the mother.
11. Strengthening Stepfamilies—developed by Elizabeth Einstein and Linda Albert; focuses on the development of the stepfamily and stepparent-child relationships.

Since it is not possible to provide an in-depth description of each strategy, only the most salient aspects will be discussed. Relevant research will be included when available. Finally, a brief comparison and evaluation of these strategies will conclude the chapter.

SYSTEMATIC TRAINING FOR EFFECTIVE PARENTING

The principles upon which Systematic Training for Effective Parenting (STEP) is based date to more than 65 years ago, when Alfred Adler, a psychiatrist, conducted open family-counseling sessions in Vienna. The sessions were open to the public as well as being designed to help the family in question. These groups were closed in the mid-1930s by Austrian fascists. Some of Adler's students came to the United States and established family centers based on Adler's principles. Perhaps Adler's best-known student was Rudolf Dreikurs, who founded child guidance and Family Education Association centers in Chicago. Parent-education study groups used Dreikurs's books *The Challenge of Parenthood* and *Children: The Challenge.* Two individuals who studied with Dreikurs, Don Dinkmeyer and Gary McKay, in 1973 published *Raising a Responsible Child* and in 1976 published a comprehensive package of parent-education materials called Systematic Training for Effective Parenting (STEP), based on Adlerian principles. The program was revised in 1997 (Dinkmeyer, McKay, & Dinkmeyer, 1997a).

Both Adler and Dreikurs advocated a democratic family atmosphere, which focused on encouragement, mutual respect, discipline that is consistent with behavior, firm limits, offering choices, making suggestions, and joint decision making by parents and children. Their emphasis was on producing socially responsible children, the basic requirements for which are listed in the Highlights.

The STEP kit, available in both English and Spanish, includes a detailed leader's manual, one parent's handbook, a video for parent educators on how to lead a successful parenting program, and two videos that demonstrate STEP principles in contemporary examples. The materials in the *Leader's Resource Guide* include detailed session guides, group-discussion guides, reproducible information sheets, 11 handouts on drugs and drug-abuse information, script for videos, supplemental activities to provide additional discussion and practice of STEP principles, 14 sheets for distribution on special topics of interest to parents, a certificate of participation, publicity aids, and a parent survey and evaluation form that may be used as

pre- and posttests (Dinkmeyer et al., 1997a). Seven sessions, lasting from 1.5 to 2 hours weekly, are recommended to be conducted with about 12 group members. In each session a specific topic or concept is presented and parents view a videotape of situations and solutions.

The 1997 version of *The Parent's Handbook* (Dinkmeyer, McKay, & Dinkmeyer, 1997b) uses less academic language than the previous versions and includes all essential topics covered in the seven sessions—understanding yourself and your child, understanding beliefs and feelings, encouraging your child and yourself, listening and talking to your child, helping children cooperate, discipline that makes sense, and choosing your approach. In addition, the handbook includes topics on single parents, stepfamilies, cooperation in the family, schoolwork and homework, drugs, violence, and gangs. It also provides at-home activities for parents and family members.

The Goals of Misbehavior

Implicit in the Adlerian approach to understanding behavior is the notion that behavior is purposive

---

HIGHLIGHTS

Basic Requirements for Producing Socially Responsible Children

Democratic relationships based on mutual respect; a feeling that the child deserves to be treated with both firmness and kindness

Encouragement that communicates respect, love, support, and valuing the child as a person

The use of natural and logical consequences to replace reward and punishment, which enables the child to develop responsibility, self-discipline, and judgment

A basic understanding of human behavior that helps parents to maintain a consistent approach to human relationships

Source: Dinkmeyer, D., & McKay, G. (1996). *Raising a responsible child* (Rev. ed.). New York: Fireside.

and best understood in terms of its social consequences (Dinkmeyer et al., 1997a). Dreikurs expanded on this notion by identifying the four goals of misbehavior: attention getting, power, revenge, and display of inadequacy. Since misbehavior serves a purpose, it is best understood by observing the consequences—observing the parent's reaction to the misbehavior. The child's response to the parent's attempts at correction serve to reveal the purpose of the misbehavior, which usually stems from the child's major goal in life—to belong. According to these authors, misbehaving children are discouraged; they do not believe they can belong in useful ways. Therefore they seek to belong through misbehavior (Dinkmeyer et al., 1997b).

Dreikurs's four categories of misbehavior are seen as "goals" in the sense that the misbehavior achieves something for the child. The first goal, attention, is almost universal in young children. If children cannot gain attention in constructive ways, they will seek it in destructive ways, especially if they feel that they can belong only by receiving attention. When this occurs, STEP advises parents to either ignore the misbehavior or pay attention to it in ways the child does not expect.

The second goal is power. Children who seek power may feel that they are important only when they are the boss. When children seek power, STEP recommends that parents refrain from becoming angry and disengage themselves from the power struggle. If the struggle for power continues, children may alter their desire and pursue the third goal.

Revenge is a goal that children pursue when they feel they must hurt others as they believe they have been hurt. The child finds a place by being cruel and disliked. Parents need to realize that vengeful behavior stems from discouragement, and they should avoid retaliation. Remaining calm and showing goodwill are necessary to improve the parent-child relationship.

When children continue a war of revenge with their parents, they may sometimes give up and seek to be excused for their misbehavior by displaying the fourth goal, inadequacy. These children are extremely discouraged and have given up hope of succeeding. Normally parents, too, feel despair, and children will respond to parents passively or fail to respond at all. When displays of inadequacy occur, parents need to eliminate criticism and focus on the child's strengths and assets, encouraging any efforts to improve.

Since children usually are unaware of their goals, their behavior and intentions toward their parents will change only if parents change their approaches. Before parents can change, it is important for them to understand more about their children and themselves. For example, STEP emphasizes that emotions are based on beliefs, and children learn to use their emotions to achieve one or more of the four goals. Often, beliefs are faulty because interpretations of experiences are inaccurate. Factors that contribute to beliefs are family atmosphere and values, sex roles played by parents, family constellation, and parents' attitudes and behavior toward children. The last factor is a significant one. STEP differentiates between "good" parents, who are so involved with their children that they believe they must do everything for them, and "responsible" parents, who give their children choices and let them experience the results of their decisions.

Reflective Listening

STEP emphasizes both the receptive and the expressive aspects of communication in effective, responsive parenting. The parent attempts to ascertain what the child is feeling when she communicates. Reflective listening, then, involves analyzing a child's "feeling" message and putting the feeling word into a response. For example, C (child): "That teacher is unfair! I'll never do well in that class!" and P (parent): "You're feeling angry and disappointed, and you've given up" (Dinkmeyer et al., 1997b).

Closed responses deny children a right to their feelings by demonstrating the listener's unwillingness to accept and understand; on the other hand, open responses acknowledge the child's right to his feelings by demonstrating that the listener both accepts and understands the feeling and the message.

Expressive Aspects of Communication

The expressive aspects of communication that are emphasized in STEP are the following: (1) problem ownership, (2) "I" messages, and (3) exploring alternatives.

Problem Ownership. The principle of problem ownership described by Thomas Gordon (1975) in his Parent Effectiveness Training (PET) program states that child behaviors fall into three categories: (a) behaviors that are unacceptable to the parent because they interfere with the parent's rights or prevent the parent from having his or her needs met (the parent owns the problem); (b) behaviors that indicate the child's needs are not being met or that the child is unhappy, frustrated, or in trouble (the child owns the problem); and (c) behaviors that cause neither parent nor child a problem (the no-problem area). The contention is that differentiation of problem ownership is critical because a different set of skills is used in each case. When the parent owns the problem, he or she uses "confrontation skills" in its solution; when the child owns the problem, the parent uses "helping skills" in its solution.

"I" Messages. Equally important to listening effectively to children is talking effectively to them. Most parents use ineffective methods of communicating, such as sending a "solution message" or a "put-down message." The emphasis on "I" messages (a confrontation skill) rather than on "you" messages helps parents to understand that if they give the child a statement of fact about how the parent is feeling in a given situation, they are less likely to be met with resistance and rebellion. For example, when a child has a messy room, a "you" message might be: "You are so lazy; this room is a mess." An alternative "I" message might be: "I get frustrated when I'm trying to keep the house clean and I see that you haven't done your share." The second alternative avoids implying that the child is "bad" and places the responsibility with the child for modifying her behavior. "I" messages have three components: (1) a statement of feeling; (2) a nonjudgmental description of the child's behavior; and (3) a description of the tangible effects of the child's behavior on the parent. Gordon (1975) suggested using active listening when the child owns the problem and "I" messages when the parent owns the problem.

The original "I" message described by Gordon has been expanded to include the "appreciative I-message" designed to express positive feelings and the "preventive I-message" to inform others ahead of time about things that are desired or needed (Burr, 1990). Burr recommends the use of "we" statements when the problem is one of mutual concern to parent and child. An "I" statement indicates an individual has a problem; a "we" statement indicates that someone thinks a group or a relationship has a problem. For example, a parent who is trying to help solve a family dispute about which TV program to watch may observe that the children are being too inconsiderate of one another. She might say, "We have a problem bigger than just what program to watch tonight. It's that we're not being considerate of one another."

"We" statements, then, are declarative sentences that try to locate tendencies, patterns, problems, thoughts, feelings, or other experiences in a relationship or a group rather than in a person. These statements usually create less defensiveness and resistance than compound "I" messages. They foster the cooperative, mutually facilitating aspects of the relationship rather than a somewhat competitive or adversarial situation that leads to defensiveness. The concept of "we" messages adds to rather than replaces the "I" messages, and a combination of "I" and "We" statements facilitates communication.

Exploring Alternatives. There are times when reflective listening and "I" and "we" messages do not solve problems; that is, children need help in considering various courses of action. This process should not be confused with giving advice. STEP outlines the process of exploring alternatives. See the Highlights for steps in using this problem-solving approach.

In addition, STEP emphasized the importance of friendly conversation in a calm atmosphere in the face of conflict; avoiding sarcasm, ridicule, pressure, and labels that indicate lack of confidence; and communicating faith in the child through words, gestures, and tone of voice.

Natural and Logical Consequences

A key element in the STEP approach is the utilization of natural and logical consequences as an alternative to reward and punishment. Natural consequences are those that occur naturally as a result of behavior. For example, a child who refuses to eat goes hungry or a child who refuses to wear mittens gets cold hands (Dinkmeyer et al., 1997b). Logical consequences are those that are imposed as a result of behavior but are logically related to the behavior. They express the reality of the social order and acknowledge mutual rights and mutual respect. For example, a child who does not put his dirty clothes in the hamper by wash time must wash them himself. The purpose of allowing natural consequences to occur and of designing logical consequences is to encourage children to make re-

sponsible decisions, not to force their submission (Dinkmeyer et al., 1997b). Several principles are given in STEP to guide the use of natural and logical consequences. See the Highlights for these principles.

There are three steps in applying consequences: (1) Provide choices and accept the child's decision; (2) as a consequence is followed through, assure the child that there will be an opportunity to change the decision later; and (3) if the child repeats the misbehavior, extend the time that must elapse before the child may try again.

STEP points out that there are some major differences between applying logical consequences and punishment. First, logical consequences express the impersonal reality of the social order and acknowledge mutual rights and mutual respect, whereas punishment expresses the power of personal authority. Second, logical consequences are logically related to misbehavior, whereas punishment rarely is. Third, logical consequences imply no element of moral judgment, whereas punishment tells the child she is bad. Fourth, logical consequences focus on present and future behavior, whereas punishment focuses on what is past. Fifth, logical consequences are based on goodwill, and punishment is associated with threats or retaliation. Finally, logical consequences permit choice, whereas punishment demands obedience (Dinkmeyer et al., 1997b). STEP includes excellent examples of applying logical consequences in common situations.

The Family Meeting

The final component of democratic family relationships outlined in STEP is the family meeting. There is a regularly scheduled meeting of all family members where beliefs, values, wishes, complaints, plans, questions, and suggestions are discussed. All members participate as equals in the family meeting, the goals of which are communication and agreements. If suggested guidelines for family meetings are met, then they can provide a resource for solving problems, giving encouragement, and planning family recreation.

Other STEP Programs

Since the publication of STEP, the Dinkmeyers and McKays have developed several other programs. STEP/Teen, originally designed in 1983 and revised in 1998 (Dinkmeyer, McKay, McKay, & Dinkmeyer, 1998), was designed for parents of junior high and high school youth. The format of the program is similar to that of STEP in that it brings parents together in a structured framework of group discussions led by a leader, readings are assigned, recordings dramatizing true-to-life teen/parent situations are used, and activities with the goal of changing negative family behavior are provided. The guide for parents focuses on topics of the weekly meetings and provides exercises to do at home.

Vignettes are available on video- or audiocassettes that depict everyday problems such as smoking, low grades, and curfews, as well as more difficult scenarios, including unwanted pregnancy,

an overprotective single parent, building self-esteem, gangs, and using drugs. See the Highlights for more information about topics included for group discussions. The complete STEP/Teen kit includes a leader's guide, *Parenting Teenagers* (a 10-chapter text for parents), two video- or five audiocassettes, a booklet entitled "STEP for Substance Abuse," a discussion-guidelines poster, certificate of participation blackline master, publicity materials, and a storage box.

The Next STEP (Dinkmeyer, McKay, Dinkmeyer, Dinkmeyer, & McKay, 1987) was designed as a follow-up to STEP and has the goal of enhancing parental skills learned in STEP and STEP/Teen. Like the two earlier programs, this one is designed to show parents how to help children learn to be responsible, but the focus is on parents' needs and rights and on helping parents change their own behavior. The program is implemented in six sessions. The parents' handbook, *The Effective Parent,* provides reading material and activities for implementing concepts. An opportunity is provided for parents at each session to present a problem they are having in implementing their STEP skills at home. Using a seven-step process, the group analyzes the problem and offers suggestions for solving it. Three-segment videocassettes demonstrate how a problem-solving group works and models effective family meetings. Topics included in the Next STEP are found in the Highlights.

Early Childhood STEP, designed by Dinkmeyer, McKay, McKay, Dinkmeyer, and Dinkmeyer (1997), adopts and expands the proven principles and techniques of STEP for infants,

Topics in STEP/Teen

Understanding yourself and your teenager
Changing your response to your teen
Communicating respect and encouragement
Encouraging cooperation and solving problems
Using consequences to build responsibility
Deciding what to do—Parts I and II

HIGHLIGHTS_____

Topics Included in the Next STEP

Building your own self-esteem
Realizing you're not perfect and don't have to
    be
Reducing stress in yourself and your child
Choosing to change beliefs
Asserting your rights
Controlling the situation, not the child

toddlers, and preschoolers. The program follows the same format as other programs, implemented in seven sessions. The materials include a *Leader's Resource Guide;* a parent's handbook, titled *Parenting Young Children;* two videocassettes that model skills; a video for leaders; and other materials for parents, for publicity, and for evaluation. Materials also are available in Spanish. See Highlights for topics included in the program.

Research Relating to the Adlerian Approach

Systematic research relating to the effects of parent education using the Adlerian approach, and STEP specifically, has been sparse. The *Leader's Guide* (Dinkmeyer et al., 1997b) lists 41 studies relating to the various STEP programs. However, a full reference was not provided for any study. Information regarding the research conducted can be obtained from American Guidance Service. There is incon-

HIGHLIGHTS_____

Topics Included in Early Childhood STEP

Understanding young children
Understanding young children's behavior
Building self-esteem in the early years
Listening and talking to young children
Helping young children learn to cooperate
Discipline for young children
Young children's social and emotional development

sistent evidence concerning its potential value in the lives of children whose parents have been trained.

Several early studies indicated that following the implementation of the STEP Program, participants perceive their children's behavior more positively and demonstrate greater acceptance of and trust for their children. The children of participants perceive themselves as being more accepted by their peer group and as more capable of helping others in social situations (Dinkmeyer, 1979; Summerlin & Ward, 1978; Williams, Omizo, & Abrams, 1984).

ACTIVE PARENTING TODAY

Active Parenting TODAY, a video-based parent-education program, originally was published in 1983 and was revised in 1993 by Dr. Michael Popkin (1996). The complete program kit includes videotapes, a leader's guide, a parent's handbook and action guide, a promotion packet, promotional brochures, and announcement posters. Workshops to train Active Parenting leaders in building skills in parent-education and small-group leadership are conducted regularly in several locations across the United States.

Concepts included in the Active Parenting program are based on ideas proposed by Alfred Adler, Rudolf Dreikurs, and Carl Rogers. Since many of these concepts, included in STEP, have been discussed earlier, they will not be discussed here. Concepts and parenting skills in 40 vignettes are presented in six 2-hour sessions. Popkin published a Spanish version of the Active Parenting TODAY program in 1999. Topics include The Active Parent; Developing Responsibility: Discipline; and Winning Cooperation. The leader presents new information; a video demonstrates concepts; participants engage in group activities to practice skills; and parents implement skills in home activities. See the Highlights for more information.

Since the original Active Parenting program was developed, Popkin, Gard, and Montgomery (1996) have developed 1,2,3,4 Parents, a video-based discussion program for parents of children 1

HIGHLIGHTS

Topics for Active Parenting TODAY Sessions

The Active Parent	Styles of parenting What kind of children do we want to raise? "Freedom within limits" Family-enrichment activities
Understanding Your Child	The ABCs of behavior Four goals of misbehavior Parenting and anger Developing self-esteem
Instilling Courage	Avoiding discouragement Four methods of encouragement The encouragement circle exercise
Developing Responsibility	Who owns the problem? "I" messages Natural and logical consequences Mutual respect
Winning Cooperation	Avoiding communication blocks Active communication Listening for feelings Expressing love
The Democratic Family in Action	The family council meeting Handling parents in a group Emphasizing the family unit Raising a "we" generation

Source: Popkin, M. (1993). *Active Parenting TODAY.* Atlanta: Active Parenting.

to 4 years of age. Although it was designed for all parents, it especially targets low-income parents, parents experiencing family problems, parents determined to be at risk, parents without partners, and/or parents with several children.

Active Parenting of Teens (Popkin, 1990) uses a similar format to the original Active Parenting program and is implemented in six sessions. See Highlights for topics included in this program. The materials include a parent's handbook, a leader's guide, and two videos.

Parents on Board, a parent involvement program for parents of 4- to 14-year-olds, was designed to teach parents how to build academic success in their children. It is a video and discussion program implemented in three 1-hour ses-

sions. The parent's handbook accompanying the program, *Helping Your Child Succeed in School,* consists of eight chapters that are covered in the three group sessions: Preparing your Child to

HIGHLIGHTS

Topics Included in Active Parenting of Teens

The active parent
Instilling courage and self-esteem
Developing responsibility
Winning cooperation through communication
The challenge of alcohol and drugs
Parenting and teen sexuality

Succeed, Encouraging Positive Behavior, and Re-inforcing your Child's Academic Skills (Popkin, Youngs, & Healy, 1995). Other Active Parenting programs include Windows: Healing and Helping through Loss, a video-based education program for parents experiencing loss; Active Christian Parenting; Free the Horses, a video-based self-esteem curriculum; and Active Teaching.

Active Parenting also publishes a magazine through which interested people may keep up with the activities of leaders and the director; locations of workshops; materials offered by Active Parenting, Inc.; and the other resources that may be used in parent education.

HOW TO TALK SO KIDS WILL LISTEN

How to Talk So Kids Will Listen is a unique parent-education program because it is a self-contained course designed to be used and administered by parents themselves. Any motivated person can serve as the chairperson, or the leadership role can be shared. No one needs special training, since the chairperson merely has to read simple directions, distribute materials, and operate the cassette player. It is a seven-session multimedia approach for use by a group of 6–12 parents who get together and discuss the problems of typical families. The program was designed by Adele Faber and Elaine Mazlish (1980), each a parent of three children, and it is based on 10 years of their experiences with parent-guidance groups led by Haim Ginott.

The kit includes a framework for each meeting, and the authors conduct each session on tape. Parents have their own workbooks, and two books by the authors (*How to Talk So Kids Will Listen and Listen So Kids Will Talk* [Faber & Mazlish, 1980] and *Liberated Parents: Liberated Children* [Faber & Mazlish, 1974]) are required for each participant. Discussions and role-playing are incorporated. See the Highlights for the topics included in the program.

In each session, parents glean information about how to speak to and act toward children in ways that communicate acceptance, respect, worthiness as an individual, and empathy. Practical ex-

"Saying it with a word" is a strategy to engage cooperation of children.

amples of dialogue between parent and child to communicate these feelings are provided, as well as examples of inappropriate methods of communicating. See the Highlights for selected examples of skills for engaging cooperation and inappropriate methods that may deter cooperation.

HIGHLIGHTS

Topics for How to Talk So Kids Will Listen

Helping children deal with their feelings
Engaging cooperation
Providing alternatives to punishment
Encouraging autonomy
Using praise effectively
Freeing children from playing roles

Inappropriate Methods That Deter Cooperation

METHOD	EXAMPLE
Blaming and accusing	"Look at the dirty footprints you put on my clean kitchen floor. You never consider how hard I work."
Name-calling	"You are the sloppiest person. Just look at your room!"
Threats	"If you don't start doing your share around here, I'm going to cut your allowance."
Commands	"Take the garbage out this minute, and no back talk, young man."
Lecturing and moralizing	"Now, do you think that was a nice thing to say about your friend? You should learn to treat your friends the way you want to be treated."
Warnings	"Don't step off the sidewalk. You'll get hit by a car."
Martyrdom statements	"Why are you doing this to me, hard as I work?"
Comparisons	"Why can't you try as hard in school as your sister does?"
Sarcasm	"You knew you had to get up early, but you were so smart and stayed up until midnight."
Prophecy	"If you continue in the same manner, you'll never amount to anything."

Source: Adapted from Faber, A., & Mazlish, E. (1980). *How to talk so kids will listen.* New York: Avon.

Skills for Engaging Cooperation

SKILL	EXAMPLE
Describe (what you see or the problem).	"Your dirty clothes are on the floor in your room."
Give information.	"The battery in the flashlight will last longer when you turn it off after each use."
Say it with a word.	(when milk is left out of the refrigerator) "Susie, the milk."
Talk about your feelings.	"I am frustrated because you are making so much noise that I can't hear your father on the telephone."
Write a note.	(taped to basket of clean laundry) "Marlin, please fold me."

Many experts have regarded praise as an effective motivator of behavior. However, Ginott believed that often the most well-meaning praise could bring unexpected reactions. For example, praise can lead to doubt of the praiser (for example, you look awful but someone tells you how nice you look), can lead to immediate denial ("I know I look awful"), can be viewed as a threat ("I probably won't look good the next time, either"), can cause one to focus on his weaknesses ("I'm not really that attractive"), can create anxiety and interfere with activity ("I'll never be able to do that well again"), or can be seen as manipulation ("I wonder what she wants of me.").

Instead of using praise, Faber and Mazlish recommend that the adult describe with appreciation what she feels or sees. ("Your room looks so clean. I see that you've put everything away, vacuumed, and made your bed. It's such a pleasure to see how attractive your room looks.") In this way the child is able to praise herself ("I really did a good job of getting my room clean.").

Faber and Mazlish (1987) developed an additional program for parents, Siblings Without Rivalry. In this program parents are taught how to help children deal with their feelings about one another, how to keep children separate and unequal, how to assist siblings in roles, what to do when kids fight, and how to use problem-solving techniques. These two programs, based on the ideas of Haim Ginott, are relatively inexpensive and appear to be more appropriate for middle-class parents, since parents must have the resources and motivation to implement the program. The material can be easily understood by middle-class parents and includes many cartoon-type drawings to illustrate concepts. However, research relating to the effectiveness of these strategies is unavailable.

PARENTS AS TEACHERS

The Parents as Teachers (PAT) program was established by the Early Childhood Development Act, passed by the Missouri Legislature in 1984, which authorized state funding to support parent-education services (birth through age 4) and child

screening (ages 1 through 4) in all local school districts (Parents as Teachers National Center, 1993). The first funds were appropriated in the 1985–1986 school year, and by the year 2000 all families in the state with children under the age of 3 who wish to participate were included. PAT has been replicated in more than 1,000 sites in the United States, and programs also have been established in five foreign countries. Adaptations include PAT programs designed for use in child-care centers and in the workplace, for teen parents, for Native Americans, for disadvantaged families, for families with special needs, for military families, and for families making the transition from homelessness.

Through PAT, parent educators help parents recognize everyday learning opportunities in their children's lives, beginning at birth. Parents may enroll during the last trimester of pregnancy. Ideally, the program reaches first-time parents, but different sorts of families have been enrolled, regardless of the number and age of the children. Parent educators provide parents with practical information and guidance in helping their children develop skills in the areas of language, social, and cognitive development. Further, practical ideas are provided to help parents stimulate curiosity in their children.

Personal visits, preferably in the home, are key components of the program. The parent educator observes the child in the natural setting and gives appropriate input to the family. The purpose and content of the home visits vary over the 3-year span. During pregnancy and the first 8 months after birth, parents are introduced to the program, goals are defined, child-rearing practices are recommended, parents are taught observational skills and how to talk to babies, and written materials related to the baby's development are discussed and left in the parents' homes.

In the 8- to 18-month period, four foundations of educational development form the core of the curriculum for the home visits: curiosity, social development, language, and intellectual development. Parents are urged to see themselves in three roles: as designer (designing a safe and stimulating environment that will stimulate the child's curiosity and allow for exploration and practice of developing skills), as consultant (responding promptly and enthusiastically to the child's overtures with appropriate language), and as authority figure (setting firm and consistent limits).

From 19 to 36 months, the abilities of a well-developed child serve as the basis for personal-visit discussions. Families are urged to view themselves as the child's educational managers, making decisions about alternative care situations. Practical aspects of child rearing such as child-proofing, selection of appropriate toys, toilet training, discipline, and sibling rivalry are topics of interest to many parents.

Throughout the 3-year period, parent educators keep records of the home visits, which are used to document the child's and family's progress. Each parent educator has a caseload of about 30 families.

Group meetings are scheduled approximately once each month to provide other staff in the program an opportunity for input, to present outside speakers (such as pediatricians and child psychologists), and to create opportunities for families to share successes and common concerns about their children's behavior and development. Some of these group meetings are held at night and on Saturdays to allow fathers and mothers who work outside the home to participate. Some PAT sites have parent resource centers where parents can bring their children to play, talk informally with the parent educator, use the materials and equipment, and visit with other parents.

Another component of PAT is the monitoring of each child's development. Developmental screening is conducted annually, beginning at age 1. Parents are reassured if children are developing on target and alerted if any developmental problems are identified. If necessary, parents are assisted with appropriate interventions. Parents also are taught how to monitor the child's development themselves.

Evaluations of 350 families who participated in the pilot phase of PAT found that when the program children reached age 3 and were compared with a matched comparison group, they were sig-nificantly more advanced than control children in language development, significantly ahead in problem solving and other intellectual abilities, and significantly advanced in demonstrating coping skills and positive relationships with adults. The pilot children were followed as they entered public school; after completing first grade, they scored significantly higher on standardized measures of reading and math achievement than did comparison children and were rated higher by their teachers in all areas evaluated, and a significantly higher proportion of PAT parents initiated contacts with teachers and school officials and took active roles in their children's learning.

Owen and Mulvihill (1994) evaluated the effectiveness of PAT for middle-class parents. Outcomes were assessed for mothers, fathers, and children when the children were 1, 2, and 3 years of age. No significant differences were found between PAT children and control children on a set of cognitive and language measures. Though all parents received high evaluations for the quality of parenting, PAT families were found to provide more developmentally stimulating environments for their children than the comparison group, even after controlling for baseline parent knowledge differences. These researchers concluded that the PAT program was effective in increasing qualities of parenting and the home environment. They proposed that the higher quality of the home environment of PAT families could have later significance for children.

The PAT program is implemented by the Parents as Teachers National Center, Inc., located at the University of Missouri in St. Louis. The center conducts institutes on program implementation. The week-long institutes cover organization and management, marketing and recruitment, home visits, group meetings, monitoring children's progress, and program evaluation. Educators and other professionals from across the United States, Canada, England, Saudi Arabia, Australia, and New Zealand have attended these institutes. The center also provides consultant services and in-service training. A national advisory board, consisting of leading educators and child-development specialists, assists in directing the center's activities.

NURTURING PROGRAMS

The Nurturing Programs originally were developed in the 1980s by Family Development Resources, founded by Stephen Bavolek (Bavolek & Bavolek, 1988). Both home- and group-based programs have been developed for parents and children from birth through adolescence, teen parents and their families, Hispanic families, parents of children with special learning needs, and foster and adoptive parents. Goals of the program are to help parents improve their nurturing in the following four areas: appropriate expectations of children, empathy, nonviolent behavior management, and appropriate family roles. Originally, the program was designed to treat and prevent child and adolescent maltreatment.

Professionals and paraprofessionals may be trained to develop and implement Nurturing Programs by attending workshops held in various locations in the United States, Canada, and Europe. Participants in these 2- to 3-day workshops learn about the Nurturing Program philosophy, how to help families develop appropriate expectations, empathic awareness, self-esteem, and alternatives to physical and emotional abuse, and how to implement the various programs.

The home-based program for parents and children from birth to 5 years consists of 45 sessions of 1.5 hours each that meet one day a week for 45 consecutive weeks. Parents meet with the home visitor for the first hour to learn a new concept regarding the self and parenting. The concept may be learned by engaging in role play, discussion, viewing an audiovisual program, or other strategies. The focus of the home sessions alternates between nurturing parenting skills and nurturing self skills. Then parents and children engage in "family nurturing time" for 30 minutes, learning new skills, discussing ideas, practicing infant and child massage (using massage techniques to teach children gentle touch), and having fun. Parents are taught appropriate activities to engage in with their children. Each home visit ends with the home visitor, parents, and children engaging in a family hug.

The group-based program for parents and children from birth to 5 years consists of 23 sessions of 2.5 hours each that meet one day a week for 23 consecutive weeks. Parents and children meet in groups concurrently. Parents as a group learn parenting skills for 40 minutes while the children engage in activities appropriate for their age level. Then parents and children engage in family nurturing time for 30 minutes, which consists of activities, games, songs, infant and child massage, and snacks. The facilitators model, instruct, and supervise parents in practicing new skills. Following the parent and children activities, parents increase their self-awareness and self-growth by learning ways to nurture themselves through discussion, role play, and art activities. Each session ends with a group hug to increase group cohesion, offer praise, and experience positive touch. Parents also are provided with home practice activities.

The Nurturing Program for parents and children ages 4 to 12 years follows the same format as the program for parents and children birth to 5 years except that the program consists of 15 sessions of 2.5 hours each that meet 1 day a week for 15 consecutive weeks. The program for adolescents consists of twelve 3-hour sessions. Parents and their teenage children (ages 12 to 19 years) attend the program together. Adults and adolescents meet in two separate groups for the first 70 minutes, followed by a 20-minute snack time. Then the next hour and a half is spent with parents and adolescents together in one large group. Activities for nurturing the self and for developing parenting and communication skills, relaxation exercises, and home practice applications are included. Each session ends with everyone participating in a large group hug.

Programs for the specialized groups include the same components, with activities and materials designed to meet their special needs. Materials have been developed in Spanish, for adults with moderate learning disabilities, and especially for African American families. Other available materials include an infant massage manual and instructional video, multicultural parenting guides, and an excellent pamphlet on child-centered coaching. Materials are published for either the home- or the group-based program. Evaluation tools also are provided. Four types of evaluation measures are used: affective (assessment of parenting attitudes), cognitive (tests of knowledge acquired), process (participants' feedback, self-assessment, self-reports, satisfaction ratings, facilitator observations), and retention/attendance rates (number finishing course).

ASSERTIVE DISCIPLINE

The Assertive Discipline strategy was developed by Lee Canter, a family-child counselor, and Marlene Canter, a teacher. Originally their ideas were aimed at educators to help with discipline in the classroom when they wrote *Assertive Discipline: A Take Charge Approach for Today's Educator* (Canter & Canter, 1976). Based on their successful training workshops for educators that implemented this approach, *Assertive Discipline for Parents* (Canter & Canter, 1985) was developed. Since then, workshops for parents have been conducted across the United States.

The Canters define *discipline* as "corrective action designed to help teach children more appropriate behavior." Under no circumstances, they claim, should discipline violate the physical or emotional well-being of children. They feel that assertive discipline is warranted when other approaches have failed to work. They believe that a parent needs to take charge in problem situations and let children know that the parent is the "boss." The message that a parent should get across is that he or she loves the child too much to let him misbehave; therefore, problem behavior must stop. Further, the Canters feel that it is equally important for parents to provide their children with direct and positive feedback when they change the

problem behavior. These strategists recognize that many parents are reluctant to "come on strong" with their children, and most do not know how to take charge.

Before parents are taught to implement an assertive discipline plan, the typical inappropriate responses that many parents use are discussed. Nonassertive responses are inappropriate because parents are not stating clearly what they want the child to do or they are not reinforcing their words with actions. These responses, then, communicate to the child that parents do not "mean business." Hostile responses usually result in negative feelings between parent and child and communicate to the child that the parent is out of control.

Once parents have learned to recognize inappropriate responses, they are ready to learn how to put an assertive discipline plan into action. The assertive discipline plan has three basic steps: communicate assertively, back up words with action, and lay down the law. According to the authors, to communicate effectively a parent must address the child with direct, assertive statements and "praise a child at least three times a day." The parent must back up her words with action by using disciplinary consequences for behavior, such as separation, taking away privileges, or grounding. However, the parent also should provide positive support when he "catches the child being good." Laying down the law includes setting up a systematic assertive discipline plan, using a "parent-saver" technique, and conducting a "lay-down-the-law" session. The assertive discipline plan includes specific behaviors to be changed, consequences for misbehavior, reinforcement to be used for positive behavior, and ways to monitor the child's actions. "Parent-saver" techniques, include establishing a discipline hierarchy with increasingly severe consequences, developing a contract, and marble mania. A "lay-down-the-law" session is a no-nonsense approach asserting parental authority in which the parents demand that the child change her problem behavior. [*Note:* The authors do not necessarily endorse these techniques.]

"Marble mania" is a parent-saver technique whereby children earn marbles to trade as rewards for "good" behavior.

Research Related to Assertive Discipline

No research could be located evaluating the effectiveness of assertive discipline as a parenting strategy. Although the approach incorporates some positive techniques from other strategies (reinforcement for "good" behavior, utilizing choices, selecting logical consequences, and developing a contract), the emphasis seems to be on a more authoritarian approach. Because the strategy incorporates aspects of several strategies—STEP, PET, and behavior modification—it is difficult to generalize from results related to any single strategy.

However, there is no question that assertive discipline is an extremely popular approach in school classroom management across the country. In many school systems, all teachers are expected to use this approach and receive in-service training in implementing it. Nevertheless, there is little research related to its success in schools. Even though the model stresses a reward system for appropriate behavior, it is the intervention procedures that make it popular as well as controversial.

Among the criticisms of the approach made by Gartrell (1987) and Hitz (1988) are the following:

1. The model does not facilitate the development of a positive self-concept, especially for young children, 4 to 8 years of age.

2. Desirable behavior is forced through power-assertion techniques rather than through developing responsible behavior rooted in ethical purposes. It appears that children learn only that behavior is good because it is rewarded or bad because it is punished.

3. Positive attitudes toward schoolwork and oneself are inhibited. The atmosphere seems to be one in which the attention is focused on who gets his name placed on the chalkboard rather than on academics. The fear and stigma of public punishment cannot be overestimated. As adults, our recollections of school often are those of only a negative nature.

4. The approach tends to turn teachers into managing technicians rather than to assist them in the development of problem-solving guidance techniques or professional judgment in altering curriculum. It overlooks the fact that appropriate curriculum and methods often prevent discipline problems.

5. Although positive reinforcement is recommended in the model, it is often ineffective and can be coercive and manipulative.

These criticisms may seem harsh, but no data to date have refuted them. Both Gartrell and Hitz emphasize the need for further research.

THE NATIONAL EXTENSION PARENT EDUCATION MODEL

The National Extension Parent Education Model was developed by a group of extension specialists to assist parent educators in developing and focusing their parent-education efforts (Smith, Cudaback, Goddard, & Myers-Wall, 1994). The model is not a parenting curriculum but, rather, an overview of parenting essentials. It includes sample objectives, reviews of the literature, and a list of available Extension parenting programs. The model, which became available in 1994, consists of the following components and critical parenting practices:

Take Care of Self—manage personal stress, manage family resources, offer support to other parents, ask for and accept support from others when needed, recognize one's own personal and parenting strengths, have a sense of purpose in setting child-rearing goals, and cooperate with one's child-rearing partners.

Understand—observe and understand one's children and their development and recognize how children influence and respond to what happens around them.

Guide—establish and maintain reasonable limits, provide children with developmentally appropriate opportunities to learn responsibility, convey fundamental values underlying basic human decency, teach problem-solving skills, monitor children's activities, and facilitate their contact with peers and adults.

Nurture—express affection and compassion; foster children's self-respect and hope; listen and attend to children's feelings and ideas; teach kindness; provide for the nutrition, shelter, clothing, health, and safety needs of one's children; celebrate life with one's children; and provide children with a name and a sense of heritage.

Motivate—teach children about themselves, others, and the world around them; stimulate curiosity, imagination, and the search for knowledge; create beneficial learning conditions; and help children process and manage information.

Advocate—find, use, and create community resources when needed to benefit one's children and the community of children; stimulate social change to create supportive environments for children and families; and build relationships with family, neighborhood, and community groups.

There are a variety of ways to implement this model. See Highlights for suggestions. The curriculum guide for this program includes a description of parent-education resources developed in various states and ordering information.

Materials to assist parent educators in developing parenting programs are available through county Extension offices throughout the country. County Extension specialists use these materials with individual parents and with groups of parents in developing more effective parenting skills.

PARTNERS FOR FRAGILE FAMILIES

Partners for Fragile Families was developed in 1990–1991 by Pamela Wilson and Jeffery M. Johnson to address young fathers' real experiences. In 25 sessions, support, information, and motivation on issues involving parenthood, relationships, sexuality, employability, and manhood are provided. The format of each session is guided discussion. Five sessions of approximately 1.5 hours are devoted to personal development, including topics such as values, manhood, stereotypes

Suggestions for Implementing the National Extension Parent Education Model

Parent-education groups

Newsletters

Home visits

Hospital programs

Community forums

Support groups

Learn-at-home activities

Social-change groups/liberation pedagogy

Parent-education resource centers

Radio programs

Mentor mother/grandparent programs

Newspaper articles/tabletop messages

Interagency support/collaboration

Community coalitions/task forces

Parent advisory groups

Source: Smith, C., Cudaback, D., Goddard, W., & Myers-Wall, J. (1994). *National extension parent education model of critical parenting practices.* Manhattan, KS: Kansas State University.

and manhood, and becoming self-sufficient. Another five sessions deal with life skills, including communication, decision making, dealing with stress, and coping with discrimination. Responsible fatherhood is discussed in seven sessions that include the following topics: fatherhood today, understanding the child-support system, understanding children's needs, a father's influence on his children, coping as a single father, building your child's self-esteem, and helping children learn. Four sessions are devoted to relationships, with discussion centering on expectations of relationships, conflict resolution/anger management, obtaining help from the support network, and male/female relationships. The last five sessions focus on health and sexuality. These discussions deal with men's health, substance abuse, sexuality, reducing sexual risks, and putting it all together.

Since 1997 the National Center for Strategic Non-profit Planning and Community Leadership (NPCL) in Washington, D.C., has provided training for using the curriculum. All materials in the program may be purchased from this agency. Materials include goals and objectives for each session, a materials checklist, handouts, suggested activities, and questions for discussion. An assessment package has been developed, which includes

baseline and interim checklists that connect program goals to participant interests and skills, knowledge and attitude assessment forms that can be used for pre- and posttests.

GROWING TOGETHER

This program for teen mothers was developed in 1992 by American Guidance Service. It was designed to teach positive behaviors to young mothers, such as setting goals; seeking help in the family, school, and community; and developing pride in themselves and their new role as parents. Further, it focuses on practical methods to help teen mothers cope with their own needs and those of their infants.

The program consists of six videos, each focusing on one topic of interest to teen parents. Program 1—"Just Like You"—deals with self-esteem. It presents ways to develop a solid foundation for the emotional health of the baby and ways to help the mother develop her own self-esteem. Program 2—"Out of Danger"—outlines and discusses the vulnerability of babies and steps their mothers can take to protect them. "Good Food for a Good Start" is the focus of Program 3, which teaches the fundamental principles of proper infant feeding. This session explains and encourages a healthy diet for both the baby and the mother. Program 4—"Strong and Healthy"—presents basic information the mother should know about maintaining the infant's health and her own. The program emphasizes a positive approach to healthy living and when to call the doctor in case of illness. "What My Baby Can Do" is the focus of Program 5. This session covers physical development, what to expect at each age, and how to foster normal infant development. The last session, Program 6—"Feelings, Family, and Friends"—focuses on social and emotional development through positive play activities, interaction with family, and finding support from friends.

A program format is included for each of the six sessions. Suggestions for in-class and out-of-class activities, reproducible blackline masters for handouts that may be used to reinforce concepts outlined in the videos, and minicharts also are provided. The program may be purchased from American Guidance Service.

ACHIEVE! SUCCESS FOR YOUNG FATHERS

This program was designed for teen fathers and includes information for those not married and not living with the child's mother. It is a documentary series of four videos of 15 minutes each. Videos depict men who have succeeded as young fathers, serving as mentors, who share ideas on how to fill the essential role of father in a baby's life. Ways to overcome stereotypes and peer pressure that can interfere with success are presented. Information provided is based on principles and components of successful programs throughout the country.

The following topics are included in the videos: Deciding to Succeed—Your Baby Needs You focuses on respecting self and baby and the joys of being a father; Practical Skills—How to Do Baby Care discusses sleep and feeding schedules, appropriate play, dealing with crying, health and safety, and handling visitation; Successful Communication—How to Talk and Listen focuses on talking with the mother of the baby, her parents,

the young father's parents, and communication skills; and the last session, Responsible Fatherhood: Taking Control of your Future, emphasizes the importance of finishing school, getting help with starting a career, and sexual responsibility to secure the future. The program may be purchased from American Guidance Service (no date).

STRENGTHENING STEPFAMILIES

This program was designed by Elizabeth Einstein and Linda Albert. It includes readings, recordings, discussion, and at-home activities focusing on stepfamily structure, strengthening couple relationships, effective relationships with stepchildren, children's adjustment, and developmental stages of the stepfamily. It is implemented in five 1.5- to 2-hour sessions. The complete program includes a leader's guide; a participant's handbook, *Strengthening Your Stepfamily;* an encouragement packet with 30 at-home activities; three audiocassettes; wall charts; blackline masters; publicity aids; and certificates of participation. It may be purchased from American Guidance Service.

COMPARISON AND EVALUATION OF CONTEMPORARY STRATEGIES

Similarities

Selected strategies for parenting described in this chapter share several similarities and some differences, which are summarized in the Highlights. [*Note:* Strategies designed for special populations are not included.] The most obvious similarity is the emphasis on a democratic relationship between parents and children, with the child's needs and feelings respected as being valid and as being highly correlated with behavior. Only in the case of assertive discipline are power-assertion techniques emphasized. Punitive techniques (shouting, threatening, ridiculing, shaming, and physical punishment) are not advocated, whereas inductive techniques, use of encouragement, and development of self-control are emphasized. Parenting behaviors are manifested in a context of warmth, nurturance, and acceptance in all the strategies, again with the exception of assertive discipline techniques, and most strategies recommend imposing certain limits.

Communication is seen as the major component of a positive parent-child relationship in most of the strategies. PAT emphasizes understanding the baby's cues and the importance of listening and demonstrates to parents ways to stimulate language development. STEP encourages reflective listening and open responses. Assertive discipline emphasizes assertive communication, and Active Parenting emphasizes active listening, avoiding communication blocks, and "I" messages. The Nurturing Program encourages the use of "I" statements when the parent wants to send a message about her feelings, thoughts, and needs; and "you" messages when the parent wants to give the child a choice, to praise her, or to gain clarification of the child's feelings (such as "Stephen, you have a choice. You can clean your room now, or you can clean your room later. However, if your room is not cleaned by 6 p.m., you can't watch TV tonight. It's your choice.") (Kaplan & Bavolek, 1996). The National Extension Parent Education Model encourages parents to listen and attend to children's feelings and ideas. In How to Talk So Kids Will Listen, the emphasis is on what the parent says rather than on listening to the child.

Identifying the causes of children's behavior is emphasized in all the strategies except assertive discipline. STEP, especially, emphasizes that all misbehavior has a goal that is based on faulty beliefs, and parents need to understand the beliefs and identify the goals before they can effectively deal with the behavior. PAT and the Nurturing Program provide parents with information on children's development in order for parents to gain an understanding of developmentally appropriate behavior and to understand how children respond to what happens around them. Active Parenting, which includes STEP concepts, emphasizes problem ownership and goals of misbe-

havior to understand both the parent's and the child's behavior. In assertive discipline no concern for the cause of children's behavior is demonstrated, but parents decide what specific behavior they want to change.

Finally, most strategies have as their goal the raising of a responsible child. The goals that are implicit in most of the strategies are helping parents and children resolve conflict in ways that assist children in becoming more responsible, providing choices, promoting decision making, being consistent in demands, and emphasizing the needs of parents as well as children. Further, modeling of responsible behavior of the child is advocated as a way to foster responsibility in children.

Differences

The major difference among the strategies seems to be the degree of emphasis given to various principles. STEP and assertive discipline stress changing the child's behavior, but the mechanism for doing so is different in each strategy. Assertive discipline uses explicit rewards and punishments to change behavior, whereas STEP focuses on changing children's behavior by the use of natural and logical consequences. Even though other strategies focus less on changing children's behavior, they address the issue through the use of problem-solving sessions or changes in communication techniques.

The use of parental power is the technique that separates assertive discipline techniques from the remaining strategies. Whereas other strategies seek to reduce the power of the parent and to create a more egalitarian relationship, assertive discipline enhances the parent as the powerful authority figure. Further, this strategy forcefully employs the use of punishment more than other strategies. The Nurturing Program strongly discourages the use of physical punishment and demonstrates many ways to touch the child appropriately. Parents are taught ways to be nurturing in routine activities such as feeding, bath, and bed times. However, the program does encourage parents to use time-out for

Similarities and Differences among Selected Strategies

Approach	STRATEGY					
	STEP	PAT	Nurturing	Active Parenting	How to Talk So Kids Will Listen	Assertive Discipline
Minimizes use of parental power and emphasizes democratic relationships.	×	×	×	×	+	0
Warmth, nurturance, and acceptance are manifested by parent.	+	×	×	×	+	0
Limits are implemented.	×	×	+	×	+	×
Communication is emphasized.	×	×	×	×	×	0*
Parents learn causes of children's behavior.	×	×	+	×	+	0
Raising a responsible child is a major goal.	×	×	+	×	×	×-0**
Emphasizes changing child's behavior.	×	NA	0	×	×	×
Uses explicit reward/ punishment to change child's behavior.	0	NA	0	0	+	×
Emphasizes use of punishment.	0	NA	0	0	0	×
Emphasizes use of praise.	0	NA	+	×	×	×

× = Strongly
+ = Moderately
0 = Little or not at all
N/A = not applicable
* = Emphasis on parent communicating
** = Authors' claim may not be accurate

certain inappropriate behaviors, such as when the child deliberately breaks something, throws objects in the house, ignores a request to stop doing something, or demonstrates abusive behaviors to others (Kaplan & Bavolek, 1996).

Most strategies advocate the use of praise, but the way in which it is used varies. STEP differen-tiates between praise and encouragement and rec-ommends the use of only the latter. It is contended that praise focuses only on the outward manifesta-tion of a specific behavior (the product), whereas encouragement focuses on the child's motives and efforts (the process). The Nurturing Program en-courages parents to use praise to point out the worth of the child's abilities, traits, or achievements. Parents are encouraged also to promote self-praise in children by describing to the child how good her action must have made her feel. Parents are warned that praise can be inappropriate if it is followed by a negative statement. How to Talk So Kids Will Listen focuses on the kind of praise that builds a positive self-image—praising efforts rather than children's personalities. Active Parenting stresses the instilling of courage by providing encouragement and avoiding discouragement.

The National Extension Parent Education Model differs from other strategies in its emphasis on parents caring for themselves through managing stress and the resources available to the family. It encourages families to recognize their strengths and to cooperate with their child-rearing partners. Further, parents are challenged to become advocates for community resources that support children and families.

Obviously, these similarities and differences in approach result in slightly differing parental behavior in certain situations and in similar parental behavior in other situations. Examples of parental behavior by strategy for selected situations are given in the Highlights.

Strengths and Limitations

It appears that each of the strategies previously described has unique strengths and limitations. In general the skills described in the strategies are relatively simple for parents to learn. If parents apply them over a period of time with success and see that they actually cause either their children or themselves to change behavior, then they are likely to become encouraged and develop a more positive relationship with their children.

Further, being trained in a specific strategy of parenting may give parents some concrete ideas of how to deal with specific problems in the parent-child relationship. As we have already mentioned, parents are now more isolated from sources of support in parenting than they once were, and many of them are eager for sources of ideas and advice.

Finally, most of the strategies take into account the parents' feelings as well as the children's. Becoming aware of one's own anger, discouragement, satisfaction, needs, desires, and concerns may be the first step in becoming a more effective parent. And improving communication between parents and children can be mutually satisfying to both.

One must recognize, however, that strategies for parenting have limitations, both individually and collectively. First, most strategies do not account for either age or sex differences in children. Most research indicates that there are subtle differences in the behavior of boys and girls and differences in the ways both mothers and fathers interact with each sex. Further, although the strategies make some attempt to differentiate between the application of methods for younger children and teenagers, a precise differentiation is absent. The impression one gets is that the strategists assume that all parenting behaviors are applicable equally to all age groups. Obviously one cannot engage in active listening with an infant. Parents need a bit more guidance in understanding the effects of both gender and the developmental level of children in their application of specific methods or skills. Hills and Knowles (1987) pointed out that many programs need teaching strategies that provide opportunities for parents to bring their experiences and concerns into all phases of learning the skills. This would promote transfer of the skills taught to actual family situations. They suggested that parents should be asked to describe their understanding of a concept and then to use their own judgment and words in implementing the skill.

Another assumption that seems to be made by strategists is that a given strategy is applicable equally to all cultures and socioeconomic classes. Therefore, strategies fail to take into account variation in cultural attitudes and values and complex issues related to poverty. In fact, most strategies are oriented to middle-class Anglo-Americans. One cannot help but wonder how motivated Native Americans would be to learn and implement some of the skills set forth in strategies that ignore

Parental Behavior in Given Situations by Selected Strategies

Situation	STRATEGY				
	STEP	Nurturing	Active Parenting	How to Talk So Kids Will Listen	Assertive Discipline
Child does not clean room by agreed-on time.	"I" message; logical consequence; family meeting	"I" statement	"I" message; logical consequence; family meeting	Expresses strong disapproval; engages cooperation	States assertively that child is to clean room; uses "broken record"; applies disciplinary consequence
Child forgets to take gym clothes to school.	Natural consequence	Natural consequence	Natural consequence	Encourages autonomy and assumption of responsibility	Consequence stipulated by school; no action by parent
Child complains about a particular teacher.	Reflective listening	Active listening	Active communication	Feedback techniques—helps child cope with negative feelings	No action
Children argue about assigned chores.	Family meeting	Loss of privilege, or time-out	Family meeting	Includes children in decisions about chores	Communicates assertively; reinforces words with action; "lays down the law"
Preschool child colors on the wall.	Logical consequence	Logical consequence	Logical consequence; "I" message	Expresses strong disapproval	Communicates assertively; reinforces words with action; "lays down the law"; uses parent-saver technique
Child does poorly in school.	Identifies goal; logical consequences	Active listening; identifies goal	Identifies goal; logical consequence	Encourages responsibility for action; expresses strong disapproval	Establishes discipline hierarchy; utilizes positive contract; tries marble mania
Child comes home on time for dinner after several instances of being late.	Encourages	Praise or "you" statement	Encourages; "I" message	Encourages efforts; builds on strengths; praises	Applies positive reinforcement, such as praise, especially in the presence of others

Note: Situations are not applicable for all the programs included in this chapter, since some programs target selected populations with very young children.

the preservation of their cultural heritage—or how it would be possible in the ecological context of poverty for mothers or fathers to practice "I" messages or reflective listening.

Thompson, Grow, Ruma, Daly, and Burke (1993) noted that the number of low-income children has increased and pointed out that these children are more prone to behavioral problems because of the combination of economic stress, environmental forces, and other critical events. They indicated that many parenting programs have not been successful with low-income parents. Those that have been successful have used methods designed especially for low-income families—home visits to individualize the support, make-up sessions for families unable to be present for all treatment sessions, and financial incentives for completing the program. They stated that lecture/discussion/reading approaches do not work with low-income parents, but a modeling/role-playing approach has been found to be more successful for teaching new skills to low-income parents. Further, low-income parents are more likely to remain in parent-education programs if family management training is provided first in the sequence of activities. This group of researchers recommended that the following approaches be used with low-income parents: Focus on very practical skills that can be implemented immediately at home; help parents learn to observe and define specific behaviors to be changed; teach parents to reinforce positive behaviors and to prevent problem situations; teach parents to respond to negative behaviors with nonaversive consequences; teach parents to help children set goals and solve problems; and assist parents in establishing family rules, meetings, and traditions.

A glaring deficiency in all the strategies is the assumption that if parents learn and use the techniques accurately, then all parent-child relationships will be positive. Each strategist seems to think she or he has all the answers. Some attempts have been made to combine various aspects of several strategies, but few have been made to help parents evaluate aspects of strategies and select those techniques that appear most appropriate and most successful for them. In short, a few qualifiers must be placed on the effectiveness of the skills described in each strategy.

Some critics have contended that parents would probably benefit more from a basic, adequate knowledge of child development than from "glib guidelines." Contemporary strategies appear to be cookbook approaches even though they are based on theoretical or philosophical perspectives. A parent who relies on a single overall framework might achieve consistency in his or her relationships with children, but the chances are that a single approach will not serve the parent adequately in all respects. Further, the expectation that the specifically prescribed behaviors for parents will result in predictable behavior in children fails to consider the complex nature of the parent-child relationship and other variables that undoubtedly affect that relationship. Therefore, it seems that more emphasis must be placed on putting into the hands of parents child-development literature that is understandable.

Lest we appear too negative, let us hasten to add that we believe there is some value in teaching specific skills to parents. At the same time, one must strive to develop in parents attitudes that are consistent with the techniques being used, and knowledge and understanding of child development and behavior.

Brems, Baldwin, and Baxter (1993) have pointed out that research has indicated few differences in outcomes as a result of specific programs. However, it has identified several theory-free program components that are particularly relevant to program effectiveness: assessment of parental needs along with the incorporation of strategies that address those needs; active participation of parents with their children; parental support; and individualized tailoring of programs to parents. Critics of traditional parenting programs have noted that they are of help only to parents who do not have many problems with their children; they tend to decrease the self-confidence of parents who already have problems with their children or who come from the lower economic strata. Though these criticisms have been used to argue against the use of parenting education programs altogether, they also may be used as a rationale for designing alternative programs that are more sensitive to parental needs.

Several theoretical models have been used and tested to measure outcomes of parent-education programs. The phenomenological approach described by First and Way (1995) was used to assess the outcomes of a parent-education program by examining both the structure and the experiences of the participants. This qualitative study used intensive interviews, and the stories participants told were analyzed. These researchers concluded that transformative learning, which helps participants see their lives in fundamentally different ways and to act on those perceptions, had occurred. The cognitive development model was used by Thomas (1996) to design, implement, and evaluate a parent-education program. This model, which focused on parent development in the areas of parental awareness and interpersonal interaction themes, also proved to be an effective approach. Programs developed by these researchers were described in Chapter 1.

Another theoretical model was developed and tested by Rueter, Conger, and Ramisetty-Mikler (1999). This model was designed to evaluate a parenting-skills training program focusing on teaching skills to parents and middle-school students to reduce a child's risk for drug and alcohol use. The model identified two variables that can moderate the benefits that parents might receive from the training: pretreatment skills of parents and life context. It was hypothesized that family stress resulting from marital difficulties or financial concerns would reduce the benefits of the program, and that strong preprogram skills (e.g., parental communication, parental negativity, or parent-child relationship quality) would increase benefits. Results were different for mothers and fathers, with fathers responding in the expected direction. However, mothers with the weakest

preprogram communication skills and reported marital difficulties benefited the most. These researchers proposed that variables that could mediate program outcomes should be considered when assessing a program.

It is suggested that new parenting programs need to become more conceptually comprehensive, procedurally interactive, and topically relevant to parental backgrounds and needs. The application of any one particular "canned" approach no longer appears warranted, and, instead, an integration of strategies seems necessary.

In summary, no one strategy is a panacea for parent-child relationships. It seems wise to take a more eclectic approach in parent education. We should provide parents with a broad base from which to function and allow them more freedom to choose from a number of strategies whose methods the parents feel comfortable with and that seem to be successful for them and their children.

SUMMARY

In an effort to assist parents in becoming more effective in a rapidly changing society, a number of professionals have developed strategies of parent education. Some of the strategies have been developed and packaged so that parents participate in structured training sessions over a given period of time, whereas others are simply outlined in reading and video materials so that parents can be self-taught. All the strategies are allegedly designed for "normal" parents and children, providing support rather than crisis intervention.

Contemporary strategies share several similarities, and each has its strengths and weaknesses. Unfortunately, little research exists that test the long-term effects of change in either parents' or children's behavior as a result of parent training using a particular strategy. Therefore, the effectiveness of these contemporary strategies must be assumed rather than known. Nevertheless, the availability of such resources for parents seems to be a positive force in today's society.

REFERENCES

AMERICAN GUIDANCE SERVICE. (n.d.). *Achieve! Success for young fathers.* Circle Pines, MN: American Guidance Service.

AMERICAN GUIDANCE SERVICE. (1992). *Growing together.* Circle Pines, MN: American Guidance Service.

BAVOLEK, S., & BAVOLEK, J. (1988). *Nurturing program for parents and children birth to five years: Parent handbook.* Eau Claire: WI: Family Development Resources.

BREMS, C., BALDWIN, M., & BAXTER, S. (1993). Empirical evaluation of a self psychologically oriented parent education program. *Family Relations, 53*(1), 26–30.

BURR, W. (1990). Beyond I-statements in family communication. *Family Relations, 39*(3), 266–273.

CANTER, L., & CANTER, M. (1976). *Assertive discipline: A take-charge approach for today's educator.* Seal Beach, CA: Canter and Associates.

CANTER, L., & CANTER, M. (1985). *Assertive discipline for parents* (Rev. ed.). New York: Harper & Row.

DINKMEYER, D. (1979). A comprehensive and systematic approach to parent education. *Journal of Family Therapy, 7*(2), 46–50.

DINKMEYER, D., & MCKAY, G. (1996). *Raising a responsible child* (Rev. ed.). New York: Fireside.

DINKMEYER, D., MCKAY, G., & DINKMEYER, D. (1997a). *Leader's resource guide.* Circle Pines, MN: American Guidance Service.

DINKMEYER, D., MCKAY, G., & DINKMEYER, D. (1997b). *The parent's handbook.* Circle Pines, MN: American Guidance Service.

DINKMEYER, D., MCKAY, G., DINKMEYER, D., DINKMEYER, J., & MCKAY, J. (1987). *The next STEP.* Circle Pines, MN: American Guidance Service.

DINKMEYER, D., MCKAY, G., MCKAY, J., & DINKMEYER, D. (1998). *STEP/Teen.* Circle Pines, MN: American Guidance Service.

DINKMEYER, D., MCKAY, G., MCKAY, J., DINKMEYER, J., & DINKMEYER, D. (1997). *Early Childhood STEP.* Circle Pines, MN: American Guidance Service.

EINSTEIN, E., & ALBERT, L. (n.d.). *Strengthening stepfamilies.* Circle Pines, MN: American Guidance Service.

FABER, A., & MAZLISH, E. (1974). *Liberated parents, liberated children.* New York: Avon.

FABER, A., & MAZLISH, E. (1980). *How to talk so kids will listen & listen so kids will talk.* New York: Avon.

FABER, A., & MAZLISH, E. (1987). *Siblings without rivalry.* New York: Negotiation Institute.

FIRST, J., & WAY, W. (1995). Parent education outcomes: Insights into transformative learning. *Family Relations, 44,* 104–109.

GARTRELL, D. (1987). Assertive discipline: Unhealthy for children and other living things. *Young Children, 42*(2), 10–11.

GORDON, T. (1975). *Parent effectiveness training.* New York: New American Library.

HILLS, M., & KNOWLES, D. (1987). Providing for personal meaning in parent education programs. *Family Relations, 36*(2), 158–162.

HITZ, R. (1988). Assertive discipline: A response to Lee Canter. *Young Children, 43*(2), 25–26.

KAPLAN, F., & BAVOLEK, S. (1996). *The nurturing program implementation and resource guide.* Park City, UT: Family Development Resources.

OWEN, M., & MULVIHILL, B. (1994). Benefits of a parent education and support program in the first three years. *Family Relations, 43,* 206–212.

Parents as Teachers National Center & Missouri Department of Elementary and Secondary Education. (1993). *Program planning and implementation guide.* St. Louis, MO: Parents as Teachers National Center.

POPKIN, M. (1990). *Active parenting of teens.* Marietta, GA: Active Parenting Publishers.

POPKIN, M. (1993). *Active parenting TODAY.* Marietta, GA: Active Parenting Publishers.

POPKIN, M. (1996). *Active parenting.* Atlanta: Active Parenting Publishers.

POPKIN, M. (1999). *Active parenting TODAY* (Spanish version). Marietta, GA: Active Parenting Publishers.

POPKIN, M., GARD, B., & MONTGOMERY, M. (1996). *1,2,3,4 Parents.* Marietta, GA: Active Parenting Publishers.

POPKIN, M., YOUNGS, B., & HEALY, J. (1995). *Helping your child succeed in school.* Marietta, GA: Active Parenting Publishers.

RUETER, M., CONGER, R., RAMISETTY-MIKLER, S. (1999). Assessing the benefits of a parenting skills training program: A theoretical approach to predicting direct and moderating effects. *Family Relations, 48,* 67–77.

SMITH, C., CUDABACK, D., GODDARD, W., & MYERS-WALL, J. (1994). *National extension parent education model of critical parenting practices.* Manhattan, KS: Kansas State University.

SUMMERLIN, M. L., & WARD, G. R. (1978). The effect of parental participation in a parent group on a child's self-concept. *Journal of Psychology, 100,* 227–232.

THOMAS, R. (1996). Reflective dialogue parent education design: Focus on parent development. *Family Relations, 45,* 189–200.

THOMPSON, R., GROW, C., RUMA, P., DALY, D., & BURKE, R. (1993). Evaluation of a practical parenting program with middle- and low-income families. *Family Relations, 42*(1), 21–25.

WILLIAMS, R., OMIZO, M., & ABRAMS, B. (1984). Effects of STEP on parental attitudes and locus of control of their learning disabled children. *School Counselor, 32,* 126–133.

WILSON, P., & JOHNSON, J. (1991). *Partners for fragile families.* Washington, DC: National Center for Strategic Non-profit Planning and Community Leadership.

CHAPTER 6

Parenting in Diverse Cultures

The term *culture* refers to the sum total of the attainments and learned behavior patterns of a specific people, regarded as expressing a traditional way of life. The behavioral patterns of a given culture are believed to be transmitted from one generation to the next, subject to gradual and continuous modification. In the United States, many diverse groups exist that manifest distinct behavioral patterns and can be clearly designated as subcultures. These include racial/ethnic groups, religious groups, socioeconomic classes, and geographic populations. In most subcultures certain aspects of the lifestyle deviate to some extent from that of the dominant culture. However, it is important to note that subcultures within the United States are probably similar in more ways than they are different. Socioeconomic differences are included in the following discussion of cultural diversity because poor families may display cultural behavior patterns that are different from expectations implicit in the larger middle-class culture. Class differences exist in all racial minority groups and are believed to be a more fundamental barrier than race or ethnicity to structural integration into American society.

SOCIOECONOMIC DIFFERENCES IN PARENTING

A serious contemporary concern is the growing number of children in the United States, especially younger ones, who live in poverty. The proportion of children living in poverty has increased steadily since 1975 and only recently has begun to level off. In 1997, 19 percent of all dependent children (under age 18) and 22 percent of children under the age of 6 lived in families below the poverty line, a rate almost twice as high as that in most other industrialized nations. Of all children under 18 in 1997, approximately 37 percent of African American, 36 percent of Hispanic, and 11 percent of White children were poor. Figures were not provided for Native American children, but based on older data, the figure probably is close to 40 percent. Ten percent of all children in married-couple families are poor, whereas 49 percent in female-headed households are poor. A staggering 63 percent of Hispanic and 55 percent of African

American children living in female-headed households are poor. Eleven percent of the nation's families live below the poverty line, and an additional 15 percent live at 125 percent of the poverty level (Forum on Child & Family Statistics, 1999; U.S. Bureau of the Census, 1998).

The three groups of families significantly represented in the poverty population are single-mother families, minority-group families, and families with preschool children. Other factors related to family poverty are young parents, low level of educational attainment, and unemployed status.

The largest percentage of poor families are single-parent families. Single parents have a 40 percent poverty rate, but the low number of poor single-parent men masks the high rate for single-parent mothers. Families headed by single-parent females are three times more likely to be in poverty than those headed by single-parent men. The majority of poor single mothers live independently with their children rather than cohabiting or living with relatives or friends, and at least 25 percent of those who have children under the age of 6 are not receiving any kind of government benefits. For those who are, benefits account for less than 7 percent of their aggregate income (U.S. General Accounting Office, 1992).

Three reasons have been given for the increase in child poverty rates: Economic changes have eliminated many blue-collar jobs that pay well; the percentage of children living in single-mother families has increased; and government benefits have steadily declined. Poverty is a conglomerate of conditions and events that amount to a pervasive stressor, often including exposure to poor health conditions, inadequate housing and homelessness, environmental toxins, and violent or unsupportive neighborhoods. The impact of poverty, however, can vary with race, gender, and ethnicity. The employment of one, or even two workers, is not necessarily sufficient to bring family income above the poverty line because the minimum wage is too low (Garrett, Ng'andu, & Ferron, 1994; Huston, McLoyd, & Coll, 1994).

For several decades researchers have been investigating differences in parenting practices among lower, middle, and upper socioeconomic classes. Particularly in the 1960s, in conjunction with the federal government's War on Poverty, there was a multitude of research on children from low-socioeconomic-status families and how best to help them. One of the difficulties of these studies was that socioeconomic status often was confounded with race or minority-group membership. Nevertheless, the picture that emerged, and subsequently the services that were provided, assumed a generalized image of poor families and poor children. Specifically, the emphasis was on the detrimental effects of early experiences of "deprived" children. The terms *progressive retardation* and *cumulative cultural deficit* were commonly used to describe what would ultimately happen to poor children in an academic setting if intervention did not occur. Programs were designed to assist poor children in "catching up" so that they could match middle-class standards. Little attention was given to the strengths of poor families, and indeed poor children were assumed to be lacking in cognitive and affective strengths altogether.

Much of the research in the 1960s has been criticized for its biases, assumptions, and faulty methodology. The current perception is that social-class groups are not homogeneous and that social-class levels differ from one section of the United States to another. Some researchers contend that there is as much variation in child-rearing patterns within a given social class as there is between social classes. It has been concluded that assertions on the effects of social class on child development represent probabilities, not inevitabilities. More recent research has introduced statistical sampling controls for socioeconomic status when assessing the effects of race or ethnicity in an attempt to untangle the two variables, and little research has focused on differences within ethnic groups. However, evidence for variability within a given social class or a given ethnic or racial group is beginning to emerge.

Quality of the Home Environment

Research in the 1960s and 1970s focused on the differences in mother-child interaction between low- and middle- to upper-income families, especially in the areas of language patterns and discipline techniques. Fairly consistent differences emerged. Lower-class mothers were found to be less instructive and more imperative than middle-class mothers in their control systems with children, more critical, more restrictive, and less sensitive to their children's needs. Middle-class mothers were found to be less intrusive and to give more reinforcement to their children's behavior and responses, and these behaviors were reflected in their language patterns and those of their children. The most consistent differences were found in the degree and quality of verbal interaction (Bee, Van Egeren, Streissguth, Nyman, & Leckie, 1969; Clarke-Stewart, 1977; Hess & Shipman, 1965).

Several more-recent researchers have focused on differences in the quality of the home environments of low-income and middle- and upper-income children because this variable has been consistently related to school success. It has been asserted that the more time children live in families with incomes below the poverty line, the lower the quality of the home environments, and improvements in income have the strongest effects on the home environments of chronically poor children (Huston et al., 1994). McLeod and Shanahan (1993) found that the length of time spent in poverty was an important predictor of children's health even after current poverty status was taken into account. Stress was a function of the duration of poverty, and harsh discipline, including paternal abuse, was more prevalent in persistently poor families, accounting for children's mental-health problems. Persistent poverty significantly predicted children's internalizing symptoms above and beyond the effect of current poverty, but only current poverty predicted externalizing symptoms. These researchers concluded that poor children appeared to experience the same parenting disadvantages regardless of race.

The availability of stimulating toys and books, and encouragement and support for intellectual accomplishments, factors known to contribute to a child's language development and later school performance, have been reported to occur less often in the homes of families living in poverty. Low-income parents are also reported to play fewer language games that are conducive to early language learning and to press their children for language less often. To further exacerbate the problem, teachers in some schools with large numbers of low-income children devote less daily time to instruction in basic academic skills, such as reading. Variations in exposure to language in the home and academic instruction in the school as influenced by socioeconomic status over time are predictors of subsequent child language, IQ, and achievement (Walker, Greenwood, Hart, & Carta, 1994).

Results of a study that was a 5-year extension of a 10-year longitudinal study showed that cumulative language spoken in the home was a key predictor of later school outcome. Children reared in lower socioeconomic environments had fewer early language experiences associated with later optimal language outcomes. The constraints placed on their language development in the context of early parenting may have compromised their growth in both early language and intelligence, as well as later success in reading and spelling achievement, in particular. The elementary school results showed that the earlier differences were predictive 7 years beyond the initial measures. Children from low-income families continued to demonstrate lower performance on language and reading-related achievement across grades in the elementary school, suggesting that initial differences were further maintained in the context of schooling. The authors pointed out that the differences found in this study were attributable to socioeconomic status factors and not specifically to their minority or cultural background (Walker et al., 1994).

Kaiser and Delaney (1996) confirmed that impoverished children exhibit poorer language development and facility and poorer cognitive functioning—which translates into lower academic achievement, more mental and physical health problems, and poorer social adjustment. Bolger, Patterson, Thompson, and Kupersmidt (1995) studied outcomes associated with persistent economic hardship among a group of children over a 4-year period. Children who experienced persistent family economic hardship started out behind other children on every measure of school-based competence and generally stayed behind throughout the study. Overall, the greatest difficulties in adjustment were

shown by children whose families experienced intermittent economic hardship; the fewest difficulties were shown by those families who did not experience economic hardship. Children who experienced persistent economic hardship had difficulties in peer relations, showed conduct problems at school, and reported low self-esteem. Both White and African American boys were more affected than were girls by family economic hardship, at least in externalizing behavior problems. However, to some extent parental characteristics mediated the effects. For example, maternal involvement was predicted by mothers' own levels of educational attainment, which in turn predicted children's intelligence scores.

Miller and Davis (1997) examined the relationship among depth or timing of poverty, mother's marital history, and quality of the home environment for children 6 to 9 years of age. They found that the quality of the home environment was substantially lower for poor children than for children who were not poor and that the quality of the home environment increases with increasing income up to approximately three times the poverty level, even when other sociodemographic attributes are taken into account. Low educational level of the mothers in this study was significantly and negatively associated with the quality of the home environment, even when poverty history was controlled, although the estimated effects of maternal education were notably smaller than the poverty effects. The number of children in the household and minority identification also were negatively associated with home-environment quality. Results suggested that poverty has a more important effect on the provision of material and other learning resources than on the quality of the parents' interactions with the child. Further, children who had experienced marital disruption had markedly lower home-environment quality, especially on emotional support, and children of never-married mothers fared less well than children of married mothers.

Neighborhood quality, as well as family income, appears to affect cognitive development and IQ. Klebanov, Brooks-Gunn, McCarton, and McCormick (1998) found that as early as age 1, the accumulation of family risks was associated with lower infant-development test scores. By age 3, neighborhood income entered as the third strongest environmental influence on test scores, just after family poverty.

Another study found that neighborhood income level was found to influence IQ by age 5. Living in more affluent neighborhoods raised IQ 1.6 points for each 10 percent increase in the proportion of affluent neighbors. Conversely, living in a poor neighborhood did not negatively affect age-5 IQ. These authors noted that the effects of persistent poverty on children are 60–80 percent greater than the effects of transient poverty, and the apparent effects of female headship of families on child cognition are due mostly to the lower incomes of female-headed families rather than to family structure (Duncan, Brooks-Gunn, & Klebanov, 1994).

These and other studies emphasize the importance of a home environment for young children that is stimulating, both in materials (toys and books) and in interactions with adults that are rich in language experiences. The pattern, first noted in the 1960s, of lower academic achievement and early school failure that is disproportionately experienced by children of poor families was confirmed by research in the 1990s. And it appears that many children are at risk for progressive and cumulative poor performance in elementary school as a result of early home environments that fail to stimulate language and cognitive development, and the risk is compounded when children grow up in poor-quality neighborhoods.

Parenting Behaviors

The impact of poverty on children is mediated by the behavior of adults—how they react to inadequate financial resources structures the consequences of poverty for children. The same level of income or material comfort may be perceived quite differently, depending on whether parents communicate worries about economic insecurity or whether children often are denied objects and experiences because the family lacks money (Garrett et al., 1994; Huston et al., 1994). Nevertheless, a large body of data indicates that poverty has pro-

found effects on parenting, largely because of high levels of stress.

There has been little emphasis in the literature on the parenting behaviors of low-income fathers, but it has been suggested that loss of income for fathers may result in their becoming punitive and unnurturing, which results in children developing socioemotional problems, somatic symptoms, and reduced aspirations and expectations. Parents may react to financial stress by overemphasizing obedience, withholding affection, relying on corporal punishment as a means of control, and failing to be responsive to the socioemotional needs of children (Garrett et al., 1994). Using a national sample, Hashima and Amato (1994) found that the likelihood of punitive parental behavior decreased as household income increased. Parents at low-income levels were especially likely to report behaving in a punitive and unsupportive fashion toward their children.

Conger, Ge, Elder, Lorenz, and Simons (1994) found that aversive behavior toward children is a spillover effect of marital conflict. Earlier research had suggested that economic stress may increase conflict and irritability in family interactions. The study by Conger and his associates found that economic pressure is associated directly with parent-adolescent financial conflicts as well as indirectly through parent depressed mood and hostile interactions in the marriage. Both marital conflict and financial conflict were found to be significantly related to parent hostility toward the child.

There is far more emphasis in the literature on the parenting behaviors of low-income mothers and how they affect children. Many studies of diverse samples report that mothers experiencing high emotional stress exhibit diminished nurturance and sensitivity toward their children and, in disciplinary encounters, rely less on reasoning and loss of privileges and more on aversive, coercive techniques. Economic loss has adverse, indirect effects on children's behavior and socioemotional functioning through increasing negative parenting behaviors, which is consistent with the evidence that children of parents who use harsh, punitive, and inconsistent discipline are prone to a number of behavioral and psychological problems (Kalil & Eccles, 1998; McLoyd, Jayaratne, Ceballo, & Borquez, 1994).

Epidemiological researchers have found consistent relationships between low socioeconomic status and early-onset behavior problems in childhood. It has been speculated that low-income mothers employ harsh disciplinary practices at a high rate because of urgent needs to try to prevent their children from becoming involved in antisocial activity, either as victims or as perpetrators. Stress induced by economic disadvantage may lead to increased coercive exchanges between parent and child. Many researchers have found that harsh and punitive parenting is associated with child aggressive behavior, and this relationship holds in diverse cultural groups and with children in five different countries. The stresses of socioeconomic disadvantage may cause a parent to be less attentive to the child's needs and thus less warm toward the child. Some studies have found maternal warmth to be negatively correlated with low-socioeconomic status, which is associated with child aggressiveness. Children also may learn aggression from models; violence often is readily observed in low-socioeconomic marital dyads and neighborhoods, and observation of adult conflict is associated with both immediate and long-term adverse effects on children (Dodge, Pettit, & Bates, 1994).

Researchers have found that children in the lowest socioeconomic class received teacher-rated externalizing problem scores significantly above the national mean; more than 60 percent of the low-status children received a score in the clinical risk range at some time during elementary school. In fact, the lower the socioeconomic status, the greater the behavior problems. Low-status children were more likely than their more advantaged peers to receive harsh discipline from their parents, to observe violence in their extended families and neighborhoods, and to have unstable peer groups and friendships. They received less cognitive stimulation in their home environments; mothers were less warm and experienced more life stressors, perceived less social support and greater isolation, and were more likely to believe that aggression is an appropriate and effective way to solve problems. These find-

ings held even when the effects of single parenthood were controlled statistically, revealing their direct relationship to economic disadvantage. Harsh discipline was the strongest predictor of behavior problems (Dodge et al., 1994).

Felner, Brand, DuBois, Adan, Mulhall, and Evans (1995) found that young adolescents from families characterized by lower levels of occupational status reported greater maternal rejection, less sense of belonging at school, and greater exposure to major stressful events than their more advantaged peers. Parental education had a different and more pervasive pattern of association with risk experiences. Specifically, adolescents from homes in which neither parent had graduated from high school reported more developmentally negative experiences, including higher levels of rejection from both parents, less social support and emphasis on intellectual-cultural issues in their families, more negative feelings about school, and heightened levels of exposure to both major and relatively minor stressors. These findings suggested that household occupational status and parental educational attainment each had unique influences on children's academic performance and achievement. Further, parental education also associated significantly with several other indices of socioemotional functioning where household occupational status did not.

Because it appears to inhibit the capacity of families with adolescents to achieve informal social control, poverty increases the likelihood of delinquency. Strong family social controls may serve as an important buffer against structural disadvantage in the larger community. The fundamental causes of delinquency are consistent across time and rooted not in race but in generic family processes—such as supervision, attachment, and discipline—that are systematically influenced by family poverty and structural disadvantage (Sampson & Laub, 1994).

When economic hardship is accompanied by social isolation, parents are more likely to become neglectful of and abusive toward their children. The reported incidence of maltreatment is disproportionately large among families living in poverty, and socially isolated families have higher rates of child abuse than other families do (Hashima & Amato, 1994). Several studies have pointed out the buffering effects of social support on the negative parental behaviors associated with the stresses of economic deprivation. Social support appears to have a positive effect on parenting behavior by making mothers feel less isolated and overwhelmed by their parenting situation, more gratified with the maternal role, and more satisfied with their children (McLoyd et al., 1994).

The preceding evidence suggests rather strongly that there are documented differences between the home environments and the parenting behaviors experienced by poor children and their more economically advantaged peers. This contemporary research has used statistical controls that help to untangle the variables of income/socioeconomic status and race/ethnicity. The results, therefore, point more clearly to differences in income as the major factor influencing these differences. Lack of financial resources causes increased stress, leading to negative parenting behaviors, which result in adverse outcomes for children.

However, parenting behavior may be related to other factors, such as education, health status, and biological differences. We conclude that con-sistent differences have been observed among different social-class levels but that many other factors influence children's behaviors and abilities. Further, conditions associated with poverty, such as slum neighborhoods, inferior employment, poor health, unstable marriages, and high birthrates, serve to devastate the child's well-being as much as specific parenting behaviors.

Finally, there appear to be "within-class" differences that might be as significant as "between-class" differences. Clearly, lower-class parents lack resources in parenting equal to those of middle- and upper-class parents—financial, educational, psychological, and medical resources. And this lack of resources surely has some impact on the way in which they interact with their children.

PARENTING IN AFRICAN AMERICAN FAMILIES

In 1997 there were approximately 8.5 million African American families and more than 34 million African Americans in the United States. Most reside in the inner-city sections of the largest cities (U.S. Bureau of the Census, 1998). According to many researchers, African Americans constitute a distinctive culture that represents an interaction be-

---

HIGHLIGHTS

Positive Home and Parental Characteristics

QUALITY OF HOME ENVIRONMENT

Provision of stimulating toys and books
Encouragement and support for intellectual accomplishments
Early language stimulation
Living in an affluent neighborhood
Low level of financial stress

PARENTING BEHAVIORS

High levels of nurturance and maternal warmth
Low likelihood of punitive behavior toward children
Reliance on reasoning and loss of privilege as discipline techniques
Absence of violence in home and neighborhood
Social control, e.g., supervision, guidance, attachment
Economic security

tween strong African cultural derivatives and the influence of American cultural imperatives (Greene, 1995). The tendency to have dual or even several social systems or structural arrangements for access to, and receiving, resources and for enforcing laws has reinforced the development and continuance of a distinct African American culture. However, as a group, African Americans are geographically and socioeconomically diverse, but they share cultural origins and negative racial barriers in a variety of ways (Greene, 1995).

Demographics

There have been enormous changes among African Americans over the past two decades: a rise of their underclass, a rise of their middle class (more than one-third of African Americans are classified as middle-class), and the demise of their stable blue-collar working class. Social scientists have emphasized the underclass, manifested by increased unemployment, poverty, and female-headed families. African American poverty was dramatically reduced between 1959 and 1979 by

the combination of an expanding economy, greater educational opportunity, more government programs for the poor, and the enforcement of civil rights and affirmative action. Since 1979, however, these trends have been reversed, and by 1985 poverty among African Americans had reached unprecedented levels. More than half of all African American households earned less than $25,000 in 1996. Twenty-eight percent of all African Americans now live below the poverty line. The situation is worse for children. Thirty-seven percent of African American children in all family types live in poverty, and more than half who live in mother-only families live below the poverty line. The younger the child, the more likely she is to be impoverished (U.S. Bureau of the Census, 1998).

The exceptionally high rate of unemployment for African Americans and their relatively low level of education account for the fact that their median household income is approximately 59 percent of Whites'. African American males have almost three times the rate of unemployment that Whites males do. At the present time the median

One of the major functions of African American parents is to transmit their cultural heritage to their children.

family income in constant dollars for African Americans is only $2,000 per year more than it was in 1970. Although African American women make a much greater contribution to the economic standing of their families than White women do, even when both groups are married to working husbands, African American women earn less than White men and women and African men (U.S. Bureau of the Census, 1998). Even when African Americans complete 4 years of college, their incomes do not equal those of some other racial groups with comparable education.

Traditionally, African Americans have begun their childbearing much earlier than other racial groups; they continue their childbearing longer and have a higher average number of children ever born than Whites or Hispanics do. Further, African American females are more likely to be never-married mothers and to divorce if they do marry than Whites or Hispanics and are less likely to re-marry than Whites. Separation and divorce occur at younger ages for African Americans than for other groups, and the period of separation before divorce is longer. Even so, African American families are represented by great diversity in lifestyle. In their struggle for equality and justice, African Americans have survived by living in a variety of family forms—two-parent households, common-law marriages, extended families, male-headed families, and female-headed families.

Since the 1970s, however, there has been a dramatic increase in both teenage pregnancies and out-of-wedlock births among African Americans of all social classes. Seventy percent of all African American babies are born out of wedlock; nearly one-fourth are born to teenagers, and most of those teens are unmarried. Births to single African American women are two and one-half times higher than to single White women even though these rates in the White population have risen drastically in the past 6 years (U.S. Bureau of the Census, 1998). Research has pointed out, however, that "multiple mothering" is commonplace in African American families. That is, aunts, cousins, close friends, and fictive kin provide mothers with a range of modeling and tangible support, so that these families may be unlike the typical White model of a single parent (Greene, 1995).

Diverse Viewpoints of the African American Family

African American families have immense differentiation in cultural values and regional differences. Several viewpoints of the African American family have been held by social scientists and have influenced research, policy, and programs. Until 1965–1970 the major image of these families, particularly of poor African American families, was one of pathology and deviance. Most of these ideas developed because researchers failed to distinguish between factors of culture and class in family lifestyles. For many years it was believed that family structure determined social achievement.

Amuzie Chimezie (cited in Hale-Benson, 1986) believes that theorists of African American culture are divided broadly into two categories—negative and affirmative. Negative theorists deny the existence of an African American culture and attribute differences to class position; degree of poverty; and attendant social pathologies, that is, the *cultural deviant* approach.

In 1965 Daniel Patrick Moynihan published a report, *The Negro Family: The Case for National Action.* Moynihan's position was that slavery had destroyed African cultures and family patterns. The efforts of African American males to protect and support their families were so undermined that the men were not authority figures in their families; therefore, a matriarchal family emerged. The bond between the mother and the child became the most durable and meaningful feature of African American family life. The African American male did not have an opportunity to become acculturated to the dominant nuclear family form. The huge migration of African Americans to northern cities before World War I and later to inner-city sections of large cities in the United States only created more difficulties as African American men were thrown into highly competitive and racially discriminating situations. The family structure was further weakened, and desertion and divorce, sexual promiscuity, illegitimacy, crime, delinquency, and welfare dependency were thought to be characteristic of African American families.

Other writers, such as Frazier (1939) and Rainwater (1966), also contributed to the unfortunate idea that African American families were unstable, structurally weak, socially disorganized, and handicapped in performing essential family functions. In addition, African American families were said to be seriously deficient in necessary resources and competencies. It was felt that the extremely persistent negative conditions in which these families lived caused them to resort to adaptive strategies that produced expressive and violent behavior within the family as well as tendencies toward depression and a sense of fatalism. These attitudes were perpetuated from one generation to another. The idea of a cycle of poverty was a prevalent one in the 1960s. Those individuals who still hold to the viewpoint that African American families in general are deviant and pathological feel that the situation is growing steadily worse, because the number of African American divorces, out-of-wedlock births, and unemployed are increasing (Frazier, 1939; Moynihan, 1965; Rainwater, 1966; Staples & Mirandé, 1980).

On the other hand, the affirmative theorists subscribe to at least four different viewpoints. The first is the African Heritage theory, which is based on the assumption that certain African traits have been retained by African Americans and are evidenced in kinship patterns, marriage, sexuality, child rearing, and so forth (Hale-Benson, 1986). This viewpoint is sometimes referred to as the *cultural variant* approach and views African American families as culturally unique units.

The affirmative New World Experience theory attributes distinctiveness to the experiences of blacks in America rather than to African traditions. The Biculturation theory views African American culture as composed of African American and Euro-American elements in that African American children are socialized in both African American and Euro-American culture. However, there is lack of consensus about the importance of each culture to them.

The Eclectic theory recognizes a distinctive African American culture and attempts to identify the salient factors that are theoretically responsible for its cultural elements. These theorists believe that certain aspects of African American culture are African retentions and others arise from American experience. They emphasize that many factors influence and affect Black ways of life (Hale-Benson, 1986). Finally, some subscribe to the *cultural equivalent* approach, in which African American families are seen as culturally equivalent if they adhere to the White, middle-class lifestyle.

If one subscribes to the African Heritage theory, then one would contend that the development and behavioral styles of African American children differ as a result of growing up in a distinct culture. Hale-Benson (1986), an African Heritage theorist, pointed out a number of characteristics unique to African American culture that have roots in West Africa, which have resulted in the emergence of a distinct language system and particular behavioral characteristics. Apparently the aspects of African culture that have survived and been transmitted have occurred without conscious effort and so subtly that they are not thought of as Africanisms but may influence the manner in which African American children are parented (see Highlights).

Functions of African American Families

African American families are varied and complex. Depending partly on socioeconomic status, some families are adaptable and stable and are effective socializers of their children; others are marginal, operating close to their limits. The families who live in poverty have few resources and may demonstrate some of the negative characteristics that have been attributed to them. On the other hand, many families are resilient and resourceful, even in the absence of adequate financial resources (Greene, 1995).

Many people believe that the major function of African American parents is to transmit the cultural heritage of Africa and African America to their children, often in the form of accounts of the struggles, achievements, and defeats of African

HIGHLIGHTS

Unique Traits of African American Families

Funerals	Motor habits—walking, speaking, dancing,
Magical practices	burden carrying, and so on
Folklore	Hairdressing—wrapping, braiding, cornrowing
Dance	Respect for elderly
Song	
Wearing of kerchiefs, scarves	

Source: Hale-Benson, J. (1986). *Black children: Their roots, culture, and learning styles* (Rev. ed.). Provo, UT: Brigham Young University Press.

American heroes. Bicultural socialization often occurs, whereby both the aspects of African heritage and the realities of America are integral aspects. When rearing children, African American parents may have to resolve basic conflicts between European and African views, often being forced to ignore White child-rearing norms that are irrelevant to the existing situation of their children. Clearly, ethnic image is critical to promoting self-image (Greene, 1995; Hale, 1991; Julian, McHenry, & McKelvey, 1994).

Most African Americans have a large network of relatives and fictive kin (Padgett, 1997). Upward mobility does not seem to erase the sense of reciprocal obligation to kin, which suggests that the extended family is a cultural rather than an economic phenomenon. One study, controlling for income, found extended living arrangements twice as common among African American as among White households (cited in Taylor, Chatters, Tucker, & Lewis, 1991).

African Americans are more likely to socialize children without strict differences determined by the gender of the child and to share in child care and in decision making about child rearing (Allen & Majidi-Ahi, 1989). A study of rural two-parent African American families showed that fathers often are involved in child rearing, and men and women are beginning to share household tasks, even though the women still assume a greater share of the responsibility. However, a 1997 study by Padgett found that African American married women do two-thirds of the housework as compared to their husbands' one-third, and the division of labor was not affected by children's involvement in household work. Nevertheless, research has emphasized the gender-role flexibility of African American families as an important adaptive strategy that derives from valuing interdependence among group members (Greene, 1995).

Finally, African American families historically have valued education, hard work, achievement, and social mobility, though the gap is widening between those who are able to take advantage of educational opportunities and those who are not even aware of them.

Characteristics of African American Culture That Affect Parenting

Because of the emphasis on affective, interpersonal relations and the emotional, people-oriented characteristics of African American people, children are likely to grow up to be feeling- and people-oriented and more proficient in nonverbal communication skills than White children are. White children are more likely to be object-oriented, since they have had numerous opportunities to manipulate objects and to discover their properties and relationships. African American babies experience considerable human interaction with people of all ages. Babies often are encouraged to feel or to rub the holder's face, and a game of "rubbing each other's face" ensues. Infants and young children often sleep with their parents. There is a rhythm of sleeping and eating, with each activity being of short duration and the pattern repeated frequently.

Many African American parents expect early assumption of the child's responsibility for his bodily functions and personal feelings (Julian et al., 1994). Therefore, toilet learning is normally begun early and is stringent. This pattern is in startling contrast to that experienced by White infants whereby, after many months of paying no attention to wet and soiled diapers, the mother suddenly interferes and begins the toilet-learning process.

Verbal communication during infancy may be less important than other types of communication, such as looking deeply into the child's eyes and caressing the baby. Looking into the eyes is used by the mother to impress a point on the child. When African American school children refuse to look at their teachers, they may be trying to sever an intense level of communication that is typically shared among their people. Or, the child may feel that it is disrespectful to an authority figure to look him or her in the eye.

Cultural-specific values of African American families have been found in such areas as discipline, expectations regarding age- and sex-appropriate responsibilities, kin network, and awareness of racism. There is special emphasis in child rearing on respect for authority figures; strict discipline; a high value on a variety of responses, abilities, and talents; open receptivity to multiple environmental stimuli; and expression of emotions

by both males and females. Many writers have emphasized that African American families use corporal punishment more than White families. However, many of these studies generalized the child-rearing behaviors of low-income African American mothers to all African American mothers, suggesting that African American families were a monolithic group (Bradley, 1998). Further, historically, models of child rearing developed with respect to the ethnic majority have been used as standards in comparing or evaluating minority parenting practices. Only recently have studies begun to focus on within-group differences. Bluestone and Tamis-LeMonda (1999) found that substantive variation existed among African American parents in disciplinary strategies. The most common disciplinary strategy used with working- and middle-class African American mothers was reasoning—a characteristic of authoritative parenting. Physical punishment was reported relatively infrequently. Maternal depression and negative child-rearing histories were negatively associated with child-centered parenting styles, and higher levels of maternal education were positively associated with child-centered parenting.

Bradley (1998) also found that the middle-income African American parents (mothers and fathers) in her sample preferred to use nonphysical forms of discipline. However, parents did use an "order child not to" disciplinary technique that seems more associated with an authoritarian style. Several scholars have suggested that demanding obedience from African American children in some cases is imperative, given the life circumstances imposed on African American youth in a discriminatory society. Parents in this study used as disciplinary techniques only the belt and spanking with an open hand in severe contextual situations. In fact, physical punishment was used only when a child directly challenged the authority of the parent. This finding is consistent with the African American value of respecting elders and authority figures. Another study examined the parenting practices of low-income, White urban mothers with children 3 to 6 years old. The results indicated that

HIGHLIGHTS

Characteristics of African American Culture That Affect Child Rearing

Feeling orientation
People orientation
Proficiency in nonverbal communication skills
High degree of human interaction
Biculturation
Multiple environmental stimuli

all these mothers could not be characterized as "parent-centered" as opposed to "child-centered," a distinction often made between African American and White mothers. Some did use authoritarian control practices and demonstrated attitudes emphasizing obedience, but the correlations between these two characteristics were not significant—that is, they existed independently. Mothers who took the child's perspective in disciplinary encounters were as likely to use power assertion as those who were parent-centered, but mothers varied widely in their attitudes toward physical punishment. In this study, religious mothers were more likely to be child-oriented. Younger, less educated mothers who were raising their children alone and were less involved in religion placed more emphasis on respect for obedience and were more likely to use a parent-oriented approach, whereas older, more educated married mothers appeared to emphasize more autonomous behavior and use a more child-oriented democratic approach (Kelly, Power, & Wimbush, 1992).

Therefore, it appears that the most significant factors in differentiating parenting styles of African American parents are socioeconomic status, level of education, their own parenting histories, and presence or absence of depression.

African American Mothers

A strong bond seems to exist between African American mothers and their children. African American heritage emphasizes that children represent the continuity of life, and the mother role is highly valued. Whereas some researchers have described the African American family structure as matriarchal, with a domineering, pathological female as head, others have described the African American mother as strong, particularly in the sense that she has been able to maintain the dual role of wage earner and manager of a household. Contrary to the dominant cultural norm of women remaining at home to raise children, African American women have always worked outside the home (Greene, 1995).

The increasing out-of-wedlock birthrate may suggest that more young African American women desire to achieve the status of parenthood without becoming involved in the marital role. Even though most African Americans do not view childbearing outside of marriage as socially desirable, long-term shame and stigma are uncommon. In addition, African American females have a more restricted field of marriage eligibles and often marry less-educated men (Littlejohn-Blake & Darling, 1993). The accessibility and assistance of the kin network is particularly important to African American single mothers, especially if they are young and/or poor.

However, a recent study concerning African American mothers and grandmothers found surprising results that are in marked contrast to results of studies a decade ago (Chase-Lansdale, Brooks-Gunn, & Zamsky, 1994). The study included African American multigenerational families living below the poverty line. Contrary to expectations, the researchers found that grandmothers' parenting was not superior to that of the mothers, despite their age and experience. For mothers and grandmothers that co-resided, the correlations between mothering and grandmothering behaviors involved only the negative dimensions of parenting, especially for the younger childbearers and grandmothers. Harsh parenting showed continuity across generations, suggesting that negative ways of treating children are readily learned and modeled. However, mothers and grandmothers who lived apart were somewhat more likely to be similar in the positive dimensions of parenting. Co-residence seemed to have negative consequences on the quality of both mothers' and especially grandmothers' parenting for the sample as a whole. However, the age of the mother at first birth was a factor: When the mother was very young, co-residing grandmothers offered higher-quality parenting than non-co-residers—for example, positive emotional expression, more expert teaching skills, greater involvement and support, and warmth combined with appropriate discipline. But when mothers were older at first birth, the grandmothers' parenting quality was higher when their daughters lived independently with their children. It appears, then, that co-residence of mothers and grandmothers does not always have positive results.

Despite the large percentage of African American single-mother families, there has been considerable misinformation about the causes and consequences of this family type and a tendency to focus on their problems, ignoring the diversity that exists among African American families and their resilient, adaptive characteristics. Sudarkasa (1993) pointed out the importance of understanding the earlier African extended families out of which contemporary family structures evolved. Households headed by single parents, mostly women, were embraced as well as households headed by couples. The notion that female-headed households are the major cause of the deplorable conditions of poverty, crime, and hopelessness found among African Americans in many inner cities must be refuted. African American female-headed households have always had bases of support in other households and received critical support from brothers, sons, and uncles.

The frequent African American practice of informally "adopting" children not biologically related probably stems from the days of slavery when children often were separated from their parents without regard for family ties. These extended networks of kinship between biological and unrelated family members still exist today and carry with them networks of obligation and support (Greene, 1995).

Even though much has been written about the matriarchal theme in African American families and its consequences, in reality the egalitarian family pattern is common in intact families. Although it is not clear how prevalent the egalitarian pattern is, it does appear to be the norm for middle-class African American families.

African American Fathers

African American fathers have been neglected in the research on African American families, proba-

bly because they have not been as accessible as White fathers and have been perceived as being less significant persons to their families. Historically, African American fathers have been depicted as peripheral to family and as performing poorly in the family roles of spouse and father. However, some investigators have found that the role of economic provider was a frequently cited role among both middle-income and blue-collar African American men. For middle-income fathers, central to their self-perceptions of being better providers for their families is the goal of exceeding the socioeconomic status of their own fathers. Personal income and age have been found to be associated with the likelihood that African American men will perceive themselves as good providers for their families. Having a higher personal income is associated with being married among African American men and satisfaction with family life among African American husbands (Taylor et al., 1991).

McAdoo (1993) has noted that when African Americans marry, they are expected to work cooperatively for the good of the marital unit; the family's survival depends on spousal cooperation. His research has found that couples share equally in decision making, demonstrating the same kind of decision-making pattern as other groups. Other research has shown that both fathers and mothers are involved in the racial socialization of their children (cited in Taylor et al., 1991).

Fathers' involvement in the basic caregiving of their preschool children in intact middle- to lower-income African American families was examined by Ahmeduzzaman and Roopnarine (1992). Their data revealed that fathers spent about one-third as much time as their wives in primary caregiving, and fathers' educational level, family income, communication, extrafamilial support, and length of time married were the chief variables associated with different dimensions of men's involvement with children. Men with higher incomes and better education and who had been married for longer periods of time were more likely to be involved with their preschoolers than those who had lower incomes and less education and who had been married for shorter periods of time. Men's ability to communicate in productive ways within the family was positively linked to their involvement with children. The stronger the commitment to the family, the more likely fathers were to rate their overall involvement and participation in child care as being greater. The more support fathers received from extrafamilial members, the more invested they were in the socialization and care of their children.

African American adolescent fathers are a diverse group in terms of age, timing of fatherhood in relation to work and education, number of children, length of fatherhood experience, relationship with the child's mother, and marital experience. One study found that young African American men were more likely than Hispanics or Whites to have had a nonmarital first birth and were least likely to live with that child. However, in comparison with other adolescent fathers, African Americans were more likely to complete high school. Another researcher suggested that the father's absence from the home of the mother and child does not necessarily reflect noninvolvement with parenting; minority fathers were more likely to be involved than were White fathers (cited in Taylor et al., 1991).

The recent research on African American fathers, though limited, does not support the stereotypical view that they are invisible and uninvolved with their children. In fact, African American married men are more likely to share housework and child care than White men are; there is more egalitarianism in household tasks between couples when the wife's employment status, earning power, and sex-role attitudes are controlled for. The greater the economic security of the family, the more active the father becomes in child rearing (Ahmeduzzaman & Roopnarine, 1992).

Rearing African American Children

African American children today are more likely than ever before to be born into devastating conditions of poverty and to be born to a mother who is not married and who lacked adequate prenatal care. These children are twice as likely as White children to die in the first year of their lives and three times as likely to be misplaced in classes for educable mentally retarded. They are twice as likely as White children to have a parent who is unemployed and to live in substandard housing. African American teenagers are more likely today than 10 years ago to drop out of high school and to be unemployed. They are four times as likely as White teens to be incarcerated (Goduka, 1990).

These risks to the healthy development of children, especially those in inner cities, seem overwhelming. Yet, despite the odds, many African American children grow up to be well adjusted. The literature and the media do not emphasize the diversity of African American youth as individuals who come from different families, neighborhoods, communities, and socioeconomic backgrounds, but instead have focused on the problems identified earlier. As a result, little is really known about various aspects of the development and socialization of African American children (Taylor et al., 1991).

African American parents, like all other parents, play a crucial role in helping their children learn to participate successfully in society. As in other cultures, male and female African American children are reared differently. By the age of 3, most of them are no longer treated as babies. Early independence is valued, and many children assume responsibility for the care of younger siblings. For males the peer group is more important in the socialization process than for females. Male children are socialized into the peer group earlier and more completely than are females.

An important rite of passage into manhood by African American males is that of "playing the dozens," a verbal duel in which two males make derogatory comments about each other's family. Onlooking peers urge each on. The skills of each player are appreciated and judged by the peer group. To master this game, the boy must control his emotions so that he can think quickly and counter with an even more clever remark about a family member of his opponent. Learning to control one's emotions is an important aspect of socialization of the African American male (Hale-Benson, 1986). Urban youth have developed other ritualized games, such as "ribbin," "jivin," and "shuckin," possibly to cope with the stresses and strains of their environment.

In traditional families African American girls usually are given responsibility for the care of younger siblings and the household at an early age. Daughters are expected to be independent and capable of shouldering family responsibilities very early. African American mothers advocate acceleration of development. This emphasis helps to develop a strong motherhood orientation. Girls are not expected to have jobs outside the home until adolescence. The most frequent jobs for younger African American girls are baby-sitting and other domestic duties. In many families there is a strong emphasis on personal uniqueness. Girls are taught to develop their own style, sexuality, and personal distinctiveness. What one does and how it is done are both viewed as important. Personal attributes are considered more important than status or office.

Stevens (1997) noted that the socialization experiences of African American families are anchored in an African American cultural idiom. The girls in her study were observed employing ritual insult games, mostly verbal, to organize the context of their social environments. Most of these games centered on boys and were a means of exercising some control over their environments. The girls' assertive behavior was an emotive stylistic expression that is cultural, and they saw "arguing" as a demonstration of self-assertiveness and a sense of power. Self-esteem concerns were salient in the management of sexuality and gender development. Girls saw themselves competing with one another for a boy's attention or interest, and as a result, they engaged in physical fights and verbal insult games with their female peers. Stevens concluded that many African American females, at the onset of adolescence, experience a normative crisis of connection/disconnection with parents and their fictive kinship group as they try to negotiate relationships within the dominant culture for cultural/bicultural competence.

The peer group exerts a strong influence on both African American boys and African American girls. The peer group is critical for the continuation of the socialization process begun by the parents. It is a much more significant influence in families in which the father is absent or unemployed. African American fathers have been found to have somewhat distinct influences on the development of their sons and daughters. Father involvement is relevant for helping sons to avoid problem behaviors, whereas for daughters involvement helps to prevent psychological distress (Salem, Zimmerman, & Notaro, 1998). Identification with the peer group is achieved earlier and more completely for boys than for girls. For both sexes it is a significant influence during the teen years. Boys, particularly, affiliate with informal gangs and are likely to be dependent on and influenced by them greatly. Concepts of womanhood and manhood are learned from the peer group. Friends are viewed as the source of rewards, both material and nonmaterial. In many families, dating has begun by age 12, as well as a heavy commitment to a peer group of the same sex. By adolescence an intensely sexual, frequently exploitative, web of informal social relations may have developed between the sexes.

In summary, African American parents instill in their children respect for authority figures, a strong work ethic, emphasis on achievement, a sense of duty and obligation to kin, a strong religious orientation, self-esteem and pride in their cultural heritage, and the importance of coping skills and resiliency (Julian et al., 1994; Kane, 1998).

Resources for African American Families

A number of researchers have pointed out that one of the strengths of African American families is the extensive support system provided by a network of relatives, friends, and neighbors. This system provides emotional support and economic supplements, better enabling the family to handle adverse external forces. Since the majority of both African American men and African American women work, this support system is even more important.

The kin network has been vitally important as a coping strategy for large numbers of these families. The extended network is a more salient structure for African American than for White families. African Americans see more of their kin other than their parents than do White families. More Whites have living parents than African Americans do. Aunts frequently become mother substitutes in African American families (McAdoo, 1993).

Even though many African Americans are reared in nuclear families, a large number still receive instrumental or task-oriented help from a significant adult other than the parents. The unmarried, divorced, or widowed are most often integrated immediately into the extended-kin network. Some of the services provided by this expanded network system include assistance with finances; help in making important decisions; assistance in planning and carrying out special occasions; and providing clothing, food, furniture, and transportation to various places. Usually help is extended in the areas of greatest need. Among poor African Americans, the extended family assists in the socialization of children (McAdoo, 1993).

Kinship networks may be declining. The size of African American families is decreasing. Young women giving birth out of wedlock are more likely now to move into their own households than to stay with their families. In addition, greater numbers of divorced or widowed men and women who can support themselves are living by themselves.

Some African American researchers have noted that the extended family also can be a liability for the African American family. In some instances it may deter upward mobility. Once a family has achieved a higher status, the family may be expected to provide help for other extended-family members. Thus, professional and social upward mobility may be limited to some extent because of the necessity of providing physical and financial resources to members of the larger family. The dilemma of upward mobility versus meeting the everyday needs of extended-family members is a very real one.

It is felt by some experts that if the welfare of African American children in this country is to be significantly enhanced, a national commitment will have to be made to full employment, a guaranteed minimum income, a comprehensive program of child development and child care, meaningful education, decent housing, a restructuring of the health-care system, and reconsideration of foster-child placements. Further, this commitment will have to be translated into public policies and comprehensive programs at the national level. Most of these ideas were debated in the 1990s, but little progress has been made.

In sum, varying viewpoints of African American families in the United States are represented by the cultural deviant, cultural equivalent, and cultural variant approaches. Despite the lack of agreement among these approaches, it seems clear that the families are characterized by a number of behavior patterns and traditions that are significantly related to child-rearing practices.

There is considerable evidence to refute the persistent image of the African American family as being matriarchal. Egalitarianism in family roles seems to be more common than once believed, especially among the middle class. Nevertheless, African American mothers seem to be especially close to their children, and the differences in child-rearing patterns for male and female children seem to be especially visible. The network of relatives, friends, and neighbors who provide a support system for the families is seen as being a particular strength, but some believe that it has been a factor in limiting upward mobility.

Clearly it can be concluded that many African American families have been the victims of racism, poverty, and limited education, which accounts for many of the stereotypes that have held sway, and both future research and new programs are needed to completely replace these attitudes.

Future Research Needs

Over the last two decades a more balanced depiction of African American family life has emerged, with growing appreciation of the diversity of these families in both status and form. The tendency to compare African American families with the

White middle-class family norm is just beginning to be replaced by research that examines differences within African American families. Research must consider the impact and interrelationships among factors that operate at varying levels and potentially manifest themselves through diverse behaviors and phenomena—for example, linkages between changes in family structure and alterations in family relationships and functioning. Research must occur within expanded disciplinary frameworks to avoid viewing African American family phenomena in isolation and separate from other perspectives. The tendency to view African American families as a collection of the problems and challenges they face has diverted attention from important and basic issues of family functions, structure, and relationships and has largely restricted the research focus to that of "problem Black families." Critics of African American family research have noted that simply making racial comparisons in which White behaviors are designated as the standard of baseline research invariably indicates the presence of deficiencies in African Americans. Future research must avoid this temptation (Taylor et al., 1991).

PARENTING IN MEXICAN AMERICAN FAMILIES

The principal origins of Hispanic people in the United States are Mexico, Puerto Rico, and Cuba, and the descendant population of all three groups is scattered widely. High immigration rates and birthrates have increased considerably the nation's Hispanic population in the last two decades. In 1996 Hispanics in the United States totaled more than 27 million, almost doubling since the 1980 census. Hispanics are concentrated in nine states, led by California and Texas (U.S. Bureau of the Census, 1997). Census data have often failed to distinguish the three Hispanic populations from one another by identifying a Hispanic as one with a Spanish origin, one with a Spanish surname, and/or one who uses the Spanish language. However, it has been pointed out that Hispanics of Mexican descent are considerably

different on a number of characteristics from non-Mexican Hispanics.

In 1995 there were almost 18 million Mexican Americans, representing by far the largest Hispanic subgroup in this country. Ninety percent of Mexican Americans live in the West and the South. Though recent data suggest that Hispanics, especially those between the ages of 25 and 34, are getting much closer to non-Hispanics in completing high school and college, data reported in 1996 indicated that Mexican Americans (both males and females) complete fewer years of formal education and are less likely to graduate from high school than other Hispanics. Fifty-three percent of Mexican Americans have less than a high school education. Further, they are considerably lower on the occupational scale than other Hispanics, with Mexican Americans having higher percentages of manual laborers and farmers. Median incomes of Mexican American women are lower than those of all other, non-Mexican Hispanic women, and Mexican American men earn less than Cubano men (U.S. Bureau of the Census, 1997). It has been said, however, that Mexican Americans represent the nation's second largest and most rapidly growing ethnic group. Because of the differences among Mexican Americans and other Hispanics and because of the large number of Mexican Americans in this country, we have chosen to limit our discussion to parenting in Mexican American families.

Demographics

There are a number of demographic characteristics that differentiate the Mexican American family from the dominant White family in the United States. The first is its high fertility rate. Mexican Americans have the highest fertility rate of any major ethnic and racial group in the United States (U.S. Bureau of the Census, 1998). Attitudes and normative beliefs (what others think one should do) of significant others, combined with motivation to comply with those reference groups, have a relationship to whether Mexican American women will or will not have more children. Those with lower incomes, less education, lower parity, and of the Catholic faith are more influenced in fertility by their normative beliefs. Further, evidence suggests that the church's influence on the fertility of Mexican American women is considerably less than might be expected.

In 1996, 72 percent of Mexican American children under 18 lived with both parents in intact families, a figure higher than the population in general, but down from 81 percent in 1980. In 1996, 21 percent of Mexican American families with children under 18 were headed by females, and 7% were headed by males. Recent data have challenged the long-held notion that Hispanic families have lower rates of marital disruption than others. Though the actual divorce rates for Mexican Americans are lower than for non-Hispanic Whites, when separations are included, the differences disappear. Marital stability is inversely related to level of education among Mexican Americans (U.S. Bureau of the Census, 1998).

In 1996, 76 percent of Mexican American males earned less than $25,000 per year, and the majority of females earned less than $20,000 per year. Thirty-one percent of all Mexican Americans and 34 percent of all Mexican American children live below the poverty line (U.S. Bureau of the Census, 1997).

Family Roles and Relationships

Many descriptions of Mexican American family life have presented negative, stereotypical views, with little optimism for the ultimate fate of Mexican American children. That image persisted for some time, but beginning in the late 1970s, a number of researchers began to challenge it. First, earlier researchers may have been guilty of using the dominant family structure as a yardstick by which to measure "deviant" family patterns in minority groups, failing to be sensitive to other cultural or ethnic systems. Second, many recent researchers have contended that earlier research was based on persistent traditional stereotypes rather than on convincing empirical evidence. Even when differences from the traditional images were found, they were attributed to the Mexican American family's

acculturation or modernization, as if an acculturated family was somehow "more correct." Or data that did not fit the picture were ignored, discarded, or considered irrelevant (Mirandé, 1977; Zinn, 1979). In fact, one writer concluded that the works he reviewed on Mexican American culture and family life constituted an exercise in social science fiction and presented a distorted view of Mexican Americans as passive, masochistic vegetables controlled by traditional culture (Romano, 1973).

A very different image of Mexican American family life has emerged. Mexican American writers argue that *la familia* is a warm and nurturing institution rather than an unstable, pathological one. The traditional concept of *machismo* has been redefined in terms of family pride, respect, and honor rather than in terms of male dominance. In fact, this view asserts that the family is the most important unit in life and individuals are likely to put the needs of the family above their own. The family, then, is depicted as a stable structure in which one's place is firmly established and cooperation among family members is emphasized. An important part of the concept of machismo is seen as the father's using his authority within the family in a fair and just manner. If he misuses his authority, he risks losing respect within the family and the community (Staples & Mirandé, 1980).

The family orientation of Mexican Americans has been a consistent theme in the literature for decades and has led to the traditional extended-family stereotype. In attempting to clarify many of the assumptions and interpretations that have produced pejorative images of these families, recent researchers have maintained that despite the adaptive requirements of acculturation and urbanization, Mexican Americans still enjoy large extended-family networks. It has been found that they participate in relatively large kin networks and engage in high rates of visiting and exchange. They are more willing than some other ethnic groups to agree that the family should be the resource for dealing with problems. Because of geographic closeness, kin are available and are used for meeting instrumental and affective needs. Whereas non-Hispanics have a tendency to migrate away from kin networks, Mexican

Americans have a tendency to migrate toward them. Kinship ties seem to be an enjoyable and expected set of practices and attitudes (Vega, 1991).

Education and income have been reported to be the best predictors of more available support and more contact with network members. Historically, a case has been made for kinship networks as exchange systems for people who are economically marginal, but researchers have noted emotional support as the main outcome of familism (the tendency to favor interaction and social support over other alternatives). Several researchers have reconfirmed the familistic orientation of Mexican Americans by noting that the family is the major source of advice and help across generations, but the acculturation process has created distinctive intergenerational expectations (Vega, 1991).

There is both evidence for continuity in traditional cultural gender expectations and evidence of more egalitarian relationships. In fact, studies have found a range of gender roles, from a patriarchal, role-segregated structure to an egalitarian, joint-role structure, with many combinations of these two polar opposites evident (Vega, 1991). It has been found that the availability of employment is the most important determinant of whether Mexican American women work. Chilman (1993) noted that a woman's power in relationships within and outside the family tends to increase when she is employed outside the home and has acquired a high level of education and independent income. When these roles shift, there may be considerable stress involved. Many investigators emphasize, however, that Mexican American families, like other Hispanic families, are adaptive, and gender-role expectations change as social conditions require.

Some scholars have described Mexican American family systems as extended, enmeshed, dense, and self-reliant (Vega, Kolody, & Valle, 1986). Recent studies have indicated that familism, and hence the availability of social support, increases with each generation living in this country. These findings contradict earlier views that the highest degrees of familism correlate with "Mexicanness" and Mexican birth and would become weaker in subsequent generations (Vega et al.,

1986). Nevertheless, the consequential role of familism among Mexican Americans, especially with regard to expressive support, cannot be overemphasized. Mexican American families have been described as "closed systems," with intense, multiplex relationships and with members who underutilize mental-health services. Perhaps this is due to the stress-buffering qualities of an endogenous support system. Familism is a basic source of emotional support for children. "Family" includes not only parents but also aunts and uncles, grandparents, cousins, and even friends. In fact, there is little distinction made between relatives and friends—often they are one and the same. The custom of compadres that dates to the colonial times remains intact in many families, with Mexican American adults reporting at least one, two, or three such relationships. Often these friends serve as godparents to the children. This kinship web imposes the obligation of mutual aid, respect, and affection (Ramirez, 1989).

Few important differences have been found between non-Hispanic Whites and Mexican Americans on marital satisfaction, wife labor-force participation, role expectation, family dynamics, or conjugal power (Vega et al., 1986). Further, few major differences have been found between Whites and Mexican Americans on dimensions of family functioning, such as cohesion and adaptability. Mexican American families are well functioning and resilient. Cohesion has been found to be highest at the early stages of the family life cycle, to decrease as children reach adolescence and thereafter, but to rise again as children leave home. Adaptability also decreases as families move through the child-rearing years and increases again when children leave home (Vega et al., 1986).

It is important to emphasize that there is no one typical Mexican American family, just as there is no one typical White family. Obviously such factors as education, income, age, geographic location, and time of migration to the United States contribute to a diversity of family types. In fact, time of immigration seems to have a fairly significant impact on the socialization of children (Buriel, 1993).

Rearing Mexican American Children

Only a few studies have been conducted on the child-rearing attitudes and practices of Mexican American parents, and those that exist fail to provide consistent conclusions. Some researchers have concluded that Mexican American parents are primarily permissive, whereas others have suggested that traditional values and authoritarian practices are more prevalent. Still others describe Mexican American families as nurturing and affectionate within a patriarchal, authoritarian family structure, with unusual respect for males and the elderly (Martinez, 1988).

One writer (Ramirez, 1989) noted that *el amor de madre* (motherly love) is a greater force in Mexican American families than wifely love; that is, the parent-child relationship is more important than the spousal relationship. Most homes are child-centered when children are young. Though there is an emphasis on good behavior, much nurturance and protection are provided to young children. There is a basic acceptance of the child's individuality and a relaxed attitude toward achievement of developmental milestones. As children approach the latency period and later (age 5 or so until puberty), parents begin to expect more responsible behavior from children; they are assigned tasks or responsibilities in accordance with their age and ability.

A recent observational study of predominantly lower-class mothers and their young children found few permissive Mexican American mothers, and authoritative and authoritarian mothers were about equal in number. Authoritative parents use rational, issue-oriented discipline techniques and set firm limits within a loving context. This style of child rearing is characteristic of White middle-class mothers but is thought to be inconsistent with the communal values of Mexican Americans. Although these results suggest that at least some Mexican American mothers resemble White mothers in their child-rearing patterns, others clearly do not (Martinez, 1993).

Dumka, Roosa, and Jackson (1997) examined mothers' parenting and children's adjustment in

Characteristics of Mexican American Families

Strong family ties
Migration toward kin networks
Emotional support
Two-parent participation in child rearing
Range of gender roles
Mutual aid, respect, affection
Authoritative, authoritarian, and permissive child-rearing styles
Differences in child rearing according to gender of child
Deference and respect accorded to fathers

low-income Mexican immigrant and Mexican American families. Mothers' supportive parenting was found to partially mediate the effects of family conflict on children's depression. High levels of supportive parenting were linked to low levels of children's depression and low levels of child conduct disorders, whereas high levels of inconsistent parenting were related to higher levels of children's depression and conduct disorder. Further, higher maternal acculturation was related to greater consistency in discipline, which then led to reduced depression in children.

The home environment of Mexican American children may vary according to their generation status. Shared cultural variables, particularly Spanish-language background and achievement aspirations, vary as a function of generational status. Surprisingly, first- and second-generation children often perform better in school than their third-generation counterparts, suggesting that immigrant parents, particularly mothers, may pass on high aspirations to their children (Buriel, 1993). Further, there is substantial variation in the degree of Spanish retention in each generation. One study found that personal aspirations were by far the most potent predictors of first, second, and third generations of Mexican American students, and that socioeconomic status was unrelated to most measures. These results seem to suggest that the strength of the relationship of socioeconomic status to achievement may be greater for White students than for Mexican American students (Buriel & Cardoza, 1988).

However, Buriel (1993) later found that child-rearing orientations of Mexican Americans differed with parents' education and income, but significantly with whether children were first-, second-, or third-generation immigrants. On average, years of schooling and family incomes are highest in the third generation. Further, changes in language usage may correlate with changes in child-rearing styles. Buriel found that mothers born in Mexico (where children were first- and second-generation immigrants) stressed early autonomy, productive use of time, strictness, and permissiveness more than mothers of third-generation children. Fathers of first- and second-generation children are similar to their spouses in areas of autonomy, strictness, and support. By contrast, fathers of third-generation children expect early autonomy of daughters only and less strictness of sons. Further, foreign-born parents score high on valuing responsibility, whereas U.S.-born parents score high on concern. Emphasis on a concern style reflects a shift toward the child-rearing norms of mainstream Euro-American society, arising from acculturation. However, the author concluded that a child-rearing style resembling responsibility may be crucial in fostering healthy social and academic development in Mexican American adolescents because delinquency and school achievement seem to be two serious problems among Mexican American adolescents who are third-generation immigrants.

As with other ethnic minority groups, there appear to be gender differences in the rearing of Mexican American children that become especially prominent at adolescence. Mothers seem to be particularly close to their daughters, and this closeness extends into and beyond puberty. The mother-son relationship is close but not as strong as that of mother and daughter. Fathers appear warm and affectionate when children are young and are playful companions. Some evidence suggests, however, that fathers become more aloof as children approach puberty, assuming the role of primary disciplinarian. Sons often are pampered and indulged more than daughters during childhood, and at adolescence they have far more freedom than girls do. Males often are encouraged to gain worldly knowledge outside the home, whereas females are likely to remain close to home and be protected and guarded in their contacts outside the family to preserve femininity and innocence (Ramirez, 1989).

One study suggested that Mexican American adolescents undergo the identity process somewhat differently from the way White adolescents do. Specifically, Mexican Americans have been found to be more "foreclosed" than Whites are on ideological identity, even when socioeconomic status is held constant; that is, they tend to adopt wholesale the commitments of others, usually their parents, without first testing the fit for themselves. Males are inclined to be more foreclosed and less "identity achieved" than females. This phenomenon may be due to the fact that minority status exposes Mexican Americans to a narrower range of available occupational and ideological roles and commitments than Whites, or there may be actual cultural differences in ways the two groups develop identity because of parental socialization techniques. The differences between the two groups in resolving difficulties such as sex roles, dating, friendship, and recreational preferences were less than differences related to issues of political and religious ideology, philosophical lifestyle, and occupation. Foreclosure is associated with warmth and support, but also a highly controlling parental style is optimal for effectively guiding youth into preconceived roles (Abraham, 1986).

Peers contribute significantly to the socialization of adolescent males, whereas adolescent females are more confined to the home and rely more heavily on mothers and sisters. The value of premarital chastity for females still exists, but its enforcement is more difficult than in the past. Even though strong role differentiation for males and females has persisted, there is evidence that many young Mexican Americans are challenging their traditional roles, thereby establishing more equality among males and females, especially among middle-class urban families.

In sum, when attempting to summarize the cultural aspects of parenting in Mexican American families, we are struck by several factors: (1) the lack of empirical data to support the stereotyped traditional view of the Mexican American family as rigid, patriarchal, and damaging to children; (2) the lack of control in research for socioeconomic status and level of education variables, thereby often confusing cultural values with social conditions; and (3) the tendency to generalize that Mexican American families are homogeneous in their family interaction and child-rearing patterns and to ignore the evidence of diversity among these families, taking into account structural family variables.

It does appear that there are some cultural differences in values between Mexican Americans and other cultural groups that account for differences in parenting. Probably the most important of these are familism (identification with the family) and the normative deference and respect formally accorded to the father. Other differences may well be the result of low socioeconomic status, lower levels of education, and structural components of the family itself. It should be remembered that the Mexican American family has experienced change, just as the Euro-American family has changed. Much of this change has occurred without rejection of the cultural heritage or assimilation into mainstream White society.

Future Research Needs

Because Mexican Americans are a rapidly growing ethnic group in this country, careful research still needs to be undertaken to give keener insight into these family relationships. Further, demographic data are needed that differentiate between Hispanics of Mexican and non-Mexican descent. Convincing empirical evidence, with socioeconomic status and educational variables controlled, would facilitate the elimination of stereotypes. Overgeneralization from idiosyncratic samples should be avoided. Especially important are data

regarding the way in which traditional values influence family relationships and parenting, attention to the diversity among Mexican American families, and in-depth studies of intergenerational relationships.

PARENTING IN NATIVE AMERICAN FAMILIES

According to the U.S. Census, Native Americans include American Indians, Eskimos, and Aleutians. Our discussion refers only to American Indians, by far the largest percentage of Native Americans. It appears that Native Americans currently have few, if any, ties to any particular geographic area. The majority currently reside in the southern and western portions of the United States (Pipes, Westby, & Inglebret, 1993). Unlike other minorities, however, Native Americans are more diverse than they are similar. For example, researchers report approximately 250 languages among Indians in the United States, complicated by phonetic variations. Further, the number of reported tribal groupings ranges from 300 to 400, with many subgroupings. The population of American Indians consists of distinct tribal and native groups with significant observable

---

_____ TIPS _____

For Professionals Working with Parents from Diverse Cultures

Avoid using White middle-class standards for assessing parenting behaviors.

Provide access to support services for families with children living in poverty.

Become familiar with the cultural characteristics of all families with whom you work—traditional rituals, language patterns, family members' roles and responsibilities.

Arrange for families to communicate with professionals in their home language.

Be aware of within-group differences in parenting styles to avoid stereotyping.

Respect families' goals in the bicultural socialization of their children.

customs, governance, language, income, and religion. Therefore, there are no absolute universal cultural norms for Indians (Dykeman & Nelson, 1995; Pipes et al., 1993).

Demographics

Contrary to popular belief, Native Americans are not a dying breed. At the present time, they number 2.3 million and are expected to reach 4.6 million by the year 2050. Between the 1980 and 1990 census, there was an increase of 38 percent in the Native American population. Approximately 35 percent of American Indians live on reservations or other tribally controlled land (U.S. Bureau of the Census, 1997), and an additional 13 percent live near or adjacent to Indian reservations (Pipes et al., 1993). The Bureau of Indian Affairs (BIA) has noted that more Indians have recently been returning to the reservations and that fewer are leaving. This phenomenon—combined with fewer infant deaths, better health services, and high fertility rates—accounts for part of the increase in population. Though American Indians can be found throughout the United States, five states contain the majority of Native Americans residing on reservations: Arizona, New Mexico, South Dakota, Montana, and Washington. American Indians have the longest tenure in this country of all racial minorities.

In 1996, 66 percent of family households were married couples, 26 percent were headed by single females, and 8 percent were headed by single males. In 1990 the average family size was 3.6, with household size varying on the reservations from 3.5 (Blackfeet) to 4.6 (Zuni). Rural Indian families are larger than urban ones, sometimes having five or more children, and Indian families as a group have more children under the age of 18 than does the general U.S. population. About half of Indian households include other relatives, and about one-fourth include individuals unrelated to the family (U.S. Bureau of the Census, 1993, 1997).

American Indians are among the most impoverished groups in the United States. Median income varies across tribes, ranging from just over $13,000 (Navajo) to just under $25,000 (Cherokee), with an average median income being $21,619. Thirty-one percent of Native American individuals and 27 percent of families are below the poverty line (U.S. Bureau of the Census, 1997). The 1990 census reported that more than half of American Indians living on reservations were below the poverty line, but there are vast differences among the reservations. For example, 49 percent on the Hopi reservation were poor as compared with 67 percent on the Pine Ridge reservation. In 1990 the per capita income for Native Americans living on reservations was $4,478, ranging from a low of $3,113 to a high of $4,718. It is estimated that 50 percent of families maintained by females are below the poverty line (U.S. Bureau of the Census, 1993).

In 1990, 69 percent of all American Indian males older than 16 were employed, but the figure fell to 62 percent on the reservations, again with considerable variation among the reservations. The proportion of females in the labor force increased from 48 percent in 1980 to 55 percent in 1990. Educational attainment has increased; in 1980, 56 percent of the population had graduated from high school, and in 1990, 67 percent had diplomas. On the 10 largest reservations, the figure for high school graduates drops to 54 percent, with a high of 66 percent (Blackfeet) and a low of 37 percent (Gila River) (U.S. Bureau of the Census, 1993).

Native Americans have an alcoholism rate 3.8 times that of other ethnic groups; cirrhosis of the liver is 4.5 times higher. The homicide rate is 2.8 times higher than in other groups, and the suicide rate is 2.3 times higher. The mortality rate from motor vehicle accidents is 5.5 times higher, and the infant mortality rate is twice the national average. One-third of Native Americans are classified as illiterate (LaFromboise & Low, 1989). Native Americans have the highest birthrate in the United States and the highest mortality rate. In 1990 only 8 percent of the American Indian population was 60 years or older, which is about half the proportion for the total U.S. population.

Housing, sanitation, and health characteristics are significantly inferior for many Native Americans, especially those that live on the reservations. Some dwellings lack water and electricity, and at least one-fifth of reservations lack complete plumbing. On the Navajo and Hopi reservations, respectively, 49 percent and 47 percent of the homes still lack complete plumbing (U.S. Bureau of the Census, 1993). Marginal incomes, substandard housing, poor transportation, and inadequate nutrition make American Indians more vulnerable to a variety of health problems. In 1955 the Indian Health Service assumed responsibility for Indian health care. Although death rates due to health problems are considerably higher than for the U.S. population as a whole, there has been a marked decrease since 1955. It can be concluded that even though conditions are improving for American Indians, as a group they are the most in need of services of all groups in this country.

Family Structure

Native American families are extremely diverse. Family structure, values, and roles and relationships differ from tribe to tribe. Actually, little is known about Native American families, and the knowledge is fragmented, anecdotal, descriptive, and often overpowered by poor understanding of tribal cultures. However, there is little disagreement among researchers that the family remains the basic unit of Native American society and community. Extended-family ties are very strong (Dykeman & Nelson, 1995). Native American families represent a combination of traditional beliefs, languages, and practices. They are characterized by a unique history and lifestyle and are supported by the strengths of their individual and tribal identity.

The traditional Native American family system is vastly different from other extended-family units in this country. These networks are structurally open, assume a village-type characteristic, and are usually composed of clans, which include several households of relatives. "Family" is defined by some tribes in terms of household composition, the extended family through second cousins, and clan membership (Carson, Dail, Greeley, & Kenote, 1990). The roles of family members and the structure of the extended family vary across tribes. Traditionally, they live in relational net-

works that serve to support and nurture strong bonds of mutual assistance and affection. Many engage in the traditional system of collective interdependence, with family members responsible not only to one another but also to the clan and the tribe (LaFromboise & Low, 1989).

Relationships between family members and the community can be complex. The degree of social and governing control exhibited by women or men depends on the tribe. Some tribes are more matriarchal, and others, patriarchal (LaFromboise & Low, 1989). Although the extended-family network is rapidly changing on many reservations, it is still a major factor contributing to family strengths. Guidance and wisdom received from elders facilitate family cohesion and resiliency, and the personal support from extended-family members and the community, especially during times of crisis, contributes immensely to family strengths (Carson et al., 1990).

Some Native American family systems can cover a broad geographic region and in fact represent an interstate family structure, with several households in each of several states. Still other family structures represent a small community in an urban area; for example, several households of the same family may be in close proximity to one another within an urban community. Finally, family households may be spread among several communities or cities of a metropolitan area. All these types of family structure represent lateral extension. Nevertheless, the family remains a repository of values and guides behavior through all stages of the life cycle (London & Devore, 1988).

Native Americans view their extended family as a source of strength and perennial support, offering multiple opportunities for the effective socialization of children, but some feel that the extended-family system is greatly misunderstood by human-service professionals. There have been numerous attempts to impose the traditional Western model of the nuclear monogamous family on Native Americans, but they have struggled continuously to maintain their tribal identities and at the same time their special relationships with the federal government. Generally, Native Americans have not wanted or acquiesced to acculturation and assimilation into mainstream society. Instead of being viewed as a culturally variant but well-functioning society, they have largely received societal ridicule for their resistance to the norms and models of middle-class American society.

Value Orientation

The value systems of Native Americans as a group have consistent themes, with tribal-specific expectations. Common among all tribal groups are tribal loyalty, respect for elders, reticence, humility, avoidance of personal glory and gain, giving and sharing with as many as three generations of relatives, precedence of group goals over individual goals, rich oral traditions, group cohesion and consensus, and an abiding love for their land (Dykeman & Nelson, 1995; London & Devore, 1988; Pipes et al., 1993).

Other values include responsibility, courage, patience, optimism, and contentment that is derived from a cosmic identity, a spiritual orientation to life, and traditional religious practices. Living in harmony with all of nature, including human beings, is paramount, and the world of nature often is used as a tool for learning both within and beyond the family (Carson et al., 1990). Native Americans may feel indifferent toward acquiring material goods. Traditionally, the acquiring of "things" for the sake of ownership or status is not as important as being a good person (Little Soldier, 1992).

Many Native Americans tend to view time as flowing and relative—things are done as the need arises rather than by the clock or according to some future-oriented master plan. Time is perceived as flexible and geared to the activity at hand. There is a tendency to live in the present and seek immediate gratification (Little Soldier, 1992).

Most Native Americans value noninterference. Any kind of intervention (for example, by social workers) is contrary to Indians' strict adherence to the principle of self-determination. The less assimilated and acculturated the individual, the more important this principle is to him or her. Further, the majority culture norm of quick self-

disclosure in therapeutic intervention does not extend to American Indians (Dykeman & Nelson, 1995). These phenomena characterize Navajos; the tribes of the northern and southern plains; and, to some extent, other tribes and the Pueblo Indians. It is not clear from the literature how much can be generalized based on these values (Strauss, 1986).

Parent-Child Interactions

Perhaps because of the diverse nature of American Indians, there is little systematic knowledge about parenting styles and how they vary from tribe to tribe. Further, because few widely used developmental tests have been standardized for American Indian populations, we have little insight into the development of American Indian children. However, child-rearing practices are shaped largely by Indian worldviews, which regard children as beloved gifts. Native Americans are described as having a "beautiful blindness" toward children with disabilities (Pipes et al., 1993). Time spent caring for, playing with, and admiring children is cherished. Native Americans celebrate milestones in early childhood, such as the first steps, first smile, first word, and so forth, but no pressure is

HIGHLIGHTS

Characteristics of Native American Families

High poverty rates
Diverse values, roles, and relationships across tribes
Family is the basic unit of society and community
"Family" includes household residents, extended family, and clan members
Relational networks support and nurture strong bonds of mutual assistance and affection
Elders provide guidance and wisdom
Many individuals participate in child rearing
Living in harmony with nature is valued
Participation in tribal ceremonies and rites of passage
Group-oriented philosophy

felt over the timing of these events (LaFromboise & Low, 1989).

The most striking difference in child rearing and socialization is the exposure of children to a wide array of persons to whom they can become attached—parents, siblings, aunts, uncles, cousins, and grandparents—thus protecting children and providing them with the assurance of love (Dykeman & Nelson, 1995). Grandmothers and aunts, and in some tribes men, share in child care. The extended family plays as much a role in child rearing, supervision of children, and the transgenerational transmission of teachings and customs as do parents. Grandparents perpetuate the oral tradition—they are safekeepers of tribal stories. They engage in purposeful activities with grandchildren that are geared toward passing on cultural values and beliefs and educating children about the physical, social, and spiritual world. There also are indirect lines of communication about children's behavior—for example, from the mother to the aunt or uncle—that serve to protect the bonds between parents and youth (Carson et al., 1990; LaFromboise & Low, 1989).

Children are regarded as important to the family and are accorded as much respect as adults—adults rarely hit children. In fact, physical punishment usually is not condoned. Parents more often use facial expressions and other body language to indicate disapproval, or they use social shame (embarrassment). Shouting when correcting a child is disapproved of. Autonomy is highly valued, and children are expected to make their own decisions and to operate semi-independently at an early age. Parents give children choices and allow them to experience the natural consequences of them. The impact of the child's behavior on others is emphasized. Children are not socialized to expect praise for that which is already required of them; parents reserve praise for special accomplishments. It is these characteristics of parenting that sometimes are perceived as overly permissive or negligent by nontribal social workers.

Families encourage children and youth to participate in tribal ceremonies, and parents devote considerable time and effort to making items for children to wear or to use in ceremonies. Traditional rites of passage that are symbolic of entrance into adulthood are common, and these practices are an integral part of the maintenance of individual, family, and tribal identity (Carson et al., 1990).

Native American children demonstrate lower school achievement than most other groups, and they have the highest dropout rate. These problems are due to a number of factors, including health and family problems, geographic distances from schools, absenteeism (sometimes because of tribal ceremonies), and lack of culturally relevant instructional materials and approaches to learning. White teachers who are unfamiliar with tribal cultures frequently interpret language and cultural differences as deviant. For example, most White teachers focus on verbal instruction, whereas most Indian children learn better through visual means. Lack of eye contact is the most notable difference frequently cited between White and Native American children. Some tribes consider it rude and disrespectful to make direct eye contact with authority figures. A bowed head is a sign of respect (Pipes et al., 1993).

As Indian children enter school, they often feel stranded between two cultures. Many speak a first language other than English, practice an entirely different religion, and hold different cultural values, yet they are expected to perform successfully according to conventional White criteria. Native American children in the upper elementary grades often are perceived as uncommunicative, but silence is comfortable in traditional Native American culture. Further, when there is pressure for a right answer, Native American children would rather remain silent than risk being called upon and being embarrassed and ridiculed. Since these children have grown up with a group-oriented philosophy, striving for individual achievement is foreign to their world outside of school. They prefer anonymity, harmony, and cooperative rather than competitive learning. Because children are likely to feel marginal in both cultures, biculturalism must become an educational priority (Little Soldier, 1992). During the past two decades, Indian education has come under increasing tribal control, and there is more emphasis on tribal history, Indian languages, and increased self-esteem.

The Indian Child Welfare Act

The Indian Child Welfare Act (ICWA) became law in 1978, after 4 years of congressional lobbying. The intent of Congress was to increase the probability that tribal children would grow up in tribal environments. Research had indicated a high correlation between children's removal from tribal cultural settings and subsequent problems with parenting, alcoholism, and suicide (Blanchard & Barsh, 1980). However, passage of the act has caused concern, controversy, and misunderstanding among social workers, particularly between Indians and non-Indians. They cannot agree on how much American Indian children and families benefit by provisions of the act.

American Indians themselves have been gravely concerned about the barriers that have existed to the reunification of American Indian families after separation of a staggering percentage of children from their families. Placing children in non-Indian homes, not allowing parents to visit their children while the children are in substitute care, placing children at great distances from their homes, a series of foster-care placements over a short time, and the disruptive responses of children following visits by their parents have all been viewed as obstacles to family reunification. Thus, the ICWA was initiated. The law returns to tribes the responsibility for and jurisdiction over American Indian children.

According to Goodluck (1989), the enactment of the ICWA brought about the following improvements: an increase in tribal family and children's programs, an increase in tribal service delivery systems on the reservation for abused and neglected children, and an increase in ICWA training and leadership opportunities for direct staff and administrators. In addition, significant case law has been developed that confirms the original act's goals and objectives, specifically to promote the security and well-being of children within the tribal context and to prevent the unnecessary breakup of extended families. The findings of three national centers that have researched and surveyed the impact of the act indicate that it has made a difference, but many problems continue. Their findings show that Native American children are still being placed at a higher rate, but the placements are at the direction of the tribal systems, under the supervision of tribal workers, and within Native American homes, which encourage tribal value systems.

In sum, it is difficult to make generalizations about parenting in American Indian families. Because of their diversity, family lifestyles cannot be studied easily; and because of Native Americans' resistance to being studied by non-Indian researchers who are critical and biased, even less data are available. To be sure, there are strengths in traditional Native American values and practices that have not been emphasized in the literature by those with little understanding of this minority culture. And further, the status of Native American families is in a state of transition. Nevertheless, it seems imperative that educators, social workers, psychologists, and health personnel make an effort to understand and appreciate the heritage of Native American families so that those children can experience a sense of competence and self-satisfaction in on- or off-reservation situations.

Future Research Needs

There is no doubt that adaptive behavior must be understood within a sociocultural environment. Future research must test treatments that are adaptable to both tribal and nontribal environments. Researchers require deeper insight into the Native American heritage of values and family structure and the role of culture in the child's overall development. Assistance programs must provide support to Native American families in the form of child care, counseling, homemaker services, alcohol- and drug-abuse programs, respite care, foster-care and adoption subsidies, legal counseling, and protective services programs for children. And, finally, Native Americans themselves must be given greater opportunity to prepare for careers as psychologists, health personnel, social workers, and anthropologists so that the body of really insightful data can be enlarged.

PARENTING IN ASIAN AMERICAN FAMILIES

The literature on Asian American families is scant in comparison with the research on other cultural groups, especially African American and Mexican American families. Asian Americans have been described as the "model minority." In fact, they represent a diverse, heterogeneous population, including Japanese Americans, Chinese Americans, Filipino Americans, Korean Americans, Vietnamese Americans, and other Southeast Asian refugees. Therefore, there is considerable variation among these groups in demographic characteristics, values, family traditions, and parent-child interactions. Further, the time of immigration to the United States seems to affect the degree of acculturation and assimilation into mainstream American culture, with third- and fourth-generation Asian Americans demonstrating more similarity to the majority culture than first- and second-generation immigrants. This section will focus primarily on Japanese Americans and Chinese Americans, the two groups for whom the most data exist.

Historical Perspectives

Chinese immigrants came to the United States in two streams of different character: The first began in the 1820s when impoverished rural Chinese came to work on the railroads and in the mines; the second began in 1847 and consisted of middle- and upper-class Chinese who came to seek higher education or to join relatives who had professional degrees (Young-Shi & McAdoo, 1993). Another influx of Chinese immigrants into the United States began to occur in the 1960s.

Early Japanese immigration to California was similar to that of the Chinese. Large-scale emigration of Japanese people to America began in the late 1880s. After the passage of the Chinese Exclusion Act in 1882, Japanese laborers were brought in to replace the departing Chinese laborers.

The Chinese system of patrilineal descent divided household property and land equally among adult sons, usually upon the marriage of the youngest son. Responsibility for the support of aging parents was shared by all the sons. Conversely, daughters married out of the village, did not inherit property, and were not responsible for the support of elderly parents. For those fortunate enough, ownership of property and land provided a strong tie to the Chinese village of emigration. Therefore, to ensure a continuing bond to family and village, emigrating Chinese men were expected to leave their wives and children behind. "Without the establishment of families in America, there was little incentive for early Chinese immigrants to invest in acquiring the cultural and social skills necessary to get on in Anglo society" (Nee & Wong, 1985, p. 289).

Like the Chinese, early Japanese immigrants came to America as temporary residents, to earn the higher wages available here and to return to Japan upon completion of their work contracts. However, differences in Japanese and Chinese rural social structure resulted in a weaker tie to family and village for Japanese immigrants. The Japanese inheritance system was one in which one son, usually the oldest, inherited the property and land and was responsible for the care of aging parents. Younger sons could pursue their fortunes elsewhere; therefore, the extended-kinship system in Japanese villages was much weaker than in Chinese villages. By the second decade of sustained Japanese immigration, the formation of families became important. The weaker tie to family and village in Japan permitted the early formation of Japanese family life in America, and by 1920, there was a sizable second generation of Japanese Americans in this country.

These differences had implications for the well-being of the two groups in America. As long as the Chinese viewed their American experience as temporary, failing to establish families and produce a large second generation, they retained the characteristics of low educational attainment and high illiteracy. To make matters worse, a strong anti-Chinese movement emerged, characterized by ethnic antagonism and violence, culminating in the passage of the Chinese Exclusion Act in the early 1880s. Thus, it was more than 80 years after the beginning of large-scale immigration of Chinese and the formation of immigrant families in America before significant socioeconomic gains occurred (Nee & Wong, 1985).

On the other hand, by 1920 the sizable second generation of Japanese American children began to enter American public schools and to achieve the high educational goals that still characterize this population. The transition from Japanese sojourner to settler was much more rapid, then, than that for Chinese immigrants. Nevertheless, both groups experienced considerable discrimination and hostility. Since World War II, all Asian Americans have made significant socioeconomic gains. However, the large influx of Chinese immigrants in the 1960s has had the effect of lowering the overall socioeconomic profile of Chinese Americans, compared with that of Japanese Americans (Nee & Wong, 1985).

Demographics

Chinese Americans—the largest Asian American population, numbering approximately 2.3 million—are an extremely heterogeneous group socially, politically, and culturally. They emigrated from a number of provinces in China and countries in Asia and thus speak a variety of dialects. The majority of the population now resides along the East and West coasts and around metropolitan areas. Chinese Americans have among the highest incomes of many ethnic minorities, with the median family income being approximately $38,000 in 1990 (U.S. Bureau of the Census, 1993). However, many are unemployed or underemployed, receiving lower wages than their peers for comparable work, especially recent immigrants. Therefore, they span the range of socioeconomic status. Even though education is highly valued, there is still a high percentage of Chinese American illiterates (Huang & Ying, 1989). Seventy-four percent of Chinese Americans 25 years and older have finished high school, and 41 percent have bachelor's degrees or higher (Lee, 1998).

Japanese Americans are the third largest Asian American population—numbering approximately 925,000, behind Chinese Americans and Filipino Americans—and are concentrated in the West and in Hawaii. However, the Japanese American population has been declining—from 21 percent of all Asian Americans in 1980 to 10 percent in 2000. The outmarriage rate of Japanese Americans (rate of marriages to persons outside their population) is greater than 60 percent. With the declining population and the increasing outmarriage rate, many worry that the Japanese American culture and values will disappear altogether. Hawaiian Japanese Americans live in an environment with many Asian Americans and tend to preserve their Japanese culture to a greater degree than their mainland counterparts. Differences also exist between those in Los Angeles, where there is a concentrated population, and those in Chicago, where they are widely dispersed (Lee, 1998).

Both education and family interdependence are valued by Asian American parents.

Educationally, Japanese Americans are above the national average, with almost all of the population finishing high school. Not surprisingly, they have one of the highest incomes of all groups (median family income was nearly $52,000 in 1990) and one of the lowest poverty rates (7 percent in 1990). In fact, it has been reported that Japanese American households have the second highest income in the country, second to Jews, presumably because of outstanding achievement in educational attainment. Another factor contributing to their economic status is low rates of separation and divorce, resulting in 85 percent of children under 18 living with two parents. Still, some Japanese Americans are underemployed, making less than their non-Asian peers. Japanese Americans have low rates of delinquency, and they are underrepresented in child-abuse statistics (Lee, 1998; Nagata, 1989).

Chinese American Families

Family Characteristics.   The historical and cultural antecedents of Chinese family characteristics derive from Confucian traditions, passed from one generation to the next, which still impose an Eastern philosophy on Chinese American families. Confucian philosophy dictated a sense of order and prescribed role relationships in Chinese society. Guidelines were provided for specific family relationships and patterns of communication. Negotiations with the outside world were delineated, with the goal of harmonious existence in society.

There was strong emphasis in traditional Chinese society on specific family roles and the proper behavior associated with each. The role structure was vertical and hierarchal, with the father as the undisputed head of the family. The obligations, responsibilities, and privileges of each role were clearly delineated. The father's authority was unchallenged, and he received total respect and loyalty from all family members. In return, he assumed maximum responsibility for the family's social status and economic well-being. The mother was responsible for emotional nurturance of family members and for their psychological well-being, her primary role being to serve her husband and rear the children. Though she was less removed and distant than the father, she was accorded respect by the children. She was discouraged from working outside the home. In traditional Chinese families, there also were gender and birth privileges, with sons more highly valued than daughters. Lineage was passed through the male, whereas females were absorbed into the families of their husbands. The role of female was less rewarding because females did not gain status and respect until they became mothers-in-law (Huang & Ying, 1989; Yau & Smetana, 1996).

As China has modernized, these roles have changed radically, and only derivatives of them may be found in Chinese American culture. For example, contemporary fathers may be figurative heads of families, with the mother as the driving force and the decision maker behind the scenes. Male/female role distinctions are far less glaring. Many Chinese Americans have attempted to reconstruct the kin network, with the extended family as the primary unit, but these relationships often have become disrupted. Some still see the extended family as an important source of social and sometimes financial support, but others see it as a burden and a restriction of autonomy.

In traditional Chinese families, gender and age governed the degree of open expression allowed, as well as the structure of the language used and the topics discussed. Even now, expression of emotion generally is frowned upon and suppression of undesirable thoughts or emotions is highly valued, views that are in stark contrast to the American value of speaking one's mind. Reciprocity in interaction that is obligatory and unspoken is still of paramount importance. Behavior is often dictated by a sense of obligation or, conversely, to avoid being in a situation of obligation. Shame and loss of face are guiding principles of behavior and powerful motivating forces for conforming to family and societal expectations. Even honesty and truthfulness are secondary to saving face for self and for others. Interdependence is the foundation of Chinese culture, with group values being more highly valued than individual desires (Huang &

Ying, 1989; Miller, Wiley, Fung, & Hui Lang, 1997; Yau & Smetana, 1996).

Parent-Child Interactions.   Individuals in Chinese society are believed to have the potential from within to achieve fulfillment and happiness. A sincere effort to conduct oneself morally and to develop one's potential brings personal satisfaction. *Filial piety* is a central Confucian concept and has governed intergenerational Chinese families for centuries. It is a complex system that involves a series of obligations of child to parent—most centrally to provide aid to, comfort to, affection to, and contact with the parent and to bring glory to the parent by doing well in educational and occupational areas, that is, achieving success in the outside world. It means that children are expected to satisfy their parents, to respect and to show reverence for elders in all situations (Kelley & Tseng, 1992; Lin & Liu, 1993). The concept of filial piety, or *hsiao*, is deeply ingrained in Chinese culture and has served as the moral foundation of interpersonal relationships in China for centuries: "To encourage the hsiao of a son to his parents is also to encourage the loyalty of the people to the ruler" (Lin & Liu, 1993, p. 272).

Miller et al. (1997) described how storytelling functions as a means of socialization, but in different ways, for Chinese and American parents of 2-year-olds. Chinese parents were much more likely than American parents to tell stories about their children's transgressions, apparently viewing the child's transgressions as a way of teaching young children the appropriate rules of conduct. American parents were more likely to use the child's past experiences in stories for entertainment and affirmation. Other research has noted the subtle nature of Chinese American mothers' interactions with their children.

Chinese parents are very concerned about the education of their children and want them to do well academically. Traditional parents frequently insist that children learn a Chinese language. The parents' attitudes toward their heritage in a dominant society have always been considered to play a significant role in the children's cognitive develop-

ment and mental health. Young-Shi and McAdoo (1993) found that parents' attitudes toward Chinese culture and language usage with children were significantly correlated with boys' self-concept.

According to Kelley and Tseng (1992), Chinese parents tend to be warm, affectionate, and lenient toward infants and young children, but once they reach the "age of understanding," discipline becomes much more strict. Children are taught mutual dependence, group identification, self-discipline, and good manners, as well as the importance of education. Departure from parental goals is seen as a reflection on the parents; therefore, parents take complete responsibility for the development of their children and are very involved in child rearing. They view the parenting role mainly as one of teacher.

Gorman (1998) noted that even though Chinese parenting historically has been seen as more authoritarian than mainstream American parenting, some research suggests that authoritarian parenting may be a Western concept that does not accurately depict Chinese socialization. Gorman found little rule setting for adolescents among the Chinese mothers in the study, suggesting that these mothers did not characterize their roles as including domination and control. Rather, these mothers perceived that they were training their children, giving them guidance, and helping them to make good decisions; that is, they provided pertinent information and arguments but left the final decision in their children's hands. This approach is consistent with the Chinese cultural value of individual responsibility. Expectations for their children were based on mothers' deep desires for children's successful adjustment rather than on a need to dominate their children. Mothers were concerned about making sure their children became productive members of society and were not negatively influenced by their peers. Lack of concern over their children's academics was striking. Few mothers reported problems with their children's academic behavior, suggesting that influences on academics may be more indirect and subtle than traditionally identified means of involvement and influence. Mothers preferred the indirect approach to dealing with differences of opinion, rather than badgering, arguing with, or coercing their children. This style of interaction appears to reflect the cultural value of self-sufficiency and the importance of reaching the "age of understanding."

The author concluded that Chinese parenting is characterized by an interaction of expectations and filial obligation rather than parental control and child submission. Though the expectations were communicated in subtle ways, they appeared to be understood clearly by the children. This balance between subtle expression of parental expectations and compliance stemming from a deep sense of filial obligation appears to be at the root of many of these mothers' interactions with their adolescents.

Yau and Smetana (1996) examined adolescent-parent conflict in lower-class Chinese early, mid-, and late adolescents. They noted that adolescent-parent conflict reflects the development of autonomy during adolescence in both Chinese and American cultures. Conflicts over everyday issues of family life occurred frequently and were of moderate intensity. Conflicts emerged primarily over issues of exercising or maintaining personal jurisdiction. In this study, conflicts over homework and academic achievement and over teen behaviors (smoking, leisure activities, relations between parents and themselves) were reported more frequently by Chinese than American adolescents. Further, Chinese teenagers were more subtle and indirect in expressing disagreements with parents than American adolescents. Girls reported more conflicts than boys, and conflicts were primarily with mothers rather than fathers. Chinese adolescents reported their parents as warm but controlling, and mothers were warmer than fathers.

The father-son dyad is prominent in Chinese society, and parents often have a strong voice in the son's selection of a spouse. Even into adulthood, Chinese children remain emotionally and often financially attached to their parents. It is common for the adult child to move into an occupational position provided by family contacts. Whereas cooperation and obedience are highly valued, independence training is not. There is frequent giving and receiving of help between the generations—an indication of family solidarity. The Chinese maintain their self-esteem by having someone to depend on. The Chinese elderly are highly influential and highly valued; their experience is the major source of knowledge to children, and they are seen as a link to the gods (Lin & Liu, 1993).

Kelley and Tseng (1992) compared the child-rearing practices of immigrant Chinese and White mothers. The results suggested that the two groups had similar child-rearing goals, but immigrant Chinese mothers relied on traditional Chinese methods of socialization to achieve those goals. These mothers were maintaining strong bonds to Chinese culture, as evidenced by their participation in a church where Chinese was spoken and their children's attendance at a Chinese-language program. Chinese mothers reported a higher degree of physical control over their children, including the use of harsh scolding. However, both groups of mothers reported reliance on rule setting, with White mothers relying more heavily on this approach. Chinese mothers also reported less nurturance, responsiveness, and consistency and were more restrictive with their children than White mothers.

The use of reasoning was reported by both groups. The authors believe this approach to be uncommon in traditional Chinese families and suggest that this finding represents a shift in younger-generation Chinese away from traditional child-rearing patterns. Again, contrary to historical perceptions, no differences were observed in the degree to which mothers emphasized obedience. Also contrary to the results of previous research, abrupt changes in Chinese parenting behavior did not occur when the child entered primary school.

The subjects in the Kelly and Tseng study were first-generation Chinese Americans. Even so, some departure from traditional parenting practices was found. A complete understanding of parent-child relationships in these families will not be possible without continued research that includes second-, third-, and even fourth-generation Chinese American families from a range of socioeconomic levels.

Japanese American Families

Family Characteristics. Japanese American adults typically have been perceived to be successful, well acculturated, and mentally healthy, and their children often are seen as being obedient and educationally successful. Though these families have tended to remain intact, generational changes and outmarriage rates have affected the nature of family characteristics. Families vary enormously in the extent to which they have maintained the characteristics of the traditional family, which are as follows: emphasis on the household as the most important entity for early socialization and upbringing; emphasis on the group rather than the individual; loyalty; importance of rank and status; emphasis on ascribed and contractual obligations; vertical relationships (meaning that relationships are clearly defined to those above or below one's social status); conformity to societal norms; and social control based on shame and guilt. Authority of the traditional family is vested in the father and older male children (Nagata, 1989).

It has been said that Japanese American values, skills, attitudes, and behavior do not differ markedly from those of the average American. A possible explanation is that as white-collar and professional jobs opened to Japanese Americans in post–World War II, they moved into White residential suburbs and assimilated into American society. Their dispersed pattern reduced visibility as a racial minority and promoted higher outmarriage rates. Further, the concentration of family-run small businesses provides the economic basis for stable family life and resources to support high educational attainment. The combination of values compatibility, high educational attainment, and family stability account for the socioeconomic parity that Japanese Americans have achieved with middle- and upper-class Americans, despite a history of discrimination, and that is quite unlike the status of other minorities (Lee, 1998; Nee & Wong, 1985). Each successive generation of Japanese Americans is more acculturated than the last, and today's Japanese Americans probably are more influenced by American society than by their parents and grandparents (Nagata, 1989).

Parent-Child Interactions. Both middle-class White mothers and Japanese American mothers are child-centered; however, they tend to perceive and treat very young children in fundamentally different ways. The Japanese mother is likely to organize her interactions with her infant so as to consolidate and strengthen a mutual dependence

---

HIGHLIGHTS

Characteristics of Asian American Families

CHINESE AMERICANS	JAPANESE AMERICANS
Father is undisputed head of family	Authority vested in father and older male children
"Saving face" an important guiding principle	Emphasis on group as opposed to individual
Role differentiation	Loyalty
Gender and birth privileges	Child-centeredness
Obligatory reciprocity in interactions	Emphasis on prolonged dependency, obedience, conformity, and nonconfrontational parenting techniques
Interdependence/group values	
Filial piety (*hsiao*)	High educational and achievement expectations
High achievement expectations	High family stability
Value on cooperation and obedience	High level of parental education and income
Elders are highly valued	

between herself and her infant, and her goal is a passive, accommodative, placid baby. Some researchers maintain that in traditional Japanese families, training in behavioral deportment begins in infancy. Cross-cultural researchers have concluded that because of different patterns of interaction with their mothers in the United States and Japan, infants have learned how to behave in different and culturally appropriate ways by 3 to 4 months of age (Bornstein, 1989).

Japanese American mothers expect early mastery of emotional maturity, self-control, and social courtesy in their preschoolers. Culturally specific goals that Japanese American parents have for their school-age children include patience, persistence, and accommodation. There is an emphasis on prolonged dependency, obedience and conformity, and indirect, nonconfrontational techniques of parenting that rely on nonverbal communication. There is a reluctance to praise achievements and a hesitancy to speak out or to ask questions. Emotions tend to be repressed or internalized rather than expressed (Nagata, 1989).

A pervasive Japanese cultural value is to know one's role, accept one's place in society, and work hard to perform faithfully one's assigned task. Okagaki and Sternberg (1993) noted that both Japanese and White middle-class mothers value independence in children. For White mothers, the independence takes the form of assertiveness; for Japanese mothers, independence means that the child is able to enter into relationships of mutual sympathy, trust, and consideration—consistent with the central values of interdependence, cooperation, and collaboration. In their recent study, these researchers found that both White and Japanese American mothers gave higher importance ratings to the goals on teaching first and second graders socially conforming behaviors (e.g., following directions and obeying school rules) than to teaching socially autonomous behaviors (e.g., how to make friends and how to make decisions). However, unlike White parents, the Japanese American parents saw noncognitive attributes (such as motivation, social skills, and working hard) as important as or more so than cognitive skills.

One can conclude that middle-class White parents and traditional Japanese parents share many of the same goals for their children, notably educational achievement and economic security, but differ dramatically in the ways in which they reach those goals. However, generational status and acculturation level apparently influence the degree to which contemporary Japanese Americans maintain traditional child-rearing philosophies.

Summary

The Asian American population in the United States, which represents about 4 percent of the total population, consists of Chinese Americans, Filipino Americans, Japanese Americans, Korean Americans, Vietnamese Americans, and other Southeast Asian refugees. They are, then, a diverse and heterogeneous population, speaking many different languages and dialects. This section has focused on Chinese Americans and Japanese Americans, whose emigration patterns were very different, which accounts for some of the differences between the two groups today.

Emphasis on education and achievement in both groups has resulted in a high standard of living, at least for Japanese Americans. Families tend to remain small (1.1 to 1.4 children per family) and intact, and great emphasis is placed upon interdependence in family relationships, creating prescribed obligations of children to their parents. Fathers and sons (especially eldest sons) are the authority figures, and the social structure is vertical.

Although the child-rearing values between Asian American parents and middle-class American parents are similar in some ways, the particular child-rearing patterns used between the groups appear to differ. However, the longer Asian American families have resided in the United States, the more likely they are to be influenced by American behaviors. It is important, however, to emphasize that in some families, there is uncertainty about identification with the old and new cultures, and role relationships may become confused. Identifying differences in values and social norms among cultural groups and explicitly acknowledging the difficulties of simultaneously living in two social worlds may help children to succeed in creating a way of life that reflects the traditions, values, and languages of both cultures (Okagaki & Sternberg, 1993).

SIMILARITIES AND DIFFERENCES AMONG CULTURES

Because there are many subcultures in the United States, we do not have a single identifiable pattern of parent-child interactions or child-rearing techniques. Because we are a democratic society that values freedom of religion, freedom of speech, freedom of the press, and freedom of unique family values, cultural differences in parent-child interactions are evident. Each subculture has unique language patterns, each has traditional rituals, and each has its own perceptions of family structure, roles, and functioning.

In many ways the similarities among cultures are striking. Children are valued and respected, but the outward manifestations may be quite different. White cultures seem to value individualism over familism, whereas African Americans, Mexican Americans, Native Americans, and Asian Americans demonstrate strong relational bonds with family members. The traditional stereotype of African American families as matriarchal and of Mexican American families and Asian American families as patriarchal has been replaced by a more contemporary attitude of egalitarianism. Many members of African American, Mexican American, Native American, and Asian American cultures have become acculturated to the degree that they resemble the majority culture more than they do their own minority culture.

Most differences in parenting style are related less to ethnic background than to geographic location, level of education, and income. Recently there has been an attempt to preserve much of the cultural heritage of these minority groups. Surely one's cultural heritage affects one's life in many ways, regardless of the effort to become "assimilated" or "acculturated" into mainstream society. Even greater emphasis may need to be put on the preservation of language, values, rituals, and ethnic traditions in our pluralistic society. At the least, greater effort should be made to understand, appreciate, and cultivate the unique characteristics of our minority populations.

SUMMARY

Variations in parenting attitudes and styles are evident among the diverse cultural groups in the United States. This chapter has addressed the characteristics of and similarities and differences among four such groups—African Americans, Mexican Americans, Native Americans, and Asian Americans. Many other cultures exist in this country; unfortunately, space prohibits the discussion of additional groups.

A key variable relating to parenting practices in any ethnic or cultural group is the socioeconomic status of the families constituting that group. The literature of the 1960s and the early 1970s identified significant differences among lower- and middle-class parents in several areas. Contemporary research has found that the quality of the environment in low-income families is generally lower than for middle- and upper-class families. Fairly consistent differences in parental behavior also have been found. Many observers have emphasized that within-class differences may be as great as between-class differences.

The four ethnic groups discussed in this chapter clearly have distinctive characteristics; some derive from the cultural heritage of the group itself, and some are more related to the minority status the group has experienced for an extended period of time. However, those families that have been assimilated into the majority culture and have achieved middle-class status tend to use parenting practices that are similar to those of White middle-class society.

More objective research and support are needed to emphasize the strengths of culturally diverse groups and to determine how best to preserve these strengths through healthy parent-child relationships. Only then will damaging stereotypes be eliminated.

REFERENCES

ABRAHAM, K. (1986). Ego-identity differences among Anglo-American and Mexican-American adolescents. *Journal of Adolescence, 2,* 151–166.

AHMEDUZZAMAN, M., & ROOPNARINE, J. (1992). Sociodemographic factors, functioning style, social support, and fathers' involvement with preschoolers in African-American families. *Journal of Marriage and the Family, 54*(3), 699–707.

ALLEN, L., & MAJIDI-AHI, S. (1989). Black American children. In J. Gibbs et al. (Eds.), *Children of color* (pp. 148–178). San Francisco: Jossey-Bass.

BEE, H., VAN EGEREN, L., STREISSGUTH, A., NYMAN, B., & LECKIE, M. (1969). Social class differences in maternal strategies and speech patterns. *Developmental Psychology, 1,* 726–734.

BLANCHARD, E., & BARSH, R. (1980). What is best for tribal children? A response to Fischler. *Social Work, 25,* 350–357.

BLUESTONE, C., & TAMIS-LEMONDA, C. (1999). Correlates of parenting styles in predominantly working- and middle-class African American mothers. *Journal of Marriage and the Family, 61*(4), 881–894.

BOLGER, K., PATTERSON, C., THOMPSON, W., & KUPERSMIDT, J. (1995). Psychosocial adjustment among children experiencing persistent and intermittent family economic hardship. *Child Development, 66,* 1107–1129.

BORNSTEIN, M. (1989). Cross-cultural comparisons: The case of Japanese-American infant and mother activities and interactions. What we know, what we need to know, and why we need to know it. *Developmental Review, 9,* 171–204.

BRADLEY, C. (1998). Child rearing in African American families: A study of the disciplinary practices of African American parents. *Journal of Multicultural Counseling and Development, 26*(4), 273–282.

BURIEL, R. (1993). Childrearing orientations in Mexican American families: The influence of generation and sociocultural factors. *Journal of Marriage and the Family, 55*(4), 987–1001.

BURIEL, R., & CARDOZA, D. (1988). Sociocultural correlates of achievement among three generations of Mexican-American high school seniors. *American Education Research Journal, 25*(2), 177–192.

CARSON, D., DAIL, P., GREELEY, S., & KENOTE, T. (1990). Stresses and strengths of Native American reservation families in poverty. *Family Perspective, 24*(4), 383–400.

CHASE-LANSDALE, P., BROOKS-GUNN, J., & ZAMSKY, E. (1994). Young African-American multigenerational families in poverty: Quality of mothering and grandmothering. *Child Development, 65*(2), 373–393.

CHILMAN, C. (1993). Hispanic families in the United States. In H. McAdoo (Ed.), *Family ethnicity: Strength in diversity* (pp. 141–163). Newbury Park, CA: Sage.

CLARKE-STEWART, A. (1977). *Child care in the family: A review of research and some propositions for policy.* New York: Academic.

CONGER, R., GE, X., ELDER, G., LORENZ, F., & SIMONS, R. (1994). Economic stress, coercive family process, and developmental problems of adolescents. *Child Development, 65*(2), 541–561.

DODGE, K., PETTIT, G., & BATES, J. (1994). Socialization mediators of the relation between socioeconomic status and child conduct problems. *Child Development, 65*(2), 649–665.

DUMKA, L., ROOSA, M., & JACKSON, K. (1997). Risk, conflict, mothers' parenting, and children's adjustment in low-income, Mexican immigrant, and Mexican-American families. *Journal of Marriage and the Family, 59,* 309–323.

DUNCAN, G., BROOKS-GUNN, J., & KLEBANOV, P. (1994). Economic deprivation and early childhood development. *Child Development, 65*(2), 296–318.

DYKEMAN, C., & NELSON, J. (1995). Building strong working alliances with American Indian families. *Social Work in Education, 17*(3), 148–159.

FELNER, R., BRAND, S., DUBOIS, D., ADAN, A., MULHALL, P., & EVANS E. (1995). Socioeconomic disadvantage, proximal environmental experiences, and socioemotional and academic adjustment in early adolescence: Investigation of a mediated effects model. *Child Development, 66,* 774–792.

FORUM ON CHILD & FAMILY STATISTICS. (1999). *America's children: Key national indicators of well-being, 1999.* [On-line]. Available: http://www.childstats.gov/.

FRAZIER, E. (1939). *The Negro family in the United States.* Chicago: University of Chicago Press.

GARRETT, P., NG'ANDU, N., & FERRON, J. (1994). Poverty experiences of young children and the quality of their home environment. *Child Development, 65*(2), 331–345.

GODUKA, I. (1990). Racialization of poverty—American apartheid: Where does it leave the black child? *Family Perspective, 24*(4), 373–382.

GOODLUCK, C. (1989). Social services with Native Americans: Current status of the Indian Child Welfare Act. In J. Gibbs et al. (Eds.), *Children of color* (pp. 217–226). San Francisco: Jossey-Bass.

GORMAN, J. (1998). Parenting attitudes and practices of immigrant Chinese mothers of adolescents. *Family Relations, 47,* 73–80.

GREENE, B. (1995). African American Families. *National Forum, 75*(3), 29–33.

HALE, J. (1991). The transmission of cultural values to young African American children. *Young Children, 46(6),* 7–15.

HALE-BENSON, J. (1986). *Black children: Their roots, culture, and learning styles* (Rev. ed.). Baltimore: Johns Hopkins University Press.

HASHIMA, P., & AMATO, P. (1994). Poverty, social support, and parental behavior. *Child Development, 65*(2), 394–403.

HESS, R., & SHIPMAN, V. (1965). Early experience and the socialization of cognitive modes in young children. *Child Development, 36,* 869–886.

HUANG, L., & YING, Y. (1989). Chinese American children and adolescents. In J. Gibbs et al. (Eds.), *Children of color* (pp. 30–66). San Francisco: Jossey-Bass.

HUSTON, A., MCLOYD, V., & COLL, C. (1994). Children and poverty: Issues in contemporary research. *Child Development, 65*(2), 275–282.

JULIAN, T., MCKENRY, P., & MCKELVEY, M. (1994). Perceptions of Caucasian, African-American, Hispanic, and Asian-American parents. *Family Relations, 43,* 30–37.

KAISER, A., & DELANEY, E. (1996). The effects of poverty on parenting young children. *Peabody Journal of Education, 71*(4), 66–85.

KALIL, A., & ECCLES, J. (1998). Does welfare affect family processes and adolescent adjustment? *Child Development, 69*(6), 1597–1613.

KANE, C. (1998). Differences in family of origin perceptions among African American, Asian American, and Hispanic American college students. *Journal of Black Studies, 29*(2), 93–106.

KELLEY, M., POWER, T., & WIMBUSH, D. (1992). Determinants of disciplinary practices in low-income black mothers. *Child Development, 63*(3), 573–582.

KELLEY, M., & TSENG, H. (1992). Cultural differences in child rearing. *Journal of Cross Cultural Psychology, 23*(4), 444–455.

KLEBANOV, P., BROOKS-GUNN, J., MCCARTON, C., & MCCORMICK, M. (1998). The contribution of neighborhood and family income to developmental test scores over the first three years of life. *Child Development, 69*(5), 1420–1436.

LAFROMBOISE, T., & LOW, K. (1989). American Indian children and adolescents. In J. Gibbs et al. (Eds.), *Children of color* (pp. 114–147). San Francisco: Jossey-Bass.

LEE, S. (1998). Asian Americans: Diverse and growing. *Population Bulletin, 55*(2), Washington DC: Population Reference Bureau.

LIN, C., & LIU, W. (1993). Intergenerational relationships among Chinese immigrant families from Taiwan. In H. McAdoo (Ed.), *Family ethnicity: Strength in diversity* (pp. 271–286). Newbury Park, CA: Sage.

LITTLEJOHN-BLAKE, S., & DARLING, C. (1993). Understanding the strengths of African American families. *Journal of Black Studies, 23*(4), 460–472.

LITTLE SOLDIER, L. (1992). Working with Native American children. *Young Children, 47*(6), 15–21.

LONDON, H., & DEVORE, W. (1988). Layers of understanding: Counseling ethnic minority families. *Family Relations, 37*(30), 310–314.

MARTINEZ, E. (1988). Child behavior in Mexican-American/Chicano families: Maternal teaching and childrearing practices. *Family Relations, 37*(3), 275–280.

MARTINEZ, E. (1993). Parenting young children in Mexican American/Chicano families. In H. McAdoo (Ed.), *Family ethnicity: Strength in diversity* (pp. 184–192). Newbury Park, CA: Sage.

MCADOO, J. (1993). Decision making and marital satisfaction in African American families. In H. McAdoo (Ed.), *Family ethnicity: Strength in diversity* (pp. 109–119). Newbury Park, CA: Sage.

MCLEOD, J., & SHANAHAN, M. (1993). Poverty, parenting, and children's mental health. *American Sociological Review, 58,* 351–366.

MCLOYD, V., JAYARATNE, T., CEBALLO, R., & BORQUEZ, J. (1994). Unemployment and work interruption among African American single mothers: Effects on parenting and adolescent socioemotional functioning. *Child Development, 65*(2), 562–589.

MILLER, J., & DAVIS, D. (1997). Poverty history, marital history, and quality of children's home environments. *Journal of Marriage and the Family, 59,* 996–1007.

MILLER, P., WILEY, A., FUNG, H., & HUI LIANG. (1997). Personal storytelling as a medium of socialization in Chinese and American families. *Child Development, 68*(3), 557–568.

MIRANDÉ, A. (1977). The Chicano family: A reanalysis of conflicting views. *Journal of Marriage and the Family, 39*(4), 747–756.

MOYNIHAN, D. (1965). *The Negro family: The case for national action.* Washington DC: U.S. Government Printing Office.

NAGATA, D. (1989). Japanese American children and adolescents. In J. Gibbs et al. (Eds.), *Children of color* (pp. 67–113). San Francisco: Jossey-Bass.

NEE, V., & WONG, H. (1985). Asian American socioeconomic achievement: The strength of the family bond. *Sociological Perspectives, 28*(3), 281–306.

OKAGAKI, L., & STERNBERG, R. (1993). Parental beliefs and children's school performance. *Child Development, 64*(1), 36–56.

PADGETT, D. (1997). The contribution of support networks to household labor in African American families. *Journal of Family Issues, 18*(3), 227–250.

PIPES, M., WESTBY, C., & INGLEBRET, E. (1993). Profile of Native American students. In L. Clark (Ed.), *Faculty and student challenges in facing cultural-linguistic diversity.* Springfield, IL: Thomas.

RAINWATER, L. (1966). The crucible of identity: The lower class Negro family. *Daedalus, 95,* 258–264.

RAMIREZ, O. (1989). Mexican American children and adolescents. In J. Gibbs et al. (Eds.), *Children of color* (pp. 224–250). San Francisco: Jossey-Bass.

ROMANO, O. (1973). The anthropology and sociology of Mexican-Americans: The distortion of Mexican-American history. In O. Romano (Ed.), *Voices: Readings from El Grito, a journal of contemporary Mexican-American thought* (pp. 43–56). Berkeley, CA: Qunto Sal.

SALEM, D., ZIMMERMAN, M., & NOTARO, P. (1998). Effects of family structure, family process, and father involvement on psychosocial outcomes among African American adolescents. *Family Relations, 47,* 331–341.

SAMPSON, R., & LAUB, J. (1994). Urban poverty and the family context of delinquency: A new look at structure and process in a classic study. *Child Development, 65*(2), 523–540.

STAPLES, R., & MIRANDÉ, A. (1980). Racial and cultural variations among American families: A decennial review of the literature on minority families. *Journal of Marriage and the Family, 42*(4), 887–903.

STEVENS, J. (1997). African American female adolescent identity development: A three-dimensional perspective. *Child Welfare, LXXVI*(1), 145–172.

STRAUSS, J. (1986). The study of American Indian families: Implications for applied research. *Family Perspectives, 20*(4), 337–350.

SUDARKASA, N. (1993). Female-headed African American households. In H. McAdoo (Ed.), *Family ethnicity: Strength in diversity* (pp. 81–89). Newbury Park, CA: Sage.

TAYLOR, R., CHATTERS, L., TUCKER, M., & LEWIS, E. (1991). Developments in research on black families: A decade review. In A. Booth (Ed.), *Contemporary families: Looking forward, looking back* (pp. 275–296). Minneapolis: National Council on Family Relations.

U.S. BUREAU OF THE CENSUS. (1993). *Statistical abstract of the United States: 1993* (113th ed.). Washington, DC: U.S. Department of Commerce.

U.S. BUREAU OF THE CENSUS. (1997). *Statistical abstract of the United States: 1997* (117th ed.). Washington, DC: U.S. Department of Commerce.

U.S. BUREAU OF THE CENSUS. (1998). *Statistical abstract of the United States: 1998* (118th ed.). Washington, DC: U.S. Department of Commerce.

U.S. GENERAL ACCOUNTING OFFICE. (1992). *Poverty trends, 1980–88: Changes in family composition and income sources among the poor.* Washington, DC: Author.

VEGA, W. (1991). Hispanic families in the 1980s: A decade of research. In A. Booth (Ed.), *Contemporary families: Looking forward, looking back* (pp. 297–306). Minneapolis: National Council on Family Relations.

VEGA, W., KOLODY, B., & VALLE, R. (1986). The relationship of marital status, confident support, and depression among Mexican immigrant women. *Journal of Marriage and the Family, 48*(3), 597–605.

WALKER, D., GREENWOOD, C., HART, B., & CARTA, J. (1994). Prediction of school outcomes based on early language production and socioeconomic factors. *Child Development, 65*(2), 606–621.

YAU, J., & SMETANA, J. (1996). Adolescent-parent conflict among Chinese adolescents in Hong Kong. *Child Development, 67,* 1262–1275.

YOUNG-SHI, O., & MCADOO, H. (1993). Socialization of Chinese American children. In H. McAdoo (Ed.), *Family ethnicity: Strength in diversity* (pp. 245–270). Newbury Park, CA: Sage.

ZINN, M. (1979). Chicano family research: Conceptual distortions and alternative directions. *Journal of Ethnic Studies, 7*(3), 59–71.

CHAPTER 7

Parenting in Single-Parent Families and Stepfamilies

Dramatic changes began to occur in the marital behavior of American adults during the decade of the 1970s, and many of the trends have continued into the present. Specifically, the likelihood of marriage has declined or marriage has occurred later, divorce has increased to a record high and then leveled off, and significant changes have occurred in the living arrangements of both adults and children. A majority of households in the United States are not nuclear families with both biological parents living with their offspring. There has been a gradual, steady increase in the percentage of adults and children residing in single-parent, blended, or other households that frequently include nonrelated individuals (U.S. Bureau of the Census, 1997).

In 1996, 86 percent of the households in the United States were family households, with 40 percent of these being married couples living with their own children under 18 years of age. Only 2 percent were male households and 10 percent were female households with their own children under 18 years of age. Table 7.1 shows the number and percent change in types of households from 1980 to 1996. As noted, the actual number and percent change in male households increased considerably from 1980 to 1990 and continued to rise between 1990 and 1996. The greatest percent change was in female households from 1980 to 1990, with a significant

increase also occurring in these households from 1990 to 1996 (U.S. Bureau of the Census, 1997).

The growth in the number of single-parent families is significant. In 1980 there were 32,150,000 single-parent families in the United States. This number had increased to 37,077,000 by 1996. Almost 30 million of these families were White, 3.5 million were African American, and nearly 2 million were of Hispanic origin. Sixty-two percent of all African American families, 38 percent of all Hispanic families, and 26 percent of all White families are single-parent. The number of single-parent families almost doubled between 1980 and 1996 for both African Americans and Hispanics (see Table 7.3). During roughly the same period, the percent of married couples declined and the percent of single individuals increased.

Delayed marriage and divorce accounted for the increase in single individuals. Never-married persons make up the largest share of unmarried adults and a sizable portion of the total adult population. In 1996 nearly 27 percent of men and 20 percent of the adult population over 18 years of age had never married. Divorce still accounts for a significant number of single people. However, between 1980 and 1995, the rate of divorce per 1,000 people declined from 5.2 to 4.4 (see Table 7.2). Further, the number of divorced people who re-

TABLE 7.1

	1980*	% Change 1970–1980	1990*	% Change 1980–1990	1996*	% Change 1990–1996
HOUSEHOLDS 1980, 1990, 1996						
Family	59,550	16	66,070	11	69,594	5
Nonfamily	21,226	78	27,257	28	30,033	10
FAMILY HOUSEHOLDS 1980, 1990, 1996						
Married couples	49,112	10	52,317	7	53,567	2
Male households**	1,733	29	2,884	40	3,513	18
Female households**	8,705	36	10,890	20	12,514	16

Source: U.S. Bureau of the Census. (1997). *Statistical abstract of the United States: 1997* (117th ed.). Washington, DC: U.S. Department of Commerce.

*Number in thousands.

**No spouse present.

TABLE 7.2   Divorces 1980, 1990, 1995

	1980	**1990**	**1995**
Number 1,000 population	1,189	1,182	1,169
Rate 1,000 population	5.2	4.7	4.4

Source: U.S. Bureau of the Census. (1997). *Statistical abstract of the United States: 1997* (117th ed.). Washington, DC: U.S. Department of Commerce.

marry has declined from about 80 percent to approximately 57 percent. Approximately half of those who remarry are predicted to experience another divorce (U.S. Bureau of the Census, 1997).

Divorce, separation, and out-of-wedlock births have been responsible for the shift in the living arrangements of children. Not surprisingly, the percentage of children under 18 living with both parents has declined. In 1980, 79 percent of all children lived with both parents, whereas in 1996, 68 percent did (U.S. Bureau of the Census, 1997). Children tend to move from one family type to another—from a two-parent family to a single-parent family, to a stepfamily, and perhaps to a nonparental family. Aquilino (1996) examined the life course and transitions of children born to unmarried parents. He found that the respondents in a national sample experienced a variety of childhood living arrangements. Although the single-parent family was by far the most common by age 15, about one-fourth had never lived in a single-parent household before age 16. More than one-third lived in a stepfamily at some point, and one in four had lived with a grandparent or a relative with no parent present. Nearly one in four lived with two legal parents (either two biological or two adoptive parents) before age 16. When children were 3 years old and younger, most lived in two-parent family situations, with four out of five other living arrangements occurring fairly steadily throughout childhood.

This chapter will explore some of the problems experienced by families residing in single-parent and blended households. Parenting styles and suggestions for resources and supports for these family structures also will be examined.

SINGLE-PARENT FAMILIES

There are a variety of types of single parents, and no one label is strictly definitive. A single-parent family implies that a mother or a father is parenting primarily alone, but in many cases the noncustodial parent may be highly involved at least part-time in child rearing. In the definition we will be using, *single-parent family* refers to the living arrangements of the family structure consisting of one parent with dependent children living in the same household.

Single parents are not a homogeneous group; they exist in all social classes, in all racial and ethnic groups, and in all age groups from younger than 15 to older than 50. Divorces, separations, desertions, out-of-wedlock births, incarcerations, hospitalizations, military duties, out-of-state employments, and single-parent adoptions result in single parenthood. However, the rise in the divorce rate during the last quarter of the twentieth century and the increasing number of never-married persons account for most of the single parents in the United States today. Table 7.3 shows the number of single-parent households and the percentage of all family groups with children under 18 in the United States by race and Hispanic origin in 1980, 1990, and 1996.

Researchers have long been interested in the single-parent family. In the 1930s, 1940s, and 1950s, sociological studies of the single parent multiplied. Most of these studies, however, were related to father absence and its resulting effects. In reality, these studies were about single mothers and their problems and the effects of father absence on

TABLE 7.3   Single-Parent Households with Children under 18, by Race and Hispanic Origin 1980, 1990, 1996

SUBJECT	1980		1990		1996	
	*No.**	*%***	*No.**	*%***	*No.**	*%***
All Races	32,150	100	34,670	100	37,077	100
Maintained by mother	6,230	19	8,398	24	9,855	27
Maintained by father	690	2	1,351	4	1,862	5
White	27,294	100	28,294	100	29,947	100
Maintained by mother	4,122	15	5,310	19	6,329	21
Maintained by father	542	2	1,079	4	1,440	5
African American						
Maintained by mother	1,984	49	2,860	56	3,171	58
Maintained by father	129	3	221	4	320	6
Hispanic						
Maintained by mother	526	24	1,003	29	1,483	53
Maintained by father	120	3	138	4	219	5

Source: U.S. Bureau of the Census. (1997). *Statistical abstract of the United States: 1997* (117th ed.). Washington, DC: U.S. Department of Commerce.

*Number in thousands.

**Percentage of all family groups with children under 18 years of age.

children. Much of the controversy and contradiction regarding single-parent families centers on faulty or questionable conceptualizations and methodological issues in research. Until recently, single-parent families headed by males had been largely excluded from research considerations, and when they were studied, sample sizes were almost always small.

In the 1960s and 1970s, considerable data were collected on unwed teenage mothers. More recently, single fathers, other single parents, and the adjustment processes of single parents and their children have received increased attention.

Single parenthood, regardless of its origin, cannot be considered as a single event; rather, it is the process or the chain of events set into motion that determines the effects on the adults and children involved. Single parents are faced with a number of changes, including decreased financial resources; changes in residence; assumption of new roles and responsibilities; establishment of new patterns of intrafamilial interaction; reorganization of routines and schedules; and, eventually,

the introduction of new relationships into the existing family. The nature of these changes demands resources that are most often beyond those immediately accessible to individual family members (Hetherington, 1992). The following sections will examine some of these changes for mothers, fathers, and children.

Single Mothers

The vast majority of single-parent households are maintained by mothers—75 percent. Mother-child families are disproportionately concentrated among African Americans, with approximately 90 percent of their single-parent families headed by mothers. Of all children living in single-parent families, approximately 75 percent live with their mothers (U.S. Bureau of the Census, 1997).

Figure 7.1 indicates the percentage of single mothers according to race and Hispanic origin with children under 18 years of age who achieved single status because they never married or through divorce, widowhood, or absence of husband. As can

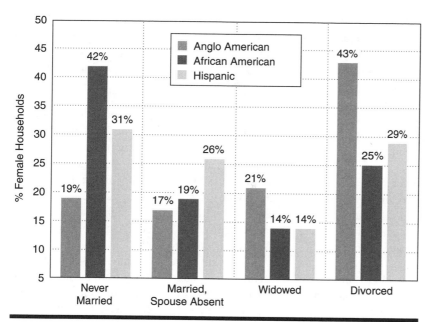

FIGURE 7.1 Types of Mothers with Children under 18 Years of Age, 1992
Source: Rawlings, S. (1993). *Household and family characteristics: March, 1992.* U.S. Bureau of the Census, Current Population Reports, P20–467. Washington, DC: U.S. Government Printing Office.

be noted, the largest percentage of both African American and Hispanic mothers had never been married, whereas the largest percentage of White mothers became single by divorce. Across all races, the percent of single mothers who were never married is approaching the percent who are divorced.

Given the importance of the family as a social institution, it is not surprising that researchers as well as policymakers have responded to the rise in the single-parent family structure with interest and concern. Some view the single-mother family as an indicator of social disorganization, signaling the "demise of the family." Others regard it as an alternative family form consistent with the emerging economic independence of women. However one views the change, the mother-only family has become a common phenomenon that has already begun to alter the social and economic context of family.

Sources of Stress for Single Mothers. Previous research has indicated that single mothers share common concerns, including income inadequacy, role overload, parenting and child care, social isolation, and emotional and psychological problems (Goldberg, Greenberger, Hamill, & O'Neil, 1992; McLanahan & Booth, 1991; Olson & Banyard, 1993). More recent research has continued to explore the problems of single motherhood. In particular, the economic plight of single mothers has been extensively documented. About half of all single mothers are poor. During the 1990s, more than 3.5 million custodial single mothers were living below the poverty line, and only one-third of these had child-support agreements. In contrast, only 207,000 single custodial fathers lived in poverty during the same period (U.S. Bureau of the Census, 1997).

Although many single mothers who live below the poverty line were poor before becoming single mothers, a sizable majority become poor at the time of marital dissolution. It has been estimated that the income of single mothers and their children 1 year after divorce is only 67 percent of their predivorce income, whereas for divorced men it is 90 percent of predivorce income. Therefore, children whose parents divorce often experience a dramatically reduced standard of living. Single-mother families are more likely than two-parent families to be poor because they have a low earning capacity, they often do not receive child support from the nonresidential father, and they receive meager benefits from the state (McLanahan & Booth, 1991).

Remarriage is the most common way out of poverty or financial distress for divorced mothers with children. Nevertheless, not all children whose mothers remarry return to the standard of living they experienced when their parents were together (Ganong, Coleman, & Mistina, 1995). There are racial differences as well. Folk (1996) noted that the mean income for African American single mothers was only slightly above the poverty threshold, whereas for White mothers it was twice the poverty threshold.

Earnings by the single mother constitute the major source of income for her family. Thus, her earning capacity is the most important factor in determining the family's economic status. Unfortunately, single mothers earn considerably less than other primary breadwinners, partly because they have a lower hourly wage and partly because they work fewer hours. Even those women who work full-time, year-round earn only about 60 percent as much as full-time male workers, suggesting that a large portion of the earnings gap may be due to gender discrimination in the labor market (McLanahan & Booth, 1991).

Hao and Brinton (1997) noted the divergence in labor force participation and school attendance in single and married mothers. Over the last two decades, employment has increased steadily for married mothers, especially those with young children, but employment of single mothers has been stagnant. Welfare reform probably will force more single mothers than ever before into attempting a speedy transition from welfare to work. However, neither welfare recipients nor low-wage working mothers seem to be able to make ends meet on their main income sources alone. Edin and Lein (1996) found that although working mothers had

more income left over after paying for housing and food, their overall budget deficits were larger because working was more expensive than relying on welfare. Specifically, welfare recipients in their study had a shortfall of $131 per month, compared with $411 for working mothers.

Aside from low wages, a major barrier to employment for most mothers is child care. Whereas in two-parent families the second parent can provide child care or share its cost, the single mother has no such support. Thus, she is doubly disadvantaged with respect to earning capacity; her wage rate is lower than that of the higher earner in a two-parent family, and her child-care costs are higher (McLanahan & Booth, 1991).

A second source of income for single mothers is child-support and alimony from the nonresidential father. However, most poor mothers do not even have a child support agreement, and when they do, only about one-third of them receive the full amount. Whatever they receive is not enough to bring women and children out of poverty (Pirog, Klotz, & Byers, 1998). Thus, those women and children most in need of support do not receive it. It is too early to determine the effects of increased efforts by all states to identify "deadbeat dads" and attempts to collect child support.

A final source of income for single mothers is public transfers. In 1996 the Opportunities Reconciliation Act (known as welfare reform) created sweeping changes in the nation's social safety net for poor women and children. It replaced Aid to Families with Dependent Children (AFDC) with Temporary Assistance to Needy Families (TANF) so that low-income families no longer receive benefits if they meet certain income criteria. Rather, work requirements and other stipulations must be met before applicants can receive benefits. Further, federal legislation created a 5-year maximum time limit for receiving benefits. States have wide discretion in the provision of public-assistance benefits, including reducing the time limit below 5 years (Pirog et al., 1998). By 2002, 50 percent of those receiving public assistance must be working. If the legislation is fully implemented, virtually every single mother who is not disabled will be expected to work after 2 years on the welfare rolls, regardless of her educational preparation. Mothers who fail to sustain their families with their wages will, after this lifetime limit of 5 years, have no safety net to fall back on (Edin & Lein, 1996).

Under the AFDC program, most mothers who entered welfare exited relatively quickly; 60 percent left the program within 2 years. Most left for employment, but more than half of those who left for work returned for a subsequent period. Not surprisingly, those mothers most vulnerable to repeated welfare use had the least work experience and education (Edin & Lein, 1996). The new welfare legislation imposes many restrictions. For example, it requires states to deny benefits to single mothers under age 18 unless they live with their parents and are enrolled in school or a job-training program (Hao & Brinton, 1997).

Past research documents that social stigma is associated with receiving public-assistance benefits. Jarrett (1996) interviewed African American single mothers receiving benefits and found that these women experienced stigma in numerous ways from various sources. They felt welfare recipients generally are characterized as rejecting the American work ethic; that the public views single mothers as having more children to increase welfare benefits; that the public views nonmarital childbearing as an intentional means to secure welfare income; and that welfare recipients are viewed as inadequate parents.

Being poor places single mothers at extremely high risk for anxiety, depression, and other health problems. Feelings of helplessness and despair are common and understandable (Davies, Avison, & McAlpine, 1997). Simons, Beaman, Conger, and Chao (1993) reported research that emphasized that single mothers are at greater risk for psychological problems. The findings of their study suggested two routes to poor adjustment among single parents. The first consisted of the ramifications of inadequate resources, whereas the second involved the consequences of antisocial orientation. Single mothers with little education and low access to social-support networks and those who were under severe economic pressure reported both high exposure to negative life events and low social support. Meager income and attendant economic hardship

increased the mothers' likelihood of experiencing negative life events, whereas low education reduced their chances of having access to social-network support. These reduced means served to increase exposure to stressful events while limiting the availability of important coping resources, the ultimate result being psychological distress.

Regardless of income, single mothers experience higher rates of life stress than do married women (Olson & Banyard, 1993). In addition to income loss following divorce, mothers and their children experience many other changes, some of which involve the loss of social status as well as social support. Changes in residence are perhaps the most common forms of instability in newly formed single-mother families.

However, the current context of single parenthood may be only partially responsible for the mental health of single mothers (Davies et al., 1997). These researchers found that single mothers, whether never married, separated, or divorced, were three times more likely than married mothers to have previously experienced a depressive disorder. Higher rates of depression in single mothers was linked, in part, to greater exposure to stress in the family of origin that, in turn, increased the likelihood of an early onset of depression and subsequent depressive disorders. The childhood experiences associated with depression were having an alcoholic, depressive, or abusive parent and/or a significantly poor attachment to their mothers. In contrast, those women whose childhoods had been relatively free of adversity were more likely to report either absence or later onset of depression in their current context.

Job/family role strain also is a source of stress for employed single mothers of young children. Campbell and Moen (1992) found that certain characteristics associated with the work role were related to job/family role strain. Higher strain was associated with more hours spent working and with less positive attitudes toward employment, lower levels of work satisfaction, and less control over work schedules. Attitude toward employment was the most important work variable explaining strain, followed by work time and work satisfaction. The number of children and the child's age were the most important variables explaining strain. As the number of children in the family increased, the likelihood of role strain increased. Younger mothers experienced greater strain than older mothers. Income inadequacy also was related to higher role strain. Single mothers in one study (Folk, 1996) worked 40 hours per week and spent 30 additional hours per week on household chores, not including child care. Mothers who lived with their parents spent from 5 to 10 hours per week less in household work than mothers in other living arrangements. Children of White mothers contributed 6 hours of household work time, and African American children spent 8 hours helping with household work.

Having a child with a disability creates additional stress for single mothers. Gottlieb (1997) found that the extent of the mother's employment responsibilities was a critical factor for her overall well-being. Mothers who had income sources in addition to earnings experienced less stress, less depression, and fewer health problems than other mothers, and those with intimate nonspousal partners reported greater psychological well-being and less depression than those with no partner or with nonsupportive partners.

Olson and Banyard (1993) noted that ongoing problems of money, parenting, inadequate and/or dangerous living arrangements, and intimate relationships present daily stressors for single mothers. The child stressors involved negative challenging behaviors on the part of the child such as noncompliance, irritating behaviors, defiance, temper tantrums, rule violations, conflict with siblings, making messes, demanding attention, illness, school failure/misbehavior, dawdling, and stressful interactions with child-care providers. Stressful interactions with adults included conflicts with boyfriends, crises in friends' lives, friends making difficult demands, and family crises and conflicts. Financial stressors included not having enough money to buy food or supplies or to pay bills. Household stressors were day-to-day maintenance, a messy house, and/or the breakdown of appliances. Conflicts with bosses and co-

workers and reprimands for staying home with a sick child were work stressors reported by these single mothers. Negative affect included depressive thoughts, anxiety over child's happiness, and feelings of being overwhelmed by fatigue and stress. Personal illness and concern over the family's ecological situation were reported also as stressors.

Coping Strategies Used by Single Mothers. Several studies have explored coping strategies used by single mothers to alleviate financial strain, improve their status, and receive support (Driscoll et al., 1999; Edin & Lein, 1996; Hao & Brinton, 1997). About one-third of poor mothers move their families out of poverty by marriage, and another one-third through employment. With welfare reform, fewer mothers will be receiving public assistance, and for those who do, it is not enough to alleviate poverty. However, single mothers face a small pool of marriage partners, partly because of the reluctance of males to marry them and partly because many males do not or cannot sustain employment. The latter situation is especially prevalent among African Americans. Evidence indicates that divorced women at higher socioeconomic levels are more likely to marry than poor women. Therefore, women in the most disadvantaged economic situations are the least likely to improve their situations by marriage (Driscoll et al., 1999).

In an interesting study by Edin and Lein (1996), low-income mothers in four cities were interviewed to identify the survival strategies they used to manage inadequate income. They found that between 30 percent and 60 percent of the welfare recipients used employment to supplement their welfare benefits, but fewer than 10 percent who worked side jobs reported their earnings. Between 2 percent and 19 percent sold sex, drugs, or stolen goods to generate extra money; 25 percent to 44 percent received cash assistance from a community group, a local charity, or some other nonwelfare agency. Most also used network-based strategies to obtain extra money. Between 40 percent and 55 percent received cash help from a family member; 24 percent to 32 percent received cash assistance from a boyfriend; and 27 percent to 41 percent received cash help from a child's father.

Nine out of 10 working mothers not receiving welfare reported at least one noncash resource (a free baby-sitter, living with a relative or friend, walking or receiving a ride to work, health insurance paid by an employer or a child's father), and nearly half had three or more such resources. Working mothers, then, had more cash network support and more access to noncash resources than welfare recipients had, providing a much stronger safety net (Edin & Lein, 1996).

The extended family, especially the single mother's mother, is an important part of the single mother's support system. Living with kin can provide normative supervision and encouragement, potential in-kind transfers (room and board, child-care assistance, housework assistance), and possible role modeling. These researchers found that living with kin initially promoted movement to more productive activities (i.e., work or school) for single mothers, but the specific characteristics of work or school influence continued productivity more than family did. For example, low-paying jobs significantly contribute to employment instability. Folk (1996) found that single mothers who lived in a parent's home were significantly less likely to receive public assistance because they received room and board, child care, and some additional cash assistance. Further, living in a parent's home significantly reduced the household workload for all these mothers.

Over time, increased education provides the most important way for single mothers to increase their incomes. Folk (1996) found education to be positively related to income adequacy for both African Americans and Whites, with each year of education adding more than $1,000 to income per adult equivalent. Being older and having fewer children also had a significant effect on income adequacy for White mothers. Folk concluded that focusing on increasing education and employment of all single mothers would have longer-lasting ef-

fects for both mothers and their children than mandatory co-residence with parents.

Social-support networks contribute to positive coping by single mothers, and these networks vary by ethnicity. Schaffer and Wagner (1996) noted that White women report having more close friends, interacting with friends more frequently, and relying on friends for advice and social support more often than Mexican American women. On the other hand, Mexican American women generally have larger extended families, live closer to their relatives, and maintain family relationships more actively than Whites through frequent visiting and mutual aid, resulting in more internally cohesive support networks. Further, the authors found the longer the Mexican American single mother had been single, the greater the cohesiveness of her support network. Finally, women who were employed had significantly more friends.

In their study of family support to single African American mothers, Jayakody, Chatters, and Taylor (1993) found that kin support in the financial, emotional, and child-care arenas was present and functioning for their sample. The majority of mothers lived in close proximity to their families, had daily contact with them, and reported feelings of closeness to and satisfaction with their families. The prevalence of support from their kin networks was not as extensive as had been suggested in some earlier studies. In this study, about one-quarter of never-married mothers received financial assistance and less than a fifth received child-care assistance. In contrast, the most extensive support provided these mothers was emotional assistance, reported by four out of five mothers. Analysis demonstrated that all four dimensions (support, proximity, interaction, and affinity) were important in specifying kin networks and their degree of viability. Family satisfaction and the proximity of immediate family were predictors of family assistance.

Though single mothers appear to have reasonable access to social support, they are notably disadvantaged with respect to psychological resources. This is noted by studies that report a high level of depression and a low level of psychological well-being in single mothers, indicating that single mothers are not receiving the services they need (McLanahan & Booth, 1991).

Parenting by Single Mothers. Since single mothers are vulnerable to stress resulting from a variety of contextual and personal variables, parenting is difficult. Ineffective parenting practices and poor parent-child relationships may result. Numerous studies have linked single mothers' psychological adjustment to their ability to parent (Amato & Booth, 1996; Arditti & Bickley, 1996; Bank, Forgatch, Patterson, & Fetrow, 1993; Barratt, Roach, & Colbert, 1991; Simons et al., 1993). Barratt et al. (1991) found that mothers' psychological symptoms were linked to caregiving environments provided by the mothers. Significant negative correlations were found between psychological symptoms and mothers' organization of the physical and temporal environment, maternal involvement with the child, and the provision of age-appropriate toys.

Simons et al. (1993) found that negative life events in the lives of single mothers and inadequate social support were associated with psychological stress that precipitated ineffective parenting. Bank et al. (1993) found that the negative contextual factors of diminished social status and financial resources and the antisocial personality of the mother influenced antisocial child behavior. Machida and Holloway (1991) found that mothers' beliefs concerning internal control were associated with the child's level of self-esteem and physical and psychological symptoms. Those mothers with higher scores on controllability measures had children with higher levels of self-esteem and fewer physical and psychological problems.

Amato and Booth (1996) noted that during the period of separation and the first 2 years following divorce, there is typically a marked disruption in the mother-child relationship. In this period, a preoccupied and/or emotionally disturbed mother and a distressed, demanding child are likely to have difficulty supporting or consoling each other, and one may even exacerbate the problems of the other. Custodial mothers frequently become temporarily

erratic, uncommunicative, unsupportive, and inconsistently punitive in dealing with their children. Bank et al. (1993) noted that single mothers initially are ineffective in their discipline practices, are more negative, issue more commands, and employ more dominating and hostile styles in interacting with their children. Difficulty in controlling and monitoring children's behavior is the most sustained parenting problem faced by divorced mothers.

Johnston (1990) noted that role reversal and boundary problems often exist in single-mother families, resulting in negative outcomes for children. He concluded that appropriate role structure in single-parent families implies consistent management, discipline that is sensitive to children's needs, and realistic expectations for performance and coordination of family members' activities. The findings of this study confirmed the benefits of authoritative parenting, which was more likely to be found in families where there was a better co-parental alliance and fewer parental boundary problems.

Various child factors have been found to affect single mothers' caregiving. For example, Barratt et al. (1991) found significant negative associations between infant difficulty and mothers' emotional and verbal responsiveness. Interestingly, the single mothers living apart from their own parents or other adult relatives exhibited more emotional and verbal responsiveness and greater involvement with their infants than did those who were currently living with their adult relatives. Arditti and Bickley (1996) also found that parenting stress increased with perceptions that the child was temperamentally difficult.

Disruption in parent-child relationships are most marked and enduring for custodial mothers and their sons, who are likely to become involved in escalating coercive interchanges (Mott, Kowaleski-Jones, & Menaghan, 1997). Machida and Holloway (1991) found that single mothers of girls reported fewer health and behavior problems in their offspring than mothers of boys did. Bank et al. (1993) also stated that boys are at significant risk for antisocial behavior problems in single-

_____ Tips _____

For Divorced Single Parents

Make every attempt to work out mutually agreeable custody and visitation decisions, and honor agreements.

Use authoritative parenting techniques.

Make as few life changes as possible—e.g., moving, changing schools/churches.

Continue children's regular relationships with both parents.

Do everything possible to maintain children's predivorce standard of living.

Stop fighting and minimize conflict.

Attend classes or programs for single parents.

Expect children of all ages to demonstrate some behavior changes. Exercise patience and support.

Maintain or create a strong support system—family, friends, etc.

Seek help for yourself and your children if necessary.

Reorganize priorities or lower standards to prevent role overload.

Seek high-quality child-care programs, if applicable.

Maintain regular communication with children's teachers to support school performance.

_____

mother families. However, these researchers concluded that it is not divorce per se that causes antisocial behavior in boys; rather, it is the combined effects of negative contextual variables that lead to reduced parenting effectiveness—such as socioeconomic disadvantage and maternal antisocial qualities, which are likely to be exacerbated through the demands and stresses experienced by divorced and single parents.

Mott et al. (1997) explored the short- and long-term implications of father absence for children 9 to 11 years old. For boys, particularly, there was a clear, systematic relationship between father absence and less satisfactory behavior, including both internalizing and externalizing behaviors. The strongest effects were found for children of fathers who had recently left, and these effects were largely independent of prior family conditions that could be linked with both family disruption and child misbehavior. Father absence had far fewer effects on girls. For example, both long- and short-term effects were less systematic and tended to lose significance when background variables were controlled. The researchers also found negative effects on both boys and girls when a new man entered the home.

Some evidence suggests that the mother-child relationship becomes closer and/or less hierarchical after divorce. There is disagreement about whether this nonhierarchical relationship is beneficial or whether it can oversensitize the child to feelings of adults and interfere with psychological development (McLanahan & Booth, 1991). Hetherington (1992) concluded that greater autonomy and decision-making power of children may be associated with earlier acceptance of responsibility and social maturity or with an unwillingness to accept parental direction and restraints, particularly in adolescents.

Divorced mothers have been found to be more liberal than nondivorced mothers with respect to attitudes and behaviors relating to independence and nontraditional roles. Divorced mothers hold less restrictive attitudes about premarital sex than do continuously married mothers and are less likely to monitor adolescents' social activities. Further, single mothers have been found to provide less help to their adolescents with their homework and with planning their high school curriculum than do mothers of adolescents living with both parents (McLanahan & Booth, 1991). Hetherington (1992) reported that mothers' attempts to control adolescent daughters' acting-out behavior may result in a higher level of conflict and that these reactive attempts on the part of the mother do not seem to be successful.

Research on children in single-parent and other types of nontraditional families has emphasized that transitions to single-parent, stepparent, and nonparental living arrangements are linked to lower academic performance, lower probability of high school completion, behavior problems, decreased probability of postsecondary education, earlier movement toward residential independence, earlier marriage and subsequent divorce, and cohabitation (Aquilino, 1996). Some of the problems have been attributed to reduced parental involvement and less stringent supervision of children. Other researchers have linked negative outcomes to increased stress in children moving from one family type to another. Educational attainment of mothers appeared to mediate some of the problems of children, especially school achievement.

However, in spite of the period of diminished parenting in the immediate aftermath of divorce, single mothers become increasingly competent and authoritative parents with time. After about 2 years, the parent-child relationship and parenting practices have improved so that many families have stabilized and are functioning more effectively.

Never-Married Single Mothers.   Births to unmarried mothers account for nearly one-third of all births in the United States and three-fourths of births to teenagers (Driscoll et al., 1999). However, more unmarried women between the ages of 20 and 24 are giving birth than women under the age of 20 (Foster, Jones, & Hoffman, 1998). In fact, births to unmarried women in their early twenties are more than 50 percent higher than births to teens and roughly 30 percent higher than births to women in their late twenties. The older women become, the less likely they are to bear children out of wedlock. Researchers have begun to take an interest in the life course of children born under these circumstances. Previous research typically has not differentiated these children from those of divorced parents.

Driscoll and associates (1999) examined the outcomes of births to unmarried women. They noted that these women are less likely than other women to marry by age 35 and are less likely to work; and if they do marry, their husbands earn less than husbands of other women. The particularly high rate of poverty experienced by these mothers affects their children's quality of life and their life chances. Unstable living arrangements are common, and nearly three-fourths of the children experienced at least one transition—for example, from a single-parent family to a stepfamily or to living with a grandparent. Girls who experienced frequent changes in family structure were at increased risk for both premarital sex and a premarital birth during adolescence.

The women in the sample who had premarital births, as opposed to those who were married, were more likely to be young; to have unplanned pregnancies; to be undereducated and receive less income; to be disproportionately Black or Hispanic; to be less likely to have lived with both parents, and to be more likely to have received welfare while growing up relative to the general population. In addition, 42 percent of the women who had one premarital birth had another. Overall, women who married after the birth of a child more closely resembled women with marital births than those who did not marry.

Children in these families also seem to be at risk. Aquilino (1996) found that children experiencing informal adoption and numerous transitions had the worst outcomes, and those experiencing the two-parent biological or adoptive family demonstrated the best outcomes. Nearly 40 percent of the children in his study made their first attempt at residential independence by age 18; 50 percent made their first transition to the labor force by the same age. Multiple transitions and multiple family types were related to lower child educational attainment. Mothers' education had strong positive effects on their children's educational outcomes, which emphasizes the importance of keeping teen mothers in school. Growing up with a grandparent or without a relative present was associated with markedly lower chances of high school completion and post-secondary school enrollment, and indirectly with a likelihood of residential independence by age 18. A very different picture emerged if the parent and the child both lived with the grandparent. This three-generation living arrangement was associated with higher educational attainment.

Foster and associates (1998) examined the economic and demographic characteristics and outcomes for children of unmarried mothers age 20 and older. They found that 61 percent of births to women older than 20 involved non-White women, and 41 percent of these women began childbearing as teenagers. Only 11 percent of births to these older, unmarried women were to women who were cohabiting at the time of birth. The economic status of these older unmarried mothers was much closer to that of teen mothers than to that of married mothers of the same age, and those who began having children as teenagers were much more economically depressed than women who delayed childbearing until their twenties.

Older unmarried mothers in this study experienced a 16 percent drop in income after giving birth, and labor force participation decreased. In contrast, the income of teen mothers was unaffected by birth, and labor force participation increased. Welfare use increased for both groups—64 percent for teen mothers and 22 percent for older mothers. Unmarried cohabiting mothers, who accounted for 10 percent of the sample, fared better, having higher levels of income and lower levels of public assistance.

Gringlas and Weinraub (1995) examined a sample of unmarried mothers and their children, whom they had studied 7 years previously when the children were preschoolers. In the earlier study, the single mothers differed from demographically matched, married counterparts in stress levels and social supports, but no differences in child outcomes were observed. However, 7 years later when the children were preadolescents, important differences were found between them and their matched counterparts reared in two-parent families. The children of single parents who had experienced neither family disruption nor marital discord during the intervening years showed more social-emotional and academic problems than those children reared in two-parent homes, particularly boys. Children in single-parent high-stress families demonstrated the highest incidence of behavior problems, the lowest social competence ratings, and the lowest reports of academic performance. Children from single-parent low-stress households were rated no differently from the children from two-parent homes. These findings are consistent with findings of studies of children from all types of single-parent families, underscoring the impact of stress and negative life events on the vulnerability of children, especially as they approach adolescence. Taken together, it appears that children who grow up with never-married mothers generally are at risk for social/emotional maladjustment and lowered academic performance.

Single Fathers

A single-father family is one that consists of an unmarried male and his minor child or children who live in the same household. Single fathers include widowers, divorced or separated fathers, never-married males, and single adoptive fathers who have primary responsibility for care of their children. The phenomenon of single-parent fathers is not new, but the incidence of this family type increased significantly in the last quarter of the twentieth century.

Table 7.3 shows the number of households with children under 18 years of age maintained by single fathers. Five percent of all households with minor children were headed by single fathers in 1996, whereas only 2 percent were households of this type in 1980. Of that 5 percent, 2,096,000 were White, 504,000 were Black, and 384,000 were Hispanic (U.S. Bureau of the Census, 1997). Even though single-father households have increased rapidly, single-mother households are still about four times more prevalent than single-father ones (U.S. Bureau of the Census, 1997).

Because state custody laws are becoming more gender-neutral and many divorcing parents mutually work out their arrangements, more fathers are receiving custody of their children. As noted in Table 7.3, the number of African American and Hispanic single-father households has increased dramatically since 1980, but the actual number remains small when compared with White single fathers. Further, it is common for children to move back and forth between parents even if one parent is awarded custody. The swelling numbers of single fathers also are due to the behaviors of mothers and fathers themselves. With an increasingly "female-friendly" job market, mothers have more attractive employment options. Thus, a mother may be more willing than before to relinquish custody or to agree to joint custody in order to pursue a career. Finally, fathers are more willing now than before to be full-time caregivers of their children (Greif, 1995; U.S. Bureau of the Census, 1997).

The demographic profile of single fathers in the research shows them to be fairly homogeneous—White, middle-class, Protestant and Catholic, with slightly-higher-than-average incomes and some college education. They tend to be in their thirties and rearing one or two children, usually older than 5 years. Some researchers have found that single fathers are slightly more likely to have a male than a female child.

Sources of Stress for Single Fathers. The onset of single fatherhood, regardless of the manner in which the status is achieved, produces a psychological crisis for the father and for his children, at least temporarily. Sources of stress for single fathers include negative affect, job/family conflict, financial concerns, and parenting issues. Both custodial and noncustodial fathers experience stress, varying somewhat in source and degree. For example, noncustodial fathers often experience considerable stress relating to visitation with their children, and custodial fathers more than noncustodial fathers experience stress relating to issues of child care and job/family conflict.

Though single fathers do experience financial problems, they are better able to realize economic security than single mothers are. On the whole, they have higher incomes than single mothers do. It is estimated that the income of divorced men is 90 percent of predivorce income. Single fathers are more likely than single mothers to be in the labor force, to earn higher wages, and to work more hours. Although many noncustodial fathers pay child support, the amount is generally low and much less than either the actual cost of rearing a child or the amount borne by custodial mothers (Smock & Manning, 1997).

Although single fathers are better off economically than single mothers are, some do experience a decrease in income following divorce, and some even experience impoverishment. A significant portion of the decrease in income is due to indirect loss. The hidden contributions previously made by the wife are important—household tasks performed, child care, and so on (Greif, 1995). Another problem associated with the financial status of single fathers is disagreements with ex-spouses concerning finances, such as alimony and custody payments. Divorced fathers are more likely than married fathers are to increase their workloads in an attempt to increase their incomes, thereby increasing stress. Some fathers report that they are unable to work overtime because of parental responsibilities, and other fathers report difficulties with budgeting. Some studies have indicated that financial status is the key to a man's performance and satisfaction as a single father. Other studies have not found income to have a significant direct effect on parent-child relationships or on a variety of parenting experiences. However, job-related problems could have an indirect effect (Greif, 1995).

Although it is unusual, some women pay child support to their custodial ex-husbands. Greif (1995) found that women who pay child support are usually women who (1) earn a higher-than-average income, (2) continue to be involved with their children after divorce, (3) are less likely to be living with any of their children, and (4) do not give financial reasons for not having custody. The reasons given by women for not paying support are related to the financial and societal expectations of women.

Potentially, the noncustodial father faces a number of problems, many of them psychological. He is at risk for increased adjustment difficulties, depression, lowered self-esteem, anxiety, and loss of influence in making the child feel a part of the family. Although some custodial mothers encourage involvement of the father, more commonly fathers face resistance and anger from their ex-spouses, difficulties in maintaining contact with their children, and problems with visitation procedures. These ordeals cause considerable stress, and excessive stress causes depression, anxiety, and guilt. Men who can bend to the complex logistics of their visitation rights, who can deal with the anger of their ex-wives, and who can manage the capriciousness of their children experience less stress and adjust more satisfactorily to single fatherhood (Devlin, Brown, Beebe, & Parulis, 1992; Greif, 1995).

Further, the single noncustodial father is likely to experience feelings of loss, self-doubt, and ambivalence, and a generally diminished sense of importance as a parent (Wilbur & Wilbur, 1988). Buehler (1988) noted previous research that has emphasized that divorced adults report lower levels of well-being than do married adults. However, the literature is inconsistent about whether single mothers or fathers experience higher levels of social and emotional well-being. This researcher and others have concluded that relationships among marital status, gender, and well-being may be mediated by socioeconomic status.

Buehler's (1988) study of the social and emotional well-being of single custodial parents found some differences between single mothers and single fathers. Fathers were more bothered than mothers by high blood pressure and frequent drinking and drug use, whereas mothers seemed more bothered than fathers by insomnia, fatigue, and crying spells. Mothers more often than fathers reported improved health following divorce and higher levels of family esteem. Both fathers and mothers in this study were dissatisfied with their personal growth since the divorce. Buehler concluded that custodial mothers and fathers reported similar levels of social, emotional, and familial well-being, and there were no gender differences on psychosomatic symptomatology, life satisfaction, life-area rankings, family cooperation, social support from relatives, and satisfaction with contact with their former spouses.

Custodial fathers are subject to job/family conflict similar to the ways in which single mothers are. Conflicts between child-care responsibilities and vocational responsibilities are likely to occur. Business trips, job mobility, working hours, earnings, promotions, and relations with co-workers and supervisors may be limited. The problems relating to employment, finances, and child care tend to interact and to impinge on the family at a time when emotional resources are likely to be at the lowest ebb.

The synchronization of work, supervision of children, and household management seems to be a major problem for most single fathers. For example, they state that they have no chance to shop for bargains, are seldom able to cook economically, and do not have time to perform housekeeping tasks properly. However, divorced fathers especially seem able to perform such homemaking tasks as cooking, cleaning, and shopping without considerable difficulty. In fact, homemaking is a major part of the single-father role. This may imply that fathers today are more familiar with roles in home management and child care than men were in the past. The stress associated with these tasks appears to stem from role overload rather than inability to perform tasks.

Parenting by Single Fathers.   Relationships with children, child rearing, and child care present adjustment problems for single fathers (Wilbur & Wilbur, 1988). Both custodial and noncustodial fathers must redefine relationships with their children. The custodial father finds that he is required to make a major shift in lifestyle and priorities as a result of being the primary caregiver of the child. The bond between father and child becomes a new focal point for self-direction and sets the criteria for organizing the more traditional spheres of male functioning—work and social life. Some research has indicated that initially single fathers seek reassurances from their children to an unhealthy degree. Failure to understand their children's feelings when children cry or become unmanageable may cause them to seek help from friends, family members, or professionals. With time, however, most single fathers move past the need to rely on their children for validation (Greif, 1995). Tillitski (1992) reported that custodial fathers were found to have greater concern about the nurturing aspects of the parental role than mothers and fathers in dual-parent settings. The father's level of comfort with parenting depends upon the number of years of custody, satisfaction with his social life, not having a religious affiliation, an increased income, rating himself as a good parent, a positive relationship with his children, and an amicable visitation arrangement, if applicable.

Many fathers report that the child-care arrangements they have made for their young children are unsatisfactory. These fathers feel that the children are not supervised properly and not well liked by their caretakers. Many school-age children and adolescents are unsupervised after school.

Evidence provided by Greif (1995) and Tillitski (1992) indicates that single fathers can fulfill the primary parenting role satisfactorily. Tillitski noted that research consistently has found that children's postdivorce adjustment is not directly related to the gender of the custodial parent but in large measure is due to the parenting skills of the residential parent. In general, single fathers report a fairly high level of comfort with their roles. Over time, they show improvement in their skills, but they become more challenged by other problems. Although managing housework and child care becomes easier as children become more responsible and independent, rearing older children poses new challenges. Adolescent sexuality and peer pressure challenge many parent-child relationships in new ways. Further, loneliness may increase if there are no prospects for a new marriage. Fortunately, in many cases the co-parental relationship with the ex-wife becomes more satisfactory.

In general, children in single-father families have been shown to demonstrate favorable levels of adjustment. Most researchers suggest that children who have frequent, high-quality contact with their noncustodial parents (usually fathers) have more favorable adjustment than those who have less frequent or poor-quality contact, and that the quality of visitation is influenced significantly by relation-

ship between spouses. The co-parental relationship with ex-wives is critical. This relationship, when functioning well, can be a cornerstone of the family's adaptation (Greif, 1995; Wolchik, Fenaughty, & Braver, 1996). Unfortunately, many noncustodial parents gradually reduce and eventually cease their active roles in their children's lives, causing most children to experience a strong sense of loss. These disengaging fathers report that decreased contact is due to difficult and painful visitation experiences. Wolchik et al. (1996) examined the type, frequency, and stability of visitation problems for both residential and nonresidential parents during the first 3 years following divorce. They found visitation problems to be extremely common. Across the three waves of assessment, the overwhelming majority of residential parents reported a variety of visitation problems. A smaller, but still substantial, percentage of nonresidential parents also reported several visitation problems (see Highlights). These problems were not related to the extent of visitations but stemmed from the hurt and anger associated with the divorce and concerns about the ex-spouses' parenting abilities. Other researchers have confirmed these findings.

The quality of the relationship with the ex-spouse is critical for the noncustodial father's involvement with his children, not only for the father's functioning, but also for the children's healthy adjustment. Evidence indicates that the relationship with the former wife influences visitation outcomes. Hostile relationships between ex-spouses,

---

Visitation Problems of Noncustodial Parents

Ex-spouse spoils the child.
Ex-spouse is inflexible with visitation schedule.
Ex-spouse is a negative role model.
Ex-spouse changes visitation on short notice.
Visitation with ex-spouse results in more difficulties with child.
Ex-spouses argue about visitation issues.

Source: Wolchik, S., Fenaughty, A., & Braver, S. (1996). Residential and nonresidential parents' perspectives on visitation problems. *Family Relations, 45,* 203–237.

poor relationship quality, and little discussion regarding child rearing tend to be negatively associated with father involvement and contact with children. Other factors affecting involvement are custody status and proximity of the father's residence to the children's residence (Arditti & Bickley, 1996).

Dudley (1991) confirmed that a large percentage of noncustodial fathers have infrequent or no contact with their children. He examined the obstacles a group of divorced fathers faced in being active in the parenting of their children. A large percentage of the fathers identified former spouses as the obstacle. Some accused their former spouses of directly interfering with established visitation arrangements; others stated that former spouses would say negative things about them that affected the children's attitudes. Some fathers felt that the courts had failed to enforce or expand their visitation agreements. Most of the fathers who felt the major obstacle was their spouse had experienced considerable conflict with their wives when they separated and were likely to have used adversarial divorce proceedings. They also perceived their former wives as uncooperative in implementing their schedules with their children both at the time of the divorce and at the time of the study. Two-thirds had returned to court, indicating that such issues as visitation and child support had not been resolved fully. Most of these fathers wanted considerably more time with their children currently than they had.

The second obstacle to regular visitation with their children in this sample of divorced fathers was related to personal reasons. The personal problems varied widely but included substance abuse, job demands, personal leisure, health problems, girlfriends, and a gay orientation.

Older children who could no longer find time for them was the third obstacle reported by these fathers. The children preferred to be with their friends and some had part-time jobs that demanded much of their time. Fathers with older children reported that they had in the past been more active with their children, and their greatest loss was not living in the same household with them. The absence of daily contact excluded them from some of the daily happenings and decisions that they wished they could have shared with their children.

Of the fathers who reported long distance between them and their children as the major obstacle, most had made numerous efforts to stay connected, for example, through telephone calls and short summer vacations of a week or less. Many of these fathers felt anguish because of their separation from their children, and most wanted substantially more time with them.

Some research has also found that fathers' involvement with children following divorce varied with the circumstances of the children's birth and their current living arrangements. Fathers whose children were born outside marriage were less involved with their children on all dimensions—paying support, visiting, and decision making—than those fathers whose children were born within marriage. If fathers do not live with mothers and children, their presence in children's lives is frequently marginal and, even when active for a while, tends to become fragile over time. In one national study of unwed fathers, approximately three-fourths of those who did not reside with their children at birth never lived in the household with the mother and child. About 50 percent of the total sample visited once a week, but 20 percent never visited. The pattern over time was toward less contact as the children became older. African American unmarried fathers were more likely than White and Hispanic fathers to live close to their children and to see them frequently. However, another reported study involving 18- to 22-year-olds found that only 13 percent of the African Americans whose fathers were married to their mothers at birth had a strong bond with their fathers. Mothers and grandmothers serve as gatekeepers for young unmarried fathers' presence in their children's lives. Further, institutional practices create barriers, and many of these fathers relinquish involvement (Doherty, Kouneski, & Kouneski, 1998).

Higher socioeconomic status and geographic proximity were found by Seltzer (1991) to increase involvement, whereas time since separation decreased involvement. This researcher found that

Maintaining relationships with both parents is an important factor in children's adjustment to divorce.

separation may have long-term effects on continued involvement throughout childhood.

Issues Related to Single Parenting

Several issues of single parenting have received considerable attention in the literature—short- and long-term effects of divorce on children and growing up in single-parent families, child custody, and child support. These issues will be explored in the subsequent sections.

Effects of Divorce on Children. The impressive consensus of research on the effects of divorce on children is that divorce results in negative stresses and long-term adjustment of children to continued changes in environment. Widespread behavioral problems of children at the time of separation have been documented. Children of divorce consistently have been found to perform poorly on a wide variety of social, academic, and physical health criteria. Symptoms vary according to the situation and developmental level of children at the time of divorce. Further, the degree of risk to the child of suffering problems induced by divorce varies with different personal histories, demographic characteristics, the child's coping skills, and family interaction characteristics (Portes, Haas, & Brown, 1991). Differential outcomes appear in relation to children's developmental stages at the time of divorce (Wallerstein & Blakeslee, 1989) (see Highlights).

Children are likely to experience and/or demonstrate anger; fear about the future; diminished physical health; depression, moodiness, and withdrawal; lower perceived social competence; increased school problems, including absences, low popularity ratings, and lower academic achievement; and acting out, aggression, and temper tantrums.

Negative changes are most marked for younger children, since older children are more socially and cognitively skilled and have greater personal and extrafamilial resources for coping with their parents' divorces. About one-third of late preadolescents and adolescents cope by disengaging from the family and becoming involved in activi-

even among those fathers who visited their children at least once during the past year, fewer than two-fifths saw their children weekly. And even among those who paid child support, the annual payment was a small fraction of a child's expenses for the year. Seltzer concluded that if nonresident fathers are encouraged to participate more in child care, either through more rigorous child-support enforcement or through changes in visitation and custody administration, other aspects of involvement might increase as well. However, longitudinal studies show an increasing alienation of divorced fathers from their children. Sixty-four percent of adult children in one study reported poor relationships with their custodial fathers (Doherty et al., 1998). The stability of paternal roles for those divorced for shorter and longer periods also suggests that increasing fathers' economic ties to children in the early years after

Typical Reactions of Children to Divorce

PRESCHOOL	SCHOOL-AGE	ADOLESCENTS
Feelings of contributing to divorce	May be immobilized by suffering	Become either overburdened or encouraged in breaking away from family
Intense guilt	Difficulty obtaining relief	Feelings of betrayal
Use of denial as a means of coping	Preoccupation with longing for absent parent	Sorrow
Fear of disruption of nurturance and possible abandonment	Inability to use denial as a way of coping	Anxiety about parents' sexuality, loneliness, and regression
Impaired ability to master tasks and secure relief through play	Either avoidance and silence or strong verbal denial of sadness	Anger toward parent with whom not allied
Aggression and acting-out behaviors	Compulsive behavior	Avoidance
Regression to infantile behaviors	Desire for reconciliation	
Signs of shock, anger, and depression	Feelings of rejection and abandonment	
	Painful loyalty conflicts	
	Displacement of anger to teacher, siblings, peers	
	Either performance in school suffers or school becomes source of gratification	
	Worry about selves and parents; feelings of shame	
	Demanding and aggressive behaviors	

ties outside the home (Hetherington, 1992). Portes et al. (1991) found that child coping skills emerged as a powerful factor in child adjustment. It appeared that children's insight into the divorce process is inextricably intertwined with their adjustment capabilities.

Father-Absence Hypothesis. A review of the literature regarding children's adjustment to divorce reveals several hypotheses explaining ways in which divorce may affect children. Kalter, Kloner, Schreier, and Okla (1989) have delineated some of these, noting that among the earliest models for explaining the effects of divorce on children was the father-absence hypothesis. Although the research based on this hypothesis did not often differentiate among the reasons for father absence, it was used to explain the effect of divorce, especially for boys. Presumably, boys need a regular, ongoing relation-

ship with their fathers to develop a valued sense of masculinity, to be able to internalize controls over behavior, to achieve appropriate development of conscience, and perform up to their abilities academically. Failures in these developmental accomplishments were seen as being responsible, in large measure, for aggressive acting-out behavior problems, poor academic work, and social isolation from peers. Kalter et al. (1989) found that boys, as reported by their mothers and teachers, had significantly more difficulties adjusting to divorce than did girls. Other researchers (Demo & Acock, 1991; Kline, Johnston, & Tschann, 1991; McLanahan & Booth, 1991) also noted that boys suffered more severe and long-lasting adjustment problems following divorce than did girls.

Kurtz (1995) found that mothers were more encouraging of positive coping strategies for sons than for daughters. Perhaps this divergent behavior is because boys characteristically exhibit overt maladaptive behaviors (e.g., aggression) and are more likely to become involved in disputes with parents. Mothers' perceptions of sons' vulnerability may compel them to provide male children more direction and encouragement in coping efforts. Further, some research indicates that children influence the stressors they experience (Sandler, Tein, & West, 1994). Possibly, boys who act out more overtly than girls actually increase negative events in the family.

Though there is a long-standing belief that boys, especially before adolescence, are more vulnerable to divorce than girls, a substantial body of research has found no gender differences in adjustment following divorce. For example, Sandler et al. (1994) found no differences between younger and older children or between boys and girls on measures of negative life events, coping strategies, and psychological symptoms. However, adolescence, for both males and females, seems to be a particularly critical time. Adolescent girls of early divorce are more likely than girls in nondivorced families to demonstrate antisocial behavior, depression, and withdrawal, in addition to difficulties in sexual behavior and relationships with boys that may indicate the need of a father's support and advice. Puberal changes and heterosexual relationships in boys also may be problematic. Both boys and girls need consistent relationships with their fathers as they are growing up. This need is more obvious at some developmental stages than at others (Chase-Lansdale, Cherlin, & Kiernan, 1995).

Economic-Distress Hypothesis. A second hypothesis explaining effects of divorce on children is the economic-distress model (Kalter et al., 1989). As noted earlier in the section on single mothers, considerable evidence points to the fact that divorce brings substantial economic deprivation to mother-only households and that poverty either directly or indirectly accounts for many problems of the children of divorce. Thus, the lack of economically based advantages and the socio-cultural factors associated with being poor may themselves account for low academic performance and for antisocial, undercontrolled behavior problems, quite apart from other effects of divorce.

Multiple-Stress Hypothesis. The third hypothesis, proposed by Kalter et al. (1989), was the multiple-life-stress view, which includes economic distress but adds other possible sources of stress, such as residential shifts, deaths in the family, loss of a job, and parental remarriage. Initially, this notion was based on the relationship between stressful events and the development of mental or physical health. Recently, emphasis has been on the aggregation of multiple stressful life circumstances that results in enduring psychopathology. Therefore, a divorce characterized by numerous psychosocial stressors would be more likely to cause adjustment problems in children than one in which stressors are minimal.

Parental-Hostility Hypothesis. More recent research has focused on the idea that interparental hostility is a key factor in negative divorce sequelae for children. Parents who engage in acrimonious battles and mutual derogation stimulate anxiety and anger in their children, who love both parents. Further, even parents who fight inadvertently are modeling aggression as a way of resolving interpersonal conflicts and frustration. The aggressive behavior problems so commonly seen among children of divorce may be the result of anger, conflicted loyalties, or learned aggression stemming from exposure to high levels of parental conflict. Numerous studies have found a significant pattern showing that adjustment is adversely affected by parental discord. Much research reports that children's adjustment is facilitated under conditions of low parental conflict, both before and after the divorce (Amato & Booth, 1996; Ehrenberg, 1996; Shifflett & Cummings, 1999; Wolchik et al., 1996). Amato and Booth (1996) found that the problems of children after divorce actually were evident 8 to 12 years before the divorce. Further, low quality of parents' marriages affected both father-child and mother-child affection. Consequently, both mothers' and fathers' relationships with children are vulnerable to the ill effects of parental discord.

Parent Adjustment Hypothesis.   Another hypothesis explaining the effects of divorce on children is the parent adjustment hypothesis. This thesis suggests that when parents, especially primary custodial parents, can adjust well to adversity, they can continue to provide effective care, guidance, and support for their children. It is the continuity of effective parenting that is seen as facilitating healthy child development. Further, a supportive parent-child relationship is seen as buffering the child from divorce-related stresses. On the other hand, when parents are distraught and unable to continue as effective parents, children's developmental progress may be compromised and psychological problems are likely to emerge. Support for the parent adjustment hypothesis for both boys and girls was found by Kalter and associates (1989). The single mothers in their study appeared to be less well adjusted when compared with the norms. Mothers who scored high on measures of total problems, internalizing, externalizing, aggression, and depression, had children with significantly

more problems than other mothers. These researchers concluded that mothers' psychological adjustment was important in the face of stresses caused by divorce. When mothers experienced economic deprivation, interparental hostility, and the burdens of single parenting, children tended to fare less well. Further, these researchers emphasized that when parental adjustment and its effects on the existence of a developmentally facilitating parent-child relationship are taken into account, they will carry more predictive weight than the individual psychosocial stressor usually associated with divorce.

Other researchers also have found support for the parent adjustment hypothesis. Portes et al. (1991) found that single-parent families who were unable to function cohesively following divorce were likely to have a parent who feels isolated, uses more alcohol, and becomes punitive with the children. These researchers found that external support systems (extended family, churches, friends) were a significant factor in mediating the negative effects on the child's adjustment.

There are a variety of ways by which parents and professionals can assist children in adjusting to divorce. Suggestions can be found in Tips for Parents.

TIPS

For Parents Helping Children Adjust to Divorce

Discuss family problems with the child. Use simple, honest explanations on the child's level.

Tell the child in advance that a divorce will occur.

Assure the child that he is loved and will continue to be loved by both parents.

Tell the child the primary issues and reasons for the divorce at the level the child can understand. Be truthful.

Avoid placing blame for the divorce.

Express positive feelings and confidence about the future.

Do not ask a young child to make the decision concerning which parent will assume custody.

Avoid disrupting the child's routine as much as possible.

Encourage the child to express her feelings and concerns.

Expect the child to feel and express negative emotions.

Avoid arguments concerning money, custody, visitations, and so forth.

Plan for continuous contact with the absent parent and the extended family.

Kurtz (1995) found significant relationships among parental coping strategies, level of cohesion in the family, and children's coping strategies. Positive parental strategies, such as acquiring or bolstering informational, instrumental, and emotional support from others, decreased the probability of problem behaviors in children. Conversely, escape-avoidant coping strategies, such as wishful thinking, escape, and avoidance behaviors, increased the probability of children's maladaptive behaviors. The degree of commitment, help, and empathic support in the home environment was inversely related to escape-avoidant coping strategies. This study indicated the need for assisting parents and children in developing appropriate strategies for coping with the stresses of divorce.

Some family-court judges across the country are requiring divorcing parents to take a course to learn how to help children cope with divorce before the divorce is granted. The course is designed to assist parents in seeing their divorce through the eyes of their children and to understand that divorce can have lasting effects on the children's lives. Parents receive printed information about ways to assist children in the transition from a two-parent to a one-parent home, pitfalls to avoid, and strategies to make children feel a part of one family even though their parents no longer live together (Palmer, 1993). A short, two-session parent-education program that specifically focused on divorce and parental conflict was designed and tested by Shifflett and Cummings (1999). Evaluative results indicated that participation in the program had positive effects on parents' self-reported knowledge and behavior with regard to interparental conflict, including conflict with ex-spouses. Moreover, parents reported a high level of satisfaction with the program.

Considerable research has emphasized that for a large portion of children, the initial difficulties associated with divorce dissipate over time. After about 2 years, single parents become increasingly more competent and more authoritative (Hetherington, 1992). However, other research has pointed out that for a significant number of children, the effects of divorce can persist for 10 or more years, even into adulthood (Chase-Lansdale et al., 1995).

The first cohort of children who experienced extremely high divorce rates in the 1960s and 1970s has reached adulthood. Several studies have found modest long-term negative effects of divorce during childhood or adolescence on adult well-being: lower levels of satisfaction with certain dimensions of life, higher levels of psychological distress or depression, and higher rates of seeking counseling. Chase-Lansdale et al. (1995), using an extensive longitudinal data set, examined the relationship of parental divorce to adolescent socioemotional adjustment, school performance, and family economic standing at age 16. Then they assessed the links between the age-16 indicators and adult mental health at age 23. All the participants' families were intact when the children were 7 years of age. Those adolescents whose parents divorced between the time they were 7 and 16 years of age showed greater emotional maladjustment than did those adolescents whose parents were still married. Females demonstrated more problems than males did. Further, those children who had more emotional problems and lower school achievement at age 7 also had poorer mental health at age 23, after controlling for socioeconomic status. These findings suggested that a parental divorce during childhood and adolescence affected mental health at age 23.

Concern about the effects of divorce on children's well-being has not been unfelt by unhappily married couples themselves, and a substantial number of later-divorcing couples claim to have postponed their divorce until children were older. Popular reasoning seemed to be that parental divorce is easier and less disruptive for offspring who are older (Cooney, Hutchinson, & Leather, 1995). Several recent studies have exploded this myth (Amato & Booth, 1996; Chase-Lansdale et al., 1995; Cooney et al., 1995). In fact, Chase-Lansdale and associates (1995) found that a divorce when the child was between 11 and 16 years of age led to more deleterious effects than did a divorce when the child was between 7 and 11 years of age, suggesting that later divorces may be more harmful than earlier ones. Adolescents often respond to divorce with egocentric concerns and consider divorce in terms of how it affects them personally, academically, and financially (Cooney et al., 1995).

Amato and Booth (1996) reported that adult children of divorced parents felt less affection for their parents, had less contact with them, and engaged in fewer intergenerational exchanges of assistance than other adults did. Both Amato and Booth and Cooney et al. (1995) found that relationships with fathers are especially vulnerable after divorce. At least some of the erosion in relationships between parents and adult children postdivorce was associated with situations arising after the divorce and aspects of the divorce process itself, rather than with predivorce family dynamics. Parental drinking was the only postdivorce factor that was significantly associated with lower levels of parent-child intimacy.

Sometimes divorcing parents involve their adolescent and adult children in the divorce process, perhaps because of the stress, negativity, and pressure to form alliances that often accompany such actions. Daughters usually are more affected than sons, probably because they have greater emotional connectedness and behavioral involvement with their parents during adolescence and beyond. Further, these researchers found that postdivorce parent-child intimacy was positively associated with children's perceptions that a given parent was a potential source of financial assistance to them.

It can be concluded from the body of research on the effects of divorce on children that divorce in childhood is significantly related to more emotional problems, lower school performance, and poorer family economic standing during adolescence. These variables at 16 years of age are predictive of adult mental health. Divorce during adolescence and adulthood produces emotional problems for children and strained parent-child relationships. Although the group that is seriously affected is small, it does represent a sizable group of the young adult population that may require clinical intervention. It seems clear that some type of intervention needs to occur at every developmental stage when divorce occurs.

Although most of the research has focused on the negative effects and outcomes of divorce, some positive effects have been noted. The tendency for children in single-parent families to display more androgynous behavior and higher levels of maturity and perceived self-efficacy in adolescence may be interpreted as beneficial effects. Children in single-mother households are not pressured as strongly as their counterparts in two-parent families to conform to traditional gender roles. Children in single-parent families frequently assume a variety of domestic responsibilities to compensate for the absent parent (Demo & Acock, 1991; Lauer & Lauer, 1991).

Hilton and Haldeman (1991) studied gender differences in the performance of household tasks by children and adults in single-parent, two-parent, and two-earner families. They found that family type made a difference in the degree to which household tasks were shared by family members. Boys in single-parent families shared the household-work role less than did boys in two-parent families. Girls in single-parent families, on the other hand, were very undifferentiated in their household-task behavior. More than half the time they performed tasks that were classified as male. In the two-parent families, parents were highly sex segregated in their household-task behavior, and household tasks primarily were the domain of the female parent. Overall, the children were much less segregated than were parents in the performance of household tasks.

Summary. In sum, divorce clearly has an impact on children and requires moderate to significant adjustment. Research has indicated that the first year following divorce seems to be particularly stressful for both children and their parents, with parent-child relationships being less than optimal. However, over time the majority of children become socially and psychologically better adjusted, depending on their age and sex at the time of the divorce and on family characteristics such as parental harmony, the parents' educational level and socioeconomic status, the family processes, and the presence or absence of another adult in the home. Although some negative effects have been seen in children's personal adjustment, their self-concepts, their cognitive functioning, their social behaviors, and their interpersonal relationships, some positive effects also have been found.

Child Custody.   Child-custody laws have experienced a variety of changes throughout history. Before the 1800s, fathers were given custody because they were better able to support children, and when they were denied custody, their financial responsibility to support the children terminated. In the early 1900s, however, it was recognized that fathers were responsible for their children even if they did not have custody. As the women's movement progressed and more women entered the labor force, greater attention was given to the mother's role in caring for her children. This emphasis gave rise to the "tender years" philosophy—when children are young, the mother is the preferred custodial parent; but for older children, equal rights of mothers and fathers were considered. More recently the trend has shifted away from favoring mothers, and the "tender years" presumption was viewed as a violation of fathers' constitutional rights of equal protection. By 1995, 45 states and the District of Columbia had adopted by statute or case law a gender-neutral custody decision-making process. The use of the "tender years" doctrine has decreased substantially, but it still exists to some extent with older, more traditional judges (Buehler & Gerard, 1995). Equality in custody adjudication has emerged in the form of the concept of acting in the "best interests" of the child.

The notion of "best interests" of the child is included in all state codes but is often difficult to determine. It is considered to be the most important consideration in a custody suit. It has been interpreted to mean that a child has a right to a loving, stable home with adequate provision for her maintenance, education, and continued contact with the noncustodial parent. The same standard is applied when determining the frequency and circumstances with which the noncustodial parent

will be permitted to exercise visitation privileges with the child.

In general, the custody of children involves both physical custody and legal custody. *Sole legal custody* is the legal authority arrangement in which only one parent has the right and responsibility to make decisions related to the health, education, and welfare of the child. *Sole physical custody* is a living arrangement in which the child resides with and is under the supervision of one parent, with the court having the power to order visitation with the other parent. *Joint* or *shared legal custody* is defined as a continuing mutual responsibility of and involvement by both parents in decisions regarding the child's welfare in matters of education, medical care, and emotional, moral, and religious development. *Joint* or *shared physical custody* means that each parent has significant periods of physical custody to ensure a child frequent and continual contact with both parents. *Visitation* means the conditions under which a parent (or another designated adult) has the right to physical interaction with the child and has the right and responsibility during these placements to make routine decisions about the child's care consistent with the major decisions made by the person having legal custody (Buehler & Gerard, 1995).

Most states emphasize that parents should be encouraged to arrive at custody decisions privately (as long as children are not in harm's way) and that when disputes occur, they should be resolved on a case-by-case basis using the best interests of the child standard. Another trend in child-custody decision making is an increased effort to move the process from the courtroom to the mediation office. Some evidence indicates that the substantial majority of cases can be resolved through mediation.

The quality of parent-child relationships is very important in determining the best interests of the child, but a preference for the psychological parent does not exist in any state statute. Some state courts view the primary caregiver as the most logical parent to have primary custody for several reasons. It is relatively easy to identify who the primary caregiver is, and this identification is based on past behaviors rather than future-oriented suppositions. Theoretically, this preference generally favors mothers. Many judges seriously consider the preferences of older children (older than 14 years) in making custody decisions. Still, in some cases, the court arranges postdivorce custody to resemble the predivorce living arrangement, taking into consideration the relative amount of time the child shared with each parent. An example is a recent contested custody case in Florida in which the father was awarded primary custody of the children and the mother was awarded liberal visitation rights. The mother, a prominent lawyer, often spent 14 hours a day working while the father, an unemployed architect, stayed at home with the children and did volunteer work at school. Similar cases of fast-track career women losing custody to former husbands have occurred across the United States (Petersen, 1998).

Other factors that strongly influence custody decision making include the following: the occurrence of domestic violence (child and spouse), substance abuse, parents' sexual promiscuity, and the cooperative- or friendly-parent factor (e.g., a parent who is willing to promote a strong committed nonresidential parent-child relationship). Other than the judge, key players in determining the best interests of the child are mental-health professionals and attorneys who serve as guardians ad litem (Buehler & Gerard, 1995).

The interest in joint physical/legal custody arose as part of the social-equality movement of the 1970s with the intent of encouraging frequent and continuing contact with both parents and encouraging both parents to share the rights and responsibilities of child rearing. By 1995, 19 states had enacted statutes with a preference for joint custody, and the remaining states had statutes with joint custody as an option (Buehler & Gerard, 1995). See Highlights for criteria to determine if joint custody is likely to be in the best interests of the child.

Joint physical/legal custody allows parents to plan creatively the residential arrangements that will best meet the child's needs. Joint physical custody does not mean a rigid 50/50 division of residence. Although the actual physical arrangements

are varied, joint custody has been defined as any custody or visitation arrangement that allows both parents to have adequate and normal day-to-day interaction with the children and provides that each adult participate in both the responsibilities and the rewards of child rearing. Time-sharing arrangements have been found to vary according to the particular needs of children and parents. Some children alternate between parents' homes on an equal-time basis. Other families have a more traditional arrangement, in which children spend the week with one parent and weekends with the other parent. The children's ages and school situations, as well as the parents' employment and availability, must be considered when planning an appropriate physical-custody arrangement.

Most studies have shown that fathers and children are together more often in joint-custody than in sole-maternal-custody arrangements. These findings hold for both legal and physical joint custody. Further, joint custody has been linked to increased collaborative parenting and greater child-support compliance. However, studies also indicate that very few differences in children's adjustment (e.g., self-esteem, behavior problems) are evident between those in joint custody and those in sole custody. Most parents arrange children's custody privately, but state custody statutes seem to shape parents' decisions about legal custody much more than their decisions about physical custody. It appears that joint legal custody and maternal physical custody is a reasonable and fairly common option, because it allows shared responsibility without imposing a physical arrangement that may be untenable for some families (Buehler & Gerard, 1995; Wilcox, Wolchik, & Brever, 1998).

Buehler and Gerard recommended public policy that protects parent-child relationships, minimizes hostile parental conflict, and ensures adequate economic support for children. They supported a requirement that parents forward to the judge their preference for legal-custody arrangements (shared or sole), for physical-custody arrangements (shared or sole), and for access arrangements. A presumption that honors an agreement arranged mutually by parents minimizes state

Criteria for Joint Custody

Joint custody is in the best interests of the child when:

Parents are committed to making joint custody work
Parents want to actively parent their child
Parents can separate their interpersonal difficulties from their parenting decisions
Parents have a reasonable level of communication and a willingness to cooperate
Parents are able to give priority to their child's needs
Parents are psychologically stable
Parents are seen by the child as sources of security and love
Parents are flexible enough to make changes as developmental needs of the child
    change

Joint custody is not in the best interests of the child when:

Evidence of family violence exists
Evidence of child neglect exists
Parent(s) have psychological problems
The child is upset or unresponsive to the shared-custody arrangement
Intense, hostile interparental conflict exists
Parents strongly oppose shared custody
Great geographic distances exist and financial resources are few

Source: Buehler, C., & Gerard, J. (1995). Divorce law in the United States: A focus on child custody. *Family Relations, 44,* 439–458.

intrusion and recognizes that most parents will arrange their lives in ways that serve children's best interests. In contested cases, these researchers favor shared legal custody, sole physical custody to the primary caregiver, and children's substantial access to the nonresidential parent.

Some researchers have observed gender differences in satisfaction with legal-custody arrangements. For example, fathers are very satisfied with joint legal-custody; however, mothers are more satisfied with sole-custody outcomes. Since one of the central tasks of the divorce process is renegotiation of family relationships, custody choice might be viewed by parents as a way to either limit future interactions or maintain ongoing relationships with one's ex-spouse, Further, custody choice may be a way to limit or augment one's own role as a parent. Resistance by a mother to joint legal custody may represent a desire to restrict the father's

postdivorce involvement with the child or to maintain parental control. Thus, custody often becomes a win-lose battle over parental rights rather than a postdivorce reframing of parental responsibilities (Wilcox et al., 1998).

Wilcox and associates (1998) found that mothers were more likely to prefer joint custody when they were experiencing fewer problems— low levels of conflict with their ex-husbands, low levels of anger or hurt over the divorce, few visitation problems, little psychological stress, social support for maintaining father-child relationships, and perceptions of ex-husbands as competent parents. Most of the demographic variables (e. g., child's age, gender, race, mother's religion or education) did not significantly predict mothers' custody preferences.

It is important to note that in some cases, the custody of the child is not awarded to either biological parent but to a third party. However, in 44 states a natural parent is preferred over a third party. Third parties seeking custody usually must provide a preponderance of evidence that the natural parents are unfit. In the case of death of a custodial parent or abandonment by a noncustodial parent, custody may be awarded to a long-standing residential stepparent or grandparent. Otherwise, grandparents and stepparents have limited ability to obtain custody. Most states allow courts to grant stepparents visitation rights if the arrangement is in the best interests of the child. All states grant grandparents visitation rights. However, at time of this writing, a grandparent's right to visitation when the mother objects is before the U.S. Supreme Court.

Child Support.   Child support is the mechanism by which economic resources are transferred from noncustodial parents (mostly men) to custodial parents (mostly women) (Teachman, 1991). In 1984 and 1988, the federal government passed legislation aimed at more effective enforcement of child-support orders. An important impetus behind this legislation was the belief that child-support enforcement would reduce poverty, or at least reduce the cost of public assistance to women and children. (Pirog et al., 1998; Pirog-Good & Brown, 1996). Based on these statutes, each state was required to develop a specific numeric formula to determine the amount of child-support obligation. Although the history of state support guidelines is relatively short, it has been a turbulent period affected by the increasing incidence of child poverty in single-parent households, mushrooming state budget deficits, the upheaval of America's social safety net, and the growth of fathers' rights advocacy groups. The 1996 Personal Responsibilities and Work Opportunities Reconciliation Act (welfare reform) greatly affected the safety net for many poor women and children, so that many women receiving TANF were no longer eligible for cash assistance. Given the fact that the federal and state governments have limited their roles in supporting poor children, the amount of child support ordered for the lowest-income children takes

on increased importance (Pirog et al., 1998). Therefore, it appears that at the present time, the main beneficiaries of the child-support legislation are non-TANF women and their children. In almost all cases, the revenue collected from noncustodial parents of TANF children, even if it were paid directly to the ex-family, would not raise the family's income enough to get off welfare. Rather, the support collected goes into the general budget and may be used to finance administrative costs of local government, used to offset the costs of specific programs, or put to other uses. Depending on the way local governments use this revenue, TANF mothers and children may or may not benefit indirectly from support monies. Thus, the effects of the support enforcement program for contributing to the welfare of poor children or alleviating the feminization of poverty are indirect at best. Although there may be some microlevel redistribution of wealth from middle-class fathers to the less affluent female-headed households in which their children live, the program does little to improve the income level of the poorest women and children (Pirog et al., 1998).

Since more minority women are poor, it is not surprising that data reveal that African American and Hispanic women are at a disadvantage in being awarded child support and alimony (Peterson & Nord, 1990). Child-support, when it is received, is not nearly enough to pay for the cost of rearing a child. Child-support orders across states were examined by Pirog and associates (1998). They found that child-support payments to low-income families varied from zero to an average of $126 per month. In many states, child support for very-low-income women and children is inadequate to replace cash assistance from TANF.

Researchers have found that the amount of child-support payments varies from 36 percent to 59 percent of the typical average costs of rearing children. Sorensen (1997) found that the average amount of child support that nonresident fathers paid was between $1,675 and $1,881 per year, which represented from 6 percent to 7 percent of these fathers' personal incomes. She estimated that between 46 percent and 54 percent of nonresident fathers did not pay any child support. Many state guidelines for setting child-support awards require that at least 17 percent of the nonresident parent's income go to child support. Empirical research has shown that the cost of rearing two children in a household is at least 19 percent, and possibly as much as 39 percent, of family income. These estimates led Sorensen to conclude that nonresidential fathers in 1996 could have paid between $32 billion and $34 billion more in child support than they paid, an increase of 65 percent to 300 percent, depending on the standard used.

In 1997, states collected a record $13.4 billion in court-ordered support payments, up 63 percent in 5 years. Still, an estimated $7 billion remains uncollected each year, plus $40 billion owed from past years. The 1996 legislation allows delinquent fathers' wages to be garnisheed and their professional licenses to be revoked. A better approach to get fathers involved would seem to be implementation of fatherhood programs, based on the knowledge not only that fathers are important in their children's development but also that involved fathers are more likely to support their children (Meckler, 1998).

It can be concluded that child-support orders are insufficient to meet the needs of very low-income children, especially as low-income families reach their time limits for public assistance, and that both child-support orders and child-support collection rarely provide a fair proportionate share of the noncustodial parents' contributions to typical expenditures on children. One of the biggest challenges facing the enforcement system is to establish child-support orders for the millions of children who are eligible for but do not have child-support orders.

Various factors have been found to affect receipt of child support: characteristics of mothers, fathers, and children; the structure of the divorce settlement; and the nature of the legal environment. Several researchers have found that the most prominent predictor of receiving any child support is having a legal child-support agreement at the time of divorce (Smock & Manning, 1997; Sorensen, 1997). The findings of the Smock and

Manning study indicated that the amount of child support awarded was related to pre- and postdivorce earnings. Those men with higher incomes, with more education, who were older, who had resided with their spouses longer, and who had more children paid the most. The majority of fathers paying child support are White, have graduated from high school, are 30 years of age or older, do not have a new family to support, and are working year-round (Sorensen, 1997). Fathers least likely to pay child support are Black, Hispanic, poor, undereducated, young, and unemployed or underemployed. When fathers with these characteristics do pay child support, the amount is very minimal.

Table 7.4 shows the total number of custodial mothers and fathers receiving child support, the number below the poverty line, and the percent distribution of those who received the full amount and those who received no payments. It also shows the number who were not awarded child support. As noted, only about half of all custodial parents in 1995 received a child-support agreement. Of these, less than half actually received the full amount, and approximately 25 percent received no payment at all. For parents below the poverty line, the picture is even more bleak. Less than half of poor custodial parents had a child-support agreement, and a little over one-third received no payment at all.

Table 7.5 shows the number of households, according to race and ethnic origin and income, who received alimony and child support. As noted, alimony is almost a phenomenon of the past, and those families who need child support the most are the ones who do not receive it.

These findings suggest that children from less privileged homes suffer the most serious economic consequences of divorce. The most vulnerable children (those from the least advantaged families) are the least protected economically following divorce, both in terms of living with a mother who has a child-support award and in terms of the size of the award.

Paasch and Teachman (1991) examined the gender of children and receipt of assistance from absent fathers. They asked custodial mothers what types of assistance other than child support fathers

TABLE 7.4 Child Support—Award and Recipiency Status of Custodial Parent: 1991*

AWARD & RECIPIENCY STATUS	% DIST.	ALL CUSTODIAL PARENTS			% DIST.	CUSTODIAL PARENTS BELOW POVERTY LINE		
		Total	Mother	Father		Total	Mother	Father
		11,502	9,918	1,584		3,720	3,513	207
With an agreement		6,190	5,542	684		1,438	1,368	71
Received full amount	51.5	2,742	2,552	189	39.7	499	497	2
Received no payment	24.8	1,320	1,156	164	31.7	398	355	43
Child support not awarded		5,312	4,376	936		2,282	2,145	136

Source: U.S. Bureau of the Census. (1997). *Statistical abstract of the United States: 1997* (117th ed.). Washington, DC: U.S. Department of Commerce.

*Per 1,000.

provided to their children—purchase of clothing and gifts, provision of medical care, involvement in school activities, and other types of assistance. The findings indicated that the percentage of absent fathers providing assistance other than child support was quite small. For seven of the eight types of assistance, the majority of fathers had never contributed. For the types of assistance that did not require direct contact but required monetary contributions, such as paying for dental care, uninsured medical expenses, medical insurance, and so on, a higher percentage of fathers provided. But for direct assistance, such as helping with homework, attending school events, and taking children on vacations, a lower percentage of fathers provided. There were no significant differ-

ences in the amount and kind of assistance provided to sons and daughters. These researchers concluded that policies aimed at increasing child-support payments are not misdirected. That is, in attempting to minimize their child-support payments, fathers cannot claim that they are providing assistance to their children in other ways. A more general participation on the part of fathers might increase the socioemotional well-being of children as well as their welfare.

Several researchers have examined the effects of remarriage on child support (Folk, Graham, & Beller, 1992; Hill, 1992). Hill found that remarriage alters child-support payments only when it is the custodial mother remarrying, and the changes in the family income of the noncustodial father are

TABLE 7.5 Number of Households Receiving Alimony and Child Support by Characteristics of Householder and Family Income: 1995*

	TOTAL NO. OF FAMILIES UNDER 65	WHITE	BLACK	HISPANIC	UNDER $15,000	$15,000 TO $24,999	$25,000 TO $34,999
Total	69,597	58,872	8,055	6,287	9,723	10,040	9,828
Alimony	287	210	33	12	38	31	46
Child support	4,378	3,645	664	307	1,054	801	774

Source: U.S. Bureau of the Census. (1997). *Statistical abstract of the United States: 1997* (117th ed.). Washington, DC: U.S. Department of Commerce.

*Per 1,000.

relevant, but those of the custodial mother are not. The authors concluded that substantial increases in the fathers' incomes would have to occur to prompt any detectable changes in the economic well-being of their children. Child-support levels have not been sensitive to changes in the financial needs of the custodial mother. Hill found that the remarriage of the mother was a strong predictor of change in child-support payments. This event led to a persistent reduction in per-child support of about $360. On the other hand, the absent father's remarriage and his addition of children prompted no appreciable change in child-support levels. Teachman (1991) found that, contrary to expectations, fathers who had remarried were more likely than those who had remained single to pay support. Folk et al. (1992) found little evidence that simply having a child-support award had any systematic effect on the single mother's remarriage, but there was some evidence that larger-than-average awards may delay marriage. Mothers who received any support were more likely than those who received none to remain single for longer periods of time.

Little research has focused on noncustodial mothers who pay child support. Smock and Manning (1997) found that 19 percent of their sample were resident fathers who received child support from their ex-wives, and the amount collected was less than that of mothers. In an earlier study, Christensen, Dahl, and Rettig (1990) examined the differences in the treatment of noncustodial mothers and noncustodial fathers by courts at the time of the divorce. Their findings also showed that noncustodial mothers were required to pay child support less frequently than were noncustodial fathers (33.3 percent versus 83.9 percent). They, too, found that the amount that noncustodial mothers paid was less than half that required of noncustodial fathers. However, mothers' incomes were 62 percent of noncustodial fathers' incomes. The support awards were 20 percent of the mothers' incomes and 25 percent of the fathers'. Further examinations revealed that trade-offs made between spouses in divorce agreements regarding property and child support were likely to jeopar-

dize the mothers' futures while providing a slightly improved level of living in the present. Further, more of the noncustodial mothers had incomes closer to the poverty level than did noncustodial fathers, and many did not have jobs that provided fringe benefits. If the single variable of child support is considered, it would appear that noncustodial mothers had an economic advantage over noncustodial fathers. Further examination, however, revealed that noncustodial mothers were in more economic danger than noncustodial fathers, even before the transfer of child support. These researchers concluded that the relative economic disadvantage of women warrants changes in the treatment of noncustodial mothers and fathers.

Services and Support
for Single-Parent Families

The literature overwhelmingly notes that one of the greatest needs of single mothers is adequate income. Since a large portion of single mothers lives below the poverty level, much debate has occurred over how to reduce poverty in mother-only households. It is not clear whether the reforms to the welfare system will be successful in helping single mothers with young children become productive, self-sufficient members of society.

McLanahan and Booth (1991) proposed that a mix of public and private programs is needed to reduce poverty and income insecurity in single-mother families. They suggested the implementation of a publicly guaranteed child-support minimum benefit accompanied by a strengthening of the private child-support system. According to these researchers, the best way to protect poor fathers from economic hardship is to make child-support obligations a percentage of current income and to designate a minimum income that is not subject to the child-support tax.

Bryner (1992) also made recommendations, which included the following. Programs aimed at assisting TANF recipients can merge with those aimed at women who are working full- or part-time and still remain poor. A wider range of services to include prenatal health care, child care, and parental leave would reduce the problems that women face when they are trying to support their families. The personal exemption for each child in low- and middle-income families could be raised so that the government does not tax away that portion of a family's income needed to rear its children. An increase in tax credit aimed at families with children would be an effective, direct means of assuring that women who work are given the help they need to take care of their families.

Bryner (1992) further noted that working women who head households are victimized by divorce laws that contribute to poverty. No-fault divorce laws have been a disaster for women with children, and courts need to fashion divorce settlements that ensure children and their guardians an adequate income.

Employers should be encouraged to support working women. Though family- and medical-leave legislation has been passed, the United States is well behind other industrialized nations in providing basic family policies. Some companies and government employers are experimenting with flexible work hours and job-sharing arrangements, child care, and home-based employment, but government mandates would further these inevitable accommodations to working mothers.

Affirmative action can play an important role in assisting mothers who work and, in particular, African American families. Though affirmative action has helped African American workers in occupational advancement, significant numbers have not been placed in senior management positions.

Assistance should be provided that strengthens families, keeping them together. Prevention is far superior to treatment. Home-visiting programs are particularly effective when combined with community centers that provide support groups, development-oriented child care, and other programs for women.

The final suggestion made by Bryner (1992) was that a concerted effort be made to reclaim urban areas from the violence, crime, and decay that affect them. Housing policy, educational reform in urban schools, increased police protection, encouragement of investments, and job creation in eco-nomically depressed areas should all be a part of the policy agenda. Training and education programs must be combined with a commitment to guarantee a job for every person who seeks one.

The development of an adequate and appropriate support system is crucial to single-parent families. This system may be composed of extended family; friends; employment and child-care resources; and community resources such as schools, churches, clinics, or social-service agencies. Families may need help in identifying, contacting, and developing relationships with an appropriate support network. Neighborhood resources would be beneficial and convenient. This kind of support system facilitates the parenting role and is associated with life satisfaction, personal growth, and less distress for both men and women.

Several types of services for single parents have been suggested (see Highlights). In addition, individuals need information about single parenthood and knowledge about rearing children without a co-parent before experiencing this lifestyle. High school students, both male and female, need to be taught homemaking, including budgeting and marketing. Knowledge about child development and criteria for quality alternative child care is of critical importance.

The resources available for children in coping with divorce and adjusting to a single-parent family have been studied less than those for adults. Resources available to children vary with the gender of the child and his or her developmental level. Older children have access to more out-of-home resources than do younger ones. The peer group can serve as a source of support and gratification. The school, the neighborhood, and the workplace (for working adolescents) can help to counter the deleterious effects of an adverse home situation. Boys may not receive as much support as girls do—generally because boys are viewed more negatively by parents, peers, and teachers. Boys confront more negative sanctions, inconsistency, and opposition and less responsiveness to their needs, particularly from divorced mothers. Grandparents offer support to their grandchildren, and where

Services Needed by Single Parents

More part-time work for mothers and fathers who wish to combine parenting and work or who desire to supplement their income.

Adequate child-care services that are affordable, are convenient to either work or home, have an extended day, provide drop-in care, and have after-school care for school-age children.

Transportation for children to child-care centers.

Child care in shopping centers.

Baby-sitting cooperatives.

Organized, registered housekeeper services to provide quality help when needed.

Increased tax deductions for child care and housekeepers.

Greater acceptance of single fathers in public housing.

"Big Sister" programs for fathers rearing daughters.

School holiday programs by public schools and child-care centers.

Increased counseling services for parents and children.

Flextime by employers to allow more flexible hours for work and family sick-leave benefits. It is clear that the demands of work and family must be integrated more successfully for single-parent families to survive.

Additional supportive organizations, especially for low-income families.

Additional research on needs of single parents and how institutions and policies can be altered to meet those needs.

---

there is a grandmother available, children have shown better adjustment (Hetherington, 1992).

Professionals developing programs for recently singled parents should have the following goals for these families: to resolve conflict, to reduce the psychological stress felt by family members, to improve parenting skills in managing and setting limits for children's behavior, to establish new coping strategies and methods for adapting to new roles for family members, to provide a network of resources available for continual support, and to help families cope with specific issues.

STEPFAMILIES

The blended family is one that contains children from a previous marriage of either parent or both parents (Ganong, Coleman, Fine, & McDaniel, 1998). By definition, a blended family cannot exist without children. A common name for this type of family structure is stepfamily. The term *stepfamily*

does not appear in the dictionary, but terms for individual family members do. The terms *stepmother* and *stepfather* merely imply the occupation of the mother's or father's position by virtue of marriage. There is no explanation of the roles or responsibilities that either is to perform. The old English term *steop,* from which the present prefix *step-* is probably derived, means "bereaved" or "orphaned" (Webster's New Encyclopedic Dictionary, 1994). Therefore, the term *stepparent* may be appropriate when the death of a biological parent occurs, but in the case of divorce, the adult is an additional parent rather than a replacement.

The phenomenon of stepfamilies is certainly not new, but a quantitative increase and qualitative changes have occurred in the last two decades in this family system. As children, we enjoyed such stories as "Hansel and Gretel," "Snow White and the Seven Dwarfs," and "Cinderella," all of which depicted a wicked and cruel stepmother. The stepfamily concept dates at least to Greek mythology, and stories about this family structure are found worldwide (Visher & Visher, 1989).

To avoid the negative connotations of the label *stepfamily,* this family form has been referred to as the reconstituted, blended, merged, remarried, multimarried, sequential, recoupled, or combined family (Coleman & Ganong, 1991).

Blended families vary both in composition and in the manner in which they are formed. The most frequent combination is a mother, her children, and a stepfather. But the family may be composed of a stepmother, a father, and his children; or a mother and a father may bring together two sets of children. One researcher described six family types based on where a child lives that capture the "linked family systems" and the interrelationships of people living in different households. Another researcher identified nine structural types of stepfamilies based on the presence or absence of and child custody by husbands and wives from present and prior marriages. The number could extend further by considering three or more marriages and grandparents who have divorced and remarried (Giles-Sims & Crosbie-Burnett, 1989). Thus, the many variations of blended families provide complex family environments—structurally, interpersonally, and emotionally. This complexity distinguishes blended families from other family forms and is a major cause of difficulty for its members' adjustment and adaptation. Much of the research has tended to ignore this complexity.

It is estimated that 35 percent of children born in the last decade will live with a stepparent before they are 18 years of age (Fine, Voydanoff, & Donnelly, 1994; Visher & Visher, 1998). In 1992 more than 11 percent of children in the United States lived with a parent and a stepparent (Ganong et al., 1998). It is estimated that 1,300 new stepfamilies are formed every day in the United States, and it is projected that by 2010 stepfamilies will outnumber all other family types (Visher & Visher, 1998). Most stepfamilies include stepfathers, but 18 percent of stepfamilies are stepmother families. Two factors seem important in predicting an increase in stepfamilies. Although divorce leveled off in the 1990s, with an increased lifespan more couples have more years to diverge as they mature. Further, there is a growing focus on quality of life, so that people who are in domestically violent and verbally abusive relationships are likely to divorce. Of those who divorce, 75 percent will remarry and 60 percent of these will take children into the remarried family. One half of all marriages involve at least one previously married partner.

Sweeney (1997) found a significant relationship between socioeconomic prospects and the propensity to remarry. Her research indicated that good socioeconomic prospects (reflected in high occupational status) delay remarriage for women in general but hasten it for women divorcing at relatively older ages. This finding suggests that women separating at younger ages may use good socioeconomic prospects to finance a longer search for a partner, but older women with good socioeconomic prospects my be better able to attract mates. Thus, at least among older women, patterns of remarriage will tend to increase the concentration of poverty among divorced women. For these women, those with the least ability to support themselves also will be least likely to remarry. Findings also supported the prediction that socioeconomic prospects are very important for the remarriage of women, but with few exceptions, they are not related to the remarriage of men.

In the case of divorce, more mothers receive custody of their children than fathers do. This accounts for the predominance of blended households composed of mothers, their children, and stepfathers. Blended families represent the most common alternative family structure.

Table 7.6 reflects the number and percentage of various types of stepfamilies compared with all married-couple households with children. As noted, there were approximately 5,254,000 stepfamily households in 1990, with the largest percentage composed of the biological mother and a stepfather. The next largest type of stepfamily was the joint biological family and stepfamily, in which there was at least one child of both parents and one or more stepchildren, or biological children of both parents (and therefore stepchildren for both parents). In fact, this type of stepfamily is almost as

TABLE 7.6   Married-Couple Family Households with Children: 1980, 1990

	1980		1990	
TYPE OF FAMILY	*No.**	*% Distribution*	*No.**	*% Distribution*
Biological mother–stepfather**	1,818	7.5	2,619	10.3
Biological father–stepmother†	171	0.7	152	0.6
Joint biological–step††	1,862	7.7	2,475	9.8
Joint step–adoptive‡	12	—	8	—

Source: U.S. Bureau of the Census. (1992). *Statistical abstract of the United States: 1992* (112th ed.). Washington, DC: U.S. Department of Commerce.

*Number in thousands.

**All own children of biological mother and stepchildren of father.

†All own children of biological father and stepchildren of mother.

††At least one child is biological child of both parents, at least one child is biological child of one parent and stepchild of the other; or a combination of biological children of mother and biological children of father.

‡At least one child is biological child of one parent and stepchild of the other, and at least one child is an adopted child of both parents.

prevalent as the biological mother–stepfather structure (U.S. Bureau of the Census, 1992). It must be mentioned, however, that most census data were collected on households rather than families; consequently, nonresidential relationships are not included (Coleman & Ganong, 1991).

Table 7.7 shows the number and percentage of children living in stepfamilies by race and Hispanic origin of the mother. As noted, approximately 31 percent of African American married-couple households were stepfamilies composed of

the biological mother and a stepfather, and 15 percent of Hispanic married-couple households were of that structure, followed by 13 percent of White married-couple households. For each racial and ethnic group, this stepfamily structure increased from 1980 to 1990, whereas the structure composed of the stepmother and biological father declined (U.S. Bureau of the Census, 1992).

It is predicted that 40 percent of children born in the 1990s will live in a stepfamily before they reach the age of 18 (Fine, Donnelly, & Voydanoff,

TABLE 7.7   Children under 18 Years of Age Living in Stepfamily Households by Race and Hispanic Origin of Mother: 1980, 1990

	Biological Mother–Stepfather				*Biological Father–Stepmother*			
	1980		1990		1980		1990	
	No.*	*%*	*No.**	*%*	*No.**	*%*	*No.**	*%*
White	4,382	10.3	5,258	13.2	644	1.6	549	1.4
African American	877	23.2	1,147	31.3	46	1.2	38	1.0
Hispanic	N/A		699	15.3	N/A		38	0.8

Source: U.S. Bureau of the Census. (1992). *Statistical abstract of the United States: 1992* (112th ed.). Washington, DC: U.S. Department of Commerce.

*Number in thousands.

1991; Hetherington, 1992). Furthermore, because the divorce rate is slightly higher for second than for first marriages, many adults and children will be exposed to a series of marital transitions and household reorganizations. It is estimated that 1 out of every 10 children will experience two divorces of the custodial parent before turning 16 years of age (Hetherington, 1992). Approximately 8 million children in 1990 lived in stepfamilies. More than 5 million of these were White children, but a higher percentage of African American and Hispanic children live in stepfamilies than White children.

Issues for Stepfamilies

Nearly all of the empirical research on stepfamilies has been published in the last two decades. Before the 1980s, most data were collected on clinical populations, which led to the view that stepfamilies and steprelationships were problem-oriented (Coleman & Ganong, 1991). More recent stepfamily models have addressed the diversity and the complexity of the stepfamily suprasystem and have focused on healthy stepfamily development rather than on the deficit comparison with first marriages. These models draw heavily on the subsystem structures and processes, which within the overall stepfamily network define who is part of what group and who performs which roles and tasks.

Healthy stepfamily development requires responding to the challenges of remarriage, which include old myths and persistent stigmas; experiences of loss, isolation, and discontinuity from the past; financial discontinuity; lack of a common family paradigm; unrealistic expectations; and problems of boundary ambiguity. Moving from stage to stage in the developmental process depends on the successful completion of tasks associated with previous developmental stages. Remarrieds often struggle to resolve prior losses and competition between sequential spouses, make room for new family members, realign loyalty and power, recommit to becoming a family, rebalance relationships, relinquish feelings of deprivation and burden, grow toward a new integration, and improve relationships among stepfamily members (Ganong et al., 1998).

Using a national survey, Shapiro (1996) investigated the differences in psychological distress between remarried and divorced adults. He found significantly lower rates of economic distress and psychological distress in single adults who had remarried than in those who were divorced. The remarried subjects reported higher incomes than those who were divorced, and divorced women experienced the greatest economic distress. Although remarried women had lower rates of depression than divorced women, their depression scores were higher than scores on all other psychological and economic measures. Accessibility to financial resources of the remarried subjects appeared to facilitate coping with stressful events, thus affecting psychological well-being. Shapiro concluded, however, that both economic and interpersonal factors were important in explaining differences in psychological distress between divorced and remarried adults.

Marital Relationships. The remarried couple, not having had time to consolidate their marital relationship without children, find that the many time-consuming, child-related concerns make it extremely difficult for them to solidify their relationship and strengthen the family bond (MacDonald & DeMaris, 1995). A primary challenge lies in developing and sustaining the marital bond in this instantly formed family with children. Spouses must establish their relationship within a family system that is structurally more complex than experienced in a first marriage and that may include ex-in-laws and noncustodial children as well as nonresidential parents and grandparents; thus, family boundaries are often not well marked. Our society provides few norms to guide remarried family members in adjusting to their newly adopted complex roles and relationships. Moreover, family members bring with them previous histories and experiences of marriage and family life that can affect their adjustment to the new marriage. The typical starting point for the new marriage is a tenuous couple relationship, a tightly bonded parent-child alliance, and potential interference in family functioning from an outsider (the new stepparent)—a situation that would be considered pathological in a newly first-married pair.

In most first marriages, a close marital relationship serves as the foundation for positive relationships among other family members and may promote the psychological well-being of spouses. Especially in the early stage of remarriage, however, a positive marital relationship has sometimes been associated with behavior problems in children and difficulties in parent-child interaction. Stepchildren often view the new stepparent as a competitor for the affection and attention of their biological parent, and they resent a close relationship. It is not surprising, therefore, that, among married couples in stepfamilies, the most frequently reported area of stress, and the one that interferes most with marital satisfaction, is that of parent-child relationships (Fine & Kurdek, 1995).

Researchers studying stepfamilies generally have found positive relationships between perceived marital quality and perceived quality of each of the parent-child relationships, but some variables may moderate these perceptions. Based on previous research, Fine and Kurdek (1995) examined the relationship between perceived marital quality and the quality of stepparent-child relationships in both stepmother and stepfather families. They found that the relationship between perceived marital quality and quality of the stepparent-child relationship was stronger for stepparents than for biological parents. Findings also supported the notion that, for spouses in stepfamilies, the boundary between the marital subsystem and the stepparent-stepchild subsystem is more permeable than that between the marital subsystem and the biological parent-child subsystem. Stepparents' relationships with their spouses and stepchildren are affectively linked because these relationships begin and develop simultaneously. Whereas biological parents may consider marital problems to be separate from difficulties arising from the parent-child relationship, stepparents are likely to believe that there is a link between marital difficulties and problems with their stepchildren.

MacDonald and DeMaris (1995) tested the hypothesis that marital conflict is more frequent in stepfamilies than in biological families. Differences in perceived marital conflict for three types of stepfamilies were assessed—those with at least one stepchild and one biological child of one or both partners, those that included no children from previous marriages but only children from the present marriage, and those that included at least one stepchild and no biological children. Further, differences in conflict were examined in three types of marriages—those that were first marriages for both partners, those that were remarriages for only one partner, and that those were remarriages for both partners. These researchers found that for those families with only one remarried partner, the frequency of conflict did not differ significantly from two-partner first marriages. However, contrary to expectation, marital conflict in families with two remarried partners occurred less frequently than in all other family types.

The findings with respect to child type also were contrary to expectations. The frequency of conflict was no different in families with both biological children and stepchildren and families with biological children only. However, as marital duration increased (6 years or more), conflict increased for stepchildren-only couples and decreased for couples with only biological children, and eventually conflict surpassed that found in couples with only biological children. These findings are consistent with the notion that many stepfamilies experience an initial "fantasy" stage, followed by an "immersion" stage, in which fantasies generally meet with disappointment.

Interestingly, some research has indicated that the primary way remarried couples prepare for their remarriage is by living together (Ganong & Coleman, 1989). The next most frequent way of preparing themselves for stepfamily life was found by these researchers to be counseling. About one-third of the women and a quarter of the men in their study received counseling before remarriage. Few couples were found to have discussed before remarriage any issues deemed important by family experts. The reasons given for remarriage were more pragmatic than romantic—social pressure, convenience, and practical considerations. Cohabitation did seem to have a positive effect on adjustment, especially for husbands. It was found that for men, the frequency of disagreements, marital problems, and feelings for the spouse were significantly lower for those who had cohabited than for those who had not. For women, the only significant differences were found in the number of disagreements.

Boundaries. Boundaries in stepfamilies often are ambiguous and not well marked (Hetherington, 1992). Boundary ambiguity is conceptualized as the uncertainty of family members regarding their perceptions about who is in or out of the family and who is performing what roles and tasks within the family system. Boundaries have psychological dimensions that foster a sense of identity that differentiates the members of a family from one another and from other groups. Boundary ambiguity has been shown to be related to family stress and overall family dysfunction. Recent research found support between high boundary ambiguity and measures of family health and individual well-being in stepfamilies.

Pill (1990) examined stepfamily cohesion and adaptability, the process of revising basic assumptions about family life, and the development of stepfamily identity. The results indicated that the stepfamilies in his study had low levels of family cohesion. However, it was hypothesized that stepfamilies with low to moderate levels of cohesion would feel more satisfied than stepfamilies with higher levels. It was apparent that these couples made purposeful efforts to both provide for and promote psychological distance by broadening the context of their immediate families. Extended-family members and/or friends were invited to family celebrations. For vacations, children were urged to invite friends, engage in separate activities, choose whether to participate, or go and come as they pleased if circumstances allowed. More than 90 percent of the families who used these approaches reported satisfaction with them, whereas only about half of those families who restricted these activities were satisfied with the outcomes.

Other results of the Pill (1990) study indicated that couples reported the closest relationships between biologically related family members. However, most of these couples were very matter-of-fact and viewed this situation as natural and understandable. Family members frequently showed emotional support, encouragement, and warmth toward one another, but steprelationships were less intimate than biological relationships, and maintaining respect for these differences was reported to be important.

Roles of Stepparents. Earlier research indicated that the absence of well-defined, appropriate, and acceptable roles for stepparents clearly distinguishes blended families from nuclear families. The role definitions of stepparents in this society both are poorly articulated and imply contradictory functions of "parents," "stepparents," "nonparents," and "friends." The use of the label *stepparent* reflects a variety of beliefs, including that the stepparent should function in some parentlike ways and yet assume a secondary, "hands-off" role in other dimensions of child rearing. The use of the parent label has been used to reflect the belief that stepparents do and should function like biological parents. The use of the friend label reflects the belief that stepparents should function in a supportive and nurturant way rather than taking an active disciplinary and decision-making role (Fine, Coleman, & Ganong, 1998). In the study conducted by these researchers, about half of the parents and stepparents identified "parent" as the ideal stepparent role, whereas less than 20 percent chose "stepparent" or "friend" as the ideal role. The parents and stepparents did not differ significantly, but children identified "friend" as the ideal descriptor. Only 18 percent of the children identified "stepparent" and 29 percent chose "parent" as the ideal stepparent role.

A stepparent cannot totally assume the role of father or mother; he or she is a nonparent. Some of the most obvious roles of natural fathers are those that are biological, financial, and educational. Stepfathers cannot assume a biological role; they frequently share the financial responsibilities with the natural father; and they certainly share socialization of the child simultaneously or temporally. The three roles (parent, stepparent, friend and nonparent) in most cases are interwoven, and the question "How much should I parent?" seems to persist (Fine, 1995; Fine et al., 1998).

This lack of clarity and content in the stepparent role has been confirmed by a number of researchers, and currently there is no social consensus about expectations for appropriate behavior (Fine, 1995; Fine et al., 1998). This confusion seems to plague all members of the stepfamily. Several variables have been identified that appear to relate to stepparent clarity. The first is gender of stepparent. Some evidence indicates that the role of the stepmother is more ambiguous than that of the stepfather, possibly because stepmothers have fewer socially accepted role prescriptions than stepfathers do. Second, the role seems more ambiguous when the nonresidential parent is highly involved with his or her child, particularly if the nonresidential parent is the mother. Third, the residential status of the stepparent seems to influence role ambiguity. For example, nonresidential stepmothers experience greater stress than stepmothers living with their stepchildren because the limited amount of contact with their stepchildren may provide little opportunity to develop clear roles, thus leading to greater role ambiguity. Fourth, the type of stepfamily—complex versus simple—appears to affect role ambiguity. In complex stepfamilies (those with each spouse bringing children to the remarried family), each parent is simultaneously assuming the roles of biological parent and stepparent, which leads to ambiguity and confusion. Fifth, the length of time that the stepfamily has been together is a factor. Two competing forces seem to be at work in this regard. The longer the stepfamily is together, the more time family members have to develop consensus about roles. On the other hand, as the stepfamily develops, members enter new developmental stages, causing a waxing and waning of the degree of role clarity. Finally, the age of the stepchild seems to be associated with the extent of stepparent role ambiguity. Younger stepchildren contribute to and experience less role

ambiguity than older children because they have had less time since the divorce of their parents to become socialized to a family without the stepparent. Further, the more mature cognitive abilities of older children lead to a greater potential for experiencing role ambiguity than in younger children (Fine, 1995).

Research also has shown that stepparents' roles are less active than biological parents' (Fine, 1995). Societal perceptions suggest that stepparents as opposed to biological parents should demonstrate less warmth, fewer controlling behaviors toward stepchildren, and a more disengaged parenting style characterized by low levels of involvement, parental monitoring, and discipline. However, the stepmother role is constructed to be more active than the stepfather role. Women are expected to be heavily involved in and assume primary responsibility for the well-being of children. Further, one might expect stepparents to assume a more active disciplinary role over time, and then become less active as children reach adolescence, particularly in families with stepsons. However, evidence indicates that stepparents do not reduce their disciplinary roles as stepdaughters reach adolescence.

It seems, then, that the most difficult interpersonal challenge in stepfamilies lies in developing a constructive relationship between parents and children. The child must renegotiate his relationship both with the noncustodial parent and with the custodial parent and establish a new relationship with the stepparent. Parents must establish relationships with their stepchildren and redefine relationships with their biological children. This process usually involves considerable confusion and ambivalence.

Research findings suggest that the ambiguity of the stepparenting role is reflected in less familial cohesiveness, poorer communication and parental discipline, less control and monitoring, and more disengagement on the part of the stepparent. Moreover, after initial attempts to form a positive relationship with the stepchild and to enhance the new family unit, many stepparents increasingly become disengaged from their stepchildren. Stepmothers are less able to disengage than stepfathers, since they are more likely to have to remain involved in routine child care. The stepparent's disengagement and eventual withdrawal may be a response to persistent resentment and resistance on the part of some stepchildren (Hetherington, 1992).

In Fine et al.'s (1998) study, there was not agreement among family members about the stepparent's role. Stepparents reported that they should and did exhibit more warmth and control than stepchildren thought they should and did engage in. Further, stepchildren were more certain about the stepparent than stepparents were. When consensus in families existed, it was positively related to fewer mental-health symptoms for stepparents, stepchildren's perceived closeness of the stepparent-stepchild relationship, the parent's perception that the stepparent was functioning successfully, and stepparents' perceptions of greater family strengths.

Hetherington (1992) suggested that with younger children, the most successful strategy for a new stepparent is to build a warm, involved relationship with the stepchildren initially and to support the discipline of the biological parent but to avoid assuming the role of a controlling disciplinarian rapidly. Even authoritative stepparenting (involving high warmth, effective communication, and firm but responsive control) may at first lead to resentment and resistance on the part of stepchildren. Authoritative parenting should be gradual, but with some stepchildren (especially adolescents), it may remain undesirable or impossible. Other suggestions for developing the stepparent role may be found in the Highlights.

It is clear that the stepparent role is distinct from the parent role in some respects. The role most be developed over a period of time and, to a degree, earned. There are no societal norms to assist stepparents in this development. It appears that stepparent roles and responsibilities vary widely and seem to take longer to work out than do stepsibling roles. Months of trial and error by most stepparents are needed when many roles, such as consultant, coach, mediator, and friend, are tried.

Although stepparents have been found to feel more like friends than like parents, some research indicates that both stepparents and stepchildren are more accepting of stepparents assuming a child-rearing role than nuclear-family members

---

HIGHLIGHTS

Tips for Developing the Stepparent Role

Allow ample time to work out grieving for old relationships and restructuring new ones.

Know yourself and family members.

Work to help each family member find his or her place in the new family.

Develop a distant but cordial relationship with each partner's ex-spouse and their new partners.

If possible, move to a new house, or renovate the old, so new spouse and stepchildren have the opportunity to establish their own territory.

Communicate, negotiate, compromise, make more joint decisions, respect and accept what cannot be changed.

Include children in discussions according to developmental level.

Understand the legal obligations involved with the new marriage—wills, child support, and/or alimony.

Attempt mutual courtesy but do not expect stepchild's love.

Respect the special biological bond between biological parent and child.

believe is appropriate. Although a sizable portion of remarried couples expect to share equally in rearing children, these expectations may not materialize. In one study (Coleman & Ganong, 1991), even though 50 percent of newly remarried parents planned to share equally in child-rearing responsibilities, only about one-third actually did so.

Emotional bonds between stepparents and stepchildren have been found to be less close than biological parent-child ties and are somewhat more likely to be characterized by conflict. Some stepparent-child relationships are quite positive, however, especially if the child has little contact with the noncustodial parent. Stepfathers are more likely than stepmothers to have positive relationships with children. Generally, when both adults bring children into the new family, stepparent-child relationships are more distant (Coleman & Ganong, 1991).

Schwebel, Fine, and Renner (1991) had college students describe how biological, adoptive, and stepparents should respond to specifically described parenting situations. These researchers concluded that subjects in the study viewed the roles of stepparents as less clear than those of biological and adoptive parents. The lack of conventional wisdom about what is appropriate for stepparents was evident. There was greater variability, or lack of agreement, among respondents on how stepparents, in contrast to biological and adoptive parents, would and should respond. These researchers concluded that lacking conventional wisdom, stepparents must make their own unguided decisions about the division of role responsibilities, and the lack of guidance leads to differences of opinion, disappointments, conflict, stress, and unrealistic expectations.

Pill (1990) concluded that stepparents enter into remarriage with unrealistic expectations concerning their role. He found that 41 percent of the stepfamilies in his sample entered remarried life with the anticipation that their stepfamily would become closely bonded like a nuclear family. However, the realities of stepfamily bonding did not match earlier expectations in 75 percent of the fam-

ilies. Additionally, the hope of many parents that noncustodial children would be incorporated more closely into the stepfamily did not occur, and this situation was universally experienced with sadness. Another theme that emerged in this study was that living in a stepfamily requires a continual and deliberate effort. Though many adults assumed that the beginning stages of stepfamily formation would require attention, most were unprepared for the unrelenting nature of the demands placed on them. See Highlights for potential areas of conflict in stepfamilies.

Financial Issues.   Money is a common source of conflict for stepfamilies. Some couples rank it as the number one problem. Economic integration is one of the developmental tasks of remarried families. Often the stresses associated with remarriage, particularly finances, are related to the presence of children from previous marriages. Many of the financial problems related to children can be traced to the necessity to maintain communication with a former spouse. Inability to depend on the receipt of child support and resentment of child- and/or spousal-support obligations are potential areas of conflict for remarried spouses.

Spouses have revealed that they are reluctant to discuss financial matters with each other. Men feel torn between the financial demands of two families and hesitate to accept financial responsibility for their stepchildren. Women are reluctant to reveal their financial affairs and are concerned that their children might be a burden for their new husbands. Stepfamilies need to seek help with financial problems, and financial-management workshops should be provided for stepfamilies to assist them with these concerns.

An interesting study on the normative beliefs about parents' and stepparents' financial obligations to children following divorce and remarriage was conducted by Ganong et al. (1995). They found that participants perceived fathers to be financially obligated to support their children following divorce, but whether they should pay for extra costs such as tutoring was based primarily on their ability to pay. Stepfathers were perceived to

Potential Areas of Conflict in Stepfamilies

Discipline by stepparent
Sharing parenting duties
Relationships with ex-spouses
Awkward development of bonds between stepparents and stepchildren
Establishing interactional patterns in the absence of common past history
Financial issues

have total primary control over stepchildren as long as they were married to the children's mothers, including paying for educational services. But if they divorce, stepfathers no longer have control or obligations. Visher and Visher (1998) noted that stepparents often are held responsible for financially supporting their stepchildren, and their income is taken into account when stepchildren apply for college scholarships, even though stepparents have no legal rights.

Legal Issues Relating To Stepparent Roles. Since the mid-1980s, the rights and responsibilities of stepparents have become clearer, since many states have developed statutes that either specifically address stepparents or refer to "third parties" in general, a category that is often interpreted to include stepparents. Recently, it has become easier for stepchildren and stepparents to maintain postdivorce relationships through custody or visitation (Fine & Fine, 1992). Visitation following termination of the remarriage allows stepparents physical access to their stepchildren but excludes them from the decision-making and child-rearing responsibilities of legal custody.

However, states vary in both their statutes and their case law, and in some states there is still little clarity because stepparents are not specifically identified and because courts and legislatures have been slow to recognize that stepparents and stepchildren can have meaningful and enduring relationships.

Only a few states have statutes that require stepparents to support stepchildren who live with

them during marriage (Fine & Fine, 1992). Typically, these state statutes do not require continued support after termination of the marriage between the stepparent and the child's biological parent. In the absence of statutes that directly address stepfamily members' support responsibilities, some states rely on common law to make such determinations. In some states, the doctrine of *in loco parentis* may lead to support obligations. Under this doctrine, a person who deliberately acts as the child's parent (e.g., supports the child financially, presents himself or herself as the child's parent in the community) may be considered to have a direct obligation to support a stepchild. However, parents may terminate the *in loco parentis* relationship and its corresponding financial responsibilities at any time, most often at the time of divorce. Further, the stepparent can prevent the application of a support duty by clearly indicating that he or she does not intend to financially support the stepchild. The common-law attempts to impose obligations have met with little success.

Generally, stepfamily members who have not had their relationships legally sanctioned through adoption cannot inherit from one another unless stipulated in a will. Thus, unless the stepfamily member is specifically included in a will, he or she cannot inherit from the deceased. In a few states, stepchildren are permitted to inherit in instances in which they are the only next of kin and the property otherwise would go to the state. Similarly, courts generally do not recognize stepchildren as "children" under wrongful death statutes (Fine & Fine, 1992).

In 1996 changes in Social Security benefits were enacted into law. Two restrictions on a stepchild's eligibility for benefits from a stepparent were included in this legislation. The stepparent must have provided 50 percent of the stepchild's support immediately before death, and if the stepparent and the natural parent divorce, benefits are terminated (DiSimone, 1996).

Until recently, under divorce statutes a nonparent did not have standing to seek custody of a child following divorce, even when a close relationship had been established. This situation has now changed in many states. Specific statutes have been enacted so that under certain circumstances a "fit" nonbiological parent may obtain custody of the child if that is in the child's best interests (Buser, 1991).

Although 44 states have a preference or presumption for placing a child in custody of a natural parent, third parties (which include stepparents) may receive custody if preponderant evidence exists that natural parents are unfit. Although grandparents and stepparents have limited ability to gain custody, most states allow courts to grant them visitation rights if the arrangement is in the best interests of the child. Seven states specifically address stepparent visitation in their statutes by providing for this option; seven other states provide an opportunity for visitation of third parties but do not specifically mention stepparents. The emotional bond between stepchild and stepparent and the duration of the relationship are important when determining the best interests of the child in this context (Buehler & Gerard, 1995).

Visher and Visher (1998) labeled stepparents as the forgotten family members who receive little attention from the media, from educators, and from many segments of society, including policymakers and the legal system. They noted that mediators, attorneys, and judges often want to avoid dealing with stepparents, considering them as sabotaging obstructionists. These researchers suggested that stepparents be included in the legal process and be perceived as allies who often can be more objective than biological parents in making decisions about children. Further, they believe that

well-conceived legal recognition of the stepparent role could be very helpful in the emotional and financial security of the children in stepfamilies.

Some stepparents choose to adopt their stepchildren. Although the actual number of adopted stepchildren is not known, it is estimated that 100,000 stepchildren are adopted by their stepparents every year. Ganong et al. (1998) examined the factors that stepfamily members consider when contemplating stepchild adoption. They found that a common motive was the desire to become as much like a nuclear family as possible. Adoption was seen as a way to solidify the stepparent-stepchild relationship and to reflect its closeness. For some, it was a way to disconnect the nonresidential parent from their lives. For others, adoption was seen as a way to remove some of the daily hassles of being in a stepfamily, such as having different last names. Another motivation stemmed from the concern about custody decisions when the residential parents die while children are still minors. Interestingly, inadequate legal protection for stepparents who do not adopt was not a motive in most of these families. Stepparents and stepchildren thought more about adoption than did biological parents, but stepchildren did not always understand what adoption would mean to their relationships with parents and stepparents.

The study also revealed several barriers to adoption. For example, adoption was considered less often when the children and the nonresidential parent had a good relationship. Some families were reluctant to engage in hostile legal proceedings and angry interactions surrounding requests that nonresidential parents relinquish their parental rights. Financial concerns were common barriers to seeking adoption. The loss of financial provisions for children from nonresidential parents, such as child support or money for college, was relevant for some families. Other concerns were the ongoing financial commitment of adoptive parents if remarriages ended and the actual costs of adoption, such as court costs and attorney fees.

These researchers proposed that public policy be implemented that legally recognizes the role of stepparents in the lives of stepchildren without severing relationships with natural parents. Stepfamilies need more flexibility to construct new creative roles. Attempting to replicate a nuclear family ordinarily does not foster positive development of the stepfamily.

In summary, legislatures and courts have not generally recognized the stepparent-stepchild relationship as one that is potentially enduring beyond the marriage of the biological parent and stepparent. Depending to some extent on the state in which one lives, stepparents are unlikely to have legal obligations to support stepchildren following divorce and may have difficulty maintaining relationships with stepchildren through visitation or custody. If stepparents are allowed visitation or custody, it is not because of any particular rights that they are entitled to but, rather, because the courts have determined that this is in the best interests of the child. Although these recent changes reflect greater sensitivity to the possible enduring nature of steprelationships, further efforts are recommended by many family and legal experts.

Stepmothers

As noted earlier, research has indicated stepmothering to be more difficult than stepfathering and revealed greater acceptance by children of stepfathers than of stepmothers. Historically, the stepmother has received negative press, and she has had to combat the myth of the wicked and cruel stepmother. Research has found, however, that only a small percentage of stepmothers actually reject their stepchildren. The distorted conceptions of stepmothering have been explained partly by the fact that stepmothers spend more time with the children, thus incurring more opportunity for disharmony because of proximity and the nature of the maternal role. In addition, it has been assumed that children in our society have been closer to their mothers, and therefore no one could follow easily in the steps of a natural mother (MacDonald, & DeMaris, 1996).

Dainton (1993) examined some of the impediments to the identity-management strategies enacted by stepmothers in the face of two competing myths—that a stepmother is evil and that she will instantly love her stepchildren. Despite the increasing number of stepfamilies, Dainton found that these two myths show few signs of losing strength. She also found that the role of stepmother elicited more negative connotations than any other family position. Stepmothers were perceived as less affectionate, good, fair, kind, loving, and likable and were thought to be more cruel, hateful, unfair, and unloving. The myths surrounding stepmothers negatively affect their experiences and contribute to the stress they suffer. Further, they promote unrealistic expectations and interfere with family integration.

In the stepmother role, identity management involves not only maintaining preferred perceptions but also preventing unwanted perceptions associated with a preconceived evaluation. A stepmother's behavior might be interpreted as negative even if by objective measures it is not, simply because her behaviors are expected to be negative. Her dilemma is whether or not she should attempt to use corrective strategies, because any efforts to actively repair others' perceptions might be interpreted unfavorably. She is faced with a no-win situation (Dainton, 1993).

Another identity-management difficulty stepmothers face is related to the extent to which they play an active parenting role. In attempting the stepparent role, stepmothers are in a double bind. On the one hand, they are expected to love the children as if they were her own, but on the other hand, they are often sanctioned against adopting a bona fide parental role. Thus, becoming a stepmother requires a careful balancing act, wherein a woman must regulate perceptions of involvement without being perceived as overinvolved or uncaring (Dainton, 1993).

Dainton (1993) found that stepmothers use a couple of strategies to manage these problems: (1) concealing the fact one is a stepmother—masquerading as a natural mother; and (2) confronting and breaking through—acknowledging one's status and working to frame the identity in a constructive and commendable context. Several alternatives have been suggested. One is that the remarried couple first establish the solidarity of the marriage in the children's minds, then use that solidarity to establish the credibility of the stepparent as a valid parental authority. Such efforts are clearly corrective in nature. Others suggest that the stepmother remove herself from the parenting role altogether by insisting that the biological father take on all the parenting responsibilities. This removal does not mean that the stepmother cannot be supportive or nurturing to the stepchildren, but this approach avoids the negative expectations associated with the role and frees the stepmother to work on positive, nonparental relationships with her stepchildren. Another approach is to focus on alternative role enactment. Since there is no prescribed accepted role, stepparents should feel free to try on various roles until they find one that fits—primary mother (only works if biological mother is dead to the child), other mother, and friend. Simply finding a name that the child feels comfortable calling the stepmother might assist in establishing the stepmother's identity—the stepmother's first name, a mutually agreed-upon nickname, or a variation of "mother" not used for the biological mother (Dainton, 1993).

Stepmothers have been found to have a more optimistic attitude toward stepparenting than do stepfathers. They are less likely to endorse myths regarding stepfamilies, and they report greater satisfaction with the stepparent-child relationships than stepfathers (Kurdek & Fine, 1991). Further, these researchers found that for stepmothers, low role ambiguity, high optimism, and few myths were related to high satisfaction with family, marital, and personal life, but they were unrelated to parenting satisfaction.

Fine et al. (1991) found that stepmothers, more than stepfathers, were optimistic about remarriage, had more stability in their beliefs about romance following remarriage, perceived themselves as both agreeing with their spouses in making child-rearing decisions and having fewer difficulties in rearing children, and reported greater satisfaction with their lives. Conversely, these researchers found that depression and anxiety were related to negative perceptions of oneself, one's future, and one's environment. They concluded that the stepmother's ability to remain optimistic in the face of changing circumstances may be a coping strategy that facilitates stepfamily adjustment.

Any mother's ability to give and relate to her child is at least partially dependent on the nurturing, cooperation, and mutual problem-solving assistance she receives from her spouse (Fine et al., 1991). A stepmother is even more dependent on, and in need of, her husband's support. She is a newcomer to an already formed relationship between father and child and may be seen as both rescuer and intruder. The stepmother may feel she has to make up for past hurts. Because the stepmother's role and status are so dependent on the support of her husband, the level of his self-confidence is important. If he disengages from his role and leaves all the decisions to her to make alone, her job is much more difficult (Fine et al., 1991).

Ganong and Coleman (1989) found that the stepmothers in their study had concerns about the quality of their marriage, their partners' former spouses, the discipline of the stepchildren, finances, and in-laws. These researchers also found that stepmothers' expectations for the stepparent-child relationship held before remarriage were generally optimistic, and they expected to fulfill a parent role with the children. Further, these mothers expected their new partners to have good relationships with the children.

In summary, stepmothers have a harder time adjusting to their roles than stepfathers do. They appear to make a better adjustment if they are under 40 years of age, have been married before, bring any children they may have with them into the remarriage, inherit stepchildren who are under 13 years of age, have sufficient ego strength and self-esteem, have the nurturance and support of their husbands, and have willingness to accept not being loved for a while.

Stepfathers

Residential stepfathers outnumber stepmothers because most blended families are formed because of divorce rather than death, and most mothers retain custody of their children. Adjusting to the role of stepfather is easier than adjusting to the role of stepmother. Stepfathers have their problems, too, but they are not perpetuated in mythology and fairy tales. Therefore, stepfathers do not have to overcome negative press. Being a stepfather does not entail the same expectation as being a stepmother, largely because our culture expects less love and nurturing from a man than from a woman (Coleman & Ganong, 1991).

However, Deal, Hagen, and Anderson (1992) reported that the marital subsystem in a stepfamily is operating from a position of less strength than that in an intact family. Therefore, the new stepfather is often, at least initially, in a position of greater marginality than either the mother or her biological children. As a result of this and the mother-child bond first formed in the biological family and strengthened in the single-parent family, it is important for the stepfather to establish a positive relationship with his new wife's children. Such a relationship may be necessary not only to cement the spousal bond but also to prevent the husband-wife relationship from being viewed as threatening by the children.

A stepfather's role is ambiguous with children at any age, but building a new relationship with a teenage stepchild is likely to be fraught with pitfalls. Younger children are more likely to accept the stepfather as a parent figure, whereas older children can accept a stepfather as a companion and support for their mother. Adolescent stepchildren may resist being responsive and obedient to someone they sometimes view as an intruder at the very time when their own development requires that they become more autonomous from the family, test limits, and establish their independence (Hagan, Hollier, O'Connor, & Eisenberg, 1992).

In Hagan et al.'s longitudinal study of the adaptation of family members and changes in the functioning of family subsystems over a 2-year period following remarriage, stepfather-stepchild relationships were found to be awkward initially. Stepfathers felt alienated from adolescent stepchildren, and although they exhibited little overt nega-

tivity, they were less positive and involved in controlling and monitoring their children's behavior than were nondivorced fathers. These differences, though less negative, were still evident 2 years after remarriage. Further, stepfathers became more disengaged as the study progressed. By the end of the 2-year study, two-fifths of the stepfathers were disengaged compared with one-fifth of nondivorced fathers, and they were less authoritative in their child-rearing orientation (Hagan et al., 1992).

Kurdek and Fine (1991) found that stepfathers were less optimistic about stepparenting and their relationship with the children than were stepmothers. Further, the level of optimism was associated with the stepfathers' satisfaction with stepparenting. Marsiglio (1992) found that stepfathers had diverse perceptions about the various aspects of stepfathering. A significant proportion of the stepfathers in his study perceived themselves as having positive, fatherlike role identities, although many also believed the identity as a father was tenuous. Some felt that it was harder to love stepchildren than their own children; others felt that they were more like a friend than a parent to their stepchildren; and about one-third reported that it was harder to be a stepparent than a natural parent.

Marsiglio found that several factors affected stepfathers' perceptions of their roles. Stepfathers co-residing in households in which only stepchildren were present were less likely than fathers living with both step- and biological children to have perceptions consistent with a fatherlike role identity. In addition, stepfathers whose children were younger when the parents married or began to cohabit were more likely to have fatherlike perceptions. Stepfathers also were more likely to report fatherlike perceptions if they were happier with their spouses. Extensive contact with the biological father seemed to be detrimental to stepfathers' establishing fatherlike role identities when the oldest stepchildren were boys.

Claxton-Oldfield (1992) examined the perceptions of adolescents and young adults of stepfathers' behaviors in disciplining and showing affection to their stepchildren. The results indicated that stepfathers were perceived more frequently than biological fathers to be unaffectionate, unfair, cruel, unloving, and unlikable. Although these feelings were not on the extremely negative side, they were certainly significantly less positive than those for biological fathers. On the whole, the young people felt positive about affectionate roles for stepfathers but at the same time thought they would feel uncomfortable if stepfathers demonstrated affection.

Fine, Ganong, and Coleman (1997) investigated stepfathers' perceptions of their adjustment in relation to several dimensions of the stepparent role—beliefs about how stepparents should behave, level of certainty of those beliefs, and behaviors performed to fulfill in the role as stepparent. In general, stepfathers who reported that they frequently engaged in warmth and control parenting behaviors and who believed that they should do so reported better adjustments. Further, little role discrepancy between what stepfathers believed others thought they should do and the actual standards of behavior was related to more stepfamily involvement, more satisfaction with stepparenting, greater life satisfaction, perceived success as a stepfather, more closeness with stepchildren, more marital satisfaction, more perceived family strengths, and less stepparent shame. Discrepancy scores on the warmth parenting dimension were significantly more highly correlated with adjustment scores than were discrepancy scores on the control dimension.

The researchers concluded that stepfathers were more satisfied with several dimensions of their marital and family lives when they perceived that they frequently engaged in authoritative parenting behaviors (both warmth and control). However, those stepfathers who believed that they should be active on the control dimension were more likely to have higher levels of depression. The length of time as a stepfamily did not affect any of the role perception and adjustment variables.

Hetherington (1992) concluded that the complexity and ambiguity of society's definition of the stepfather's role as well as the multiple challenges that stepfathers encounter suggest that the course of adjustment is difficult. In the longitudinal study of marital transitions and their effects, stepfathers were trying to maintain gratifying marital relationships while confronting wives who were perceived as exhibiting little control over their adolescent children, quarrelsome siblings, and suspicious, resentful, antisocial stepchildren. It is not surprising, then, that stepfathers in this study disengaged from parenting and demonstrated low levels of involvement and rapport, little control over the stepchildren's behavior, lack of awareness of their activities, and little exertion of discipline. No doubt different findings would have emerged if the stepchildren had been younger. Further, more than 2 years, which was the approximate length of the study, may be necessary for stepfathers to establish positive relationships with adolescent stepchildren.

In summary, stepfathers may have an easier time establishing a relationship with their stepchildren than stepmothers do. They experience stress because they often are uncertain about how much discipline to exercise and how much affection to show stepchildren. Stepfathers and stepchildren may be accustomed to different household rules, activities, and ways of doing things; children may be jealous of stepfathers and see them as rivals for the attention of their mothers. Further, children may feel loyal to their noncustodial fathers and experience guilt and a sense of betrayal if they like their stepfathers. Other adjustments stepfathers must make include the resolution of problems with finances and not being a full-time father to their own children. Most of these adjustments can be made over a period of time, and after about 3 years it is likely that relationships with stepchildren will be more positive.

Children in Stepfamilies

Studies have shown that children in stepfamilies exhibit similar adjustment problems to children in single-parent families and more problems than children in original two-parent families. It might be expected that remarriage would dramatically increase children's well-being as economic and social resources increase. Yet, empirical research does not support this expectation (Hanson, McLanahan, & Thomson, 1996). Following their parents' remarriage, children of all ages show initial increases in problem behavior and disruptions in relationships with other family members. In both home and school settings, behavioral, social, emotional, and learning problems have been found to be more characteristic of children in stepfamilies than of children in nondivorced families. The effects of the parents' remarriage are most marked by increased frequency on the part of the children of externalizing, antisocial, and noncompliant behavior. Though it has been speculated that girls may show more internalizing (e.g., depression and anxiety) than boys in response to family conflict and their parents' remarriage, research has shown that externalizing—fighting, poor peer relations, school-related problems such as absences and expulsions—is the most common response of both boys and girls, although some findings may be age specific (Coleman & Ganong, 1991; Hetherington, 1992).

In the longitudinal study of effects of remarriage on children, Lindner, Hagan, and Brown (1992) found that early-adolescent children in intact families were perceived as more socially and scholastically adjusted and as exhibiting fewer problems in adjustment than children in stepfamilies. Parents and teachers tended to see girls as better adjusted than boys. Girls were perceived as having these characteristics even though observers detected few gender differences in the way in which these adolescent children adjusted to their parents' remarriage.

In general, the academic performance of stepchildren has been found to be slightly lower than that of biological children. On measures of intelligence, few differences between children in stepfamilies and other children have been found. Overall, it can be concluded that stepchildren's self-esteem is similar to that of other children (Coleman & Ganong, 1991).

Some investigators have argued that the high incidence of behavior problems in stepchildren can be attributed to stresses that preceded the remarriage, stressors of the divorce itself, and stresses caused by living in a single-parent family. Certainly, some of the legacy of past family experience is carried over into children's response to the custodial parent's remarriage; however, the remarriage itself also seems to present new adaptational challenges (Hetherington, 1992).

Although the biological mother may take her children into the new marriage and have a stable, positive relationship, a temporary period of disruption and an increase in conflict and negativity usually occur. However, these appear to be temporary, and some research has shown that by 2 years following remarriage few differences are found between the relationships of nondivorced mothers and the relationships of remarried mothers and their children except for less effective control and monitoring of the children by the remarried mothers (Hetherington, 1992).

Previous research reported that children in stepfamilies had more household responsibilities than children in intact families. Ishii-Kuntz and Coltrane (1992) found that children in families with stepchildren only were likely to receive twice as many hours of housework per week as children in stepfamilies with biological children only (7.5 hours per week versus 4 hours).

Though little is known about sibling relationships in stepfamilies, the meager research available suggests that following divorce and remarriage, rivalry, disengagement, and hostility among siblings are more likely to occur than positive, mutually supportive behaviors. However, during times of marital transitions such as divorce and remarriage of parents, sisters are more able than brothers to act as buffers for each other and to fill the emotional void left by unresponsive parents. Brothers are less likely to be mutually supportive under such circumstances, and sisters are unlikely to be emotional resources for brothers (Hetherington, 1992).

Anderson and Rice (1992) found that adolescent children in stepfamilies displayed more negative and less positive behavior toward their siblings than did children in nondivorced families. However, the magnitude of these differences was not large. Further, girls displayed more positive behavior toward their siblings than did boys. Mothers and children in the study indicated that girls, more than boys, offered more positive behavior such as support, empathy, and involvement toward their siblings. However, this effect was tempered by the fact that fathers and observers did not report this difference. During the course of this 2-year longitudinal study, both positive and negative behaviors toward siblings decreased.

Consistently research has shown that the greatest difficulty in adjustment to parental remarriage occurs during adolescence, particularly for girls. Although girls may have developed close bonds with their mothers earlier, as they approach adolescence, greater conflict and problems in parent-child relationships emerge. Boys seem to develop a negative coercive relationship with their divorced custodial mothers during the single-parent stage, and they may have more to gain and little to lose by the introduction of warm, supportive stepfathers. In contrast, girls—who usually have better relationships with their divorced mothers—may have more to lose in the remarriage and have been found to exhibit more enduring antagonism and resistance to new stepfathers (Hetherington, 1992).

Some of the deviant behavior in adolescent boys and girls in stepfamilies has been attributed to the greater autonomy of adolescents in making decisions and a permissive parenting style in the stepfamily (Crosbie-Burnett & Giles-Sims, 1994). Other developmental tasks confronting early adolescents make adaptation to parents' remarriage particularly difficult, including coping with pubertal sexual fantasies and feelings. Children who have experienced precocious power and independence in single-parent households may be particularly sensitive to infringements on their autonomy by stepparents at this time, and coping with changing adolescent perceptions of parents and an increasing preoccupation with sexuality may render the presence of biologically unrelated adults distressing. The introduction of a stepparent in early adolescence may result in troubles with intimacy, sexuality, and the appropriate display of affection between family members. In contrast, late adolescents may not be averse to the entry of stepparents into their families because they are anticipating leaving home and entering new young adult roles and relationships; in fact, remarriage may relieve them of emotional and economic responsibility for

their custodial parents (Crosbie-Burnett & Giles-Sims, 1994; Hetherington, 1992).

Other researchers have examined the effects of adolescent adjustment in stepfamilies. Adolescents in stepfamilies earn lower grades and have lower educational expectations and attainment than adolescents in intact, nuclear families, and stepparents are less active than biological parents in school affairs. Further, teachers' reports of children's behavior problems indicate that stepchildren have more behavior problems than children in nondivorced families, yet stepparents have less face-to-face contact with teachers than do parents in intact and in divorced families. In addition, school counselors report more contact with stepchildren than with children in other family structures (Crosbie-Burnett & Giles-Sims, 1994).

Adolescents in stepfamilies reported less warmth, more conflict, and more permissive parenting than adolescents in nondivorced families (Kurdek & Fine, 1993). Some research has found that adolescents living with stepfathers had higher self-esteem, and fewer reported social problems than those living with stepmothers (Fine & Kurdek, 1992). These researchers also found that girls had higher grades and more health problems than did boys. The complexity of the stepfamily was not related to adjustment. Self-mastery and family process variables were strongly related to adjustment, particularly among girls living with stepmothers. The results of this study suggested that process more than contextual variables is strongly related to adolescent adjustment in stepfamilies.

Previous research has shown that stepparents are less active in both the control and the support dimensions of parenting than are parents in nuclear families. Some studies have shown that adolescent adjustment was lower when stepparents punished more and was higher when parents were more rewarding. Adolescent adjustment, particularly for girls, seems to be positively related to supervision and warmth by parents and stepparents. Further, adjustment is negatively related to the authoritarian style and positively related to the authoritative style of parenting. Thus, previous research noted the dangers of too much control without support and of too little control, and the benefits of support and warmth. Building on this research, Crosbie-Burnett and Giles-Sims (1994) investigated adolescent adjustment and stepparenting styles. Findings indicated that the highest level of adolescent adjustment was associated with the supportive style and the authoritative style. The lowest level of adjustment was associated with the disengaged styles. Results generalized across gender of adolescents and complexity of stepfamilies. Findings suggested that stepparents who are not involved effectively in the control dimension may be more likely to disengage altogether when adolescents are younger and when they are anxious, unhappy, or resentful. These researchers concluded that the support dimension of stepparenting is more salient for adolescent adjustment than the control dimension, and that adolescents will accept some controlling behavior from stepparents if it is combined with support.

Some research has shown that parents' remarriage does not affect children's attitudes toward marriage, but stepchildren have been found to be more positive toward divorce than children from nuclear or single-parent families. Although living in a single-parent household has predicted greater chances of having a premarital birth, living in a stepfamily has not. Nor has living in a stepfamily been found to be related to adolescent marriage, divorce, and remarriage later in life. Adolescents in stable stepfamilies are no more likely than those in nuclear families to have had premarital sexual intercourse. However, research indicates that adolescents in stepfamilies are more prone to peer influence and more willing to engage in antisocial behavior than children living in nondivorced families. Further, adolescents in stepfamilies have been found to use more alcohol than children in intact and in single-parent families (Coleman & Ganong, 1991).

It must be pointed out, however, that not all children exhibit negative behavior in response to parental remarriage; some children function quite well. Most research has found that even for those who have initial negative reactions, a large percentage adapt to the stepfamily situation over time,

with patterns that vary somewhat with children's gender and age (Crosbie-Burnett & Giles-Sims, 1994; Hetherington, 1992; Wallerstein & Corbin, 1989). Younger children have been found to make satisfactory adjustment within a 2- to 3-year period (Hetherington, 1992). However, Lindner et al. (1992) found that adolescent children in their longitudinal study, while showing declines in problem behavior, continued to demonstrate more than 2 years later greater problems in adjustment than children in intact families. Hetherington (1992) proposed, however, that the lack of evidence for positive adaptation may have been because adolescents take longer to adjust to stepparents and 2 years following remarriage may not be enough time for satisfactory adjustment to occur.

The effects of remarriage will vary according to the developmental stage in the family life cycle. Remarriage, like divorce, is not seen as a single event but as a series of changes in the family organization, functioning, and life experiences. Each family member is part of this interactional, interdependent family system in which the behavior of each individual or subsystem modifies that of the other. Thus, the marital, parent-child, or sibling subsystem modifies that of other subsystems. Individuals and subsystems are linked in a network of feedback loops, and a change in one leads to changes in the others. Remarriage involves alterations in family organization and functioning that are associated with a period of disequilibrium followed by gradual restabilization of the relationships in the new family system.

The joint biological-step family structure makes up about 10 percent of all married-couple households. Though the children of these families (the "ours" children) represent a significant number of children in stepfamilies, very little research has been conducted on them and how they affect stepfamily functioning. The data that are available indicate that they help solidify the stepfamily in that they are the only family members who are biologically related to each person in the family.

MacDonald and DeMaris (1996) examined parenting in stepfamilies with both stepchildren and common biological children. Findings revealed that stepmothers, more often than stepfathers, experienced greater difficulty in rearing their stepchildren than in rearing their biological children, regardless of whether biological children were from a previous marriage or from the current marriage. However, adding joint biological children to the stepfamily had no effect on stepparents' perceptions of the relative difficulty of rearing their stepchildren but in some cases affected their satisfaction with stepchildren. Both stepmothers and stepfathers were less satisfied with stepchildren than with their biological children only when the joint children were firstborns. This suggests that frustration of stepparents who add joint biological children to their families probably is related to becoming a new parent rather than to role conflict.

Factors Associated with Children's Adjustment in Stepfamilies.

A number of factors have been found to be associated with children's adjustment in stepfamilies. The marital adjustment of the husband and wife is important. In a longitudinal study of the effects of marital transitions, the quality of the marital relationship was linked to the quality of both the mother's and the father's relationship with their children (Anderson, Lindner, & Bennion, 1992). Satisfaction with remarriage and low marital conflict have been found to be positively associated with the quality of the stepparent-child relationships (Coleman & Ganong, 1991).

Fine et al. (1994) found that the relationship between husbands' marital satisfaction and child well-being were stronger for older than for younger children. Weak relationships were found between positive child well-being and parental depression and marital satisfaction. No differences were found among the various types of stepfamilies in child well-being. The gender of the child was not related to child well-being, nor was it related to parental depression or marital satisfaction.

Satisfaction with remarriage and low marital conflict lead to quality of the stepparent-stepchild relationship.

It appeared that, particularly relative to stepfather families, the difficulties and stress inherent in the less complex stepfamily arrangements did not lead to appreciably greater adjustment problems for children. The researchers concluded that it is erroneous to assume that children in stepfamilies experience substantial adjustment difficulties.

The parenting orientation of stepparents appears to be a significant factor in children's adjustment. The pervasively beneficial effects of authoritative parenting, especially for adolescents, already have been discussed. Regardless of the gender of the child or parent, warmth, support, involvement, and monitoring have been consistently related to high levels of social competence, and absence of coercion, conflict, and negativity has been associated with lower levels of externalizing behavior and higher levels of social and scholastic competence. Thus, warm, supportive, noncoercive parents who monitored their children's behavior but granted them considerable autonomy had the most well adjusted children. Further, researchers have reported that the quality of sibling relationships also was consistently associated with children's adjustment (Anderson et al., 1992).

The way children respond to their current family situation depends on preceding family relationships. Children who enter a stepfamily face yet another in a series of family transitions. Many such children, particularly boys, may still be showing adjustment problems associated with the previous transition of divorce and life in a single-mother home (Hetherington, 1992). Further, the level of parental conflict in stepfamilies seems to be related to children's adjustment. Children in stepfamilies not only have a higher risk of exposure to conflict but also may be more adversely affected by conflict than other children. Since they experienced at least one marital disruption, they may find marital conflict more threatening. Hanson et al. (1996) found that children in stepfather households were exposed to more parental conflict overall than children in other types of households. High conflict has similar negative effects on children's well-being regardless of the type of family structure.

Children in stepfather families who experienced no parental conflict or very low levels (about 25 percent of all children in stepfather families) did as well as average children in two-parent families with respect to grade point average, externalizing or internalizing behavior, and overall quality of life. In other areas of well-being—school performance, school behavior problems, initiative, and sociability—they performed worse, despite the absence of parental conflict. The well-being of about 40 percent of children in stepfather families was at risk. These researchers concluded that factors other than parental conflict influence children in stepfamilies.

Some research indicates that the custodial mother's number of dating partners, the remarriage courtship length, and the timing and sequence of typical courtship stages affect the child's adjustment and her relationship with the residential parents after remarriage (Montgomery, Anderson, Hetherington, & Clingempeel, 1992). Previous research has found that during the period following divorce, custodial mothers and their children are faced with the tasks of redefining their roles and relationships and establishing new rituals and routines, all of which may take several years. When the custodial mother begins courtship for remarriage, the introduction of a courting partner may influence these processes of adjustment and restructuring. Further, the timing of maternal courtship and the point at which remarriage occurs during the postdivorce coping process are likely to influence the child's adjustment and relationships within the remarried family. A long courting relationship in which the future stepfather gradually increases contact may necessitate a different adjustment pattern from that of a courting relationship that proceeds more rapidly. Other research has indicated that the longer the period of time custodial mothers and their children have spent living together in divorced households, the greater will be the disruption at remarriage. Established relationships may be more difficult to renegotiate than relationships that are in flux.

In the Montgomery et al. (1992) study, a longer time spent in a divorced, mother-custody household was associated with continuing difficulty in step-father-stepchild relationships and lower levels of the child's social competence during the initial months following remarriage. In addition, children whose custodial mother cohabited before remarriage appeared to be more socially competent throughout the 2 years after remarriage, while also experiencing less negative family relationships. These researchers speculated that cohabitation may provide a more gentle transition to remarriage, with the future stepfather gradually being incorporated into family routines and a longer period of adaptation, making remarriage seem less abrupt.

The number of dating partners before meeting the future spouse was negatively correlated with child competence. Remarried women who had previously dated many partners showed less warmth and involvement with their children in the first months after remarriage, and their children appeared to be less socially competent during the first year of remarriage.

Social support continues to be found as important for parents and children experiencing stress related to marital transitions. Coleman and Ganong (1991) reported that social support was found to be related to remarriage satisfaction as well as being important to children, especially adolescents. With further advance into adolescence, many youngsters may find supports outside the home—in the neighborhood, school, the workplace, or peer groups—that are not available to younger children and that are able to buffer the experience of multiple family reorganizations or adverse family relationships. These support systems allow the adolescent to disengage and may be a constructive way of coping with a stressful family situation. A grandparent, a teacher, or a neighbor may offer support, having a positive effect on the adolescent's adjustment. If the adolescent's disengagement is accompanied by high involvement in peer activities with no concomitant adult monitoring, deviant behavior may develop (Hetherington, 1992).

Support for Stepfamilies

The variability of stepfamilies has posed significant problems in designing systematic studies and in providing services. Books written especially for blended families began to appear in the late 1970s. Various community agencies have instituted self-help groups for stepfamilies so that comfort and support from sharing common problems and feelings might be provided. In one aspect, the support by the extended family may be greater for stepfamilies than that experienced by single parents, since the possibility exists for an additional set of parents. Friends and co-workers often are additional sources of support for blended families.

It has been suggested that programs for adults who are planning to form a blended family would assist in the process of structuring a new family. Knowing what to expect of the new spouse, typical reactions of children to the stepparent, and areas likely to produce conflict would assist in developing more realistic expectations. The essential ingredient in such programs should be the process by which couples are encouraged and taught to discuss specific problems of remarriage openly and constructively (see Highlights).

One example of a program designed for remarried couples is the Personal Reflections Program evaluated by Kaplan and Hennon (1992). This program encourages self-insight about remarriage and stepfamily roles. Self-insight and communication of this insight are sought to facilitate role crystallization, thereby reducing role strain. Focus is placed on finding as much congruence as possible in the expectations of both partners for the new marriage. It is predicted that the greater the shared definition of norms for remarriage and/or stepfamily roles, the greater will be the individual feelings of well-being, the extent of satisfaction with role performance, and the degree of dyadic adjustment and remarriage satisfaction.

Nelson and Levant (1991) evaluated the effectiveness of a skills training program for parents in stepfamilies. The purpose of this program was to increase communication and parenting abilities by teaching generic skills and applying them to stepfamily-specific situations. Communication skills included attending, listening, and responding to content; listening and responding to feelings; self-awareness; and genuineness. Parenting skills included communicating rules and consequences, the

Group-Discussion Topics for Couples Planning to Remarry

1. Feelings related to the previous marriage and divorce. Discussion should allow for expression of feelings about the first marriage and the legal settlement, involving custody, visitation, and financial arrangements.
2. Remarriage adjustment, including adjustments between the children and the parent's new spouse, to a new lifestyle, to a new family group, to different expectations for household management, to new kin, and to a new individual position in family.
3. Division of labor in present marital household.
4. Perception of role relations, including those of the new partner to the children and the children to the new partner.
5. Responsibilities of the new partner to the children (financial, disciplinary).
6. Exchange of views between the present couple on child rearing.
7. Perceptions of what constitutes a "happy family life" and perceptions of ways the second marriage's family life is viewed as different from that of the first.
8. Feelings about financial arrangements.
9. Feelings about continued relations between the ex-spouse and/or the ex-spouse's kin; and between the children and the absent parent and kin.
10. Feelings about the partner's children living with ex-spouse who visit regularly in the present household.
11. Discussion allowing for recognition of difficulties of acquiring an "instant family" and the time factor for privacy for a couple relationship.

family meeting, and an integration session. The program was implemented in four 6-hour sessions over a 4-month period. The results indicated that trained parents improved their communication by learning to better reflect and express feelings. However, they still relied on undesirable parenting responses such as lecturing, providing answers, questioning, and giving orders. It was concluded that these approaches were well entrenched as parenting techniques and were not amenable to short-term intervention. Children did not perceive increased acceptance and decreased rejection from the trained parents. Parents' and spouses' perceptions of stepfamily adaptability or cohesion were not changed. Further, no changes were found in stepfamily satisfaction for focal parents or spouses.

Visher and Visher (1989) recommended parenting coalitions after remarriage to foster cooperation between stepparents and biological parents in meeting the needs of children. They pointed out the following advantages to these coalitions. Cooperation rather than competition between the

parenting adults helps meet the needs of the child as well as the adults by reducing antagonism between the adults. Cooperation between households can reduce children's fears of losing contact with one of their parents and can alleviate many of the loyalty conflicts that arise for children when their bioparents are divorced and additional parenting figures have entered their lives. Also, the responsibility of rearing children is shared among more adults; children's self-esteem is enhanced and they are easier to be with as a result; and the power struggles between households are decreased. Most of all, everyone finds relief from the heavy burden of negative feelings that previously controlled their thoughts and behaviors.

Obstacles that must be resolved before parenting coalitions can function effectively include the following: inadequate psychological separation between the divorced parents, hostility between the adults, lack of commitment between the couple, failure to include stepparents in the coalition, fear of more loss in the parent-child relationships when children go back and forth between households and develop bonds with stepparents, anxiety caused by a family system in which the linkage of the households through the children reduces the autonomy of the individual households. These researchers suggested that therapists work with families in assisting them to resolve these obstacles and in forming and using the parenting coalition.

In sum, the phenomenon of blended families is increasing in frequency and importance and with such rapidity that it is essential for both the social sciences and the helping professions to focus significant effort on its problems and many ramifications. There is a need to provide continuing services to these families. It appears that providing opportunities to share experiences with others who have the same feelings and problems is helpful. Professionals who work with blended families need to know as much as possible about the individual history of each family member. It is important for the professional to understand the stresses related to the new situation and to help each family member identify and understand them. The needs of each individual should be recognized, and efforts aimed at effective adjustment must take into account what is tolerable for all, so that no one is the object of attack. The professional's task is to help free family members emotionally so that they can direct their energies to the new family situation.

It is apparent from the preceding discussion that blended families are more dissimilar than similar to nuclear families. Because they possess unique strengths and weaknesses, they are in need of understanding and support.

The evidence suggests that the stepparent role may be one of the most difficult assumed by adults in today's society, and children in blended families experience considerable confusion during the readjustment process. Recognizing the stresses may help prepare family members for the realities of their new family structure.

Adults in the new blended family need time alone to develop a positive spousal relationship. Building other relationships takes time. Instant love should not be expected. Divided loyalties, different histories of values and lifestyles, and the ex-

panded network of new relationships are factors that may interfere with rapid adjustment.

It seems important for children in blended families to continue relationships with noncustodial biological parents. If stepparents do not compete with natural parents but attempt to establish their own roles with stepchildren, stepparenting will be more effective and more rewarding.

SUMMARY

Dramatic structural changes in families began to occur in the United States during the decade of the 1970s, and some of these trends continued through the millennium. Most of these changes were due to the increase in single-parent and stepfamilies. The high divorce rate and the large number of people who remarry account for the increase in these family structures.

Although the stereotypical image of the single-parent family as deviant and pathological is being replaced by a healthier image, single parents experience considerable stress, which affects adjustment, such an inadequate income, difficulties with child care and child rearing, and synchronization of family and work responsibilities. Issues facing single parents include child custody, child support, and effects of living in a single-parent family on the child. Recent research on the effects of divorce on children has provided information about the complex process of adjustment following divorce. Most children suffer temporary negative effects in many areas of development, including interpersonal and peer relationships, school performance, and self-esteem, and exhibit various levels of antisocial behavior. Several hypotheses have been generated to explain the effects of divorce on children: father absence, economic distress, multiple life stress, interparental hostility, and parent adjustment.

Several factors mediate the degree of stress and length of the adjustment period. These include parental harmony, the gender of the child, and the parents' educational and income levels. Further, contact with noncustodial parents is important. Problems tend to be more severe and long-lasting for boys. Adjustment is affected by the presence or the absence of these variables, and some psychological problems may continue for years.

The phenomenon of stepfamilies is not new, but the quantitative increase and the qualitative changes in functioning have brought more attention to the needs of parents and children residing in these families. Blended families have become the most common alternative family structure, representing about 22 percent of all married-couple households. Current estimates are that 40 percent of all children will be a part of a stepfamily before their eighteenth birthdays.

Research in the 1990s indicated that there is better understanding and greater acceptance of blended families than in the past. Stepfamilies function very differently from nuclear families, utilizing different organizational and integration processes. Blended families face a number of issues that affect the adjustment of family members: establishing a solid marital relationship, redefining the boundaries of the new family, establishing a constructive stepparent-child relationship, eco-

nomic integration, and understanding the legal issues surrounding the blended family.

Remarriage, as does divorce, represents a period of transition in which family roles, rules, and relationships are redefined and new patterns of resource allocations are established. All family members are faced with a period of adjustment, with the first year after remarriage being the most difficult and effective family functioning being achieved in about 3 years. Various factors affect the adjustment of children: the marital adjustment of the parents, parenting orientation, previous family experiences, the custodial mother's courtship patterns, and the amount of social support provided.

Clearly, single-parent and stepfamilies represent unique problems and needs for the parents and children involved. This does not, however, imply that these family structures are weaker than the traditional nuclear family. It does suggest that understanding and support may be needed. Undoubtedly these families possess unique strengths, as well, most of which are yet to be documented by research.

REFERENCES

AMATO, P., & BOOTH, A. (1996). A prospective study of divorce and parent-child relationships. *Journal of Marriage and the Family, 58,* 356–365.

ANDERSON, E., LINDNER, M., & BENNION, L. (1992). The effect of family relationships on adolescent development during family reorganization. In E. M. Hetherington & G. Clingempeel (Eds.), Coping with marital transitions. *Monographs of the Society for Research in Child Development, 57*(2-3), 178–199.

ANDERSON, E., & RICE, A. (1992). Sibling relationships during remarriage. In E. M. Hetherington & G. Clingempeel (Eds.), Coping with marital transitions. *Monographs of the Society for Research in Child Development, 57*(2-3), 149–177.

AQUILINO, W. (1996). The life course of children born to unmarried mothers: Childhood living arrangements and young adult outcomes. *Journal of Marriage and the Family, 58,* 293–310.

ARDITTI, J., & BICKLEY, P. (1996). Fathers' involvement and mothers' parenting stress postdivorce. *Journal of Divorce & Remarriage, 26* (1-2), 1–23.

BANK, L., FORGATCH, M., PATTERSON, G., & FETROW, R. (1993). Parenting practices of single mothers: Mediators of negative contextual factors. *Journal of Marriage and the Family, 55*(2), 371–384.

BARRATT, M., ROACH, M., & COLBERT, K. (1991). Single mothers and their infants: Factors associated with optimal parenting. *Family Relations, 40*(4), 448–454.

BRYNER, G. (1992). Policy options for reducing poverty in female-headed families. *Family Perspective, 26*(2), 183–200.

BUEHLER, C. (1988). The social and emotional well-being of divorced residential parents. *Sex Roles, 18*(5-6), 247–257.

BUEHLER, C., & GERARD, J. (1995). Divorce law in the United States: A focus on child custody. *Family Relations, 4,* 439–458.

BUSER, P. (1991). Introduction: The first generation of stepchildren. *Family Law Quarterly, 25*(1), 1–18.

CAMPBELL, M., & MOEN, P. (1992). Job-family role strain among employed single mothers of preschoolers. *Family Relations, 41*(2), 205–211.

CHASE-LANSDALE, P., CHERLIN, A., & KIERNAN, K. (1995). The long-term effects of parental divorce on the mental health of young adults: A developmental perspective. *Child Development, 66,* 1614–1634.

CHRISTENSEN, D., DAHL, C., & RETTIG, K. (1990). Non-custodial mothers and child support: Examining the larger context. *Family Relations, 39*(4), 388–394.

CLAXTON-OLDFIELD, S. (1992). Perceptions of stepfamilies: Disciplinary and affectionate behavior. *Journal of Family Issues, 13*(3), 378–389.

COLEMAN, M., & GANONG, L. (1991). Remarriage and stepfamily research in the 1980s: Increased interest in an old family form. In A. Booth (Ed.), *Contemporary families: Looking forward, looking back* (pp. 192–206). Minneapolis: National Council on Family Relations.

COONEY, T., HUTCHINSON, M., & LEATHER, D. (1995). Surviving the breakup? Predictors of parent-child relations after parental divorce. *Family Relations, 44,* 153–161.

CROSBIE-BURNETT, M., & GILES-SIMS, J. (1994). Adolescent adjustment and stepparenting styles. *Family Relations, 43,* 394–399.

DAINTON, M. (1993). The myths and misconceptions of the stepmother identity: Descriptions and prescriptions for identity management. *Family Relations, 42*(1), 93–98.

DAVIES, L., AVISON, W., & McALPINE, D. (1997). Significant life experiences and depression among single and married mothers. *Journal of Marriage and the Family, 59,* 294–308.

DEAL, J., HAGAN, S., & ANDERSON, E. (1992). The marital relationship in remarried families. In E. M. Hetherington & G. Clingempeel (Eds.), Coping with marital transitions. *Monographs of the Society for Research in Child Development, 57*(2-3), 73–93.

DEMO, D., & ACOCK, A. (1991). The impact of divorce on children. In A. Booth (Ed.), *Contemporary families: Looking forward, looking back* (pp. 162–190). Minneapolis: National Council on Family Relations.

DEMO, D., & ACOCK, A. (1996). Singlehood, marriage, and remarriage. *Journal of Family Issues, 17*(3), 388–407.

DEVLIN, A., BROWN, E., BEEBE, J., & PARULIS, E. (1992). Parent education for divorced fathers. *Family Relations, 41*(3), 290–296.

DiSIMONE, R. (1996). Program legislation enacted in early 1996. *Social Security Bulletin, 59*(2), 64–67.

DOHERTY, W., KOUNESKI, E., & KOUNESKI, M. (1998). Responsible fathering: An overview and conceptual framework. *Journal of Marriage and the Family, 60,* 277–292.

DRISCOLL, A., HEARN, G., EVANS, J., MOORE, K., SUGLAND, B., & CALL, V. (1999). Nonmarital childbearing among adult women. *Journal of Marriage and the Family, 61,* 178–187.

DUDLEY, J. (1991). Increasing our understanding of divorced fathers who have infrequent contact with their children. *Family Relations, 40*(3), 279–285.

EDIN, K., & LEIN, L. (1996). Work, welfare, and single mothers' economic survival strategies. *American Sociological Review, 61,* 253–266.

EHRENBERG, M. (1996). Cooperative parenting arrangements after marital separation: Former couples who make it work. *Journal of Divorce & Remarriage, 26*(1-2), 93–115.

FINE, M. (1995). The clarity and content of the stepparent role: A review of the literature. *Journal of Divorce & Remarriage, 24*(1-2), 19–34.

FINE, M., COLEMAN, M., & GANONG, L. (1998). Consistency in perceptions of the step-parent role among step-parents, parents, and stepchildren. *Journal of Social and Personal Relationships, 15*(6), 810–828.

FINE, M., DONNELLY, B., & VOYDANOFF, P. (1991). The relation between cognition and maternal satisfaction in stepfather families. *Family Perspective, 25*(1), 19–26.

FINE, M., & FINE, D. (1992). Recent changes in laws affecting stepfamilies: Suggestions for legal reform. *Family Relations, 41*(3), 334–340.

FINE, M., GANONG, L., & COLEMAN, M. (1997). The relation between role constructions and adjustment among stepfathers. *Journal of Family Issues, 18*(5), 503–525.

FINE, M., & KURDEK, L. (1992). The adjustment of adolescents in stepfather and stepmother families. *Journal of Marriage and the Family, 54*(4), 725–736.

FINE, M., & KURDEK, L. (1995). Relation between marital quality and (step)parent-child relationship quality for parents and stepparents in stepfamilies. *Journal of Family Psychology, 9*(2), 216–223.

FINE, M., VOYDANOFF, P., & DONNELLY, B. (1994). Parental perceptions of child well-being: Relations to family structure, parental depression, and marital satisfaction. *Journal of Applied Developmental Psychology, 15,* 165–186.

FOLK, K. (1996). Single mothers in various living arrangements: Differences in economic and time resources. *American Journal of Economics and Sociology, 55*(3), 277–292.

FOLK, K., GRAHAM, J., & BELLER, A. (1992). Child support and remarriage: Implications for the economic well-being of children. *Journal of Family Issues, 13*(2), 142–157.

FOSTER, E., JONES, D., & HOFFMAN, S. (1998). The economic impact of nonmarital childbearing: How are older, single mothers faring? *Journal of Marriage and the Family, 60,* 163–174.

GANONG, L., & COLEMAN, M. (1989). Preparing for remarriage: Anticipating the issues, seeking solutions. *Family Relations, 38*(1), 28–33.

GANONG, L., COLEMAN, M., FINE, M., & MCDANIEL, K. (1998). Issues considered in contemplating stepchild adoption. *Family Relations, 47*(1), 63–72.

GANONG, L., COLEMAN, M., & MISTINA, D. (1995). Normative beliefs about parents' and stepparents' financial obligations to children following divorce and remarriage. *Family Relations, 44,* 306–315.

GILES-SIMS, J., & CROSBIE-BURNETT, M. (1989). Stepfamily research: Implications for policy, clinical interventions, and further research. *Family Relations, 38*(1), 19–23.

GOLDBERG, W., GREENBERGER, E., HAMILL, S., & O'NEIL, R. (1992). Role demands in the lives of single mothers with preschoolers. *Journal of Family Issues, 13*(3), 312–333.

GOTTLIEB, A. (1997). Single mothers of children with developmental disabilities: The impact of multiple roles. *Family Relations, 46,* 5–12.

GREIF, G. (1995). Single fathers with custody following separation and divorce. *Marriage & Family Review, 20*(1-2), 213–231.

GRINGLAS, M., & WEINRAUB, M. (1995). The more things change…Single parenting revisited. *Journal of Family Issues, 16*(1), 29–52.

HAGAN, M., HOLLIER, E. A., O'CONNOR, T., & EISENBERG, M. (1992). Parent-child relationships in nondivorced, divorced, single-mother, and remarried families. In E. M. Hetherington & G. Clingempeel (Eds.), Coping with marital transitions. *Monographs of the Society for Research in Child Development, 57*(2-3), 94–148.

HANSON, T., MCLANAHAN, S., & THOMSON, E. (1996). Double jeopardy: Parental conflict and stepfamily outcomes for children. *Journal of Marriage and the Family, 58,* 141–154.

HAO, L., & BRINTON, M. (1997). Productive activities and support systems of single mothers. *American Journal of Sociology, 102*(5), 1305–1344.

HETHERINGTON, E. M. (1992). Coping with marital transitions: A family systems perspective. In E. M. Hetherington & G. Clingempeel (Eds.), Coping with marital transitions. *Monographs of the Society for Research in Child Development, 57*(2-3), 1–14.

HILL, M. (1992). The role of economic resources and remarriage in financial assistance for children of divorce. *Journal of Family Issues, 13*(2), 158–178.

HILTON, J., & HALDEMAN, V. (1991). Gender differences in the performance of household tasks by adults and children in single-parent and two-parent, two-earner families. *Journal of Family Issues, 12*(1), 114–130.

ISHII-KUNTZ, M., & COLTRANE, S. (1992). Remarriage, stepparenting, and household labor. *Journal of Family Issues, 13*(2), 215–233.

JARRETT, R. (1996). Welfare stigma among low-income African American single mothers. *Family Relations, 45,* 368–374.

JAYAKODY, R., CHATTERS, L., & TAYLOR, R. (1993). Family support to single and married African American mothers: The provision of financial, emotional, and child care assistance. *Journal of Marriage and the Family, 55*(2), 261–276.

JOHNSTON, J. (1990). Role diffusion and role reversal: Structural variations in divorced families and children's functioning. *Family Relations, 39*(4), 405–413.

KALTER, N., KLONER, A., SCHREIER, S., & OKLA, K. (1989). Predictors of children's postdivorce adjustment. *American Journal of Orthopsychiatry, 59*(4), 605–617.

KAPLAN, L., & HENNON, C. (1992). Remarriage education: The Personal Reflections Program. *Family Relations, 41*(2), 127–134.

KLINE, M., JOHNSTON, J., & TSCHANN, J. (1991). The long shadow of marital conflict: A model of children's postdivorce adjustment. *Journal of Marriage and the Family, 53*(2), 297–309.

KURDEK, L., & FINE, M. (1991). Cognitive correlates of satisfaction for mothers and stepfathers in stepfather families. *Journal of Marriage and the Family, 53*(3), 565–572.

KURDEK, L., & FINE, M. (1993). The relation between family structure and young adolescents' appraisals of family climate and parenting behavior. *Journal of Family Issues, 14*(2), 279–290.

KURTZ, L. (1995). The relationship between parental coping strategies and children's adaptive processes in divorced and intact families. *Journal of Divorce & Remarriage, 24*(3-4), 89–110.

LAUER, R., & LAUER, J. (1991). The long-term relational consequences of problematic family backgrounds. *Family Relations, 40*(3), 286–290.

LINDNER, M., HAGAN, M., & BROWN, J. (1992). The adjustment of children in nondivorced, divorced single-mother, and remarried families. In E. M. Hetherington & G. Clingempeel (Eds.), Coping with marital transitions. *Monographs of the Society for Research in Child Development, 57*(2-3), 35–72.

MACDONALD, W., & DEMARIS, A. (1995). Remarriage, stepchildren, and marital conflict: Challenges to the incomplete institutionalization hypothesis. *Journal of Marriage & the Family, 57*(2), 387–398.

MACDONALD, W., & DEMARIS, A. (1996). Parenting stepchildren and biological children: The effects of stepparent's gender and new biological children. *Journal of Family Issues, 17*(1), 5–25.

MACHIDA, S., & HOLLOWAY, S. (1991). The relationship between divorced mothers' perceived control over child rearing and children's post-divorce development. *Family Relations, 40*(3), 272–278.

MANNING, W., & SMOCK, P. (1997). Children's living arrangements in unmarried-mother families. *Journal of Family Issues, 18*(5), 526–544.

MARSIGLIO, W. (1992). Stepfathers with minor children living at home: Parenting perceptions and relationship quality. *Journal of Family Issues, 13*(2), 195–214.

MCLANAHAN, S., & BOOTH, K. (1991). Mother-only families: Problems, prospects, and politics. In A. Booth (Ed.), *Contemporary families: Looking forward, looking back* (pp. 405–428). Minneapolis: National Council on Family Relations.

MECKLER, L. (1998, July 4). Government looks at new ways to get fathers involved with their children. *The Tuscaloosa News*, p. A3.

MONTGOMERY, M., ANDERSON, E., HETHERINGTON, M., & CLINGEMPEEL, G. (1992). Patterns of courtship for remarriage: Implications for child adjustment and parent-child relationships. *Journal of Marriage and the Family, 54*(3), 686–698.

MOTT, F., KOWALESKI-JONES, L., & MENAGHAN, E. (1997). Paternal absence and child behavior: Does a child's gender make a difference? *Journal of Marriage and the Family, 59*, 103–118.

NELSON, W., & LEVANT, R. (1991). An evaluation of a skills training program for parents in stepfamilies. *Family Relations, 40*(3), 291–296.

OLSON, S., & BANYARD, V. (1993). Stop the world so I can get off for a while: Sources of daily stress in the lives of low-income single mothers of young children. *Family Relations, 42*(1), 50–56.

PAASCH, K., & TEACHMAN, J. (1991). Gender of children and receipt of assistance from absent fathers. *Journal of Family Issues, 12*(4), 450–466.

PALMER, R. (1993, September 25). In Lauderdale County: 'No course, no divorce.' *The Tuscaloosa News*, p. B4.

PETERSEN, M. (1998, July 26). The short end of long hours: A woman's job puts child custody at risk. *The Tuscaloosa News*, pp. D1, D3.

PETERSON, J., & NORD, C. (1990). The regular receipt of child support: A multistep process. *Journal of Marriage and the Family, 52*(2), 539–551.

PILL, C. (1990). Stepfamilies: Redefining the family. *Family Relations, 39*(2), 186–193.

PIROG, M., KLOTZ, M., & BYERS, K. (1998). Interstate comparisons of child support orders using state guidelines. *Family Relations, 47*, 289–295.

PIROG-GOOD, M., & BROWN, P. (1996). Accuracy and ambiguity in the application of state child support guidelines. *Family Relations, 45*, 3–10.

PORTES, P., HAAS, R., & BROWN, J. (1991). Identifying family factors that predict children's adjustment to divorce: An analytic synthesis. *Journal of Divorce & Remarriage, 15*(3-4), 87–101.

Rawlings, S. (1993). Household and family characteristics: March, 1992. U.S. Bureau of the Census, Current Population Reports, P20–467. Washington, DC: U.S. Government Printing Office.

SANDLER, I., TEIN, J., & WEST, S. (1994). Coping, stress, and the psychological symptoms of children of divorce: A cross-sectional and longitudinal study. *Child Development, 65*, 1744–1763.

SCHAFFER, D., & WAGNER, R. (1996). Mexican American and Anglo single mothers: The influence of ethnicity, generation, and socioeconomic status on social support networks. *Hispanic Journal of Behavioral Sciences, 18*(1), 74–86.

SCHWEBEL, A., FINE, M., & RENNER, M. (1991). A study of perceptions of the stepparent role. *Journal of Family Issues, 12*(1), 43–57.

SELTZER, J. (1991). Relationships between fathers and children who live apart: The father's role after separation. *Journal of Marriage and the Family, 53*(1), 79–101.

SHAPIRO, A. (1996). Explaining psychological distress in a sample of remarried and divorced persons. *Journal of Family Issues, 17*(2), 186–203.

SHIFFLETT, K., & CUMMINGS, E. (1999). A program for educating parents about the effects of divorce and conflict on children: An initial evaluation. *Family Relations, 48,* 79–89.

SIMONS, R., BEAMAN, J., CONGER, R., & CHAO, W. (1993). Stress, support, and antisocial behavior traits as determinants of emotional well-being and parenting practices among single mothers. *Journal of Marriage and the Family, 55*(2), 385–398.

SMOCK, P., & MANNING, W. (1997). Nonresident parents' characteristics and child support. *Journal of Marriage and the Family, 59,* 798–808.

SORENSEN, E. (1997). A national profile of nonresident fathers and their ability to pay child support. *Journal of Marriage and the Family, 59,* 785–797.

SWEENEY, M. (1997). Remarriage of women and men after divorce. *Journal of Family Issues, 18*(5), 479–502.

TEACHMAN, J. (1991). Who pays? Receipt of child support in the United States. *Journal of Marriage and the Family, 53*(3), 759–772.

TILLITSKI, C. (1992). Fathers and child custody: Issues, trends, and implications for counseling. *Journal of Mental Health Counseling, 14*(3), 351–361.

U.S. BUREAU OF THE CENSUS. (1992). *Statistical abstract of the United States: 1992* (112th ed.). Washington, DC: U.S. Department of Commerce.

U.S. BUREAU OF THE CENSUS. (1997). *Statistical abstract of the United States: 1997* (117th ed.). Washington, DC: U.S. Department of Commerce.

VISHER, E., & VISHER, J. (1989). Parenting coalitions after remarriage: Dynamics and therapeutic guidelines. *Family Relations, 38*(1), 65–70.

VISHER, E., & VISHER, J. (1998). Stepparents: The forgotten family members. *Family & Conciliation Courts Review, 36*(4), 444–452.

WALLERSTEIN, J., & BLAKESLEE, S. (1989). *Second chances: Men, women, and children a decade after divorce.* New York: Ticknor & Fields.

WALLERSTEIN, J., & CORBIN, S. (1989). Daughters of divorce: Report from a ten-year follow-up. *American Journal of Orthopsychiatry, 59*(4), 593–604.

WEBSTER'S NEW ENCYCLOPEDIC DICTIONARY. (1994). New York: Black Dog & Leventhal.

WILBUR, J., & WILBUR, M. (1988). The noncustodial parent: Dilemmas and interventions. *Journal of Counseling and Development, 66*(9), 435–437.

WILCOX, K., WOLCHIK, S., & BRAVER, S. (1998). Predictors of maternal preference for joint or sole legal custody. *Family Relations, 47,* 93–101

WOLCHIK, S., FENAUGHTY, A., & BRAVER, S. (1996). Residential and nonresidential parents' perspectives on visitation problems. *Family Relations, 45,* 230–237.

CHAPTER 8

Parenting in Families
with Diverse Lifestyles

Lifestyles among families in the United States are more diverse than they are similar. Within each family structure—nuclear, extended, single-parent, or blended—exists a variety of lifestyles, and the freedom to choose among this variety is one of the strengths of the nation.

This chapter will explore only a few family lifestyle variations. These include dual-career and dual-earner families, families with a cohabiting parent, and families with a homosexual parent. These are far from exhaustive but represent those that have been researched to some extent and those that, in some way, have an impact on parent-child relationships. The traditional stereotype of a family consisting of a breadwinner father, a homemaker mother, and two or more children is being replaced gradually by a recognition that families are diverse, representing a range of lifestyles as well as a variety of structures.

DUAL-CAREER FAMILIES

Among Americans, especially upper-middle-class individuals, there is a widely held belief that educated, bright, and talented women should not bury their talents in domestic and child-rearing concerns. Instead, these women should ardently pursue careers and compete with men in the world of work. At the same time, however, these career women are expected to maintain their femininity, get married, have children, and manage households. In response to these incongruent and impossible cultural expectations, many families are attempting a lifestyle in which both partners are engaged in dual roles. These families have been labeled dual-career. This family form has become relatively common in recent years. In 1991 almost 24 percent of the total population had 4 or more years of college, with the percentage of Whites being almost twice that of African Americans, and 2.5 times that of Hispanics (U.S. Bureau of the Census, 1997). Most men and women with college degrees are pursuing professional careers. Men and women with technical training, or with less education, are working at lower-level jobs, but most families with two parents are those with two wage

earners. Only a small minority of U.S. households reflect the traditional nuclear family: an employed husband, a homemaker wife, and children.

The dual-career family was first defined by Rhonda and Robert Rapoport (1976) as one in which both partners pursue careers and, at the same time, maintain a family life together. The concept of dual career is different from that of dual work in that a high degree of commitment and continuous development characterize a career. Work, on the other hand, may involve any kind of gainful employment. The practice of women working outside the home because of economic necessity has been accepted for some time, but the focus on couples who are each committed to a career emerged in the 1970s. Dual-worker, or dual-earner, families considerably outnumber dual-career families.

Although it is difficult to ascertain the number of dual-career families in the United States, it is reasonable to assume that the percentage has increased significantly along with the general labor force participation rates of women and number of women earning college degrees. Swiss and Walker (1993) reported that the number of women entering the labor force with a college degree was rising 1.5 times faster than the number of degreed men entering the labor force. Women now constitute more than half of the population entering the professions of business and law and 40 percent of those entering the field of medicine.

Figure 8.1 shows the increase of working women with children under 18 years of age from 1975 through 1996 (U.S. Bureau of the Census, 1997). By 1996 approximately 72 percent of married women with children aged 6 to 17 were in the workforce, and nearly 63 percent had children under 6 years of age. These figures represent more than an 80 percent increase since 1970.

A sizable percent of the new entrants into the workforce are now women, and most of these women will bear at least one child during their working years. A larger percentage of married Black women with children under 18 years of age (79 percent) than of White women (70 percent) were employed. An even larger percentage of widowed, separated, or divorced women of all races

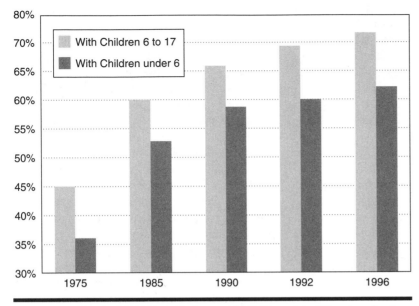

FIGURE 8.1   Married, Working Mothers with Children 6 to 17 and under 6
Source: U.S. Bureau of the Census. (1997). *Statistical abstract of the United States: 1997.* Washington, DC: U.S. Department of Commerce.

with minor children worked in 1996. Approximately 81 percent with children aged 6 to 17 years were in the labor force, and 69 percent with children under 6 years of age were employed. Thus, it may be concluded that the dual-earner family is the norm rather than the exceptional lifestyle. A number of factors have contributed to the increase in career-oriented women, including increased numbers of women who have college degrees or technical training, greater demand for skilled labor, increased awareness of sex-role equality, the women's movement, and federal legislation prohibiting discrimination.

Evidence indicates that greater numbers of young collegiates are planning for dual-career lifestyles. Most collegiate women feel it is very important to have a career, but at the same time, they plan to marry and have two or three children. They plan to interrupt their careers for 1 to 5 years to have children and do not feel that this interruption will disadvantage them at work.

Characteristics of Dual-Career Families

Although there is great diversity among dual-career couples, some generalizations can be made. Dual-career couples tend to be highly educated and working in professions such as law, medicine, and business. Both husband and wife often are in fast-track careers. In approximately 20 percent of these households, the wife earns more than her husband. Even though women are gaining increasing influence and power in the workplace, only 11 percent of corporate officers in 1998 were women. Only two female CEOs were listed in Fortune 500 that year (Joyce, 1999).

Dual-career couples tend to share the same values; have fewer needs for affection, inclusion, and control; and are self-reliant. They tend to have only one or two children and to delay childbirth until wives are well established in their careers. On the other hand, traditional couples generally have their children before wives enter the workforce.

Recently, the tendency to delay parenthood has been reported extensively by the media. More women are having their first child in their thirties and early forties. Ranson (1998) found that the kind of college education selected by women affects the timing of first childbirth. Of the 185 college graduates he surveyed, whose average age was 30, 70 percent were married, were employed, and had no children 7 years after graduation. In a sample of women aged 28 to 38, those with degrees in education and nursing were more likely to have children than were women with degrees in business and engineering. The women gave several reasons for determining the timing for initiating birth: age, financial security, job security, and achievement of professional goals. Those who were teachers mentioned having a permanent teaching certificate, a permanent contract, a full-time position with maternity benefits, and a support group of women with similar experiences. These reasons suggested that education graduates enter a specific labor market in which the organization of work significantly facilitates combination with childbearing.

Women without children reported that they had voluntarily postponed pregnancy for several reasons: incompatibility of work and family life, delay and difficulty in establishing careers, few models, and few incentives for combining work and family life. The researcher concluded that educational choices followed by occupational opportunities seemed to exert considerable influence on the timing of the transition to motherhood. Traditional career choices such as teaching and nursing expose women to serious practical disadvantages, such as lower pay and fewer promotion prospects, but they are far more responsive to the needs of women with children. Women who make nontraditional career choices may enjoy the benefits of increased pay and promotion prospects but at the price of prolonged postponement of pregnancy and considerably more struggle in combining work and family demands.

Most dual-career women are confident that the demands of combined career and family responsibilities can be managed well, even though advancement in a profession requires a weekly work commitment exceeding 40 hours, as well as overnight travel in many professional situations. These women usually are highly invested in both the parental role and the work role. Motherhood may be one of several roles that must be balanced and integrated rather than the primary role. Most adopt less traditional gender roles (Wille, 1995).

Dual-career mothers often have different perceptions from other mothers of the value or importance of child care and household chores. For example, they are more likely to emphasize the positive rather than the negative outcomes of alternative care for young children and are less committed to the importance of exclusive maternal care for children. Their standards for care may be more relaxed, and many deem it acceptable to be less than perfect as a mother and a housekeeper. Roles often are redefined—many adopt a less traditional definition of the maternal role, making it possible for them to view themselves as exemplary mothers even if they do less household work and child care than homemaker mothers. These attitudes may make it possible for employed women to cope with the potential of role overload and conflict (DeMeis & Perkins, 1996).

DeMeis and Perkins (1996) found that full-time homemakers spent almost twice as many hours caring for their homes as mothers who were employed full-time. However, the two groups spent most of their time at home doing similar chores, except that twice as many homemakers as employed mothers reported doing yard work. Similarly, the two groups engaged in the same number and types of child caregiving behaviors, except that more homemaker mothers than employed mothers watched educational television with their children. However, employed mothers perceived all child-care activities as less typical of mothers than did homemaker mothers.

Most dual-career fathers establish a stable successful career before having children. They are likely to have more flexibility in their work roles, higher salaries, and more freedom than other fathers, which enables them to be more involved in family activities. In fact, some studies show that as many as two-thirds of dual-career fathers also have routine child-care responsibilities. As a rule, dual-career fathers also have stronger identities, more self-confidence, greater maturity, and more experiences to share with their children than other fathers have. As a result of more education, more life experiences, and more unconventional timing of parenthood, these fathers are likely to value success in all areas of child behavior and to be more nurturing and less controlling than other fathers (Heath, 1994).

Berry and Rao (1997) found that dual-career fathers were clearly involved with their children in a variety of ways that affected their work roles and caused varying levels of stress. The more child-related events in which fathers engaged that affected their workplace roles, the more stress they experienced. Family activities contributed more to stress than did either the workplace or the father's personality. Those fathers who reported the most stressful events were more involved in general child care and experienced stress related to being a parent. Workplace flexibility and work hours were significantly related to stress and family conflict. Those fathers who worked longer hours were less involved with their children, and less flexible work schedules predicted stress and role strain.

It appears that many dual-career couples strive for an egalitarian relationship, with both partners seeking both professional and family rewards. In fact, each is psychologically vested in both professional and parenting roles. Often the details of parenting and working must be fine-tuned. However, because these families usually have relatively high incomes, they are able to hire-out household and yard work and to afford high-quality care and education for their children. But the evidence suggests that balancing these multiple roles can be stress inducing. (See the Highlights for a summary of the characteristics of dual-career couples.)

DUAL-EARNER FAMILIES

The career concept has experienced rather dramatic revision in recent years, so that it is now broadly defined as a pattern of work-related expe-

HIGHLIGHTS

Characteristics of Dual-Career Couples

Both partners possess highly qualified job skills.

Parents share similar values.

Parents have fewer needs for affection, inclusion, and control.

Both partners are self-reliant.

Families have small number of children (one or two).

Parents delay childbearing.

Family has higher income than other families.

There is a mutual understanding of and appreciation for each other's career needs.

Both partners are psychologically vested in both professional and parenting roles.

riences that spans the course of a person's life. Most two-parent families are dual-earner rather than dual-career. Families in which one or both partners are involved in noninvolving, nondevelopmental work roles are often designated dual-earner, dual-income, or two-paycheck families.

Today, the majority of married women and mothers are in the labor force. Before 1940, the typical employed woman was young and single. Between 1940 and 1960, older married women entered the labor force, whereas the rates of participation for young women did not increase sharply until 1960. By 1970, employment had become the modal status among mothers of school-age children. The most striking change since 1980 is in the increased employment of mothers of babies and preschool children. Women are now firmly established in the labor market, as indicated by reduced turnover and by higher proportions of women working full-time, year-round, as opposed to part-time and/or part of the year (Glass & Estes, 1996; U.S. Bureau of the Census, 1997).

The 150-year-old normative American ideal for child-rearing families of a married couple with complementary roles—the husband with an occupation outside the household that provided for the family's economic needs and the wife with primary responsibility for the household, the children, and the emotional well-being of all—was adequate only when the wages of the husband/father were sufficient to support his wife and children. For many families, this ideal was out of reach even before the economy structurally changed from one based primarily on manufacturing to one that was service-based. Changes in available employment prompted many families to increase their number of earners to avoid real decline in family income. Between 1940 and 1980, married women's economic dependency on their husbands declined substantially.

Even though most families have two earners, some families are not able to rise above the poverty line, especially if both are earning minimum wage. In 1996, 12 percent of all families earned less than $10,000 a year—8 percent of White families, 23 percent of African American families, and 17 percent of Hispanic families (U.S. Bureau of the Census, 1997). Several studies have indicated that women return to work soon after the birth of children primarily for economic reasons (Glass & Estes, 1996). Even though many mothers work out of necessity, many work because of preference. One study found that the number of women working because of preference increased from 31 percent in 1970 to approximately 47 percent in 1990 (Herring & Wilson-Sadberry, 1993). Career development and personal enjoyment also contributed to women's employment decisions.

Most of the research on work and the family has been conducted with middle-class, husband-wife families, ignoring minority and single-parent families. Even for husband-wife middle-class families, the dual-earner family is the norm. The share of two-earner family income contributed by wives' earnings is significant for all income groups. Wives provide an average of 31 percent of family earnings, and when wives work year-round, they contribute 40 percent or more (Spitze, 1991), with wives' share being significantly higher in low-income and African American families (Hanson & Ooms, 1991). Even though women earn less than 60 percent of the amount men earn (U.S. Bureau of the Census, 1997), it is clear that employed wives and mothers have a major impact on family in-

come levels. They often raise their family income to the level of their "life cycle reference group" and provide alternatives to husbands' occupational mobility. Further, they relieve the unusually high expenses associated with "life-cycle squeezes." Wives are most likely to be in the labor force when they are in a position to improve family status (Seyler, Monroe, & Garand, 1995).

Two-earner couples spend slightly more on consumption of nondurable items, including employment-related expenses and time-saving goods and services, and spend little or no more on durable items than do single-earner families. It has been calculated that a two-earner family would need 30 percent more income to maintain the same standard of living as a one-earner family (Spitze, 1991). Women in Brannen's (1992) study expected to bear the brunt of the costs of the dual-earner lifestyle, including child-care costs, operating the second car, and paying domestic help. Substantial work-related costs are incurred in dual-earner families, the largest being child care and baby-sitting.

Working mothers enjoy more than just economic benefits. Studies show that working mothers have higher self-esteem and fewer occasions of depression than housewives. Other studies have shown that employment has positive effects for both men and women on their well-being. Earned income also enhances a sense of mastery and personal fulfillment, which in turn increases overall well-being (Rogers, 1996; Windle & Dumenci, 1997).

Integration of Work and Family Roles and Responsibilities

Much of the recent literature on work and family issues has investigated how parents' employment experiences affect their own well-being, their marital relationships, and the interaction patterns in their families, with consequences for children. A number of studies have examined the coping strategies used by dual-career and dual-earner families in response to work/family conflict. This section will discuss these issues for both dual-career and dual-earner families.

Sharing household work relieves some of the stress from overload in dual-career families.

Role Conflict and Role Overload. Role conflict and role overload generate considerable stress for dual-career and dual-earner families. Both men and women experience work/family conflict, but women experience a greater degree of conflict and role overload than men do. Both men and women who have high role conflict experience greater depression, anxiety, and somatization, as well as greater dissatisfaction with their marriages. However, it is mainly women who experience high job dissatisfaction and absenteeism as a result of significant role conflict, which causes greater disruption in their lives than in their husbands'.

The signs of role overload include guilt, stress, fatigue, questions about competence, and professional burnout. Guilt can plague dual-career and dual-earner mothers at work and at home— guilt for leaving the office early to attend a soccer game; regret for delegating the care of a sick child to someone the child barely knows; worrying at work about the children's day; worrying at home about unfinished work at the office while trying to

create "quality time" with the children. In neither job can women have a sense of "a job well done."

Once role strain is experienced, its influence is pervasive. Regardless of gender, high role strain is associated with significant emotional stress and physical symptomatology. Windle and Dumenci (1997) examined the influence of parental and occupational stress on depressive symptoms of both husbands and wives in dual-earner families. They found that high levels of occupational and parental role stress were related to depressive symptoms in husbands and wives in similar ways. Results did not support the notion that occupational stress is more highly related to depressive symptoms among men or that parental stress is more highly related to depressive symptoms among women. Lower levels of marital satisfaction, more years of marriage, and lower perceptions of family cohesion also were found to be statistically significant predictors of depressive symptoms for both husbands and wives. Although some coping strategies have been found to reduce stress for both men and women, coping responses and resources have not been found to attenuate significantly the impact of role strain.

Tiedje et al. (1990) examined how women who combined the roles of mother, spouse, and professional perceived their multiple roles. Some women viewed their roles as a source of both conflict and enhancement, sometimes occurring simultaneously; others derived either conflict or enhancement; still others derived comparatively little conflict or enhancement. Women experiencing high enhancement and low conflict scored the highest on measures of mental health and role satisfaction, whereas those experiencing high conflict and low enhancement scored the lowest. Regardless of their perceptions of enhancement, women who perceived their roles as conflicting were more depressed and less satisfied as parents. Women who perceived high role rewards and low conflicts seemed more able to enjoy parenting.

Cultural Attitudes. Cultural attitudes toward working mothers have changed significantly. Although some people may still view working mothers negatively and believe that maternal employment causes family problems, recent research has refuted these negative impressions, and women's employment is viewed more positively and analyzed with almost the same degree of complexity as is men's employment.

Blain (1994) found some of the old stereotypical ideas about women emerging in the family discourse of the dual-earner families she studied. She found that women were doing most of the work in the homes and men's optional contributions were often restricted to physical household maintenance. Several reasons surfaced for women carrying these responsibilities: Women seemed to have more training by practice and example than men do; women have a natural gift for organization; women have more time; women are closer to the children; and distribution of work is the result of personal preferences and choices.

The researcher concluded that although many women appear to want their husbands to assume more responsibility for housework and child care,

they often feel that they are more competent because of training and practice and/or have a natural ability for motherhood. Similarly, many fathers feel less knowledgeable and able than their wives and are reluctant to upset the balance of the household as they see it. With their child-care activities defined as "help," they alternately accommodate and resist their wives' requests for more help.

Research has noted that some wives in dual-earner families, as well as husbands, resist more collaborative arrangements of family work. Allen and Hawkins (1999) noted that 21 percent to 25 percent of women were maternal "gatekeepers" of the home, resisting increased involvement of their husbands in family work. They defined maternal gatekeeping as "the mother's reluctance to relinquish responsibilities for family matters by setting rigid standards, wanting to be ultimately accountable for domestic labor to confirm to others and to herself that she has a valued maternal identity, and expecting that family work is truly a woman's domain" (p. 205). The authors noted that specific cultural ideas of mothering make it difficult for some women to relinquish responsibility for some of their cherished and practiced maternal behaviors, and they feel both relieved and displaced by paternal involvement.

In a national study of gender ideologies and the division of household labor in dual-earner couples, Greenstein (1996) found considerable gender segregation in household tasks. Wives performed about 74 percent of the total hours spent on traditionally female tasks, and husbands contributed about 20 percent. On the other hand, husbands contributed about 70 percent of the total hours spent on traditional male tasks, and wives about 19 percent. As husbands' hours of employment increased, the proportion of hours they spent in domestic labor decreased. As wives' hours of employment increased, husbands' contributions to household labor increased. The gender ideologies of men who were married to the most traditional women had little effect on the percentage of domestic labor they performed. Egalitarian men married to the most nontraditional or egalitarian women did the largest percentage of housework, and egalitarian men married to traditional women did much less. Greenstein concluded that husbands perform relatively little domestic labor unless both husbands and wives are nontraditional in their beliefs about gender and marital roles. Thus, the interaction of gender ideologies of husbands and wives appears to affect the division of household labor.

Work Environment.   Considerable research has focused on the importance of the work environment in creating or inhibiting work/family conflict and stress. When maternal employment leads to time and role conflicts, family conflict increases and family members are negatively affected. Support from co-workers and supervisors, job involvement and autonomy, and work demands can influence parenting functioning and thus child functioning. Work stressors can erode family and child adaptation, whereas work support and satisfaction can enhance it. Fathers in high-conflict work environments experience more tension in family relationships, less marital satisfaction, and less involvement in the family. In contrast, job satisfaction has been found to be associated with low family conflict.

The alienating nature of work for blue-collar men, as well as financial pressures and lack of opportunities for upward mobility, leave little energy for constructive family involvement. Such conditions promote harsher discipline and greater physical punishment for children, and wives are isolated from men's work roles (Menaghan & Parcel, 1991).

Research on working mothers indicates that women who have better work environments tend to report more favorable family relationships and better child adaptation. Unpleasant and demanding work climates have been associated with more family conflict and less family cohesion.

Glass and Estes (1996) examined job turnover of employed mothers of infants in relation to workplace support and child-care satisfaction. Results indicated that intentions to change jobs were negligibly affected by background and family status variables. Being older and married significantly inhibited job-change intentions. Further, father care

as the primary child-care arrangement seemed to impede changing jobs.

Both partners' incomes and traditional gender-role attitudes increased the odds of terminating employment, whereas child-care satisfaction and child-care cost decreased the odds; that is, women who earned more and paid more for child care exhibited stronger job attachment. Respondents' wages did not predict the odds of leaving the labor force, but social support from supervisors and co-workers decreased the odds for both changing jobs and withdrawing from the labor force entirely. Other workplace characteristics, such as the ability to work at home and the availability of sick leave for family members, decreased intentions to leave the labor force.

Warren and Johnson (1995) investigated the relationship between work-related coping resources and work/family role strain for employed mothers of preschool children. Results indicated that lower work/family strain was associated with higher work-environment support, higher supervisor support, and greater use of family-oriented benefits. The more supportive the organizational culture of employees with family responsibilities was perceived to be, the less the strain between work and family issues. Supervisor flexibility was significantly related to worries about adequately performing the demands associated with work and family roles.

The most beneficial aspects of the work environment were permitting employees to come in late or leave early, to take occasional days off without pay, and to receive phone calls from family members at work. The five most frequently used benefits were flextime, leave in lieu of overtime, short-term leave (personal/family), sick-child days, and personal days with pay. These results and others clearly demonstrate that a family-friendly atmosphere at work is strong support in balancing work and family obligations.

Discrimination in the workplace is a problem, particularly for women. Swiss and Walker (1993) found that the professional women in their study encountered the so-called glass ceiling, which limits how far a woman can advance. The women in

Swiss and Walker's study were penalized for their choice to have children, no matter how well they performed on the job. Women encountered obstacles to taking maternity leaves or denied themselves leaves for fear of repercussions on the job; had serious problems with reentry after taking maternity leaves; encountered hostile, career-derailing behavior from colleagues and bosses in response to the decision to become a mother; and faced a constant uphill struggle for acceptance and equality in the still-male-dominated professions. Piller (1998) found that women are leaving or avoiding computer careers in large numbers, citing discrimination by male co-workers, few role models, family-unfriendly work environments, and a general sense that the field is irrelevant to their interests. The extreme demands of the job have been found to be incompatible with responsible parenting. Further, women are more concerned with putting technology to use, whereas men are interested in technical skills. A further illustration of the gender gap in this field is the lack of computer products designed with women in mind. The number of women computer professionals decreased from 35 percent to 29 percent during the 1990s.

An analysis from 1985 through 1990 found that new mothers are 10 times more likely to lose their jobs after taking disability leave than employees taking other kinds of medical leaves. Yet there is no foundation for the fear that women of childbearing age are a risky investment for company resources and training.

Joesch (1997) investigated the work interruptions for women bearing children. Using a national data set, he found that the majority of women in the survey worked until late in their pregnancies. Two percent returned to work the month the baby was born, and by the end of the second month after delivery, 50 percent had returned. Only 11 percent did not return to work at all. African American women resumed working sooner than White women, as did women who had been with their employers for a longer period of time. Working part-time during pregnancy was associated with resuming work later. Paid leaves as part of maternity benefits provided by employers accounted for two-thirds of the leaves taken for birth. Clark, Hyde, Essex, and Klein (1997) examined the association between the length of maternity leave and the quality of mother-infant interactions when the infants were 4 months of age. The length of the leave was found to interact significantly with maternal depressive symptoms and infant temperament. The combination of higher levels of maternal depressive symptoms and shorter maternity leaves was associated with less maternal positive involvement, sensitivity, and responsiveness to one's infant. Further, length of maternity leave and infant temperament were positively correlated. For those mothers who view their infants as prone to distress or having a difficult temperament, early return to work may be especially stressful, contributing to poorer quality of interactions between the two. Nondepressed women who remained on leave longer had more positive interactions with their infants.

The findings of these researchers underscore the importance of parental-leave policies that appreciate individual differences and allow for individual choices based on the emotional and physical needs of women and their families. The authors recommended that the current medical-leave policy be expanded to 4 to 6 months, providing partial wage replacement and flexible work schedules, and include employers with fewer than 50 employees. The passage of the Family and Medical Leave Act of 1993 (discussed later in the chapter) was designed to protect parents' jobs during maternity or sick leave.

It is clear that many characteristics of the work environment can contribute to role conflict and overload. The stress that results from work/family conflict is more likely to spill over into the home than into the workplace. A recent national study found that more than three times as much "job-to-home spillover" as "home-to-job spillover" occurs in response to work/family conflicts (Cohen, 1993).

Strategies for Coping with Work/Family Conflict. Both men and women use a variety of strategies for coping with role conflict and overload. Women use a greater number and variety of strategies than men do, and coping strategies vary according to the stage in the family life cycle (Schnittger & Bird, 1990).

Sharing of Household Labor and Child Care. The sharing of domestic labor and child care by fathers as a strategy for relieving the role overload of working mothers has received considerable attention. Data show that 90 percent of wives and 82 percent of husbands agree that when both work full-time, they should share household work and child care equally. Because of the inconsistency between this shift in public attitudes and the persistence of inequality in the division of household labor among full-time working spouses, research has begun to focus on perceptions of fairness in the division of household labor. A striking finding is that a relatively small percentage of spouses, especially wives, define inequality in the division of labor as unfair (Gager, 1998).

Aldous, Mulligan, and Bjarnason (1998) used longitudinal data to examine changes in fathers' participation in child care. Data indicated that fathers spent less time in child care than did mothers, for both younger and school-age children. When children were preschoolers, fathers contributed about one-third of the child care that mothers did. When children were older, fathers' time increased to two-thirds of mothers' time.

More work hours for fathers regardless of children's ages resulted in less parenting. More work hours for mothers with preschoolers resulted in more physical care by fathers. However, the fathers' work schedules had precedence over mothers'. It was found also that early participation in child care led to fathers' continued involvement as the child grew older. Mothers' earnings, fathers' personal sentiments of marital satisfaction, and both partners' perceptions of the fairness of the division of child care were not related significantly to the extent of fathering. Interestingly, the more attention a child received from one parent, the more she received from the other. Consistent with previous research, older sons especially benefited from increased paternal attention. Finally, the study found that fathers' early participation in child care led to their continued involvement as children grew older.

Gager (1998) interviewed dual-career couples about the division of household labor and perceived fairness of labor division. Most of the respondents, both men and women, reported that housework made them feel frustrated, tired, bored, or stressed out, with a few describing it as relaxing, meditative, or therapeutic. The most valued outcome of completing household tasks cited by both men and women was a sense of satisfaction or accomplishment. Wives who perceived their marriages as happy were less apt to view inequitable division of labor as problematic. Child care was the most valued household task for both men and women, and when a task was valued, the importance of fairness in division of household labor was minimized. Fewer than one-fourth of the couples sought a 50/50 division of tasks. For the most part, husbands were able to avoid tasks they disliked, whereas wives were not. The majority of wives simply wanted their husbands to provide a little more help so that they felt less overwhelmed. As in previously mentioned research, some women felt that their heavier role in household management was justified because they were more efficient than their husbands. Others believed that their husbands' lesser participation was justified because the husbands earned more or spent more hours at paid work. Those men who had more egalitarian role models and who had performed household tasks as children were more likely to engage in household tasks as adults. Kleiman (1999) found that people who exercise power in the workplace also exercise power in the division of household work. Men who perform managerial duties do significantly less housework, whereas female managers persuade their husbands to participate more in household maintenance. Kleiman also found that, overall, the number of hours that men care for children has increased by half an hour per week—from 1.8 hours to 2.3 hours over the last 20 years.

Interestingly, the perceptions of husbands and wives about the distribution of both household tasks and child care seem to differ. Cohen (1993) reported that only 5 percent of the dual-earner men and 71 percent of the women in the National Study of the Changing Workforce perceived that they assumed the major responsibility for the care of their children. Forty-three percent of the men and 19 percent of the women perceived that they shared responsibility for children's care. (See Figure 8.2.)

Sullivan (1997) investigated the division of housework among remarried and cohabiting couples. She found that married women contributed considerably more housework than cohabiting women (81 percent compared with 70 percent). Women in their second-plus partnerships contributed a lower proportion of time (76 percent) to the overall housework than did women in first partnerships (80 percent). Interestingly, number of previous partners for men had no effects. Presence of dependent children in the household meant that mothers did proportionately more of the housework than nonmothers. Women who earned more than their partners contributed significantly lower proportions of total housework than those who earned half as much as their partners.

Sullivan concluded that the interactive processes involved in partners' negotiations about housework are complex, including such factors as men's willingness to engage in discussions of division of labor and their appreciation of the housework performed by women. Remarried men who have lived alone for a period of time may have performed some female-type tasks and thus may be more willing to share household labor.

Research indicates, then, that the increased involvement of men in both household tasks and child care is evolving rather slowly, with child care being a more salient activity than household work for fathers in dual-earner families. Many variables seem to affect how these responsibilities are divided, and perceptions of fairness seem to vary.

Social Support. A support network for dual-earner and dual-career parents is crucial for resolving family/work conflict—from husbands, friends, and work supervisors. The literature clearly reveals the importance of social support in protecting people from the negative consequences of extensive stress. Supportive relationships also are seen as critical social resources in dealing with work/family issues. Taylor and Spencer (1989) pointed out that spousal support has three components: emotional support (husband's attitude toward wife's career), domestic support (his help with household labor and child care), and economic support (his ability to meet family financial needs). Each of these components has been shown to be related to women's

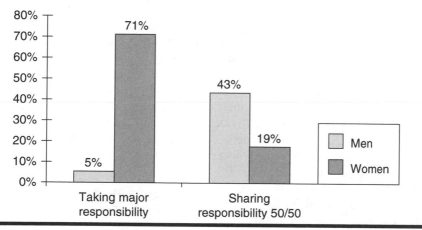

FIGURE 8.2 Perceptions of Dual-Earner Parents about Their Share of Responsibility for Child Care

Source: Cohen, D. (1993, September). Stress in balancing work and family more likely felt at home, study finds. *Education Week*, p. 10.

career and family decisions. Women whose husbands are supportive of their careers have higher job commitment. In dual-earner families, the more financially able the husband is to support the family, the less inclined women may be to devote high levels of time to the job. Women make different career decisions in the presence or absence of various forms of spousal support. The effects of support may be moderated by personal lifestyle orientation. A woman whose career is prioritized over family may be more likely than others to accept a promotion requiring more time and travel, even with limited spousal support.

Supportive relationships extend to friends and other couples living similar lifestyles. Friendships with others in dual-career lifestyles serve to insulate dual-career couples from societal expectations (Schnittger & Bird, 1990).

As previously indicated, support from co-workers and supervisors reduces stress associated with work/family conflict. Other types of support in the form of needed changes in workplace policies will be discussed in a subsequent section.

Other Coping Strategies Used by Dual-Career and Dual-Earner Couples to Balance Work and Family. Trade-offs are made by dual-career and dual-earner families, especially mothers in these families, to balance the demands of work and family. One example is reducing the workload, which may be accomplished in several ways—sharing with the father, hiring domestic help, utilizing child care, simply ignoring home maintenance tasks, and delegating responsibilities to children (Schnittger & Bird, 1990). Families with teenage children delegate more duties to the children than those families with younger children. Many dual-earner women are working in lower-status positions and cannot afford to hire others to clean their homes. Even middle-class working women often do not have outside help. Hochschild (1989) found that 85 percent of the women in her study did not employ regular household help. Strain in the working-class family is exacerbated by the absence of enough money to pay for needed services, economic insecurity, poor child care, lack of dignity, and boredom

in each partner's job. Strain in dual-career families is exacerbated by the instability of paid help and the enormous demands of the career system in which both partners have become willing believers.

Compromises with respect to career aspirations are another important way in which dual-career families cope with work/family conflict. Passing up promotions and relocations, reducing work hours, and avoiding extensive business travel all have been used as strategies (Schnittger & Bird, 1990; Taylor & Spencer, 1989). Izraeli (1989) found that the women physicians in her study compromised their careers by working fewer hours a day, and they were less likely to hold a second job or make after-work home calls. In addition, they were more likely than their physician husbands to be in a specialization that permitted greater control over their work time and involved fewer emergencies.

Among the coping strategies used by the professional women in Swiss and Walker's study (1993) were moving from full-time employment to part-time, self-employment, and putting careers on hold and staying at home. Most part-timers are bargains for their organizations, working at peak efficiency and handling more than their fair share of the load. Among the women who became self-employed, many opened small, home-based businesses, working more than 40 hours per week, and earning less than they did when pursuing their corporate careers. Women who put their careers on hold sometimes were viewed inaccurately as dropouts or cop-outs.

Obviously, no single solution will work for all families. The most well adjusted couples believe that their arrangements are fair, both for their individual and shared careers and for their family goals. Other strategies couples use may be found in the Highlights.

Marital Relationships in Dual-Career and Dual-Earner Families

Although earlier research suggested negative effects on the marital relationship when wives worked, recent studies have reported no effects of the wife's employment, occupational commitment,

Coping Strategies Used by Dual-Career Women and Men

WOMEN

Cognitive restructuring (defining dual-career patterns as favorable)

Establishing priorities among roles

Compartmentalizing work and family roles

Compromising career aspirations

Defining roles structurally (changing attitudes and perceptions)

Redefining personal role

Delegating

Using social support

Limiting avocational activities

Limiting time for meeting personal needs

Turning child care over to others

Keeping children awake later to be with them

MEN

Organizing work life and family life

Cognitive restructuring (maintaining a positive perspective on lifestyle)

Attending to personal needs

Redefining roles

Delegating

Dissociating from tasks

or higher occupational status on the marital satisfaction of either husband or wife. Rogers (1996) found that for continuously married families with children, there was a weak, but nonsignificant, association between maternal employment and mothers' reports of marital quality. As the number of children in the household increased, full-time employment was associated with less marital happiness and more marital conflict. In stepfather families, however, mothers' full-time employment was associated with greater marital happiness and less marital conflict when there were more children in the family. The author concluded that when mothers bring more children to the remarriage, the symbolic importance of their employment, regardless of the financial contribution, may contribute to more positive marital relationships.

Wives' employment may improve marital relations or solidarity by providing spouses with similar experiences and concerns. Only small differences between dual- and single-earner couples have been found in the time they spend together. However, negative effects may result from specific aspects of the wife's employment, such as long hours or dissatisfaction with her job (Spitze, 1991). When wives work, usually the balance of

power in the relationship changes, with women gaining greater power (Menaghan & Parcel, 1991).

Kluwer, Heesink, and Van de Vliert (1997) found that both constructive and destructive conflict outcomes were predicted by spouses' overt expressions of discontent with the division of household labor. An important predictor of destructive conflict outcomes was wife demand/husband withdrawal interaction, which was, in turn, predicted by wives' discontent with labor division. When husbands reported little discontent with housework, wife demand/husband withdrawal interactions were less likely. Or husbands might react to wives' demanding behavior. Traditional wives and wives with traditional husbands were more likely to avoid conflict or to withdraw from discussions of discontent with the division of labor than were egalitarian wives or wives with egalitarian husbands. Thus, a lack of reported conflict over the division of labor may not mean that conflict does not exist. Discontent may be suppressed to avoid the risk of negative consequences. Marital interaction only partially mediated the wives' discontent.

Kluwer, Heesink, and Van de Vliert (1996) confirmed that wives' dissatisfaction about household labor division plays a crucial role in marital conflict. Consistent with other research, their findings were that husbands spend less time on household chores and more time on paid work than do their wives. Both partners preferred that wives spend less time on household labor, but similar feelings about paid work were not noted except when husbands worked long hours. Dissatisfaction with household labor was greater than dissatisfaction about time spent in paid work. A majority of wives wanted their husbands to do more housework than they actually did, and wives' dissatisfaction predicted the frequency of conflict about household labor. When husbands spent longer hours in paid work, both partners were dissatisfied, and longer work hours increased the frequency of conflict about paid work. However, couples reported more conflict about household labor than about paid work.

A survey conducted by Yankelovich Partners ("Juggling Act," 1999) revealed that although parents find it hard to balance work and family, 52 percent of working parents believed that they are more productive because they have children. Only 11 percent felt that they are less productive. It may be that parents try harder to be more efficient so that they have more time to spend with their children.

Research suggests positive effects on marital relationships when husbands share domestic labor and child care. Several studies have shown that both employed and nonemployed wives were less distressed when husbands thus shared (Menaghan & Parcel, 1991). However, Guelzow, Bird, and Koball (1991) found that men and women who worked long hours reported being supportive in their marriages, doing favors for each other, listening and offering advice, and altering habits and ways of doing things to please each other.

The previous research indicates that working women assume most of the responsibility for home care and child care. The strain of women working "second shifts" often affects men nearly as much as it affects women. Women who work these extra hours experience fatigue, illness, and emotional exhaustion, but the strain extends to men as well. Men in Hochschild's (1989) study who shared the second shift were affected directly; and if they did

not share it, they were affected through their wives. Izraeli (1989) found that dual-career men in her study who supported their wives both in the home and in their professional roles had important payoffs for themselves. These men experienced less burnout in their professions than those men who were not supportive. In Swiss and Walker's (1993) study, some of the professional women admitted deep resentment toward their husbands whose clear-cut roles somehow allowed them to set aside time to exercise during the week or to play golf on the weekends. Many of these dual-career women had no time or energy for their mates and virtually none for themselves.

The balance between two high-powered careers and family demands was so tenuous for most couples in the Swiss and Walker (1993) study that if parenting negotiations fell apart, the marriage became vulnerable. Marital strain became an even greater problem than the stresses faced as parents. Anger was the dominant emotion for these women, who came to realize that they represented the primary parents, without choice and by default. Hochschild (1989) found that when women confronted their husbands, great emotional upheaval resulted. One-half of the women in her study tried one way or another to change the roles at home. Some tried indirect ways of changing marital roles—playing helpless or withholding sex. Others tried to be supermoms and do everything without imposing on their husbands. Menaghan and Parcel (1991) reported that wives used negative tactics to "pressure" their husbands to do more at home.

Happy, egalitarian marriages do exist. However, the women in these marriages admit that it takes hard work, the acceptance of some failures, and continual negotiation between two overburdened parents.

Children in Dual-Career and Dual-Earner Families

Considerable research has addressed the effects of mothers' employment on children. The most accurate conclusion one can draw from the research is that no consistent negative effects accrue to the children of employed mothers. In fact, many benefits may occur. Brannen's (1992) study of dual-earner households revealed that these mothers saw themselves as the principal figures in bringing about normal developmental progress in their children, primarily by giving them as much time as possible. Many admitted feeling guilty, but 80 percent were more positive than negative in balancing the costs and benefits of working. They testified to a heightened quality in their relationships with their children because they were not with them all the time, thereby suggesting yet another meaning to giving children time.

Bryant and Zick (1996) focused on how mothers' employment time affected parent-child time and whether the time was gender-related. The results of their study, which used national time-diary information from two-parent, two-child families, indicated that 85 percent of the parents shared eating time with their children; 61 percent shared leisure activities with them. Parents were least likely to share housework with the children (51 percent mothers and 30 percent fathers). Mothers in this study spent 50 percent more time in child-care activities than fathers spent, and more time was spent in caring for younger than older children. As mothers' work hours increased, the amount of household work shared with children by both mothers and fathers increased. Surprisingly, the more hours mothers worked, the greater the leisure time spent with children. Household activities shared with children were gender-related and age-related. Female children shared food preparation and household maintenance with their mothers; older male children shared yard work and car maintenance with their fathers; and younger children tended to share shopping. Both parents shared more leisure time with male than with female children.

Volling and Belsky (1993) found in their study of maternal-employment decisions in the first year of infancy that all the women, regardless of employment status, were more committed to their mother roles than they were to their work roles.

Hilton, Essa, and Murray (1991) found that fathers in two-earner families contributed a substantial amount of time to nonphysical care of the children. That is, they engaged in activities that contributed to social, emotional, and educational development, such as playing and talking with the children, joint leisure activities, and reading to the children. One-earner families were found to spend more total time on nonphysical care than other family types.

In more than 25 percent of dual-earner families with children, husbands' and wives' working schedules do not overlap, and in most of these families fathers care for their children. Mothers who are employed part-time and are on nonstandard shifts are more likely to use father care. More motivating is the active desire of both parents to create and sustain a strong father-child bond. However, father care is more likely to stem from economic pressure than from the belief that fathers have a responsibility to be involved in their children's upbringing (Glass, 1998).

Glass (1998) found that care supplied by fathers when their wives returned to work after childbirth averaged 18 hours a week at 6 months postpartum. On average, fathers covered about 59 percent of mothers' work hours when they cared for their infants. At 12 months postpartum, the amount of care provided by fathers had changed little. As mothers increased their work hours, families sought other child-care arrangements. Sociodemographic differences revealed that families using father care had lower total family incomes and paid less for child care. Father care was more common when mothers worked fewer than 20 hours per week, when one parent worked an evening or night shift, when fathers worked fewer hours, and when mothers had more education. Dissatisfaction with the quality of child care in the community and having other children under age 6 also were factors. However, over time father care was substantially unstable. Father care generally was not reported to be easier or more satisfactory than other forms of care.

Volling and Belsky (1992) examined infant-father attachment security in dual-earner and single-earner families. They found only one instance in which secure or insecure infant-father attachment differed according to family type. Fathers of securely attached infants in dual-earner families were reported to be more involved in traditionally feminine household tasks than were fathers in single-earner families. Dual-earner fathers of insecurely attached children experienced a greater increase in marital conflict and negative feelings than fathers in all other family types.

If, however, there is significant parental interrole conflict and/or role dissatisfaction, negative effects may be seen in parenting and in children's behavior. MacEwen and Barling (1991) examined the effects of maternal-employment experiences on children's behavior. They found that cognitive difficulties exerted an effect on mothers' rejecting parenting behavior; that is, parents avoided interactions with their children. After a particularly stressful day, fathers tended to withdraw from family interactions. Negative mood of parents was found to exert both rejecting and punishing parenting behaviors. Parents may punish previously acceptable behavior, selectively attend to negative behaviors, and become involved in a coercive cycle of parent-child interactions. The more negative the parent's mood, the more rejecting and punishing was the parent. The more rejecting the parent, the higher the child rated on anxiety and withdrawal. The more punishing the parent, the higher the child was rated on conduct disorder and attention/immaturity. It also was suggested that the mood of one parent affects the mood of the other. Thus, the negative effects can be increased. In addition, problem-child behavior affects parental mood. Thus, a reciprocal coercive parent-child relationship is operating.

Greenberger and O'Neil (1990) examined parents' concerns about their children's development and the implications for their well-being and attitudes toward work. They found that greater child concerns were related to greater role strain and depression on the part of mothers. Perceived quality of child care and problem behaviors were related to mothers' well-being and job-related attitudes. The well-being of mothers was poorer when they felt that substitute child-care arrangements were not meeting their children's needs. Ratings of

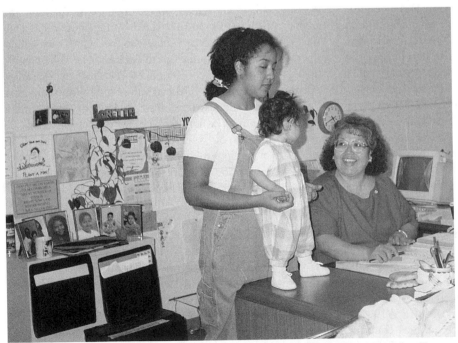

Balancing work and child-care needs is a common difficulty in two-earner families.

child behavior problems were associated with greater role strain, depression, and lower levels of commitment to jobs. Fathers who rated their children's behavior as difficult reported significantly greater role strain, depression, and symptoms of ill health. Fathers who evaluated their child-care arrangements less favorably expressed significantly lower organizational commitment. The more the fathers believed that maternal employment was damaging to children, the greater their role strain.

The National Study of the Changing Workforce (Cohen, 1993) indicated that workers with children often are stressed by concerns about their children's welfare: 62 percent of the parents in this survey cited finding high-quality child care as their biggest problem, and 66 percent lamented not having enough time to spend with their children. Although these parents felt strongly about doing a good job at work, they also yearned to spend more time with their families. The study also found that though parents take relatively little time off for child-care reasons, families bear the brunt of work/family conflicts. More than a quarter of employed parents with children younger than 13 said they had experienced a breakdown in their child-care arrangements in the past 3 months. Workers with flexible schedules or assistance with child care were found to take more initiative, were more committed to doing their jobs well, and were more loyal to employers.

Dual-career parents probably use indirect discipline and emotional support more often than conventional parents and use techniques such as reasoning and isolation frequently. Dual-career parents tend to train children to be self-reliant and independent and also seem to value the development of consideration, self-control, and curiosity. These values contrast with those of working-class mothers, who emphasize behavioral conformity, such as obedience, respect, and neatness. Mothers who work use coercive discipline less often and feel less hostility and more empathy for their children, but tend to be overindulgent. Professional women also seem to experience pleasure in their children's growing independence and to be less overprotective and less self-sacrificing.

Dual-career parents appear to be more concerned about the quality of the parent-child relationship than with the child's objective behavior. Thus, parents devise activities that are directed toward enhancing the environment of the children both at home and in educational settings. They develop hobbies and activities in which the entire family can participate. Dual-career mothers participate in the school-age child's activities by supervising the child's progress and being involved in school activities that can be coordinated with their work. These parents also set a high priority on achievement and the psychological adjustment of children.

Paulson (1996) explored the indirect influence of maternal employment on adolescent achievement through the mediating factors of parenting styles and parental involvement. Previous research has shown that several parenting

---

TIPS

For Dual-Career/Dual-Earner Parents

Make time with children quality time.

Seek high-quality child care or supervision for children during working hours; plan for backups in emergencies.

Recognize the value of both mothers' and fathers' time and relationships with children.

Examine and prioritize multiple responsibilities.

Negotiate shared responsibilities for parenting and household maintenance.

Delegate some household responsibilities to children, appropriate to their developmental levels.

Advocate for "family-friendly" policies in the workplace.

Take advantage of family and medical leave, if possible, to spend time with newborns or family members who are ill.

Support spouses in their employment/career commitments.

Allow time to invest in the couple relationship.

Participate in parenting workshops designed for dual-career parents.

Hold family meetings to make collaborative family decisions.

characteristics significantly relate to children's achievement—responsiveness, demandingness, monitoring, and parental involvement (interest in schoolwork, involvement in school activities). Participants in Paulson's study included 240 ninth-grade boys and girls and their parents. Results showed that both gender and socioeconomic status were significantly related to achievement. Girls' achievement was higher than boys', and middle-class children's achievement was higher than that of children from the working class. Other data revealed that mothers' employment had a positive effect on adolescent achievement when maternal and paternal attitudes were consistent with mothers' employment status. Maternal values and interest in schoolwork were related also to adolescent achievement. Maternal employment had a positive influence on adolescents' perceptions of maternal parenting when maternal attitudes toward employment were consistent with their employment status.

This study confirmed that maternal employment per se has no effect on adolescent achievement; rather, it is the attitudes that mothers, not fathers, have toward maternal employment that are related to achievement and to adolescents' perceptions of mothering. The researcher concluded that mothers' own satisfaction with their choices is a more important indicator of children's outcomes than whether mothers are actually employed outside the home, but parenting styles and parent involvement in children's achievement are important mediators of differences in families. Adolescent achievement is most positively influenced by high levels of maternal involvement in children's achievement.

Studies of daughters' academic achievements provide additional evidence of the positive effects of a career mother. These studies have found that achieving women and career women more often had educated and employed mothers than did women whose mothers had not made such accomplishments. Daughters of employed mothers are likely to be independent and to plan future employment. Both sons and daughters of employed mothers hold more egalitarian sex-role attitudes and view women as more competent (Spitze, 1991).

Wright and Young (1998) investigated the relationship of family structure, maternal employment, and gender-role attitudes of children. Three family types (single-mother, single-father, and intact) participated in the study. Children in single-father homes had more traditional gender attitudes, whereas those in single-mother homes had more egalitarian attitudes. However, when maternal employment and gender of respondent were controlled, family structure had no effect on male children's gender-role activities. However, both males and females who had working mothers had substantially more egalitarian attitudes. Males appeared to be more affected by the working status of their mothers than by family structure. Females, on the other hand, appeared to be affected by both the presence of fathers and the working status of their mothers. The presence of fathers increased the tendency toward more traditional gender-related attitudes that can be reversed or limited by the working status of the mother.

Benin and Edwards (1990) concluded from their research of adolescents' chores in part- and full-time dual- and single-earner families that none of these family types was likely to prepare adolescents to participate fully as marriage partners in an egalitarian division of labor. Full-time dual-earner parents in their study contributed to a perpetuation of inequality in housework by allowing sons to spend 7.5 fewer hours per week doing chores than daughters. A clear message was sent that they were not equally responsible for the household maintenance. Part-time dual-earner parents were not training either sons or daughters to participate in household labor, whereas traditional families in the sample were socializing children to perform chores along highly stereotypical gender lines.

In summary, a child in a dual-career or dual-earner family can manifest pathological behavior just as a child in any other lifestyle can do, depending on how the situations are managed and what social pressures are operating on the family. Leaving children to "fend for themselves" could fail to produce resourcefulness and, instead, arouse greater dependency. Guilt on the part of the parent(s) could lead to overprotectiveness or indulgence. A lack of appropriate child-care arrangements could confuse the child and create anxiety. In addition, the degree of work/family conflict, role overload, and role conflict affects the parent-child relationship; and gender ideologies of the parents affect not only how fathers are involved but also how responsibilities are assigned to the children.

Support for Dual-Career and Dual-Earner Parents

Neither partner is prepared fully for the potential conflict, competition, and stress accompanying a dual-career or dual-earner lifestyle. Research reviewed in this chapter indicates that conflicts between work and parental roles are especially stressful for the female spouse. Women appear to be able to handle conflicts arising from the professional role more easily than those arising from family roles. Therefore, support for families in this lifestyle should be from the preventive as well as the crisis-intervention standpoint. Effective parenting appears to depend on both parents having a positive attitude about the mother's working, her job situation, appropriate child-care arrangements, and effective resolution of work/family conflict experienced. Several approaches have been suggested to assist these families.

Group Experiences. Provision for group experiences whereby dual-career and dual-earner parents can share common problems could facilitate a sense of community with similar families, thus decreasing feelings of guilt and alienation. Sharing ideas with similar families can serve to increase coping skills. Knowledge and information regarding available quality child-care facilities and/or domestic help could be shared. Hawkins and Roberts (1992) suggested that a program designed as primary intervention to help dual-earner couples share housework and child care have the following objectives: to assist couples in developing and implementing an equitable division of do-

mestic labor; assist couples in developing a more effective system of communication; and reduce marital conflict. They suggested that intervention occur at multiple levels—biological, individual, dyadic, familial, social, structural, and cultural. Further, these authors recommended that housework and child care be connected and that the program length and spacing match the dual-earner lifestyle.

Groups composed of families in different stages of the life cycle can help inform younger couples about what to expect. Discussions that help couples understand the concept of equitable, rather than equal, opportunities and constraints would facilitate understanding and acceptance among spouses. Families need help in learning how to negotiate and implement time-limited behavior contracts. When pressures and obligations are especially acute for a particular family member, another member gives assistance, a policy that helps to develop feelings of fairness. Development of management skills can assist families with planning and organizing all the tasks associated with the dual-career role. More effective use of time can help facilitate time for leisure activities in which the entire family can participate. Developing communication skills in all family members would enhance the sharing of feelings and thoughts with one another, thereby reducing hostility.

The "family meeting" approach (described in Chapter 5) is a means of working toward the goal of equity for all family members. In this approach, each member is allowed his or her chance to speak and has a part in the development of rules that govern the family. The family meeting also provides the opportunity for families to grow and change as the family moves through the life cycle.

The problems posed by a dual-career or dual-earner lifestyle warrant preparing young unmarried people for the eventuality. Recognizing the likelihood that in their future family both parents will work, developing insight into the stresses and strains they might experience, and learning appropriate techniques for resolution would all be part of an effective preventive approach. Further, educating young people, as well as those who are already parents, in the benefits of shared parenting would be important.

Environmental/Cultural Changes. Several environmental/cultural changes have been proposed that would support the dual-career or dual-earner lifestyle. Though some men are performing household tasks and parenting roles, it is still widely believed that the mother can perform these more effectively and should do so. Nevertheless, the attitude now prevails among Americans that men are being helpful to their wives when they perform child-rearing and household tasks. Continued change in society's attitude toward promoting a more equitable reorganization of domestic responsibilities appears important. Children would benefit by having fathers who participate in the full range of parenting responsibilities.

An upgrading in the domestic-helper occupations and improvement in the whole range of services available to the dual-career family are necessary. Providing additional quality child-care alternatives and upgrading child-care occupations are important sources of support for dual-career and dual-earner families.

Construction of family housing units that meet the varied needs of families and that are located conveniently to support services and the workplace would facilitate the dual-career/dual-earner lifestyle. Families in different stages of the life cycle who live in close proximity can provide some of the same benefits that extended families have provided in the past—provision of models, assisting with child care, encouragement, and the like.

Some changes in the world of work are emerging, but progress should continue. The following assumptions must be altered before any real and lasting change in the work culture can occur: that career commitment means that the family must come in a distant second; that face time (the time one is visibly present on the job) is the best measure of dedication; that "real" professional work can only be accomplished full-time; that a job with any significant level of responsibility must always override personal life (Swiss & Walker, 1993).

To provide support for dual-career and dual-earner families, Voydanoff (1989) suggested that at the most basic level an organization should expand its conception of what it takes to be a successful employee in its environment. Organizations must recognize the nonwork consequences of different career paths. Some jobs and career paths produce more stress than others—they demand more hours and/or require more extensive travel. For these reasons, career paths may differ in the extent to which they intrude into the family lives of employees and prevent them from fulfilling family responsibilities. Organizations must be aware of these differences and make this information available to employees so that they can make career decisions compatible with their family responsibilities and their desired lifestyles. This approach further requires organizations to sanction alternative career directions and to avoid pressuring employees to pursue one route to career success. Employers should recognize, sanction, and reward alternative routes to success among employees who need to balance their work and family responsibilities. Further, organizations need to recognize that family responsibilities (and work/family conflict) vary with employees' careers and family stages.

Swiss and Walker (1993) have recommended that work/family conflicts be reduced by the following means: allowing employees to use vacation time in part-day increments for doctor's appointments, school plays, and family emergencies; flextime at all levels of an organization—core business hours, compressed workweeks (e.g., four 9- or 10-hour days); job sharing for both support staff and managers; part-time work; parental leave that is genuinely supported and encouraged for both men and women; phased work reentry after parental leave (e.g., half-time for several months before returning to a full-time schedule); telecommuting and working from the home as a short- or long-term arrangement, depending on the nature of the work; lunchtime seminars to share and address the concerns of working parents (e.g., how to select quality child care, how to plan for a maternity leave, or strategies for managing alternative work options); periodic employee focus groups to determine the most pressing dependent-care concerns and to incorporate recommendations into institutional planning; and regular family-friendly audits to gauge an organization's success in promoting and retaining women and to track the extent to which women and men use parental benefits.

The recommendations made by Swiss and Walker (1993) concerning child- and elder-care support include resource and referral for child- and elder-care options; on-site child-care centers; consortium arrangements to pool resources and support child-care centers between area businesses or between local child-care centers and public school systems; a cafeteria of benefits for child care and elder care; flexible (tax-advantage) benefits programs for dependent care and medical expenses; support for after-school care of children; school vacation programs to provide coverage while parents work when schools are closed; emergency backup child care, either in facilities or with subsidies; and sick-child care (e.g., allowing parents to use their own sick days to care for sick children, subsidizing paid in-home care, or providing a sick-child-care center).

Employer-supported benefits and policies can help dual-earner families to alleviate the stress of balancing work and family demands. Seyler, Monroe, and Garand (1995) surveyed a random sample of 290 businesses that employed more than 50 people. Results indicated that maternity leave was the most commonly offered policy, with 71 percent offering this benefit in some form. The most commonly offered form of financial assistance was pretax salary reduction, with 20 percent of companies offering this benefit. Few companies offered any type of financial aid to assist parents with child-care needs; no companies contracted with child-care providers for sick children; and fewer than 50 percent offered any type of information and referral services. Nine companies sponsored child-care centers, primarily hospitals and nursing homes, and five of these offered before- and after-school care for kindergarten and school-age children.

More than half (57 percent) of the companies did not provide personal days or emergency days for employees to stay at home with sick children. It was clear that very few companies provided a comprehensive set of family benefits. Only one in six companies offered four or more family benefits, and no company offered more than 10. Companies offering zero to three options made up 80 percent of the sample. According to these researchers, employers are likely to provide family benefits only to the extent that it is in their self-interest to do so.

Although progress has been made in some of these areas, many of the necessary changes have not occurred because of the inflexibility of social systems and internalized resistance to change on the part of individuals. Whereas some social systems can be altered by legislation, attitudinal changes are more difficult. The Family and Medical Leave Act of 1993 was passed by the U.S. Congress in February 1993 and implemented in August 1993. Under this act, employees have the following rights and obligations: A worker who has been employed for at least 25 hours per week may take up to 12 weeks of unpaid leave in any 12-month period. The reasons for the leave may include the birth or adoption of a child; the serious illness of a child, spouse, or parent; or a serious illness that prevents the worker from doing the job. An employee must be given his or her old job or an equivalent position upon returning to work. A worker on leave cannot collect unemployment or other government compensation. Employers with fewer than 50 workers are exempt, and companies may deny leave to salaried employees in the highest 10 percent of their workforce if their leave would create "substantial and grievous injury" to the business operation. Employers may require medical certification establishing the need for the leave. Employers must continue to provide health-care benefits during the leave but are not required to pay the worker's salary. If the employee does not return to work, he or she must repay any health-care premiums paid by the company during the leave. Four percent of companies in 1993 had more than 50 workers ("The law's rules," 1993). A federal jury awarded $375,000 in damages to a Maryland man who was denied 12 weeks of leave guaranteed by the Family Leave Act. The man had applied for paternal leave to care for his newborn daughter because his wife was near death from childbirth complications ("Man wins…," 1999).

Obviously, sex roles are learned early. Values and attitudes that affect one's ability to function effectively in a dual-career or dual-earner lifestyle are being formed during the preschool years. Throughout the child's development, appropriate concepts regarding this and other lifestyles should be taught so that individuals can make wise decisions concerning available options.

In summary, dual-worker and dual-career families are increasing at a rapid pace, out of both economic necessity and a desire by women to fulfill personal goals. It is true that dual-career couples have more financial resources with which to seek necessary assistance than dual-earner couples have—child care, maintenance of the home, and so on. Though children of dual-career families seem to manifest more positive than negative characteristics, career couples may need help in resolving the conflicts that arise between their professions and their families. Dual-career and dual-earner families need a strong support network—at the workplace and from spouses, friends, and the extended family.

COHABITING PARENTS

An unmarried-couple household is defined by the Census Bureau as one that contains only two unrelated adults of the opposite sex, with or without children younger than 15 years present in the home. Although this definition is intended prima-rily to identify cohabiting couples, and presumably does in most cases, it also may include households with a roomer, a boarder, or an employee living on the premises. On the other hand, it may exclude other cohabiting couples in households where there are more than two adults residing. Therefore, the numbers are approximate.

In 1996, there were nearly 4 million unmarried-couple households, more than twice the number in 1980. Two-thirds of these households had no children younger than 15 living in the home. Compared with the number of married-couple households, the number of unmarried-couple households is relatively small, but the ratio of unmarried to married couples is growing. Living together in nonmarital unions is becoming increasingly common and represents a lifestyle experienced by many individuals at some point during their lifetimes.

Between the mid-1980s and the mid-1990s, the number of marriages preceded by cohabitation quadrupled. Currently, nearly 50 percent of Americans in their twenties and thirties have cohabited (Brown & Booth, 1996).

Although the largest number of individuals who cohabit are between 25 and 45 years of age, couples who cohabit represent a wide age range, from college students to elderly people. Table 8.1 shows the number and ages of people in unmarried households. The increase in cohabitation has paralleled the sharp decline in both first-marriage rates and rates of remarriage, as well as the recent leveling off of divorce rates. The increase in the proportion of unmarried young people should not

TABLE 8.1 Unmarried Households by Age, 1980–1996

	1980	1990	1996
Total	1,589	2,856	3,958
Age of householder			
Under 25 years old	411	596	816
25 to 44 years old	837	1,775	2,315
45 to 64 years old	221	358	606
65 years old and over	119	127	221

Source: U.S. Bureau of the Census. (1997). *Statistical abstract of the United States: 1997*. Washington, DC: U.S. Department of Commerce.

be interpreted as an increase in "singlehood" as traditionally regarded. Young people are setting up housekeeping with partners of the opposite sex at almost as early an age as they did before marriage rates declined (Bumpass, Sweet, & Cherlin, 1991).

A number of reasons are given for choosing a cohabiting lifestyle. It may be a phase of courtship, a stage of marriage, or simply a relationship that is an end in itself (Oropesa, 1996). Cohabitation involves sharing a residence and personal resources, excluding intimate relationships with others, and, in a substantial number of cases, having a child (Brown & Booth, 1996). In the Bumpass et al. (1991) study, the majority of couples said they chose to cohabit because it gave them an opportunity to be sure of compatibility before marriage.

Schoen and Weinick (1993) contended that many important questions regarding cohabitation remain to be answered, including whether it is a transient stage on the way to marriage or a different type of relationship that provides an alternative to legal marriage. These researchers concluded from the couples they studied that the propensity to marry is greater than the propensity to cohabit. They discovered that cohabitors are less concerned than married people with finding a partner of a similar age, that marriages are more religiously homogamous than cohabitations, and that cohabiting couples are more homogamous with respect to education than are married couples.

Cohabitation for most couples is a temporary arrangement—ending either in termination or in marriage. For about half of cohabitors, the relationship lasts approximately two years and then ends, either because the couple get married or because they split up. Only one-third of these rela-

tionships continue 2 years without marriage or a split; one-tenth of cohabitors remain in a long-term relationship that seldom ends in marriage (Brown & Booth, 1996). Bumpass and associates (1991) and Surra (1990) concluded that cohabitation encompasses a wide variety of relationship experiences. Some cohabiting homosexual couples continue a long-term committed relationship similar to marriage for heterosexual couples.

Children are present in more than one-third of cohabiting households. In a national survey, Manning and Lichter (1996) found that 3.5 percent, or 2.2 million children, lived in cohabiting families. Of these households, one-third of the children have a parent who has never been married, and almost one-half have previously married parents. Children in cohabiting households are not all young children. One-quarter of the households have children age 10 or older, most of whose parents were previously married. Therefore, the issues of parenting and stepparenting are very much a part of the picture (Bumpass et al., 1991). Table 8.2 shows the number of cohabiting households with children under 15 years old.

Data also reveal striking racial and ethnic variations in children's experiences in cohabiting-couple households. Parental cohabitation is most common among Puerto Rican children (8 percent) and least prevalent among Asian children (1 percent). Similar percentages (about 5 percent) of Mexican American and Black children live in cohabiting families, and only 3 percent of White children do so (Manning & Lichter, 1996).

Wu (1996) studied the childbearing experiences of women after their entry into a cohabiting relationship. Results showed that within 1 year

TABLE 8.2 Unmarried Households with Children*

	1980	1990	1996
Number with children under 15 years old	431	891	1,442
Number with no children under 15 years old	1,159	1,966	2,516

Source: U.S. Bureau of the Census. (1997). *Statistical abstract of the United States: 1997.* Washington, DC.: U.S. Department of Commerce.

*Number in thousands.

after the onset of cohabitation, only 3 percent of the women gave birth, but it was twice that percentage after 3 years. The longer women stayed in these relationships, the more likely they were to bear children. Greater likelihood of birth in a cohabiting relationship was associated with women's younger age, lower educational status, and having a previously married partner. Manning and Lansdale (1996) used two national data sets to examine premarital childbearing in cohabiting relationships. They found that more than one-quarter (28 percent) of White, 75 percent of African American, and 47 percent of Puerto Rican women conceived their first child before marriage. Only 13 percent of the White women and 36 percent of the Puerto Rican women had not married before the birth of the child. Sixty-eight percent of the African American women had not married when their babies were born. Overall, most women who conceived their first child while cohabiting were still in cohabiting unions when their children were born. White, single, pregnant women were the most likely to marry before the birth of their first child, and African American women the least likely to do so. Further, cohabitation increased the likelihood of a completed premarital pregnancy for all age groups.

These researchers concluded that a nontrivial proportion of premarital pregnancies and births to U.S. women take place within cohabiting unions. Parenthood is more likely among never-married cohabiting women than among women living alone. Further, the role of cohabitation varies across ethnic groups. Whereas cohabitation operates primarily as a transitional stage before marriage for Whites, nonmarital unions are common family contexts for childbearing among Puerto Ricans—about half of babies born premaritally have parents who live together. In contrast, African American women are much less likely to be in any union (cohabiting or marriage) when they first become mothers. Socioeconomic conditions may provide a partial explanation for the relatively high rates of premarital childbearing among Blacks and Puerto Ricans, but cohabitation seems to play an entirely different role in these two groups. The importance of the cultural context in understanding the dynamics of cohabitation cannot be underestimated.

If children are born of a cohabiting union, there may be complications, but there is a trend toward increased legal protection of children living in these circumstances. These children are penalized to a greater extent than their parents are, particularly when their parents separate. An uncertain child-custody situation may result, including a significant economic loss if child support is not mandated. When a cohabiting partner has custody of a child by a prior marriage, there is a risk that the former spouse may maintain successful action to secure custody, especially if he or she is remarried and resides in a traditional family lifestyle.

Manning and Lichter (1996) used 1990 census data to determine the economic characteristics of U.S. children living in cohabiting-couple families. Parents of these children were more likely to be young, poorly educated, and unemployed than their counterparts in married-couple families. Previous research has shown that parental cohabitation has negative effects on children's well-being—these children display lower academic performance, less initiative, and more school problems than children from families with two continuously married parents. Studies have shown that the median household income is considerably lower among cohabiting couples than among married-couple families.

Apparently, there is considerable economic uncertainty for children in cohabiting-couple families, a situation that parallels the economic circumstances of children in single-parent households. Although these children have two potential economic providers, these researchers found that family resources (in the form of parental education, employment, and income) fell well short of family resources in married-couple families. Officially, 44 percent of children in cohabiting families lived below the poverty level. When the cohabiting partner's income was considered, the percentage dropped to 31 percent. A striking two-fifths of the officially defined poor children in cohabiting-couple families were lifted out of poverty by redefining family income and family size to include the cohabiting partner. Puerto Rican children, in particular, were found to benefit from a cohabiting partner's income—the poverty level was cut almost in half by this additional income. For Black children, inclusion of the unmarried partner's income reduced the poverty level from 50 percent to 39 percent. Because cohabiting unions often are unstable (i.e., ending in separation and not marriage), the additional potential source of income from an unmarried partner may be unreliable.

Using data from the National Survey of Families and Households, Brown and Booth (1996) evaluated the extent to which cohabitation is similar to marriage. Results indicated a modest but significant difference in four out of five dimensions of relationship quality between marrieds and cohabitors. Those in cohabiting unions experienced more disagreements, more fights or violence, lower levels of perceived fairness in relationships, and less happiness with their relationships relative to marrieds. However, when comparing the cohabitors who planned to marry with the marrieds, no significant differences on any dimension of relationship quality were found. Among marrieds and cohabitors who planned to marry, the presence of biological children was associated with more disagreements, more hitting and shouting, and less happiness and interaction. The effects of having been previously married on current relationship quality were the same for marrieds and cohabitors who planned to marry. Prior marriage did not significantly affect current relationship quality.

These researchers concluded that cohabitation is very similar to marriage. More than three-fourths of all cohabitors reported plans to marry their partners, which implies that most of them view cohabitation as a prelude to marriage. This study demonstrated that a majority of cohabitors are involved in unions that are little different from marriage in terms of quality.

Horwitz and White (1998) compared the mental health of cohabitors with that of married people. A sample of unmarried adults who were tested at 18, 21, and 24 years of age were retested 7 years later. The results indicated that there were no differences between cohabitors and others in levels of depression. Cohabiting men, however, reported significantly more alcohol problems than both married and single men; cohabiting women reported more alcohol problems than married women. Overall, the cohabitors were more similar to single people than to married people.

Cohabitation has some, but not all, of the mental-health benefits of marriage—advantages of an intimate relationship, a source of social support, a confidant, regular sexual activity, and some of the advantages of shared incomes. Cohabitors are not faced with the same restraints that bind the married; they have more choice and flexibility to terminate their relationships when they choose.

Several studies have examined premarital cohabitation and subsequent marital stability. Most of the studies indicated that couples who cohabit before marriage reported lower-quality marriages, lower commitment to the institution of marriage, more individualistic views of marriage, and greater likelihood of divorce than couples who did not cohabit before marriage (Brown & Booth, 1996; Horwitz & White, 1998; Wu, 1995).

In fact, 27 percent of women who cohabit before marriage divorce within 5 years after marriage, as opposed to 10 percent who never lived with a boyfriend. Other studies have shown as high as 46 percent of cohabitors divorcing after marriage. Several reasons have been proposed for the likelihood to divorce. For example, cohabitors may be more unconventional, less committed to the institution of marriage, and more open to the possibility of divorce. It also is possible that living together slowly erodes an individual's ability to commit and his or her faith in the institution of marriage (Boorstein, 1999).

Using a sample of women from the Family and Friends Survey, Wu (1995) examined the relationships between premarital cohabitation and cohabitation after marital disruption. Results indicated that 48 percent of women who had cohabited premaritally had experienced a postmarital cohabitation by the time of the survey, compared with 13 percent who had not cohabited premaritally. Fifty-seven percent of the men who had cohabited before marriage were in another cohabiting union, compared with 24 percent who had not cohabited premaritally.

The average duration of the first marriage was significantly shorter for cohabitors than for noncohabitors. Fifty-eight percent of cohabitors had children at the time of marital dissolution, as opposed to 77 percent of the noncohabitors—a difference that was highly significant. For men, the figures were 55 percent and 67 percent, respectively.

Widows and widowers were significantly less likely to enter into cohabiting relationships than were separated and divorced persons. Presence of children also was a strong barrier to forming cohabiting relationships for women, but not for men.

In summary, cohabitation has become more common in the past 25 years, especially among certain groups of individuals. The stigma once attached to cohabitation seems to be diminishing. However, when children result from cohabiting unions, especially those in which parents have psychological problems or the relationships are unstable, children are likely to suffer. Thus, it appears that there is cause for concern about the parenting practices that may exist in some cohabiting households. Certainly, parents who engage in serial cohabitation are likely to possess characteristics that prohibit effective parenting.

GAY AND LESBIAN PARENTS

Although homosexuality has always existed and the gay movement has a long history, only in the past 20 to 25 years has this phenomenon been discussed openly by the lay public and emphasized in research. Position statements by the American Psychiatric and Psychological Associations in the 1970s led to the removal of homosexuality from the list of mental illnesses. The affirmation of the rights of gay people by these professional and other groups have helped to promote considerable change in societal attitudes. The once firmly held cultural stereotypes and myths regarding homosexuality have been reexamined. However, many issues of homosexuality are still highly emotionally charged and debated. Among these issues are whether homosexual individuals should be allowed to rear their own children or, in the case of

women, be allowed to be artificially inseminated, to adopt, or to provide foster care to children.

In the late 1970s, the terms *gay* and *homosexual* were defined differently—with *homosexual* being defined as "one with an erotic preference for a member of the same gender," whereas a gay person, in addition, has managed to reject the negative stereotype associated with being homosexual (Morin & Schultz, 1978). Homosexuality as a cultural phenomenon is not simply a behavior but also a way of life. Being gay is far more than sexual behavior and includes attitudes, values, and lifestyle choices. Gay or lesbian is a way of labeling oneself as multidimensional (Blumenfeld & Raymond, 1988). Thus, the terms *gay* and *lesbian* connote a value system as well as designating group membership. These terms indicate a positive identification, but the term *homosexual* has neutral or even negative connotations.

It has been estimated that approximately 10 percent of the population, or 25 million people, are predominately homosexual, and a great many more have had sexual experiences with an individual of the same sex. The actual number of homosexual, or gay, parents is not known. Part of the reason is that a large percentage of homosexuals have not "come out of the closet," or established their identity as gay persons. Some are reflected in the data on unrelated adults living together; others are counted in the single-parents category; and many are still residing in nuclear households. Using a sample of more than 9,000 adults in five U.S. cities, Cameron and Cameron (1996) found that approximately 25 percent of gay men were fathers and 33 percent of lesbians were mothers. From their data, they projected that less than 1 percent of all parents are homosexual.

Rough estimates of the total population of lesbian mothers range from 1 million to more than 5 million, and gay fathers numbered about 2 million. Therefore, it appears that the number of gay mothers and fathers is substantial. One estimate claims that 1.5 million lesbian mothers reside with their children as a family unit. The number of households headed by gay fathers is probably much smaller. The combined number of children of gays and lesbians is somewhere between 6 and 14 million. However, many gay parents are still married, and their family members do not know that they are homosexual. Whatever the accurate figure, one cannot assume that these parents or their children are insignificant in number (Flaks, Ficher, Masterpasqua, & Joseph, 1995; Patterson, 1992).

Increasing openness among gay and lesbian adults has resulted in the visibility of a number of family forms in which one or both of a child's parents identify themselves as gay or lesbian (Baptiste, 1987; Bozett & Sussman, 1990). The largest number of these families are those in which children were born in the context of a heterosexual relationship between biological parents (Cameron & Cameron, 1996). These include families in which the parents divorce when the husband comes out as gay or when the wife comes out as a lesbian, families in which the parents divorce when both the husband and the wife come out, and families in which one or both of the parents come out and they decide not to divorce. Parental acknowledgment of a gay or lesbian identity may precede or follow the decision about divorce. The gay or lesbian parent may be either the residential or the nonresidential parent, or children may live part of the time in each home. Gay and lesbian parents may be single, or they may have same-sex partners. In addition to those who become parents within the context of heterosexual marriages or relationships before coming out, growing numbers of lesbians and gay men are becoming parents after coming out. In 1990 it was estimated that 5,000 to 10,000 lesbians have borne children after coming out (Seligmann, 1990), and that figure is probably a conservative estimate. A gay or lesbian parent's same-sex partner may or may not assume co-parenting or stepparenting relationships with the children. If the partner also has children, stepsibling relationships may develop (Patterson, 1992).

Reasons Gays and Lesbians Marry and Become Parents

Research studies have suggested a number of reasons that gays and lesbians marry and become parents. These include the desire to conceal one's true sexual orientation, testing the ability to respond heterosexually, denying homosexuality and/or eliminating homosexual impulses, yielding to social pressure, escaping an intolerable relationship with one's immediate family, fleeing from disappointing heterosexual relationships, the desire to have children, genuine affection for the prospective spouse, and believing one is bisexual (Bigner & Bozett, 1990; Bozett, 1989). However, it was reported that most of the gay fathers in one study did not identify themselves as homosexuals when they had their children. The process of self-identity and finally public identity apparently takes time for many homosexuals. A number enter marriage expecting and desiring contentment within the traditional nuclear context. Children, then, result from this attempt.

Gay Fathers

Rearing children can be as much a purpose for lesbians and gays who form families as for heterosexuals. The gay father is a fairly newly emergent figure in homosexual culture. There is little information or knowledge about these men (Bigner & Bozett, 1990). Gay fathers constitute approximately 20 percent to 25 percent of self-identified gay men—a minority within a minority in our culture. It is estimated that more than 2.3 million gay men are natural fathers, and some have adopted children (Bozett, 1989). Although approximately 10 percent of all American males are predominately homosexual in orientation, the actual number of gay fathers cannot be determined accurately because many are still married or are "closeted" for other reasons (Bigner & Bozett, 1990). A homosexual father has two diametrically opposed roles—fatherhood, which is a culturally accepted role, and his gay identity. These conflicting roles present a complex set of problems relating to self and to social acceptance that heterosexual fathers do not encounter. Thus, homosexual fathers have all the problems other fathers have plus the problem of handling the cognitive dissonance associated with dual roles (Bigner & Bozett, 1990).

Most of the recent research conducted on gay fathers to date has been carried out on men who were married, although now alternative routes to fatherhood are available (donation of sperm to surrogate mothers, adoption, and foster care) (Alpert, 1988; Ricketts & Achtenberg, 1990). The primary mode of adjustment to the married father's homosexuality is separation and/or divorce, but homosexuality may or may not be the major cause for divorce.

Establishing a Gay Identity.   Gay fathers have a unique and more complex social-psychological environment than other homosexual or heterosexual males. Their challenges of adjustment include identity concerns, acceptance of self, acceptance by family, and acceptance by other homosexuals as well as matters more specific to parenting and custody issues. The term *gay father* is contradictory in nature to some, since *gay* has the connotation of homosexuality, whereas *father* implies heterosexuality. The problem lies in determining how the two may be applied simultaneously to an individual who has a same-sex orientation and who also is a parent. The idea of a gay father is contradictory to the stereotypical image of a gay man, which implies that gays are antifamily in their lifestyle and orientation to group living.

The process of identity development for the gay father requires a reconciliation of two polar extremes—heterosexual and homosexual. And, since each identity is essentially unacceptable by the opposite culture, the task is to integrate both identities into the cognitive class called *gay father.* This process involves the man's disclosure of his gay identity to nongays and his father identity to gays, thus forming close liaisons with people who positively sanction both identities. This process is referred to as *integrative sanctioning.* It also involves the father's distancing himself from others who are not tolerant. At the same time, identity development is enhanced by participation in a gay lifestyle (Bigner & Bozett, 1990). This process usually takes years to achieve and is an invisible event for others in the family (Strommen, 1990).

Gay men have much to lose by disclosure—personal security and intimacy provided by home and family life, economic security, and social stability (Bigner & Bozett, 1990). Both gay men and lesbians face a number of social and legal sanctions in today's society, ranging from the risk of violent assault to the denial of employment and housing. The gay or lesbian parent who discloses to a spouse faces not only these problems but also unexpected legal difficulties in the courts over the issue of child custody. It has been reported consistently that if a parent's homosexuality is raised as a custody issue, it not only becomes the central issue in the custody case but also makes a ruling in favor of the gay parent significantly less likely (Strommen, 1989).

Reactions of significant others (parents, spouses, siblings, children) cannot be predicted. Parents and spouses often react to disclosure similarly—they may perceive the person as a stranger, someone whose essential wants are unrecognizable and different; they may experience powerful feelings of guilt and failure, feelings that somehow they are responsible for this new alien identity, and feelings of regret, confusion, and denial. Williamson (1998) found that family emotional reactions varied widely, but certain variables predict the most likely responses—denial, anger, bargaining, depression, and acceptance. Some researchers have labeled these responses "stages," but Williamson noted that they do not occur in any necessary order, or all may not occur, or two or more may occur simultaneously. The act of disclosure, however, will produce some degree of family crisis. Disclosure is a complex family event, not simply an individual initiative. As complex as it is, disclosure has several advantages: Secrets in families have destructive effects on the quality of family life and relationships; the level of intimacy between human beings in a relationship depends on openness, candor, and self-revelation; disclosure opens up significant new possibilities for social support from family members and significant others, even if the support is preceded by stress.

Gay fathers who come out perceive less discrimination from family, friends, and co-workers than those who are closeted. Gay fathers who have achieved a sense of psychological well-being are less anxious, less depressed, and less guilty about their sexuality. They also exhibit fewer stress-related conditions such as ulcers, substance abuse, and sleeping and eating disorders. They exhibit a stabilization of self-concept and an increase in congruence between their public and self identities (Bozett, 1989).

Divorce is the most common outcome for married gays and lesbians (Bigner & Bozett, 1990; Strommen, 1989). The extent of reintegration into the family may depend on such factors as ethnicity, individual family culture, and degree of religiosity. Moreover, since individuals who exhibit authoritarian personalities conform rigidly to middle-class values, have little tolerance for ambiguity, and have punitive attitudes concerning nonconforming sexual activity, it is likely that such individuals will have great difficulty accepting a family member as gay (Bozett & Sussman, 1990; Strommen, 1990).

For some homosexual men, resolution of the two conflicting roles and acceptance of self come only after extended therapy. Essential factors contributing to the resolution include engaging in a variety of social and sexual experiences in the gay world over a period of time, disclosing one's homosexuality to his intimate and significant others, and receiving positive sanctions in these endeavors. Self-acceptance almost always demands disclosure of sexual orientation, a hard decision for a gay father.

Bozett (1987) pointed out that parenting by gay fathers who remain married and do not disclose their homosexuality to their children is frequently of lesser quality than those who do because of the tension in the relationship; the time involved in clandestine gay activities; and the tendency to be workaholics, thereby resulting in spending minimal time at home. On the other hand, gay fathers who come out to their children frequently live in stable, domestic relationships, often with permanent partners. They tend to be dependable and to spend quality time with their children. Although many gay fathers do not reveal their homosexuality to their children, many do. Many men feel it important to do so because they want to be able to share with their children and they wish to be honest. Further, many gay fathers

feel it important for their children to have an opportunity as they grow up to become acquainted with competent and accomplished gay men and lesbian women. In this way, children will have contact with role models that they can respect. Bozett (1989) concluded that being gay is compatible with fathering, and the significance of their paternal role is all the more evident once gay men leave their marriages.

The establishment of a gay identity in the gay world is difficult because many aspects of the father role conflict with the gay life. For example, the gay world is one that is single-oriented, with few long-term commitments in time, finances, or responsibilities. It is a transient world and a very difficult one for fathers to participate in unless they have abandoned all parental responsibilities. In addition, the gay world is youth-dominated. Most gay fathers are older than other males in the group.

Many gay men are intolerant of children, and gay fathers with custody of their children may find it difficult to establish relationships with other gay men. All of these factors minimize the chances of the gay father's social success in establishing an identity in the gay world (Bigner & Jacobsen, 1989).

Parenting by Gay Fathers. Traditionally, homosexuality has been believed to be incompatible with effective parenting. However, little evidence to date supports such a belief. Gay fathers generally are similar to nongay fathers in their reasons for having children. However, some significant differences between the two groups have been found. Bigner and Bozett (1990) found that gay fathers differed from nongay fathers in two ways. Nongay fathers placed a greater emphasis on traditional values of being a parent, such as continuing the family name, ensuring security in old age by having children to care for them, and transmission of family traditions. In contrast, gay fathers responded differently by placing greater emphasis on the function of parenthood in conveying social status and gaining acceptability as an adult member of the community.

Bigner and Jacobsen (1989) studied the value of children to gay and heterosexual fathers. They found that gay fathers did not accept the notion that children improve a marriage to the same degree that heterosexual fathers did. Gay fathers also did not believe that children function to enhance the morality of one's behavior. However, gay fathers tended to agree more than heterosexual fathers that the production of children enhances one's masculinity and that parenthood provides an entrance into the adult community, as well as to being accepted by other adults in the heterosexual community. Gay fathers in this study reflected a traditional attitude toward marriage and family orientations. They saw parenthood as a way to protect against societal rejection and to attain some type of social status in one's community.

Bigner and Bozett (1990) concluded that there is no evidence that demonstrates that living with a homosexual parent has any negative effects on children. In fact, it appears that gay parents are as effective as and may be more so in some ways than nongay parents. Gay fathers are more endorsing of paternal nurturance, less endorsing of economic providing as a major ingredient of fathering behavior, and somewhat less traditional in their overall approach to parenting. Most gay fathers have positive relationships with their children, and the father's sexual orientation has little importance in the overall parent-child relationship. Gay fathers try harder to create stable home lives and positive relationships than traditional heterosexual parents are expected to.

Studies of children of gay fathers are extremely sparse. Those that exist have found that children perceive their fathers positively as parent figures. They consider them friends, confidants, and advisors. Some gay fathers report that they encourage play with sex-typed toys. Closeness to the gay father is positively related to the child's level of self-esteem, particularly for sons. However, the quality of the parent-child relationship strongly influences the closeness to the parent. Children of gay and lesbian parents also reported a greater openness to alternative lifestyles (Gottman, 1990).

Thus, it can be concluded from the research on gay fathering that being gay and fathering are compatible. Disclosure to significant others facilitates psychological well-being, which in turn facilitates effective parenting. Children seem to suffer no harmful effects of their fathers' sexual orientation, and most have positive relationships with them.

Research that has compared parenting by gay and heterosexual fathers has found no reasons to believe that gay fathers are less effective as parents (Barrett & Robinson, 1990; Bozett, 1989). One study found no differences between the two groups in problem solving, in providing recreation for children, and in encouraging autonomy. Besides demonstrating greater emphasis on nurturance, less emphasis on the role of economic provision, and less conformity in their overall paternal attitudes, the gay fathers assessed themselves significantly more positively in the paternal role than the heterosexual fathers did. The investigators concluded that gay fathers had a substantial psychological investment in their father roles (Barrett & Robinson, 1990; Bigner & Bozett, 1990; Bozett, 1989).

Lesbian Mothers

Lesbians have been having and rearing children for a long time. Today, many are having, adopting, and rearing children after "coming out." Some are parenting with their primary partners, others alone, and still others with male or female friends or a family of friends. There are many types of lesbian family situations, and lesbians have few role models for the formation of their families (Flaks et al., 1995). Data indicate that there are fewer lesbians than gay men at all ages, but more lesbians than gays are or have been married. Almost one-third of all lesbians have been married, with approximately one-half of these marriages producing children. Thus, approximately 16 percent of lesbians are mothers. Lesbians are more likely to marry than gay men because many realize their sexual preference after the popular marrying ages of 21 to 23. Further, women experience greater pressure to marry than males do, and they might not find sexual relations with men completely intolerable or impossible (Coleman, 1990).

Lesbians choose to parent for most of the same reasons as heterosexual women, primarily because they want children. They may have had memorable childhoods and they want to create the same for other young children. Or they may have had miserable childhoods and want the opportunity to do it differently for other children. Some want to share the experience of parenting with a life partner. Others want to put a spark into their relationships (Pies, 1990).

The lesbian-mother family is one of the most stigmatized and least studied types of single-parent families. DiLapi (1989), using the "motherhood hierarchy" (most appropriate, moderately appropriate, and least appropriate) as a conceptual framework, pointed out that lesbian mothers were considered by society as the least appropriate women to be mothers. According to McCandlish (1987), "Lesbian mothers raise their families in a larger society that is hostile and uncomprehending and that fails to provide role models and adequate protection" (p. 23). However, lesbian mothers now win 15 percent to 20 percent of contested custody cases, as opposed to 1 percent in 1970. Fertility alternatives for lesbians that bypass custody disputes are likely to increase significantly the number of lesbian mothers rearing children. These alternatives are discussed later in this section. Lesbian mothers try to fulfill several roles. The normal problems associated with the maternal role, whether as a single mother or as a mother in a nuclear family, are compounded by lesbianism. Single mothers, regardless of their sexual orientation, can be expected to face many of the same kind of problems, especially those related to economics and social isolation.

Unique Problems of Lesbian Mothers.   One of the major problems faced by single lesbian mothers is obtaining and maintaining custody of their children. The biggest percentage of lesbian mothers always live with the fear that a bid for custody can be made by the child's father or his extended family. This ever-present threat creates a unique problem. The legal system in the United States has long been hostile to gay men and to lesbians who already are or who wish to become parents (Patterson, 1992). Because of judicial and legislative as-

sumptions about the adverse effects of parental homosexuality on children, lesbian mothers and gay fathers often have been denied custody and/or visitation with their children following divorce. As in the case of gay fathers, decisions of the court concerning lesbians rearing their own children, foster children, or adoptive children are based on commonly accepted myths. There is concern that children reared by lesbians may be sexually molested, grow up to be lesbians themselves, and suffer from the stigmatizing process surrounding culturally labeled deviants. In spite of the evidence to the contrary, these myths still are widely believed (Patterson, 1992).

The lesbian mother must also contend with problems associated with the relationship of the lover and her children. Many of these adults view themselves as instant parents, and thus conflicts often emerge relating to child rearing, especially discipline. Some research has found that in lesbian mothers' homes where there are live-in lovers, the children relate to them in ways similar to those in which children in blended heterosexual homes do. "Stepparenting" in gay and lesbian families has similar rewards and problems to stepparenting in other families.

Lovers are viewed by the children as additional mothers, sisters, aunts, but not as fathers. Close relationships are formed, and reactions of loss, grief, guilt, and depression may follow the dissolution of the relationship. Harris and Turner (1986) indicated that both gay fathers and lesbian mothers were more likely to have live-in lovers than single heterosexual parents. Serial relations of gay parents thus present problems for children that are similar to those children experience in serial marriages or cohabitation by heterosexual parents.

There is little research on how lesbians view their potentially conflicting identities of mother, lesbian, and possible wife. It is possible that a lesbian views the mother role as an aspect of her identity as a woman and therefore does not experience the role conflict that gay men do (Strommen, 1989). Lesbian mothers may experience difficulty "coming out of the closet" and revealing their sexual orientation to their children. The unpredictability of the child's acceptance of the mother's sexual orientation and the fear that the child will experience difficulty being accepted by her peers and/or others once her sexual orientation is known are factors that inhibit disclosure. Lesbian mothers appear to be discreet in efforts to protect their children (Pennington, 1987).

Parenting by Lesbian Mothers.   Lesbian mothers have been found to be more similar to than different from single heterosexual mothers. The area of greatest commonality appears to be the salience of motherhood in their lives. Both groups of mothers have reported that motherhood influenced the conduct of their lives in ways that overshadowed the influence of other factors. Research on the effects of lesbian or gay parents on children has focused on several issues—whether children will show disturbances in sexual identity, be less psychologically healthy than children growing up in homes with heterosexual parents, experience difficulties in social relationships, and be at greater risk for sexual abuse by the parent and/or parent's friends or acquaintances. It is important to remember that the preponderance of research has focused on children who were born in the context of heterosexual marriages, whose parents divorced, and whose mothers have identified themselves as lesbians. Most studies are comparisons of these children with children in divorced heterosexual mother-headed families. Less research is available on children whose fathers have identified themselves as gay.

Gender identity among children from 5 to 17 years of age of lesbian mothers has been assessed by several investigators using projective techniques and interviews. No evidence of special difficulties in gender identity among children of lesbian mothers has emerged. Further, children reported that they were happy with the sex to which they belonged, and that they did not wish to be members of the opposite sex (Patterson, 1992).

A number of studies have examined gender-role behavior among children of lesbian mothers. When children of lesbian and of heterosexual mothers were asked to reveal toy preferences, ac-

tivities, interests, or occupational choices, no significant differences between the two groups were found (Patterson, 1992).

Sex-role behavior of lesbian and heterosexual mothers' children also was assessed by Green, Mandel, Hotvedt, Gray, and Smith (1986). Interviews with the children of both sets of mothers with respect to favorite television programs, favorite television characters, or favorite games or toys found no differences between the children of lesbian and heterosexual mothers. There was some indication that the offspring of lesbian mothers had less sex-typed preferences for activities at school and in their neighborhoods than children of heterosexual mothers. Further, lesbian mothers were more likely than heterosexual mothers to report that their daughters often participated in rough-and-tumble play or occasionally played with "masculine" toys such as trucks or guns; however, they reported no differences in these areas for sons. Lesbian mothers were no more or less likely than heterosexual mothers to report that their children often played with "feminine" toys such as dolls. In both family types, however, children's sex-role behavior was within normal limits.

In another study reported by Patterson (1992), children of lesbian and heterosexual mothers did not differ on masculinity or on androgyny, but children of lesbian mothers reported greater psychological femininity than those of heterosexual mothers. The gender-role preferences of adult daughters of two groups of heterosexual mothers (mothers who had divorced and remarried and mothers who had divorced but not remarried) and adult daughters of lesbian mothers were compared by Gottman (1990), who found no significant differences in gender-role preferences of the women in the three groups.

The sexual orientation of the children of lesbians also has been of interest. Several studies in the 1980s examined whether lesbian and gay parents have a disproportionate fraction of children who become homosexual, based on percentages in the general population (Gottman, 1990; Huggins, 1989; and Paul, 1986). In each of these studies, development of gender identity, of gender-role behavior, and of sexual preference among offspring of gay and lesbian parents was within normal bounds. Although studies have assessed more than 300 offspring of gay or lesbian parents in at least 12 different samples, Patterson (1992) noted that no evidence has been found for significant disturbances of any kind in the development of sexual identity among these individuals. However, Cameron and Cameron (1996) argued that their data provided some evidence that children reared by homosexual parents are more likely than children reared by heterosexual parents to have models, associates, and experiences that would influence them to engage in homosexuality and, therefore, become homosexual. They further contended that these children have greater probability of various forms of childhood victimization (from parents and their associates) and are more apt to be socially and psychologically disturbed. The authors admitted that their evidence was limited.

Several studies of other aspects of personal development among children of gay and lesbian parents have assessed a broad array of characteristics. Among them have been separation-individuation, psychiatric evaluations, assessments of behavior problems, personality, self-concept, locus of control, moral judgment, and intelligence. Flaks and associates (1995) evaluated cognitive functioning and behavioral adjustment of children and parents' relationship and parenting skills of lesbian couples whose children were conceived by means of donor insemination. Children's functioning and parenting were compared with those of children in matched, heterosexual families. No significant differences were found in cognitive functioning or behavioral adjustment in lesbian and heterosexual families. Comparisons between lesbian and heterosexual mothers revealed that lesbian mothers had more parenting awareness skills than heterosexual mothers, and they identified more childcare problems and solutions. Further, relationship qualities did not differ significantly between lesbian and heterosexual couples.

The researchers concluded that their results were consistent with previous research that has shown that children of lesbians and heterosexual parents are markedly similar in the areas of intellectual functioning and behavioral adjustment. Further, of the 24 comparisons made, 17 actually favored the children of lesbian parents, a factor that diminishes the likelihood that differences were found because of small sample size. Chan, Raboy, and Patterson (1998) examined parents' and children's psychological adjustment in four family structures (heterosexual couples, single heterosexual mothers, lesbian couples, and single lesbian mothers). All the children in the study had been conceived by donor insemination. Data were collected on child adjustment, parental adjustment, and parental relationship satisfaction. Results indicated no significant differences between biological and nonbiological mothers' reports of well-being as a function of relationship status or as a function of sexual orientation. All children in the sample were well adjusted, and no significant differences emerged as a function of parental sexual orientation or number of parents in the home. Thus, structural factors such as household composition and sexual orientation were not associated with significant outcomes for children or their parents.

Data revealed that children's behavioral problems as reported by parents were significantly correlated with parents' own adjustment. Children who exhibited more behavioral problems had parents who reported more parenting stress and more dysfunctional parent-child interactions. Parents' sexual orientation and relationship status were unrelated to children's behavior problems. Parents' reports of parenting distress were significantly related to teachers' reports of children's externalizing and total behavior problems. Better relationship adjustment of couples, regardless of gender of partners, was associated with fewer behavior problems among the children. In summary, the data in this study revealed that parenting stress, but not parents' sexual orientation, relationship status, or educational attainment, was significantly related to children's adjustment. Children were rated as better adjusted when their parents reported greater relationship satisfaction, higher levels of love, and lower interparental conflict.

Because of fears that children of gay and lesbian parents might encounter difficulties among their peers, some attention has been focused on peer relations. Green and his colleagues (1986) asked children to rate their own popularity among same-sex and among opposite-sex peers, and they also asked mothers to rate their children's social skills and popularity among peers. The results showed that most mothers rated their children's social skills in a positive manner, and there were no differences between the reports given by lesbian and heterosexual mothers about their children. In addition, the self-reports of the children of lesbian mothers did not differ from those of offspring of heterosexual mothers. In other studies assessing peer relations reported by Patterson (1992), no significant differences between children of lesbian and heterosexual mothers were found.

Concerns that children of gay or lesbian parents are more likely than children of heterosexual parents to be sexually abused have been addressed in the literature related to abuse. Results of work in this area show that the great majority of adults who perpetrate sexual abuse are male; sexual abuse of children by adult women is extremely rare. Lesbian mothers are thus at very low risk for sexual abuse of their children. Available evidence also reveals that gay men are no more likely than heterosexual men to perpetrate child sexual abuse. Fears that children in custody of gay or lesbian parents might be at greater risk for sexual abuse are thus without empirical foundation (Patterson, 1992). Patterson (1992) concluded that the picture of lesbian mothers' children that emerges from the results of existing research is one of general engagement in social life with peers, with fathers, and with mothers' adult friends—both female and male, both homosexual and heterosexual.

Taken as a whole, the evidence seems to suggest that lesbians differ from other mothers largely in their sexual preference. They experience problems in child rearing that are similar to those experienced by other single mothers or to those experienced in blended families.

TIPS

For Gay and Lesbian Parents

Disclose sexual preference to children and other family members as early as possible.

Be honest about the circumstances surrounding the birth of children.

Encourage children's relationships with nonresidential biological parents, if applicable.

Avoid serial relationships, especially when children are young.

Negotiate the partner's role in parenting and the family.

Seek support from friends, family, support groups, and professionals when needed.

Effects of Homosexuality on Children

The studies reported in the previous sections provide no evidence to suggest that psychological development among children of gay men or lesbians is compromised in any respect relative to that of offspring of heterosexual parents. These results led Patterson (1992), who reviewed numerous studies, to conclude that despite long-standing legal presumptions against gay and lesbian parents in many states, despite dire predictions about their children based on well-known theories of psychosocial development, and despite the accumulation of a substantial body of research investigating these issues, not a single study has found children of gay or lesbian parents to be disadvantaged in any significant respect relative to children of heterosexual parents. Indeed, the evidence to date suggests that home environments provided by gay and lesbian parents are as likely as those provided by heterosexual parents to support and enable children's psychosocial development.

Of concern, however, has been the reactions of children to first learning that a parent is gay. Most parents feel initially that children would reject them if they knew of their homosexuality.

A central issue of gay fathers is disclosure of their sexual orientation to their children. Research indicates that it is significantly more difficult for gay fathers than for lesbian mothers to acknowledge their homosexuality. Both men and women report that having children made the coming-out process more difficult. Lesbians most feared losing custody, whereas gay fathers' greatest fear was damaging their children (Bozett, 1989). Usually one of two events prompts fathers' disclosure: when parents become separated or divorced, or when the father develops an intimate relationship or partnership with another man. When children are young, the disclosure may be indirect and may occur when the father takes the children to a gay social event or when he openly shows his affection for another man. Both direct (telling) and indirect ways of disclosure are used with older children.

The responses of children to learning about parents' homosexuality range from positive with no problems, to mild reactions, to anger and confusion. Overall, parents report that their children's initial reactions are positive and constitute few if any problems. Children who are told at an earlier age have fewer difficulties than those who find out when they are adolescents or adults. Some research indicates that approximately 60 percent of the children of lesbian mothers and 21 percent of the children of gay fathers experience relationship problems with other people because of their knowledge of their parents' homosexuality, although most of the problems are not serious. An overriding fear of the children of gay fathers is what their peers will think of them if their fathers' gay identities become public knowledge. A central concern is that their peers will think of them as gay as well. Children use several controlling strategies in relation to their fathers so that they are seen by others as they want to be perceived. They may use several methods of boundary control, or they may simply not share their knowledge of their fathers' sexual orientation with others (Bigner & Bozett, 1990; Bozett, 1989).

Strommen (1990) pointed out that little research has focused on children's perceptions of homosexual identity or how they perceive that their parents' homosexuality affects them. He noted that about half of the children initially have negative or uncertain reactions to parental disclosure. Younger children, having no clear idea of what homosexuality is or its implications for personal identity, do not seem to experience the feelings of estrangement that older relatives do. A minority of these children fear "identity contamination" or being abused by others because their parents are homosexual. Some express resentment toward their parents for this social difficulty, whereas others blame society. It is not surprising, given this problem, that homosexual parents practice discretion and advise their children to do so with peers.

In summary, few studies have found any significant differences between the children of lesbian mothers and those of heterosexual mothers. The body of research supports the normality of children reared by lesbians, who do not differ from their counterparts reared by heterosexual mothers in sex-role socialization, gender identity, achievement of developmental tasks, intelligence, reaction to father absence, parental separation and divorce, and general adjustment and development (Patterson, 1992; Pennington, 1987).

Alternative Routes to Parenthood for Gays and Lesbians

Until fairly recently, more gays and lesbians became parents within the context of a heterosexual marriage or relationship than through other means. After disclosure, most left their relationships, and many lesbian mothers continued to rear their children, either alone or with same-sex partners. Now, many have chosen parenthood through a variety of alternative routes. It has been estimated that between 5,000 and 10,000 lesbians have had biological children after coming out, and hundreds more have become mothers through adoption (Flaks et al., 1995). The norm of two-parent heterosexual families is being increasingly challenged by the following alternative routes to parenthood: lesbians parenting alone through fertilization by artificial insemination by donor (AID); a gay couple hiring a surrogate mother to be fertilized by one or both partners through AID; a lesbian and a gay both becoming biological parents, through fertilization by intercourse or AID; a lesbian and her partner contracting with a gay man to parent together—the gay man not always being the biological parent (donor); and one partner from a lesbian couple and one from a gay couple conceiving, with the agreement that all four partners have equal responsibility in parenting the child. These alternative routes may sound implausible, but they are all very real, with the first alternative currently being the most common.

Little data exist on the number of children conceived by these methods and reared by their gay parents. Two recent studies by Flaks et al. (1995) and Chan et al. (1998) are exceptions. A chapter in a recent book about gay parents (Pies, 1987) raised some extremely provocative issues, including the following: who the biological parents will be; whether a surrogate mother will be used; whether the donor will be known or unknown; whether the child will know both biological parents; whether the donor or the surrogate will participate in parenting the child; how many parents the child will have; the kind of relationship the biological parent's lover will have with the child; and whether there will be a legal contract with the parenting parties.

Of course, there are no norms and few role models to assist in making these decisions. For lesbians, deciding whether to use a known or an unknown donor seems to be the most difficult initial task, and this decision is complicated by the growing concern about the transmission of acquired immune deficiency syndrome (AIDS) through donor sperm (Pies, 1987).

Even after initial decisions regarding the conception, pregnancy, and birthing have been made, more difficult ones remain. What inherent right do children have to know their biological parents? With unknown donors as biological fathers, children will never be able to exercise that right. How will children perceive the lover in relationship to the parenting role? Because gays have biologically asymmetrical relationships with children, the co-parenting relationship can become strained.

Clearly there are many questions and few answers surrounding these alternative approaches. The choices made now will have a long-term impact on children's lives, but it will be years before researchers are able to determine just what that impact will be.

Gay Adoption and Foster Care

When seeking to adopt or to become foster parents, most gays and lesbians make no mention of their sexual preference. It was not until 1979 that it was reported that an openly gay couple had adopted an infant. However, hundreds of gays and lesbians have adopted and have been licensed as foster parents without their sexual orientations being public.

All states allow adoption by unmarried persons, but few states explicitly regulate the ability of homosexuals to become foster or adoptive parents. A sizable number of states at the present time continue to have antisodomy laws on the books, and licensing of openly gay foster and adoptive parents is unlikely in these states. Even when openly homosexual men and women succeed in adopting, with few exceptions they must do so as single individuals, even if they are in couples and even if their partners are co-parenting on an equal basis. Havemann (1997) reported that a handful of states allow gay couples to adopt in a complex and expensive two-step process, in which first one parent is allowed to adopt and then the second can petition for joint rights.

Often, when gays or lesbians are approved as adoptive or foster parents, they are awarded only difficult-to-place children, older children, those who have been severely abused or neglected, or those who have serious emotional or physical disabilities. In a number of cities, social-service agencies are encouraging the placement of babies and children with AIDS to gay or lesbian parents and are beginning to view lesbian and gay homes as appropriate foster-care placements for homosexually identified youth (Ricketts & Achtenberg, 1990). In 1997 New Jersey became the first state in the nation to allow gay partners to jointly adopt children on the same basis as married couples. The new policy resulted from a settlement of a class-action lawsuit brought by a gay couple who sought to adopt a child from the state's foster-care program. They had been caring for the child, who was 2 years old, since he was 3 months of age. The child, at birth, had been addicted to cocaine and exposed to HIV (Havemann, 1997).

Screening out gay men as prospective adoptive or foster parents has been partly based on the fear of child molestation. Yet this fear has not been substantiated by research. Rather, national police data confirm that more than 90 percent of all sexual abuse to minors involves an adult male and a female child—a heterosexual crime rather than a homosexual one.

Support for Gay and Lesbian Parents

Since many homosexuals have undergone years of turmoil relating to the negative sanctions of the family and the larger society, socialization as a heterosexual when feelings and desires were homosexual, the need to "come out of the closet," and other problems relating to this sexual orientation, extensive counseling and/or psychotherapy may be needed. Obviously, support groups of gay fathers and lesbian mothers would be helpful as a means of exploring common problems and solutions, and a number of these exist today.

Changes in society and its institutions are needed to provide support for individuals engaging in this lifestyle rather than trying to stamp out homosexuality through intervention programs. It appears that these programs promote a negative identity related to homosexuality rather than a positive one and, in addition, have a high rate of failure. Intervention programs communicate that homosexuals are sick and ought to be cured. The failure, then, compounds the damage by implying that the individual is sick and cannot get better despite all that has been done.

It has been suggested that social systems must provide support and facilitate the development of a gay identity and lifestyle by informing children about the existence of this sexual orientation and providing opportunities for children to observe competent gay models. Exploring this as an optional lifestyle should help young people grow up with a greater openness and sense of freedom to be whoever they are.

It is likely, then, that this lifestyle will become more visible to the lay public, and greater numbers of professionals will be called upon to render services to these families. Gay parents are a unique group, with a special identity and special needs. They need assistance with parenting, self-disclosure, handling stigma, and with formation and maintenance of the family unit. Ricketts and Achtenberg (1990) recommended that human-services workers be educated about lesbian and gay families and that agencies and groups that work with foster children modernize their understanding of the children they serve. They noted the need for further research to show that children who have gay or lesbian parents are not adversely affected—particularly, there is a need for longitudinal studies and those that address specifically adoptive and foster children.

In conclusion, gay parents seem to be more similar to than different from other single parents and/or stepparents, and their children resemble children from heterosexual single-parent and stepparent families. Though being gay is incompatible with traditional marriage, it does not seem to be incompatible with parenting. In fact, gay fathers and mothers, especially those who have resolved their identity problems, seem to be very concerned and involved with their children. Clearly this population of families is difficult to study, and most sample sizes are small and not random. Much more research needs to be conducted.

SUMMARY

Lifestyle variations that depart from the traditional stereotype include dual-career and dual-earner families, cohabiting families, and homosexual families. Dual-earner families constitute the largest percentage of this group and, when combined with dual-career families, outnumber single-career families with children. Even so, the societal stigma of mothers working, especially when their children are young, has not been overcome entirely. Both mothers and fathers in dual-career families may feel guilty about spending too little time with their children. In any case, they face work/family conflicts as they combine their family and professional roles. However, there is little evidence to support the notion that maternal employment is, in and of itself, detrimental to children.

Cohabitation, at least openly, is one of the most recent and rapidly increasing lifestyles. Since many cohabiting couples with children present in the home become legally married, this lifestyle often is temporary. Research on cohabitation and its effects on children is severely limited. However, it is believed that parental serial relationships may have detrimental effects, and in some cases the losses children experience as a result of the breakup of these relationships may be similar to the effects of divorce. Readjustments to parents' new lovers may be similar to readjustments in blended families.

Gay and lesbian parents and their children experience considerable stigma and discrimination. The gay rights movement has reduced discrimination to some extent, and more and more gay parents are obtaining custody of children and are producing children in a variety of nontraditional ways. Homosexual parents without a live-in lover are similar to single parents with custody. They experience, however, not only the same problems as other single parents but also the problems associated with being gay. Likewise, gay parents with live-in lovers experience problems similar to those in blended families, plus the problems of being gay.

Little research has been conducted on children in gay and lesbian families. Existing studies have used small samples, most often restricted to a particular geographic area. Therefore, few generalizations can be made. However, the evidence to date suggests that children reared by homosexual parents are little different from children reared by heterosexual parents and are no more likely than other children to become gay or lesbian themselves.

REFERENCES

ALDOUS, J., MULLIGAN, G., & BJARNASON, T. (1998). Fathering over time: What makes the difference? *Journal of Marriage and the Family, 60,* 809–820.

ALLEN, S., & HAWKINS, A. (1999). Maternal gatekeeping: Mother's beliefs and behaviors that inhibit greater father involvement in family work. *Journal of Marriage and the Family, 61,* 199–212.

ALPERT, H. (1988). *We are everywhere: Writings by and about lesbian parents.* Freedom, CA: Crossing Press.

BAPTISTE, D. (1987). Psychotherapy with gay/lesbian couples and their children in "stepfamilies": A challenge for marriage and family therapists. In E. Coleman (Ed.), *Integrated identity for gay men and lesbians: Psychotherapeutic approaches for emotional well-being* (pp. 223–238). New York: Harrington Park.

BARRETT, R., & ROBINSON, B. (1990). *Gay fathers.* Lexington, MA: Lexington Books.

BENIN, M., & EDWARDS, D. (1990). Adolescents' chores: The differences between dual- and single-earner families. *Journal of Marriage and the Family, 52*(2), 361–373.

BERRY, J., & RAO, J. (1997). Balancing employment and fatherhood. *Journal of Family Issues, 18*(4), 386–402.

BIGNER, J., & BOZETT, F. (1990). Parenting by gay fathers. In F. Bozett & M. Sussman (Eds.), *Homosexuality and family relations* (pp. 155–175). New York: Harrington Park.

BIGNER, J., & JACOBSEN, R. (1989). The value of children to gay and heterosexual fathers. In F. Bozett (Ed.), *Homosexuality and the family* (pp. 163–172). New York: Harrington Park.

BLAIN, J. (1994). Discourses of agency and domestic labor: Family discourse and gendered practice in dual-earner families. *Journal of Family Issues, 15*(4), 515–549.

BLUMENFELD, W., & RAYMOND, D. (1988). *Looking at gay and lesbian life.* New York: Philosophical Library.

BOORSTEIN, M. (1999, September 3). Survey: Divorce more likely when couples live together. *The Tuscaloosa News,* A p. 1.

BOZETT, F. (1987). Gay fathers. In F. Bozett (Ed.), *Gay and lesbian parents* (pp. 3–19). New York: Praeger.

BOZETT, F. (1989). Gay fathers: A review of the literature. In F. Bozett (Ed.), *Homosexuality and the family* (pp. 137–162). New York: Harrington Park.

BOZETT, F., & SUSSMAN, M. (1990). *Homosexuality and family relations.* New York: Harrington Park.

BRANNEN, J. (1992). Money, marriage and motherhood: Dual earner households after maternity leave. In S. Arber & N. Gilbert (Eds.), *Women and working lives* (pp. 54–70). Houndsmills, England: Macmillan.

BROWN, S., & BOOTH, A. (1996). Cohabitation versus marriage: A comparison of relationship quality. *Journal of Marriage and the Family, 58,* 668–678.

BRYANT, W., & ZICK, C. (1996). An examination of parent-child shared time. *Journal of Marriage and the Family, 58,* 227–237.

BUMPASS, L., SWEET, J., & CHERLIN, A. (1991). The role of cohabitation in declining rates of marriage. *Journal of Marriage and the Family, 53*(4), 913–927.

CAMERON, P., & CAMERON, K. (1996). Homosexual parents. *Adolescence, 31*(124), 757–776.

CHAN, R., RABOY, B., & PATTERSON, C. (1998). Psychosocial adjustment among children conceived via donor insemination by lesbian and heterosexual mothers. *Child Development, 69*(2), 443–457.

CLARK, R., HYDE, J., ESSEX, M., & KLEIN, M. (1997). Length of maternity leave and quality of mother-infant interactions. *Child Development, 68*(2), 364–383.

COHEN, D. (1993, September 15). Stress balancing work and family more likely felt at home, study finds. *Education Week,* p. 10.

COLEMAN, E. (1990). The married lesbian. In F. Bozett & M. Sussman (Eds.), *Homosexuality and family relations* (pp. 119–135). New York: Harrington Park.

DARLING-FISHER, C., & TIEDJE, L. (1990). The impact of maternal employment characteristics on fathers' participation in child care. *Family Relations, 39*(1), 20–26.

DEMEIS, D., & PERKINS, H. (1996). "Supermoms" of the nineties. *Journal of Family Issues, 17*(6), 777–792.

DILAPI, E. (1989). Lesbian mothers and the motherhood hierarchy. In F. Bozett (Ed.), *Homosexuality and the family* (pp. 101–121). New York: Harrington Park.

FLAKS, D., FICHER, I., MASTERPASQUA, F., & JOSEPH, G. (1995). Lesbians choosing motherhood: A comparative study of lesbian and heterosexual parents and their children. *Developmental Psychology, 31*(1), 105–114.

GAGER, C. (1998). The role of valued outcomes, justifications, and comparison referents in perceptions of fairness among dual-earner couples. *Journal of Family Issues, 19*(5), 622–648.

GLASS, J. (1998). Gender liberation, economic squeeze, or fear of strangers: Why fathers provide infant care in dual earner families. *Journal of Marriage and the Family, 60,* 821–834.

GLASS, J., & ESTES, S. (1996). Workplace support, child care, and turn over intentions among employed mothers of infants. *Journal of Family Issues, 17*(3), 317–335.

GOTTMAN, J. (1990). Children of gay and lesbian parents. In F. Bozett & M. Sussman (Eds.), *Homosexuality and family relations* (pp. 177–196). New York: Harrington Park.

GREEN, R., MANDEL, J., HOTVEDT, M., GRAY, J., & SMITH, L. (1986). Lesbian mothers and their children: A comparison with solo parent heterosexual mothers and their children. *Archives of Sexual Behavior, 7,* 175–181.

GREENBERGER, E., & O'NEIL, R. (1990). Parents' concerns about their child's development: Implications for fathers' and mothers' well-being and attitudes toward work. *Journal of Marriage and the Family, 52*(3), 621–635.

GREENSTEIN, T. (1996). Husbands' participation in domestic labor: Interactive effects of wives' and husbands' gender ideologies. *Journal of Marriage and the Family, 58,* 585–595.

GUELZOW, M., BIRD, G., & KOBALL, E. (1991). An exploratory path analysis of the stress process for dual-career men and women. *Journal of Marriage and the Family, 53*(1), 151–164.

HANSON, S., & OOMS, T. (1991). The economic costs and rewards of two-earner, two-parent families. *Journal of Marriage and the Family, 53*(3), 622–634.

HARRIS, M., & TURNER, P. (1986). Gay and lesbian parents. *Journal of Homosexuality, 12*(2), 101–113.

HAVEMANN, J. (1997, December 18). Gays, singles win joint adoption rights. *Albuquerque Journal,* p. A12.

HAWKINS, A., & ROBERTS, T. (1992). Designing a primary intervention to help dual-earner couples share housework and child care. *Family Relations, 41*(2), 169–177.

HEATH, T. (1994). The impact of delayed fatherhood on the father-child relationship. *Journal of Genetic Psychology, 155*(4), 511–531.

HERRING, C., & WILSON-SADBERRY, K. (1993). Preference or necessity? Changing work roles of black and white women, 1973–1990. *Journal of Marriage and the Family, 55*(2), 314–325.

HILTON, J., ESSA, E., & MURRAY, C. (1991). Nonphysical care of children in single-parent, one-earner, and two-earner households. *Family Perspective, 25*(1), 41–55.

HOCHSCHILD, A. (1989). *The second shift.* New York: Avon Books.

HORWITZ, A., & WHITE, H. (1998). The relationship of cohabitation and mental health: A study of a young adult cohort. *Journal of Marriage and the Family, 60,* 505–514.

HUGGINS, S. (1989). A comparison study of self-esteem of adolescent children of divorced lesbian mothers and divorced heterosexual mothers. In F. Bozett (Ed.), *Homosexuality and the family* (pp. 123–135). New York: Harrington Park.

IZRAELI, D. (1989). Burning out in medicine: A comparison of husbands and wives in dual-career couples. In E. Goldsmith (Ed.), *Work and family: Theory, research, and applications* (pp. 329–346). Newbury Park, CA: Sage.

JOESCH, J. (1997). Paid leave and the timing of women's employment before and after birth. *Journal of Marriage and the Family, 59,* 1008–1021.

JOYCE, A. (1999, February 28). Women gaining at work, book says. *Albuquerque Journal,* p. I1.

Juggling act: The joys of parenthood. (1999, February 14). *The Tuscaloosa News,* p. E1.

KLEIMAN, C. (1999, March 20). Equality in housework inches ahead, but it's a chore. *Albuquerque Journal,* p. B1.

KLUWER, E., HEESINK, J., & VAN DE VLIERT, E. (1996). Marital conflict about the division of household labor and paid work. *Journal of Marriage and the Family, 58,* 958–969.

KLUWER, E., HEESINK, J., & VAN DE VLIERT, E. (1997). The marital dynamics of conflict over the division of labor. *Journal of Marriage and the Family, 59,* 635–653.

THE LAW'S RULES. (1993, August 15). *The Tuscaloosa News,* p. E5.

MACEWEN, K., & BARLING, J. (1991). Effects of maternal employment experiences on children's behavior via mood, cognitive difficulties, and parenting behavior. *Journal of Marriage and the Family, 53* (3), 635–644.

Man wins paternal leave case. (1999, February 3). *The Tuscaloosa News,* p. A10.

MANNING, W., & LANSDALE, N. (1996). Racial and ethnic differences in the role of cohabitation in premarital childbearing. *Journal of Marriage and the Family, 58,* 63–77.

MANNING, W., & LICHTER, D. (1996). Parental cohabitation and children's economic well-being. *Journal of Marriage and the Family, 58,* 998–1010.

MCCANDLISH, B. (1987). Against all odds: Lesbian mother and family dynamics. In F. Bozett (Ed.), *Gay and lesbian parents* (pp. 23–36). New York: Praeger.

MENAGHAN, E., & PARCEL, T. (1991). Parental employment and family life: Research in the 1980s. In A. Booth (Ed.), *Contemporary families: Looking forward, looking back* (pp. 361–380). Minneapolis: National Council on Family Relations.

MORIN, S., & SCHULTZ, S. (1978). The gay movement and the rights of children. *Journal of Social Issues, 34*(2), 137–147.

OROPESA, R. (1996). Normative beliefs about marriage and cohabitation: A comparison of non-Latino whites, Mexican Americans, and Puerto Ricans. *Journal of Marriage and the Family, 58,* 49–62.

PATTERSON, C. (1992). Children of lesbian and gay parents. *Child Development, 63,* 1025–1042.

PAUL, J. (1986). *Growing up with a gay, lesbian, or bisexual parent: An exploratory study of experiences and perceptions.* Unpublished doctoral dissertation, University of California at Berkeley.

PAULSON, S. (1996). Maternal employment and adolescent achievement revisited. *Family Relations, 45,* 201–208.

PENNINGTON, S. (1987). Children of lesbian mothers. In F. Bozett (Ed.), *Gay and lesbian parents* (pp. 58–74.) New York: Praeger.

PIES, C. (1987). Considering parenthood: Psychosocial issues for gay men and lesbians choosing alternative fertilization. In F. Bozett (Ed.), *Gay and lesbian parents* (pp. 165–174). New York: Praeger.

PIES, C. (1990). Lesbians and the choice to parent. In F. Bozett & M. Sussman (Eds.), *Homosexuality and family relations* (pp. 137–154). New York: Harrington Park.

PILLER, C. (1998, September 20). For women, interest low in high-tech occupation. *Orlando Sentinel,* p. G1.

PITTMAN, J., SOLHEIM, C., & BLANCHARD, D. (1996). Stress as a driver of the allocation of housework. *Journal of Marriage and the Family, 58,* 456–468.

RANSON, G. (1998). Education, work and family decision making: Finding the "right time" to have a baby. *Canadian Review of Sociology & Anthropology, 35*(4), 517–534.

RAPOPORT, R., & RAPOPORT, R. N. (1976). *Dual-career families re-examined.* New York: Harper & Row.

RICKETTS, W., & ACHTENBERG, R. (1990). Adoption and foster parenting for lesbians and gay men: Creating new traditions in family. In F. Bozett & M. Sussman (Eds.), *Homosexuality and family relations* (pp. 83–118). New York: Harrington Park.

ROGERS, S. (1996). Mothers' work hours and marital quality: Variations by family structure and family size. *Journal of Marriage and the Family, 58,* 606–617.

SCHNITTGER, M., & BIRD, G. (1990). Coping among dual-career men and women across the family life cycle. *Family Relations, 39*(2), 199–205.

SCHOEN, R., & WEINICK, R. (1993). Partner choice in marriages and cohabitation. *Journal of Marriage and the Family, 55*(2), 408–414.

SELIGMANN, J. (1990). Variations on a theme. *Newsweek* (Special Issue: "The 21st Century Family," Winter/Spring 1990), pp. 38–46.

SEYLER, D., MONROE, P., & GARAND, J. (1995). Balancing work and family. *Journal of Family Issues, 16*(2), 170–193.

SPITZE, G. (1991). Women's employment and family relations. In A. Booth (Ed.), *Contemporary families: Looking forward, looking back* (pp. 381–404). Minneapolis: National Council on Family Relations.

STROMMEN, E. (1989). "You're a what?": Family members reactions to the disclosure of homosexuality. In F. Bozett (Ed.), *Homosexuality and the family* (pp. 37–58). New York: Harrington Park.

STROMMEN, E. (1990). Hidden branches and growing pains: Homosexuality and the family tree. In F. Bozett & M. Sussman (Eds.), *Homosexuality and family relations* (pp. 9–34). New York: Harrington Park.

SULLIVAN, O. (1997). The division of housework among "remarried" couples. *Journal of Family Issues, 18*(2), 205–223.

SURRA, C. (1990). Research and theory on mate selection and premarital relationships in the 1990s. *Journal of Marriage and the Family, 52*(4), 844–865.

SWISS, D., & WALKER, J. (1993). *Women and the work/family dilemma.* New York: John Wiley.

TAYLOR, J., & SPENCER, B. (1989). Lifestyle patterns of university women: Implications for family/career decision modeling. In E. Goldsmith (Ed.), *Work and family: Theory, research, and application* (pp. 265–277). Newbury Park, CA: Sage.

TIEDJE, L., WORTMAN, C., DOWNEY, G., EMMONS, C., BIERNAT, M., & LONG, E. (1990). Women with multiple roles: Role-compatibility perceptions, satisfaction, and mental health. *Journal of Marriage and the Family, 52*(1), 63–72.

U.S. BUREAU OF THE CENSUS. (1997). *Statistical abstract of the United States: 1997.* Washington, DC: U.S. Department of Commerce.

VOLLING, B., & BELSKY, J. (1992). Infant, father, and marital antecedents of infant-father attachment security in dual-earner and single-earner families. *International Journal of Behavioral Development, 15*(1), 84–97.

VOLLING, B., & BELSKY, J. (1993). Parent, infant, and contextual characteristics related to maternal employment decisions in the first year of infancy. *Family Relations, 42*(1), 4–12.

VOYDANOFF, P. (1989). Work and family: A review and expanded coneptualization. In E. Goldsmith (Ed.), *Work and family: Theory, research, and applications* (pp. 1–22). Newbury Park, CA: Sage.

WARREN, J., & JOHNSON, P. (1995). The impact of workplace support on work-family role strain. *Family Relations, 44,* 163–169.

WILLE, D. (1995). The 1990s: Gender differences in parenting roles. *Sex Roles, 33*(11/12), 803–817.

WILLIAMSON, D. (1998). Disclosure is a family event. *Family Relations, 47,* 23–25.

WINDLE, M., & DUMENCI, L. (1997). Parental occupational stress as predictors of depressive symptoms among dual-income couples: A multilevel modeling approach. *Journal of Marriage and the Family, 59,* 625–634.

WRIGHT, D., & YOUNG, R. (1998). The effects of family structure and maternal employment on the development of gender-related attitudes among men and women. *Journal of Family Issues, 19*(3), 300–314.

WU, Z. (1995). Premarital cohabitation and postmarital cohabiting union formation. *Journal of Family Issues, 16*(2), 212–232.

WU, Z. (1996). Childbearing in cohabitational relationships. *Journal of Marriage and the Family, 58,* 281–292.

CHAPTER 9

Parenting in High-Risk Families

Numerous factors influence the degree of risk that might be involved in parenting for any particular family or any specific group of families. Risk factors may be related to health, medical, psychological, structural, economic, developmental, or social aspects of family life, or to any combination thereof. It is probably accurate to say that some risks exist in every family situation. Many families are able to minimize the risk factors by a network of support systems, but others are unable to do so with any degree of success.

Certain groups of families attempt to function in relatively high-risk situations and are therefore in greater need of support services than other families. Three such families—those with teenage parents, abusive or neglectful parents, and homeless parents—will be discussed in this chapter. In the discussion of adolescent parents, we do not mean to imply that these family types are pathological. We do mean to emphasize, however, that optimal parenting is considerably at risk. Abusive parents, on the other hand, represent a risk situation for children and their parents that is clearly serious—and often deadly, at least for the children involved. Homeless parents with children are growing in number, and these families are at risk economically, socially, psychologically, and educationally. These three types of families have unique needs and require special kinds of support and intervention services.

ADOLESCENT PARENTS

Teenage parenthood is not a new social phenomenon, but in the last 30 years public concern has been expressed about the extent of adolescent childbearing and the problems associated with it. Adolescent sexuality, pregnancy, and parenthood have generated intense debate. Although early marriage and premarital pregnancy were of minor public concern during the baby boom era, teen pregnancy and childbearing drew little public notice. The trend became a troubling one only in the late 1960s, but by the mid-1970s it had become an urgent social crisis. Since then, it has attracted considerable attention by scholars, policymakers, and the public at large. In the 1990s, interest seemed to ebb, yet many teenagers were having babies, rearing them, and suffering the consequences of early childbearing (Furstenberg, 1991). By the late 1990s, data indicated that the rate of teen pregnancy had declined to its lowest level since 1973 (Meckler, 1999). Research and policy interest in adolescent sexual behavior, pregnancy, and parenting is important, since these behaviors are critical in the process of family formation and because their precocious timing often makes them problematic for the individual and society (Miller & Moore, 1991). A teenage pregnancy is clearly an event that has considerable personal consequences and costs for individual adolescents and their families.

The Problem

Looking at the statistics, one can hardly disagree that teenage childbearing raises serious social, economic, and health concerns. In 1980 the total number of births to teenagers was more than half a million. These numbers decreased fairly significantly by 1985, but by 1990 they had escalated again. However, by 1994 the number was approximately 50,000 less than in 1980 (see Table 9.1). Rates of births to Black and Native American teenagers were four to five times higher than to Whites (Dalla & Gamble, 1997). Asian Americans tend to have low teen birthrates, whereas Hawaiians have high rates (U.S. Bureau of the Census, 1997). Additional data have shown a 21 percent overall decrease in births to teens between 1991 and 1996 and an additional 3 percent from 1996 to 1997. Among 16-year-olds, births decreased by 30 percent during that time period, and 1997 saw a record low for births to unmarried Black women and continued decline in all out-of-wedlock births. Further, the number of teen mothers having a second child also decreased dramatically. In fact, second babies decreased 22 percent between 1991 and 1996. Although decreasing rates are positive, some advocates worry that the nation will become complacent about teen pregnancy, whereas many more prevention efforts are warranted (Meckler, 1998, 1999).

A total of 880,000 teenagers (97 out of every 1,000) became pregnant in 1996. Approximately one-third of these aborted, a decrease of 31 percent from 1986. The decrease in teen pregnancy and

TABLE 9.1 Births and Birthrates to Teenagers by Race and Age, 1980 to 1994

NUMBER OF BIRTHS	1980	1985	1990	1994
All races, total*	552,161	467,485	521,826	505,488
15–17 years	198,222	167,789	183,327	195,169
18–19 years	353,939	299,696	333,499	310,319
White	393,564	324,590	354,482	348,081
15–17 years	129,341	107,998	114,934	126,388
18–19 years	264,223	216,597	239,548	221,693
Black	147,378	130,857	151,613	140,968
15–17 years	65,069	55,656	62,881	62,563
18–19 years	82,309	75,201	88,732	78,405
Birthrates**				
All races, total*	53.0	51.0	59.9	58.9
15–17 years	32.5	31.0	37.5	37.6
18–19 years	82.1	79.6	88.6	91.5
White	45.4	43.3	50.8	56.1
15–17 years	25.5	24.4	29.5	30.7
18–19 years	73.2	70.4	78.0	82.1
Black	97.8	95.4	112.8	104.5
15–17 years	72.5	69.3	82.3	79.8
18–19 years	135.1	132.4	152.9	148.3

Source: U.S. Bureau of the Census. (1997). *Statistical abstract of the United States: 1997* (117th ed). Washington, DC: U.S. Department of Commerce.

*Includes races other than White and Black.

**Per 1,000 births.

childbirth has been attributed to a combination of reasons—more reliable contraceptives, less sexual activity, fear of AIDS, a focus on abstinence, and even a strong economy.

Estimates of total societal costs of teen parenthood range from $9 billion to $29 billion annually. The lifetime cost just to one teen has been estimated at $109,000. Teen pregnancy also serves as a marker of sexual behavior that brings a substantial risk of contracting AIDS and other sexually transmitted diseases (Allen, Philliber, Herrling, & Kuperminc, 1997).

Although adoption may be an option for unmarried adolescents who are unwilling or unable to care for their babies, few who carry their babies to term enter into an adoption plan or arrange for their babies to be cared for by relatives or friends.

An increasing percentage of teens are choosing not to marry to resolve their pregnancies. These young women, then, are keeping their babies and rearing them with or without the help of mates or their parents and with whatever support services they can secure (Donnelly & Voydanoff, 1991; Furstenberg, 1991).

Factors Associated with Adolescent Pregnancy

Miller and Moore (1991) presented an extensive review of the literature on teenage pregnancy and parenthood. They found the factors listed in the Highlights to be associated with the incidence of teenage fertility. Clearly, multiple factors interact in complex ways to explain the high rates of teen pregnancy.

Factors Associated with Teenage Fertility

Lowered age of reproductive maturation

Social extension of the adolescent stage of development

Changing attitudes toward sexuality

Early initiation of and increased sexual activity

Failure to use contraceptives

Social factors

Parent-adolescent communication

Psychosocial factors

Outcomes

The adverse consequences of teenage childbearing to the mother, the child, and the extended family have been well documented.

Outcomes for the Teen Mother. It was concluded by a panel of the National Research Council—after reviewing hundreds of studies on the economic, educational, social, and health effects of teenage pregnancy and parenthood—that teen parents are at greater risk of social and economic disadvantage throughout their lives than those who delay childbearing until their twenties. These women are less likely to be employed, to earn high wages, or to be happily married, and they are more likely to have larger families and receive welfare (Furstenberg, 1991).

Seventy-five percent of all teen mothers are single, and at least 40,000 drop out of school each year because of pregnancy and childbirth (DeJong & Cottrell, 1999). Teen mothers account for 40 percent of all African American children living in poverty (Solomon & Liefeld, 1998). Though pregnant and parenting teens by law can continue their education, many find the burdens of parenthood coupled with the developmental tasks of adolescence and the policies imposed by schools to be too burdensome to manage. Educational and employment opportunities may be foreclosed. Repeat pregnancies and subsequent children are likely to occur. Many drop out of school, but even those who finish high school face barriers to self-sufficiency, including low wages, inadequate job skills, and difficulty obtaining child care (Chase-Lansdale, Brooks-Gunn, & Paikoff, 1991).

On the other hand, teen mothers who finish high school and seek additional schooling, education, or training, and who have a strong support system are more likely than other teen mothers to hold stable jobs and have brief or no dependency on welfare (Harris, 1991).

A large majority of adolescent mothers continue to reside with their families following the birth of their first child. In fact, the 1996 welfare reform law mandates that teens receiving benefits live with their parents and be either in school or in a job-training program. Actually, grandmothers offer the most consistent support to adolescent mothers in the form of residential, child-care, and financial aid (SmithBattle, 1996). A list of negative outcomes for the teen mother may be found in the Highlights.

Furstenberg (1991) concluded that teens derive some benefits from parenthood, but that does not mean that early childbearing is the result of a rational choice. Parenthood is frequently the result of the unanticipated and unwelcome outcome of having sex without using birth control. Many teenagers are able to salvage their lives after childbearing occurs, but most evidence leads to the conclusion that teenagers do measurably better when they delay parenthood. Few who give birth in their teens regard it as an optimal time for parenthood.

Chase-Lansdale et al. (1991) reported that many teen mothers are able to eventually move out of the cycle of poverty. However, a significant diversity of outcomes have been found. The reasons for this diversity over time were traced to different ecologies, individual characteristics, and family systems. Family systems that positively influenced teenagers' changes over time were co-residence with family of origin until completion of school or a job-training program and the formation of a new family by getting and remaining married.

Outcomes for the Child. A combination of factors can compromise the healthy birth and continued appropriate development of infants born to teen mothers. Many teen mothers live in poverty

Outcomes of Teenage Pregnancy for Mothers

MATERNAL HEALTH

Poor nutrition
Less mature reproductive system
Poor prenatal care
Improper weight gain
High incidence of toxemia
Higher risk of death

MATERNAL STRESS

School, peer group, parents—may result in alcohol and drug use, depression
Major transition to pregnancy
Poor coping mechanisms

PREMATURE DECISION MAKING

Immature cognitive skills
Narrow range of alternatives
Neglected consideration of long-term consequences
Distorted outcomes
Egocentricity
Primacy of own needs

ECONOMIC CONSEQUENCES

Low educational attainment
Low wages
Lifetime economic stress and limited opportunities

Opportunities to remain in school and to receive job training are crucial for pregnant and parenting teens.

and have other characteristics and behaviors that place their children at risk. They are likely to have poor nutritional habits and status and a lifestyle that does not produce healthy babies. Pregnant teens are less likely than older pregnant women to gain adequate weight during pregnancy or to receive prenatal care, but 1997 was a record year for early prenatal care. They are more likely to have risk conditions such as anemia and pregnancy-associated high blood pressure. Russell (1993) reported that although smoking declined, overall, for pregnant women in 1990, teen mothers had the highest rate of smoking of all pregnant women. Babies born to smoking mothers face about double the risk of low birth weight, increasing the likelihood of illness and death during infancy. Previous studies estimated that the number of infant deaths could drop by 10 percent if pregnant women did not smoke. Additional outcomes for the child may be found in the Highlights. It is important to note that the younger the mother, the poorer the outcomes for the infant.

Evidence indicates that as the children of teen mothers grow, they are at a developmental disadvantage when compared with children of older mothers. During infancy, differences are minimal, but slight problems in cognitive development emerge in the preschool years and continue into elementary school. Similarly, difficulties in socioemotional functioning appear in the preschool years, particularly in the domains of impulse control and externalizing behavior. Preschoolers of teenagers

Outcomes of Teenage Pregnancy for the Child

Increased risk for prematurity and low birth weight
Potential congenital malformations, neurological defects, perinatal mortality,
    growth failure
Less parental knowledge about child development
Punitive attitudes toward child rearing
Inappropriate social stimulation
Few options for quality care
Inadequate knowledge of support services

---

seem to be more active, aggressive, and undercontrolled than children of older mothers. In both cognitive and social development, differences are more pronounced for boys than for girls (Brooks-Gunn & Chase-Lansdale, 1991). The major disadvantages for children of teen mothers are attributed to a host of problematic conditions—low socioeconomic status, limited educational attainment, high family instability, disadvantaged neighborhoods, and poor-quality schools. The majority of research indicates that it is the ecological situation rather than the mother's young age per se that poses risks to child development (Chase-Lansdale et al., 1991).

Specific risk factors are associated with specific adjustment problems. Poverty and low maternal self-esteem are related to child behavior problems, whereas urban residence and low maternal educational level are related to child academic test scores. Poverty and maternal adjustment are related to how sensitive the mother is to meeting the social and emotional needs of the child and the level of communication and coercion used in disciplinary encounters. Maternal level of education influences the degree to which experiences in the home complement school experiences. Children with multiple stressors are at greatest risk for low achievement and behavior maladjustment. However, some children of teen parents fare well. Research has shown that children of adolescent parents who are successful in school and who exhibit few behavioral problems tend to have mothers who are relatively well adjusted, who finish high school, who limit further childbearing,

and who eventually become economically self-sufficient. Most of these children have experienced supportive home environments (Luster, Perlstadt, McKinney, Sims, & Juang, 1996).

Outcomes for Mothers and Sisters of Parenting Teens.

Research has documented that a first birth creates and transforms intergenerational connections (SmithBattle, 1996). Recently, a number of studies have focused on the young grandmothers who have moved into their grandparenting role as a result of their daughters' early entry into motherhood. This phenomenon will become more pronounced as a result of welfare policy. More African American teen mothers live with their mothers than do White teen mothers. Studies focusing on the psychological well-being of women who become young grandmothers have indicated that they are upset and disappointed upon learning of their adolescent daughters' pregnancies. However, despite this initial reaction, grandmothers in the African American community almost universally provide support to their daughters and grandchildren. Women in their twenties and thirties who become grandmothers find the role change to be burdensome, stressful, and in conflict with the tasks of adult midlife, which involve marriage, parenthood, productivity, and leisure. Research is needed that examines how grandmothers' employment, education, and marital status intertwine with their psychological development over time.

Studies are just emerging that examine the impact on children of child care provided by grandmothers. Research has shown both positive and detrimental effects of grandparent assistance on teen parenting, practices, and child outcomes. Positively, adolescent mothers are more likely to remain in school, to develop more skillful and less restrictive parenting practices, to provide more verbal stimulation, and to produce more securely attached infants. Other studies have shown that too little or too much grandparent assistance with child care makes it more difficult for adolescent mothers to develop responsive caregiving. Families have been categorized according to the roles that the grandmother and the adolescent mother assume— parental replacement, parental supplement, supported primary parent, and parental apprentice (SmithBattle, 1996).

A longitudinal naturalistic study (SmithBattle, 1996) found that in some families, issues of authority and control entangled family members in competition and conflict over "Whose baby is this?" That led to the grandmothers taking over infant care, with the mothers submitting, rebelling, and/or withdrawing from care. However, in other families, grandmothers provided responsive caregiving without taking over, which regarded the adolescent mothers' capabilities. They approached conflicts through dialogue, and they shared caregiving responsibilities in a highly fluid manner.

Little research has been conducted on the outcomes for sisters of childbearing adolescents, but limited research has shown that sisters of childbearing adolescents are two to six times more likely to bear children as adolescents themselves than are sisters of adolescents who do not give birth. Further, evidence has shown that younger sisters of childbearing adolescents are more sexually active and are younger at sexual onset than other girls of their same age, race, and socioeconomic status.

East (1996) examined the precursors of early childbearing among the younger sisters of adolescent mothers. Results indicated that the younger sisters of childbearing adolescents were consistently different from their counterparts whose older sisters had not borne children. They were more accepting of nonmarital adolescent childbearing, ascribed younger ages to typical life-course transitions (i.e., best age to get married, have first child), had more pessimistic school and career expectations, and were more likely to have engaged in problem behaviors (e.g., smoking cigarettes, skipping school). These characteristics were associated with a nonvirgin sexual status and with high closeness and rivalry with the childbearing sister, but they were not associated with mothers' permissiveness or lack of mother-daughter communication. Therefore, it seems that adolescent childbearing can affect the entire family.

Parenting by Adolescents

There is strong consensus in the developmental literature that children's emotional and cognitive development are enhanced by actively involved, nurturing, and responsive parenting. Adolescents who become parents face the demands of parenting concurrently with the developmental tasks of adolescence.

Leitch (1998) pointed out that the role of the adolescent in achieving developmental tasks must be reorganized to accommodate the role of parenthood. The requirements of parenthood can conflict with the characteristics and needs of adolescents. For example, body image is a common concern of adolescents, and it is likely to influence choices about breast-feeding. Other needs that conflict are the development of self-identity, seeking peer acceptance, seeking relationships with the opposite sex, and striving for independence. These conflicts must be considered when designing programs for pregnant and parenting teens.

The early research on adolescent parenting reported teen mothers to be less aware of and less knowledgeable about infants' and children's developmental milestones, less sensitive to infant signals and needs, less aware of how to stimulate children's development, less inclined to spontaneous play, and less likely to spend time looking at and talking to their infants, while being more ambivalent toward motherhood and more prone to use physical punishment. However, it became evident that when adolescents are compared with older mothers, the age of the parent is almost unavoidably confounded with other variables, especially education and economic resources. Diversity in parenting behavior and multiple trajectories in the life courses of adolescent mothers are central themes reported in the long-term longitudinal follow-up of adolescent mothers who are now in midlife (Miller & Moore, 1991).

Some researchers argue that environmental and family factors associated with young parenthood may influence parenting more than the age of the mother. Adolescent mothers are often at risk for distress, which makes it difficult to provide nurturant, stimulating care. Other researchers have suggested that an integrated model of parenting that incorporates the unique circumstances of young parents, including familial, maternal, and child factors, affects the parenting a child receives. Maternal characteristics include learning ability, cognitive readiness for parenting, psychosocial adjustment, maternal health, and the social context in which the parent-child relationship is embedded (Whiteside-Mansell, Pope, & Bradley, 1996). Leitch (1998) concluded that teen pregnancy is a multifaceted problem that requires clinicians and researchers alike to draw upon multifaceted strategies in their approaches.

Whiteside-Mansell et al. (1996) attempted to determine whether there were identifiable patterns of parenting among a sample of young mothers 15 to 24 years of age. Results showed that maternal IQ was a significant discriminating factor among the mothers, with higher maternal IQ associated with more positive parenting behavior. Among mothers with low IQs, birth of additional children was associated with less than optimal parenting. On average, scores of the young mothers in this study on the HOME inventory, an instrument that measures the quality of the home environment, were lower than scores for mothers older than 25. The patterns of parenting were related to children's cognitive and social development in the expected ways, with children of mothers with the most positive parenting behaviors having higher scores on both cognitive and social measures. Although none of the groups of mothers exhibited high-quality care, those who exhibited adequate behaviors in acceptance, responsivity, and involvement had the lowest percentage of maternal, familial, and child risk factors.

Maternal age had only a weak negative relationship with the quality of the home environment, and living with the family of origin was not a protective factor for parenting behavior. The mothers with the highest quality of parenting behavior usually were not living in poverty, but poverty was not always associated with low-quality parenting behavior. The researchers concluded that parenting is dynamic. Target families should be screened to determine risk status, and intervention must include an approach that focuses both on stress reduction and on competent development.

Peeples (1994) asked a group of teenage mothers in a YWCA (Young Women's Christian Association) support program what they wanted to tell their peers about being mothers. Parental stress was a common thread. These teen mothers indicated that stress occurs when they do not have money, adequate housing, child care, and medical care. It occurs from encountering school and employer prejudice against teen mothers, uncertainty about child discipline, concern for their children's future, problems between themselves and their families, and a desire to continue their education. Some want the father to be involved with the child. Most worried about outside influences on their children that they cannot always control—gangs, drugs, and alcohol.

Barratt, Roach, Morgan, and Colbert (1996) investigated adjustment to motherhood by single adolescent mothers. Adolescent mothers were compared with adolescent nonmothers, single adult mothers, and married adult mothers. Results showed that adolescent mothers scored significantly higher than adolescent nonmothers on the personal-enjoyment scale, but they did not differ significantly in personal enjoyment from single or married adult mothers. On measures of mental health, adolescent mothers did not differ significantly from adolescent nonmothers or single adult mothers, but adolescent mothers had higher scores on the interpersonal sensitivity, phobic anxiety, and paranoid ideation subscales. Comparisons on the well-being scale revealed significantly higher scores for adolescent mothers than for adolescent nonmothers, but adolescent mothers' scores were significantly lower than those for married adult mothers.

Results also showed a significantly positive relationship between the mental-health status of adolescent mothers and the amount of assistance they received in caregiving. Findings suggested that motherhood may represent an important contributor to White adolescent mothers' self-identity and enjoyment of life. Further, maternal age alone does not appear to be a significant contributor to psychological adjustment. These researchers concluded that single marital status and poor psychological adjustment might be critical screening variables for identifying mothers in greatest need of assistance.

Factors relating to parenting competence among Navajo teenage mothers were explored by Dalla and Gamble (1997) in two studies. An examination of Navajo myths, cultural symbols, and practices suggests that motherhood per se is highly valued within the culture, and female fertility often is celebrated through a 4-day sacred ceremony, the Kinanlda. Results of the first study indicated that self-esteem and school functioning were highly and significantly related to perceived competence, and school functioning was marginally and negatively associated with role restriction. Surprisingly, child risk factors had low association with each of the predicted parenting variables. Women who reported feeling more positive about themselves also reported experiencing fewer problems in the academic context. Women reporting greater support from network members also indicated more positive relationships with male partners.

In the second study, one group of mothers reported a high degree of identification with the maternal role, and these mothers were intensely committed to that role and to their children. The other group of mothers described a clear lack of child-rearing involvement or responsibility. Instead, they relied on their own mothers for the daily care and rearing of their children. Most mothers reported being committed to their partners, the fa-

thers of their children, for an extended period of time before becoming pregnant, but half reported being in the process of separating from their long-term partners, mostly because of the partners' use of alcohol, inability to find employment, or lack of support. Most mothers reported extensive support from family members. Only mothers highly committed to the maternal role reported being influenced in their parenting attitudes and behaviors by traditional knowledge. These two studies found extreme diversity among the young mothers. Personal resources, such as self-esteem and the mothers' perceptions of their role as mother and attitude toward children, emerged as significant predictors of competent parenting behavior.

Barratt (1991) identified factors contributing to competent parenting by adolescent mothers and optimal outcomes for their school-age children. Results of his work indicated that the mother's level of education, her intelligence, and her observed involvement with her child were positively associated with the provision of reading and enrichment activities for her child. More contact with the father (or father figure) was associated with the provision of more reading and enrichment activities.

Mothers with numerous children were less involved and more punitive than those who had only one child. Further, children's math and reading achievement and overall scholastic aptitude were associated with a higher level of education on the part of the mothers' mothers and with levels of maternal intelligence. The three background factors as a set (mother's age at child's birth, mother's education, mother's intelligence) enabled significant prediction of each of the child-outcome assessments—math, reading, and scholastic aptitude. In addition, the set of factors evolving since birth (number of children, mother's education level, household poverty, marital status, mother's employment, contact with father) significantly predicted math achievement and scholastic aptitude performance.

Stern and Alvarez (1992) found that adolescent mothers who had received parent education had more knowledge of child development and were more realistic in their developmental-milestone expectations of their children than were pregnant and nonpregnant teens who had not received these services. These researchers also found that pregnant and parenting adolescents who reported the use of self-blame and avoidance as coping strategies held more negative attitudes toward caretaking. Adolescents with poorer self-image adjustment also were found to express more difficulties associated with caretaking.

Luster et al. (1996) examined factors associated with the quality of home environment for 1-year-old infants of teen mothers who were involved in the Family TIES Support Program. Half of the mothers received more intensive support through weekly home visits by paraprofessional family advocates, whereas the other half received the regular TIES program. Results indicated that mothers who received weekly home visits had higher scores on

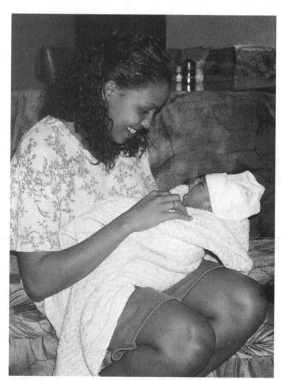

Teen mothers with knowledge of child development and parent education are more realistic in their expectations of children.

the HOME inventory than those in the comparison group. Further, data showed that teen mothers who provided relatively supportive environments for their infants were less depressed and more empathic, received more support from the fathers of their babies, and lived in safer neighborhoods. Their infants were heavier at birth and less irritable at 12 months.

Research has focused on the sources of support. Findings indicate that husbands of adolescent mothers may be important sources of support for teen parents. Yet many teen mothers are not married. Kin are a major source of both tangible and instrumental support for teen mothers. Friends, community agencies, and school personnel may be at various times influential sources of support, especially for the unmarried young mother.

Other research has focused on the types of support. Some evidence has indicated that the most effective type of support may be dependent on the needs created by stressors experienced by teen mothers. Certain types of stress create a need for emotional support, whereas other stressors create a need for instrumental or financial support. For example, problem-solving assistance has been found to be helpful for adolescent mothers facing financial and child-centered problems.

Kin networks clearly extend beyond the immediate nuclear family, and they can improve the quality of life for some young mothers. More than one-third of all working mothers turn to kin for assistance in low-cost child care and income support. For a small majority, financial assistance from others (seemingly kin) also covers half or more of all living expenses. For both child care and income support, those most in need, the currently unmarried, receive the greatest benefits. However, Parish, Hao, and Hogan (1991) concluded that the deficits of early motherhood, particularly unwed motherhood among teenage children, remain difficult to overcome. Some academicians as well as policymakers in recent years have implied that family networks provide alternatives to direct government support and intervention. The findings from their research suggest that kin networks, valuable as they may be, are a thin reed on which to build any program for the long-term problems of early motherhood. Much of the help by kin depends on these kin themselves, male and female, being employed and having the income to provide occasional cash assistance.

Nath, Borkowski, Whitman, and Schellenbach (1991) noted that the amount of support required, or even desired, may vary according to the individual characteristics of the mothers. Many young mothers derive considerable support from their social networks, but evidence also indicates that interference is experienced from the same networks. Negative input has been found in the areas of child rearing and emotional/personal concerns. Kin networks also have been found to have limitations. A rapid thinning of the kin network occurs in women's early twenties as they establish households separate from their own parents and other nearby kin. The consequences are the most severe for child care, but to some extent for income support as well. Distance continues to inhibit much in-kind aid and many cash flows.

Social support plays a critical role in shaping the life of teen mothers. In developing intervention programs, it is important that a lifespan perspective be taken in evaluating the teen mother's social-support needs. This suggests that the amount and kind of support for most adolescent mothers typically change over time and must be taken into account. In addition, the individual characteristics of teen mothers should be dynamically reflected in the planning process (Nath et al., 1991).

Teenage Fathers

The National Survey of Adolescent Males estimated that the prevalence of teen fatherhood was 2 percent for White males, 5 percent for African American males, and 2 percent for Hispanic males. Probably the percentages are higher; some experts estimate 5 percent for Hispanic males and 11 percent to 15 percent for African American males (Thornberry, Smith, & Howard, 1997). Using data from the Rochester Youth Development study, Thornberry et al. (1997) identified the risk factors of teen fatherhood. Data indicated that seven out of the 615 young, urban men in the study became fathers at age 15, and from that point on, the rate increased steadily until it reached 28 percent by age 19. Thus, slightly over a quarter of the young men in this study became teen fathers. Significant correlations between potential risk factors for teen fatherhood were found for minority status (41 percent of Hispanic males and 31 percent of African American males, as opposed to 8 percent of White males): neighborhoods characterized by poverty, female-headed families, high arrest rates, and social disorganization. Further, certain family characteristics were found to be significant—growing up in lower-class families; parents who themselves were teen parents; low levels of support from parents and friends; low achievement in school and parents who did not expect them to attend college; early sexual activity; and frequent involvement in drug use, general delinquency, and violence. As the number of risk factors increased, the probability of becoming a teenage father increased exponentially. One risk factor led to 2 percent becoming teen fathers; two risk factors led to 6 percent; and four risk factors led to 12 percent. After that point, the risks of teen fatherhood virtually exploded, with almost one-third of those with five risk factors and about half with six or more risk factors becoming teen fathers.

Despite the increased emphasis on the needs of unmarried pregnant adolescent females, adolescent fathers have received less than adequate attention (Kiselica & Sturmer, 1993; Robinson, 1988). Most people believe that teenage fathers' first impulse is to walk away from their parental responsibilities. In the popular media, they are likely to be pictured as self-centered "ne'er-do-wells," the "macho" type interested only in sexual gratification, who have fleeting, casual relationships with their girlfriends and leave town at the first hint of pregnancy. This perception of teenage fathers is at odds with the present cultural expectation that fathers accept the responsibilities of emotionally and financially supporting their children. Findings from recent research on teen fathers has challenged such stereotypical views of this population. In a study reported by Kiselica and Sturmer

(1993), most teen fathers in that sample planned to provide financial support, sustain contact with the mother, and develop a relationship with the baby.

Allen and Doherty (1996) interviewed a small sample of African American teen fathers to ascertain what being a father meant to them. They found a positive correlation between partner relationship and paternal involvement. The fathers were especially influenced by childhood memories of their own fathers and, to a lesser degree, other male relatives or father figures. Most felt that they were better fathers than their own fathers. The significant aspects of fatherhood included "being there" at the births of their children and being actively involved in the lives of the children after birth. Further, these young men saw fathers as very important to families and perceived themselves as the primary disciplinarians of their children in the future. Many obstacles to their involvement emerged: strained relationships with the mother, nonsupport by family and friends, and hindrances posed by social institutions (schools, hospitals, social-service agencies).

In reality, many young men experience the same emotional confusion and struggles that young mothers do. Most have had relationships with their girlfriends for more than a year and report feelings of affection and love. Most often they are not consulted when decisions are made about their babies—decisions usually made by the mother and her parents (Nath et al., 1991).

Some research has focused on the concerns expressed by adolescent fathers and their perceived needs. Hendricks (1988) found that the teen fathers he studied tended to worry about their financial responsibilities, competence as parents, and relationships with the mothers of their children. He discovered that they had diverse needs, including information, practical help, and counseling. The majority of the teen fathers indicated an interest in receiving preparation for fatherhood, including training in the responsibilities of being a young father and child-care training. Ketterlinus, Lamb, and Nitz (1991) found that the most common concerns of White adolescent fathers involved vocational/educational issues, interpersonal relationships,

health, and future parenting abilities. Overall, these studies show that adolescent males express many concerns about fatherhood.

Pirog-Good (1996), using data from the National Longitudinal Survey of Labor Market Participation, examined the educational and labor market outcomes of adolescent fathers. School satisfaction for White teen fathers, was significantly lower than that for other White males, but this difference did not hold between Black teen fathers and non-fathers. However, teen fathers were disillusioned with school before the birth of their first children and became even more dissatisfied after becoming parents. Teen fathers had acquired less education and expected to complete fewer years of education than their nonfather counterparts.

Teen fathers were significantly more likely to indicate a willingness to enter job training, to apply for food stamps, and to shoplift than their counterparts, but willingness to work did not differ between the two groups. Teen fathers earned more per hour than other males below the age of 21, but by the time they were in their early twenties, no difference in wages existed. By the time they were 27 years of age, they earned significantly less than those males who had children after age 20. The same pattern emerged for annual income.

The researcher concluded that the educational disadvantages of teen fathers should not be minimized, because these deficiencies are likely to lead to fewer and less lucrative opportunities in the labor market in adulthood, reducing the ability of these men to support themselves and their children. Family-background variables—educational attainment of parents and the availability of cultural capital in the home—were significant predictors of high school completion.

Pirog-Good (1996) also examined family background and attitudes of teen fathers. She found that White, but not Black, teen fathers had an external locus of control—the belief that one's future is controlled externally. This belief may hinder White teen fathers from being involved in the lives of their children or from paying child support. She further found that self-esteem of

Black teens was unrelated to whether they had fathered children, but becoming teen fathers initially improved self-esteem in Whites. However, these improvements were no longer evident 7 years later.

Some recent research suggests that teen fathers are more willing to be involved in the lives of their offspring than most scholars suspect, especially if they can provide economic support (Hawkins, 1992). The degree to which teen fathers are involved after the births of their babies seems to be related not only to whether they can contribute economically but to other factors as well. For example, fathers with employment experience interacted more and fathers from minority groups had higher rates of paternal involvement than did White fathers (Danziger & Radin, 1990).

It is obvious from the research that there are significant differences in the attitudes of teenage fathers and the degree to which they function as parents. Clearly they can provide effective support for mothers and can contribute to the development of their children. Like teen mothers, young fathers must deal with the stressful demands of adolescence and parenthood simultaneously rather than sequentially. Therefore, they are in great need of support and services.

In spite of the expressed concerns of teen fathers, and in spite of repeated assertions by numerous authorities on teenage parents that adolescent fathers are an at-risk group who require the same services deemed to be essential for teenage mothers, it appears that the needs of teenage fathers largely go unnoticed. Societal responses to teenage fathers traditionally have been limited to punitive measures, such as denying them counseling services unless they are seriously intent on marriage. Kiselica and Sturmer (1993) found that teenage fathers were underserved relative to teenage mothers. These researchers concluded that society is giving teenage fathers a mixed message: You are expected to be a responsible parent, but you will not be provided with the guidance and assistance necessary to become one. In light of these findings, service providers are challenged to examine their attitudes toward teenage fathers, to divest themselves of prejudices against such youths, and to assist teenage fathers in becoming responsible parents.

Programs for Teen Pregnancy and Parenthood

Programs relating to teen pregnancy and parenthood are aimed at three target groups, with the focus and content differing for each group. The first group are children and young people who are not pregnant but desire to be parents in the future. The major emphasis is on the prevention of early pregnancy by focusing on the challenges facing parents

---

TIPS

For Teen Mothers

Participate in a teen parent program.
Continue education as long as possible to enhance earning potential.
Encourage the father's participation in child rearing.
Secure quality child care.
Assume major responsibility for child rearing.
Value the child's needs over own needs.
Balance peer activities with caring for the child.
Seek counseling from appropriate adults and professionals.
Identify and use community resources.
Participate in a support group (friends, family, peers).
Delay future pregnancies.

TIPS

For Teen Fathers

Maintain a positive relationship with the child's mother.
Provide feasible financial support for the child and the mother.
Be actively involved in the rearing of the child.
Participate in a teen parent program.
Continue education for as long as possible to enhance earning potential.
Delay fathering other children.

and the maturity required for effective parenting (physically, socially, psychologically, and economically), decision-making and problem-solving skills, and the effects of socioeconomic status on both mothers and children. Further, information on parental and child development and family relationships is appropriate. Most programs of this nature are being conducted in public schools. However, they often are fragmented and do not provide in-depth knowledge about parenting.

A considerable amount of money has been spent by federal, state, and local governments to implement intervention programs to prevent teen pregnancy. Title XX, the Adolescent Family Life Act (AFL), passed by Congress in 1981, funds programs aimed at helping young people to postpone sexual activity and provides services to pregnant teens. Since 1986, AFL programs have operated under a continuing resolution, and the appropriate focus of governmental policy has been a matter of ongoing debate (Miller & Moore, 1991).

Many abstinence-only programs, in which certain topics such as abortion and contraception are not dealt with, have been implemented widely. Controversy surrounds these programs. Christopher (1995) concluded, after reviewing numerous pregnancy-prevention programs, that there is little compelling evidence that purely abstinence programs are effective in changing coital or contraceptive behaviors that would have an impact on teen pregnancy.

Another pregnancy-prevention strategy is school-based clinics with family-planning services. Findings from evaluations of these programs show that the presence of school clinics is unrelated to sexual behavior of students. Further, it appears that clinics increase the use of effective birth control among youth who already are sexually active, but they have little impact on pregnancy rates (Christopher, 1995).

Several researchers have reached similar conclusions about characteristics of successful pregnancy-prevention programs. Franklin, Grant, Corcoran, Miller, and Bultman (1997) analyzed the effectiveness of 32 outcome studies on the primary prevention of adolescent pregnancy. Three outcomes were analyzed—sexual activity, contraceptive use, and pregnancy rates or childbirths. Results indicated that pregnancy-prevention programs had no effect on the sexual activity of adolescents. However, programs increased the use of contraceptives. Some evidence showed that programs were effective in reducing pregnancy rates, but the researchers concluded that comprehensive approaches would have greater impact. These must include problem-solving skills and building skills to resist social and peer pressure to engage in sexual intercourse.

An interesting example of such a program is the Teen Outreach Program, evaluated by Allen et al. (1997), consisting of 25 national sites. The program combines volunteer community service and classroom-based discussion of future life options. Topics include understanding yourself and your values, life skills, coping with family stress, human growth and development, and issues relating to social and emotional transitions from adolescence to adulthood. One of the more striking features of the program is its lack of explicit focus on the problem behaviors that it seeks to prevent; rather, it focuses on enhancing participants' competence in decision making, interacting with peers and adults, and recognizing and handling their own emotions.

Evaluation results showed that the risk of school suspension was less than half that of the control group. Participants' risk for course failure was 39 percent of that of the control group, and risk of pregnancy was only 41 percent of that of the control group.

The second target group consists of pregnant teens and, it is hoped, the prospective fathers. These teens, for the most part, have not planned to be parents and are not ready to assume the impending role. Although it is not possible during the pregnancy period to prepare teenagers adequately for parenthood, the focus should be on providing services so that both the mother and the father can remain in school and on preventing future pregnancies. Several researchers have concluded that program investment in education for pregnant teens, prospective teen fathers, and teen mothers and fathers pays far greater returns than the costs in reducing the welfare dependency of women giving birth during their teen years.

The content of a comprehensive program should include prenatal development, nutrition and its relationship to the health of the mother and the developing baby, appropriate prenatal care, medical facilities, labor and delivery procedures, care of the newborn, development during infancy, goal setting for parents' and child's development, counseling to solve psychosocial problems that may have led to the pregnancy, and available social services. Many programs for pregnant teens are conducted by community agencies and often are focused only on the medical care of the mother. Creative and innovative approaches are needed to secure the involvement of the prospective fathers.

The third group for whom programs should be provided is teens who already are parents. The primary emphasis of these programs should be on the continued educational development of both fathers and mothers (see Highlights).

HIGHLIGHTS

Components of Comprehensive Programs for Teen Parents

Comprehensive services involving extensive interagency coordination

Provisions for child care, transportation, personal counseling to alleviate problems associated with pregnancy

Sympathetic and supportive atmosphere

Mechanism for peer-group support

Provisions for continuation of schooling and/or training for employment

Services offered for extended period of time

Sensitive, caring, nonjudgmental staff

Involvement of teen's parents and father of baby or father figure

Information on nutrition, child growth and development

Development of effective parenting skills

Diversified funding sources

Further, research has provided support for emphasis on family involvement. Data from Hanson's study (1992) showed that family involvement, regardless of how it was defined, had a strong correlation with positive outcomes for teens and their children. Factors that showed a strong relationship to family involvement included educational status, relationship with family, and welfare status.

Research also has emphasized the need for programs and services for the children of teen parents. Chase-Lansdale et al. (1991) emphasized that these programs need to take a life-course perspective and that particular attention should be paid to the interaction of children's lives with the timing and sequencing of events in their mothers' lives. At the very least, services for the children of adolescent mothers should focus on elementary and school-age children in addition to infants and toddlers. The long-term implications of adolescent childbearing—severe school failure, school behavior problems, early sexual activity, pregnancy—occur when children of teenage mothers are older. Intervention programs should use an ecological approach, and services to mothers and children should be provided simultaneously. Preschool children should be in developmentally oriented child care at the same time that their mothers are in a comprehensive program. Further, services for children of teenage mothers need to take a three-generation family perspective, involving children, mothers, and grandmothers.

Solomon and Liefeld (1998) evaluated a community-based family support center based on an ecological model that recognizes the contexts of family and neighborhood as two of the most important influences on adolescents' lives. Results indicated that significant differences in repeat pregnancies occurred between the intervention and control groups (3 in the intervention group and 11 in the control group at 2 years; 7 in the intervention and 14 in control at 3 years). Data also showed that significantly fewer participants in the intervention group than in the control group dropped out of school. This is one of the first reports documenting the effectiveness of a family support center for adolescent mothers and their infants. Satisfaction surveys revealed that adolescent mothers were satisfied with caseworkers' care and availability, assistance with obtaining social services, availability of child care, and recreational programming.

High schools that offer child-care services provide an incentive for teen parents to remain in school. Most experts agree that child-care programs are most effective if they are designed to improve parenting skills. Highly effective programs require parent involvement, including that of the father, and parenting classes. The best possible programs for teen parents and their children involve ongoing collaboration among professionals in the child-care, health, education, social-services, and governmental sectors. Further, they must be adequately funded, school-based, prevention-oriented, and multidimensional (DeJong & Cottrell, 1999).

Sustaining participation in parent-education programs for young parents has been a major concern for program organizers, who have cited high levels of attrition, with half of the participants dropping out before completion. McCarthy, Sundby, Merladet, and Luxenberg (1997) identified factors that predicted attendance in a parenting-skills program. These included number of group sessions, whether parents were on welfare, number of children in the family, and whether the program included goals of learning to relax and meeting other parents. Programs whose participants were likely to have a regular attendance had the following characteristics: The group had fewer sessions; goals of meeting other parents and learning how to relax were included; participants were receiving welfare; and participants had one child. Barriers to attendance included working, lack of reliable transportation and child care, unstable living environments, and criticism from friends and family.

In summary, substantial research has documented the problems associated with early childbearing. Most of the research on teen pregnancy and motherhood has emphasized the negative outcomes for both mother and child, but some research has pointed out that teen pregnancy can stimulate positive change in the adolescent's life. Research suggests that developmental level interacts with psychological, sociocultural, economic,

family, and health variables to create a context in which teenage pregnancy can be either an inhibitor or an enhancer of maturation. Current research is examining these various interrelationships to increase the understanding of the effects of teen parenthood and to provide information to alleviate some of the negative effects. It is clear that the issues of teen pregnancy are complex and that adolescent parents are not a homogeneous group.

Intervention programs will be effective only if they are geared to the individual differences of target groups, if premature pregnancies are prevented, and if adequate support services are provided, including quality child care and enhancement of parenting skills once parenthood occurs. Programs must take into account the parents' developmental level, their socioeconomic status, their race/ethnicity, and available support systems. Meeting the needs of pregnant teens and parents probably presents the greatest challenge to professionals who develop parent-education programs.

ABUSIVE PARENTS

The maltreatment or abuse of children by their parents is not a new phenomenon. Today one would certainly consider infanticide, allowing or requiring young children to work for long hours in factories, and even "treating children as miniature adults" as child abuse. Yet in previous years these were common practices. It has been more than 30 years since research on children with multiple bone injuries judged these to be due to assault and ascertained that the children had also suffered additional trauma such as malnourishment, burns, and head injuries. Only since the 1960s has child abuse been of such public concern that reporting statutes have been enacted. Currently, all 50 states and the District of Columbia have passed statutory provisions for mandatory reporting of nonaccidental injury or neglect of children (Besharov & Laumann, 1996).

Child maltreatment came into public focus because of both the seriousness of the acts and the great extent of the problem. Concern for abused and neglected children has never been more intense in the United States than it is today. It has been recognized that abuse not only is a tragedy for the child and his abusive family but also is a community problem.

For many years, advocates, program administrators, and politicians have joined to encourage reports of child abuse and neglect. Their efforts have been spectacularly successful, with about 3 million cases of suspected cases reported in the mid-1990s. However, large numbers of endangered children still are not reported (Besharov & Laumann, 1996).

The national Child Abuse Prevention and Treatment Act (PL 93-247, passed in 1974) defined child abuse and neglect as "the physical or mental injury, sexual abuse, negligent treatment, or maltreatment of a child under the age of eighteen by a person who is responsible for the child's welfare under the circumstances which indicate that the child's health or welfare is harmed or threatened thereby" (U.S. Department of Health, Education, & Welfare, 1975, p. 3). Thus, it can be seen that the spectrum of maltreatment of children has a wide range. Both acts of commission and acts of omission are included, so that physical abuse, sexual abuse, emotional abuse, as well as neglect, are considered maltreatment. Abuse may appear as emotional or nutritional deprivation without any evident physical signs—acts of omission (neglect)—or abuse may be incipient or insidious maltreatment, mild deprivation with verbal abuse, and/or premeditated trauma with permanent injury or death—acts of commission.

Types of Child Abuse/Neglect

Abuse is an active, hostile, deliberate, and aggressive act carried out by an adult with the intent of willfully injuring the child. Child neglect, on the other hand, is a more passive type of treatment characterized by a lack of interest in the welfare of the child. Categorizing the various types of abuse is beneficial only from a diagnostician's point of view. From the child's standpoint, it does not make any difference; it is all maltreatment.

Neglect is the omission of the parent(s) to provide for normal growth and development of children. It can further be delineated into three subcategories: physical neglect, educational neglect, and emotional neglect. Physical neglect includes refusal to provide or delay in providing needed health care; abandonment; expulsion of the child from the home and other custody issues; inadequate supervision; and other physical neglect, such as inadequate nutrition, clothing, hygiene, and shelter. Physically neglected children frequently are unclean, unkempt, inappropriately dressed, underweight, and in need of medical attention. Educational neglect includes failure to enroll a child in school and to require a child to attend school and failure to attend to special-education needs. Emotional neglect includes inadequate nurturance, domestic violence in the child's presence, permitting substance abuse by the child, and refusal to obtain or delay in obtaining needed psychological care for the child (Cates, Markell, & Baettenhausen, 1995; Martin & Walters, 1992). Forty percent of cases reported are cases of children who are physically neglected (Whipple & Wilson, 1996).

Physical abuse or neglect is the easiest to detect and the most often reported. In this case, the parent (or caregiver) inflicts physical injury on the child through beating, whipping, branding, scalding, shaking, or even torture. Common weapons are hairbrushes, belts, sticks, light cords, or whatever is at hand. Frequently cigarette burns or burns caused by scalding water or open flames are inflicted. Gouges in the skin caused by belt buckles, sticks, or other implements are common evidences of physical abuse, as are welts, lesions, and severe bruises. X-rays frequently reveal bone scars where previously unattended breaks have occurred (Cates et al., 1995; Gillmer, 1992). Of all reported cases of maltreatment, 29 percent are cases of suspected physical abuse (Whipple & Wilson, 1996).

Sexual abuse is the exploitation of the child or adolescent for the sexual gratification of another person. It includes behaviors such as intercourse, sodomy, oral-genital stimulation, verbal stimulation, exhibitionism, voyeurism, fondling, and involving a child in prostitution or the production of pornography (Cates et al., 1995; Gillmer, 1992).

Concern for the victims of sexual abuse has become a national issue only during the last 15 years. Seventeen percent of all reported cases of abuse are cases of suspected sexual abuse (Whipple & Wilson, 1996).

Emotional abuse occurs when the parent (or adult caregiver) inflicts damage on the child through behaviors other than physical or sexual. These behaviors include systematically ignoring the child; continually shaming, ridiculing, teasing, or shouting at the child; and isolating or scapegoating the child. Emotional neglect is the consistent failure of a parent or caregiver to provide a child with appropriate support, attention, or affection (Cates et al., 1995; Gillmer, 1992). Emotional abuse and neglect are difficult to detect and are rarely reported, constituting 14 percent of all cases reported (Whipple & Wilson, 1996).

Abuse is rarely a single event but, rather, a pattern of behavior that is repeated over time. In addition, a specific type of abuse does not occur in isolation. Psychological maltreatment occurs in conjunction with physical abuse, physical neglect, and sexual abuse. There is growing consensus that psychological maltreatment is at the core of negative developmental outcomes for children. Not only does psychological maltreatment co-occur with other types of abuse, but also many of the negative short- and long-term effects of maltreatment are psychological in nature (Claussen & Crittenden, 1991).

Incidence.   No one really knows the accurate incidence of child abuse. What is known is the number of cases reported. In 1992 nearly 3 million children were reported as suspected victims of abuse or neglect, an increase of 8 percent in 1 year (Cates et al., 1995). By 1997 the number of reported cases was 3.2 million (Srinivasan, 1999). Gootman (1996) noted that nearly half a million children have been abused or neglected before they enter kindergarten. About 1,100 childhood deaths per year occur as a result of abuse and/or neglect, down from an estimated 3,000 to 5,000 during the past 20 years. Even at this level, maltreatment is the sixth leading cause of death for children under

14 years of age (Besharov & Laumann, 1996). Most experts agree that reports have increased over the past 30 years because professionals and laypeople have become more likely to report apparently abusive and neglectful situations. Still, large numbers go unreported, probably more than half a million each year. Besharov and Laumann (1996) stated that the more serious the case, the more likely it is to be reported. They estimated that more than 85 percent of fatal or serious physical-abuse cases, 72 percent of sexual-abuse cases, and 60 percent of moderate physical-abuse cases are reported. Nevertheless, there is no reason for complacency. Obtaining and maintaining a high level of reporting requires a continuation of public education and professional training that began 30 years ago.

The original child-protection laws were received by the public with mixed reactions. Often people were opposed on the grounds of intrusion into the private domain of the family. The problems faced by agencies today, however, are quite different. Workers are not facing a lack of clout, inadequate laws, or community resistance; rather, the obstacle is the sheer magnitude of the problem. There are too many cases for too few trained and qualified caseworkers and inadequate services for the victims and their parents. Nationwide, the average caseload is twice that considered reasonable.

Nationwide, between 60 percent and 65 percent of all reports are closed after initial investigations determine that they are "unfounded" or "unsubstantiated." As a result, some children in real danger are lost in the press to eliminate inappropriate cases. Forced to allocate a substantial portion of their limited resources to unfounded reports, child-protective agencies are less able to respond promptly and effectively when children are in serious danger. Some reports are uninvestigated for as long as 2 weeks or more, decision making suffers, and caseworkers become desensitized to the obvious warning signals of immediate and serious danger (Besharov & Laumann, 1996). Further, the resources for abused children have increased only a fraction compared with the increase in incidence.

Factors Contributing to Abuse

Family Characteristics. Numerous studies have documented that the most likely person to abuse children is the primary caretaker. Biological parents have been shown to be the perpetrators in the largest percentage of reported cases. Specifically, parents constitute 75 percent of perpetrators, other relatives 10%, and nonrelated individuals 6% (Srinivason, 1999).

Why do parents abuse their children? The answer to this question is not simple. Early research sought to identify the personality characteristics of abusive parents, the social/environmental factors, the child characteristics, and the parent-child interaction patterns in an attempt to identify the risk factors of abuse. Methodological problems with these studies have been cited as a severe limitation to generalizing the characteristics of abusive parents and children. Recent theories emphasize abuse as complex and multidetermined. Interactions between environmental, interpersonal, parental, and child factors are the focus of recent research. As the knowledge of child maltreatment has grown, it has become clear that attempting to understand maltreatment as a single homogeneous category is not useful. Numerous studies have indicated that multiple transactions among environmental forces, parental characteristics, and child characteristics make joint contributions to maladaptive parenting practices and child maltreatment. However, a few common characteristics of parents who have been found in numerous studies to inflict physical abuse, neglect, or sexual abuse can be found in the Highlights.

Baumrind (1994) provided a helpful discussion of family factors associated with child abuse and neglect from an ecological perspective. The primary caregiving environment—the family—is embedded in a complex ecosystem that affects family processes through conditions that exist in the larger society. Economic stress is the most insidious condition. Poor families are more likely than more affluent families to be reported for abuse and neglect. The highest incidence of child neglect and the most severe physical injuries have been found in families living in the most extreme poverty. From an ecological perspective, not only the child but also the perpetrators are viewed to be victimized by poverty and prejudice. Objective economic conditions, including unstable work, are related to parents' emotional states and behavior through their perceptions of economic pressure and limited resources to cope with pressure. Economic stress generates depression and demoralization, which in turn results in marital conflict and poor parenting.

Abusive parents under economic stress are more likely to have the following attitudes and negative parenting techniques: power-assertive and harsh discipline; little support, responsiveness, and affection; irritability; attributing misbehavior to willfulness or stubbornness; lack of involvement; and rating their children as aggressive and hyperactive. Environmental factors that buffer the negative effects of poverty include commitment, family support and cohesive neighborhoods. Baumrind emphasized the importance of recognizing and appreciating subcultural differences in child-rearing norms and practices, such as indulgent, harmonious mother-child relationships in Japanese families and the value of obedience and respect for authority that sometimes result in corporal punishment in African American families. It also is important to consider the circumstances surrounding the maltreatment—family circumstances that influence the capacity to parent and predispose parents to abuse their children, such as parental youth and inexperience, marital discord and divorce, and presence of difficult children.

A widespread perception is that mothers primarily are responsible for child neglect. This belief has been at the expense of an understanding of, and efforts to change, the social and economic context in which child neglect occurs. Throughout history, most conditions that have brought families to agency attention on grounds of neglect have been confined almost exclusively to the female domain of home and child care. The highest incidence of neglect has been confirmed in low-income, marginalized, and mother-headed families. Therefore, child-welfare workers and scholars continue to

Characteristics of Parents Who Abuse Children

PHYSICAL ABUSE

Intrapsychic disorders such as marital discord, drinking problems, mental illness

Family discord, poor spousal relationships

Modeling of aggressive behavior as preferred mode of interaction

History of family violence

Low self-esteem, low family satisfaction (mothers)

Little understanding of child's needs

Low family interaction—emphasis on negative aspects

Intolerance

Aversive behavior (mothers)

Multiple life stresses; economic problems

Likelihood of emotional problems

Likelihood of having been abused themselves as children

NEGLECT

Social disorganization

Low family interaction; emphasis on negative aspects

Environmental factors and parental inadequacies such as unemployment, low income, poor housing, separation, and divorce

Psychic disorders—high stress, anxiety, depression

Withdrawal from environment (mothers)

Intellectual inadequacies

Larger families

Resistance to rehabilitation

Inability to access support system

Poor parenting skills

SEXUAL ABUSE

Family disruption, psychopathology

Perpetrators commonly males who live with and/or are related to child (stepfathers living in home five times more likely to abuse stepdaughters than biological fathers)

History of parent-child problems

Likelihood of alcohol and substance abuse

Intellectual inadequacies

Parental illness

Likelihood of mother having been sexually abused

---

dwell on the personal responsibility of parents and have sought explanations for poor-quality child care primarily within the realm of mothering, failing to address the social and economic factors related to child neglect (Swift, 1995).

Community Characteristics. Coulton, Korbin, Su, and Chow (1995) concluded that child maltreatment is as much a function of community characteristics as of family characteristics. The most significant community indicators of abuse were poverty and unemployment. Other community variables included signs of lack of investment in communities, such as vacant housing, large numbers of female-headed households, and a large

Black population. Other indicators were the childcare burden, including the high ratio of children to adults; few elderly residents; a small proportion of adult males; and high mobility. Concomitant conditions were violent crime, drug trafficking, juvenile delinquency, and teen childbearing.

Lack of Social Support. Moncher (1995) examined four primary factors of social support in relation to physical abuse of children by mothers: direct aid provided for caretaking; support for emotional needs and individual growth of the caretaker; education in and feedback about parenting efforts; and structural aspects of the support network. Results indicated that the perceived availability of concrete support was significantly correlated with abuse risk, but the exchange of child-rearing services was not. Perceived availability of emotional support and the level of criticism arising from network relationships were significantly related to abuse risk, whereas relationship closeness and listening availability were not. Feedback and education from the network and structural aspects of the support network were not significantly related to abuse risk.

The researcher concluded that social support is a complicated and multifaceted construct. The availability of concrete and emotional support and lack of criticism from significant others were important components in the relationship between social isolation and abuse risk, and these relationships were qualified by important network-composition variables.

Culture. Several studies have noted that perceptions of abuse differ among various professionals and laypeople and that perceptions vary by culture. Rose and Meezan (1996) examined the perceptions of the seriousness of specific aspects of neglect held by mothers from three cultural groups (Latin, Caucasian, and African American) and public-welfare workers (protective-service investigators and caseworkers). Findings suggested that members of minority groups perceived some types of child neglect as more serious than their Caucasian counterparts did, that investigative workers perceived most types of child neglect as more serious than service workers did, and that workers of all types viewed child neglect as more serious than mothers did. Comparisons revealed that various groups perceived the dimensions of neglect differently with respect to their potential harm to children.

Dubowitz, Klockner, Starr, and Black (1998) also compared views on child neglect among African American and White community members and professionals in the field. Results indicated small, but significant, differences between middle-class African American and White community groups, with both groups showing greater concern with psychological care than lower-class African American groups. Both African American groups were more concerned than middle-class Whites

about physical care. Overall, all groups were consistent in their views of the circumstances that are harmful to children. Findings suggested that the standards of professionals may be considerably lower than those of the community members.

Effects of Abuse on Children

The short- and long-term effects of abuse on children vary, depending on a number of factors—the specific type of abuse, the length and degree of abuse, and various mediating variables.

Gootman (1996) noted that abused and neglected children often react to everyday events in ways that make no sense to casual observers. Some become hyperactive when they have flashbacks to their trauma; some act out, regress academically when a theme emerges that is reminiscent of their trauma or holds intense personal meaning for them. They may flit from one activity to another or try to disrupt the classroom. Their hyperactivity may represent attempts to keep their minds busy so that frightening thoughts and images do not intrude. Other children become hypervigilant, fearful, suspicious, and mistrustful—always on the lookout for potential dangers. Abuse is unpredictable; children never know when they are going to get it. Therefore, they must remain on guard so that feelings of helplessness and panic do not occur. Some abused children daydream frequently, becoming trancelike and appearing "spacey" and forgetful. Some read and do not seem to be processing what they are reading. Many dissociate or hypnotize themselves, separating their minds from their bodies to escape overwhelming thoughts, emotions, and sensations experienced during abuse. Children who are closely guarding family secrets also may exhibit severe learning problems.

Because of the behaviors abused children exhibit in school, many are mistakenly labeled learning disabled (LD), as having a behavioral disorder (BD), or as having attention deficit/hyperactivity disorder (ADHD). The practices associated with managing and teaching children so labeled can be extremely detrimental to the treatment of abused children. Finding the source of the abused child's dysfunction often is blocked, and abused children are not provided with the compassion and skills they need to overcome the effects of maltreatment (Gootman, 1996).

Effects of Physical Abuse and Neglect. Children may carry the scars of physical abuse forever, with the psychological scars being even more debilitating than the physical ones (Martin & Elmer, 1992). Numerous studies have indicated that physically abused and neglected children suffer from a complex set of psychological, interpersonal, social, and intellectual deficits. The effects are both short- and long-term. Among these are problems reflecting the abused individual's inability to deal in an effective way with feelings. These include a basic mistrust of self and others, followed by inability to establish meaningful interpersonal relationships, ingrained feelings of low self-worth, and a sense of helplessness. Thus, it can be expected that such psychological impairment would create long-term difficulties in the more concrete tasks of living, such as obtaining and keeping a job, maintaining adult relationships, and successfully rearing children (Martin & Elmer, 1992).

Research indicates that physically abused and neglected children have a variety of difficulties, including developmental delay, behavioral problems, and excessive hostility (Martin & Elmer, 1992).

Alessandri and Lewis (1996) examined the differences in the expression of shame and pride in maltreated and nonmaltreated preschool children by presenting them with easy and difficult tasks in which their emotional responses could be observed. Failure on easy tasks produced more shame than failure on difficult tasks; similarly, success with more difficult tasks produced more pride than success with easy tasks. In general, girls exhibited more shame than boys, and boys showed more pride than girls. Maltreated girls showed significantly more shame than nonmaltreated girls. In fact, girls showed more shame than both abused and nonabused boys. Across emotions, abused boys showed less emotional expression than both nonabused boys and both groups of girls. Boys received more positive maternal behaviors and abused children received more negative feedback than nonabused children. Abused girls received the highest negative feedback of all groups. This study illuminates the interaction of the effects of gender and abuse.

Martin and Elmer (1992) studied a group of adult individuals who had been abused as children to ascertain the long-term effects of physical abuse or neglect. They found a range of variability of adaptation. However, the investigators' appraisal was that few were adapting with high degrees of flexibility or reliability. The adults had many deficits, especially in the economic sphere. Some of the subjects showed evidence of retardation, thought to be due to central nervous system damage identified many years before. Severe emotional difficulties showed up in a variety of ways. A high proportion had physical handicaps and cosmetic disfigurement. Twenty-six percent had alcohol problems. Although there was little incidence of aggressiveness, there were many signs of suspicion and resentment. Most, however, were more satisfied with their present lives than with their childhood experiences. Additional effects of physical abuse and neglect may be found in the Highlights.

Graziano and Mills (1992) noted that the effects of maltreatment on psychological functioning may be mediated by several important interactive variables. These include the overall quality of the parent-child relationship; the general socioeconomic condition of the family; the type, duration, and severity of maltreatment; the child's developmental stage at the time maltreatment occurs; the completeness and soundness of the child's earlier development; and the degree to which development is disrupted by the maltreatment. Thus, an older child with a stable and healthy early development might suffer fewer and/or less severe psychopathological effects of abuse than a younger child with a tenuous developmental history, even if the abuse is the same.

Effects of Sexual Abuse. Clinical observations of sexually abused children indicate a variety of behavioral and emotional problems, including depression, guilt, learning difficulties, sexual

Effects of Abuse on Children

PHYSICAL ABUSE

Psychological and behavioral problems in all areas of development

Impulsive, disorganized, inconsistent behavior

At risk for forming abnormal patterns of attachments

Poor affective expression

Abnormal moral development

Difficulty with self-control

Difficulty in school—increased frequency of learning disorders, language delays, and other neurologically based handicaps; lower cognitive functioning; lower academic performance

Poor social skills—heightened aggression toward peers and adults; absence of appropriate conflict resolution skills; low sensitivity; little empathy and concern for distress of other children; avoidance and withdrawal of interaction; at risk for becoming violent juvenile delinquents and demonstrating criminal behavior

NEGLECT

Poor coping skills; noncompliant; easily frustrated

High negativity toward and reliance on mother

Inattention, uninvolvement, and difficulty with schoolwork

Poor peer relations—aggressive, immature

At risk for demonstrating deficits in auditory comprehension and verbal ability

Insecure attachment

Low levels of self-esteem, self-assertion, ego-control, flexibility, creativity

Developmental delays in social, emotional, cognitive areas; unready to learn

SEXUALLY ABUSED

PRESCHOOL CHILDREN

Inappropriate sexual (or sexualized) behavior—heightened interest in or preoccupation with sexuality manifested in sexual play, masturbation, seductive or sexually aggressive behavior

High passivity during play

Withdrawal behaviors

Less disturbance than older sexually abused children

SCHOOL-AGE CHILDREN

Behavioral and academic problems, leading to grade retention

Poor performance in schoolwork as rated by teachers

Developmental immaturity as rated by teachers

Emotional problems such as depression, internalizing

Sexually inappropriate behavior

ADOLESCENTS

Depression, low self-esteem, suicidal ideation

Drug abuse

Prostitution

Physical fights; delinquent /criminal behavior

Acting-out behaviors—running away, hostility

Compulsive masturbation

Gender-identity disturbances—bisexuality or homosexuality

promiscuity, runaway behavior, somatic complaints, sudden changes in behavior, phobias, nightmares, compulsive rituals, self-destructive behavior, or suicidal behavior (Banyard & Williams, 1996). Further, sexually abused children have been found to display significantly higher scores than nonabused children on measures of dsyfunction, including concentration problems; aggression; withdrawal; a characteristic personality style of being too nice, pleasant, or anxious to please; antisocial behavior; nervousness and anxiety; behavioral regression; self-esteem and body-image problems; fear; and symptoms of posttraumatic stress. Sexually abused children are more likely than nonabused children to report symptoms of muscle tension and gastrointestinal and genitourinary difficulties.

Beitchman, Zucker, Hood, DaCosta, and Akman (1992) reviewed research on the long-term effects of child sexual abuse. They noted that the short-term effects may be different from the long-term effects. The majority of adults sexually abused as children report sexual problems in adulthood: frigidity, confusion about sexual orientation, promiscuity, decreased sex drive, sexual dissatisfaction, and other sexual disturbances. The highest rate of sexual disturbances has been found in victims of father-daughter incest, or abuse involving penetration. Abuse by stepfathers also is very traumatic. Abuse by a parent involves greater betrayal and loss of trust than abuse by others. Parental sexual abuse also is likely to reflect a significant level of family disturbance with little emotional support of the child and is likely to occur over a longer period of time and with greater frequency than abuse by others.

Whether childhood sexual abuse contributed to greater risk for teen pregnancy was investigated by Roosa, Tein, Reinholtz, and Angelini (1997). Although the women who were sexually abused as children and those who had teen pregnancies had similar developmental influences or experiences, the results of their study did not support arguments that sexual abuse is a major contributor to the risk of teenage pregnancy.

Some evidence exists that shows a relationship between childhood sexual abuse and later homosexual behavior. There appears to be a higher rate of homosexuality among individuals who were sexually abused as children than would be expected in the average population; however, the studies have been conducted using clinical populations and the conclusions are tentative (Beitchman et al., 1992).

Some research indicates that women with a history of childhood sexual abuse, as compared with nonabused women, suffer from generalized emotional symptoms such as fear, anxiety, and depression. Further, fear of men, anxiety attacks, and problems with anger also have been described. Women with a history of sexual abuse are significantly more likely than nonabused women to experience depression and to think of self-harm, attempt suicide, and have personality disorders. Revictimization during adolescence and adulthood is about three times more likely to occur when women have been abused as children (Banyard & Williams, 1996). It was concluded by Beitchman and his associates (1992) that the severity of long-term effects depended on how long the abuse lasted (continued for 2 or more years), whether force and violence were used, whether the father or the stepfather was the perpetrator, and whether penetration or oral-genital contact had occurred.

Banyard and Williams (1996) tested the hypothesis that sexual abuse involving the use of physical force, genital penetration, and perpetration by a close family member will produce greater or more extreme symptomology among survivors. Results indicated that both the experience of physical force and older age at the time of abuse were related to higher reported symptomology. Physical force was associated with depression, anxiety, and sleep problems. Greater force was more prevalent among those who experienced penetration, and younger age was associated with victimization by a family member. Sexual abuse by a family member was associated with greater sleep problems and more dissociation.

Cole, Woolger, Power, and Smith (1992) studied the parenting practices of women who had been sexually abused as children. They found that women with a history of father-daughter incest as children reported difficulty in parenting their own children. These women reported less confidence and less sense of control than nonrisk mothers. In addition, they reported significantly less support in the parental partnership with their spouses, and reported being less consistent and organized, and making fewer maturity demands on their children. Even though many sexually abused women report positive attitudes toward child rearing, they are often hostile, resentful, and jealous when describing their actual parenting situations. Many feel overwhelmed and inadequate, and blame themselves for being poor parents and their children for being difficult.

The factors that mediate the long-term effects of sexual abuse have been outlined by Beitchman and associates (1992). These include the woman's present perception of her abuse as a child, the mother's response to the abuse at the time it occurred, the degree of support the child received, and the perception by the adult of the child's role in the abuse.

Beitchman and his associates (1992) reviewed the short-term effects of child sexual abuse. They concluded that family breakdown was evident in families in which sexual abuse occurred. Further, as indicated earlier, these researchers noted that the frequency and duration of the abuse, the father or the stepfather as perpetrator, and abuse involving force and/or penetration were associated with greater trauma in the child.

Familial Aspects of Abuse

Results of research in the late 1980s and 1990s suggested that children exposed to family violence had adjustment difficulties that resembled the problems shown by abused children. These studies showed that children exposed to family violence demonstrated internalizing and externalizing problems, attention problems, anxiety, and withdrawal. Siblings typically experienced the same type of maltreatment as the reported child (Jaffe, Wolfe, Wilson, & Zak, 1986; Jean-Giles & Crittenden, 1990).

The belief that abused children become abusive parents has been widespread. In fact, Baumrind (1994) stated that the most important predictor of maltreatment by a parent is prior abuse of the parent. The frequent explanation of intergenerational transmission of maltreatment comes from attachment theory. The child who is abused constructs, at an early age, a model that best fits the reality that she experiences, and that model is resistant to contrary experiences that occur as she gets older. However, Kaufman and Zigler (1987) proposed that unqualified acceptance of this hypothesis is unfounded. They reported that mediating factors affect the rate of intergenerational transmission of abuse and estimated it to be about 30 percent. Some studies have indicated that environmental factors (poverty, stress, and isolation), family structure, available social supports, and feelings about their abuse as children are related to the intergenerational transmission of abuse. Those who are poor, are isolated, and have fewer social supports are more likely to repeat the abuse with their children. Nonrepeaters more often reported a supportive relationship with one parent when growing up, had greater awareness of their history of being abused and vowed not to repeat the pattern, and had fewer current stressful life events.

Several other researchers have reported high percentages of intergenerational abuse. Gelles and Conte (1991) have conducted several studies on the intergenerational transmission of child abuse. In one study, 70 percent of the parents who were identified as having experienced child abuse were observed to maltreat or provide borderline care of their children. In another study, 47 percent of those parents who were abused as children abused their own children. The continued cycle of violence was further substantiated by the fact that abused children as they grew into adolescence and adulthood had a higher percentage than the matched controls of arrests for delinquency, adult criminality, and violent criminal behavior. Evidence indicated that those mothers who were able to break the cycle of abuse were significantly more likely to have received emotional support from a nonabusive adult during childhood; to have participated in therapy during some period in their lives; and to have a nonabusive, stable, emotionally supportive, and satisfying relationship with a mate.

A substantial number, then, of all individuals who are physically abused, sexually abused, or extremely neglected are projected to subject their offspring to one of these forms of maltreatment. The rate of abused parents who abuse their children is approximately six times higher than the base rate for abuse in the general population (5 percent). Although being maltreated as a child puts one at risk in the etiology of abuse, the path between these two points is far from direct or inevitable. It is of critical importance to assess the multiple factors and their relationships and to use comparison groups when examining intergenerational transmission of abuse (Kaufman & Zigler, 1987).

In summary, recent research highlights the importance of careful selection of abusing populations and use of adequately matched control groups in the examination of factors contributing to child abuse. Further, it is important to evaluate the characteristics of mothers and fathers separately, and the interactions of environmental, interpersonal, parental, and child factors needs to be studied.

Reporting Abuse

The child-abuse and -protection laws in all 50 states require certain professionals to report known and suspected incidents of child abuse and neglect. Included are teachers, child-care workers, doctors, nurses, social workers, and anyone who renders services to children under 18 years of age. These laws are aimed at protecting children and are not meant to punish those who neglect or abuse them but to rehabilitate them. To ensure the protection of children, reporters do not have to be certain that the child is abused or neglected; rather, one "has cause to believe" or is "reasonably suspect" that abuse or neglect is occurring. The use of these terms affords legal protection to those who do report suspected

cases. Reporters are immune from civil or criminal liability as long as the report is made in good faith.

Reports of suspected abuse and neglect should be made to the local departments of human services or to the police. It is the local child-protection-services division that ultimately receives and investigates reported cases. Individuals who work with children should make themselves aware of the symptoms of abuse so that they have reasonable bases for reporting. Cates et al. (1995) noted that teachers are in a particularly strategic position to detect child abuse. Because children are required to attend school, teachers and other educators are faced with the responsibility of maintaining a protective and vigilant posture in relation to students' well-being. Since children will not report abuse directly, teachers need to be aware of specific behavioral and physical indicators that may indicate that abuse has occurred. See the Highlights for physical and behavioral indicators of abuse.

In attempting to detect abuse, it is important to note that children who are motorically delayed or impaired may be prone to accidents and as a result have bruises, scrapes, cuts, or other minor injuries. Therefore, it is important for teachers who serve these children to be familiar with the child's condition as well as acquainted with the child's family. A teacher who is equipped with knowledge of the symptoms of abuse and neglect and the characteristics of the child and family will be better able to determine whether an at-risk child with a disability is a victim of abuse. Teachers should make note of consistent behaviors or physical evidence, being aware that one incident may not be evidence of abuse.

Few people fail to report because they do not care about an endangered child. Instead, they may be unaware of the danger the child faces or of the protective procedures that are available (Besharov & Laumann, 1996). Others are not sure what constitutes abuse and neglect, do not know how or to whom to make a report, are reluctant to get involved for fear of prosecution by the child's parents, and lack confidence that a report will ultimately do any good.

Indicators of Abuse

PHYSICAL	BEHAVIORAL
Emotional Abuse and Neglect	
Height and weight significantly below age level	Begging or stealing food
Inappropriate clothing for weather	Constant fatigue
Poor hygiene, lice, body odor, scaly skin	Poor school attendance
Unsupervised, abandoned child	Chronic hunger
Lack of safe and sanitary shelter	Dull, apathetic appearance
Unattended medical or dental needs	Running away from home
Developmental lags	Child reports that no one cares or looks after him
Habit disorders	Sudden onset of behavioral extremes (conduct
Depression	problems)
Physical Abuse	
Frequent injuries such as cuts, bruises, or burns	Poor school attendance
Wearing long sleeves in warm weather	Refusing to change clothes for physical
Pain despite lack of evident injury	education
Inability to perform fine motor skills because of	Finding reasons to stay at school and not go home
injured hands	Frequent complaints of harsh treatments by
Difficulty walking or sitting	parents
	Fear of adults
Sexual Abuse	
Bedwetting or soiling	Excessive fears, clinging
Stained or bloody underclothing	Unusual, sophisticated sexual behavior/
Blood or purulent discharge from genital or	knowledge
anal area	Poor school attendance
Difficulty walking or sitting	Finding reasons to stay at school instead of going
	home

Besharov and Laumann (1996) expressed concern about the large number of unfounded reports of abuse. Determination that a report is unfounded can be made only after an unavoidably traumatic investigation that inherently is a breach of parental and family privacy. To determine whether a particular child is in danger, caseworkers must inquire into the most intimate personal and family matters. Each year, about 700,000 families experience investigations of unfounded reports. Few of these reports are made maliciously, and after investigation many families are referred to other agencies for services. As a result of unfounded reports, overextended caseworkers devote time that could be spent more effectively in responding promptly and effectively when children are in serious danger and monitoring known dangerous home situations.

These researchers contended that many unfounded reports could be eliminated by shifting priorities away from merely seeking more reports toward encouraging better reports. They made the following suggestions: Clarify child-abuse reporting laws—rewrite existing laws so that conditions are clear about what should and should not be reported, described in terms of specific parental behaviors or conditions that are tied to severe and demonstrable harms (or potential harms) to children; provide continuing public education and professional training; screen reports—adopt policies that provide explicit guidance about the kinds of cases that should not be assigned for investigation; modify liability laws to include professionals who in good faith decide that a child has not been abused or neglected and hence should not be reported; inform individuals who report as to the outcome; and adopt an agency policy about reporting.

Support for Abusive Parents

Each reported case is investigated, and decisions are made concerning the most appropriate way to assist the family. Since some abusive parents can be rehabilitated, it is important that a plan for this rehabilitation be developed as soon as possible. Some parents seek help on their own.

Various organizations are available to assist abusive families. Parents Anonymous is a nationwide organization that provides group therapy, ego-building sessions, and a 24-hour "hotline." The aim of the organization is to change behavior through modification. Local groups of this organization are found throughout the United States.

Most organized services have been established to help the child and family after the abuse pattern has been established and the parent has been reported to the authorities—tertiary intervention. These services include supportive, supplementary, substitutive, and protective approaches. Most programs have focused on rehabilitating parents; few have been aimed at the abused child (Graziano & Mills, 1992).

Recent research emphasizes the need for treatment programs for abusive parents to be directed toward a specific homogeneous group—the type of maltreatment (abusive, neglectful), the sex of the perpetrator, and the socioeconomic status. The focus of any intervention strategy is to stop the current abuse and prevent future maltreatment (Gelles

& Conte, 1991). A variety of approaches have been used. For example, Graziano and Mills (1992) reported that behavior modification had been attempted to help parents who physically abused their children to gain control of their aggressive behavior and increase anger control.

In discussing strategies for rehabilitating neglectful parents, Martin and Walters (1992) stressed that treatment programs must provide a wide array of intervention services that include tangible aid as well as parent-skills development and social support. Home-health visitors have been found to be effective in providing services to prevent child neglect. Tangible aid in the areas of housing, health care, financial management, homemaking skills, nutrition, and transportation, is effective. Assisting the family in identifying and utilizing social support is important. The provision of parent education is also a clear need. Mental-health services for those parents suffering from depression and other problems must be provided.

Graziano and Mills (1992) have noted that most of the parent-intervention programs are largely uncontrolled, work only with a small number of questionably representative families, and focus on corollary behavior rather than directly upon the parents' maltreating behavior. One limitation has been the lack of attempts to monitor the physical signs of abuse. Thus, although parents may improve in some ways, there is little direct evidence that abuse has decreased. These researchers reported that in one study that reviewed 89 treatment programs, one-third or more of the parents continued to maltreat their children even while in treatment.

Although some families benefit from intervention programs, a number of studies (Gelles & Conte, 1991; Graziano & Mills, 1992; Heap, 1991) show that despite great investments in improving parental functioning, a fairly high percentage of cases consistently show no improvement. The numbers are variously reported at 20 percent to 66 percent. Longitudinal changes in family functioning have not been mapped in detail. Some research has indicated that global family functioning upon entry to the program was strongly associated with family functioning at the end of the program. In fact, some studies reported that from 3 percent to 25 percent of the parents increased their maltreatment despite the intervention.

Ayoub, Willett, and Robinson (1992) have suggested that it is important to identify the families most likely to benefit from intervention programs. They noted that the belief has been challenged that short-term early intervention can prevent child abuse or neglect for all families. Research suggests that the length of treatment should differ from family to family and that the outcomes of treatment will vary for families with different problems and patterns of change. Some families may not benefit from intervention and others may not need it. Some families may do well in one treatment program, or for a short length of time, whereas other families may require longer-term treatment in a different type of intervention program. In general, positive change in family functioning seems difficult to achieve and even harder to maintain.

Guterman (1997) synthesized the rapidly expanding empirical base on early prevention of physical abuse and neglect. He examined 18 studies that revealed a promising yet complex picture regarding successful intervention. Several trends emerged: (a) Parenting education support is essential; (b) it is important to link families to formal and/or informal supports; (c) it is important to couple longer-term interventions and those that employ paraprofessional helpers with a moderate to high degree of service intensity; (d) there is a clinical advantage for programs that employ universalistic intake procedures over those that screen for psychological risk; (e) health education is important to reduce medically related maltreatment risks. Guterman recommended that future program design and study should address parental powerlessness in the makeup of physical abuse and neglect risk.

Early interventions support families during the initial phases of the parent-child relationship, a period when families frequently face both their highest risk for physical abuse and/or neglect and their greatest opportunities for establishing lasting positive parent-child interaction patterns. Most early-intervention programs contain the following core principles: early identification and/or screening of families referred through a universalistic service system; initiation of supportive services during pregnancy or shortly after birth; voluntary participation; in-home service provision; case-management support; and provision of parenting education and guidance (Guterman, 1997).

Gootman (1996) concluded that early childhood classrooms provide an optimal setting for counteracting and overcoming the problems of many abused and neglected children. A warm, caring teacher can plant seeds of successful survival that will continue to grow and flourish in maltreated children. An early-childhood curriculum that attends to the intellectual, social, emotional, and physical growth of children and is flexible enough to adapt to the individual needs can provide children with the skills they need to successfully overcome their maltreatment. An early-childhood approach that treats the source of problems, rather than their manifestations, can counteract the effects of maltreatment by providing an appropriate antidote.

Graziano and Mills (1992) have recommended that parent-intervention approaches be continued and improved but emphasized that maltreated children benefit from professional intervention. Because of the variability among the children and their family conditions and the complexities of each case, individualized approaches to evaluation, education, and treatment are necessary. These researchers suggested that the effectiveness of intervention strategies for the children may depend on an appropriate combination of methods because the effects of abuse on the child vary according to the type of abuse. For example, they recommended that the focus for children who have been physically abused be on the reduction of overt aggression and impulsivity, anger management, and improvement of social competence and cognition. For school-age children, deficits in academic performance can be improved through special education/training programs. Social-skills training is another focus area—improving empathy, social sensitivity, and peer relationships. Improving self-esteem has been accomplished through contingency-management methods.

Since intervention programs for parents after the abuse has occurred have not been very successful, some experts are emphasizing the need for a focus on prevention. For example, Jones and McCurdy (1992), who found a strong association between child neglect and poverty, suggested the need for family policy changes that would help alleviate neglect of children. Their findings suggest a need for a strong commitment to working with and providing services to families in poverty. A big step toward preventing neglect would be to provide health care, especially prenatal care, to all families. Other policies aimed at reducing poverty also should be implemented.

Garbarino and Kostelny (1992) emphasized that child maltreatment is not just an individual family problem but a neighborhood and community problem as well. Their research noted the importance of an ecological perspective on child maltreatment. They indicated that the child maltreatment field needs to identify and explore the critical elements of community development that would benefit from a reduction in child abuse. Identifying "prevention zones" that can become targets for comprehensive, sustained intervention by a wide range of public and private agencies would be a course to follow. They noted that major resources have to be committed to make a better community for children.

Community-based programs that focus on low-income children, in particular, are one method of reaching families at risk for abuse. These programs offer parent training and education, home visits, support groups, counseling, parent-child play groups, drop-in centers, and case management. Whipple and Wilson (1996) evaluated the effectiveness of a community-based parent-education support program in ameliorating risk factors associated with physical child abuse. The program offered a continuum of services. Results indicated that stress and depression decreased significantly for the highly involved parents (involved in three to five programs), especially for those who had

used the services for the longest period of time. The researchers concluded that parent-education programs that work in conjunction with other community resources, especially income-maintenance and job-training programs, are promising methods for meeting the needs of multiproblem families. Essential community services include child care, early childhood education, drug-abuse prevention, and teen peer support. Improvements in overall social structure—such as reducing poverty and social injustice, ensuring basic economic opportunity, jobs, and adequate houses—are essential.

Much more research needs to be done regarding programs for children victimized by all kinds of abuse. Obviously the child's cognitive level must be considered. The kind of abuse also must be considered, since children are affected in different ways by different types of abuse. It appears that the entire family must be involved if rehabilitation programs are to succeed.

Obviously the number of reported cases of child abuse and neglect is increasing. The problem is one with which parents, teachers, family-services personnel, and researchers need assistance. Additional information concerning family processes in abusive and neglectful families, effective approaches to rehabilitating parents, and methods of assisting the abused children themselves are clearly needed. It is difficult to determine the extent to which child abuse has long-term effects on children, but the pattern is learned early and may continue.

HOMELESS FAMILIES

Homelessness has become one of the most visible and persistent social problems in the United States. Even as economic conditions improve in many sections of the country, the number and diversity of homeless people continue to grow. Decent and affordable housing has long been considered a basic human right. That it is not available to large numbers of individuals, families, and children is of concern to researchers, policymakers, and the general public. Several researchers (Bassuk et al., 1997; Letiecq, Anderson, & Koblinsky, 1996;

Steinbock, 1995) have found that the lack of affordable housing is a major factor in homelessness. Some research has been focused on housing issues, shelter problems, the needs of the homeless, the process of becoming homeless, and the effects of the experience on the families and children who experience it. There is a growing consensus among social scientists that homelessness is one of the more complex and serious social problems facing contemporary American society and an acute tragedy for the families and children who become homeless (Dail, 1990).

Debate has occurred over how to define homelessness. Typically the term refers to persons living in areas not designated as habitats (Dail, 1990). The United States Department of Housing and Urban Development (HUD) considers persons to be homeless if their nighttime residence is in public or private emergency shelters; in the streets, parks, subways, bus terminals, railroad stations, airports; under bridges or aqueducts; in abandoned buildings without utilities; in cars or trucks; or in any other public or private space that is not designated a shelter (Berger & Tremblay, 1989). Sometimes those who are living temporarily in hotel rooms, as well as those residing in social- and health-service facilities without a permanent address, are defined as homeless. The operative definition has a significant impact on the numbers arrived at by anyone attempting to count the homeless (Dail, 1990).

Incidence

The National Law Center (1993) reported that by conservative estimates, on any given night more than 770,000 men, women, and children are homeless in America. In 1992 an estimated 2 million people were homeless. By 1993 women and children represented the fastest-growing segment of the homeless, constituting 43 percent of all homeless individuals. As many as 100,000 children are homeless on any given night (Anderson & Koblinsky, 1995; Letiecq et al., 1996; Letiecq, Anderson, & Koblinsky, 1998). Only about 1 percent of the total homeless population is made up of men with children (Kurtz, Jarvis, & Kurtz, 1991).

The homeless population is quite diverse—homeless men, homeless women (with or without children), runaway youth, families, individuals who are employed, and the chronically mentally ill—but homeless women with children constitute the largest percentage of the homeless population. Nine out of 10 homeless families with children are female-headed, with a mean of two children per family. Three-fourths are families of racial and ethnic minority status; the mean age of the mother is late twenties; approximately half have never been married; and half have not completed high school (Anderson & Koblinsky, 1995).

Domestic violence is the precipitating factor for roughly one-half of homeless women seeking shelter (Steinbock, 1995). They are usually socially isolated and alienated from social-support systems, including the extended family. Some are victims of adverse economic conditions that may have been triggered by divorce, unemployment, or illness.

Causes of Homelessness

Eviction is the most immediate reason that families become homeless. Loss of a place to live, however, often is the culmination of long-term financial problems related to joblessness, underemployment, illness, unmanageable medical costs, and family breakups (Letiecq et al., 1998).

Homeless mothers have been found to experience high prevalence of disruptive family events, including divorce, illness, and physical and/or sexual abuse. The vast majority are homeless for economic reasons—they were poor before becoming homeless, frequently struggling to pay bills. Many lived in neighborhoods characterized by violence, persistent unemployment, poor schools, and limited access to medical and social services. Although eviction or relationship problems precipitate homelessness for many single-parent households, the reality is that neither federal assistance nor minimum-wage earnings of these low-skilled women are sufficient to pay the rent, cover child care, and meet health-care and other living expenses. Such economic problems may increase feelings of hopelessness, dependency, and depression and contribute to family dysfunction (Anderson & Koblinsky, 1995). A lack of social support may facilitate homelessness and limit the family's efforts to return to permanent housing (Letiecq et al., 1998).

As the gap between increasing housing costs and decreasing income widens for poor Americans, the homeless population continues to rise. Thousands of low-cost housing units have been destroyed because of urban redevelopment projects, which have not made adequate provisions for replacement housing.

Poor families deal with the housing shortage most frequently by doubling or tripling up in a single-family housing unit. Pooled resources may allow families to meet basic needs. Further, another adult in the house may be a source of support, especially for young mothers in need of child-care assistance as they seek employment or attempt to further their education. This arrangement has its drawbacks. It is often temporary, and the overcrowding causes conflicts, making the situation stressful as well. Often landlords threaten to evict the primary resident. Some evidence indicates that doubling up is a precursor to families seeking shelter (Letiecq et al., 1998).

Other families are forced to settle for substandard housing conditions with major structural flaws, no heat or hot water, rodent infestation, and so forth, since decent housing is unaffordable. Frequently, the family has no alternative to the shelter system other than the streets. Long-term shelter has in some large cities, such as New York, most commonly been in welfare hotels or motels that provide private rooms, generally with private bathrooms but no kitchen or other cooking facilities. Usually beds are shared by two or more family members. There is no space for children to play, and not enough floor space for infants and toddlers to crawl. Many of these housing conditions are deplorable. Often shelters are found amid centers of pornography, drug trafficking, and prostitution. Drug-related violence often is high (Anderson & Koblinsky, 1995; Letiecq et al., 1998). The trip to the local shelter is a family's final, desperate attempt to remain intact.

In the 1980s there were virtually no shelters for homeless families and little demand for such shelters. But the number of poor families without options increased, forcing more into homelessness. Demand for shelter increased 49 percent from 1990 to 1992 (Thompson, 1993). In general, emergency shelters provide from one night to several months of shelter. During the day, families are "on their own" to report to the welfare office, search for affordable housing, seek employment, pursue education, or engage in related activities. Generally, cooking is not available, and thus parents must eat in a shelter cafeteria or find other ways to feed their families. Some research has found that as many as one-half of homeless preschoolers go to bed hungry several times a month. Emergency shelters often lack support services and restrict families to short stays.

In addition to shelter shortage, overcrowding of the existing shelters can lead to family separation, as some members of the family, usually fathers and older children, split off so that the rest of the family can stay together. Further, because of the lack of shelter space, the close physical arrangement of many family shelters leads to restrictions on the age and sex of clients. Forced to split off from their families because of the restrictions, fathers and older children will go either to single-sex shelters, to relatives, or to the streets. This makes it difficult for homeless families to stay together. In the National Law Center study (1993), one-half of the agencies surveyed did not accept men or teenage boys. When shelters are full, families are threatened with charges of child neglect unless they can find alternative housing arrangements. If they are unable to, the children may be placed in foster care. These factors combine to threaten the unity and stability of homeless families.

In recent years, some cities have developed transitional-housing programs that offer families reduced-rent apartments for 1 to 2 years while parents complete school or job-training programs. Such programs may provide homeless families with supportive services such as child care, employment counseling, GED classes, job training, health care, and/or substance-abuse counseling (Anderson & Koblinsky, 1995; Letiecq et al., 1998).

Characteristics of Homeless Parents

By definition, the homeless lack shelter. And, without shelter, homeless families have no place in which to conduct the daily activities necessary to function as self-sufficient members of society or in which to find protection from the elements or criminals. Without an address, the homeless find it difficult to secure a job or obtain welfare benefits. They lack privacy and a place to keep possessions. Further, the lack of shelter contributes over time to other problems, such as poor nutrition, poor physical and/or mental health, victimization, apathy, loneliness, and dejection. Families with minor children are in jeopardy of losing custody. Many families are alone, without knowledge of how and where to find a support system.

Letiecq and associates examined the social support of homeless mothers in 1996 and 1998. They found that homeless mothers saw or talked with significantly fewer relatives or friends weekly than did housed mothers. These mothers had fewer people they could count on for help and fewer people who could care for their children during periods of need than other mothers. Homeless mothers found their parents and relatives, their partners, professionals, and (if employed) their co-workers to be significantly less helpful in rearing their children than did housed mothers. They found also that mothers who had spent more time in temporary housing received less total support than mothers with shorter stays. The longer the mother had lived in the same place of residence, the greater the helpfulness of her social network.

Lindsey (1998) explored mothers' perceptions of how homelessness and shelter life affected family relationships. Results showed that the quality of parent-child relationships and the parental role were affected by homelessness. Almost all the mothers reported that relationships with their children became closer while living in a shelter. This closeness seemed to develop because of the amount of time they spent together and the bonding during a time of crisis. Even though mothers became closer to their children, the almost constant interaction required by shelter life became a burden for some women. All but one of the mothers found it difficult to parent their children while in a shelter. Specifically, it was hard for them to be disciplinarians and to fulfill the provider/caretaker role because they were unable to meet their children's basic needs for shelter, food, safety, and emotional nurturance. Mothers tended to attribute disciplinary problems to shelter rules that prohibited corporal punishment and to interference of other residents. Participants cited three main factors that influenced their family relationships while in a shelter: conditions of shelter life; their own emotional state; and their children's emotional state.

Shelter conditions that had a negative influence on parenting were requiring mothers and children to leave the shelter during the day, regardless of weather; rules and regulations involving curfews, rigid mealtimes and lack of access to kitchen facilities; and the requirement that children always be with the parents while in the shelter. Residents and staff were not always understanding of children's normal activity levels or misbehavior. Interference by other residents, fearing for child's safety, and unhealthy sanitary conditions were other concerns relating to shelter conditions. The mothers' emotional state—being depressed, full of despair, and impatient with their children—were reported to make parenting difficult.

Steinbock (1995) noted that placing children in foster care is a major response to homelessness. Foster-care policies continue to disrupt the fragile mother-child relationship by characterizing homelessness and substance abuse as neglectful situations requiring foster-care placement of children.

Characteristics of Homeless Children

The greatest tragedy of homeless families is the impact on children, whose outlook on themselves and the world is being shaped by insecurity, fear, and isolation (Hunter, 1993). Homeless children can be classified into three categories—runaways, throwaways, and those living with one or both homeless parents. The runaways have chosen not to live with their parents because of economic stress, family violence, drug and alcohol abuse, divorce, and physical or sexual abuse. The throwaways are children whose parents have essentially discarded them, usually because of divorce or economic stress. More than 40 percent of the homeless population now consists of families with children.

Most shelter children are younger than 5 and already show delays in language, social skills, gross and fine motor skills, and other characteristics that could lead to life-long emotional, social, and cognitive problems (Hunter, 1993). Grant

Characteristics of Homeless Parents

WOMEN

Mild to severe depression (one-third)
Mental-health and substance-abuse problems (one-fourth)
Psychiatric problems
Acute stress
Victims of sexual and physical violence
Insurmountable problems of single parenting—poverty, lack of extended family support, lack of child care
Failure to establish selves as functional, self-sufficient, autonomous adults
Long histories of economic and interpersonal problems
Pattern of residential instability
Little or no prenatal care and inadequate nutrition during pregnancy

MEN

Separated from family
Many are Vietnam veterans, employed and married—not typical "skid-row bums"
Street skills—less vulnerable than women
Chemical and/or alcohol dependency
Frequent violence

(1990) studied preschool children in shelters. He found that most were unserved for primary health care, community health ties having been broken as the family relocated. The children who had been in shelters since infancy and who had experienced intervention programs had the fewest problems. Grant concluded that three out of four preschool children he studied exhibited signs of emotional disturbance and/or speech and language delay, frequently in combination. Approximately the same percentage were restless, distractable, overactive, and unable to attend to a task for 5 minutes or longer. The health status and functional and behavioral characteristics of these preschool shelter children may be found in the Highlights.

Fox, Barnett, Davies, and Bird (1990) studied shelter children 4 to 10 years of age. Their results indicated that nearly all the children showed some difficulties. Sixty-one percent had receptive verbal functioning at or below the first percentile for their age, 29 percent were functioning at the fifth percentile for age in psychomotor ability, and 38 percent exhibited emotional and behavioral problems. One-third of the children were not attending school and one-third had repeated a grade. Other characteristics of homeless school-age children may be found in the Highlights.

Kurtz et al. (1991) studied the problems of homeless youth who sought help at runaway shelters. When compared with nonhomeless youth, they were found to have substantially more school and personal problems, especially more family difficulties. Although the homeless youths received more services from shelters than nonhomeless youths, the prognosis for the former was grim. Most lacked a stable, supportive family to which they could return. Many were already victims of a fragmented child-welfare system that offered bleak alternative living arrangements.

Support for Homeless Families

The majority of programs for homeless families have begun at the local level through private contributions and local government support—emergency shelters, clothing and food distribution centers,

Characteristics of Homeless Children

PRESCHOOL CHILDREN

Under- or nonimmunized

Chronic health conditions, such as frequent serious upper-respiratory problems, dehydration, and diarrhea

Numerous functional and behavioral disorders, such as separation problems (characterized by hysterical crying, vomiting, and severe anxiety)

Inappropriate physical pseudo-intimate relationships with adults unknown to them—indiscriminate friendliness

Superficial relationships

Little or lack of concern for classmates and teachers

Sleep disturbances (try to avoid napping, have nightmares, unable to sleep because of noise, often have to sleep with parent)

Signs of emotional disturbance—severe tantrums; dangerously aggressive and destructive behaviors; extreme withdrawal; mood swings; oppositional and manipulative behavior; lack of internalized behavior controls; dependent upon adults to structure immediate environment

Very short attention span

Random self-activity and absence of goal direction

Restricted expressive language

Delayed vocabulary development

Articulation disorders

Delayed cognitive development

Immature motor skills

Spatial difficulties

SCHOOL-AGE CHILDREN

Depression and suicidal thoughts

Intense anxiety

Higher incidence of sleep problems, shyness, withdrawal, aggression (similar to behaviorally disordered children)

Low self-esteem

Nonattendance at school

School failure and/or underachievement; special education

Mental retardation or borderline retardation

Impaired cognitive development (similar to that of abused children)

job-services programs, and health treatment initiatives. Fragmentation and inadequate funds have limited such efforts.

In 1987 President Reagan signed the first major piece of federal legislation to deal with the needs of the homeless in a comprehensive manner—the Stewart B. McKinney Homeless Assistance Act, which was reauthorized in 1988. In the 1990s Congress passed legislation that increased funds for shelters and housing, job training, health and counseling services, and education for homeless children and adults. However, it has been argued that changes in federal social policies have played a significant role in the rise in homelessness. Fewer families are qualifying for public assistance, and those who do have received drastic reductions. A large percentage of homeless work full- or part-time, but low wages cannot provide for rent and other living expenses. Only about half of the states in 1995 provided emergency-assistance funds (Anderson & Koblinsky, 1995; Steinbock, 1995).

Danseco and Holden (1998) concluded that clinical work with homeless families could be more effective if families that are more seriously affected by homelessness and who carry higher rates of emotional and behavioral symptoms could be identified. These families should be targeted for more intensive intervention, such as psychotherapy for parents, child-management training, and intensive case-management services. The more resilient homeless families may need access to resources but less direct support and encouragement in their problem-solving efforts. Those families most at risk should be identified early and intervention efforts begun as soon as possible.

On the basis of his research, Lindsey (1998) proposed that shelters should be more family-friendly, allowing parents to have as much authority and control as possible over daily routines. Requiring families to leave the center during the day actually exacerbates parent-child conflicts. Policies preventing boys over a certain age from staying with the family should be changed. Parenting classes should help parents learn appropriate disciplinary techniques. Service providers should be particularly aware of emotional needs of parents and children and promote constructive interactions among shelter residents.

Anderson and Koblinsky (1995) argued that there is a need to consider family principles when designing homeless-family policy that recognizes the diversity of family life and reinforces marital, parental, and family commitment and stability. Many current policies focus on outcomes for individuals rather than for the family unit. Moreover, the majority of these policies are short-term and crisis-oriented. In homeless policymaking, the absence of a family perspective that addresses prevention as well as short- and long-term intervention may result in policies and programs that have negative effects on family life. Further, homeless policies must address the diversity of homeless-family life. Homeless families differ on many dimensions, including family structure, family size, racial/cultural background, housing history, and pathways to homelessness. Other family factors that need to be considered are extent of parental education, intergenerational interaction, family cohesion, family conflict, life stress, and amount of social support. Further, policy must consider how policy alternatives foster or discourage family contact. Policy should recognize and provide for family diversity, empower families to become self-sufficient, encourage involvement in parenting, recognize interdependency of family members, build social-support networks, and strengthen neighborhoods and communities. Policies must address such issues as wage levels, unemployment, illiteracy, welfare assistance, mental-health care, fair-market rentals, and the availability of low-income housing.

HIGHLIGHTS

Criteria for Successful Programs for Homeless Families

A broad spectrum of services are offered, including attention to the most immediate needs (medical care, food, clothing).

Services are rendered that are coherent and easy to access.

Severe but sometimes unarticulated family needs are responded to (i.e., the most pressing and immediate problem is addressed).

Bureaucratic limitations are circumvented when necessary to meet the needs of the families being served.

Labor-intensive and manpower-affluent services are provided, including direct, one-on-one assistance.

The needs of each family are responded to.

The problems faced by families in the context of the larger community environment are understood and addressed.

SUMMARY

Teenage parents, abusive parents, and homeless parents represent families in high-risk situations, but the type and degree of risk are vastly different for each group. Teenagers are immature, both physically and psychologically, and represent, in reality, children rearing children. From a physical standpoint, very young mothers are likely to have inadequate nutrition, poor prenatal care, and labor and delivery complications. From a psychological perspective most are still in the process of developing their own sense of identity and therefore are unable to experience a positive sense of generativity. A large percentage are single parents. These conditions make effective parenting more difficult than for other parents.

The lack of preparation for parenthood and the limited knowledge and skills of child care that most teenage parents possess frequently cause unrealistic expectations to be made of children. On the other hand, spontaneity, flexibility, and a high energy level may be seen as strengths in the parenting process. The assistance of other adults, such as the teenager's own parents, continued education, preparation for parenthood, and early prenatal care, seem to mitigate some of the deleterious effects on children of teenage parents.

Abusive parents pose considerable threat to the health, safety, and welfare of children. However, the majority of parents who abuse or neglect their children are hurt, lonely, and guilt-ridden. Many are young, impoverished, socially isolated, unemployed, and/or victims of child abuse themselves.

Considerable evidence supports the fact the abuse may be perpetuated from one generation to the next. Often, abusive parents make unrealistic demands on their children, and children try to comply to avoid being harmed. Our society has yet to find an effective system for the prevention of child abuse and neglect or for the rehabilitation of abusers. Clearly these issues need to be high priorities.

Homelessness has become one of the most visible and persistent social problems in the United States. The complexity of the processes leading to homelessness makes intervention difficult. Effective strategies and policies that support homeless parents are yet to be developed. The fastest growing population of homeless individuals is single women with children under 6 years of age. Homeless parents and children are the most at risk of all families and children. They face almost insurmountable problems related to housing, unemployment, and poverty, and they experience a host of psychological and social effects. Homeless children have been found to suffer serious difficulties in all areas of development. In response to the increasing numbers of homeless individuals and their particular problems, intervention programs are just beginning to emerge. Research is needed that focuses on the variables predictive of homelessness and the interaction among these variables; the effects of homelessness on the children who experience it; the special needs of homeless parents; and community resource development for meeting the needs of homeless families.

REFERENCES

Alessandri, S., & Lewis, M. (1996). Differences in pride and shame in maltreated and nonmaltreated preschoolers. *Child Development, 67,* 1857–1869.

Allen, J., Philliber, S., Herrling, S., & Kuperminc, G. (1997). Preventing teen pregnancy and academic failure: Experimental evaluation of a developmentally based approach. *Child Development, 64*(4), 729–742.

Allen, W., & Doherty, W. (1996, March). The responsibilities of fatherhood as perceived by African American teenage fathers. *Families in Society:* *The Journal of Contemporary Human Services,* pp. 142–155.

Anderson, E., & Koblinsky, S. (1995). The need to speak to families. *Family Relations, 44,* 13–18.

Ayoub, C., Willett, J., & Robinson, D. (1992). Families at risk of child maltreatment: Entry-level characteristics and growth in family functioning during treatment. *Child Abuse and Neglect, 16,* 495–511.

Banyard, V., & Williams, L. (1996). Characteristics of child sexual abuse as correlates of women's adjustment: A prospective study. *Journal of Marriage and the Family, 58,* 853–865.

BARRATT, M. (1991). School-age offspring of adolescent mothers: Environment and outcomes. *Family Relations, 40*(4), 442–447.

BARRATT, M., ROACH, M., MORGAN, K., & COLBERT, K. (1996). Adjustment to motherhood by single adolescents. *Family Relations, 45,* 209–215.

BASSUK, E., BUCKNER, J., WEINREB, L., BROWNE, A., BASSUK, S., DAWSON, R., & PERLOFF, J. (1997). Homelessness in female-headed families: Childhood and adult risk and protective factors. *American Journal of Public Health, 87*(2), 241–248.

BAUMRIND, D. (1994). The social context of child maltreatment. *Family Relations, 43*(4), 360–369.

BEITCHMAN, J., ZUCKER, K., HOOD, J., DaCOSTA, G., & AKMAN, D. (1992). A review of the short-term effects of child sexual abuse. *Child Abuse and Neglect, 15,* 537–556.

BERGER, P., & TREMBLEY, K. (1989, Fall). Homelessness: Strategies for education, advocacy, and research. *Journal of Home Economics,* pp. 27–32.

BESHAROV, D., & LAUMANN, L. (1996). Child abuse reporting. *Society, 33*(4), 40–47.

BROOKS-GUNN, J., & CHASE-LANSDALE, P. (1991). Teenage childbearing: Effects on children. In R. Lerner, A. Petersen, & J. Brooks-Gunn (Eds.), *Encyclopedia of Adolescence* (pp. 103–106). New York: Garland.

CATES, D., MARKELL, M., & BETTENHAUSEN, S. (1995). At risk for abuse: A teacher's guide for recognizing and reporting child neglect and abuse. *Preventing School Failure, 39*(2), 6–10.

CHASE-LANSDALE, P., BROOKS-GUNN, J., & PAIKOFF, R. (1991). Research and programs for adolescent mothers: Missing links and future promises. *Family Relations, 40*(4), 396–403.

CHRISTOPHER, F. (1995). Adolescent pregnancy prevention. *Family Relations, 44,* 384–391.

CLAUSSEN, A., & CRITTENDEN, P. (1991). Physical and psychological maltreatment: Relations among types of maltreatment. *Child Abuse and Neglect, 15,* 5–16.

COLE, P., WOOLGER, C., POWER, T., & SMITH, K. (1992). Parenting difficulties among adult survivors of father-daughter incest. *Child Abuse and Neglect, 16,* 239–249.

COULTON, C., KORBIN, J., SU, M., & CHOW, J. (1995). Community level factors and child maltreatment rates. *Child Development, 66,* 1262–1276.

DAIL, P. (1990). An essay on homelessness: American's gravest poverty. *Family Perspective, 24*(4), 419–430.

DALLA, R., & GAMBLE, W. (1997). Exploring factors related to parenting competence among Navajo teenage mothers: Dual techniques of inquiry. *Family Relations, 46,* 113–121.

DANSECO, E., & HOLDEN, E. (1998). Are there different types of homeless families? A typology of homeless families based on cluster analysis. *Family Relations, 47,* 159–165.

DANZIGER, S., & RADIN, N. (1990). Absent does not equal uninvolved: Predictors of fathering in teen mother families. *Journal of Marriage and the Family, 52*(3), 636–642.

DEJONG, L., & COTTRELL, B. (1999, January). Designing infant child care programs to meet the needs of children born to teenage parents. *Young Children,* pp. 37–45.

DONNELLY, B., & VOYDANOFF, P. (1991). Factors associated with releasing for adoption among adolescent mothers. *Family Relations, 40*(4), 404–410.

DUBOWITZ, H., KLOCKNER, A., STARR, R., & BLACK, H. (1998). Community and professional definitions of child neglect. *Child Maltreatment, 98*(3), 235–244.

EAST, P. (1996). The younger sisters of childbearing adolescents: Their attitudes, expectations, and behaviors. *Child Development, 67,* 267–282.

FOX, S., BARRNETT, J., DAVIES, M., & BIRD, H. (1990). Psychopathology and developmental delay in homeless children: A pilot study. *Journal of the Academy of Adolescent Psychiatry, 29*(5), 733–735.

FRANKLIN, C., GRANT, D., CORCORAN, J., MILLER, P., & BULTMAN, L. (1997). Effectiveness of prevention programs for adolescent pregnancy: A meta-analysis. *Journal of Marriage and the Family, 59,* 551–567.

FURSTENBERG, F. (1991). As the pendulum swings: Teenage childrearing and social concern. *Family Relations, 40*(2), 127–138.

GARBARINO, J., & KOSTELNY, K. (1992). Child maltreatment as a community problem. *Child Abuse and Neglect, 16,* 455–464.

GELLES, R., & CONTE, J. (1991). Domestic violence and sexual abuse of children: A review of research in the eighties. In A. Booth (Ed.), *Contemporary Families: Looking forward, looking back* (pp. 327–340). Minneapolis: National Council on Family Relations.

GILLMER, V. (1992). *A cry for action: Support for families in New Mexico.* Albuquerque: Task Force of the New Mexico Children, Youth, and Families Department.

GOOTMAN, M. (1996). Child abuse and its implications for early childhood educators. *Preventing School Failure, 40,* 149–153.

GRANT, R. (1990). The special needs of homeless children: Early intervention at a welfare hotel. *Topics in Early Childhood Special Education, 10*(4), 76–91.

GRAZIANO, A., & MILLS, J. (1992). Treatment for sexually abused children: When is a partial solution acceptable? *Child Abuse and Neglect, 16,* 217–228.

GUTERMAN, N. (1997). Early prevention of physical child abuse and neglect: Existing evidence and future directions. *Child Maltreatment, 2*(1), 12–35.

HANSON, S. (1992). Involving families in programs for pregnant teens: Consequences for teens and their families. *Family Relations, 41*(3), 303–311.

HARRIS, K. (1991). Teenage mothers and welfare dependency: Working off welfare. *Journal of Family Issues, 12*(4), 492–518.

HAWKINS, A. (1992). Critical components or peripheral parts? Fathers in and out of families. *Family Perspective, 26*(2), 219–234.

HEAP, K. (1991). A predictive and follow-up study of abusive and neglectful families by case analysis. *Child Abuse and Neglect, 15,* 261–273.

HENDRICKS, L. (1988). Outreach with teenage fathers: A preliminary report on three ethnic groups. *Adolescence, 23*(91), 711–720.

HUNTER, L. (1993). Sibling play therapy with homeless children: An opportunity in the crises. *Child Welfare, 62*(1), 65–74.

JAFFE, P., WOLFE, D., WILSON, S., & ZAK, L. (1986). Similarities in behavior and social maladjustment among child victims and witnesses to family violence. *American Journal of Orthopsychiatry, 56*(1), 142–145.

JEAN-GILLES, M., & CRITTENDEN, P. (1990). Maltreating families: A look at siblings. *Family Relations, 39*(3), 323–329.

JONES, E., & McCURDY, K. (1992). The links between types of maltreatment and demographic characteristics of children. *Child Abuse and Neglect, 16,* 201–215.

KAUFMAN, J., & ZIGLER, E. (1987). Do abused children become abusive parents? *American Journal of Orthopsychiatry, 57*(2), 186–191.

KETTERLINUS, R., LAMB, M., & NITZ, K. (1991). Developmental and ecological sources of stress among adolescent parents. *Family Relations, 40*(4), 435–441.

KISELICA, M., & STURMER, P. (1993). Is society giving teenage fathers a mixed message? *Youth and Society, 24*(4), 487–501.

KURTZ, P., JARVIS, S., & KURTZ, G. (1991). Problems of homeless youth: Empirical findings and human services issues. *Social Work, 36*(4), 309–314.

LEITCH, M. (1998). Contextual issues in teen pregnancy and parenting: Refining our scope of inquiry. *Family Relations, 47,* 145–148.

LETIECQ, B., ANDERSON, E., & KOBLINSKY, S. (1996). Social support of homeless and permanently housed low-income mothers with young children. *Family Relations, 45,* 265–272.

LETIECQ, B., ANDERSON, E., & KOBLINSKY, S. (1998). Social support of homeless and housed mothers: A comparison of temporary and permanent housing arrangements. *Family Relations, 47,* 415–421.

LINDSEY, E. (1998). The impact of homelessness and shelter life on family relationships. *Family Relations, 47,* 243–252.

LUSTER, T., PERLSTADT, H., McKINNEY, M., SIMS, K., & JUANG, L. (1996). The effects of a family support program and other factors on the home environments provided by adolescent mothers. *Family Relations, 45,* 255–264.

MARTIN, J., & ELMER, E. (1992). Battered children grown up: A follow-up study of individuals severely maltreated as children. *Child Abuse and Neglect, 16,* 75–87.

MARTIN, M., & WALTERS, J. (1992). Child neglect: Developing strategies for prevention. *Family Perspective, 26*(3), 305–314.

McCARTHY, P., SUNDBY, M., MERLADET, J., & LUXENBERG, M. (1997). Identifying attendance correlates for a teen and young adult parenting program. *Family Relations, 46,* 107–112.

MECKLER, L. (1998, December 18). Survey of teen births finds encouraging trend. *The Tuscaloosa News,* p. D1.

MECKLER, L. (1999, April 29). Teen pregnancy plunges to lowest level since 1973. *The Tuscaloosa News,* pp. A1, A5.

MILLER, B., & MOORE, K. (1991). Adolescent sexual behavior, pregnancy, and parenting: Research through the 1980s. In A. Booth (Ed.), *Contemporary families: Looking forward, looking back* (pp. 307–326). Minneapolis: National Council on Family Relations.

MONCHER, F. (1995, September). Social isolation and child-abuse risk. *Families in Society: The Journal of Contemporary Human Services,* pp. 421–433.

NATH, P., BORKOWSKI, J., WHITMAN, T., & SCHELLENBACH, C. (1991). Understanding adolescent parenting: The dimensions and functions of social support. *Family Relations, 40*(4), 411–420.

NATIONAL LAW CENTER. (1993). *No way out: A report analyzing options available to homeless and poor families in 19 American cities.* Washington, DC: Author.

PARISH, W., HAO, L., & HOGAN, D. (1991). Family support networks, welfare, and work among young mothers. *Journal of Marriage and the Family, 53*(1), 203–215.

PEEPLES, A. (1994, January 16). Teen mothers' message to their peers: It's a stressful life. *Birmingham News,* p. 5E.

PIROG-GOOD, M. (1996). The education and labor market outcomes of adolescent fathers. *Youth and Society, 28*(2), 236–262.

ROBINSON, B. (1988). *Teenage fathers.* Lexington, MA: Lexington Books.

ROOSA, M., TEIN, J., REINHOLTZ, C., & ANGELINI, P. (1997). The relationship of childhood sexual abuse to teenage pregnancy. *Journal of Marriage and the Family, 59,* 119–130.

ROSE, S., & MEEZAN, W. (1996). Variations in perceptions of child neglect. *Child Welfare, 75*(2), 139–161.

RUSSELL, C. (1993, July 26). One-third of pregnant teen dropouts smoke. *Albuquerque Journal,* p. B1.

SMITHBATTLE, L. (1996). Intergenerational ethics of caring for adolescent mothers and their children. *Family Relations, 45,* 56–64.

SOLOMON, R., & LIEFELD, C. (1998). Effectiveness of family support center approach to adolescent mothers: Repeat pregnancy and school drop-out rates. *Family Relations, 47,* 139–144.

SRINIVASAN, K. (1999, April 2). Feds say reports of mistreated kids down. *Albuquerque Journal,* p. A9.

STEINBOCK, M. (1995). Homeless female-headed families: Relationships at risk. *Marriage and Family Review, 20*(1-2), 143–159.

STERN, M., & ALVAREZ, A. (1992). Knowledge of child development and caretaking attitudes: A comparison of pregnant, parenting, and nonpregnant adolescents. *Family Relations, 41*(3), 297–302.

SWIFT, K. (1995). An outrage to common decency: Historical perspectives on child neglect. *Child Welfare, 74*(1), 71–92.

THOMPSON, T. (1993, August 12). Report focuses on side effect of homelessness: Splitting of families. Washington Post, p. B3.

THORNBERRY, T., SMITH, C., & HOWARD, G. (1997). Risk factors for teenage fatherhood. *Journal of Marriage and the Family, 59,* 505–522.

U.S. BUREAU OF THE CENSUS. (1997). *Statistical abstract of the United States: 1997* (117th ed.). Washington, DC: U.S. Department of Commerce.

U.S. DEPARTMENT OF HEALTH, EDUCATION, AND WELFARE, OFFICE OF HUMAN DEVELOPMENT/OFFICE OF CHILD DEVELOPMENT, CHILDREN'S BUREAU/NATIONAL CENTER ON CHILD ABUSE AND NEGLECT. (1975). *Child abuse and neglect: The problem and its management.* (DHEW Publication No. OHD 75-30073).

WHIPPLE, E., & WILSON, S. (1996, April). Evaluation of a parent education and support program for families at risk of physical child abuse. *Families in Society: The Journal of Contemporary Human Services,* pp. 227–239.

WHITESIDE-MANSELL, L., POPE, S., & BRADLEY, R. (1996). Patterns of parenting behavior in young mothers. *Family Relations, 45,* 273–281.

CHAPTER 10

Parenting Children with Exceptionalities

An exceptional child, as labeled for education purposes, is one who is different in some way from the "normal" or "average" child. The term *exceptional children* includes those with special problems related to physical handicaps, sensory impairments, communicative disorders, emotional disturbances, learning disabilities, and mental retardation, as well as those who have special talents, that is, the gifted. Most exceptional children require special-education and related services if they are to reach their full potential of development.

Just over 10 percent of children are receiving special-education services in schools or community-based programs, not including those children in gifted programs. More than 12 percent of non-institutionalized children have difficulty performing one or more daily activities (Kraus, Stoddard, & Gilmartin, 1996). The number of unidentified, and therefore unserved, children is not known, nor is the number who are misserved. It is difficult to determine the number of exceptional children in a given category for the following reasons: The definitions of disabilities often are ambiguous; the diagnosis of a condition may overlap with another condition or diagnoses may change over time; many exceptional children remain undetected; and often parents resist having their children identified as exceptional because of the stigma attached to labeling (Hallahan & Kauffman, 2000).

REACTIONS OF PARENTS AT BIRTH

The birth of a child with disabilities into a family no doubt requires considerable adjustment on the part of family members. Most parents plan for and expect healthy, happy babies. When an impairment is immediately obvious, the acknowledgment of it is traumatic. The initial reaction of parents may be one of disbelief, and the degree of disbelief is related to the degree of the visibility of the handicap. When parents receive the initial diagnosis of a disability, a dream is shattered, and they may begin to grieve for the loss of a healthy child and the expectations they held for the child.

Some experts (e.g., Moses, 1983) believe that grieving is the process by which an individual can separate from a significant lost dream. Grieving facilitates personal growth through a reevaluation of basic values and attitudes. Grieving begins spontaneously—it appears to require no learning period. According to Moses, there are several states of grieving, which have no time limits:

Denial: The existence of, the permanence of, or the impact of the disability may be denied. Denial buys time for parents to gain the internal strength and the external supports necessary to cope and as such requires enormous energy.

Anxiety: A feeling of internal imbalance occurs. Anxiety facilitates the restructuring of attitudes concerning responsibility and serves as a mobilizer of energy.

Guilt: This is the most disconcerting of all grief states. Normally, it is expressed in three ways: (1) The parent feels that he or she has caused the disability; (2) the parent feels that having a child with a disability is a just or fair punishment for some specific or awful action committed in the past; or (3) the parent feels generalized or unspecified guilt because the disability exists. Nothing seems to accelerate the course of guilt feelings, and thus parents are given the opportunity to reevaluate the functions, effectiveness, and values of their central life commitments.

Depression: Self-anger, or anger turned inward, causes depression. If parents have the support needed to deal with the depression, it can help them to rework a definition of competence for their child.

Anger: People have an internal sense of justice. The anger they feel when their child is born with a disability can be frightening and can result in aggression, overprotection, or overpunitiveness toward the child.

All parents do not experience the states of grieving in the same way. Sometimes the feelings overlap or occur simultaneously; some are intense, whereas others may be mild. Therefore, these findings are referred to as *states* rather than *stages*.

The authors wish to express sincere appreciation to Bobbye Krehbiel, Ph.D., for her insight and assistance in the preparation of this chapter.

Feelings that parents may experience that are related to depression include rejection, isolation, hopelessness, resentment, and antagonism (Wallace, 1992). Parents must generate new dreams; otherwise, the child with a disability will be nothing but a disappointment to them. Coping occurs simultaneously with grieving. Parents first conceptualize the worst before they deal with reality, and confrontation of reality is facilitated by the acceptance of both the child's and the parents' limitations (Moses, 1983).

Several variables affect the degree and intensity of grief: cultural attitudes; social class; religious beliefs; the number, sex, and age of siblings; the nature and visibility of the disability; the coping strategies of family members; the degree of marital stability; and the availability and use of support systems.

TYPES OF EXCEPTIONALITIES

Children may be born with one or more disabilities, and they may acquire disabilities later in life because of accident or disease. The causes of congenital disabilities (i.e., those that children are born with) may be genetic or chromosomal, teratogenic (caused by prenatal exposure to drugs or other toxic substances or radiation), nutritional (due to maternal malnutrition), or infectious (the result of maternal infections or diseases before and/or during pregnancy). Some congenital disabilities are caused by trauma during the birth process, such as oxygen deprivation. The following discussion is a

brief description of the most common types of disabilities for which children receive special educational services. Table 10.1 provides definitions and estimated percent of children receiving special-education services in each category.

Physical Disabilities

Children demonstrate a broad range and variety of types of physical disabilities. It is estimated that 0.5 percent of all children, or approximately 200,000, have one or more physical disabilities that cause them to be in need of special-education services. Of all children receiving special-education services, about 1.2 percent have orthopedic impairments (Kraus et al., 1996). Children with physical disabilities also may have mental retardation, learning disabilities, emotional disorders, communication disorders, or special gifts and talents. Medically based categories include the following: neurological impairments, such as cerebral palsy, epilepsy, spina bifida, polio, and multiple sclerosis; musculoskeletal conditions, such as muscular dystrophy, rheumatoid arthritis, clubfoot, scoliosis, osteomyelitis, and congenital malformation of the hip, extremities, and heart; and accidents, diseases, and other conditions such as asthma, diabetes, rheumatic fever, tuberculosis, and hemophilia (Hallahan & Kauffman, 2000).

The causes of neurological impairments include congenital malformations, infectious diseases, lead poisoning, oxygen deprivation, and trauma caused by accidents or severe abuse. The causes of musculoskeletal conditions are either genetic or unknown. Maternal infectious diseases and the use of drugs during pregnancy are additional causes of some musculoskeletal conditions. Accidents (vehicular, burning, poisoning) also can cause previously normal children to acquire skeletal disabilities.

Physical disabilities, unlike learning disabilities and some forms of mental retardation, are visible, and often children require the use of prosthetic or adaptive devices to assist them in performing routine activities such as walking or eating; sometimes surgery is warranted. However,

Parents' Reactions to the Birth of a Child with Disabilities

Loss	Rejection
Denial	Isolation
Anxiety	Hopelessness
Guilt	Resentment
Depression	Antagonism
Self-anger	

TABLE 10.1 Definitions and Types of Exceptionalities

Disability	Definition	Percent of population receiving special-education services
Physical disabilities	Physical limitations that interfere with school attendance or learning to such an extent that special services, equipment, training, or facilities are required; does not include children whose primary characteristics are visual or hearing impairments.	1.2%
Mental retardation	Significantly subaverage general intellectual functioning (below 70–75 IQ) existing concurrently with deficits in adaptive behavior and manifested during the developmental period. May be mild, moderate, or severe.	12%
Learning disabilities	Substantial academic difficulties with intelligence in the normal range, creating significant discrepancy between expectations for performance and actual performance; primary cause of school-related problems; not a single condition; may be coupled with behavioral problems.	52%
Communicative disorders	Speech impairment (voice, articulation, and fluency disorders) and language impairment in the areas of form (phonology, morphology, syntax), content (semantics), and use (pragmatics).	21%
Hearing impairments/ Deafness	Hearing impairment—Hearing is impaired, but the individual can process information from sound, usually with the help of aids. Deafness—Individual has little hearing even with aids; cannot use hearing to gain information.	1.3%
Visual impairment/ Blindness	Visual impairment—Individual can read print with the use of large-print books and/or magnifying devices. Blindness—Vision is so impaired that the individual must learn to read Braille or use audiotapes and records.	0.5%
Emotional/ behavioral disorders	Behaviors adversely affect educational performance and are exhibited to a marked degree over a long period of time; includes schizophrenic children but not socially maladjusted unless severely emotionally disturbed; excludes children with mild forms of behavior.	9%
Developmental delay (discretionary category for service eligibility)	Significant delays in one or more domains of physical, cognitive, communication, social/emotional, and adaptive development that warrant special-education and related services.	
Giftedness	Evidence of high performance capability in intellectual, creative, artistic, or leadership capacity or in specific academic fields; children require services not ordinarily provided by the school to develop such capabilities fully.	Not available

Source: Kraus, L., Stoddard, S., & Gilmartin, D. (1996). *Chartbook on disability in the United States,* 1996. Washington, DC: U.S. National Institute on Disability and Rehabilitation Research.

many children with physical disabilities have no sensory or learning impairments and can learn to do most of the things that children without disabilities can do, but they do them in different ways. The more visible or grotesque a physical disability is, the more likely the child is to experience insensitivity by society at large.

Mental Retardation

Approximately 12 percent of all children receiving special-education services are said to have mental retardation (Kraus et al., 1996). There are varying degrees of mental retardation: mild, moderate, severe, and profound. Both definitions and classifications of mental retardation have changed. Now both intellectual functioning and adaptive skills are taken into consideration for diagnosis, and the lower-limit IQ score has been reduced to 70. The

Parents of children with disabilities are faced with special challenges.

American Association of Mental Retardation recently has classified students with mental retardation by the degree of support they need to function as competently as they can. These categories are intermittent, limited, extensive, and pervasive, roughly corresponding to mild, moderate, severe, and profound. Most individuals have mild retardation and are capable of functioning adequately in society with little or no assistance (Hallahan & Kauffman, 2000).

Mental retardation rarely is caused by a single factor; typically there is complex interaction of factors. Causes can be grouped into four major categories: (1) socioeconomic and environmental factors, (2) injury, (3) infections and toxins, and (4) biological causes. It has been asserted that there are more than 250 causes of mental retardation. Down syndrome (mental retardation caused by a chromosomal abnormality) and fetal alcohol syndrome (mental retardation caused by maternal alcohol use during pregnancy) are two of the leading causes. Fragile X syndrome has been reported as the most common inherited form of mental retardation, especially for boys, since two-thirds of girls with Fragile X syndrome have IQs within the normal range (Freund, 1994).

Mental retardation usually is not detectable at birth unless there is an obvious birth defect associated with retardation, such as an unusually large head (hydrocephaly), an unusually small head (microcephaly), or the physical characteristics of Down syndrome. It may be undetected for months or even years. The more severe the retardation, the earlier it is detected. Delays in normal developmental milestones, such as walking and talking, may be the first signs of moderate retardation. Most children with mild to moderate retardation are identified by kindergarten or the primary grades.

Learning Disabilities

Of all the categories of exceptional children, that of the learning disabled is the most ambiguous and ubiquitous. Until the mid-1960s, there was a confusing variety of labels used to describe children with particular types of learning problems.

These labels included the minimally brain-injured, the dyslexic, slow learners, and the perceptually disabled. In 1966, 99 characteristics were attributed to children labeled learning disabled. It has been noted that this figure allows for 4,851 possible pairings of any two characteristics—a possibility that emphasizes the heterogeneity of the learning-disabled population. As late as 1989, 38 different definitions of learning disabilities had been identified (Smith & Luckasson, 1992), and 11 definitions have had some degree of acceptance since the 1960s (Hammill, 1990). Learning disabilities have been diagnosed in 52 percent of all children receiving special-education services (Kraus et al., 1996).

Almost everyone agrees that learning disabilities are not a single condition. The following four characteristics have been included in most definitions: IQ-achievement discrepancy, presumption of central nervous system dysfunction, psychological-processing disorders, and learning problems not due to environmental disadvantage, mental retardation, or emotional disturbance. The federal definition describes the disorder as being in one or more of the psychological processes involved in understanding or in using spoken or written language (Individuals with Disabilities Act, 1997). Children who are learning disabled may have difficulty listening, thinking, speaking, reading, writing, spelling, and/or performing mathematical calculations, and these learning problems may occur concomitantly with other disabilities. The children also may be inattentive, impulsive, and/or hyperactive. Most are not identified accurately until school age, and ordinarily parents do not suspect a problem until difficulties in school arise (Hallahan & Kauffman, 2000; Smith & Luckasson, 1992). Some professionals argue for early diagnosis of learning disabilities, but we agree with the position of other professionals, who caution against labeling a preschool child learning disabled, since it tends to lower teacher expectations and thereby discourages the child from reaching his real potential. In lieu of premature labeling of children as learning disabled, Haring et al. (1992) have advocated identifying clusters of characteristics that might indicate that a child is at risk for later academic difficulty. These clusters can be found in the Highlights.

Children with learning disabilities account for 50 percent of all children requiring special education, and their incidence has more than doubled since 1977–78, when prevalence figures were first calculated. The causes are elusive but tend to fall into three general categories: biological, genetic, and environmental. Central nervous system dysfunction is considered to be the primary biological cause. Learning disabilities, especially with reading, tend to run in families, but little information is available about the exact nature of the genetic component. One study (Oliver, Cole, & Hollingsworth, 1991) found that familial learning problems are more powerful predictors of learning status in children than any other factors. Because environmentally disadvantaged children have a high incidence of learning disabilities, environmental experiences seem to play a role, but their exact nature is unknown. It is likely that environmental experiences interact with biological and genetic factors to produce at least some forms of learning disabilities.

HIGHLIGHTS

Characteristics Identifying Children at Risk for Academic Difficulties

Lack of concept development
Speech delays
Receptive- and expressive-language delays
Directionality problems
Gross and fine motor delays
Attentional problems
Hyperactivity
Immature reasoning abilities
Visual and/or auditory perceptual problems
Lack of academic-readiness skills (e.g., alphabet knowledge, quantitative concepts)
Social and/or affective skills deficits

Source: Haring, K., et al. (1992). Labeling preschoolers as learning disabled. *Topics in Early Childhood Special Education, 12*(2), p. 157.

Attention Deficit/Hyperactivity Disorder. Attention deficit/hyperactivity disorder (ADHD) recently has captured enormous attention among professionals and the general public alike. Even though individuals currently identified as having ADHD are recognized as having a disability under Section 504 of the Rehabilitation Act, controversy still is raging over the advisability of making this disorder a separate legal category. Many professionals feel that existing categories are adequately serving the needs of children identified as having ADHD, and the disorder can be considered a type of learning disability (Reid, Maag, & Vasa, 1993). The American Psychiatric Association describes three types of ADHD: the Predominantly Inattentive Type, the Predominantly Hyperactive-Impulsive Type, and the Combined Type. Symptoms for the first two types vary, and the third type represents a combination of symptoms for Type I and Type II (American Psychiatric Association, 1994).

ADHD is the label that has been given to a set of symptoms in children reflecting excessive inattention or overactivity and impulsive responding, within the context of developmentally appropriate behavior for the child's age and gender group. Unable to sustain responses long enough to accomplish assigned tasks, these children show considerably less persistence than their peers. The same set of symptoms has been described in several different ways over the past few years—as minimal brain dysfunction, hyperkinetic reaction to childhood, attention deficit disorder with or without hyperactivity, and finally ADHD. Its prevalence is estimated at 3 percent to 5 percent of the child population, with boys outnumbering girls 6 to 1. According to some sources, more than half of these children also meet the criteria for behavioral disorders, including such behaviors as extreme stubbornness, noncompliance, hostility, rule violations, aggressive acts, untruthfulness, and taking things from others without permission (Landau & McAninch, 1993). One study found that 80 percent of the children identified as ADHD also were identified as having either behavioral disorders or learning disabilities (Reid et al., 1993).

It is important to point out that although ADHD has been presented by many as an accepted pathological condition, its validity as a distinct diagnostic entity is by no means accepted universally (Reid et al., 1993). There are significant problems with diagnosing the condition accurately, which is done most often through the use of behavior scales. Despite pressure from parents, serious questions remain about whether an accurate diagnosis can be made in preschool children. Concerns about behavior management peak about age 3. Such behaviors as inattention, overactivity, and aggression cannot be taken as definitive evidence of ADHD. These behaviors are normal for 3- and 4-year-olds. In parent-referred problematic preschoolers, 50 percent did not exhibit significant behavior problems at age 6. Early diagnosis of ADHD can lead to misdiagnosing in significantly large numbers of young children (Tynan & Nearing, 1994), who are, therefore, labeled unnecessarily.

Further, there is no consensus on the causes of ADHD. Twenty-eight hypothesized causes have been advanced—as varied as anxiety and depression, head trauma, and boredom. Many professionals cling tenaciously to the notion of a biological cause and thus support the use of medication to help control the child's behavior (Reid et al., 1993). Probably the most commonly accepted cause is neurological dysfunction, which often is linked to hereditary factors (Hallahan & Kauffman, 2000). Other professionals support the use of behavior modification, cognitive mediational techniques, and/or social-skills training to improve the child's behavior.

Communicative Disorders

Speech is the vocal production of language, and language is a formalized method of communication. Communication is either impaired or unsuccessful if the sender or the receiver cannot use the signals or symbols adequately. Communicative disorders have the potential to influence most aspects of a child's life, including social interaction. It is useful to distinguish between speech disorders and language disorders.

A speech disorder is an impairment of voice, articulation of speech sounds, and/or fluency. Voice disorders occur when there is an absence or an abnormal production of voice quality, pitch, loudness, resonance, and/or duration. Articulation disorders are the abnormal production of speech sounds. Fluency disorders are defined as the abnormal flow of verbal expression, characterized by impaired rate and rhythm that may be accompanied by struggle behavior. A language disorder is the impairment or deviant development of comprehension and/or use of a spoken, written, and/or other symbol system. This disorder may involve the form, the content, and/or the function of language (Hallahan & Kauffman, 2000).

It is difficult to estimate the prevalence of communication disorders because they are widely varied, are often difficult to identify, and occur in tandem with other disabilities, such as mental retardation, learning disabilities, or sensory impairments. It is estimated that nearly one-fourth of all children identified for special education receive services primarily for communicative disorders, and speech/language therapy is one of the most frequently provided services for children with other major disabilities.

The causes of many communicative disorders are unknown, but in many cases, the causes are multiple and interrelated. Hallahan and Kauffman (2000) categorized them in the following way: Central factors are causes related to central nervous system dysfunction; peripheral factors are sensory or physical impairments that are not caused by brain injury but that contribute to language disorders; environmental and emotional factors refer to disorders that have their origin in the child's physical and/or psychological environment; and mixed factors are any combination of the preceding factors. Communication disorders must be understood within the context of normal language development, and for young children, there is great variability in the age at which children demonstrate specific language skills. Therefore, often it is difficult to determine whether a child is demonstrating delayed language development or a language disorder.

Hearing Impairments

There are two groups of hearing-impaired children: those who are deaf and those who are hard of hearing. The distinctions between these two groups are not always clear, since different professionals define them in different ways. In general, however, a child is considered deaf if she cannot process language information by auditory means, either with or without a hearing aid. A child is hard of hearing if, with a hearing aid, she has enough residual hearing to process successfully language information through auditory means. Deafness also is categorized as *prelingual* (occurring at birth) or *postlingual* (occurring at some point after the development of speech and language). It has been estimated that 95 percent of the children who are identified as deaf are prelingually deaf (Hallahan & Kauffman, 2000; Smith & Luckasson, 1992).

The causes of hearing impairments are classified on the basis of the location of the problem within the hearing mechanism: the inner ear, the middle ear, or the outer ear, with the most severe impairments being associated with the inner ear. The most frequent cause of inner ear problems resulting in deafness is genetic. Acquired causes include both bacterial and viral infections (e.g., meningitis, mumps, measles), prematurity, oxygen deprivation at birth, prenatal infections of the mother, mother/fetus Rh incompatibility, blows to the head, and excessive noise levels (Hallahan & Kauffman, 2000). Nine out of 10 deaf children have hearing parents.

Severely hearing-impaired children have great difficulty in the comprehension and production of spoken language. It is more difficult for children who are prelingually deaf to speak than it is for children postlingually deaf because they have never had a spoken-language model and they are unable to receive feedback on the sounds they attempt to produce. Therefore, it is important for deaf children to be taught an effective communication system. Most educators use a total communication approach, which is a combination of oral production and manual production (sign language).

Though deaf children are not necessarily intellectually deficient, often their academic achievement suffers because so much of academic work, especially reading, depends on mastery of spoken language. Social interaction, too, is difficult for deaf children who have no way of communicating with their hearing peers unless they learn American Sign Language. This need for social interaction may be the reason that deaf individuals, both children and adults, seek to associate with other deaf individuals with whom they can communicate (Hallahan & Kauffman, 2000).

Visual Impairments/Blindness

Like hearing impairments, visual impairments fall into two categories: the blind and the partially sighted. Further, as with hearing impairments, there is more than one definition of the categories. Children are declared legally blind if their visual acuity is 20/200 or less in the better eye, even with the use of glasses, or if their field of peripheral vision is extremely narrow. Partially sighted children have visual acuity between 20/70 and 20/200 in the better eye with glasses. Educators prefer the definitions noted in Table 10.1; that is, blind children must learn to read Braille or use aural methods such as tapes and records, whereas partially sighted children are able to read using glasses and/or magnification.

Visual impairment/blindness is one of the least prevalent disabilities in children. The most common visual problems, such as nearsightedness, farsightedness, and astigmatism, may be serious enough to cause significant impairment, but most can be corrected with glasses or contact lenses. The more serious impairments are caused by glaucoma, cataracts, and diabetes, all of which are more common in adults but which also occur in children, especially cataracts and diabetes. Most of the visual impairments that affect children are due to prenatal causes, many of which are hereditary. Other causes are excessively high levels of oxygen administered to babies born premature and maternal prenatal infectious diseases such as syphilis and rubella (German measles) (Hallahan & Kauffman, 2000).

Children who are visually impaired are not significantly disabled in their ability to understand and use language, but their early language development may be restricted by the lack of visual experiences, making their language more self-centered. There is no evidence to suggest that blindness results in lower intelligence, but children who are blind rely more heavily on the senses of hearing and touch to perceive and learn about their world. Perhaps the greatest challenge for blind children is developing mobility skills that enable them to move about effectively. Further, blind infants possess a limited range of behaviors for initiating and maintaining social interactions because of lack of contact and absence of smiling (Erwin, 1994; Hallahan & Kauffman, 2000; Smith & Luckasson, 1992).

Emotional/Behavioral Disorders

It is particularly difficult to arrive at both a label and a definition for children who have extreme social-interpersonal or intrapersonal problems. These children variously have been described as abusive, defiant, irritable, destructive, quarrelsome, withdrawn, irresponsible, jealous, hostile, aggressive, and unpredictable. There have been many labels—emotionally impaired, behaviorally impaired, socially/emotionally handicapped, emotionally disturbed, socially maladjusted, and so on. For some time, the term *seriously emotionally disturbed* was the favored one, but *behaviorally disordered* has been preferred by some professionals because it focuses on observable aspects of the child's problems—behavior. Currently the term *emotional or behavioral disorder* appears to be the generally accepted one. Despite definition difficulties, most experts agree that children who fit this category demonstrate extreme behavior that is unacceptable within the social and cultural context and the problem is chronic rather than situational. Often the phrase "[the behavior] adversely affects educational performance" is added as a qualifier. However, the issues of definition and which children are included and excluded are far from settled (Hallahan & Kauffman, 2000; Smith & Luckasson, 1992).

Two types of disordered behavior have been described—externalizing and internalizing (Achenbach, Howell, Quay, & Conners, 1991; Walker & Severson, 1990). Externalizing behavior consists of aggressive behaviors expressed outwardly toward others, whereas internalizing behaviors are expressed in a more socially withdrawn fashion and include anxiety and depression. The most common behaviors of children being served by special education are externalizing—aggressiveness, acting out, disruption. Boys with these behaviors outnumber girls 5 to 1. Several researchers have described other specific behaviors that represent the following dimensions: conduct disorder, socialized aggression, attention problems/immaturity, anxiety/withdrawal, psychotic behavior, and motor excess. Children may demonstrate several behaviors that represent more than one dimension. For example, a child might exhibit behaviors considered to be in the conduct-disorder dimension, such as disruption, temper tantrums, and fighting, and at the same time show motor-excess behaviors, such as inability to sit still and excessive talkativeness (from Hallahan & Kauffman, 2000).

Behavioral disorders range from mild to severe, and most students who receive services for them are not psychotic. Prevalence estimates vary considerably because both definition and screening are difficult. Four factors are believed to contribute to emotional/behavioral disorders: biological disorders, dysfunctional family relationships, contextual influences, and negative school experiences. Rarely can the disability be linked to a single cause. Biological factors such as difficult temperament, disease, malnutrition, substance abuse, and brain trauma all may be contributing factors. Neurological and genetic factors are especially associated with severe behavioral disorders such as autism and schizophrenia.

Dysfunctional family relationships, especially negative parent-child interactions, often are associated with behavioral disorders, but the nature of these associations is complex and unclear. The same is true for school experiences, which can influence a child's behavior in either negative or positive ways. Contextual factors, such as poverty, exposure to violence and drugs, and standards and expectations for behavior, are potential influencers. Very few children with emotional/behavioral disorders have high intelligence, and their ability to interact effectively with adults and peers is limited severely (Hallahan & Kauffman, 2000).

Developmental Delay

In 1991 a new discretionary category of eligibility for preschool children was introduced. It includes children from 3 to 5 years with significant delays in one or more domains of physical, cognitive, communicative, social and emotional, and adaptive development who, as a result of their delays, need special education and services. No categorical disability label (e.g., mentally retarded, learning disabled) is necessary. The rationale for avoiding premature categorical diagnosis is based on concern about the predictive power of assessment measures, professional hope for spontaneous improvement, and concern about the negative effects of labeling. Some professionals have expressed concern about the utility of the new discretionary category of eligibility when categorical labels are required for children entering elementary school to receive services (Bernheimer, Keogh, & Coots, 1993).

Using two longitudinal studies, Bernheimer et al. (1993) found that, as a group, children did not "outgrow" their developmental delay; rather, their cognitive/developmental scores remained stable and delayed. Behavior problems also remained stable, but there was a trend for reported physical and speech/language problems to decrease at elementary school age. In the two studies, 74 percent and 83 percent of the children, respectively, were placed into special education in elementary school. Ten percent did not require special education.

The authors concluded that *developmental delay* is a useful category for ensuring early services. The label itself is an acceptable and nonpejorative term that will allow children access to services they need without the improper labeling of *handicapped.* The label also minimizes the possibility of inaccurate diagnosis in young children because of the wide variability in development and limited predictive power of assessment tools.

Giftedness

Giftedness is the only exceptionality not included in the category of disabilities. Contrary to other exceptionalities, giftedness and special talents are characteristics to be nurtured. There is little agreement about the definition of giftedness, except that children identified as gifted excel in some way(s) when compared with their peers. The federal definition appears in Table 10.1. However, federal laws do not require special services for gifted students as they do for students with disabilities. Most states mandate programs for gifted students, and each state has its own definition of gifted. The most common features of these state definitions are general intellectual ability, specific academic aptitude, creative-thinking ability, advanced ability in the fine arts and performing arts, and leadership ability (Hallahan & Kauffman, 2000).

Assessment measures to determine giftedness vary, as do definitions. Therefore, prevalence estimates vary, depending on the definition. The most common methods of identification are IQ tests (group and individual); achievement tests; teacher, parent, peer, and self nominations; and evaluations of students' work and performances. It is important to use multiple assessment tools and instruments that are not biased against children of color to avoid identifying only White, upper-middle-class children.

Giftedness is the result of the interaction of genetics, biology, and environmental experiences. Nongenetic biological conditions that contribute to intelligence are nutritional and neurological factors. Environmental influences include those of the family, the school, the peer group, and the community. Socioeconomic status, education of parents, degree of stimulation in both home and school environments, support and encouragement from parents and teachers, the design of the curriculum, and access to gifted role models all are factors that nurture the potential for giftedness.

Gifted children seem to be superior in almost every aspect of their development—physical/motor, social/emotional, and language/cognitive. However, it is more difficult to provide the enriching experiences and services for gifted children than it is to provide services for children with disabilities because funding is more limited and the public is less sympathetic to gifted children than to children with disabilities. Gifted children from affluent families are more likely to have their talents nurtured by their families than are gifted children from low-income and/or minority families, who often are overlooked in the identification process. A variety of educational models exist for gifted children, but research on the effectiveness of these models is sparse.

In summary, exceptional children may have one or more of the following disabilities: physical defects, mental retardation, learning disabilities, communicative disorders, hearing impairments, visual impairments, emotional/behavioral disorders, or developmental delay. Children also may be gifted. A child who has a learning disability in addition to being gifted is referred to as *twice exceptional*. The extent of disability may range from mild to severe. Many conditions have both definitional and identification problems, making the accuracy of prevalence estimations difficult. The majority of disabilities in children are congenital, but some are acquired after birth.

OTHER AT-RISK OR DISABLING CONDITIONS

A variety of other conditions place children at developmental risk or result in chronic illness or disability. The degree of risk is determined by both biological and environmental factors. Biological factors include prematurity, respiratory distress, and maternal prenatal substance use. Environmental risks include poverty, lack of nurturance, and nonsynchronous interaction between child and parent. These two types of risk combine to determine the actual risk to a child (Thurman & Gonsalves, 1993). Children born with less than optimal neonatal status and poor environments have the worst long-term prognosis.

A study conducted by Bendersky and Lewis (1994) identified two types of environmental risk: social class (based on the education and occupation of the parents) and family risk, which included the size of the social-support network, the quality of the home environment, the quality of mother-child interaction, minority status, presence or absence of the father in the home, positive and negative stressful life events, and the number of children in the household. Although a family's social class tended to remain stable over the 1-year time period of the study, family risk was clearly more likely to change as a function of the changing nature of the family situation.

The results indicated that the two environmental risk factors represented different aspects of the environment and had differential influences on specific aspects of the child's development. When the effect of medical status was removed from the analyses, the family risk factor had greater impact on language and cognitive development than did social class. The higher the family risk, the worse the outcome. Biological risk variables continued to have a significant relation to sensorimotor, gross and fine motor skills and, to a lesser extent, communication skills, through the second year of life. These results suggest that the environment has the greatest impact on cognitive skills, as opposed to abilities that are predominantly motoric. The following are examples of conditions that place children at risk, both biologically and environmentally.

Prematurity

Babies who are born preterm are less active, initiate fewer interactions, and provide less feedback to their caregivers than babies who are born at term. Though premature babies are born at risk biologically, they also may be at risk environmentally. Preterm neonatal behaviors such as maintaining less eye contact, averting their gaze, smiling less, using more unclear signals, and resisting cuddling may discourage inexperienced mothers from initiating interactions. Further, if the preterm baby is born to a teenager, in addition to lacking experience, the teen may feel depressed, angry, scared,

guilty, and incompetent, which will have significant impact on her interactions with her infant (Thurman & Gonsalves, 1993).

Babies who are extremely premature require care in the Neonatal Intensive Care Unit (NICU), sometimes for weeks, even months. This experience is stressful for parents and may result in distancing, creating a feeling of lack of control over the situation and the baby's fate. Parents often need help with ways to touch and hold their babies who are attached to wires, intravenous lines, and tubes (Krehbiel, Munsick-Bruno, & Lowe, 1991). Designing family-focused intervention becomes a challenge for medical staff.

Prenatal Substance Use

Prevalence rates for maternal alcohol and drug use before delivery range from a low of 8 percent to a high of 31 percent (Gottwald & Thurman, 1994; Poulsen, 1994). Prenatal substance use crosses all community, racial, and socioeconomic groups. Children born to alcohol- and drug-using women are at high risk for developmental, behavioral, and/or learning problems. In addition to substance use, other maternal considerations include nutrition, physical and mental health, intellectual abilities, education, age, economic resources, parenting skills, parental esteem, and social supports. The greater the number of maternal vulnerabilities, the greater the risk to the child. Children of substance-abusing parents also are at greater risk for child abuse and neglect. Child factors, too, influence developmental outcome—physical and mental health, developmental and neurodevelopmental intactness, and postnatal factors such as health care, nutrition, and illness (Johnson & Left, 1999).

The group of infants most compromised are those with fetal alcohol syndrome (FAS)—1 to 3 in 1,000 births. Possible effects include central nervous system dysfunction/disorder, growth retardation, and facial dysmorphology, all of which may be permanent. The developmental effects depend on the amount, timing, and condition of the fetus's exposure to alcohol, as well as the characteristics of the mother and the child's genetic susceptibility to alcohol effects. There has been no documented safe level of drinking during pregnancy (Olson, 1994; Poulsen, 1994).

Neurodevelopmental immaturities are characteristic of children exposed to both alcohol and other drugs prenatally, including poor sleeping and feeding patterns, poor regulation of behavior, hypersensitivity to stimuli, inconsolability, depressed interactive behaviors, and poor organization of behavior. Some children outgrow these immaturities; others do not. The goodness of fit between the child's needs and constitutional characteristics and the parent's expectations, demands, and provision of opportunities will affect developmental outcomes. Especially important are parental emotional availability and responsiveness to the child's bids for attention, parental experience and skill, and parental belief in his or her power of influencing the child's development (Johnson & Left, 1999; Poulsen, 1994).

Recent concern has been expressed over the large numbers of women who use cocaine during pregnancy. The neurobehavioral functioning of newborns of mothers who use cocaine includes tremors and irritability in addition to sleeping and feeding difficulties. These babies may exhibit a set of behaviors that influence the nature of the mother-infant relationship. Studies have found that these mothers may feel less than competent interacting with their children, divert their energy from interacting with their infants to finding their next "high," lead chaotic lives with little access to social-support networks, and are more depressed than their peers, leading to unresponsiveness, inattentiveness, and negative perceptions of the child (Gottwald & Thurman, 1994).

In a study comparing mothers who used cocaine and mothers who were drug-free in their interactions with their newborns within 48 hours after birth, Gottwald and Thurman (1994) found several differences. Mothers who used cocaine spent more time merely looking at their infants and more time disengaged from their infants than did the mothers who were drug-free. Infants who were prenatally drug-exposed were more often asleep, more drowsy, and more distressed than their drug-free peers. The difficulty in organization of states of arousal made the drug-exposed infants less accessible for interaction with their mothers; they were less alert, less active, and less responsive to social interaction. These early behaviors of both infants and mothers may set in motion an interaction pattern that could have negative long-term outcomes unless intervention occurs.

It should be pointed out that both alcohol and drugs have differential effects on fetuses. Not all children prenatally exposed to alcohol are born with FAS. Not all babies of mothers who use drugs show neurological disturbances. The complex interaction of an array of biological and environmental factors determines developmental outcomes. However, evidence of both short-term and long-term negative outcomes in large numbers of children suggests that pregnant women should refrain from using any amount of drugs—either prescription or over-the-counter—and from consuming any amount of alcohol.

Acquired Immune Deficiency Syndrome

Acquired immune deficiency syndrome (AIDS) was first diagnosed in children in 1983. Between 1993 and 1997, there were 2,768 cases of AIDS reported for children age 5 and younger; 926 cases reported for children ages 6 through 12; and 2,087 cases reported for young people 13 through 19 years of age. For every year since 1993, the numbers have gradually declined for the oldest group, and for every year except 1994, the numbers have declined for the youngest and middle groups (U.S. Bureau of the Census, 1998). However, because of the rigid criteria for classifying AIDS cases and the many pediatric AIDS cases mistaken for other immune disorders, it has been estimated that actual cases vastly exceed reported cases. Both African American and Hispanic children are overrepresented in the AIDS population. New York State reported in 1990 that AIDS was the leading cause of death in children 1–4 years of age in these minority groups (Johnson, 1993; Lesar & Maldonado, 1994).

Between 12 percent and 35 percent of children born to mothers infected by human immunodeficiency virus (HIV) are infected themselves. Infection that is passed perinatally from mother to child accounts for the largest number of new cases. Maternal intravenous drug use is reported in more than 50 percent of congenitally infected children; in another 30 percent, mothers report being partners of either intravenous drug users or partners of drug users of individuals with HIV infection. By 1 year of age, approximately 25 percent of HIV-infected children will have developed AIDS (Johnson, 1993).

This epidemic has tragic consequences for children, parents, families, and communities. Survival time for children after diagnosis depends on the timing of the infection during gestation, premature birth, presence of malnutrition, route of transmission, and type of infections acquired. Often parents live with the fear that their children will experience rapid deterioration, dying precipitously after apparently stable neurologic courses. However, children with AIDS are now living longer and coping with a chronic illness. Developmental outcomes for young children include motor delays or increasing spasticity; delays or regression in the social smile; delays or regression in vocalization/speech; and generalized developmental delay. For older children, developmental outcomes include psychomotor slowing, emotional lability, social withdrawal, attentional difficulties, and visual/spatial dysfunction (Bruder, 1995; Johnson, 1993). These difficulties are due to the effect of the virus on the central nervous system.

The child with AIDS becomes a victim of ignorance and fear, experiencing loneliness, rejection, and inability to participate freely in daily life activities. Though there are no documented cases of a teacher, a child-care provider, or an uninfected child contracting HIV from a child who is HIV-positive or who has AIDS, these children still experience discrimination from society. Care for infected children presents extraordinary medical, psychological, and financial demands that strain the caretaking capabilities of any family (Johnson, 1993; Lesar & Maldonado, 1994).

CHALLENGES FOR FAMILIES WITH EXCEPTIONAL CHILDREN

Parenting is challenging for all families, but families with exceptional children are faced with special challenges. At least two characteristics have been reported in the literature that differentiate families with exceptional children from families with children without disabilities. The first is that the caregiving demands associated with children with disabilities are substantially greater than those associated with children without disabilities. These demands include not only the additional caregiving time needed by children with disabilities but also the increased difficulty of routine tasks such as feeding, bathing, and dressing.

Stress and Family Environment

The second characteristic is that parents of children with disabilities experience significantly more stress in child rearing than other parents do (Floyd & Gallagher, 1997). In fact, there is considerable literature related to stress and coping in these families, and most of it supports the finding of increased stress. However, there is substantial variation in the nature and extent to which individual families report stress. Further, in most cases increased stress does not lead to family dysfunction (Dyson, 1996; Judge, 1998). This fact is an important one, because in the past, families of children with disabilities have been viewed as pathological—stress and dysfunction have been assumed to be concomitant.

Research has identified several potential causes for increased stress in these families: the increased caregiving demands, the need to feel normal, lack of information about their children's condition, uncertainty and disappointment about their children's future, severity/type of disability, increased financial burden, lack of available and appropriate child care, single parenthood, and lack of support systems (Dyson, 1996; Freedman, Litchfield & Warfield, 1995; Gottlieb, 1997; Judge, 1998). One study found that 23 percent of the mothers of young disabled children had given up paid employment to remain in the home to care for the children, and 41 percent of mothers had declined offers of paid employment for the same reason (Trute, 1990). Another study of mothers with children with severe disabilities found that 62 percent never received help with household chores, and 60 percent had never or only sometimes had baby-sitters for their disabled children. Further, 30 percent said they never received help in understanding the child's needs, and almost 19 percent reported that they never received information about available programs or services (Marcenko & Meyers, 1991).

Despite these stress-inducing conditions, families with children with disabilities appear to adapt remarkably well. Innocenti, Huh, and Boyce (1992) investigated two aspects of parental stress: stress resulting from the parent's perception of what the child brings to the parent-child relationship (referred to as child stress) and the impact of parenting this child on other aspects of the parent's life, such as spousal relationship and physical well-being (parent stress). They found that parents of children with disabilities reported significantly more stress than other parents and that the highest stress was related primarily to issues dealing directly with the child rather than to parent-related factors.

Several studies have indicated that the environments of families differ little between those with disabled children and those without. As assessed by the Family Assessment Measure in one study, the levels of organization and functioning were similar for the two types of families. The factors that were related to functioning in the families of children with disabilities were age of the child, number of children in the family, and marital adjustment. A key element in positive family adaptation was the level of dyadic cohesion between the two parents—as cohesion increased, family strength increased (Trute, 1990).

The research conducted by Mahoney, O'Sullivan, and Robinson (1992) found that the families of children from birth to 6 with disabilities participated less frequently in recreational activities and had a stronger moral/religious orientation than general population. Interestingly, overall, interpersonal relationships as measured by family cohesion, conflict, and expressiveness appeared slightly more favorable for families of children with disabilities. There were no significant relationships between the severity of children's disability and each of the 10 subscales of the Family Environment Scale, but the more severe the child's disability, the more likely the family was to have scores suggestive of distressed family functioning. The results suggested that families of children with disabilities have family environments comparable to those of families without disabled children and apparently adapted to their problems.

Dyson's (1991) study included parents from 110 families, half with typically developing children and half with children with disabilities. She found strong evidence of stress in families with disabled children, but family groups did not differ on general family functioning. However, families with children with disabilities showed a distinct style of functioning along family dimensions. These families emphasized achievement and moral/religious beliefs and valued set rules and procedures for operating family life more than families with typical children. Although her findings suggested that a child with disabilities may have differential effects on various family psychological dimensions, parental stress did not necessarily predict family dysfunction.

Comparison of Mothers and Fathers.   Few efforts have been made to explore the differences of family members in their perception of the effect of a child with disabilities; most research has focused on mothers. Beckman (1991) used both questionnaires and interviews with mothers and fathers of children with and without disabilities. In general, mothers reported more stress than did fathers. The results suggested that mothers and fathers clearly had different perceptions of the impact of their child on their lives. Whereas mothers reported more depression, more difficulties with their sense of competence, more restrictions of the parental role, more effects on their relationships with their spouses, and more effects on their health, fathers reported more problems with attachment. There was considerable variability within each type of disability, and high levels of stress were reported across a variety of disabilities. Forty-four percent of fathers and 78 percent of mothers of children with disabilities reported stress scores in the high range.

Another study included only fathers—20 fathers of autistic children, 20 fathers of children with Down syndrome, and 20 fathers of developmentally normal children. Although fathers of children with developmental disabilities reported more disruption in family planning and increased financial burden because of their disabled children, their reported levels of perceived parenting competence, marital satisfaction, and social support were comparable to those reported by fathers of developmentally normal children. The hypothesis that fathers of autistic children would report more adjustment problems than fathers of children with Down syndrome was not supported. Overall, relative to the severe deficits observed in the sample of children, fathers demonstrated healthy levels of psychological adaptation to rearing children with disabilities. The three groups of fathers did not differ significantly in their degree of perceived parenting efficacy and satisfaction, and fathers of sons perceived parenthood as more satisfying than fathers of daughters. Reported concerns about family finances and disruptions in family planning did not appear to have a negative impact on observed father-child interactions in the autism and Down syndrome groups. It should be noted that all fathers in this study were White, middle- to upper-middle-class, and members of parent/advocacy support groups, making them a fairly select group. Fathers who had no access to support groups might have reported differently (Rodrigue, Morgan, & Geffken, 1992). Heller, Hsieh, and Rowitz (1997) found highly uneven contributions from mothers and fathers of children with mental retardation. Mothers invested more time and obtained more types of support. They were, in turn, more affected than fathers by the health and behaviors of their children. Floyd, Gilliom, and Costigan (1998) found that fathers of children with mental retardation who were happily married were more involved in parenting than fathers who were unhappily married.

Sparling, Berger, and Biller (1992) noted that recent research has suggested that fathers of children with disabilities are not necessarily depressed. One study found that fathers' maintenance of self-esteem, psychological stability, and social support were significantly associated with the child's health status (weight gain, improved functioning). Another study found that better communication of children with Down syndrome predicted both fathers' and mothers' adjustment scores, and fathers' early adjustment predicted mothers' long-term adjustment. Even though fathers have been shown to be sensitive to the condition of their children, it has less influence on their daily lives than on that of mothers. Studies have shown that fathers experience less stress than mothers with respect to depression, role restrictions, personal health, and marital problems.

The Impact of Support.   The research literature is unequivocal about the positive impact of support on families of children with disabilities. The greater the level of social support, especially informal support, the lower the level of stress. Spousal support seems especially critical. Mothers of children with disabilities have been reported to spend twice as much time in caretaking than mothers of children without disabilities (Innocenti et al., 1992), yet fathers do not always share the burden of caretaking. Several researchers have concluded that how well mothers of children with disabilities function with regard to depression, marital adjustment, and parenting appears to be related to their partners' capacity to be supportive, both instrumentally and expressively. Suarez and Baker (1997) found that a strong and satisfying marital relationship with mutual support buffers the negative effect of children's behavior problems. For mothers, spousal support moderated the effects of children's difficult behaviors on social relationships, whereas for fathers spousal support resulted in less negative perceptions of parenting.

Several other studies have noted the mediating effects of support on stress and family functioning.

Beckman (1991) found that increased informal support was significantly associated with decreased stress, and fathers and mothers reported similar levels of informal support. Formal support, however, was not significantly associated with lower stress levels, but fathers found formal support useful as a way of mediating general life stress. Mahoney et al. (1992) found that mothers' satisfaction with support consistently was associated with their perceptions of more positive family environments. Herman and Thompson (1995) found that the helpfulness of social supports, combined with children's characteristics and income, was related to parents' perception of resource adequacy. Half of the parents in their study did not have access to parent-support groups or other self-help groups. However, when parents had access to other parents who were seen as helpful, they saw their basic and child-related resources as more adequate. The researchers concluded that formal support services should complement informal support. Finally, Trivette and Dunst (1992) found that greater informal social support was associated with more parental positive emotional and physical well-being, decreased time demands, better-integrated family units, more frequent interactions with children, and perceptions of children's behavior as less troublesome. The researchers concluded that parent, family, and child functioning all are affected by intrafamily role sharing and support from extrafamily sources.

Parent-Child Relationships

As we discussed earlier, the impact of a child with disabilities on parents and other family members can be substantial. From a systems perspective, each family member is part of a system of interdependent parts. Situations and events that affect one family member affect all others, and each part of the system affects each of the other parts. In fact, a family is the central microsystem through which an individual develops, fulfilling his needs for identity, relatedness, intimacy, and growth. The family mediates between the individual and the society, and the microsystem interacts with the macrosystem—the various institutions and individuals outside the family, such as school personnel, community agencies, and churches. A child's development, then, is the result of interactions with both the microsystem and the macrosystem and the contribution of his own unique characteristics.

Throughout this book, we have discussed parent-child interactions in a variety of types of families. There are many elements or characteristics common to all families that facilitate positive outcomes. On the other hand, each family type has its particular challenges, and each family within those types has its unique characteristics. Families with children with disabilities share similar challenges, regardless of the type of disability. Some already have been mentioned, such as the grieving process, the increased burden of caregiving, financial pressures, guilt, uncertainty about the cause of the child's disability, and uncertainty about the child's future, all of which contribute to added stress. However, each type of disability brings with it additional special challenges, which will be described briefly below.

Physical Disabilities. The burden of care for a child with physical disabilities depends on the type and severity of the particular disability. When a child has severe neurological problems that prevent independent locomotion, she remains dependent on her parents long after the infancy stage. Lifting and transporting become more difficult as the child matures, and toilet learning and self-feeding may occur much later than usual. Parents may become socially isolated if they are reluctant or unable to take their disabled children to public places. This reluctance may be especially strong when the child's disability is extremely visible. Increased demands by children and fewer rewards to parents may cause angry feelings toward the child and subsequent guilt.

Many physical disabilities require the use of special equipment or prosthetic devices, which may create logistical problems. If the child has difficulty getting around, parents may be tempted to be overprotective and/or intrusive, doing things for the child that he may be able to do for himself if given time and patience and thereby encouraging unnecessary dependence. This dependence may be exacerbated if the child is unable to enter into extracurricular activities with his peers because of his physical limitations. Parents should be encouraged to nurture the child's self-concept and body image, focusing on his strengths.

Mental Retardation. The initial diagnosis of mental retardation may be especially difficult for parents because they must accept that the child will be forever limited in intellectual development. The infant is likely to look perfectly normal at birth (except in the cases of profound retardation and Down syndrome), only later to demonstrate that something is wrong. This delayed diagnosis, however, can have both positive and negative effects. During the early days and months of the child's life, parents will be able to get off to a good start with the child without the trauma associated with a diagnosed disability. These early positive patterns may make it easier for parents to cope with their grief at a later time. On the other hand, delayed diagnosis may be confusing and frustrating to parents if the cause of retardation is not known and if they perceive their roles in the child's optimal development as ambiguous or hopeless.

Babies who are at risk for mental retardation due to neurological sequelae may require prolonged feedings with immature sucking, failing to provide adequate reward to the mother. The child who lacks muscle tone, is floppy, and is difficult to handle will be picked up less often, which inhibits opportunities to learn and thus increases the cognitive disability (Gath, 1993). Parents of children with mental retardation experience recurring crises arising from the lack of normal developmental progression. The slowed rate of development and the discrepancy from the norm become a source for heightened stress. These crises are likely to occur at the age when children who are typically developing ordinarily would begin to walk and talk, begin regular kindergarten, experience the onset of puberty, and celebrate their twenty-first birthdays. Further, parents may experience a crisis when a younger sibling's development surpasses that of

the mentally retarded child. Interestingly, both mothers and fathers have been found to provide *more* support functions to children who have *less* severe mental retardation (Heller et al., 1997).

Finding appropriate child-care and preschool programs for children with mental retardation is difficult for many parents. If the child is severely retarded, the parent may decide to remain at home and care for her. Separation from siblings when the child leaves home for the first time can cause stress. Parents also have expressed frustration in trying to "get through" to retarded children whose communication is impaired, especially when they are older (Gath, 1993). Setting reasonable expectation levels for the child's behavior and performance can be extremely difficult for parents. Parental warmth, nurturance, and acceptance, focusing on the child's total development, are important.

Learning Disabilities. Growing evidence suggests that children who demonstrate severe academic difficulties during their school years tend to have pervasive problems throughout their lives. Yet there is no prototypic learning-disabled child; these children are characterized as much by their differences as by their similarities. Because of the diversity of characteristics, the lack of a visible disability, problems with definitions, and the inadvisability of early identification, parents may perceive these children as lazy, stubborn, or unmotivated. Parents inadvertently may push the child beyond his capabilities, and he may respond with inconsistent behavior and frequent mood changes.

Unfortunately, many children with learning disabilities develop emotional/behavioral disorders, partly because their learning problems have led to repeated experiences of failure, perhaps coupled with rejection by parents, teachers, and peers. These children have been found to have lower self-concepts, more anxiety, and lower peer acceptance than normally achieving children. One of the most insidious aspects of a learning disability is its invisibility—delayed and conflicting diagnoses are common. Consequently, parents may experience more stress than parents of children with other disabilities because of frustration and confusion about the child's true abilities.

Children with learning disabilities need an abundance of affection, praise, and approval from parents and peers. Parents need to be supported in their efforts to provide as many successful experiences for these children as possible—even a series of small accomplishments. Because of the child's distractibility and possible overactivity, she will need reasonable and flexible expectations for conformity. Instructions should be clear, simple, and well enunciated. A partnership between parents and teachers to provide appropriate intervention while setting reasonable expectations can help these children lead more rewarding lives.

Attention Deficit-Hyperactivity Disorder.   Parents of children who demonstrate some of the characteristics of ADHD may engage in "physician shopping" until they get a diagnosis of ADHD (Reid et al., 1993). This situation may occur because parents are so frustrated by the child's inattention, extreme activity, insensitivity to rules, and/or noncompliance that they are searching for a logical explanation that does not place blame on themselves. Society is much more sympathetic to conditions believed to have a medical or physical origin than to an emotional one. Medical classifications essentially are "no fault" labels (Reid et al., 1993).

Some experts contend that there is no evidence to date to suggest that parenting or child rearing is related to the primary symptoms of ADHD, but secondary symptoms may be related to the child's social environment (Landau & McAninch, 1993). Others state that it is hard to distinguish between ADHD and a parent-child interaction problem during the preschool years (Tynan & Nearing, 1994). Clearly, adequate insight into the symptoms, causes, diagnosis, and treatment of ADHD is yet to come. Thus, it seems wise to take a cautionary approach with young children in setting expectations and making demands.

Children may need behavioral treatment, such as behavior modification and/or social-skills training. The use of rewards is particularly effective, and verbal praise is crucial. Directions should be specific and brief. Seeking to control behavior through medication should be a last resort.

Communicative Disorders.   Children with communicative disorders are faced with major obstacles to social communication. An inability to convey one's thoughts and feelings can lead to frustration and often aggression. Speech and language disorders in children range from mild to severe. Many can be improved through speech therapy. Children who have little or no useful language by the time they are 3 years old usually are considered to have severe mental retardation or severe emotional disturbance (unless they are deaf) (Hallahan & Kauffman, 2000).

Early language learning occurs within the context of mother-child interactions, and all mothers and other caregivers should be encouraged to talk frequently to babies. For mildly impaired preschool children, normal language development can be facilitated by listening attentively and empathically, providing appropriate language models, encouraging children to use their communication skills appropriately, asking open-ended questions, and offering many opportunities for language learning. However, early intervention with children with communicative disorders is critical, and parental efforts may need to be augmented by the intervention of a speech therapist. Nonverbal children will require a specialist in language training to help them acquire functional language. Some children will require a system of augmentative or alternative communication, such as manual signing or utilization of communication boards or electronic devices.

Hearing Impairments/Deafness.   Deafness usually is unexpected and may be difficult to detect in infants, especially by hearing parents. The average age for detection of congenital hearing loss has been reported to be 15–16 months. However, the increased practice of screening newborns who are at biological risk before they leave the hospital can result in much earlier diagnosis for many children. Some researchers suggest that the full impact of deafness is not felt by parents until the preschool years, when the communication gap between deaf and hearing children becomes more evident (Meadow-Orlans, 1994). During the early weeks and months, there often is a circular relationship between the hearing mother or caregiver and the deaf infant. The child is unable to communicate, and the mother becomes discouraged and frustrated and subsequently diminishes her efforts. Experts report that frequent interaction with and positive feedback from family members can account for much of the impact of the deaf child's development of positive self-identity, especially in light of their risk for negative peer interactions (Guralnick, Connor, Hammond, Gottman, & Kinnish, 1996; Spencer, 1996).

Some evidence suggests that deaf children are more impulsive than hearing children and often are rated by their mothers as being overly dependent, restless, fussy, and disobedient. Thus, secure attachment from infant to mother may be compromised. Normal developmental milestones such as sitting and walking may occur later than expected, especially if the child is severely deaf. Unless an effective early communication system is established, the child's cognitive abilities may be handicapped.

Social and emotional development may suffer as well. Family conversations represent important interactive vehicles for developing social skills and a sense of belonging and, thus, for carrying out the socialization and self-identification functions of the family. Studies of interactions between young deaf children and their hearing mothers reveal that these experiences are missing many of the behaviors necessary for developing the social skills involved in communicating with peers and adults. Reports of maternal directiveness, intrusiveness, and lack of mutual enjoyment during play with preschool-aged deaf children suggest a conversational environment in which the deaf child gets few opportunities to initiate new topics or activities or to try out communicative turn-taking rules (Bodner-Johnson, 1991). This increased directiveness has been attributed to these mothers not sharing a common linguistic system with their deaf children (Jamieson, 1994).

Research has noted the interactional differences between hearing and deaf mothers and their deaf children. Deaf mothers seem better able than hearing mothers to facilitate language acquisition in their children. These mothers have been observed to use a variety of touching behaviors, producing slower and grammatically less complex signs than in adult-directed discourse, and frequently relating the signing space to the child's direction of gaze. These findings suggest that deaf mothers use a sequential visual process of communication with their deaf children, which includes the following three components: gaining the deaf child's visual attention, maintaining his attention throughout the communicative interaction, and allowing or directing the child to orient visually at some point to the object of the conversation. Hearing mothers, on the other hand, have been observed to continue using a habitual simultaneous visual-auditory approach despite the child's loss of hearing (Spencer, 1996; Spencer & Meadow-Orlans, 1996).

Clearly the biggest challenge facing the parents of deaf children is establishing an effective communication system. Hearing parents face a significant challenge in trying to unlearn habitual communication patterns and replace them with patterns more appropriate to the visual mode. Many experts advocate the use of deaf adults as models of effective sequential communicators (Bodner-Johnson, 1991).

Visual Impairments/Blindness. One of the most significant problems of parents with infants who are blind is the inability to establish eye contact. The infant's gaze is an important cue in sustaining reciprocal interactions with a caregiver, thus promoting positive social and emotional behaviors. Further, babies who are blind do not display the clearly differentiated facial expressions of sighted babies; they smile less often and often fail to smile even at the sound of the mother's voice. The signals they give to their caregivers are more subdued and motorically related. The inability of parents and other caregivers to interpret their babies' signals may lead to disruption in the bonding and attachment process. Research has shown that a blind child, during the second year, does not have a mental representation of the mother that can sustain her in the mother's absence.

Children who are blind also are inhibited in developing prehension skills. Even with intervention, blind babies do not achieve the coordination of ear and hand that matches the level of eye-hand coordination in sighted babies. Delayed development may lead parents to be overprotective of their blind children. Setting appropriate levels of expectation for these children leads to the development of a positive self-image.

Programs directed at supporting parents of children who are blind teach parents to provide many experiences that stimulate their young children's senses—hearing, touch, taste, smell, and movement. To develop communicative competence, parents learn to respond to all the child's attempts to communicate, by using alternative signals such as verbal response, soft touch, the imitation of vocalizations, and expanding on child utterances. Other helpful behaviors include minimizing the child's tolerance for communication breakdown, assisting the child in producing varied topics and references during interactions by talking about a variety of content outside the here and now, and by encouraging the child to use a variety of strategies to initiate social interaction (Erwin, 1994).

Emotional/Behavioral Disorders. This exceptionality may be the most challenging of all for parents. It is often not clear with emotional/behavioral disorders whether children behave the way they do because of parents' behavior or if parents behave the way they do because of their children's behavior. In any event, the complex interactions of parents and children can cause the child's behavior either to improve or to deteriorate. The following parental behaviors have been associated with behavioral disorders in children: unreasonable or punitive discipline, emotional deprivation or rejection, severe marital conflict, inconsistency, perfectionism, overindulgence, domination, detachment, and authoritarianism.

When young children do not respond well to usual disciplinary techniques, parents are likely to become angry, frustrated, and ineffective. When severely withdrawn children do not react or respond to parents' attempts to communicate and interact with them, parents may feel helpless, hurt, and guilty. The negative feedback from the child affects the parent and causes him or her to respond in a negative manner, so that a vicious cycle of dysfunctional behavior occurs. It is no wonder that many parents search avidly for a diagnosis to explain the child's behavior.

Six types of concerns of parents of children with autism were identified by Fong, Wilgosh, and Sobsey (1993): (1) behavioral concerns, such as aggressive, self-abusive, destructive, obsessive, impulsive, and self-stimulatory behaviors; (2) social and communicative concerns, such as unusual or inappropriate social behaviors and difficulties communicating with others; (3) family-related concerns, such as restricted personal lives, continual supervision and assistance with daily living skills, and increased financial burdens; (4) education and related services, such as finding appropriate educational programs; (5) relationships with professionals, such as ineffective communication and perceptions of parental blame for the child's condition; and (6) independence and future concerns, such as hope that their children could lead independent lives.

There are almost as many ways to deal with emotional/behavioral disorders as there are types of behaviors. Treatment often depends on one's explanation of the behavior. If it is explained through a biological/medical model, parents are likely to use medication to regulate the child's behavior. If it is explained through a psychoanalytic model, parents are likely to seek therapy to uncover the underlying causes of the behavior. If it is viewed through the behavioral lens, behavior modification techniques are likely to be used. Sometimes a combination of techniques is used. In any event, parents of children who are emotionally or behaviorally disordered need ample support to deal effectively with their children's behavior.

Giftedness. Gifted children do not present the same types of challenges to parents presented by children with disabilities. Most parents are very happy to have a gifted child. However, parents of gifted children may demonstrate behaviors that are on the opposite end of a continuum: they may fail to nurture the child's giftedness, not understanding his precocity, or they may exploit his exceptional traits and push him beyond reasonable limits. Often it is difficult for parents to find the right balance of nurturance and stimulation of giftedness and realistic expectations.

Parents of gifted children can learn to encourage original thinking, questioning, and experimentation without being overly demanding, treating the child as a normal member of the family without overresponding to her superiority. Providing a variety of reading materials and challenging experiences, avoiding interference with the child's work, and resisting the temptation to dominate or control the child's activities all are ways in which parents can nurture giftedness. Achieving gifted children come from homes in which parents neither overprotect their children nor subject them to excessive pressure to achieve but encourage initiative and independence. Further, to avoid conflict between gifted and nongifted siblings, the gifted characteristics of one sibling should not be overemphasized. All children should be encouraged to excel in the areas that are most congruent with their natural abilities and interests (Tuttle & Cornell, 1993).

AIDS.   Family responses to children with AIDS vary according to the level of basic coping abilities; physical health; availability of family, friends, and others; concrete resources; the degree of illness; and spiritual strength/beliefs (Lesar & Maldonado, 1994). Many mothers are identified as carriers only when their children are diagnosed; hence, they are confronted with the knowledge of a terminal illness in their children as well as in themselves. They experience agony on many levels: recurring guilt for giving the disease to their offspring and a deep sense of helplessness and anger at their failure to protect children from harm. It also may be a time when one partner becomes aware of the unknown drug or sexual behavior of the other (Johnson, 1993).

Among the most difficult aspects of HIV infection are the horrible sense of isolation and extreme fear of ostracism. Parents and children fear not only the disease itself but also rejection if the diagnosis becomes known to others. Often they experience anxiety and depression. An estimated 20–40 percent of HIV-infected children now require foster or group home placement, often because birth families, overwhelmed by their own illness, lack the ability and resources to care for them. For every child with perinatal HIV infection, there is a mother with infection and possibly a father who is ill.

Unfortunately, for many families the usual network of support disappears and some families opt not to disclose the information for fear of abandonment (Johnson, 1993; Lesar & Maldonado, 1994). Clearly families with children with AIDS have a critical need for support, and services should be both child-centered and family-focused. Most will need help with a variety of health, social, educational, and financial problems.

Resilient Children

Poulsen (1993) has noted that there is a continuum of potential resilience inherent in all children as a counterbalance to the zone of vulnerability recognized in children at risk or children with disabilities. Children who are healthy, easy temperamentally, developmentally competent, and born into families that can provide positive relationships, appropriate expectations, and minimal environmental stress tend to develop sufficient self-regulation to respond to and recover from environmental challenges. Because they have acquired a repertoire of responses, they have the flexibility to respond in a manner consistent with the context and intensity of the situation. Resilient children experience smooth transitions and recover from stressful events in appropriate ways.

Resilience, then, is the capacity to withstand stressors, overcome adversity, and achieve higher levels of self-mastery, self-esteem, and internal harmony. At the other end of the continuum are those children born at biological risk who are living in families overwhelmed by psychosocial and environmental circumstances and who often confront challenges that stress them beyond their capacity to cope. Children with difficult temperaments are more vulnerable to family stressors than those with easy temperaments. Unless vulnerable children receive identification and intervention early on, they will demonstrate negative developmental outcomes.

If parents and other caregivers are not emotionally overwhelmed by their interpersonal and family lives, they can contribute to child resilience. The following characteristics seem to facilitate resiliency: parental capacity to cope, high self-esteem, emotional availability, responsive caregiving, appropriate developmental expectations and opportunities, capacity to protect the child from overstimulation, family harmony, economic self-sufficiency, social supports, and freedom from racial discrimination.

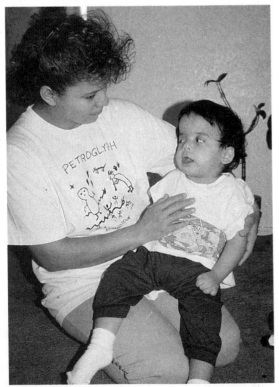

Resilient children with disabilities recover from stressful events in appropriate ways.

Poulsen (1993) contended that the best predictor of later positive interpersonal relationships, personal competence, and self-reliance is the quality of the parent-child relationship in infancy and early childhood, especially a secure attachment. The well-matched mother can help her child recover from distress through physical contact, emotional comforting, and removal of emotional and sensory overload that may contribute to distress. Reassurance, encouragement, and appropriate developmental opportunities help the child to learn resilience. Even children who are insecurely attached to their mothers can form substitute attachments to other caregivers who demonstrate these characteristics. When biological, environmental, and temperamental circumstances prevent the establishment of a rich relationship, the child probably does not develop resiliency. Both child and parent characteristics can prevent appropriate nurturance. The Highlights provide specific suggestions for helping children to develop resiliency (Poulsen, 1993).

SUPPORT FOR PARENTS WITH EXCEPTIONAL CHILDREN

Research has found repeatedly that support for parents helps to mediate some of the stress experienced in rearing children with special needs. Further, the responsibility of society at large to provide support and appropriate education for children with disabilities is reflected in both statutes and regulations at the federal and state levels and the allocation of funding for children with disabilities and their families.

Legislation

In 1975 the Education for All Handicapped Children Act (PL 94–142) was enacted by Congress, mandating a free public education for children with disabilities from ages 3 to 21. In 1986, PL 99–457 stipulated that states must provide preschool services to all children from ages 3 to 5 with disabilities and provided incentives for states to establish programs for children from birth to age 3 with

Strategies for Building Resilience

DURING INFANCY...

Availability of emotionally responsive caregivers

Appropriate maternal responses contingent on infant-initiated signals

Protection from environmental stimuli

Gradual introduction to environmental stimuli to build sensory thresholds

Swaddling to help tolerate sensory stimulation and to increase focused alertness

Handling and positioning to soothe, improve muscle tone, improve visual alertness, improve feeding, maintain posture, and encourage movement

Gradual reduction of supportive techniques with child's maturity

Recognition of infant cues for social engagement or stress relief

Appropriate speed, intensity, and tempo of maternal interactions

Appropriate response to overload signals

DURING EARLY CHILDHOOD...

Use of proximal behaviors in interaction (touch, eye contact)

Establishing personalized routines to prevent overfatigue

Protection from overstimulation

Use of rituals for daily transitions so that child can predict behavior

Setting limits on harmful behavior

Use of modeling, encouraging, acknowledging, labeling, and responding to child's feelings

Providing limited choices to encourage autonomy and decision making

Teaching and guiding social behavior

Modeling and providing time and place for relaxing activities

Modeling and encouraging representational play

Observing and intervening before behavior is out of control

Timely response to needs and initiation of social interaction

Teaching cause-and-effect relationships

Daily personalized one-to-one child-centered time

Source: Poulsen, M. (1993). Strategies for building resilience in infants and young children at risk. *Infants and Young Children, 6*(2), 29–40.

disabilities and their families. All states have elected to provide services to infants and toddlers. In 1990 the Individuals with Disabilities Act amended PL 94–142, strengthening it and changing language to ensure that free, appropriate public education is provided to children and young people regardless of the nature or severity of their disability. Public school systems are required to identify all children and youth with disabilities and provide the special-education and related services they may need. The Americans with Disabilities Act, also passed in 1990, ensures the right of individuals with disabilities to nondiscriminatory treatment in other aspects of their lives and the protection of civil rights.

As a result of these statutes, many more children with disabilities are being served and at younger ages. However, disabilities are undiagnosed in many children, and these children remain unidentified, unserved, or underserved for a variety of reasons. Though PL 94–142 stipulated that parents should be partners with professionals in developing their children's Individualized Educational Programs (IEPs), in reality these plans were developed primarily by professionals in most cases. The language of PL 99–457, however, was far more specific about the role of parents and families in the child's early-intervention services.

Family-Centered Intervention.   Public Law 99–457 was based on the beliefs that families are extremely important for promoting optimal child development and that services should evolve around and be responsive to the needs of all family members as they relate to the child's development. In fact, instead of an IEP, an Individualized Family Service Plan (IFSP) is required, targeting the whole family, not just the child, for intervention. IFSPs must be developed and written for children birth to 3 and their families by an interdisciplinary team and the parents. The IFSP must be evaluated at least once a year and reviewed every 6 months, or more often if appropriate. Families are to determine the types and extent of services to be provided. The law is very specific about what must be included in the IFSP.

Principles for a family-centered philosophy include the following: recognition that the family is the constant in the child's life; facilitation of parent and professional collaboration at all levels; sharing of unbiased, complete information with parents in a supportive manner; implementing appropriate comprehensive policies and programs that provide financial and emotional support to families; recognition of family strengths and respect for diverse methods of coping; understanding and incorporating developmental needs of children/families into health-care systems; encouragement/facilitation of parent-to-parent support; and assuring flexible, accessible, and responsive health-care delivery systems (Bruder, 1995).

The application of family-centered intervention is at different stages across the variety of early-intervention programs available. A review of the effectiveness of more than 30 early-intervention programs found that programs that adopted a joint focus on the child and the family were the most effective in achieving their goals (Graham & Bryant, 1993).

In addition to legislation that mandates services and formal support, informal support is critical to parents of exceptional children. We already have mentioned the importance of support from family members, especially from spouses. Other relatives and friends often provide both psychological and physical support to parents in caring for their children with disabilities. Further, numerous parent-support groups exist across the country on the local, state, and national levels, many specifically related to the child's particular disability. Through these groups, parents share personal experiences, learn new ways of coping, and learn how to advocate effectively for themselves and their children.

Cultural Differences.   According to Harry (1992), special-education and related services in the United States use a medical model of disability and a Western concept of service delivery. Therefore, traditional minority families may hold perceptions different from those of White families about children with disabilities and early-intervention services. In Chapter 6 of this book, we discussed briefly some differences in worldviews, conceptions of family, and codes of interaction for African Americans, Mexican Americans, Native Americans, and Asian Americans. These differences have implications for parenting exceptional children. However, it should be remembered that even though commonalities can be observed among members of a particular ethnic group, these common orientations can be expressed in vastly different ways.

For all four minority groups identified above, family extendedness is a central theme. Therefore, any intervention plan must consider the impact on and interaction of extended-family members. For traditional Hispanics, the acceptance of a severe disability may be difficult because the individual is viewed as a reflection of his or her family. Mental retardation or developmental disability may create a feeling of the family's being stigmatized. Further, respect for authority and status may strain interactions with professionals, and Hispanic family members may be alienated by the lack of personalism in the complex documentation system required by special-education programs (Harry, 1992).

Research on African American families with disabled children is minimal. Harry (1992) suggested that a severe disability in an African American child may be tied to fatalistic and religious interpretations. The concept of collective rather than individual responsibility suggests that extended-family members are likely to be involved in care for the exceptional child. Similarly, in Native American families, many adults are likely to share the care of the child. It is interesting that in most American Indian languages, there are no words for retarded, disabled, or handicapped. The belief of many traditional Native Americans that the spirit chooses the body it will inhabit also applies to children with disabilities—even though a child's body may be mutilated, a spirit chooses it for habitation nevertheless (Harry, 1992).

In traditional Asian American families, a child with serious disabilities may carry considerable stigma to the extent that the families may be reluctant to seek help. The disability may be interpreted as retribution for the sins of either parents or ancestors, a possession by evil spirits, violation of behavioral rules during the mother's pregnancy, or an imbalance of physiological functions. Families may feel that shame has been brought to the them, resulting in stoicism and dignity, which reflects their fatalistic orientation. If children have milder, school-based difficulties, parents may feel that children are lazy or they, as parents, have not trained their children properly (Harry, 1992).

Sontag and Schacht (1994) conducted an ethnic comparison of parent participation and information needs in early intervention. They found that Hispanic and American Indian parents reported more difficulty in obtaining information about their children's problems or what could be done to help their children. They were less involved in the coordinating role than were White parents. In fact, less than half of the Native Americans reported that they were engaged in coordinating their child's services. Both Hispanic and Native American parents reported a greater need to know how to obtain services, suggesting that they were not sufficiently linked to service agencies.

Further, parents from these two ethnic groups were less involved with other parents who have children with disabilities, and American Indian parents were less likely than other parents to volunteer in the programs that served their children.

These authors concluded that families with diverse ethnic and cultural experiences differ in important ways from families who identify easily with the dominant culture of health, education, and social systems. Therefore, strategies must be tailored to unique family needs so that all families will be included fully in the family decision-making process of early intervention.

SUMMARY

Parents of children with exceptionalities face many challenges. The initial diagnosis of a disability in a child shatters a dream, and most parents experience a period of grieving for the loss of a healthy child. Overwhelming evidence suggests that parenting an exceptional child is stressful. The intensity and duration of stress vary, depending on a variety of child, family, professional, and cultural factors, and increased stress may surface at various times throughout the life cycle. However, most research suggests that with appropriate support, these families are little different from other families in healthy functioning and family environment.

Families of children with disabilities share many characteristics, but each disability brings its special challenges and rewards to parents. Many children with disabilities demonstrate resilience—a remarkable capacity to adapt to stress and adversity and to achieve much higher levels of self-mastery and self-esteem than would be expected. Specific parental behaviors seem to contribute to a child's resiliency.

Early-intervention services for young children with disabilities and their families are mandated to implement a family-centered philosophy whereby parents are full partners in the decision making and in the assessment of and delivery of services to their children. Cultural sensitivity is essential if this mandate is to be achieved.

REFERENCES

ACHENBACH, T., HOWELL, C., QUAY, H., & CONNERS, C. (1991). National survey of problems and competencies among four- to sixteen-year-olds: Parents' reports for normative and clinical samples. *Monographs of the Society for Research in Child Development, 56*(3), 1–120.

AMERICAN PSYCHIATRIC ASSOCIATION. (1994). *Diagnostic and statistical manual of mental disorders* (4th ed.). Washington, DC: Author.

BECKMAN, P. (1991). Comparison of mothers' and fathers' perceptions of the effect of young children with and without disabilities. *American Journal on Mental Retardation, 95*(5), 585–595.

BENDERSKY, M., & LEWIS, M. (1994). Environmental risk, biological risk, and developmental outcome. *Developmental Psychology, 30*(4), 484–494.

BERNHEIMER, L., KEOGH, B., & COOTS, J. (1993). From research to practice: Support for developmental delay as a preschool category of exceptionality. *Journal of Early Intervention, 17*(2), 97–106.

BODNER-JOHNSON, B. (1991). Family conversation style: Its effect on the deaf child's participation. *Exceptional Children, 57*(6), 502–509.

BRUDER, M. (1995). The challenge of pediatric AIDS: A framework for early childhood special education. *Topics in Early Childhood Special Education, 15*(1), 83–99.

DYSON, L. (1991). Families of young children with handicaps: Parental stress and family functioning. *American Journal on Mental Retardation, 95*(6), 623–629.

DYSON, L. (1996). The experiences of families of children with learning disabilities: Parental stress, family functioning, and sibling self-concept. *Journal of Learning Disabilities, 29*(3), 280–286.

ERWIN, E. (1994). Social competence in young children with visual impairments. *Infants and Young Children, 6*(3), 26–33.

FLOYD, F., & GALLAGHER, E. (1997). Parental stress, care demands, and use of support services for school-age children with disabilities and behavior problems. *Family Relations, 46*(4), 359–371.

FLOYD, F., GILLIOM, L., & COSTIGAN, C. (1998). Marriage and the parenting alliance: Longitudinal prediction of change in parenting perceptions and behaviors. *Child Development, 69*(5), 1461–1479.

FONG, L., WILGOSH, L., & SOBSEY, D. (1993). The experience of parenting an adolescent with autism. *International Journal of Disability, Development and Education, 40*(2), 105–113.

FREEDMAN, R., LITCHFIELD, L., & WARFIELD, M. (1995, October). Balancing work and family: Perspectives of parents of children with developmental disabilities. *Families in Society: The Journal of Contemporary Human Services,* pp. 507–514.

FREUND, L. (1994). Diagnosis and developmental issues for young children with Fragile X syndrome. *Infants and Young Children, 6*(3), 34–45.

GATH, A. (1993). Changes that occur in families as children with intellectual disability grow up. *International Journal of Disability, Development and Education, 40*(3), 167–174.

GOTTLIEB, A. (1997). Single mothers of children with developmental disabilities: The impact of multiple roles. *Family Relations, 46*(1), 5–12.

GOTTWALD, S., & THURMAN, K. (1994). The effects of prenatal cocaine exposure on mother-infant interaction and infant arousal in the newborn period. *Topics in Early Childhood Special Education, 14*(2), 217–231.

GRAHAM, M., & BRYANT, D. (1993). Developmentally appropriate environments for children with special needs. *Infants and Young Children, 5*(3), 31–42.

GURALNICK, M., CONNOR, R., HAMMOND, M., GOTTMAN, J., & KINNISH, K. (1996). The peer relations of preschool children with communication disorders. *Child Development, 67,* 471–489.

HALLAHAN, D., & KAUFFMAN, J. (2000). *Exceptional Learners* (8th ed.). Boston: Allyn & Bacon.

HAMMILL, D. (1990). On defining learning disabilities: An emerging consensus. *Journal of Learning Disabilities, 23,* 74–84.

HARING, K., LOVETT, D., HANEY, K., ALGOZZINE, B., SMITH, D., & CLARK, J. (1992). Labeling preschoolers as learning disabled: A cautionary position. *Topics in Early Childhood Special Education, 12*(2), 151–173.

HARRY, B. (1992). *Cultural diversity, families, and the special education system.* New York: Teachers College Press.

HELLER, T., HSIEH, K., & ROWITZ, L. (1997). Maternal and paternal caregiving of persons with mental retardation across the lifespan. *Family Relations, 46*(4), 407–415.

HERMAN, S., & THOMPSON, L. (1995). Families' perceptions of their resources for caring for children with developmental disabilities. *Mental Retardation, 33*(2), 73–83.

INDIVIDUALS WITH DISABILITIES ACT (IDEA) Amendments of 1997. Public Law 105–17.

INNOCENTI, M., HUH, K., & BOYCE, G. (1992). Families of children with disabilities: Normative data and other considerations on parenting stress. *Topics in Early Childhood Special Education, 12*(3), 403–427.

JAMIESON, J. (1994). Teaching as transaction: Vygotskian perspectives on deafness and mother-child interaction. *Exceptional Children, 60*(5), 434–449.

JOHNSON, C. (1993). Developmental issues: Children infected with the human immunodeficiency virus. *Infants and Young Children, 6*(1), 1–10.

JOHNSON, M., & LEFT, M. (1999). Children of substance abusers: Overview of research findings. *Pediatrics, 103*(5), 1085–1099.

JUDGE, S. (1998). Parental coping strategies and strengths in families of young children with disabilities. *Family Relations, 47*(3), 263–268.

KRAUS, L., STODDARD, S., & GILMARTIN, D. (1996). *Chartbook on disability in the United States, 1996.* Washington, DC: U.S. National Institute on Disability and Rehabilitation Research.

KREHBIEL, R., MUNSICK-BRUNO, G., & LOWE, J. (1991). NICU infants born at developmental risk and the Individualized Family Service Plan/process (IFSP). *Children's Health Care, 20*(1), 26–32.

LANDAU, S., & MCANINCH, C. (1993). Young children with attention deficits. *Young Children, 48*(4), 49–57.

LESAR, S., & MALDONADO, Y. (1994). Infants and young children with HIV infection: Service delivery considerations for family support. *Infants and Young Children, 6*(4), 70–81.

MAHONEY, G., O'SULLIVAN, P., & ROBINSON, C. (1992). The family environments of children with disabilities: Diverse but not so different. *Topics in Early Childhood Special Education, 12*(3), 386–402.

MARCENKO, M., & MEYERS, J. (1991). Mothers of children with developmental disabilities: Who shares the burden? *Family Relations, 40*(2), 186–190.

MEADOW-ORLANS, K. (1994). Stress, support, and deafness: Perceptions of infants' mothers and fathers. *Journal of Early Intervention, 18*(1), 91–102.

MOSES, K. (1983). The impact of initial diagnosis: Mobilizing family resources. In J. Mulick & S. Pueschel (Eds.), *Parent-professional partnerships in developmental disabilities services* (pp. 11–34). Cambridge, MA: Academic Guild.

OLIVER, J., COLE, N., & HOLLINGSWORTH, H. (1991). Learning disabilities as functions of familial learning problems and developmental problems. *Exceptional Children, 57*(5), 427–441.

OLSON, H. (1994). The effects of prenatal alcohol exposure on child development. *Infants and Young Children, 6*(3), 10–25.

POULSEN, M. (1993). Strategies for building resilience in infants and young children at risk. *Infants and Young Children, 6*(2), 29–40.

POULSEN, M. (1994). The development of policy recommendations to address individual and family needs of infants and young children affected by family substance use. *Topics in Early Childhood Special Education, 14*(2), 275–291.

REID, R., MAAG, J., & VASA, S. (1993). Attention deficit hyperactivity disorder as a disability category: A critique. *Exceptional Children, 60*(3), 198–214.

RODRIGUE, J., MORGAN, S., & GEFFKEN, G. (1992). Psychosocial adaptation of fathers of children with autism, Down syndrome, and normal development. *Journal of Autism and Developmental Disorders, 22*(2), 249–262.

SMITH, D., & LUCKASSON, R. (1992). *Introduction to special education: Teaching in an age of challenge.* Needham Heights, MA: Allyn & Bacon.

SONTAG, J., & SCHACHT, R. (1994). An ethnic comparison of parent participation and information needs in early intervention. *Exceptional Children, 60*(5), 422–433.

SPARLING, J., BERGER, R., & BILLER, M. (1992). Fathers: Myth, reality, and Public Law 99–457. *Infants and Young Children, 4*(3), 9–19.

SPENCER, P. (1996). The association between language and symbolic play at two years: Evidence from deaf toddlers. *Child Development, 67,* 867–876.

SPENCER, P., & MEADOW-ORLANS, K. (1996). Play, language, and maternal responsiveness: A longitudinal study of deaf and hearing infants. *Child Development, 67,* 3176–3191.

SUAREZ, L., & BAKER, B. (1997). Child externalizing behavior and parents' stress: The role of social support. *Family Relations, 46,* 373–381.

THURMAN, S., & GONSALVES, S. (1993). Adolescent mothers and their premature infants: Responding to double risk. *Infants and Young Children, 5*(4), 44–51.

TRIVETTE, C., & DUNST, C. (1992). Characteristics and influences of role division and social support among mothers of preschool children with disabilities. *Topics in Early Childhood Special Education, 12*(3), 367–385.

TRUTE, B. (1990). Child and parent predictors of family adjustment in households containing young developmentally disabled children. *Family Relations, 39*(3), 292–297.

TUTTLE, D., & CORNELL, D. (1993). Maternal labeling of gifted children: Effects on the sibling relationship. *Exceptional Children, 59*(5), 402–410.

TYNAN, W., & NEARING, J. (1994). The diagnosis of attention deficit hyperactivity disorder in young children. *Infants and Young Children, 6*(4), 13–20.

U.S. BUREAU OF THE CENSUS. (1998). *Statistical abstract of the United States: 1998* (118th ed.). Washington, DC: U.S. Department of Commerce.

WALKER, H., & SEVERSON, H. (1990). *Systematic screening for behavior disorders (SSBD): A multiple gating procedure.* Longmont, CO: Sopris West.

WALLACE, H. (1992). Perspective: Early steps in the care of disabled children being taken in some developing countries. *Infants and Young Children, 4*(3), v–viii.

CHAPTER 11

Alternatives to Biological Parenthood

Most people become parents by biologically bearing children. However, a small percentage of individuals, for various reasons, do not wish to or cannot achieve parenthood through the ordinary methods of reproduction. Adopting children is a desirable option for some; others may wish to utilize one of the assisted-reproduction approaches; and some may elect to become foster parents. Further, biological parents often want to add children to the family and choose one of these alternatives for that purpose. Each alternative has its appealing characteristics as well as its risks. There are legal, social, economic, and moral issues associated with each, many of which are yet to be satisfactorily resolved. Especially in the case of assisted reproduction, the resolution of these issues has lagged behind the technology itself. This chapter explores these alternatives to ordinary biological parenthood.

ADOPTIVE PARENTHOOD

Adoption provides a legal process that creates a parent-child relationship between individuals who are not biologically related (Schulman & Behrman, 1993). Adoption touches the lives of few people directly (2–4 percent of American families and approximately 1 million children) but has profound significance for the lives of those it does affect. Adoption offers a means of providing a pregnant woman with an alternative home for her child, offers a solution for a couple who cannot have children of their own, and provides a child with a family that is presumably better equipped to rear the child than the one to which he was born. Despite the significance of adoption, no comprehensive national data on adoption are collected by the federal government (Stolley, 1993).

Incidence

The incidence of adoption rose dramatically between 1951 and 1970 but fell substantially in the 1970s and leveled off in the 1980s. In 1987 it was estimated that a total of 117,585 children were adopted, and in 1992 an estimated total of 127,441 were adopted, only a slight increase over 1987 (Fein, 1998).

In the United States today, adoption is characterized by a seeming paradox. On the one hand, there are large numbers of infertile couples urgently seeking babies for adoption to begin or expand their families. On the other hand, more than 85,000 children are waiting to be adopted. Most of these children are in foster care while permanent homes and families are being sought for them. The numbers of waiting children are increasing steadily. The apparent contradiction arises from the fact that most people who wish to adopt are seeking healthy infants (usually White), whereas the children waiting to be adopted are predominantly older, are children of color, are members of sibling groups, and/or may have emotional, physical, or mental disabilities (children with "special needs") (Schulman & Behrman, 1993).

These circumstances have resulted in significant changes in adoption policy and practice in recent decades. The search for healthy White infants, whose pool has diminished dramatically, has led to the evolution of and increasing interest in transracial international adoption. Only an estimated 20,000 White infants are available for adoption each year. As a result, the biggest increase in adoptions has been among children from other countries. The number of these adoptions nearly doubled from 7,093 in 1990 to 13,620 in 1997 (Fein, 1998). The urgent need to find homes for thousands of children with special needs, who in the past were considered unadoptable, has led to recruitment of adoptive parents who were previously considered unacceptable by virtue of older age, lower socioeconomic status, or being single. The roles of various placement organizations also have changed as public agencies have been required to focus on abused or neglected children waiting in foster care, whereas private agencies and intermediaries have tended to focus on finding voluntarily relinquished healthy babies for childless adults (Schulman & Behrman, 1993).

Experts postulate that the discrepancy between the number of couples seeking to adopt and the number of available healthy infants is the result of increased incidence of infertility among married couples and an absolute decrease in the number of infants placed for adoption. This last number results from the greater availability of effective methods of contraception, the rise in the rate of abortion, and perhaps most significant, the sharp increase in the tendency of unwed mothers to keep their babies rather than place them for adoption (Fein, 1998).

Children may be adopted formally (i.e., a legal recognition of a parental relationship is made) or informally (i.e., someone—usually a family member—assumes responsibility for a child without obtaining legal recognition). Further, birth parents may relinquish their parental rights to an agency that in turn consents to adoption by specific adoptive parents; or birth parents may give consent directly to adoptive parents. The latter type, independent adoption, is legal in almost all states and is attractive to some because long waiting periods may be avoided and agency standards do not apply. Both types of adoption have strengths and weaknesses. Finally, historically, adoptions were either open or closed. In open adoptions, birth parents and adoptive parents know one another, exchange information, and often continue contact and communication over time, whereas in traditional closed adoptions, the identity of birth parents is not revealed to the adoptive parents or to the children. Open adoption began to become standard practice during the 1980s because of the belief that it facilitated healthy psychological development of both adoptees and their adoptive parents.

Characteristics of Adoptive Parents

The exact numbers of people seeking to adopt a child or those who have ever sought to adopt are not known. One source reported that in 1995 nearly half a million women 18 to 44 years of age were currently seeking to adopt a child, but fewer than one-quarter of those women had applied to an agency. The largest percentage of women seeking to adopt were 35 to 39 years old. When the "never marrieds" were combined with the "formerly marrieds," single women outnumbered married women. Those with children outnumbered those without children, and the number with less than a high school education was almost twice the number who had bachelor's degrees or higher (Chadwick & Heaton, 1999).

Unrelated adoptions are more common among White women, whereas related adoptions

Open adoption facilitates healthy psychological development of both adoptees and their adoptive parents.

appear to be somewhat more common among African Americans. Hispanic women are much less likely to have ever adopted any child than are their African American or White counterparts. Also, women reporting higher levels of education or family income are significantly more likely to have adopted, especially unrelated children, whereas related adoptions are more common among those with lower levels of education and income.

Fein (1998) reported that 42 percent of adoptions in 1992 were by stepparents and other relatives. Since the 1960s, these intrafamily adoptions have increased more than any other type of adoption, both proportionately and in absolute numbers. These adoptions are the least regulated, yet they generate some of the most bitterly contested proceedings, especially when a noncustodial parent objects to a proposed stepparent adoption, when grandparents seek to maintain contact with a child over the objection of a custodial parent and adoptive stepparent, or when maternal and paternal relatives battle to adopt a child whose parents are deceased or legally unfit (Hollinger, 1993).

Ganong, Coleman, Fine, and McDaniel (1998) explored issues considered in stepchild adoption. They estimated that 100,000 stepchildren are adopted by their stepparents every year. Although there are many similarities between stepparent/ stepchild adoptions and unrelated adoptions, there also are contextual differences. In a stepchild adoption, only the stepparent is seeking to change the legal relationship to the child. Further, motivations to adopt may differ. Infertility is a primary reason for adoption by childless couples, but it is seldom the reason for stepparent adoption. Adoption by a stepparent requires the nonresidential parent to relinquish all legal ties to the child. He or she may do so voluntarily or be legally forced to do so. Termination of parental rights requires that the nonresidential parent be declared unfit and/or a judgment that termination is in the best interests of the child. The results of the Ganong et al. (1998) study were reported in Chapter 7, including the issues surrounding stepparent/stepchild adoption, motivation, and barriers.

In contrast to the increase in intrafamily adoptions is the sharp decrease, both proportionately and in absolute numbers, of adoptions of infants by unrelated adults. As explained earlier, this phenomenon is not due to the lack of interest by childless adults in finding adoptable newborns or a reduction in the number of out-of-wedlock births but is due to the lack of babies relinquished for adoption and to the number of babies classified as "special needs" babies. Foster parents often are adopters of children whom they have parented.

Overall, adoptive families of children with special needs are a diverse group of people. They include both lower- and middle-income families, most of whom have parented other children. Some are childless couples; others are single parents. However, the most dominant feature of the special-needs adoptive family is that the vast majority of them have been foster parents first. Some states report that 80 percent to 90 percent of adopters of special-needs children are foster parents first (McKenzie, 1993). Since there is considerable expense involved in adopting international children, most parents involved in these adoptions are middle-class.

Some studies have shown infertile adoptive parents to be less confident than biological parents, to feel significant anger and grief, and to worry about their ability to bond with someone else's child. These difficulties have been attributed to factors leading to the decision to adopt— unresolved grief surrounding years of infertility, uncertainty about the adoption process, and social stigma attached to infertility and adoption. However, other studies have shown few differences between biological and adoptive parents. Using a national survey, Borders, Black, and Pasley (1998) compared a group of adopted children and their parents with a matched group of biological children and their parents. Results indicated some differences between adoptive mothers and fathers— fathers had lower self-esteem, had more traditional beliefs about families, were less involved in their children's activities, and demonstrated less affection for their children than did the adoptive mothers. In the biological families, only one difference was found between mothers and fathers— fathers were less involved than mothers with their children.

Data revealed no differences between adoptive and biological parents in levels of depression, overall health, levels of self-esteem, traditional attitudes toward family life, parents' acceptance of maternal employment, importance parents placed on desirable behaviors of children, frequency of parental discipline, involvement in children's activities, parents' perceptions of children's well-being, perceived behavior problems of children, prosocial behaviors exhibited by children, and educational expectations of their children. In contrast to earlier research using clinical samples, the researchers concluded that adoptive parents and biological parents were quite similar.

Adopted Children

Only a small percentage of the total population of children under 18 years of age are adopted by non-biological adults (Brodzinsky, 1993). However, because of the increase in international adoptions, this number is rising rapidly. Slightly more children in the United States are adopted by related than by unrelated adults, and more children with special needs are being adopted.

Children with Special Needs. "Special needs" usually is used to describe those children who, because of the presence of certain characteristics and conditions, are particularly difficult to place for adoption. The category includes older children; children of color; children with physical, mental, or emotional disabilities; and children who are part of a sibling group. Recently the term has become broader in meaning to include a child-welfare service that seeks permanent homes for children in foster care who will never be able to be reunited with their birth parents. Most of these children have experienced significant trauma in their young lives, including deprivation, physical and sexual abuse, abandonment, loss, and many moves in foster care. As a result, they are prone to emotional, behavioral, and learning problems. Once these children are adopted, they are very challenging to parent. Many of these children spend years waiting to be adopted. Children of color are overrepresented in this population and are known to wait longer for adoption than White children with special needs. In addition, unmanageable numbers of infants and young children are coming into out-of-home care as a result of parental drug addiction. Infants who test positive for HIV also are increasing dramatically. Their more fragile health and uncertainty about their developmental futures make them difficult to place. Though many of these children will be able to develop normally, many prospective adoptive parents are reluctant to adopt them. Thus, they ordinarily will spend a number of years in substitute care.

Older children or children who have spent many years in foster care have a crucial need for adoptive parents. These youngsters have experienced emotional trauma, including multiple separations from their families while in foster care. Frequently they have experienced deprivation and abusive treatment. (As high as 75 percent have experienced sexual abuse.) A majority have lived in families in which drugs, alcoholism, and violence were prevalent. Many are members of sibling groups, and most are boys (McKenzie, 1993). More than 20,000 older children are adopted each year in the United States, and more than 200,000 have been adopted overall.

Transracially Adopted Children. The term *transracial adoption* means the joining of racially different parents and children together in adoptive families (Silverman, 1993). Transracial adoption

---

_____ **TIPS** _____

For Adoptive Parents

Tell the child the truth about his adoption as early as possible.

If the biological parents are unknown, respect and support the young person's desire to search for them.

If the child's race and culture differ from yours, preserve her cultural heritage.

Use an "acknowledgment of difference" style of communication about adoption.

Encourage the child to freely express feelings or ask questions related to adoption.

If the child has special needs, seek sources of support for parenting.

may be divided into two major categories: (1) the adoption of foreign-born children of different race from the adopting American families, usually White, and (2) the adoption of American-born children of different race by American families, also usually White (Schulman & Behrman, 1993). In the United States, the term is sometimes reserved for the adoption of African American children by White families, but it includes also the adoption of Native American, Asian, and Hispanic children by White families (Silverman, 1993). Many refer to the adoption of foreign-born children as international adoption.

Constituting a very important part of the total adoption picture, international adoption provides an avenue for parents in the United States who want White infants but are unable to adopt them. For other parents who are low on the list of potential eligible adopters, this avenue significantly increases the range of parenting choices. A single person or an over-40 couple, often precluded from adoption in the United States, usually can find at least some countries abroad where they can adopt. From the child's perspective, international adoption also is advantageous. For most of the homeless children of the world, international adoption represents the only realistic opportunity for permanent families of their own (Bartholet, 1993). Expenses generally range upward of $10,000, and many international adoptions cost $15,000 to $25,000 even when no major obstacles arise (Bartholet, 1993).

As a result of political pressure and rising nationalism, there has been growing hostility to international adoption in many countries that have previously been willing to free some of the homeless children for adoption by foreigners. The laws regulating adoption are varied among the "sending" countries, and numerous obstacles stand in the way of foreigners who wish to adopt. Aspects of the U.S. immigration laws pose additional obstacles in the path to the adoption of foreign-born children by American citizens (Bartholet, 1993).

A major portion of transracial adoption consists of the placement of African American children in White homes. In the late 1960s and early 1970s, more than 10,000 African American children were adopted by White parents. Subsequently, however, this practice decreased dramatically in response to strong condemnation by many African American social workers and others (Silverman, 1993). The Multiethnic Placement Act passed by Congress in 1994 was intended to reduce the length of time children wait to be adopted and to prevent discrimination on the basis of race, color, and national origin (Curtis, 1996). Currently a greater number of very young babies of African American and mixed-race heritage are being adopted by White couples; however, the definitive number of transracial adoptions cannot be determined (Silverman, 1993).

Outcomes of Adoption

Historically, adoption has been viewed as a highly successful societal solution for the problems confronting children whose biological parents could not or would not provide for them. In fact, the literature is overwhelmingly supportive of the benefits of adoption for these children, particularly when one considers the alternative caregiving options available for them. For example, research indicates that on a variety of outcome measures adopted children fare much better than those youngsters who are reared in institutional environments or in foster care. Furthermore, adoptees develop significantly better than children who are reared by biological parents who are ambivalent about caring for them or who do not want them (Brodzinsky, 1993).

However, considerable debate has arisen in the professional literature about the possibility of increased psychological risk in adopted children compared with nonadopted children. Brodzinsky (1993) reviewed the literature on the long-term outcomes of adoption. He concluded that although most adoptees are well within the normal range of functioning, as a group they are more vulnerable to various emotional, behavioral, and academic problems than their nonadopted peers living in intact homes with their biological parents. However, it must be noted that the majority of studies documenting the increased risk of psychological and academic problems among adopted children have used clinical samples.

In the Borders et al. (1998) national study, the outcomes of adopted children were compared with those of biological children. They found adopted children to be self-confident and in control and to view their adoptive parents as nurturant, comforting, predictable, and positively concerned. Further, children had strong bonds with their adoptive parents and demonstrated positive psychological health, showing no differences from biological children in adjustment or prosocial behaviors. Just as their parents were similar to biological parents, adopted children were similar to biological children.

Brodzinsky (1993) noted that there was substantial variability in the patterns of adjustment of adoptees, much of which is tied to such factors as age, gender, family structure and dynamics, and preplacement history. Most research has failed to find differences between adopted and nonadopted children in infancy, toddlerhood, and the preschool years. It is not until children are about 5–7 years of age that significant differences between these groups emerge. At this age, most children begin to understand the meaning and implications of being adopted. As children's knowledge of adoption deepens, so do their feelings of anxiety and confusion about their family status. Although the clinical literature suggests that adjustment difficulties for adoptees continue and perhaps even increase during adolescence, research data are sparse and contradictory on this issue.

Boys, adopted or nonadopted, tend to be more vulnerable than girls on a number of psychological variables, especially disruptive disorders and academic problems. In addition, some data suggest that the relative adjustment difficulties of adoptees compared with nonadoptees are greater for boys than for girls; however, at this point it is not possible to draw a firm conclusion regarding gender differences in adoption adjustment. Nor has any consistent pattern been found regarding the role of family structure. Research on the ordinal position of the adopted child also has produced mixed results (Brodzinsky, 1993).

Family communication patterns related to adoption have been linked to the child's adjustment. It has been suggested that a more open "acknowledgment of difference" style of communication about adoption among family members ultimately facilitates healthier adjustment in adoptees than a closed, "rejection of difference" approach. Research seems to be consistent with the idea that extreme styles at either end of the communication continuum—denial of differences at one end and insistence on differences at the other end—are less likely to promote positive adjustment to adoption (Brodzinsky, 1993).

Acceptance of and satisfaction with adoptive parenthood, coupled with a warm and accepting attitude toward the child, generally are predictive of more positive adoption adjustment, compared with parental rejection of the child and parental dissatisfaction with adoptive parenthood. Problems in adopted children are more likely to be manifested when there are emotional problems in one or both of the adoptive parents and/or when there is a history of death or divorce within the adoptive family.

Preplacement history involves both the prenatal and the postnatal experiences of the child before entering the adoptive family. Adverse prenatal experiences such as heightened maternal stress, poor maternal nutrition, and inadequate medical care—as well as fetal exposure to alcohol, drugs, and other teratogenic agents—are linked to increased developmental problems in childhood.

Of all the postnatal risk factors, perhaps none has been investigated as frequently as age at placement. Numerous authors have argued that the older the child at the time of placement, the greater the chance of postplacement adjustment difficulties. Critical to any underlying increased psychological risk are the specific experiences the child encounters before adoption placement. Children who experience multiple changes in caretaking environments, as well as neglect and abuse, before being placed for adoption are significantly more likely to experience adjustment difficulties, including adoption disruption (Brodzinsky, 1993).

Outcomes of Special-Needs Adoption. A number of researchers have reported a high level of parental satisfaction with adoption of children with special needs. Reported sources of satisfaction include the child's development, positive changes in other family members, and positive changes in the mother (greater tolerance, less selfishness, more sympathetic attitudes, increased compassion). Interestingly, less serious impairments appear to be more problematic in respect to parental satisfaction than are serious impairments.

The rate of disruption (giving up of children by adoptive parents) of children with special needs is between 6 percent and 20 percent, with older children being an especially vulnerable group for disruption. In fact, age is the most powerful demographic factor associated with risk for disruption. Boys are overrepresented in disruption cases. Disabilities (developmental problems and serious medical conditions) do not appear to be major risk factors. In contrast, emotional and behavioral problems are strong predictors of disruption. Aggression and acting-out behaviors—as contrasted with inhibited, withdrawn behavior—are linked centrally to disruption. Behaviors such as sexual promiscuity, fighting and physical cruelty to others, stealing, vandalizing, and threatening or attempting suicide have been found particularly to be associated with disruption. A large number of placements for a child and a strong attachment to the birth mother are other risk factors.

In general, associations of ethnicity, family structure, and income and education levels of parents to risk for disruption are weak. But adoption by foster parents consistently predicts reduced risk. Strong support systems from family and friends, as well as religious participation, predict stability.

In some cases, older-child adoption has positive outcomes, with high levels of parental satisfaction being reported. However, the most sobering finding related to the adoption of older children is the high level of behavior problems—40 percent or more in some studies. Further, children often experience behavioral problems many years after placement (Rosenthal, 1993). McKenzie (1993) reported

that many older children have been found to be difficult to parent. Their emotional problems—anger, irritability, inability to attach—continue to be the most challenging problems for adoptive families.

Excellent outcomes have been noted for adoptive nontraditional families (minority, low income and education levels, older age, and single-parent status); and minority families appear particularly resistant to potential problems. The following factors have been found to promote positive outcomes for the adoption of children with special needs: provision of accurate information about the child to the adoptive parents; financial subsidies; and other postadoption services, such as counseling, support groups, adoption education seminars, respite care, and school services.

Barth (1993) studied the outcomes of the adoption of drug-exposed young children. Even though previous research has indicated that parents who adopt drug-exposed babies often find that rearing them is vastly more difficult than experts have predicted, 84 percent of the adopted parents he studied were very satisfied with the adoption, a proportion similar to that found among parents who adopted non-drug-exposed children. These parents also indicated that they were better prepared for adoption than parents who adopted non-drug-exposed children. Barth failed to find statistically significant differences between drug-exposed children and other adopted children in behavior, temperament, and school adjustment. Further, 83 percent of their adoptive parents, as compared with 93 percent of adoptive parents of non-drug-exposed children, reported that they were in good or excellent health. This researcher also reported that compared with substitute care of drug-exposed children, adoption appears to be more cost effective. He estimated that overall savings may exceed $100,000 per child over the duration of their minority years.

Outcomes of Transracial Adoption. Nearly a dozen studies reported by Silverman (1993) consistently indicate that approximately 75 percent of transracially adopted preadolescent and younger children adjust well in their adoptive homes.

Adoptive parents report enjoying their children, feeling that their decisions to adopt were good ones, and the developing of strong bonds between themselves and their adoptees.

Studies have shown no differences in self-concept and self-esteem between transracially and intraracially adopted adolescents. Though some research has posed concern regarding African American adolescents' identities, other research seems to indicate that transracially adopted African American adolescents have developed pride in their racial heritage and are comfortable in interaction with both African Americans and Whites.

Curtis (1996) reported three-fourths of transracially adopted children to be well adjusted, and they had higher IQs than African American children adopted by same-race parents. However, for more than 20 years the National Association of Black Social Workers has argued for same-race placement for African American children in foster care and adoption. Curtis noted that evidence shows that some young Blacks in their twenties and thirties who were adopted by White parents did not have the necessary skills to cope with racism and prejudice, probably because the majority of agencies have not provided support systems for parents adopting transracial children to assist in creating racially sensitive home environments. She concluded that same-race placements are preferable and that transracial placement of African American children should be considered only when no African American families are available.

Coping Strategies Used by Children. Brodzinsky (1993) developed a stress-and-coping model of children's adoption adjustment. The primary assumption of the model is that children's adjustment to adoption is determined largely by how they view or appraise their adoption experience and by the type of coping mechanisms they use to deal with adoption-related stress. It is assumed that when children view adoption as stigmatizing, threatening, or involving loss, a pattern of negative emotions associated with stress (such as confusion, anxiety, sadness, embarrassment, and anger) is likely to be experienced. When children experience

these emotions, they consider various coping options and eventually choose one or more to reduce their distress. They may choose to talk with a friend or a parent, or they may think about adoption in a new way so that it does not sadden or anger them. Other children may attempt to put all thoughts about adoption out of their minds or to avoid anything that reminds them of adoption. Although no one pattern of coping is necessarily associated with healthier adjustment, research generally suggests that overreliance on avoidance strategies often is tied to increased maladjustment patterns.

The way children view or appraise the experience of adoption is tied to many child-related characteristics, such as the child's level of cognitive development, temperament, self-esteem, sense of personal control, and interpersonal trust. Genetic, prenatal, and birth factors also affect how children appraise their adoptions. These biological factors influence children's well-being through their impact on cognitive, social, and emotional development. The way children view their adoption experience and cope with it may be tied to the feedback they receive about their adoptive status from society, from peers, and, most important, from the family in which they live. In the last decade, adoption has become public, and increasingly children are told, even before they can fully understand, how they came to their families. Often the story is shared with family, friends, relatives, teachers, and sometimes strangers. Although adoption was once hidden, children today can belong to play groups consisting entirely of adopted children, buy storybooks about being adopted, go to summer camps for children adopted from particular foreign countries, and obtain treatment from therapists who specialize in adoption, should they need it (Fein, 1998).

Research has shown that most children view adoption more positively than negatively, although they occasionally experience stress associated with being adopted. Furthermore, those who experience the greatest stress are more likely to employ cognitive and behavioral avoidance strategies in attempting to cope with their negative feelings (Brodzinsky, 1993).

The Search by Adult Adoptees
for Birth Parents

Numerous studies have focused on the search for birth parents by adult adoptees (Andersen, 1988; Pacheco & Eme, 1993). In the early 1950s adult adoptees began to express their needs and their rights to obtain more knowledge about their backgrounds, and professionals studying adoption began to describe the adverse effects of the lack of this knowledge on adoptees, birth parents, and adoptive parents. All these forces have led to changes in the adoption policies in most states (Schulman & Behrman, 1993).

Until the 1970s adoption was shrouded in secrecy and stigma. Adoptive parents had little, if any, information about the birth parents of their adopted child, and most often children were told nothing about their adoptions. Over the last three decades, however, notable changes have occurred. Adoption practices now lie on a continuum of openness, allowing for different levels of communication between adoptive families and birth parents (Mendenhall, Grotevant, & McRoy, 1996). In confidential adoptions, no communication between adoptive families and birth parents exists. In fully disclosed, or open, adoptions, adoptive families and birth parents maintain direct, ongoing communication. In mediated adoptions, communication is relayed through third parties without exchange of identifying information. Many adoptive families move along this continuum through their life cycle. Openness changes in response to one or more members' dissatisfaction with that current level. Research has shown that adopted children, during adolescence or early adulthood, often initiate searches for their birth parents.

Carp (1995) presented a historical perspective of adoption and disclosure of family information in the United States. He reported that beginning in the 1980s, agencies adopted open disclosure policies as a result of changes in the types of children available for adoption, the increasing flexibility of adoptive parents' attitudes toward special-needs children, and the impact of the adoption movement. Mendenhall et al. (1996)

reported that couples who had changed their openness from mediated to fully disclosed demonstrated significantly better communication skills in listening, self-disclosure, clarity, continuity, tracking, and respect and regard than did the mediated couples.

Respondents in the Pacheco and Eme (1993) study gave the following reasons for initiating a search for their birth parents: pregnancy or birth of a child, medical or health concern, death of adoptive parents, engagement or marriage, and stress. Most adult adoptees who are asked why they initiated searches respond that they want more information on their medical history for the sake of their children or that they are interested in their genealogy and want to fill in their own pedigrees. The majority of adoptees who search do not do so because they have poor relationships with their adoptive parents (March, 1997; Pacheco & Eme, 1993). March found that most of her searchers were not dissatisfied with their adoptive mothers. They had positive self-concepts and had achieved their life goals and objectives. Rather, searching emerged from a need to fill the identity gaps created by secrecy in adoption. By gaining access to their birth mothers, they were able to form more cohesive identities based on complete knowledge of their genetic and genealogical roots. Concerns about the reactions of their adoptive parents often prevent adoptees from searching earlier. In fact, some adoptees even wait until their adoptive parents are dead, and others search without their adoptive parents' knowledge.

If open adoption becomes more prevalent, the need for adult adoptees to search will diminish. Some research has indicated that only about 50 percent of adoptees tell their adoptive parents before they initiate searches for their birth parents. Lichtenstein (1996) found that more than 68 percent of the searchers had told their adoptive fathers about their searches, but 66 percent had not told their adoptive mothers. It appeared that adoptive families' discussion of adoption and adoptees' feelings that their adoptive parents were open to discussing adoption were important in decisions to reveal adoptee searches.

From in-depth interviews with female adoptees, March (1997) described contact relationships between adoptees and their birth mothers. Birth mothers experienced anxiety about making contact, feelings of unworthiness, diminished self-esteem, depression, unresolved grief over the loss of their children, continued interest in their children, and latent desires to reunite. They also felt ashamed "for giving [their children] away." The major reasons for relinquishing children for adoption were financial instability and lack of parental support.

Contrary to other research, this study indicated that adoptees perceived contact with their birth mothers as having little impact on their lives. Usually an intense period of getting acquainted followed the first contact. Both adoptees and birth mothers felt that the first meeting was stressful because of uncertainty and the lack of social rules for these situations. Both adoptees and mothers feared being rejected by the other. Feelings of shame, guilt, and abandonment were common. Lack of spontaneity contributed to dissatisfaction with the reunion. Surprisingly, most adoptive parents supported adoptees' search and contact.

Pacheco and Eme (1993) studied adult adoptees' reunions with birth parents. The results indicated these reunions were rated as positive by 86 percent of the sample. Similarly, the majority of adoptees felt that the reunion improved their self-concept, self-esteem, emotional outlook, and ability to relate to others. Indeed, given the worst scenario about the reunion (rejection by the biological parent), every adoptee insisted that despite the stress involved, he or she would do it again if given the opportunity.

The principal element contributing to dissatisfaction seemed to be unrealistic expectations. Many of the adoptees found that their biological parents had an assortment of problems and needs they were not prepared to deal with, such as alcoholism, poverty, and illness. This led some to conclude that they had had a much better life than they would have had with their biological parents.

Frequency of contact following the initial encounter varied but tended to take the pattern of a period of great intensity followed by diminished frequency, with the most common present pattern being monthly/bimonthly or on holidays. Only about half of the adoptees felt that their need for emotional support from their biological parents was satisfied, and many reported more satisfying relationships with half-siblings and other relatives than with the biological parents.

Challenges to the Adoption Field

Although much has been learned about the effects of adoption procedures and the long-term outcomes of being adopted, there still are many social, ethical, and legal challenges in current adoption practice that require thoughtful attention and development of appropriate standards. Research should continue to investigate the long-term effects of adoption and identify all the variables that affect outcomes. Methodological problems have been cited as a deficiency of the research on the impact of adoption (Demick & Wapner, 1988). Many studies have failed to account for the individual differences of adoptive parents and of the children; it has been assumed that adoption is a monolithic event that affects all the participants in the same negative ways. Further, some studies have had sampling problems, and most have not taken a systems approach to conceptualizing the problem. Finally, most studies have been cross-sectional rather than longitudinal.

In summary, adoption has long been a socially acceptable way of achieving parenthood. Recent changes in society not only have been an impetus for increasing the demand for adoptive babies but also have made the number of young infants less accessible. In the past, the largest percentage of adoptive parents were middle-class established White couples who had difficulty conceiving a child, and White infants were preferred. Now more single men and women are adopting children. Older children, children of various races and minority groups, and children with disabilities are being placed. A growing trend is openness in adoption procedures, decreasing the need for adult adoptees to seek out and contact biological parents.

This procedure has been facilitated by changing laws and policies. Many experts feel that additional changes in adoption policies and procedures are needed. Certainly, more research is needed regarding adoptive children and families to resolve some of the issues surrounding this approach to parenthood.

PARENTING THROUGH ASSISTED REPRODUCTION

When the first "test-tube baby," Louise Brown, was born in England in 1978, the event was acclaimed as a revolutionary new way to become parents. More than 20 years have since passed, and great strides have been made. Artificial insemination by donor (AID or DI), in vitro fertilization, embryo transfer, and surrogate motherhood are occurring with increasing frequency. Numerous variations in noncoital reproductive techniques were perfected in the 1980s: nonsurgical ovum transfer in 1983, surrogate embryo transfer in 1984, frozen embryo transfer into a surrogate mother in 1984, ovum transfer in 1985, and intracytoplasmic sperm injection in the early 1990s. Other developments include egg donation, egg freezing, gamete intrafallopian transfer (GIFT) and zygote intrafallopian transfer (ZIFT) (see Highlights). In in vitro fertilization, the child is genetically related to both parents. In donor insemination, the child is genetically related to the mother but not to the father. In egg donation, the child is genetically related to the father but not to the mother. When both the egg and the sperm are donated, the child is not genetically related to either parent. The situation is similar to adoption but differs in that parents actually experience a pregnancy and develop relationships with the child from birth. In the case of surrogacy, the child may be genetically related to neither parent, one parent, or both parents, depending on the use of donated eggs and/or sperm. It is now possible for a child to have five "parents": a genetic and a rearing father and a genetic, a gestational, and a rearing mother, and possibly six, if one considers the partner of the gestational mother (Golombok, Cook, Bish, & Murray, 1995).

Assisted-Reproduction Developments

Artificial insemination by donor
In vitro fertilization
Gamete intrafallopian transfer (GIFT)
Zygote intrafallopian transfer (ZIFT)
Frozen embryos (cryopreservation)
Intracytoplasmic sperm injection (ICSI)

Parenthood in the laboratory rather than in the bedroom has increased for several reasons, the first of which is infertility, which has risen dramatically for both males and females. About 6 million couples in the United States have fertility problems. Since the first test-tube baby was born, the number of fertility clinics in the United States has increased from 30 to more than 300 (Wright, 1998). Male infertility is estimated to make up approximately one-third of all fertility problems, most often caused by a low sperm count or diminished motility of the sperm. Men who have low sperm counts may be assisted by pooling and concentrating sperm samples. Because of environmental hazards, male sterility is increasing. There is some evidence that approximately 25 percent of all men are affected, with low sperm counts more likely to occur among those who are exposed to various chemicals, radioactive materials, and other hazardous materials. Men undergoing chemical or radiological therapy may preserve and store their semen. Males who choose to have a vasectomy, which is usually irreversible, can save their sperm and still father children at a later date (Edwards, 1991).

In addition to infertility as a reason for increased demand for alternative parenting techniques, fewer babies are available for adoption. Historically, adoption has been the only culturally accepted way for infertile couples to achieve parenthood. Mounting evidence suggests that some of the new reproductive techniques are being adopted rapidly by normally fertile individuals. Other techniques, still in the early experimental stages, are likely to be in great demand when they are fully perfected. Among other potential uses, the new birth technologies make children possible for those with histories of genetic disease, endometriosis, hyperthyroid, and miscarriage, enabling individuals to select the sex of their offspring and to manipulate their appearance and perhaps their intellectual capacity. For gays and lesbians, the social and biological innovations provide the means of forming a family. Interestingly, they are useful in assisting heterosexual couples to defer pregnancy beyond the normal childbearing years, when problems of conception may begin to emerge (Edwards, 1991).

Artificial Insemination by Donor

AID has a long and rather successful history. It is the most commonly used alternative to parenthood, probably because it is the most frequently offered and is the least expensive. Further, it has a short waiting period and usually offers anonymity to the donor as well as to the inseminated female (Edwards, 1991). However, laws vary from state to state on whether a child conceived by AID has the right to know the identity of her biological father (Wright, 1998). In this method, semen (fresh or frozen) from a donor (known or unknown) is injected into the uterus of a fertile female. Conception then takes place in the usual manner.

AID usually is chosen when the husband is functionally sterile or if the possibility exists that he might transmit a gene for a heritable disease, such as Huntington's chorea or Tay-Sachs. Four methods of insemination are now employed: intrauterine, intracervical, vaginal, and cervical-cap. The general assumption is that the vagina presents the most hostile environment to spermatozoa, so a combination of methods frequently is used. Cervical-cap insemination is considered the method that mimics most clearly the natural process, having the added benefit of avoiding the vaginal environment. There are three types of artificial insemination: AID, artificial insemination homologous (AIH), and a combination of the former (AIC). AIH is homologous insemination with the husband's semen. It poses no significant ethical or legal problems because any resulting child is the biological offspring of the husband and wife.

However, if the husband's sperm are subgrade in number or motility, other procedures may be needed to achieve a pregnancy, assuming the wife herself is potentially fertile. AID and AIC are the available alternatives. Artificial-insemination procedures, and especially AID, are becoming more frequently practiced because of the cryobanking of semen. It is estimated that more than 30,000 donor-assisted pregnancies occur each year, but because the industry is unregulated, no one knows for sure (Gardner, 1998).

Donor inseminations are being performed for single women who want to conceive without sexual relations and without potential problems that might arise if a woman knew the biological father. Lesbians who desire a child most often use AID.

Many of the donors are unknown to the recipients. In fact, many clinics initially mixed sperm from two or more donors so that anonymity for all concerned could be maintained. Further, this procedure alleviated some of the legal problems that might have resulted. Any change in custom or practice relating to reproduction and parenthood has always elicited emotionally charged responses. In the 1950s and 1960s, when legislation became necessary, there was at first horrified negation; then negation without horror; then slow but gradual curiosity, study, and evaluation; and, finally, a very slow, steady acceptance.

In Vitro Fertilization

In vitro fertilization (IVF), the cornerstone of assisted reproductive technology (Wright, 1998), may be chosen when a woman is unable to become pregnant because of tubal blockage and/or scarring. In this method, a mature egg is fertilized outside the woman's body, most often by the husband's sperm. Patients are given fertility drugs (such as Clomid or Pergonol) to develop more than one egg at a time. Normally about 5 to 10 eggs are retrieved per patient, but as many as 40 have been produced. Blood tests and ultrasound indicate when ova are ripe. Then the eggs are extracted in a delicate operation performed under general anesthesia. Ultrasound or a laparoscope is used to guide the needle into the follicles. Eggs, which are only 1/4,000 of an inch in diameter, and the surrounding fluids are gently suctioned out. Ova are carefully washed and placed in a petri dish and incubated for 5 to 6 hours. Meanwhile, fresh semen is collected, inspected for motility, washed, and placed in a culture medium that induces sperm capacitation. After an interval of 5 to 6 hours, from 100,000 to 800,000 spermatozoa are added to the medium of the oocyte. Once fertilization has taken place, 12 to 18 hours later, the embryos are carefully monitored and assessed with respect to their size, shape, density, and the presence of fragments. Those with the proper cleavages are then transferred to the uterus, usually at the 4-cell stage of development. Up to four embryos are returned to the womb so that the chance of pregnancy begins to approximate natural fecundity—about a 25 percent chance of pregnancy rate versus a natural rate of 31 percent. The rate of successful pregnancies has been enhanced by the use of fertility drugs, making it more likely that the embryo will implant itself in the womb. The insertion of multiple embryos, combined with the use of fertility drugs, also increases the probability of multiple births (Edwards, 1991), which can compromise the health of the fetuses.

Gamete intrafallopian transfer (GIFT) is a more advanced technique with a 5 percent to 10 percent higher success rate than IVF (one live birth for every five IVF cycles). Eggs are harvested, mixed with sperm, and then returned to the fallopian tubes to fertilize. A single IVF costs between $8,000 and $10,000. Five IVFs would then cost $50,000. Only 10 states in 1998 mandated insurance coverage for infertility treatment (Wright, 1998).

The freezing of embryos (cryopreservation) is fast becoming as commonplace as IVF. With the use of fertility drugs, cryopreservation makes it possible to store the excess embryos for later use in the event that earlier attempts at implantation are unsuccessful. Moreover, many clinicians prefer cryopreservation in the belief that embryos that survive freezing and thawing may be the hardiest and most capable of producing a live birth. Cryopreservation further allows for the possibility of embryo adoption. It is estimated that frozen embryos potentially may be kept viable for 600 years and perhaps up to 10,000 years (Edwards, 1991). However, eventual disposition of unused frozen embryos can be controversial. Former spouses have waged custody battles over frozen embryos, and in at least one case, the IVF clinic claimed the embryo as its lawful property (Wright, 1998). Legally, human embryos occupy a very gray area.

In the early 1990s intracytoplasmic sperm injection (ICSI), a technique by which a single spermatozoon is injected into an oocyte, thus circumventing the selective barriers developed during evolution, was embraced as a major breakthrough for the treatment of male infertility. At first, only ejaculated sperm were injected, but later, surgically obtained immature sperm were used. By 1995 tens of thousands of ICSI children had been born by this method (TeVelde, Van Baar, & Van Kooij, 1998).

Further, choosing the sex of one's baby, especially if one desires a female child, is now more scientifically assured. Edward Fugger, a reproductive biologist at the Genetics and IVF Institute in Fairfax, Virginia, has developed a sperm-sorting technique that almost guarantees that a girl will be conceived. The X chromosomes carry a bit more (nearly 3 percent) DNA than the Y chromosomes, and the new technique can highlight the difference by labeling sperm DNA with a dye that glows in the light of a laser. The sperm are then sorted by glow. Pregnancies with female embryos can be produced more than 90 percent of the time. However, the technique for selecting sperm bearing the Y chromosome is far less discriminating. Although not foolproof, it will help families avoid bearing boys at risk for the sex-linked genetic diseases such as hemophilia. The cost of sorting sperm and flushing them into the uterus—$1,500 for sorting and $1,000 for the insemination, with no guarantee of pregnancy—will limit the procedure's use in family balancing. In addition, only a few babies have been produced by sperm sorting. It has not been tested for long-term safety (Richardson, 1999).

In vitro fertilization is the most socially accepted alternative reproductive technique, proba-

Artificial insemination by a donor has become an increasingly common alternative to biological parenthood.

bly because both the parents contribute to the conception of the child. The problems arising from parenthood through the use of this approach are not moral and legal ones resulting from the involvement of a third party. However, because IVF techniques often result in multiple pregnancies, selection reduction is an issue. Couples must decide how many eggs to fertilize and transfer at one time, whether they want to create and freeze embryos for future use, and how unused frozen embryos will eventually be disposed of.

Surrogate Mothers

The most controversial alternative reproductive technique thus far under public scrutiny is the use of surrogate mothers. The most prevalent use of this method occurs when a couple whose wife is infertile, has a disease that might be passed on through heredity, or for some reason is unable to carry a baby to term contracts with another woman to be artificially inseminated with the husband's sperm. The celebrated case of "Baby M" is an example. Elizabeth Stern, the sociological mother, had multiple sclerosis. The chosen surrogate carries the baby until he is born and then relinquishes him to the couple who contracted with the surrogate. The wife of the couple, then, according to some state laws, must adopt the child to become the legal mother. This situation is the reverse of AID—the child has the father's genes but not the mother's. The concept of surrogate motherhood is not new. Even the Bible offers an example. When Sarah was unable to give her husband, Abraham, a child, she told him to visit her handmaiden Hagar. The process, obviously, has been refined since then. With artificial insemination the mother and the father need not meet. However, in some cases a friendly relationship is formed between the couple and the surrogate mother during the pregnancy; and in some cases, the couple is present in the delivery room during the birthing.

In another type of surrogate motherhood, a woman might have her own eggs fertilized by her husband in the laboratory and then have them implanted in another woman. Thus, a busy career woman could decide to "rent the womb" of another woman by having one of her fertilized eggs implanted in the other woman. The "genetic" mother could, then, continue her work while the baby developed. After birth, the husband and wife could claim their 100 percent genetic child. Various other combinations of the use of surrogate mothers could occur—for example, with single women.

More than 20 programs have been established in the United States that make surrogate arrangements for couples, but many couples make their own. In most cases, a rather substantial fee is paid to the surrogate mother to pay for prenatal care and medical costs. When legal and/or agency fees are added, the cost can be as high as $50,000. On the other hand, private arrangements, especially if they are intrafamilial, may involve far less money. The number of babies born to surrogate mothers is unknown because of the private nature of many arrangements. The media have publicized several cases involving kin acting as surrogates, such as a sister, a mother, and even a grandmother. Several movies have been made that feature surrogate mothers as one of the main characters.

Other Innovations

Other biosocial innovations still in the experimental stage that have significant implications for alternatives to parenthood are genetic engineering, ovum transfer, and cloning and ectogenesis.

Genetic Engineering.   By separating human reproduction from the act of sexual intercourse, IVF procedures create the opportunity for further manipulation of the final product. Putting embryos into an external laboratory environment makes them directly accessible to genetic manipulation. Paralleling development in fertilization technology, significant advances have taken place over the last 20 years in recombinant DNA research and genetic engineering. Thus far, techniques have been perfected on animals but not perfected for gene insertion in humans. However, many scientists consider it only a matter of time and further experimentation before the process becomes feasible (Edwards, 1991).

Ovum Transfer.   Ovum transfer, which has been perfected in animal husbandry, is a relatively new procedure for humans. Ovum transfer consists of a donor female and a recipient female who will carry the embryo to term. It is often seen as an alternative to IVF. Ovum transfer is actually the transfer of a 5-day-old embryo rather than an ovum, and, compared with IVF, the procedure is relatively simple, less invasive, and more successful. It has the added advantage of being nonsurgical; the transfer from donor to recipient is accomplished by a specially designed catheter. This procedure need not be confined to infertile women. It can allow fertile women who are concerned about adverse genetic transmissions to have children who are not liable to them. Ovum transfer further can serve as an intermediate process to diagnose genetic makeup and to detect potential health problems early in embryonic development. Thus, this technique has a wide range of applications (Edwards, 1991).

Cloning and Ectogenesis.   Advances in IVF and ovum transfer are leading the way for other new and even more dramatic reproductive techniques such as cloning and ectogenesis. Although not yet used to reproduce humans, the possible development of these techniques in the not-so-distant future raises many ethical and legal issues, as well as fear and anxiety about the implications of such means of reproduction (Edwards, 1991).

Richard Seed, the physicist who successfully cloned the lamb Dolly, announced plans in 1998 to clone humans. Because of the medical risks involved, he decided that the first person he will try to clone is himself. His wife has agreed to carry the embryo that would be created by combining the nucleus of one of his cells with a donor egg. Cloning, even in livestock, presently carries the risk of stillbirths or abnormal fetuses. President Clinton declared a 5-year moratorium on human cloning, but in 1998 Congress failed to act on legislation to outlaw human cloning ("Would be cloner…," 1998).

Crews (1998) contended that cloning will not replace sexual reproduction for the vast majority of people desiring children. Most parents would not want a clone of another human but, rather, someone novel who would still reflect familial traits. He proposed that cloning would be useful for couples who cannot conceive on their own, single persons who want children, and parents seeking the very best DNA for their child but will not replace physical sex or biological reproduction.

Theoretically, human evolution could be halted if cloning were the only technology considered. But new technologies of education and socialization may have a greater impact on a child's intelligence than the DNA with which she is born. Parents who want a genius may decide that investing in their child's early development will vastly outweigh the gamble of attempting to replicate Einstein. Although cloning will have many uses in the future, it will likely have little effect when compared with all the other breakthroughs in physical and social evolution.

Issues Relating to Assisted Reproduction

The legal issues regarding surrogate motherhood obviously are numerous. Is surrogate mothering "baby selling"? All states in the United States have laws that prohibit trading children for money. Many people contend that surrogate motherhood does not fall into that category, but, rather, the fee is for services rendered. Many lawyers and judges feel that the right to procreate through a surrogate or other means is constitutionally protected. Is the contract between the commissioning couple and the surrogate enforceable in a court of law? If the contract is unenforceable, then who obtains custody of the child if it is challenged? What rights do the commissioner, the surrogate, and the child have? Until the "Baby M" case, these questions were not debated. They are far from settled even now. The decision by the New Jersey judge in the case—custody was awarded to the father and visitation rights were awarded to the surrogate—was based on the constitutional right to procreate by noncoital means and what he deemed were the "best interests of the child" (Rust, 1987).

To critics, surrogate motherhood constitutes "baby selling" and the commercialization of childbearing, and some state courts have agreed. Several courts, though, have upheld the legality of the practice, maintaining that it is protected by the constitutional right of privacy. The legal challenges to surrogate arrangements have slowed the practice, but they are unlikely to stop it. As long as parties to an agreement are satisfied, the practice can continue in an extralegal manner. The surrogate is plainly the gestational or carrying mother, and the contracting husband and wife are the genetic parents (Edwards, 1991).

One decision in a surrogate case is an example of how the court used existing laws to settle the issue of custody. A 4-month-old boy was awarded to the biological father, and the surrogate mother was given the right to visit the child every other weekend, some holidays, and part of each summer. The wife of the biological father was 50 years old and infertile. The surrogate, 25 years old, was married and had three other children. She agreed initially to be artificially inseminated for $25,000. However, she claimed the contract was voided when she and the biological father, to save time and money, resorted to sexual intercourse instead of insemination. The child was conceived in one of seven attempts at the father's home. The judge noted that his ruling to give legal custody to the biological father was based on the predisposition of the surrogate's husband toward violence ("Dad wins custody…," 1993).

Ultimately, the high value society places on parenthood drives the demand for new reproductive technologies. For many, the desire for children is so intense that, in the face of difficulties, they will go to any lengths to achieve their goals. Moral, ethical, legal, social, and medical issues have been raised about assisted reproduction. Reproductive technology raises questions about the definition of family and kinship and the experience of parenthood. Historically, the issue of legitimacy (in essence, to whom the child belongs) has been a central societal concern. Further, parenthood historically has been associated with both rights and obligations. If more than one kind of mother and/or father is involved, which is to have precedence? Who is the legitimate parent? What are the rights and obligations of a sperm donor, a carrying mother, or a partner in a lesbian relationship? The questions of one's origins and self-identity, and how these intersect with the adult's definition of parenthood, are pivotal issues in the life course of nonbiological families (Edwards, 1991).

Frequently newspapers carry accounts of courts making decisions regarding the issues raised above. One case, which received international attention, was that of a 59-year-old woman who gave birth to twins. Also, an Italian doctor has assisted approximately 50 postmenopausal women to give birth. Many more from a variety of countries are pregnant currently. Critics contend that middle-aged mothers will not live long enough to rear the children they bear, and they are too old for the emotional and physical strains of pregnancy. Others contend that the right of any woman to have children transcends ethical debates. Further, men can be 100 years old and have children; to prevent older women from having them is an act of discrimination (Barry, 1994).

An unusual case is that of a divorced couple who were in court to determine the "custody" of five frozen embryos. The woman sought control of the embryos to have them implanted and give birth. The ex-husband wanted them to be destroyed. The case raised legal and ethical questions about the indefinite existence of embryos. Are they to be treated as property or "children" in a divorce settlement? If treated as children, should the ex-husband be mandated to support them, born long after his divorce? ("Couple fighting...," 1994).

A number of medical concerns have been expressed about some assisted reproductive techniques. Foremost is the lack of regulation of the industry by statute and the failure of the medical profession to regulate and monitor the procedures. The introduction of new drugs for use by humans is preceded by a painstaking, highly regulated, and extremely costly process of testing—first in animals, then in human beings. However, no similar process occurs before the introduction of assisted-reproduction techniques. Recently, concerns have been expressed about the potential long-term hazards facing ICSI offspring, which could include genetic damage, cytoplasmic changes, contamination of sperm, and other damages caused by the technique itself (TeVelde et al., 1998). Bowen, Gibson, Leslie, and Saunders (1998) assessed the medical

and developmental outcomes of 1-year-old children conceived by intracytoplasmic sperm injection. ICSI children, children conceived naturally, and children conceived by IVF were compared.

Most of the ICSI children were within the normal range of intellectual development, but as a group their mean score on the Bayley Scales of Infant Development was significantly lower than the scores of the two other groups of children. Fifteen of the 89 ICSI children experienced delayed development, as compared with two of the 84 IVF children and one of the 80 children conceived naturally. However, there were no significant differences among the three groups in the number of hospital admissions, major health problems, or visits to medical practitioners since birth. The researchers felt that manipulation of human gametes or embryos and intervening with the natural process of conception may induce subtle, complex, and far-reaching changes in the genetic material of the offspring and, perhaps, of the next generation.

One of the more troubling medical issues associated with the use of fertility drugs is that of multiple births, which increases risk to both mothers and children and creates social and financial concerns for many parents. Sixty million U.S. women in 1995 used some kind of infertility service, and about one-fifth of them used fertility drugs costing $400 to $500 per month. Sometimes women progress to stronger fertility drugs requiring daily injections and extensive monitoring, which cost as much as $1,000 to $1,500 per month. Typically, one-fourth of women who become pregnant with fertility drugs can expect to have more than one baby at a time. Multiple births seem to be skyrocketing in the United States. The rate of twins grew 37 percent from 1980 to 1996; triplets, quadruplets, quintuplets, and other multiple deliveries rose 344 percent during the same period—from about 1,300 in 1980 to nearly 6,000 in 1996 (Emanuel, 1999).

Women pregnant with multiple fetuses often have considerably difficult pregnancies. They may be hospitalized or bedridden to prolong pregnancy. Babies who do survive are likely to have breathing difficulties, brain damage, and fluid imbalance—high infant mortality and long-term complications. Statistics show that 50 percent of babies weighing less than 1.7 pounds at birth have functional impairments. One study showed that 50 percent scored low on standardized tests, 21 percent were mentally retarded, 9 percent had cerebral palsy, and 25 percent had vision problems. As a result, 45 percent ended up enrolling in special-education programs. Equally important are the emotional risks that children in multiple births face because of the difficulty the parents have in meeting individual needs (Emanuel, 1999; Morrow, 1999).

Hospital and health-care costs are likely to be insurmountable. The hospital costs alone for the octuplets born in Texas in 1999 exceeded $2 million, and birth is only the beginning. Many medical personnel encourage parents to agree to "selective reduction" of the number of fetuses. Unfortunately, large multiple births receive considerable media attention (Emanuel, 1999; Morrow, 1999).

Some evidence suggests that new techniques may lead to minimizing the chances of large multiple births. For example, in 1998 a new in vitro fertilization process was announced by Stanford University researchers that extends the time in which embryos can grow before being implanted from the usual 3 days to 5 or 6 days. The extra days double the success rate and thus can minimize the chance of multiple births. The new test-tube culture, a blastocyst medium rich in amino acids and glucose, gives the organisms a better chance to survive through two key developmental stages. One or two embryos, rather than four to six, can be implanted and eliminate the risks of quadruplets or more (Schrof, 1998).

Ethical, moral, and legal questions about parenting and child rearing surround the growing trend of selling reproductive services on the Internet. The growing number of egg donors advertising on the Internet represents a dangerous journey into the commercialization of reproduction and poses profound questions about the creation of "designer" families. There is no screening of donors or checking on who is buying the eggs. The number of women donors on the Internet is uncer-

tain, but as the demand for eggs grows, the number of individuals and clinics providing the service also grows. One agency receives 20 to 60 calls a day from couples interested in finding an egg donor and 100 calls a week from individuals wanting to donate eggs. In most cases, a couple who wants an egg contacts an agency and enters into a contract. Eggs are harvested from a donor, artificially inseminated, and then implanted in the buyer. Egg donors receive an average of $2,500 to $4,000 per harvest. Those who search for eggs on the Internet are likely to be looking for donors with specific characteristics—healthy, highly intelligent, very attractive, gifted in the arts, and so forth. These individuals may pay up to double an agency fee. Often donors are not informed of risks, the side effects of fertility drugs, or consequences to their own ability to conceive. Even though some agencies carry out extensive screening of donors and recipients, it is not a common practice (Fine, 1998).

Finally, concerns have been raised about the type and extent of genetic information about the sperm and egg donors that should be shared with parents and ultimately children in cases of assisted reproductive technology (Andrews & Elster, 1998). A few state statutes require the collection of genetic information about sperm donors, and in one case egg donors, but such information generally is not for the purpose of informing the recipient or the resulting child. Rather, it is to exclude as donors those men or women with particular genetic mutations such as Tay-Sachs disease. A few states have statutes that require medical screening of surrogate mothers.

When children born of assisted reproductive technologies reach maturity and want genetic information, most states permit disclosure if good cause is given. In at least 18 states, artificial-insemination laws allow access to records under the good-cause standard or with similar proof of compelling reasons. Only one state defines what constitutes "good cause" for disclosure—a showing of a compelling necessity for identifying information. However, if records are obtained, they are unlikely to contain identifying information that would allow the resulting child, or even the physician providing the insemination, to recontact the donor for information (Andrews & Elster, 1998).

To assist parents and children of assisted reproductive technology in finding information about biological parents, one sperm bank in California is looking ahead to 2001, when the first babies born from its services will come of age and perhaps begin seeking information about their fathers. An "identity-release task force" has been established to create guidelines so that the experience will be respectful of all concerned. Gardner (1998) noted that individuals are entitled to know their true backgrounds—knowledge that, when lovingly conveyed, need not diminish their relationships with the parents who rear them.

Outcomes for Children

Since the first child was born by means of assisted reproductive technology, questions have been voiced about the outcomes for children born as a result of these methods. Only recently has research begun to assess the outcomes. Golombok et al. (1995) assessed family relationships and the social and emotional development of children conceived by in vitro fertilization and donor insemination. These families and children were compared with families with naturally conceived children and adoptive families when the children were between 4 and 8 years of age.

The researchers noted that the secrecy surrounding donor insemination and egg donation may undermine family relationships, and children conceived by gamete donation may feel confused about their identities. Children also may feel deceived by their parents if they eventually discover the facts about their conceptions. Couples may not have come to terms with their infertility, thereby experiencing difficulties relating to their children. Stress associated with a partner's infertility may result in marital difficulties. If relationship difficulties persist, problems are likely to develop for the child.

Surprisingly, results showed more marital difficulties in families with naturally conceived children and higher levels of parental anxiety and depression. Further, mothers with children conceived through assisted reproduction expressed greater warmth toward their children and more emotional involvement with them than mothers with naturally conceived children. The level of emotional involvement shown by adoptive mothers was similar to that of IVF and DI mothers. Both mothers and fathers who had used assisted reproduction interacted more with their children than mothers and fathers of naturally conceived children. Parents of naturally conceived children scored higher in stress than assisted-reproduction parents. Finally, no significant differences among the groups were found on measures of children's emotional and behavior problems.

The researchers concluded that the quality of parenting in assisted-reproduction parents was superior to that of parents who conceived their children naturally. Families that had used assisted reproductive technology were functioning extremely well. The findings suggested that genetic ties are less important for family functioning than a strong desire for parenthood. The similarity between the assisted reproductive and the adoptive parents seems to suggest that it does not matter whether a child is genetically unrelated to one parent or two; an imbalance in genetic relationships between the parents and the child does not appear to disrupt the parenting process.

There is a move toward more openness in telling gamete-donation children about their origins, which stems from the research on adoption that has demonstrated that genetic origins are important for the development of a clear sense of identity. Sparse research to date has found no evidence to suggest that children are traumatized by this information. However, very few children from assisted reproductive technology have been told about their origins, and future research will no doubt shed light on the impact of this information on children (Golombok et al., 1995).

Chan, Raboy, and Patterson (1998) assessed both parents' and children's adjustment in heterosexual-couple, single-heterosexual, lesbian-couple, and single-lesbian-mother families. All mothers had conceived their children through donor insemination, and the children were biologically related to the mothers but not the fathers. Results indicated that parents were well adjusted. No significant differences emerged from either the mothers' reports of well-being or the biological fathers' reports of well-being. Children in the sample were well adjusted. When that sample was compared with a large sample of naturally conceived children, no significant differences were found in child adjustment as a function of parental sexual orientation or number of parents in the home. Thus, neither structural factors nor parental sexual orientation was associated with significant outcomes for children or their parents.

In summary, assisted reproductive technology appears to be a continuing alternative for many infertile couples and other individuals who desire children. Although the risks associated with these methods have been minimized and new technologies continue to be developed and refined, many issues and concerns have not been resolved. The research on child outcomes is only now being conducted, and much more needs to be done before conclusions can be reached. So far, it appears that the method of conception is not important, but the parent-child interactions and family processes that occur in the family after the child is born are the major influences on development. The legal, moral, and ethical issues surrounding parenting and child rearing through assisted reproductive technology need to be dealt with, as well as screening and monitoring of the entire process.

FOSTER PARENTHOOD

Another alternative to biological parenting is to assume the role of a foster parent. Most foster parents, however, are those who have already parented their own children for a certain period of time. Foster care does not exist primarily for the benefit of adults who are seeking children but to substitute for, or supplement, families who ostensibly do not, or cannot, adequately care for their offspring. Children are placed in foster care when a local social-services agency and the courts have determined that current parental care for children

has fallen below acceptable community standards and children are at risk for harm (Barbell & Wright, 1999; Marcus, 1991). As the following discussion indicates, there are a number of rewards for parenting a foster child but also unique problems, concerns, and social issues surrounding this alternative to parenthood.

The removal of a child from his biological parents is a serious step. One can hardly imagine a greater intrusion into the lives of families by the government or society than that of separating children from their biological parents. When such separation is effected by no fault of the child, the question arises as to what conditions would warrant this extreme action. Since the 1900s, a strong commitment to and a firm policy of maintaining children in the families of origin whenever possible have existed in the United States. A statement was made at the first White House Conference on children in 1909 that home life was the highest and finest product of civilization and that children should not be deprived of it except for urgent and compelling reasons (Rosenfeld et al., 1997).

In the 1800s family poverty was a primary reason for removing children from their parents. It was believed that poverty was synonymous with unworthiness of character. But in the early 1900s a shift toward maintaining children in their own homes occurred. The federal Adoption Assistance and Child Welfare Act of 1980 (PL 96–272) provides that reasonable efforts be made to prevent or eliminate the need for removal of the child from her home and to make it possible for the child to return to it. Figure 11.1 shows the rate of placement of children in foster care from 1910 to 1997. As noted in Figure 11.1, there was a significant increase in the placement of children in foster care during the 1960s and 1970s. Several explanations account for the explosion of child placement during that time. One was the public and professional awareness of and concern about child abuse and neglect that emerged. This movement encouraged further intervention into the lives of families. The number of children placed in foster care declined in the 1980s, and by 1984 the Child Welfare Act of 1980 was showing some success in reducing the number of

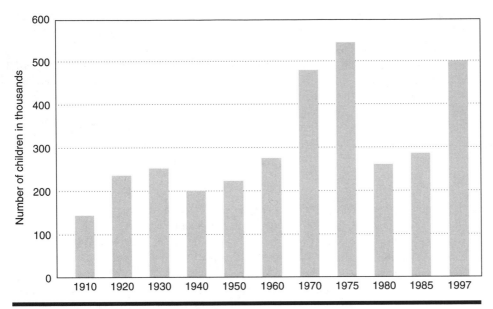

FIGURE 11.1 Children Placed in Foster Care (1910–1997)

Source: Zuravin, S., & DePanfilis, D. (1997). Factors affecting foster care placement of children receiving child protective services. *Social Work Research, 21*(1), 34–42.

children in care and the length of time spent in care. However, from the mid-1980s to the late 1990s, a dramatic 74 percent increase occurred in the number of children in out-of-home care; the length of time children remained in care and their rate of reentry into care also increased. Concurrently, the out-of-home care system found itself facing new challenges: the overrepresentation of children of color; an influx of infants and preschoolers; children with increasingly severe emotional/behavioral problems; the pervasiveness of substance abuse and its impact on families; the growing number of children infected/affected by HIV/AIDS; and the discharge of many youths from care who lacked jobs, homes, and connections to families (Barbell & Wright, 1999).

Once again, the out-of-home care system struggled to deal with the sheer numbers of children in the system and with the complex issues that brought them there. Congress, again, took action by creating the Family Preservation and Family Support program in 1993, which provided funding for a variety of services, including intensive fam-

ily-preservation services and services to reunify families with children in care. However, despite this funding, the number of children in foster care continued to increase in most states, resulting in longer periods in care, large caseloads for social-service workers, inexperienced and untrained staff, and high turnover rates of workers and foster parents. In response, Congress passed the Adoption and Safe Families Act (ASFA), which was signed into law in late 1997. This new legislation reauthorized the Family Preservation and Family Support program, renamed it the Promoting Safe and Stable Families program, and modified and clarified a wide range of policies established under the Adoption Assistance and Child Welfare Act of 1980. States now have clearer guidelines for the safety of children and the decision-making process leading to permanency (Barbell & Wright, 1999).

During the 1990s kinship foster care increased. Children placed with relatives remain connected to their birth families and cultural milieus, but evidence shows that children in kinship care have longer placements and are less likely to receive needed health services. Licensing standards are less rigorous, and children are less carefully supervised (Rosenfeld et al., 1997).

Providing appropriate services to families in foster care has been a recent effort. For example, Katz (1999) recommended concurrent planning—working with families toward reunification while simultaneously developing alternative permanency plans. This strategy is especially designed for very young, chronically neglected children from multiproblem families. It has the potential to reduce the number of temporary placements of children, decrease the length of time in care, and increase the candor and respect given to biological families and relatives by including them in the case planning early.

Barth and Price (1999) described shared family care as another innovative approach to providing services to families in foster care. In this approach, an entire family is temporarily placed in the home of a host family trained to mentor and support the biological parents as they develop the skills and supports necessary to care for their children and to live independently. Parents must demonstrate a real desire to participate in a plan to improve their parenting skills and life situations. Mentors must be knowledgeable about child development, child safety and discipline, and working with adults. They must understand substance abuse, domestic violence, and developmental disabilities. A good match between participating families and mentors is essential. The cost for this approach is higher than for basic foster care, but if more than one child is involved and placement is short, it could be cost-effective.

Testa and Rolack (1999) compared the performance of a professional foster-care program and two specialized programs with random samples of kinship and nonrelative foster homes. Professional foster care trains foster parents, most of whom care for special-needs children, and pays them an annual salary for foster parenting above and beyond board payments made by the state. Specialized foster care is the care of children with developmental, emotional, or medical needs above and beyond those of average children in out-of-home care. Specialized foster caregivers typically receive a monthly board payment that is larger than that received by foster parents caring for children not identified as special-needs. Testa and Rolack found that professional and kinship foster care consistently outperformed the specialized programs and the nonrelative care in stability, sibling placement, restrictiveness of care, and proximity to the child's community of origin. The professional foster-care program had difficulty moving children to adoptive homes or subsidized guardianship.

The Role of the Foster Parent

The foster-parent role is one that is voluntarily assumed. The assumption of any role implies evaluation of one's performance by others. The foster-parenting role is viewed positively by some people in society and negatively by others. Some segments of the community define foster parents as virtuous; other look on these role performers with suspicion.

HIGHLIGHTS

Challenges for Foster Care in the New Millennium

Meeting the needs of special populations
Recruiting and retaining high-quality foster caregivers
Continuing the promotion and use of kinship care
Assessing early infants and preschoolers in care
Increasing services to biological families
Providing immediate foster-care placement rather than temporary shelter
Identifying new models of intervention that respect, preserve, and strengthen family ties
Providing new ways of delivering services and funding
Being culture-sensitive
Improving outcomes and accountability

Source: Barbell, K., & Wright, L. (1999). Family foster care in the next century. *Child Welfare, 78*(1), 3–15.

Foster parents must attempt to stabilize a child's life despite previous emotionally damaging experiences. The child must make enormous adjustments to a new environment, which includes different adult caretakers, home, neighborhood, school, and peer relationships, all for an indeterminate period of time (Marcus, 1991; Rosenfeld et al., 1997). Foster parents should possess the same characteristics and skills that one would desire in any parent providing care and treatment to promote the child's development physically, emotionally, intellectually, socially, and spiritually (Daly & Dowd, 1992). Thus, the foster-care environment should be more than free from abuse and neglect and in compliance with legal and licensing guidelines. The foster parent should be dedicated and skilled in child care. In addition, Daly and Dowd have proposed that foster parents should have positive values, good social skills, high energy, and good judgment. In short, they must demonstrate the skills in parenting that one would want children to develop. Caregivers who lack support and training and who have too many children to nurture not only suffer burnout but also are more likely to rely on "contain and control" techniques such as early bedtimes, compulsory naps, medications, "time-outs," and restraint. In an effective, positive environment, caregivers are continually teaching new skills to children instead of focusing on problem behavior.

Marcus (1991) reported that successful child placement occurs when foster parents have had prior experience; when they function as loving, caring substitute parents; when they are tolerant of children and allow them to function as individuals; when their motives for becoming foster parents are altruistic; and when they are reliable caretakers, bonding figures, and stable figures. In other words, they are "psychological parents" to a child whose life has had no such person available in his family of origin.

People become foster parents for a number of reasons. Some indicate that they feel a sense of moral obligation, often based on religious beliefs. For others, becoming foster parents offers an alternative to adoption or an opportunity eventually to adopt a child. To many foster parents, these children fill a void created by the departure of their own children. A few enter the foster-parent program for the financial incentives offered by the agencies.

Good foster parents have always been scarce, but the number of available foster homes is shrinking. Overall, the number of foster families has declined by a third nationwide since the mid-1980s (Burry, 1999). Recruitment is exacerbated by a number of variables. First, the expenses foster parents incur in caring for foster children seldom are reimbursed fully by agency payments, and the economic reality for most families today requires that both parents work. Thus, when economic considerations are added to the advanced level of skills required to work with children and families in need of foster-care services, it is understandable that recruiting effective foster parents grows ever more difficult. Further, liability insurance is difficult to obtain (Chamberlain, Moreland, & Reid, 1992; Woolf, 1990). Not only are foster parents difficult to recruit, but also those who currently provide care drop out at alarming rates. The reasons given by foster parents for dropping out of the system include lack of training, support, and respite care, and the increasing severity of problems presented by the children placed with them.

Training of Foster Parents.   Few individuals involved in child welfare would argue against the need for effective foster-care training. Research has documented that training correlates positively with placement stability. Foster-parent training reduces the incidence of failed placements, increases desirable placement outcomes, and enriches the probability of retention of the child by the foster parents (Titterington, 1990). This researcher noted that training should facilitate mastery of subject content and provide opportunities for mutual support and empowerment. He pointed out that many foster-care training programs have been developed and implemented, the majority of which focus on child management techniques, roles and relationships in foster care, and parent-child interactions. Rosenfeld et al. (1997) pointed out that foster parents need training in providing a consistent and nurturing environment, securing appropriate services, and understanding the child's special emotional needs. Several types of training programs for foster parents have been described in the literature. Titterington (1990) developed a comprehensive networking model, with the goal of increasing support and networking for foster parents. He helped foster parents identify the networking sources most helpful to them so that their networks could be improved and expanded. This group of foster parents used friends, relatives, and neighbors more than any other persons. Titterington concluded that increased networking, along with more support and nurturance, may increase the retention of children by the foster parents with whom they are placed.

Chamberlain et al. (1992) investigated the role of enhanced services and stipends for foster parents. The foster parents were randomly assigned to one of three groups given (1) enhanced support and training plus an increased monthly payment; (2) an increased monthly payment of $70 only; and (3) neither enhanced support/training nor increased payment. Foster parents were assessed periodically during the 2-year study period.

The results demonstrated that the retention rate of parents in foster care could be increased by providing parents with enhanced training and support services and a small increased monthly stipend. For the enhanced training and support group, the foster-parent dropout rate was reduced by almost two-thirds over the 2-year study period. Foster parents in the study expressed satisfaction, accomplishment, and appreciation for being seen as experts or professional people who were contributing to a greater good. The payments for their time and efforts seemed to contribute clearly to their sense of being valued.

Burry (1999) developed a multimodel inservice training program to enhance the competency of foster parents caring for infants suffering the effects of parental substance abuse. The training curriculum was 10 hours over a 4-week period. Results indicated that parents obtained both specific skills and knowledge about caring for their infants.

The children of homeless parents often are placed in foster care. Nelson (1992) conducted an unusual pilot project in Minnesota with homeless children and their families that encompassed the whole family in foster care. The project used licensed foster families to provide community-based housing and mentorship to these homeless families for up to 6 months as they made the transition to greater stability. Host families worked with the homeless parents to meet housing, education, parenting, and self-care goals, with the support of a social worker and relevant community services.

The foster provider's role was not to be the prime parent but to share in parenting tasks by modeling nurturing and discipline and enabling the parents to claim rightful parental roles in their family. Providers performed their roles by offering direct and nonjudgmental feedback to parents about their parenting, acting as extended family to the children, setting clear family rules and boundaries, and helping families obtain services such as schooling, counseling, or economic assistance. To accomplish these tasks, the program model had four components: contracting, networking, peer support, and use of community resources.

The desired outcomes were enhanced family stability, increased competence among parents in meeting their children's physical and emotional needs, and a move to affordable permanent housing where foster families could continue to serve as sources of support to the client families when needed. At the time of this writing, program evaluation had just begun.

Training for Biological Parents. The importance of the connectedness of the biological family to children in substitute, out-of-home care has been well established. Parents must be helped to develop their capability for a continual role in decision making about their children; be encouraged to sustain regular, quality contact with their children; and be linked to other resources and services that can remediate the problems that brought them to their current status. Training in parenting often is required of biological parents in the process of regaining custody of their children. Schatz and Bane (1991) proposed several ways to assist biological parents in improving their functioning in order to regain custody of their children. One approach is through programs and services that promote family and parent competencies and the provision of social support. Probably the most widely used services for parents are therapeutic services that include mental-health and alcohol/drug-related clinical therapy programs. Generally parents are referred to a system outside the protective-service unit, with some therapeutically oriented intervention. The caseworker is responsible for management of the family in need. Other approaches and techniques include parent-support groups, family rights groups, parent-education groups, parent groupwork, social-support networking, and intensive treatment programs. The techniques and skills used to facilitate change in biological parents include contracting, communication skills, decision making, problem solving, behavior modification, and role modeling.

Training and self-help programs also provide assistance to biological parents. Self-help programs are designed to build on the strengths of families and to make available to all families the respect and resources needed for reunification. The major goal is to help parents learn to act responsibly on behalf of their children as quickly as possible. These programs include neighborhood parent-support groups, community networking, and group work with parents.

An empowerment-based approach has been advocated by Schatz and Bane (1991). This approach is based on the belief that parents whose children are in out-of-home care must sustain involvement with and responsibility for their children if at all possible; they must feel empowered in their roles as caregivers to preserve and possibly reunify their families; they must become advocates for their children's needs; and they must believe that they can be good parents for their children while they are in substitute care. To accomplish these goals, the researchers provided parents with pertinent information, skill development, and social-support opportunities to increase their capacity to understand the steps necessary for maintaining responsible involvement with their children and achieving the necessary growth and development that would result in the family's reunification.

While parents are being rehabilitated, contacts with their children in foster care are encouraged. Visits between noncustodial parents and their children are crucial for successful reunification. Some visits are supervised because parents have abused or neglected their children. Visits often are difficult because parental ability to participate in such visits is overestimated; parents may feel that they must compete with foster parents; and children may experience conflict of loyalties between the two families.

Nevertheless, there are a number of benefits of visiting. Visits provide support for families in coping with changes in relationships, help children express their feelings, reassure children about parents' well-being, help children deal with reality, help children relate more effectively to foster parents, calm separation fears, empower parents and allow them to practice new behaviors, facilitate transitions to new living arrangements, and afford staff opportunities to observe and assist parental capacity (Loar, 1998; Perkins & Ansay, 1998).

Perkins and Ansay (1998) analyzed the effectiveness of a supervised visitation program. They concluded that supervised visitation programs are effective in providing safe environments for visiting, in providing opportunities for families to maintain and foster their relationships, and in facilitating the reunification process. Cases of the families who participated in the supervised visitation program were significantly more likely to be closed than those of families not participating (71 percent versus 43 percent). Of the closed cases, the most frequent outcome was child and parent reunification.

Interestingly and unfortunately, fathers/partners and the children themselves often do not participate in the placement process, from the beginning of contact with the child-welfare system to sometime after placement. Kahkonen (1997) found that social workers concentrated mainly on working with mothers, partly because of fathers' or partners' own choices. Most marital relationships were described by social workers as chaotic, destructive, and unstable. Contacts with the children were rare until the point of placement, and therefore parent-child relationship before placement was difficult to assess.

Children in Foster Care

The process of placement itself, even if necessary to protect the child, is an additional source of distress for most children. During placement, children experience the loss of a familiar environment and the rupture of relationships in the family and the community. Along with the challenge to the child's identity as a member of her family of origin, the child also is likely to feel anxiety about other family members still at home and sometimes guilt at being in a more nurturant environment than other family members. In the new home, there are additional issues and stresses, including adaptation to a new context; possibly a poor match of personalities, resources, and needs between those of the foster family and those of the child; and, in the worst cases, retraumatization from abuse or neglect in the foster home. The demand for rapid adjustment during a period of separation and loss may exacerbate existing problems for the child or

contribute to the development of new emotional and behavioral problems (Rosenfeld et al., 1997).

Consideration of the emotional needs of foster children has focused on the issues arising as the immediate consequences of placement, blame, and loss. Children in foster care often blame themselves for their separation from their parents. Self-blame may have been internalized by children through experiences with their natural parents. Foster children may need to grieve their losses, but they may be inhibited from doing so out of their fear that the expression of grief and anger will alienate the foster family. They may not feel the support and security necessary to open themselves to expression of loss. Instead, they may experience a "honeymoon" period with underlying autonomic distress before being able to grieve (Rosenfeld et al., 1997).

A number of researchers have addressed the health status of children in foster care (Altshuler & Gleeson, 1999; Rosenfeld et al., 1997; Zlotnick, Kronstadt, & Klee, 1998). Changes in family policy, particularly regarding poor children and families, likely will mean that more poor children will enter foster care with significant health problems, including physical injuries resulting from abuse or neglect, chronic health problems, mental-health disorders, birth defects, and physical growth disorders. More will require hospitalization with longer stays, special-education services, mental-health services, and supportive care from health professionals (Silver et al., 1999).

Studies have shown that foster children have three to seven times more acute and chronic health conditions, developmental delays, and emotional adjustment problems than other poor children. For example, one study showed that 60 percent of preschool foster children had developmental delays, 35 percent had chronic medical problems, 15 percent had birth defects, and 15 percent were of short stature. Many have lost parents to HIV, and increasing numbers are infected as well. Often, they have not received routine health care, have not been immunized, and continue to have unmet health needs after placement (Rosenfeld et al., 1997). Altshuler and Gleeson (1999) noted that 20 percent of all children in out-of-home care exhibit some type of disability and that 45 percent to 80 percent have some chronic or significant physical problem. A significant number of children in kinship care suffer from obesity. Almost two-thirds of homeless children have health problems, with 28 percent having two or more (Zlotnick et al., 1998).

Foster children also have extensive mental-health needs. Nearly half have some psychological disorder and more have behavior problems. One study found that 84 percent had emotional problems. Another investigator found that 44 percent of young adults who had been foster children had been involved in delinquent activities that led to court charges. Those with multiple placements often displayed criminal behavior. Those abused and neglected children who have been placed in foster care are most often at risk for psychiatric disorders and adult criminality. On average, foster children have more than 14 risk factors (poverty, perinatal stress, mothers with little education, family discord or divorce, parental alcoholism, parental mental illness, and so forth). Further, young foster children are likely to blame themselves for their plight and feel that they are "throwaways" (Rosenfeld et al., 1997). Exacerbating these problems is the fact that most children in foster care do not receive the health care they need, even after placement (Silver et al., 1999).

Behavioral problems such as attention seeking, aggression, and delinquency are more common for foster children than for other children. Behavioral problems have been found to be positively associated with the number of placements, marital instability of biological parents, infrequent parental visits, abuse by biological parents, and the child's gender. Estimates of the prevalence of emotional disturbance (e.g., withdrawal, anxiety, depression, somatic complaints, difficulties with attachment) range from 25 percent to 96 percent. Some research indicates lower rates of emotional disturbance for children living in kinship care than for those in nonrelative care (Altshuler & Gleeson, 1999).

In general, at entry foster children have been shown to score 10 points below the normal population on cognitive tests; minority children and children from lower socioeconomic levels score significantly lower. Scores improve over time for minority children in foster care, whereas Caucasian children's scores decline. About half of foster children in one study were rated by their teachers as having specific skill deficits on problem solving and reasoning (Altshuler & Gleeson, 1999). Rosenfeld et al. (1997) reported that approximately one-third of foster children under age 5 and 52 percent of school-age children have cognitive deficits. Many have attended school sporadically before entering care. Often they have moved from school to school. Emotional trauma combined with poor school attendance inhibits learning. They essentially are placed below age-appropriate grade levels, demonstrate inappropriate school-related behaviors more frequently, and have higher retention rates than children not in care (Altshuler & Gleeson, 1999).

The foster-care system has been evaluated by examining two indicators of success—permanency and safety. Child well-being is not a variable in monitoring and evaluation. Growth and change in caseloads have placed considerable demand on the system, and accountability, expedited permanency, managed care, and outcome-based contracting has redefined the policy environment for the system. Therefore, systematic measures of child well-being rarely are used to assess the current functioning of children while in foster care or changes in their functioning as a result of receiving services (Altshuler & Gleeson, 1999).

Foster care can have some positive outcomes. After about 2 to 5 years in care, some children show significant improvement in academic achievement; many receive better medical care than before placement; and some show improvement in social development and social competence. The best predictor of a good long-term outcome is a child's ability to form at least one positive relationship with someone, not necessarily a parent or relative (Rosenfeld et al., 1997). Some research has shown that teens in kinship care function significantly better than their peers in nonrelative care (Altshuler & Gleeson, 1999).

Several studies have examined perceptions of children in foster care (Gardner, 1996; Kufeldt, Armstrong, & Dorosh, 1995; Wilson & Conroy, 1999). In one study, about half of the foster children rated their own parents as healthy and half rated them as problematic; but more than 90 percent rated their foster parents in the normal or better range. Children deprived of contact with their biological parents categorized them in the problem range. In general, the optimal arrangement, according to this study, seems to be regular but not too frequent visits with biological parents (once or twice a month) (Kufeldt et al., 1995).

Gardner (1996) examined the perceptions of foster children and found that consistently these children related to their foster families rather than to their biological kin as "family." In fact, in their ideal family representations, biological parents and siblings were excluded, suggesting some level of disconnectedness from their biological families. Research has shown that foster children are satisfied with the care they receive from foster parents (e.g., Wilson & Conroy, 1999). Most children have reported that growing up in a foster family resembled growing up in one's own family. However, foster children are aware that their families are not like others. They often express the need for more background information about their biological parents, and 50 percent in some studies have described themselves as having no roots. Children who lose contact with siblings because of out-of-home placement lose contact with a source of support for resolving their grief over parental loss as well as the potential future support of adult siblings. Many foster children express the desire to see their siblings more often (Gardner, 1996).

Factors Affecting Duration of Foster Care

Since the passage of the Adoption Assistance and Child Welfare Act of 1980, measures of success in family foster care have focused primarily on safety and timely permanence for children in care. The Adoption and Safe Families Act of 1997 places even greater demands on child-welfare systems to focus their measures of success on timely permanence; the law's requirements are intended to decrease the length of time children spend in out-of-home care and increase the number of adoptions (Altshuler & Gleeson, 1999). For the first time, states are required to develop timelines and condi-

tions for filing termination of parental rights petitions. States must file on behalf of any child, regardless of age, who has been in care for 15 of the most recent 22 months. Time frames for permanency hearings are now at 12 months after placement rather than 18 months. Determination of whether and when a child will be returned home, placed for adoption, or referred for legal guardianship or another planned permanent living arrangement must be made at a permanency hearing (Barbell & Wright, 1999).

Approximately 20 percent of children younger than 6 years of age will remain in out-of-home care for 6 years, with frequent reentry into care. Approximately one in five children who go home return to care within 3 years. The reason may be that when parents are separated from their children, they lack opportunity to learn how to interact with them affectively and to deal with the frustrations that are a normal part of parenting. Further, parent and child miss the chance to adjust to the ongoing changes that they experience as individuals in relation to each other.

It remains to be seen how effectively the new federal guidelines will be implemented. Large caseloads, inexperienced and untrained staff, and high turnover rates of workers and foster parents have made it difficult for children and families to obtain the help they need. To comply with the law, public and private agencies must initiate significant program and practice changes in the coming years.

Numerous factors affect the child's length of stay in foster care and/or the ability to return to his parents. Marcus (1991) reported that the frequency of visitation by natural parents and the number of placements the child has had were associated with length of stay. Children with initial psychological problems experience more placement changes. Poor academic progress, poor adjustment in school and community, and emotional and behavior problems when discharged from foster care also have been found to be positively related to the number of changes in placement. Changes in placement may be necessary because of the child's feelings of security and lack of attachment to his foster parents, leading to a deterioration in the relationship, progressing to the point at which daily disruptions cannot be tolerated by the foster parents, who then request that the child be transferred. Transfer also may be required because the caretaker decides not to continue as a foster parent, because of the need to group siblings together, or because of the need for transfer to a longer-term placement when attempts at reunification have been unsuccessful.

Hess and Folaron (1991) examined biological parental ambivalence to the foster-care child and its relationship to the child's reunification with her family. These researchers found that parents' ambivalent attitudes about the parental role and about reunification are a potential contributor to reunification disruption. He found that many parents express clearly their ambivalence about their children's return home. Others express interest in reunification but behave in ways that are inconsistent with their statements, such as visiting irregularly or taking no action to facilitate the return of the child. Of those children and parents studied, children with unambivalent parents were more likely to reenter foster care after reunification because of a combination of problems with the foster-care system in delivering services, such as insufficient agency guidelines and policy, heavy caseloads and high caseworker turnover, insufficient community resources, inadequate referrals to appropriate services, and impediments to services and visiting. However, the children of ambivalent parents were more likely to reenter foster care because of the parents' and/or family's problems, including the parents' attitude about reunification. Parental ambivalence contributed to reentry in more than 80 percent of the cases. Further, ambivalent parents were less likely to attend parent-education classes, to be consistent in attendance in court, and to visit with their children. Ambivalent parents were almost three times more likely than unambivalent parents to have requested that their children be placed in foster care, both initially and following reunification.

The researchers noted several factors that seemingly led to parental ambivalence—insufficient social support in the parent role, multiple stresses related to living in poverty, and unhealthy childhood experiences (many were physically or sexually abused). Hess and Folaron (1991) recommended that practitioners be willing and able to identify parents' ambivalence as relevant to risk assessment, service planning, and permanency planning and that practitioners be sensitive to the signs of ambivalence exhibited by parents when considering reunification with parents versus permanent placement.

Lie and McMurtry (1991) found that sexually abused children in foster care had characteristics that were different from those of nonsexually abused children and that the experiences in foster care were different for the two groups. They found that children in the two groups had similar profiles with respect to behavioral problems and other attributes. However, the data indicated that sexually abused children exit foster care for planned permanent living arrangements at a significantly faster rate than nonsexually abused children. Children who had been sexually abused remained in foster care approximately 8 months less than a child of similar age, race, and gender who entered care because of other types of maltreatment. Because their care was of shorter duration, sexually abused children also experienced fewer disrupted placements than their counterparts. Further, they were significantly less likely to undergo a failed reunification with their original families than children in the comparison group. These researchers concluded that sexually abused children are not necessarily ill-served in foster care. They did remain in temporary care for an average of more than 2 years, and only 44 percent had left care for a planned placement at the end of the study. Virtually all the children who had exited care successfully had done so by the end of their third year in care.

Mallon (1992) noted that gay and lesbian adolescents have been placed in out-of-home care for many years, but usually they have not been provided with the kinds of services and understanding they truly need. Long-term, systematic change to meet their needs effectively will not be possible without a sustained effort to raise the consciousness of policymakers who have the power to commit the necessary resources for services to gay and lesbian youth.

Siblings in Foster Care

Very little attention has been given to the experiences of the foster child's siblings, yet it is known that children are influenced by what happens to them (Staff & Fein, 1992). More than three-fourths of children in foster care have siblings who also are placed in substitute care. Zlotnick et al. (1998) reported that homeless children were more likely than other children to have siblings in foster care and to be placed with nonrelatives. Despite the evidence of family groups of children in the foster-care population, most of the literature focuses on foster children as individuals. Greater professional interest recently has been demonstrated in sibling relationships. This interest is due to several factors—the broadening focus on attachment to significant persons other than parents and the effects of separation from them, the number of adoptees who search for existing siblings, and the political and professional emphasis on the family unit. In addition, the legal emphasis on "best interests of the child" frequently includes consideration of ties to siblings when making placement decisions.

In fact, placing siblings together either is mandated by state laws or is the strong preference of both voluntary and public welfare agencies. Smith (1996) found that between 56 percent and 85 percent of the children in foster care also are members of sibling groups. Previous research has shown that siblings placed together were more likely to remain in their first placements and less likely to experience placement disruption than siblings who were separated. However, research on the relationship of sibling placement to child functioning has found mixed results, with some studies indicating positive results and some finding no differences. Most of the foster mothers did not feel that it was easier for foster children to integrate into the foster family if placed with siblings, but caseworkers felt that the policy of placing siblings together was an effective one.

Certain situations mandate that siblings be separated—for example, when siblings are particularly interdependent, when there is great competition for adult affection among them, and when there is overt hostility among them. There is no argument for separating siblings because they are different, or if one demonstrates a caretaking role toward the other. Like rivalry, that is a normal part of many sibling relationships. However, if the relationship is stressful for all, and if one is the consistent loser in competition for adult affection and approval, then a separate placement for that child may develop self-esteem. The siblings most likely to be separated are older, are from larger sibling groups, have developmental disabilities, have been placed in residential institutions or schools, or have come into custody at different times (Staff & Fein, 1992).

In their study of siblings in foster care, Staff and Fein (1992) found that 70 percent of siblings were placed together initially and almost half remained together throughout the study. They found that placement disruption rates did not differ between siblings and only children; that younger children were more likely to be placed together initially than were older children; and that White sibling pairs were far less likely to be together in placement than were African American, Hispanic, or mixed-race children. Further, White children had the highest sibling disruption rate. Their finding that sibling pairs who were placed together were more likely to stay in their first placement than pairs who were separated and placed separately offers strong support for siblings being placed together to reduce the likelihood of disruption.

SUMMARY

Adoption, various forms of assisted reproductive technology, and foster parenthood are potential alternatives to traditional biological childbearing. Adoption has long been a socially acceptable alternative, but with the number of available babies for adoption continuing to decline, adults are seeking other ways to achieve parenthood. With increased technology and acceptance of alternative lifestyles, in vitro fertilization, artificial insemination, and other forms of reproductive technology have become more popular. Foster parenthood has long been an alternative, and some couples choose either initially to become parents in this manner or to add children to the family by this approach.

Each approach presents specific social and legal issues that must be resolved. A recent trend is for adult adoptees to seek contact with their birth parents. Policies are being changed to accommodate this desire. Open-adoption policies are becoming the norm.

The legal issues surrounding some forms of reproductive technology have yet to be resolved. There are lingering medical risks and cost factors associated with these technologies that prohibit many couples from choosing this approach.

The foster-care system has many disadvantages for both the parents and the children involved.

Research has indicated that foster children have a range of psychological and other problems that make parenting extremely difficult. The lack of permanence in placement precludes the development of lasting parent-child relationships and attachment. Yet for many parents and children, the foster-care relationship can be extremely positive, and the development of the children can be facilitated.

More research is needed on each of these alternatives to parenthood, and particularly on the outcomes for children. Legal and social issues must be resolved so that both parents and children can benefit from their respective family situations.

REFERENCES

ALTSHULER, S., & GLEESON, J. (1999). Completing the evaluation triangle for the next century. *Child Welfare, 78*(1), 125–148.

ANDERSEN, R. (1988). Why adoptees search: Motives and more. *Child Welfare, 67*(1), 15–19.

ANDREWS, L., & ELSTER, N. (1998). Adoption, reproductive technologies, and genetic information. *Health Matrix: Journal of Law Medicine, 98*(8), 125–152.

BACHRACH, C., LONDON, K., & MAZA, P. (1991). On the path to adoption: Adoption seeking in the United States, 1988. *Journal of Marriage and the Family, 53*(3), 705–718.

BARBELL, K., & WRIGHT, L. (1999). Family foster care in the next century. *Child Welfare, 78*(1), 3–14.

BARRY, C. (1994, January 1). Doctor defends older moms. *The Tuscaloosa News,* pp. A1, A4.

BARTH, R. (1993). Revisiting the issues: Adoption of drug-exposed children. *The Future of Children: Adoption, 3*(1), 167–175.

BARTH, R., & PRICE, A. (1999). Shared family care: Providing services to parents and children placed together in out-of-home care. *Child Welfare, 78*(1), 88–107.

BARTHOLET, E. (1993). International adoption: Current status and future prospects. *The Future of Children: Adoption, 3*(1), 89–103.

BORDERS, L., BLACK, L., & PASLEY, K. (1998). Are adopted children and their parents at greater risk for negative outcomes? *Family Relations, 47,* 237–241.

BOWEN, J., GIBSON, F., LESLIE, G., & SAUNDERS, D. (1998). Medical and developmental outcomes at 1 year for children conceived by intracytoplasmic sperm injection. *Lancet, 351*(9115), 1529–1535.

BRODZINSKY, D. (1993). Long-term outcomes in adoption. *The Future of Children: Adoption, 3*(1), 153–166.

BURRY, C. (1999). Evaluation of a training program for foster parents of infants with parental substance effects. *Child Welfare, 78*(11), 197–214.

CARP, E. (1995). Adoption and disclosure of family information: A historical perspective. *Child Welfare, 74*(1), 217–240.

CHADWICK, B., & HEATON, T. (Eds.). (1999). *Statistical handbook on the American family.* Phoenix, AZ: Oryx Press.

CHAMBERLAIN, P., MORELAND, S., & REID, K. (1992). Enhanced services and stipends for foster parents: Effects on retention rates and outcomes for children. *Child Welfare, 71*(5), 387–401.

CHAN, R., RABOY, B., & PATTERSON, C. (1998). Psychosocial adjustment among children conceived via donor insemination and heterosexual mothers. *Child Development, 69*(2), 443–457.

Couple fighting over five frozen embryos. (1994, June 26). *The Tuscaloosa News,* p. A4.

CREWS, C. (1998). Let's broaden our view of cloning. *Futurist, 32*(5), 68.

CURTIS, C. (1996, March). The adoption of African American children by Whites: A renewed conflict. *Families in Society: The Journal of Contemporary Human Sciences,* pp. 156–165.

Dad wins custody in surrogate case. (1993, September 11). *The Tuscaloosa News,* p. A4.

DALY, D., & DOWD, T. (1992). Characteristics of effective, harm-free environments for children in out-of-home care. *Child Welfare, 71*(6), 487–495.

DEMICK, J., & WAPNER, S. (1988). Open and closed adoption: A developmental conceptualization. *Family Process, 27*(2), 229–249.

EDWARDS, J. (1991). New conceptions: Biological innovations and the family. *Journal of Marriage and the Family, 53*(2), 349–360.

EMANUEL, E. (1999). Eight is too many. *New Republic, 220* (4), 8–10.

FEIN, E. (1998, October 25). Secrecy, stigma no longer clouding adoptions. *The Tuscaloosa News,* p. A3.

FINE, A. (1998). Fertility business hits internet, weaving web of controversy. *Christian Science Monitor, 90*(202), 3.

GANONG, L., COLEMAN, M., FINE, M., & McDANIEL, K. (1998). Issues considered in contemplating stepchild adoption. *Family Relations, 47,* 63–71.

GARDNER, H. (1996). The concept of family: Perceptions of children in family foster care. *Child Welfare, 75*(2), 161–183.

GARDNER, M. (1998). Should children know donor parents? *Christian Science Monitor, 90*(234), p. B5.

GOLOMBOK, S., COOK, R., BISH, A., & MURRAY, C. (1995). Families created by the new reproductive technologies: Quality of parenting and social and emotional development of the children. *Child Development, 66,* 285–298.

HESS, P., & FOLARON, G. (1991). Ambivalences: A challenge to permanency for children. *Child Welfare, 70*(4), 403–423.

HOLLINGER, J. (1993). Adoption of children with special needs. *The Future of Children: Adoption, 3*(1), 43–61.

KAHKONEN, P. (1997). From the child welfare trap to the foster care trap. *Child Welfare, 66*(3), 429–445.

KATZ, L. (1999). Concurrent planning: Benefits and pitfalls. *Child Welfare, 78*(1), 71–88.

KUFELDT, K., ARMSTRONG, J., & DOROSH, M. (1995). How children in care view their own and their foster families: A research study. *Child Welfare, 74*(3), 695–715.

LICHTENSTEIN, T. (1996). To tell or not to tell: Factors affecting adoptees' telling their adoptive parents about their search. *Child Welfare, 75*(1), 61–72.

LIE, G., & McMURTRY, S. (1991). Foster care for sexually abused children: A comparative study. *Child Abuse and Neglect, 15*(1), 111–121.

LOAR, L. (1998). Making visits work. *Child Welfare, 77* (1), 41–58.

MALLON, G. (1992). Gay and no place to go: Gay and lesbian adolescents in out-of-home care settings. *Child Welfare, 71*(6), 547–555.

MARCH, K. (1997). The dilemma of adoption reunion: Establishing open communication between adoptees and their birth mothers. *Family Relations, 46,* 99–105.

MARCUS, R. (1991). The attachments of children in foster care. *Genetic, Social, and General Psychology Monographs, 117*(4), 367–394.

McKENZIE, J. (1993). Adoption of children with special needs. *The Future of Children: Adoption, 31*(1), 62–76.

MENDENHALL, T., GROTEVANT, H., & McROY, R. (1996). Adoptive couples: Communication and changes made in openness levels. *Family Relations, 45,* 223–229.

MORROW, K. (1999). Is this right? Who has the right to say? *Time, 153*(1), 41.

NELSON, K. (1992). Fostering homeless children and their parents too: The emergence of whole-family foster care. *Child Welfare, 71*(6), 575–584.

PACHECO, F., & EME, R. (1993). An outcome study of the reunion between adoptees and biological parents. *Child Welfare, 72*(1), 53–64.

PERKINS, D., & ANSAY, S. (1998). The effectiveness of visitation program in fostering visits with noncustodial parents. *Family Relations, 47,* 251–258.

RICHARDSON, S. (1999). Birth order. *Discover, 20*(1), 57–58.

ROSENFELD, A., PILOWSKY, D., FINE, P., THORPE, M., FINE, E., SIMMS, M., HALFON, N., IRWIN, M., ALFARO, J., SALETSKY, R., & NICKMAN, S. (1997). Foster care: An update. *Journal of American Adolescent Psychiatry, 36*(4), 448–457.

ROSENTHAL, J. (1993). Outcomes of adoption of children with special needs. *The Future of Children: Adoption, 3*(1), 77–88.

RUST, M. (1987, June). Whose baby is it? *American Bar Association Journal,* pp. 52–56.

SCHATZ, M., & BANE, W. (1991). Empowering the parents of children in substitute care: A training model. *Child Welfare, 70*(6).

SCHROF, J. (1998). Doubling the IVF success rate? *U.S. News & World Report, 125*(15) 71–73.

SCHULMAN, I., & BEHRMAN, R. (1993). Overview and major recommendations. *The Future of Children: Adoption, 3*(1), 4–16.

SILVER, J., DILORENZO, P., ZUKOSKI, M., ROSS, P., AMSTER, B., & SCHLEGEL, D. (1999). Starting young:

Improving the health care and developmental outcomes of infants and toddlers in the child welfare system. *Child Welfare, 78*(1), 148–183.

SILVERMAN, A. (1993). Outcomes of transracial adoption. *The Future of Children: Adoption, 3*(1), 104–118.

SMITH, M. (1996). An exploratory survey of foster mother and caseworker attitudes about sibling placement. *Child Welfare, 75*(4), 357–375.

SOKOLOFF, B. (1993). Antecedents of American adoption. *The Future of Children: Adoption, 3*(1), 17–25.

STAFF, I., & FEIN, E. (1992). Together or separate: A study of siblings in foster care. *Child Welfare, 71*(3), 257–270.

STOLLEY, K. (1993). Statistics on adoption in the United States. *The Future of Children: Adoption, 3*(1), 26–42.

TESTA, M., & ROLACK, T. (1999). Professional foster care: A future worth pursuing? *Child Welfare, 78*(1), 108–124.

TEVELDE, E., VAN BAAR, A., & VAN KOOIJ, R. (1998). Concerns about assisted reproduction. *Lancet, 351*(9115), 1524–1525.

TITTERINGTON, L. (1990). Foster care training: A comprehensive approach. *Child Welfare, 69*(2), 157–165.

WILSON, L., & CONROY, J. (1999). Satisfaction of children in out-of-home care. *Child Welfare, 78*(1), 53–69.

Would be cloner says he'll start with himself. (1998, September 6). *The Tuscaloosa News,* p. A3.

WOOLF, G. (1990). An outlook for foster care in the United States. *Child Welfare, 69*(1), 75–81.

WRIGHT, K. (1998). Human in the age of mechanical reproduction. *Discover, 19*(5), 74–81

ZLOTNICK, C., KRONSTADT, D., & KLEE, L. (1998). Foster care children and family homelessness. *Child Welfare, 88*(9), 1368–1370.

ZURAVIN, S., & DEPANFILIS, D. (1997). Factors affecting foster care placement of children receiving child protective services. *Social Work Research, 21*(1), 34–44.

CHAPTER 12

Alternatives for Child Care
and Early Education

Increasing numbers of parents are seeking part-time or full-time alternatives for assistance with parenting and child care. Parents are turning to individual caregivers who come into the home, family child-care homes, center-based care and early education, nursery schools, parent cooperatives, play groups, drop-in child-care centers, Head Start, and after-school programs for child-care assistance.

Programs for young children may be sponsored by public agencies, private nonprofit organizations, or individuals for profit. In addition to parent fees, both the federal and the state governments and a few local governments subsidize child care. Charitable organizations, such as United Way, and churches also provide support for child care. Some employers and unions sponsor or support on-site or community child-care centers, provide vouchers to parents to assist in paying for care, arrange flextime, allow shared jobs, give sick-child leave, and/or provide child-care information and referral. All told, a considerable investment is made annually in child care and early education, and the need is still largely unmet.

The services offered by programs range from care and protection of the child for part of the day while the child is entrusted to the caregiver; to child care for children of parents who work full-time, day, evening, or night; to a full range of services to the child, family, and community, based on the needs of families. The efficacy of the early care and education depends on the appropriate preparation, commitment, skill, and spirit of the adults who provide it. In privately owned centers, specific provision usually is not made for social services, but centers receiving federal funds may provide some health-care and social services and/or family support services.

Parents enroll their children in these programs for a variety of reasons, including their need for temporary relief from continual responsibility for child rearing, the desire to provide opportunities for the child to interact with peers and other authority figures, and/or so that the child can receive cognitive stimulation. However, the primary reason that increasing numbers of parents seek alternative care and education is that mothers are working. Historically, child care has been considered a service for working parents, whereas early-childhood education, or preschool, has been intended for educational or enrichment purposes for those children whose families could afford it. Recently, however, early-childhood professionals have begun to emphasize that all programs for young children, wherever they occur and for varying hours per day, should be of the same quality. The terms *care* and *education,* then, are meant to refer to programs that provide both early care and education, whether they are on a half-day or a full-day basis and whether they occur in centers, homes, schools, or churches.

NEED FOR EARLY CARE AND EDUCATION

There has been a continuing trend toward increasing numbers of women working outside the home, including mothers of very young children. Women in the workforce in 1997 included 78 percent of women with children under 6, 70 percent of women with children under the age of 1 year, 74 percent of women with children under 3, and 83 percent of mothers with children ages 3 to 5 (U.S. Bureau of the Census, 1998). For these working women, programs that provide early care and education are essential. In addition to the large numbers of working mothers, many nonemployed mothers use these programs to provide educational and social benefits for preschool children.

Today families of all social-class levels and all races use the services of early care and education programs. Because of greater educational and career opportunities for women, the battle for equal rights, and the current difficulty or impossibility for young families to live on one income, child-care and early-education programs have become a widespread necessity for a diversity of families. Before women began entering the workforce in large numbers, "day care" primarily was a social service for the small percentage of women who worked out of economic necessity; little was provided for children other than protection and physical care. Families are now demanding more from alternative care arrangements—they want their children to be in stimulating environments that maximize development in all areas. Hence, emphasis on quality has emerged, a trend that will be discussed later in this chapter.

Even though the United States is nearly alone among industrialized nations in the absence of a national family and child-care/early-education policy, the issue has become a part of the public agenda. For the first time ever, child care was a viable, visible issue in the 1988 presidential campaign and again in the 1992 campaign. Congress demonstrated its commitment in 1991 by implementing the Child Care and Development Block Grant, which authorized $2.3 billion over 3 years to help states to improve the availability, affordability, and quality of child care. In 1996 alone, the federal government spent $935 million in Child Care and Development Block Grant funds and an additional $980 million in child care for AFDC recipients and ex-recipients (U.S. Bureau of the Census, 1998).

The interest in and support of early care and education programs was fueled by the adoption of the National Goals for Education, especially Goal 1: that all children would enter school ready to learn, or better expressed, ready for school success. Early care and education programs, especially for at-risk children, were central to this goal. The Committee for Economic Development called attention to the research that links early-education programs to the productivity of the current workforce and to the future successes of the U.S. workforce. Further, a number of corporations invested significant sums of money to enhance quality and expand the supply of programs. It is apparent that the importance of quality early care and education for children is finally beginning to be recognized in the United States.

SELECTING ALTERNATIVE CARE

The kind of alternative care arrangement a family selects depends on several factors. Obviously if a mother is working full-time, all-day care is likely to be needed unless part of the child's care is assumed by other family members. During the last several years, there has been a move away from in-home care and toward out-of-home care among all socioeconomic groups. Factors affecting the choice of arrangements include the family income, the size of the family and the age of the children, the availability of service, and the family lifestyle. The Highlights show the different types of child care reported by the Census Bureau.

Families often choose family child care because they want their children in a homelike

HIGHLIGHTS

Types of Alternative Care of Preschool Children Used by Parents

PERCENTAGE	TYPE OF CARE
10.0	Grandparent in provider's home
5.5	Other relative in provider's home
16.0	Father in the child's home
6.5	Grandparent in the child's home
3.3	Other relative in the child's home
5.0	Nonrelative in the child's home
16.6	Nonrelative in another home
18.3	Group care center
11.6	Nursery/preschool
6.2	Mother cares for child while working
1.2	All other arrangements

Source: U.S. Bureau of the Census. (1996). Who's minding our preschoolers? *Current Population Reports,* P70–53. Washington, DC: U.S. Department of Commerce.

environment, with fewer children and, it is hoped, more individualized attention. Convenience also may be a factor, if the home is in their own neighborhood or close to their place of employment.

When center-based care is chosen, the selection frequently is based on the adequacy and dependability of caregivers and teachers, the location, and the cost, as well as the developmental or educational nature of the program. If every parent who needed child care were to seek a licensed center, there would simply not be enough facilities available. In 1993 nearly 10 million preschool children needed full-time child care, yet there were only 5 million licensed child-care slots available (Creighton, 1993). Many parents use unlicensed centers or family child-care homes but, ironically, appear to be satisfied with them.

TYPES OF EARLY CARE AND EDUCATION

Parents have a number of alternatives in arranging for child care and early education. Each alternative has its advantages as well as its disadvantages. The range of available alternatives is affected by geographic factors, family income, and personal belief systems.

Caregiver in the Home

Many families with young children find that a single caregiver who comes into the home can best meet their needs for the care of the child. These caregivers consist of fathers (16 percent), other relatives (10 percent), and nonrelatives (5 percent). As the number of two-parent professional families continues to grow, the number of persons seeking full-time, often live-in, care in their own home increases. In fact, over the last 15 years, several nanny-training programs have been established throughout the United States. It should be emphasized, however, that a very small percentage of families are economically able to employ a full-time nonrelative as a caregiver. Other advantages and disadvantages of this type of alternative care are enumerated in the Highlights.

Family Child-Care Homes

Family child-care homes provide care for children in the homes of the providers, who include both relatives and nonrelatives. Approximately 10 percent of children are cared for by grandparents and an additional 5.5 percent by other relatives in their homes. Securing relatives to care for the child outside the child's home may have several advantages: the preexisting relationship between the child and the caregiver; the greater likelihood of a relative being loving to the child, thus providing a higher quality of emotional care; and the possibility of less expense for the parents. More than 16 percent of children are cared for by nonrelatives in a situation where a caregiver provides care for a few children in his or her home (U.S. Bureau of the Census, 1996).

Most states require that family child-care homes be licensed, certified, registered, or otherwise approved. Regulations relate to the maximum

---

HIGHLIGHTS

Advantages and Disadvantages of Caregiver in Home

ADVANTAGES	DISADVANTAGES
Parent can choose caregiver	Finding alternative care when caregiver is ill
Child can remain in familiar home environment	Minimum or no supervision of caregiver
Opportunities for adult-child interactions are greater than in center-based care	Potential loneliness and isolation of caregiver
Children can continue to play with familiar peers in own neighborhood	Lack of experiences with peers
	Limited toys and equipment
	Limited educational experience
	More expensive than other types of care

number of children, by age, who may be cared for, as well as health and safety standards; and some states have regulations relating to the activities provided for the children, equipment, nutrition, discipline, and so on. The specified adult-child ratio and maximum number of children vary from state to state, but the ratio is approximately six children to one adult. This number may or may not include the caregiver's own children. A variation of the family child-care home that may be found in some states is the minicenter or group child-care home. In this arrangement, approximately 12 children compose the group, but the center is located in a caregiver's home, and at least two adults must supervise the group.

In spite of the prevalence of family child care and its potential for meeting the growing needs for child care, family child-care homes have been largely invisible to public scrutiny. Despite state regulations, the majority of family child-care homes operate outside the formal regulatory system. It has been estimated that 80 percent of family child-care homes are unregulated (Hofferth, West, & Henke, 1994). Even though the number of regulated homes is increasing, the percentage of chil-

dren in regulated homes has changed little in the past 15 years.

Not surprisingly, the conditions in these homes range from quality care to inadequate or intolerable care. Very little is known about the kinds of experiences that are provided for the children and the consequences of those experiences on the child's development. The difficulties in locating family child-care homes, the reluctance of caregivers to be observed, the self-selection of caregivers and child-care families, the high turnover, and the changing composition of homes have contributed to the problems of research on family child care. Obviously, responsibility falls on the parent for selecting a quality family child-care home. When parents are considering family child care, both the advantages and the disadvantages should be considered (see Highlights).

Recently a variety of types of support for family child care has emerged. Family child-care associations are now being organized at the local, regional, state, and national levels. The National Association for Family Day Care has established a voluntary accreditation system for family child-care homes; more than 30,000 family child-care

Advantages and Disadvantages of Family Child Care

ADVANTAGES

A greater likelihood that:

The homelike atmosphere will be less threatening to the child

The child will interact with a single caregiver

The child will interact with children of varying ages, thereby learning from older children and helping to teach responsibility to younger ones

The child will have to adjust to fewer children

Through a warm, "child-centered" home environment, the child will receive stimulation and learn through daily home chores and activities

The home will be based on lifestyles and values similar to those of the child's family

The facility will be closer to the parents' home and thus more convenient

DISADVANTAGES

A chance that:

The provider will be unsupervised and have less training

Alternative care will have to be arranged when the caregiver is ill

The home will be unlicensed or unregistered

There will be less variety in equipment, materials, and activities

The nutrition program will be inferior to that of a center

Field trips will not be a part of the program

providers have earned a Child Development Associate credential; the Child and Adult Care Food Program provides services to regulated family child-care homes; child-care resource and referral systems in every state maintain up-to-date listings of family child-care providers; a variety of corporations sponsor family child-care networks; and training and technical assistance is provided by a variety of organizations. These increasing support systems are providing ways to reduce the isolation and invisibility of family child care and, ultimately, have the potential for significant impact on the quality of the care provided (Kontos, Howes, & Galinsky, 1996). As a word of caution, data from the Families and Work Institute showed that 35 percent of the family child-care homes they studied were judged to be of inadequate quality; 56 percent were adequate; and only 9 percent were judged to be of good quality. Further, only half of the children developed attachments to their caregivers (U.S. News & World Report, 1994). Other data show that at least half of unregulated family child-care homes are of substandard quality (Kagan & Cohen, 1997).

Research on Family Child Care.   Though family child care is widely used as alternative care for children, especially those younger than 3, it is the least researched form of child care in the United States. Most existing studies focus on either the programmatic quality of the child-care experience or selected aspects of the family child-care provider's own family life. Existing research suggests that caregiver training and small groups predict more positive caregiving behaviors in family child care, and some research has shown that level of education also predicts the quality of care. Further, measures of the responsiveness of adult interactions with children have been shown to be good predictors of children's development (Kontos, 1994).

One study (Erwin, Sanson, Amos, & Bradley, 1993) compared aspects of family child care and child-care centers for a sample of children younger than 3, their families, and their caregivers. Teachers in child-care centers were significantly younger, were more educated, had more experience, worked fewer hours per week, and had stronger qualifications than family child-care providers. Eighty-five percent of teachers in centers had some formal qualifications, whereas no family child-care provider had formal qualifications. Mothers who used child-care centers were higher in socioeconomic status than mothers using family child care (FCC). The former expected their children's developmental achievements to be significantly later than the latter, but caregivers in the two settings were similar in most of their developmental expectations for children.

Family child-care providers mentioned feelings of isolation and of being trapped at home. Perhaps these feelings influence the high stress level and turnover rates in family child-care providers that seem to be common in the 2- to 8-year period following the beginning of family child care (Todd & Deery-Schmitt, 1996). As compared with teachers in child-care centers, family child-care providers reported being less encouraging of autonomy in children and placing less emphasis on the role of child care in developing language and self-control skills, protecting children's health, supporting parents with their problems, and identifying children with special needs. Where differences in developmental expectations occurred, they were as follows: Family child-care providers expected earlier development of some language and social skills and later development of some motor skills.

Johansen, Leibowitz, and Waite (1996) found that mothers who say that the educational features of child care are important in their choice of care are more likely to choose center-based than family child care. However, mothers who value their child's knowing the caregiver more often choose family child care. Another study found that in selecting child care, family child-care users emphasize the child-rearing philosophy of the provider and the homelike nature of the setting. Social support from the caregivers was the most significant predictor of satisfaction for parents using both family child care and center-based care. Agreement on child-rearing philosophies was a big factor in parents' satisfaction in family child care (Britner & Phillips, 1995).

Kontos (1994) examined the interrelationships of multiple levels of the family child-care system in an attempt to portray the ecology of family child care. Multiple measures were used with a sample of children, their mothers, and their family child-care providers. The "typical" caregiver in her study was in her middle thirties, had received some education past high school, had been caring for children in her home for 7 years, and had specialized training that was limited to workshops and conferences. Average ratings of the quality of the home environments were just above adequate; caregivers engaged in high-level interactions with the children during only 8 percent of the observation time. There was no evidence in her sample that families chose caregivers who resembled themselves with respect to socioeconomic status and child-rearing preferences, refuting a fairly common assumption.

Family child-care quality, surprisingly, was not associated with the characteristics of the caregiver but was associated with the conditions of caregiving, that is, number of children cared for in the home and whether the caregiver also cared for her own children. However, children's development varied primarily according to family background and the quality of family child care rather than caregiver characteristics or the conditions of caregiving. Both family background and child-care characteristics predicted children's IQ, scores on a receptive language measure, and sociability. Childcare characteristics alone predicted the amount of simple and complex cognitive play, language interaction, and simple social play.

Kontos concluded that family and family child-care effects on children were more likely to be additive than to be interactive. Although family and child-care characteristics were not related, both were significant predictors of children's development in the cognitive, language, and social areas and in several instances jointly contributed to a particular aspect of development.

Several researchers have attempted to describe accurately the population of family child-care pro-

viders. Walker (1992) gathered data on both licensed and unregulated family child-care providers in two states. His data showed that most providers were mothers of young children with low levels of education and skills and limited attachment to the labor market. Licensed providers had more education and experience than unlicensed providers, exhibited other behaviors that demonstrated a stronger attachment to the profession of child care, and provided a higher quality of care. Nearly three-fourths of the licensed providers cared for four or more children, and the quality of care increased when fewer children were cared for. Most family child-care providers do not earn a sustainable wage. In 1996 their median wage was $118 per week (Center for the Child Care Workforce, 1998).

There appears to be a need for parents to select a family child-care home carefully, especially since many parents of infants and toddlers prefer this form of care. The considerations should include the background and experience of the caregiver; the background and characteristics of others living in the home; the attitudes of the caregiver; and the number, age, and sex of the children served, since these factors seem to influence the quality of the program provided. The implications are that caregivers who care for infants and toddlers have fewer children and seem to model the family aspect. Less time is spent with the children, and housekeeping and other tasks are performed simultaneously with the care of the children. It is likely that these caregivers are not sufficiently trained to provide a stimulating environment. If family child-care homes are to provide rich and stimulating environments for young children, caregivers need specialized training, the number of children should be small, wages should approach the professional level, and models and supports should be provided. Caregivers need assistance in utilizing everyday interactions, basic care, and household routines as opportunities to facilitate the children's development. Parents need to be educated to select family child-care homes that are licensed or registered and those in which the strengths of caregivers and programs offered match objectives parents have for their children's care.

Center-Based Care and Education

Historical Perspective.   Child-care centers in the United States have been associated historically with social services for the poor. It was not until the late 1970s that middle-class parents began to demonstrate the need for alternative care as well. Recently child-care policy and programs have been involved in political and philosophical controversy and confusion. Although the role of child care has been debated, the need for alternative-care and early-education arrangements for working parents, and nonworking ones as well, continues to increase. Through the last several centuries, children have been cared for in facilities outside the home, but no commitment has been made to develop or expand programs to provide adequate care, much less high-quality care. Society sanctioned child care during the world wars and during the Great Depression but withdrew the sanction when the crises were over. Until recently the role of the mother in the home as the primary caregiver has prevailed, and efforts to resolve child-care problems by working mothers have been largely discouraged.

The historical conception of child care as a welfare service has changed, at least from the perspective of child-development and family-life specialists, and child care is presently viewed not only as a social utility needed by large numbers of non-problematic families but also as a way to supplement and enrich the family's responsibilities in the provision of child development and early educational experiences for their children. The collaborative arrangement between the early-childhood teacher and the family is just beginning to be understood by researchers and the general public. The relationships between early-childhood programs and parents are seen as dynamic, multidimensional, and developmental, and have the potential for serving many functions formerly provided by the extended family. In this sense, early-childhood programs represent a social support for, rather than a replacement of, the responsibilities of the family.

Although the number of families who select center-based programs for their children is small, the numbers are increasing and represent a substantial population. A comprehensive study conducted by the National Center for Education Statistics (Hofferth et al., 1994) found the following variables to be related to whether children were in center-based programs. Three- and 4-year-old children in low-income and lower-middle-income households were less likely than their counterparts in upper-middle to high-income households to be enrolled in a center-based program. Children who had mothers with less education were less likely than those with mothers who had attended or graduated from college to participate in center-based programs. Preschool children whose mothers were younger than 20 when they were born and children from larger families (four or more members) were less likely than children of older mothers and children from smaller families to be enrolled in center-based programs. Finally, African American children were more likely than White children and Hispanic children were less likely than White children to be in center-based programs. In other words, as family income, mother's education, and mother's age at first birth increase and as family size decreases, the likelihood of preschool children being in center-based programs increases, and ethnic background is associated with whether parents choose center-based care for their children.

Center-based care and education generally is more expensive than family child care, but less expensive than care in the child's own home by a single caregiver. The cost of full-day child care for parents ranges from $4,000 to $10,000 per year—at least as much as college tuition at a public university. The cost of center-based care is based on a number of variables: geographic area of the country, metropolitan as opposed to rural location, educational level and salaries of staff, whether the center is accredited, whether the center is nonprofit or for-profit, and so forth. The average cost for mediocre-quality center-based care in 1993 was nearly $5,000 per year, or 8 percent of the before-tax income of a full-time dual-earner household and 23 percent of the average before-tax household income of a full-time employed single parent (Cost, Quality, & Outcomes Study Team, 1995).

But parent fees do not reflect the actual full cost of care. Whereas the average expenditure by parents is $2.11 per hour, the true full cost of care is $2.83 per hour. How is the difference made up? Child-care teachers forgo $5,238 per year in wages, and teacher assistants forgo $3,582. These forgone wages represent the difference between what child-care teachers and assistants do earn and what they could earn in other female-oriented occupations. In addition to forgone wages, donations and lowered occupancy costs make up the difference between the amount parents pay for child care and the true cost of care (Cost, Quality, & Outcomes Study Team, 1995). These figures suggest that parents pay less than three-fourths of the full cost of providing center-based child care. Therefore, not-for-profit centers that are able to augment their budgets with subsidies, donations, and in-kind contributions generally are able to provide higher-quality programs for the same or less cost to parents.

When parents are considering center-based care and education as an alternative, they need to consider both the advantages and the disadvantages (see Highlights).

INFANT CARE

Before the mid-1960s it was believed harmful to separate an infant from her mother, and few infants were placed in child-care centers. A number of studies in the 1970s supported the contention that the separation of the mother and infant as a result of child care did not impede mother-infant attachment. For example, Caldwell, Wright, Honig, and Tannebaum (1970) found no differences in mother-infant attachment between center-based and home-reared infants. Subsequent research by Moskowitz, Schwarz, and Corsini (1977) supported the contention that child care does not impair children's attachment to their mothers. The research by Kagan, Kearsley, and Zelazo (1978) was probably the most comprehensive and best controlled. These investigators compared matched pairs of children; half were in child-care centers and half were being reared at home. The researchers concluded that separation anxiety may be more a function of maturational than experiential processes and thus it is inappropriate to study the effects of child care on the child-mother attachment relationship.

Belsky (1990) referred to the studies of the 1970s as the first wave of research on the developmental consequences of early child care, which focused principally on comparing young children in home care with those in high-quality, university-based infant-care centers. These studies were conducted to determine whether extensive and routine nonparental care initiated in the first years of life necessarily undermined children's psychological

Advantages and Disadvantages of Center-Based Care and Education

ADVANTAGES

A greater likelihood that:
The center will be licensed or regulated
The child will receive continual supervision
The staff will be trained
The caregiver will not experience isolation
The caregivers will always be available
The child will experience stability of place and routine
A wider variety of equipment, materials, activities, and programs will be available
An educational component will be provided

DISADVANTAGES

A chance that:
There will be less flexibility in schedules for individual differences in children
There will be less adult-child interaction
There will be multiple caregivers rather than a single, primary one
The children will be exposed to caregiver's and other children's diseases and/or infections
There will be larger groups of children
The child will have less space

development. He noted that a comprehensive review of this first wave of inquiry yielded little cause for concern, particularly with regard to socioemotional development, defined in terms of the affective bond between child and mother.

The second wave of research focused on identifying child-care factors and processes that affected the development of children. This research was remarkably successful in identifying social structural features of care—particularly group size, adult-child ratios, and caregiver/teacher training—that systematically relate to the daily processes in the early-childhood setting, such as the quantity and quality of time adults spend interacting with children and the extent of focused attention and aimless wandering that children engage in. The findings indicated that when group size is large, ratios are poor, and caregivers/teachers are untrained or unsupervised, individual attention to children is secondary to coping with overextended resources. As a result, both quality of care and child well-being are compromised (Belsky, 1990).

With the third wave of research in the 1980s, the issue of the impact of infant care resurfaced, and the debate among professionals at an international level continued throughout the 1990s. The crucial issue, once again, was whether infants with extensive early nonmaternal care were more likely than other infants to be insecurely attached to their parents. The debate was sparked by an analysis of data from two longitudinal studies by Belsky and Rovine (1988). Children's attachment was measured by using Ainsworth's Strange Situation at 12–13 months of age. The investigators claimed that the data revealed that infants who experienced more than 20 hours of nonmaternal care per week displayed more avoidance of their mothers on reunion and were more likely to be classified as "insecurely attached" than infants with fewer than 20 hours of nonmaternal care. Sons in extensive child care, particularly, were more insecurely attached to both mother and father. However, Belsky and Rovine pointed out that half of the male children with extensive nonmaternal care established secure relationships with their fathers and two-thirds established secure relationships

with at least one parent. They concluded that certain factors contribute to the development of insecurity: being male, being "fussy" or "difficult" (as described by mothers), having mothers with limited interpersonal sensitivity, having mothers with less satisfaction with certain aspects of their marriages, and having mothers with a strong career orientation.

Since the publication of Belsky's interpretations, many researchers have conducted studies and have found evidence to refute his conclusions (Field, 1991; Field, Masi, Goldstein, Perry, & Parl, 1988; Howes & Hamilton, 1992a, 1992b; Howes, Rodning, Galluzzo, & Myers, 1988; Richters & Zahn-Waxler, 1988). In general, these studies have found few, if any, differences in security of attachment between infants in child care and infants reared by their mothers. However, Egeland and Hiester (1995) found in an exploratory study that early child-care experiences may have a differentiated effect on infants who are securely as opposed to insecurely attached to their mothers.

The National Institute of Child Health and Human Development (1996) conducted a research study of infant child care to determine factors that contribute to positive caregiving. They found that positive caregiving was associated with smaller group size, fewer infants per adult, caregivers' nonauthoritarian beliefs about child rearing, and clean and stimulating physical environments.

On the basis of these and other studies, the investigators concluded first that most children with significant child-care experience are secure with both their mothers and their teachers, but the relationships of child-care children with their mothers constitute their most consistent adult relationships. The question was once again raised concerning the effects of the interactive influences of the family and child care. It now appears that infant child care per se has no impact on the security of infants' attachment to their parents. However, the quality of infant care has become an issue of grave concern for both parents and professionals. Poor or substandard infant child care can have serious long-term consequences for children's development, and high-quality care that is sensitive and responsive can facilitate the development of children, especially those who are at risk.

Clearly the issue of nonmaternal care for infants is a complex one. Recent studies have begun to focus on the quality of the caregiving environment as a variable, and although more longitudinal studies are being conducted, there still exists a need for sophisticated, well-designed, and tightly controlled research. It is unproductive to focus on whether it is good or bad for infants to be in child care; the real issue is how we can improve the quality of care so that it enhances optimal development.

SCHOOL-AGE CHILDREN IN SELF CARE

Research has pointed to the increasing number of school-age children who are without direct adult supervision for some portion of the day (Creighton, 1993; Kay, 1999; Larkin, 1998/99; Miller, 1999; Turvett, 1995). These children have for years been referred to as latchkey children. The term *latchkey* was based on the practice of children wearing housekeys on chains around their necks. More recently, to avoid the negative connotations of *latchkey* and its association with unsupervised children, the label *self care* emerged (Powell, 1987). There are many situations that complicate the description of those who are labeled self-care children. However, it seems appropriate to refer to latchkey or self-care children as those school-age children who are old enough to care for themselves for limited periods of time and yet young enough to require adult supervision most of the time. Although an absolute age range cannot be established, it has been suggested that these are children between the ages of 6 and 13 who spend time alone or with a younger sibling on a regular basis (Turvett, 1995). Although this phenomenon has created considerable anxiety for professionals and parents, little research has been conducted on the outcomes of this arrangement.

Children under self care not only are children of working parents but also are those left in charge of themselves while parents are away from home engaged in other activities. The largest percentage of children are in self care in the afternoons after

school. A smaller percentage are alone in the mornings before school, and a small number are in self care at night.

Two demographic factors, increasing numbers of mothers in the labor force and single parents, contribute to the growing numbers of children under their own supervision. In 1997, 78 percent of all married mothers and 74 percent of separated, divorced, or widowed women with children between the ages of 6 and 17 were in the labor force (U.S. Bureau of the Census, 1998). Estimates of the numbers of children in self care are between 2.5 million and 15 million (Creighton, 1993; Kay, 1999; Miller, 1999; Turvett, 1995).

No one knows how many elementary school children are home alone or with siblings before or after school, but estimates are from 7 percent to 45 percent. One national survey showed that 44 percent of 5- to 12-year-olds whose mothers worked had no care arrangements at all (Creighton, 1993). Larkin (1998/99) reported that only 25 percent of children in grades K–8 were cared for by family members while their parents were at work. The Child Welfare League of America reported that 42 percent of all 5- to 9-year-old children were home alone at least occasionally, and the percentage rose to 77 percent for older children (Willwerth, 1993).

Readiness for Self Care

Although all parents expect their children to accept increasing responsibilities as they develop, the decision to use a self-care arrangement involves a considerable increase in responsibility. When are children ready to care for themselves? The decision is obviously not an easy one for parents to make. A particular age is certainly not the criterion. Some children develop faster than others and can assume responsibility for themselves earlier than others. Family and community circumstances, the diversity of experiences that the child has had as he develops, parental attitudes toward protecting the child, and the state's legal requirements for child supervision must be considered. Most experts agree that children under 10 (some say 12) years of age should not be left alone on a

A child's readiness for self-care before and/or after school depends on physical, emotional, and social factors.

regular basis (Kay, 1999; Willwerth, 1993). Several experts have offered suggestions for parents to use in determining when children are ready to assume the responsibility for self care (see the Highlights for child's readiness and community characteristics).

Effects of Self Care

Several viewpoints currently exist in relation to children under their own supervision. Some view self-care arrangements as expecting children to assume adultlike responsibilities too soon. The pressure on children to grow up too soon can lead to unnecessary stress, with negative outcomes in such areas as achievement and socioemotional development. Yet, increasingly, families must face limited choices regarding child-care options. It is questionable whether some families can afford the lux-

ury of childhood. Although most parents who use after-school programs approve of them, poor families are unable to afford them. More than three-fourths of parents using after-school care pay full fees (Larkin, 1998/99).

What are the effects of adult-supervised situations and of self-care situations on children? Are latchkey children at risk? The research has not kept pace with the growing public use of the self-care arrangement and parents' and professionals' concerns about it. There is limited research, most of which compares children in unsupervised and adult-supervised child-care arrangements. Conclusions cannot be drawn from these studies because of the methodological problems and the limited sample sizes.

Some studies have found that children can benefit from their new independence if they are emotionally ready and well prepared. One key factor is how the child feels about the situation (Miller, 1999). Whereas some children see themselves as independent and capable, others might perceive the use of self care as abandonment and rejection. Many children find that being alone is frightening and boring. On the other hand, studies have shown that children in self care are not necessarily worse off than other children with respect to self-esteem and behavior in school (Willwerth, 1993). In the best self-care situations, children feel that parents know what they are doing even when they are not present. It is those children who have no rules or expectations, who just "hang out," who are likely to get into trouble (Turvett, 1995). Chances are high that these children will experience substance abuse, sexual activity, truancy, and poor academic performance (Creighton, 1993; Larkin, 1998/99; Rueter, 1998). Kay (1999) reported that self-care children may find that free time invites boredom, and boredom invites loneliness, fear, and trouble.

Early research conducted by Long and Long (1982) in urban areas reported fear and loneliness associated with the experience of staying home alone. Thirty percent of the latchkey children they interviewed had unusually high fears, including fear of someone breaking into the house, of

Determining Child's Readiness for Self Care

PHYSICALLY

The child must be able to:

Control her body to the degree that she will not injure herself as she moves through the house

Manipulate the locks on the doors

Safely operate any accessible equipment to which he has access

EMOTIONALLY

The child must be able to:

Be comfortable enough to be alone for the required period of time without undue fear

Cope with boredom

Follow important established rules without testing them

Handle the usual and the unexpected events without excessive fear or anxiety

Avoid a pattern of withdrawn, hostile, or self-destructive behavior

SOCIALLY

The child should:

Be able to solicit, if needed, help from friends, neighbors, or other designated persons

Understand the role of, and call on when needed, the appropriate community resources—police, fire department, rescue squads, and so forth

Be able to maintain friendships with peers and adults

Be able to resolve sibling conflicts

Sources: Miller, A. (1999). They're home alone. *Newsweek, 134*(22), 105–107; Willwerth, J. (1993). "Hello? I'm home alone." *Time, 141*(9), 46–48.

---

noises, of outdoor darkness, and of animal cries and barking. Loneliness and boredom were the chief complaints of these children. The results of this study must be viewed with caution because it

Necessary Community Characteristics in Promoting Self Care

The community must:

Be reasonably safe and be so perceived by the child and the parent

Have a variety of child-care options so that the family has choices as the child develops and family needs change

lacked precision and because interviewer bias was associated with the procedures. Further, the study was conducted with children living in an inner-city ghetto area.

In another study, Vandell and Ramanan (1991) examined relationships between types of after-school care (self care, mother care, and other adult care) in a predominantly low-income, minority, urban sample. Their results suggested that self care was associated with some behavior problems. Specifically, mothers of children in self care rated their children as more hyperactive and headstrong than mothers of other children rated theirs. However, when family income and family emotional support for the child were controlled, most of the apparent differences in child functioning associated with type of after-school care dissipated. Still, a small number of children who were in self care and living below the poverty line were reported by their mothers to have significantly more behavior problems when compared with those children in other adult care. An astonishing finding of the study was that mother care after school, presumed to be the ideal type, can be associated with children's difficulties in some families. Family incomes in mother-care families were only about 70 percent of those in families using the other types of care. Further, the quality of emotional support provided to the children was poorer in mother-care households than in self-care or other adult-care households. Children who returned home to their mothers who were single parents were reported to demonstrate more antisocial behaviors, anxiety, and peer conflicts; further, they scored lower on tests of receptive language.

One study attempted to examine the long-term effects of self care by gathering data from university students who were former "latchkey" children (Woodard & Fine, 1991). No differences were found between students who as children had been in self care and those in mother care in the areas of personality traits, emotional adjustment, cognitive development, and academic performance.

It appears that a number of factors potentially influence the effects of the self-care arrangement—the age level of the child and her unique strengths and weaknesses, the context of the setting in which self care takes place, family characteristics, and the geographic location (rural as opposed to urban or inner city). Future research must continue to focus on how the character of the parent-child relationship might mediate the effects, the important quality-of-life indicators in the neighborhood and community, the developmental processes of children and the indicators of readiness for self care, and the child's need for and conception of privacy. Further, evaluations of different approaches to supporting children in self care should be conducted. Longitudinal designs would provide developmental outcomes for children and families over time.

TIPS

For Parents Selecting Child Care

Decide on the type of child care that best meets the needs of your child and family (i.e., caregiver in home, family child care, center-based care, etc.).

Contact a local child-care resource and referral agency to obtain a list of child-care programs in your area.

Visit several programs and interview the caregiver/teacher and/or director and observe for an extended period of time.

Note adult/child ratios, group sizes, child-child interactions, and adult-child interactions (family child care and center-based care).

Notice whether children's activities are developmentally appropriate and whether the environment is responsive and stimulating.

Ask about the education and training of teachers.

Ask about the adults' philosophy of early care and education and child rearing to be sure it matches your own.

Determine if your family qualifies for child-care subsidy.

Be sure that the program you select has an open-door policy that permits parents to visit unannounced.

After enrollment, become involved with the program and communicate regularly with staff about your child's progress.

Families of Children in Self Care

Research on families of children in self care is sparse, partly because parents may define a self-care arrangement in different ways and perhaps partly because parents may not report accurately the extent to which they use self care for fear of jeopardizing their children's welfare or of being ostracized socially (Coleman, Robinson, & Rowland, 1993). Contrary to the belief that self-care arrangements are used only by families that have no other choice, one study found that higher-income and White families were more likely to use self-care arrangements for their school-age children than were less affluent or minority families.

Another study found that families using self care were diverse, single-parent, and two-parent, with diverse incomes. The majority of children were in grades 4 through 9; time alone each week varied; and most parents were satisfied or very pleased with the arrangement. Parents, especially those with younger children, expressed a need for some kind of after-school care for their children. Not all the parents in the study worked full-time. Further, the study showed that there is a discrepancy between most parents' perceptions of their children's satisfaction with self care and their own feelings about it (Coleman et al., 1993).

Other studies have examined parents' viewpoints regarding self-care arrangements. Even though parents often report positive benefits their children receive from the latchkey experience, most choose self care for their children with concern, guilt, ambivalence, and uncertainty. Several factors have been found to affect the parental satisfaction with self care: whether or not the arrangement is voluntarily undertaken, whether the child is a boy or a girl, and whether the amount of time the child has to spend alone is excessive. When self care is involuntary, involves girls more than boys, and occurs for long periods of time, parents tend to be more dissatisfied with the arrangement. The reasons cited by some parents for using self care vary—transportation problems, the expense of child care, the refusal of children to participate in formal school-age child-care programs, and the belief that the child is old enough to care for himself. Other research (Powell, 1987) has not found the cost of after-school programs to be the major barrier to their use. In fact, some of the better-educated parents who could well afford to pay for after-school programs do not use them. Low-income parents do, however, seem to be more sensitive to cost factors. The factors that Powell (1987) found to affect the choices of parents include the convenience of the location of an available program and the parental values relating to the independence of children and their ability to look after themselves.

TIPS

For Parents of Children in Self Care

Establish a routine for the child.

Maintain appropriate communication with the child and exercise some supervision even when not physically present.

Carry a cellular phone.

Be available, or designate other persons, for contact when emergencies occur.

Provide emotional security to the child.

Be home at a consistent hour.

Educate the child in the special issues of self care.

Post important phone numbers.

Rehearse with the child what to say when someone calls or knocks on the door.

Determine the community resources that are available, such as "hot lines."

Be at home in spirit—leave notes, snacks, and lights on.

Support for Children in Self Care

Several support programs have been designed for children in self care. PhoneFriend, KIDLINE, Friendly Listeners, and Grandma Please are examples. PhoneFriend, probably the best known of such programs, has created training materials to aid communities in setting up phone lines and training volunteers. About 300 chapters across the United States are known to exist (Willwerth, 1993). Most lines operate during the after-school hours for the express purpose of providing support and information for children who are without adult supervision. Most calls come from children between the ages of 7 and 10, who are bored, with many more girls than boys calling. The majority of calls for all ages deal with physical-problem situations, but as children get older, more calls are related to social and emotional problems. The number of calls to "just talk" drops off after age 8. Data on these projects indicate that children in self care need instrumental advice, opportunities for emotional expression, and companionship.

Larkin (1998/99) suggested an intergenerational approach to after-school care. She pointed out that most adults over 65 years of age are active, are eager to remain vital members of their communities, and represent an important pool of potential caregivers. They can make a real difference, especially when working with trained teachers. Studies have shown that older adults can contribute time, attention, affection, knowledge, skills, and commitment to children's well-being. They often bring particular knowledge of history and of cultural, religious, and linguistic tradition to both children and staff. The Foster Grandparent program, Care Castle, Stride Rite, and School's Out are all intergenerational programs that have been formed by communities and organizations across the country. Although child-care problems must be dealt with by leadership at all levels, older citizens are making valuable contributions to after-school care, and they are capable of making even greater contributions.

After-School Programs

It is projected that more and more parents will be making a decision regarding after-school child care. Being able to assess the available options is important for parents. Rueter (1998) raised a pointed question: Since most parents are not at home in the afternoons, why shouldn't schools stay open? He proposed that schools remain open until 7 or 8 P.M. on weekdays and be open on Saturdays and in the summers. However, some questionable practices could occur. For example, herding children into a gymnasium where the staff-child ratios are 1:100 to do homework for 3 hours can be as harmful as, or more so than, leaving children alone at home.

The overriding question with regard to programs for school-age children should not be whether harm or risk has been prevented but whether the child's development has been enhanced. The energies and commitment of program designers should be directed toward this end. Rueter (1998) recommended that coaches, counselors, and mentors provide sports and supervised activities, help with schoolwork, or provide enrichment programs.

A study conducted by Posner and Vandell (1994) documented significant positive effects for low-income children who attended formal after-school programs. The children who attended these programs were exposed to more learning opportunities than children in other forms of care; they spent more time in academic activities and enrichment lessons and less time watching TV and engaging in unstructured activities than children in other forms of care. Activities were more structured and included intensive one-on-one academic work with teachers and working on cooperative projects with peers and other adults.

Children's academic and conduct grades were positively related to time spent in one-on-one academic work with an adult but negatively correlated with time spent in unorganized outdoor activities. Emotional adjustment and work habits were positively correlated with time spent in enrichment lessons and negatively correlated with time spent in unorganized outdoor activities. For the children in self care (third graders), the more time without adult supervision was positively correlated to children's antisocial behaviors. The authors concluded that formal after-school programs are one way to alleviate some of the negative effects of urban poverty on children. Other studies have shown that high school students involved in organized activities, as compared with noninvolved students, had higher self-esteem, higher grades, higher educational aspirations, lower delinquency rates, and greater sense of control over their lives. Communities with after-school programs have been found to have lower juvenile crime rates and lower rates of juvenile tobacco and drug use. Recently Congress appropriated nearly $40 million in new grants to establish or expand after-school programs under the American After-School Act. This additional appropriation brings the amount to $450 million available for after-school programs, but it represents half the amount necessary to fund all school programs seeking support. The grant will enable 313 rural and inner-city schools to provide programs after school as well as during weekends and summers (Miller, 1999; Rueter, 1998).

In summary, more and more parents are faced with a decision regarding after-school care for their school-age children. A growing number of children are left at home in their own care or "hang out" on their own. Parents and professionals have ambivalent feelings about self care, and research has yielded conflicting results about its effects. Future efforts need to be directed toward investigating the mediating variables that affect the outcomes. Attention should be focused also on providing a variety of quality options from which parents can choose.

QUALITY EARLY CARE AND EDUCATION

The issue of what constitutes quality care and education is a complex one, and the difficulty of defining quality is compounded by the diverse opinions of parents, policymakers, caregivers, and advocacy groups. Each group has a distinct philosophy about what early care and education should accomplish for children and families. Quality may be defined in relation to the services offered and the educational, social, health, and physical activities provided for the children. The climate of the classroom—such as caregiver/teacher behavior, the social structure, and the interaction patterns of the adults and the children—is of primary concern to others. Some experts and parents are concerned about the developmental changes in children as a result of child-care experience, and others combine several or all of these factors in describing quality programs.

Parents have few, if any, resources available to assist them in selecting quality programs. One of the first criteria that parents can apply in their search for quality child care is that of licensing. States have assumed the responsibility for licensing, certifying, or registering family child-care homes, minicenters, and early-childhood centers. This licensing requirement is designed to protect children in group situations. Legally, states enact laws to provide for minimum standards that programs or homes must meet to provide services. A licensing law assigns a state agency to be responsible for developing and enforcing these minimum standards. Agencies vary across states, including the human-services department; the state department of pensions and security; the department of public welfare; children, youth, and families department; and, in some cases, the departments of health and environment and education. Licensing has been an important influence since World War II, and all states have some kind of regulation of child-care programs. Most states require licensing of child-care centers and some type of regulation for family child-care homes. States continually revise their regulations, and the minimum requirements, the types of care covered, and the enforcement practices vary considerably from state to state. States generally agree on the need for child-care regulations, but the agreement ends there.

Most states have minimum standards that relate to the building and grounds, the personnel and staffing, and the services for and care of the children. Before a center is approved for licensing and begins operation, the facility usually is inspected by the licensing agency and is reinspected from time to time thereafter for renewal of the license. In most states, licensers are not allowed to provide parents with information on the quality of specific programs unless this information is directly related to licensure. These agencies can disclose whether or not a center is licensed, what its licensed capacity is, the number of hours it operates each day, and the training and experience of the caregivers/teachers. Evaluation of the quality of the program is not allowed, and agency personnel cannot recommend one center over another. A list of licensed centers can be provided, as can a copy of licensing guidelines, and some states have developed simplified checklists for parents to use. Many states encourage agency personnel to suggest to parents that they visit and observe in a variety of centers to determine which one best meets their needs. Sometimes parents are encouraged to contact a local child-care association or resource and referral agency for information. These procedures, however, are not very helpful to parents. It cannot be assumed that parents will visit even one center before enrolling the child; many make arrangements over the telephone. Further, licensing guidelines probably would not be helpful even if parents visited. Not only are the guidelines complex, but also generally they are not designed to differentiate between programs that barely meet guidelines and those of quality. It is much easier to evaluate the plumbing, the heating, and the temperature of the refrigerator than to discover the attitudes of teachers and review the curriculum.

The first comprehensive national study on child care was the National Day Care Study completed in 1978, which was undertaken to determine the impact of variations in the staff-child ratio, the number of caregivers, the group size, and the staff qualifications on both the development of preschool children and the costs of center care. The effects of other center characteristics such as the educational program and the physical environment on the quality and cost of child care were investigated. Although the findings of this study were extensive, we will mention only a few that have been found in other studies since then to directly relate to quality. First, small groups of children provide the best care situation. Groups of 15 or fewer children as opposed to 25 or more children (3 to 6 years of age), with correspondingly small numbers of (but at least two) caregivers/teachers, were associated with higher frequencies of desirable child and caregiver behaviors and with higher gains by the children on the Preschool Inventory and Peabody Picture Vocabulary Test. Lead teachers in smaller groups engaged in more social interaction with the children, such as questioning, responding, instructing, praising, and comforting, than did teachers in larger groups. Children in smaller groups showed higher frequencies of such behaviors as considering/contemplating, contributing ideas, giving opinions, persisting at tasks, and cooperating than did children in larger groups (U.S. Department of Health, Education, & Welfare, 1978).

Second, staff specialization in child-related fields, not necessarily formal education, is linked to quality care. Teachers who had training in child development and early-childhood education engaged in more social interactions with the children than did teachers without training. Finally, some determinants of quality in center care for infants are different from those for 3- to 5-year-old children. Fewer numbers of children per adult, as well as small groups, are associated with less stress on infants and staff. One adult per three or four children is optimal. Greater education and specialization of caregivers was associated with higher staff interaction with children, more teaching of language, and more nurturance/touching of children (U.S. Department of Health, Education, & Welfare, 1978).

Similar results regarding the variables that contribute to quality in early-childhood programs have been found in later studies. For example, Howes, Phillips, and Whitebook (1992) noted that child-care quality can be defined by both structural variables (adult-child ratios, group size, training of caregivers/teachers) and process variables (the provision of activities for children and teacher behavior). Structural variables are assumed to influence process variables.

The Howes et al. study (1992) observed children from 1 through 4 years who were enrolled in a number of different child-care centers. Their study produced several interesting results. Better adult-child ratios (fewer children per adult) resulted in higher appropriate caregiving and more developmentally appropriate activities. Similarly, larger group size predicted inadequate caregiving and inadequate developmentally appropriate activities. However, extremely small group size also predicted inadequate developmentally appropriate activities. Further, children who were rated as secure with their teachers on an attachment measure were more likely to be in classrooms rated as good or very good on appropriate caregiving. Secure children also were more likely to spend more of their peer contact time in competent social play and competent social pretend play. Finally, centers that maintained adequate adult-child ratios and group sizes also tended to hire well-educated teachers and to pay relatively higher salaries.

Other research has shown consistently that child-care classrooms with a limited number of children per teacher, a relatively small group size, and teachers with strong educational backgrounds and specialized training in early childhood encourage teachers to interact with children in sensitive, nurturing, and intellectually stimulating ways (Phillipsen, Burchinal, Howes, & Cryer, 1997). One study found that the strongest predictor of classroom quality was teacher wage (Phillips, Mekos, Scarr, McCartney, & Abbott-Shim, 1995). Of course, wages are directly related to level of education and specialized training of teachers.

Phillipsen et al. (1997) found that quality was higher in infant-toddler classrooms in centers with moderately experienced directors. In preschool classrooms, quality was higher when teachers had more education, a moderate amount of experience, and higher wages. Better adult/child ratios, lower center enrollment, and a lower proportion of infants and toddlers and subsidized children in the center also predicted quality for preschoolers. Further, teacher wages are associated with the extent of staff turnover.

In both infant/toddler and preschool classrooms, higher quality was found in states with the most stringent regulations and in nonprofit centers. Results suggested that more stringent regulations for teacher education and experience and adult/child ratios have a substantial impact on child-care quality. In addition to these structural variables of quality, teacher-child relationships are an important aspect of quality, including closeness of teacher-child relationship and teacher sensitivity and responsivity (Cost, Quality, & Outcomes Study, 1999).

The NICHD Early Child Care Research Network (1997) found that the quality of care that infants experience is related to a wide range of family, economic, and child characteristics. For example, infants at the lowest and the highest income levels receive higher-quality care than those in the middle. This finding is due to the fact that the *actual* cost of child care rather than the cost *paid by the parents* predicts quality. Therefore, upper-income parents and those low-income parents who receive subsidies have greater access to quality care than middle-income parents who do not qual-

ify for subsidies. Another startling finding of this study was that boys received less responsive care at 15 months than girls received. In another portion of the NICHD Study (1996), groups with low child-adult ratios, caregivers with nonauthoritarian child-rearing beliefs, and stimulating physical environments experienced consistently positive caregiving behaviors.

There is increasing agreement among both researchers and policymakers that high-quality early-childhood programs can ameliorate some of the negative consequences of growing up in poverty. However, a recent study (Phillips, Voran, Kisker, Howes, & Whitebook, 1994) found that the quality of care provided to large proportions of low-income children is highly variable, and on some key indices barely adequate. Centers that serve predominantly high-income families provided higher quality than centers serving less advantaged populations—the teachers were better trained and more stable, were better compensated, were more sensitive, and provided more developmentally appropriate environments. Consistent with the NICHD study, this study found that the most uniformly poor quality of care, ranging from teacher training to the appropriateness of the activities in the classroom, was found in centers that served primarily middle-class children. However, in the area of teacher-child interaction, low-income children experienced the lowest quality.

Unfortunately, recent research has found that, overall, the quality of child care in the United States is mediocre at best. The Phillipsen et al. (1997) study of child care in four states found that the health and welfare of infants and toddlers was only minimally met, with mean scores on a classroom environmental rating scale falling below the average. The researchers noted a lack of warm, supportive relationships with caring adults—that is, little holding, cuddling, and talking to, and little use of toys that encourage development. Quality for preschool-age children was only somewhat better—a level considered mediocre by most professionals. In general, the level of quality required to support children's development was not being met by most centers. Further, the most comprehensive study of

High quality child care can ameliorate some of the negative effects of poverty.

child care in the 1990s was the Cost, Quality, and Outcomes Study (1999). This study has documented that the quality of child care occurring in typical settings in the United States is well below what the early-childhood profession recognizes as high quality. The average scores on scales rating quality for preschool classrooms were in the medium range. Other research has shown that as much as 40 percent of infant-toddler child care is so substandard as to potentially harm the child's development. Finally, the National Child Care Staffing Study (1997) also found that the quality of most of the centers they studied was barely adequate. These results are alarming in light of growing research that links quality to both short- and long-term positive outcomes in children.

There have been several attempts, all unsuccessful, to implement national standards for the quality of early care and education programs. In the absence of such standards, the National Association for the Education of Young Children has developed a set of standards as well as "Developmentally Appropriate Practices" for programs serving children birth through age 8. Centers may

seek to become accredited voluntarily by first undergoing an extensive self-study and finally submitting to evaluation by a national team. If the program meets all the requirements, then it may become accredited. Increasing numbers of centers are becoming involved in the accreditation process, a recognized mechanism for distinguishing high-quality centers.

In summary, research on the effects of quality as opposed to minimal child care is growing. The data thus far strongly suggest that quality care does make a difference. These findings underscore the need for widespread advocacy for quality care.

Help for Parents

Most parents believe that they are equipped to select quality care for their children, despite some evidence that suggests that parents actually do little observation and investigation of programs before enrolling their children. In an attempt to provide parent education dealing with the variables that contribute to high-quality programs, the federal Child Care and Development Block Grant

(CCDBG) mandates a consumer-education program as a condition of funding to states. Most states, at the time of this writing, have produced brochures, checklists, or guidelines on selecting quality early care and education programs, often including information about the different types of care available. This information is widely distributed in state and local government agencies, doctors' offices, and sometimes supermarkets. Further, the CCDBG requires some funds to be set aside to enhance the quality of programs. Finally, it requires that all states review their minimum standards for center-based programs. After more than a decade of lowering the minimum standards for programs, an increasing number of states are revising their standards upward. A sound regulatory process that guarantees that children will not be in substandard care, along with aggressive distribution of parent and public information about the importance of quality care, will go a long way toward changing the current face of early care and education.

EFFECTS OF EARLY CARE AND EDUCATION

Parents and experts have been concerned for years with the effects of child care on children. Before the 1970s few answers could be provided with any degree of assurance. However, during that decade research on child care increased substantially. The research was by no means flawless. For example, most of the research was conducted in high-quality centers that were not representative of most substitute care arrangements; most studies were limited to the direct effects on an individual child and have consequently ignored important questions concerning the broader impact of child care on parents, the family, and social institutions; there was nearly exclusive reliance on standardized tests to evaluate the intellectual and social development of children; some studies failed to control such variables as the caregiver/child ratios at different ages, the stability and the continuity of the caregivers, the nature of the child's daily experience, the provision of adequate conditions of nutrition and health, and the quality of the child-care experience. In addition, the long-term follow-up of chil-

dren was neglected (Belsky & Steinberg, 1978; Etaugh, 1980).

This first phase of research on the effects of child care asked whether the increasing rates of participation of young children in out-of-home care was cause for alarm. Child care was not found to be inherently or inevitably harmful. Rather, it was found to vary considerably with respect to environmental quality, and children's development was linked to that variation. Thus, the second phase of research emerged—examining specific aspects of development that are affected by varying levels of quality. (This issue was discussed briefly in a preceding section.) This phase of research is still in progress while yet a third phase is just beginning to emerge—examining how the home and child-care environments are linked in affecting the developmental outcomes of children (Hayes, Palmer, & Zaslow, 1990).

Effects on Cognitive Development

Based on studies of the effects of child care on cognitive development conducted in the 1970s and the early 1980s, it was concluded that for most middle-class children who attend centers that meet legal guidelines for quality, child care has neither salutary nor adverse effects on intellectual development as measured by standardized tests. For economically disadvantaged children, however, child care may have enduring positive effects, for it appears that quality child-care experience may attenuate the decline in test scores typically associated with high-risk populations after 18 months of age.

During the 1990s research on the effects of child care on specific aspects of child development exploded. Caughy, DiPietro, and Strobino (1994) noted that the opportunities for learning provided by nonmaternal care for children of low socioeconomic status may be as good as or better than those provided by their own homes. The results of their study of children younger than 3 who experienced routine child care (not high-quality university-based care) underscored this assumption. Specifically, child-care participation of children from impoverished environments was positively related to the subsequent development of mathematics and reading skills. The relationship was strongest for reading recognition performance if participation began before the child's first birthday. The type of child care was related to math skills—children who attended center-based care or an early-childhood program in a school had better math skills than those cared for in their own homes or in family child care.

Burchinal, Ramey, Reid, and Jaccard (1995) found that preschool experience was associated with a large boost in IQ for African American children; for both White and African American children, center/preschool experience was related to higher verbal IQs. Further, experience in high-quality structural child-care settings was particularly beneficial to intellectual development in African American children. In another study with African American infants, Burchinal, Roberts, Nabors, and Bryant (1996) found that the quality of infant care was positively related to tests of cognitive development, language development, and communication skills. Infant/adult ratio was particularly related to children's communication skills.

Perhaps the most definitive relationships between early care and education and cognitive development have been demonstrated by the Cost, Quality, and Outcomes Study (1999), still in progress at the time of this writing. This study has focused on the impact of higher-quality care and education on children. The children involved in this study have been followed through the end of second grade. Children who attended quality child-care centers performed better on both math and language measures, as well as on thinking and attentional skills. Further, children who were most at risk (i.e., those children whose mothers had less education) were more sensitive to the negative effects of poor quality and received more benefits from high quality. This survey has not found differential effects based on either ethnicity or gender alone. Although some recent research still suggests that early care and education has little effect on the cognitive development of middle-class children, the Cost, Quality, and Outcomes Study seems to suggest that all children can benefit from high-quality programs, even though children from less advantaged homes may benefit more than others.

Effects on Emotional Development

In the earlier section on infant care, the question of the quality of attachment of infants in child care to their mothers was discussed. This question continues to be debated in the literature. Part of the difficulty lies with the assessment of attachment. The most common type of measurement is the Strange Situation, in which a mother and her child are together in a strange room with toys; a stranger enters, the mother leaves, and finally the mother returns. The child's behavior, toward both the mother and the environment, is rated in each condition. Several studies using this approach have found that children were more likely to interact with their mothers than with their caregivers, and when confronted with a problem-solving task all children who requested help turned to their mothers. Neither the age of entry into child care nor the length of time in care appeared to affect the mother-child attachment bond. Additional evidence indicates that infants can develop a discriminating attachment relationship toward a familiar caregiver. However, this relationship does not supersede the child's emotional bond with her mother. Children continue to express preference for their mothers.

The NICHD Early Child Care Research Network (1997) included approximately 1,200 mothers and their infants in nine states. This study supported the validity of the Strange Situation as a measure of attachment. Further, the researchers found no significant differences in attachment security related to child-care participation. However, children who received less sensitive and responsive caregiving in child care as well as less sensitive and responsive care from their mothers had the highest rates of insecurity. The authors concluded that child care by itself is neither a risk nor a benefit for the development of infant-mother attachment. However, the *quality* of child care may have an impact.

Effects on Social Development

Research during the 1980s provided some evidence suggesting that children who entered child care before the age of 2 years were more likely than children who entered later to interact with peers in both positive and negative ways. However, later research began to make close connections between relations with adults and relations with peers. Howes et al. (1992) found that children who were more secure with their teachers were more competent with their peers than children insecure with teachers. These researchers noted that children do not become competent with peers merely through extended contact and experience but that by the provision of materials and the organization of the classroom the teacher can provide a context for the acquisition of peer social skills. They further noted that children who have daily contact with stable peer groups from fairly young ages appear most socially competent with peers. This study suggested that the quality of the early-childhood program, including the adult-child relationship, influences the way in which social development is affected.

A Swedish study followed children from 6 weeks to 4 years of age who had been in child care for more than 10 hours per week (Hagekull & Bohlin, 1995). They found differences in the quality of care to be related to children's socioemotional development both concurrently and over time. High quality was defined in terms of appropriate levels of stimulation, effective and suitable discipline measures, good physical arrangements, and a warm emotional climate between children and between children and adults. Quality of care interacted with family and child characteristics. For example, ongoing conduct behaviors (externalizing behaviors and aggression) were predicted by both socioeconomic status and home quality. Gender was not directly related to socioemotional behavior in child care except that mere exposure to child care had some beneficial effects on acting-out behaviors for boys. Age of entry into child care did not affect socioemotional aspects of behavior. Further, the better the quality of child care, the more positive the emotions of children at home.

Two-year-olds who came from homes that did not appear to support positive development reduced their externalizing behaviors when exposed to high-quality child care, and 4-year-olds from lower SES homes reduced their aggressive acting-out behaviors in high-quality care. The authors concluded that good-quality child care had general effects on positive emotional expressions. Further, high-quality child care seemed to have a compensatory effect on children from less advantaged homes, and boys seemed to gain more than girls from the experience of high-quality child care.

Volling and Feagans (1995) examined the effects of infant child care on children's social development by including family, child, and child-care characteristics. Across all measures of social competence, children's social functioning was related to multiple factors—family environment, quality of care, temperament, and so on. Children tended to engage in nonsocial activities with peers and less positive interactions with adults when group size was large and there were more children per adult, a finding consistent with other research. Further, children enrolled in more hours of center care per week engaged in less nonsocial play and more friendly interactions with peers. However, children who entered care later during their first year were less likely to interact negatively with peers. An interesting finding related to family characteristics emerged: When families stressed independence in male children, those boys tended to engage in less friendly interactions with their peers. The researchers concluded that it was the quality of the child-care environment rather than the child-care experience (e.g., hours, age at entry) that had the more pronounced effects on children's social outcomes. Further, they concluded that temperamentally vulnerable children may be at risk for social difficulties when placed in low-quality programs, and high-quality programs may actually serve to protect these children from negative social outcomes.

Taken together, current research seems to suggest that early care and education can have beneficial rather than negative effects on children's social development, as was once assumed. However, it appears that the quality of care that children experience is the key to potential benefits. Further, more sophisticated research has found that child-care quality, family characteristics, and child characteristics interact to predict child outcomes.

PARENTAL SATISFACTION WITH CHILD CARE

The National Child Care Survey (Hofferth, Brayfield, Deich, & Holcomb, 1991) found that parents' level of satisfaction with child care was quite high—96 percent of parents surveyed indicated that they were either "very satisfied" or "satisfied" with their current care arrangements. Nevertheless, slightly more than one-quarter indicated that they would prefer an alternative type of care for their youngest child, and quality was the reason most often mentioned for desiring a change. Forty-nine percent of parents desiring a change preferred center-based early care and education.

Consistent with other research, the findings of Britner and Phillips (1995) were that parental satisfaction with both center-based and family child care was high overall. On structural aspects of quality (e.g., health and safety, group size) and the quality of interactions between adults and children (e.g., adult warmth, attention to children), parents using center-based and family child care were equally satisfied. For center-based care only, teacher training and experience and group size predicted satisfaction. Although parents rated quality as more important than convenience in selection of care arrangements, they may have perceived quality on the basis of realistic options, given cost, hours, and location. Most parents in the study viewed both types of care as a source of extensive informational and emotional support. Further, compatibility of parents' and teachers' child-rearing philosophies was high in each type of care, as was their agreement on the aspects of caregiving that are important for quality care.

Even with a sample of middle-class, educated parents who should be reasonably well informed consumers, Cryer and Burchinal (1997) found that parents did not appear to match the care they selected for their infants and preschoolers to their child-care values. Although the parents indicated that they valued the same aspects of care that early-childhood professionals find important, parents overestimated the quality of their children's programs on the aspects they valued the most highly. Trained observers rated the quality of the programs and compared their ratings with parents' ratings. Possibly parents rated the quality of programs according to their hopes and desires instead of reality. The data suggested that "imperfect information" may hinder parents from demanding the aspects of high-quality child care they believe to be important for their children.

In light of the proliferation of early-childhood programs that are only barely adequate in quality, it is puzzling that such a high percentage of parents are satisfied with their current arrangements. It may be that parents overinflate their satisfaction responses because they cannot accept consciously that their children are spending considerable amounts of time in less-than-adequate environments. Too, it may be that parents are poorly informed about what constitutes quality and the importance of quality in early care and education for optimal developmental outcomes.

IN THE FUTURE

If the United States works to meet the need for early care and education services, several considerations should be taken into account. Quality cannot be conceived of as the panacea for a troubled society; overpromise can breed resentment and bitterness. However, there is enough evidence to date that quality really matters, both in the short and the long terms. Substandard environments for our most vulnerable citizens cannot be tolerated. Early care and education appear to be a good option, serving variously as substitute care while parents work or participate in vocational or educational programs; as substitute care for children whose parents are physically or mentally disabled; as a provider of enriching, stimulating, and developmental activities for children, especially children from less-than-adequate homes; and as an alternative to institutionalization for children living in dangerous home situations. Further, providing care in isolation from comprehensive services to families must be avoided. The involvement of the entire family must be achieved.

Parents seem to provide the best key for quality control and must be involved in the decision-making process. Educating parents must be an ongoing process accomplished by community and professional groups. There is a need for diversity of models and creative approaches to early care and education. Standardized equipment, buildings, and curricula are not necessary. Standardized children are not what society needs.

Credentialing of all early-childhood personnel is seen by many as a way of increasing professionalism in the field and one way to contribute to quality programs. Indeed, research has confirmed the connection between teacher preparation and quality. Few incentives for personnel exist in most states. Low wages are paid, and only a small percentage of agencies have agreed to include credentials as a recognition of achievement. Head Start has attempted through the Child Development Associate program (CDA) to recognize achievement of caregivers/teachers through training and credentialing. New regulations have increased the educational requirements for teachers. The National Association for the Education of Young Children (NAEYC) has implemented a National Institute for Professional Development and is working with individual states to develop a career lattice for all early-childhood personnel—whether they work in family child care, child-care centers, public school programs, or Head Start—with recognized credentials at varying levels. These efforts ultimately will result in a cadre of trained individuals who understand the developmental needs and learning styles of young children and who will provide high-quality programs that do more than provide baby-sitting or custodial care. Together with the Children's Defense Fund, the NAEYC has emerged as a national voice for children.

Research Needs

Continued research on early care and education from an ecological perspective is needed. Research is needed that focuses on the broader effects of child care rather than on the consequences of child care and its direct effects on the child. Few studies have examined effects on parents or parent-child relationships. Studies correlating effects of child care and family and child characteristics are just beginning to emerge.

More needs to be known about the differential consequences of center-based care, family child care, and care in the home. The issue of quality needs continuing attention. What is "good enough" for children and their families? Where is the demarcation between what is harmful, innocuous, and beneficial in early care and education? To what extent should early-childhood programs provide comprehensive services to families? What is the most effective and efficient way of educating parents about the importance of quality care and education?

Considerable progress has been made in child-care research. For example, before 1980 most research was conducted in high-quality centers only; now we have moved beyond research centers to include all types of community child care and varying levels of quality, and longitudinal studies are being conducted. We have moved from simplistic questions regarding the effects of child care to more complex questions that deal with the mediating effects of family variables and the role of quality. Despite this progress, high-quality research, as a whole, remains limited.

OTHER PRESCHOOL PROGRAMS

Head Start programs, nursery schools, play groups, parent-cooperative programs, and drop-in centers also provide alternatives for care and education for young children. With the exception of Head Start, most of these programs serve parents who are interested in child care occasionally, and they do not meet the needs of working parents.

These programs provide opportunities for children to interact socially with peers, and educational activities usually are provided. Further, they give parents some respite from continual child care. *Drop-in child-care centers* are likely to be provided by for-profit companies and may be located in shopping malls, in bowling alleys, and even in prisons. Moms' Morning Out, sponsored by some churches, is another form of drop-in care, and sometimes health clinics or community centers provide similar services. If fees are charged, parents generally pay by the hour. In *parent cooperatives,* parents perform designated roles and responsibilities for running the program, often in lieu of a portion of tuition. Sometimes parents get together and form *play groups,* another alternative for nonworking parents. These groups primarily provide opportunities for children to play together under the supervision of adults. Some are formalized and meet at the same location at designated times. Most often, mothers alternate in the supervision. In all these programs, appropriate activities, materials and toys, and warm, caring adults should be provided if children are to benefit.

Head Start was created by the Economic Opportunity Act of 1964 to "interrupt the cycle of poverty" for America's poor families. It provides comprehensive child development and support services for young children, mostly beginning at age 3, and their families—health, nutrition, education, and social services, as well as parent involvement and education. The Head Start program is administered by the Head Start Bureau, which is a part of the Administration for Children and Families (ACF) in the Department of Health and Human Services (DHHS). Grants are awarded by the ACF regional offices and the branches of the Head Start Bureau's American Indian and Migrant Programs directly to local public agencies, private nonprofit organizations, Indian tribes, and school systems for the purpose of operating Head Start programs at the community level (Administration for Children & Families, 1999a).

The Early Head Start program, which serves low-income pregnant women and families with infants and toddlers, was established in 1994 by the Head Start Reauthorization Act. In 1999 nearly $338 million was used to support these projects, which served 35,000 children below the age of 3 and their families (Administration for Children & Families, 1999b).

Head Start serves an ethnically diverse population (36 percent African American, 31 percent White, 26 percent Hispanic, 4 percent American Indian, and 3 percent Asian American). In 1999, 4 percent of Head Start children were under 3 years of age, 31 percent were age 3, 59 percent were 4 years of age, and 6 percent were 5 years old or older. Thirteen percent of Head Start enrollment consisted of children with disabilities. Since 1965, Head Start has served a total of 17,714,000 children. Fifty-five percent of all Head Start parents are single. Fifty-five percent of these families earn less than $9,000 per year and 73 percent earn less than $12,000 per year. Appropriations for the 1999 fiscal year were $4.6 billion to serve nearly 825,000 children (Administration for Children & Families, 1999b). More than half of the 4-year-olds who were eligible for Head Start did not participate. Based on the results of the Perry Preschool Project, the Early Training Project, and the Rome Head Start Study, an analysis by International Business Machines, Inc., or IBM, concluded that if all eligible children participate in a quality 2-year preschool program, their high school graduation rate could be expected to increase from 46 percent to 65 percent. The analysis also estimated that increasing the graduation rate to 65 percent would produce new revenues of $7.92 billion and reduce spending by $3.46 billion in costs avoided for welfare and incarceration. These data suggest rather strongly that quality early-childhood programs for children from low-income families have significant long-term economic impact for society (National Governors Association, 1993).

SUMMARY

Clearly our contemporary complex society requires a variety of alternatives for early care and education that support and supplement parents' roles and responsibilities. An "Aunt Jane" or

Grandma who helps with child care or who intervenes in a crisis is no longer available for many American families during their child-rearing years. We have presented several options in the present chapter for parents who need part-time or full-time care for their children or for those parents who simply wish to provide additional stimulation for their children. Alternatives include in-home care by a relative or nonrelative, family child care, center-based care and education, preschool programs, after-school programs, and Head Start.

Although alternatives for parents clearly exist in the United States, we have by no means fully met the needs of America's families. At the time of this writing, many substandard programs are operating. Middle- and lower-middle-class families cannot afford quality care for their children, and many parents choose on the basis of availability and access. Preschool programs, excluding federally funded child-care programs, consist largely of children from middle- and upper-class families. In fact, child care in the United States is put to shame by comprehensive systems in many other nations. We still have a long way to go before all parents are truly provided with alternatives for early care and education that are acceptable, are affordable, and represent high quality.

REFERENCES

ADMINISTRATION FOR CHILDREN & FAMILIES. (1999a). Head Start fact sheet. [On-line]. Available: http://www.acf.dhhs.gov/programs/hsb/about/99hsfs.htm.

ADMINISTRATION FOR CHILDREN & FAMILIES. (1999b). Frequently asked questions about Head Start. [On-line]. Available: http://www.acf.dhhs.gov/programs/hsb/laq.htm.

BELSKY, J. (1990). Parental and nonparental child care and children's socioemotional development: A decade in review. *Journal of Marriage and the Family, 52*(4), 885–903.

BELSKY, J., & ROVINE, M. (1988). Nonmaternal care in the first year of life and the security of infant-parent attachment. *Child Development, 59*(1), 157–167.

BELSKY, J., & STEINBERG, L. (1978). The effects of day care: A critical review. *Child Development, 49,* 929–949.

BRITNER, P., & PHILLIPS, D. (1995). Predictors of parent provider satisfaction with child day care dimensions: A comparison of center-based and family child day care. *Child Welfare, 74*(6), 1135–1168.

BURCHINAL, M., RAMEY, S., REID, M., & JACCARD, J. (1995). Early child care experiences and their association with family and child characteristics during middle childhood. *Early Childhood Research Quarterly, 10,* 33–61.

BURCHINAL, M., ROBERTS, J., NABORS, L., & BRYANT, D. (1996). Quality of center child care and infant cognitive and language development. *Child Development, 67,* 606–620.

CALDWELL, B., WRIGHT, A., HONIG, A., & TANNEBAUM, J. (1970). Infant day care and attachment. *American Journal of Orthopsychiatry, 40,* 397–412.

CAUGHY, M., DIPIETRO, J., & STROBINO, D. (1994). Day-care participation as a protective factor in the cognitive development of low-income children. *Child Development, 65*(2), 457–471.

CENTER FOR THE CHILD CARE WORKFORCE. (1998). *Current data on child care salaries and benefits in the United States.* Washington, DC: Author.

COLEMAN, M., ROBINSON, B., & ROWLAND, B., (1993). A typology of families with children in self care: Implications for school-age child care programming. *Child and Youth Care Forum, 22*(1), 43–53.

COST, QUALITY, & OUTCOMES STUDY. (1999). The children of the cost, quality, and outcomes study go to school. [On-line]. Available: http://www.fpg.unc.edu/~NCEDL/PAGES/cqes.htm.

COST, QUALITY, & OUTCOMES STUDY TEAM. (1995). Cost, quality, and child outcomes in child care centers: Key findings and recommendations. *Young Children, 50*(4), 40–44.

CREIGHTON, L. (1993). Kids taking care of kids. *U.S. News and World Report, 115*(24), 26–32.

CRYER, D., & BURCHINAL, M. (1997). Parents as child care consumers. *Early Childhood Research Quarterly, 12,* 35–58.

EGELAND, B., & HIESTER, M. (1995). The long-term consequences of infant day-care and mother-infant attachment. *Child Development, 66,* 474–485.

ERWIN, P., SANSON, A., AMOS, D., & BRADLEY, B. (1993). Family day care and day care centers: Career, family and child differences and their implications. *Early Child Development and Care, 86,* 89–103.

ETAUGH, C. (1980). Effects of nonmaternal care on children, research evidence and popular views. *American Psychologist, 35*(4), 309–319.

FIELD, T. (1991). Quality infant day-care and grade school behavior and performance. *Child Development, 62*(4), 863–870.

FIELD, T., MASI, W., GOLDSTEIN, S., PERRY, S., & PARL, S. (1988). Infant day care facilitates preschool social behavior. *Early Childhood Research Quarterly, 3*(4), 341–359.

HAGEKULL, B., & BOHLIN, G. (1995). Day care quality, family and child characteristics and socioemotional development. *Early Childhood Research Quarterly, 10*, 505–526.

HAYES, C., PALMER, J., & ZASLOW, M. (Eds.). (1990). *Who cares for America's children? Child care policy for the 1990s.* Washington, DC: National Academy Press.

HOFFERTH, S., BRAYFIELD, A., DEICH, S., & HOLCOMB, P. (1991). *National child care survey, 1990.* Washington, DC: Urban Institute Press.

HOFFERTH, S., WEST, J., & HENKE, R. (1994). *Access to early childhood programs for children at risk.* Washington, DC: U.S. Department of Education, OERI, National Center for Education Statistics.

HOWES, C., & HAMILTON, C. (1992a). Children's relationships with caregivers: Mothers and child care teachers. *Child Development, 63*(4), 859–866.

HOWES, C., & HAMILTON, C. (1992b). Children's relationships with child care teachers: Stability and concordance with parental attachments. *Child Development, 63*(4), 867–678.

HOWES, C., PHILLIPS, D., & WHITEBOOK, M. (1992). Thresholds of quality: Implications for the social development of children in center-based child care. *Child Development, 63*(2), 449–460.

HOWES, C., RODNING, C., GALLUZZO, D., & MYERS, L. (1988). Attachment and child care: Relationships with mother and caregiver. *Early Childhood Research Quarterly, 3*(4), 403–416.

JOHANSEN, A., LEIBOWITZ, A., & WAITE, L. (1996). The importance of child-care characteristics to choice of care. *Journal of Marriage and the Family, 58*, 759–772.

KAGAN, S., & COHEN, N. (1997). *Not by chance.* New Haven, CT: The Bush Center in Child Development and Social Policy, Yale University.

KAGAN, J., KEARSLEY, R., & ZELAZO, P. (1978). *Infancy, its place in human development.* Cambridge: Harvard University Press.

KAY, M. (1999, March). When is a child ready to stay home alone? *Family Life, 94.*

KONTOS, S. (1994). The ecology of family day care. *Early Childhood Research Quarterly, 9*(1), 87–110.

KONTOS, S., HOWES, C., & GALINSKY, E. (1996). Does training make a difference to quality in family child care? *Early Childhood Research Quarterly, 11*, 427–445.

LARKIN, E. (1998/99). The intergenerational response to childcare and after-school care. *Generations, 22*(2), 33–37.

LONG, T., & LONG, L. (1982). Latchkey children: The child's view of self care. (ERIC Document Reproduction Service No. ED 211–229).

MILLER, A. (1999). They're home alone. *Newsweek, 134*(22), 105–107.

MOSKOWITZ, D., SCHWARZ, J., & CORSINI, D. (1977). Initiating day care at three years of age: Effects on attachment. *Child Development, 48*, 1271–1276,

NATIONAL CHILD CARE STAFFING STUDY. (1997). *Who cares? Child care teachers and the quality of care in America.* Washington, DC: Center for the Child Care Workforce.

NATIONAL GOVERNORS ASSOCIATION. (1993, October). Head Start: New partnerships. *In Brief.* Washington, DC: Author.

NATIONAL INSTITUTE OF CHILD HEALTH & HUMAN DEVELOPMENT. (1996). Characteristics of infant child care: Factors contributing to positive caregiving. *Early Childhood Research Quarterly, 11*, 269–306.

NATIONAL INSTITUTE OF CHILD HEALTH & HUMAN DEVELOPMENT. (1997). The effects of infant child care on infant-mother attachment security: Results of the NICHD study of early child care. *Child Development, 68*(5), 860–879.

NATIONAL INSTITUTE OF CHILD HEALTH & HUMAN DEVELOPMENT EARLY CHILD CARE RESEARCH NETWORK. (1997). Familial factors associated with the characteristics of nonmaternal care for infants. *Journal of Marriage and the Family, 59*, 389–408.

PHILLIPS, D., MEKOS, D., SCARR, S., MCCARTNEY, K., & ABBOTT-SHIM, M. (1995). Paths to quality in child care: Structural and contextual influences in children's classroom environments. Unpublished manuscript, University of Virginia.

PHILLIPS, D., VORAN, M., KISKER, E., HOWES, C., & WHITEBOOK, M. (1994). Child care for children in poverty: Opportunity or inequity? *Child Development, 65*(2), 472–492.

PHILLIPSEN, L., BURCHINAL, M., HOWES, C., & CRYER, D. (1997). The prediction of process quality from structural features of child care. *Early Childhood Research Quarterly, 12,* 281–303.

POSNER, J., & VANDELL, D. (1994). Low-income children's after-school care: Are there beneficial effects of after-school programs? *Child Development, 65*(2), 440–456.

POWELL, D. (1987). After-school care. *Young Children, 42*(3), 62–66.

RICHTERS, J., & ZAHN-WAXLER, C. (1988). The infant day care controversy: Current status and future directions. *Early Childhood Research Quarterly, 3*(3), 319–336.

RUETER, T. (1998). An after-school haven needed. *Christian Science Monitor, 90*(153), 15.

TODD, C., & DEERY-SCHMITT, D. (1996). Factors affecting turnover among family child care providers: A longitudinal study. *Early Childhood Research Quarterly, 11,* 351–376.

TURVETT, B. (1995). The latchkey solution. *Good Housekeeping, 221*(4), 217–220.

U.S. BUREAU OF THE CENSUS. (1996). Who's minding our preschoolers? *Current Population Reports, P70–53.* Washington, DC: U.S. Department of Commerce.

U.S. BUREAU OF THE CENSUS. (1998). *Statistical abstract of the United States: 1998* (118th ed.). Washington, DC: U.S. Department of Commerce.

U.S. DEPARTMENT OF HEALTH, EDUCATION, & WELFARE, OFFICE OF HUMAN DEVELOPMENT SERVICES, ADMINISTRATION FOR CHILDREN, YOUTH, AND FAMILIES. (1978). *National day care study: Preliminary findings and their implications.* Cambridge, MA: Abt Associates.

U.S. NEWS & WORLD REPORT. (1994). Day care vs. home care. *U.S. News and World Report, 116*(15), 20.

VANDELL, D., & RAMANAN, J. (1991). Children of the national longitudinal survey of youth: Choices in after-school care and child development. *Developmental Psychology, 27*(4), 637–643.

VOLLING, B., & FEAGANS, L. (1995). Infant day care and children's social competence. *Infant Behavior and Development, 18,* 177–188.

WALKER, J. (1992). New evidence on the supply of child care: A statistical portrait of family providers and an analysis of their fees. *Journal of Human Resources, 27*(1), 40–69.

WILLWERTH, J. (1993). "Hello? I'm home alone…" *Time, 141*(9), 46–48.

WOODARD, J., & FINE, M. (1991). Long-term effects of self-supervised and adult-supervised child care arrangements on personality traits, emotional adjustment, and cognitive development. *Journal of Applied Developmental Psychology, 12*(1), 73–85.

Author Index

SUBJECT INDEX